Complex Adaptive Systems (selected titles)

John H. Holland, Christopher G. Langton, and Stewart W. Wilson, advisors

Adaptation in Natural and Artificial Systems: An Introductory Analysis with Applications to Biology, Control, and Artificial Intelligence, John H. Holland

Genetic Programming: On the Programming of Computers by Means of Natural Selection, John R. Koza

Genetic Programming: The Movie, John R. Koza and James P. Rice

Intelligent Behavior in Animals and Robots, David McFarland and Thomas Bösser

Genetic Programming II: Automatic Discovery of Reusable Programs, John R. Koza

Turtles, Termites, and Traffic Jams: Explorations in Massively Parallel Microworlds, Mitchel Resnick

Comparative Approaches to Cognitive Science, edited by Herbert L. Roitblat and Jean-Arcady Meyer

Artificial Life: An Overview, edited by Christopher G. Langton

An Introduction to Genetic Algorithms, Melanie Mitchell

Catching Ourselves in the Act: Situated Activity, Interactive Emergence, and Human Thought, Horst Hendriks-Jansen

Elements of Artificial Neural Networks, Kishan Mehrotra, Chilukuri K. Mohan, and Sanjay Ranka

Advances in Genetic Programming, Volume II, edited by Peter J. Angeline and Kenneth E. Kinnear, Jr.

Growing Artificial Societies: Social Science from the Bottom Up, Joshua M. Epstein and Robert Axtell

An Introduction to Natural Computation, Dana H. Ballard

Fourth European Conference on Artificial Life, edited by Phil Husbands and Inman Harvey

Toward a Science of Consciousness 2: The 1996 Tucson Discussions and Debates, edited by Stuart R. Hameroff, Alfred W. Kaszniak, and Alwyn C. Scott

An Introduction to Fuzzy Sets: Analysis and Design, Witold Pedrycz and Fernando Gomide

From Animals to Animats 5: Proceedings of the Fifth International Conference on Simulation of Adaptive Behavior, edited by Rolf Pfeifer, Bruce Blumberg, Jean-Arcady Meyer, and Stewart W. Wilson

Artificial Life VI: Proceedings of the Sixth International Conference, edited by Christoph Adami, Richard K. Belew, Hiroaki Kitano, and Charles E. Taylor

The Simple Genetic Algorithm: Foundations and Theory, Michael D. Vose

Advances in Genetic Programming: Volume III, edited by Lee Spector, William B. Langdon, Una-May O'Reilly, and Peter J. Angeline

Advances in Genetic Programming
Volume III

edited by Lee Spector, William B. Langdon, Una-May O'Reilly,
and Peter J. Angeline

A Bradford Book
The MIT Press
Cambridge, Massachusetts
London, England

ISSN: 1524-8828
ISBN: 0-262-19423-6

This book was printed and bound in the United States of America

Contents

Contributors

Peter J. Angeline
Natural Selection, Inc.
509 Colgate Street, Vestal, NY 13850, USA
angeline@natural-selection.com

Dana H. Ballard
Computer Science Department
University of Rochester
Rochester, NY 14627, USA
dana@cs.rochester.edu

Wolfgang Banzhaf
University of Dortmund
Department of Computer Science, LS 11
D-44221 Dortmund, Germany
banzhaf@LS11.informatik.uni-dortmund.de

Howard Barnum
Institute for Science and
Interdisciplinary Studies (ISIS)
School of Natural Science
Hampshire College
Amherst, MA 01002, USA
hbarnum@hampshire.edu

Forrest H Bennett III
Genetic Programming Inc.
Box 1669
Los Altos, California 94023, USA
forrest@evolute.com

Herbert J. Bernstein
Institute for Science and
Interdisciplinary Studies (ISIS)
School of Natural Science
Hampshire College
Amherst, MA 01002, USA
hbernstein@hampshire.edu

Robert R. Bertram
The University of Michigan
1056 W. Michigan Avenue
Adrian, Michigan 49221, USA
robertrb@umich.edu

Kumar Chellapilla
Center for Information Engineering
University of California-San Diego
La Jolla, CA 92093-4007, USA
kchellap@ece.ucsd.edu

Dong-Yeon Cho
Artificial Intelligence Lab (SCAI)
Department of Computer Engineering
Seoul National University
Seoul 151-742, Korea
dycho@scai.snu.ac.kr

Peter F. Crapper
CSIRO Land and Water
G.P.O. Box 1666
Canberra, A.C.T. 2601, Australia
Peter.Crapper@cbr.clw.csiro.au

Jason M. Daida
Artificial Intelligence Laboratory and
Space Physics Research Laboratory
The University of Michigan
2455 Hayward Avenue
Ann Arbor, Michigan 48109-2143, USA
daida@eecs.umich.edu

James A. Foster
Center for Secure and Dependable Software
Department of Computer Science
University of Idaho
Moscow, ID, 83844-1010, USA
foster@cs.uidaho.edu

Frank D. Francone
Register Machine Learning Inc.
360 Grand Ave. STE 355
Oakland, CA 94610, USA
frank@francone.com

Hitoshi Iba
Department of Information and
Communication Engineering
School of Engineering,
The University of Tokyo
7-3-1 Hongo, Bunkyo-ku, 113-8656, Japan
iba@miv.t.u-tokyo.ac.jp

Christian Igel
Institut für Neuroinformatik
Ruhr-Universität Bochum
44780 Bochum, Germany
Christian.Igel@neuroinformatik.ruhr-uni-
bochum.de

Takuya Ito
School of Information Science
Japan Advanced Institute of Science and
Technology
1-1 Asahidai, Tatsunokuchi, Nomi
Ishikawa, 923-1292, Japan
takuya@jaist.ac.jp

Laur Ivan
Department of Computer Science and
Information Systems
University of Limerick, Ireland
Laur.Ivan@ul.ie

Robert E. Keller
Systems Analysis
Department of Computer Science
University of Dortmund
D-44221 Dortmund, Germany
keller@icd.de

John R. Koza
Section on Medical Informatics
Department of Medicine
Medical School Office Building
Stanford University
Stanford, California 94305, USA
koza@stanford.edu

William B. Langdon
Centrum voor Wiskunde en Informatica
Kruislaan 413
NL-1098 SJ Amsterdam, The Netherlands
W.B.Langdon@cwi.nl

Geum Yong Lee
School of Computer and Information
Engineering
Young-San University
San 150, Ju-Nam-Ri, Ung-Sang-Eup,
Yang-San-Shi
Kyung-Nam 626-840, Korea
earthquake@netsgo.com

Jörn Mehnen
Mechanical Engineering
Department of Machining Technology
University of Dortmund
D-44221 Dortmund, Germany
mehnen@isf.mb.uni-dortmund.de

Nikolay I. Nikolaev
Department of Computer Science
American University in Bulgaria
Blagoevgrad 2700, Bulgaria
nikolaev@nws.aubg.bg

Peter Nordin
Chalmers University of Technology
Physical Resource Theory
S-412 96 Goteborg, Sweden
nordin@fy.chalmers.se

Una-May O'Reilly
The Artificial Intelligence Lab
Massachusetts Institute of Technology
545 Technology Square, Rm 937
Cambridge, MA, 02139, USA
unamay@ai.mit.edu

Riccardo Poli
School of Computer Science
The University of Birmingham
Edgbaston, Birmingham B15 2TT, UK
R.Poli@cs.bham.ac.uk

John A. Polito 2
The MEDSTAT Group
777 E. Eisenhower Parkway
Ann Arbor, Michigan 48108, USA
john.polito.ii@medstat.com

Justinian P. Rosca
Siemens Corporate Research
755 College Road East
Princeton, NJ 08540, USA
rosca@scr.siemens.com

Carolyn Penstein Rosé
Learning Research and Development Center
University of Pittsburgh
Pittsburgh, PA 15260, USA
rosecp+@pitt.edu

Conor Ryan
Department of Computer Science and
Information Systems
University of Limerick, Ireland
Conor.Ryan@ul.ie

Satoshi Sato
School of Information Science
Japan Advanced Institute of Science and
Technology
1-1 Asahidai, Tatsunokuchi, Nomi
Ishikawa, 923-1292 Japan
sato@jaist.ac.jp

Vanio Slavov
Information Technologies Lab
New Bulgarian University
Sofia 1113, Bulgaria
vslavov@inf.nbu.acad.bg

Terence Soule
Department of Computer Science
St. Cloud State University
St. Cloud, MN 56301-4498, USA
tsoule@eeyore.stcloudstate.edu

Lee Spector
School of Cognitive Science
Hampshire College
Amherst, MA 01002, USA
lspector@hampshire.edu

Stephen A. Stanhope
The University of Michigan
Artificial Intelligence Laboratory and
Space Physics Research Laboratory
2455 Hayward Avenue
Ann Arbor, Michigan 48109-2143, USA
stanhope@umich.edu

Nikhil Swamy
Box 1026
Hampshire College
Amherst, MA 01002, USA
nikhil_swamy@hampshire.edu

Astro Teller
4019 Winterburn Ave
Pittsburgh, PA 15207, USA
astro@cs.cmu.edu

Klaus Weinert
Mechanical Engineering
Department of Machining Technology
University of Dortmund
D-44221 Dortmund, Germany
weinert@isf.mb.uni-dortmund.de

Peter A. Whigham
Department of Information Science
University of Otago,
P.O. Box 56
Dunedin, New Zealand
pwhigham@infoscience.otago.ac.nz

Byoung-Tak Zhang
Artificial Intelligence Lab (SCAI)
Department of Computer Engineering
Seoul National University
Seoul 151-742, Korea
btzhang@scai.snu.ac.kr

Acknowledgments

This volume, as with the two volumes that precede it, came into being through the labors of a number of people inside and outside the genetic programming field. It is the embodiment of that coordinated effort and we hope all are proud of what was accomplished.

We thank the individual contributors whose work is the reason for this volume's existence. All of them were responsive and cooperated with our numerous and occasionally contradictory comments. Thanks are also due to all of the people who submitted manuscripts for our consideration but were not included in this volume. It was not possible to include all of the interesting and novel ideas we reviewed. Given the growth of the field and the increasing number of publications that include genetic programming work, we look forward to seeing many of the manuscripts we could not include here in other venues.

We appreciate the assistance of the numerous researchers in the genetic programming field who contributed to this book by reviewing one or more of the following chapters. In addition, John Barndon, Blake LeBaron, David Meyer, and Stan Warner provided additional expertise for papers that touched on other research areas.

We give special thanks to the following who provided technical support, disk space, and funding support for this project: the EEBIC group of the University of Birmingham School of Computer Science; Keith Marlow and Stephen Pillinger of the School of Computer Science, University of Birmingham; the Centrum voor Wiskunde en Informatica, Amsterdam; the MIT Artificial Intelligence Lab; and Natural Selection, Inc. Lee Spector is supported in part by the John D. and Catherine T. MacArthur Foundation's MacArthur Chair program at Hampshire College. William B. Langdon is funded in part by the Defence Research Agency in Malvern. Una-May O'Reilly is supported by The Office of Naval Research under contract N00014-95-1-0600.

We would also like to thank our respective family members: Rebecca S. Neimark, Eli Simon Spector, Anya Neimark Spector, Ruth Spector, Alan Spector, Blake LeBaron, Lorie Angeline, Rebecca Angeline, and Jonathan Angeline. They allowed us time away from them to bring this volume to press.

The staff at MIT Press helped considerably during the production of this book and we appreciate their professionalism and their continued support of the *Advances in Genetic Programming* series.

Finally, we would like to give a special acknowledgment to Harry Stanton, who passed away in 1997. Harry was the Executive Editor of the Bradford Books division of MIT Press and one of the initiators of the *Advances in Genetic Programming* series. His contributions as the publisher of much of the early work in genetic programming, evolutionary computation, and a number of other scientific fields, made him a significant member of the research community. We will miss his enthusiasm, wit, and wisdom.

1 An Introduction to the Third Volume

Lee Spector, W. B. Langdon, Una-May O'Reilly, Peter Angeline

Welcome to the third volume of *Advances in Genetic Programming* series. The Genetic Programming (GP) field has matured considerably since the first two volumes were produced in conjunction with workshops held at the International Conference on Genetic Algorithms (ICGA) [Kinnear, Jr., 1994; Angeline and Kinnear, Jr., 1996]. During the 1993 and 1995 ICGA conferences the interest in GP was strong but within this broader community there were only a few presentation and publication slots for GP work. The *Advances* volumes therefore provided an important outlet for creative new work in GP. Interest in GP continued to grow and there is now a separate annual conference on GP in the USA, as well as a European workshop on GP and several other conferences that regularly feature GP themes (see Section 1.2).

Since annual conferences now serve the function of quickly disseminating concise descriptions of current research, it is appropriate to update the role of the *Advances* series. As editors, we decided that this volume should be highly selective and focus solely on genuine advances that we feel are outstanding and will have broad impact on those interested in GP.

The volume consists of a combination of invited and contributed chapters. A call for contributions to the book was circulated electronically on the genetic programming mailing list[1] and in several other forums. The call for contributions stated that the "primary criterion by which submissions will be evaluated is the likely impact on the future work of other theoreticians and practitioners." We also invited a number of active researchers who previously demonstrated significant contributions to submit chapters that they felt best addressed the criteria in the call for contributions. All chapters were reviewed by the editors, sometimes with the aid of additional specialists, and only those deemed to be true advances in the field were selected for inclusion in the book. We turned away several otherwise solid and interesting papers that we felt fell short of our standards for anticipated impact. We gave the accepted chapters more pages than in previous volumes, and we conducted an intensive, iterative review/revision process in order to produce chapters of the highest possible quality. We believe that the solicitation procedure, the review criteria, and the editing process were all successful, producing an outstanding collection of chapters that will endure as being critical and influential to practitioners of GP.

For those new to GP we start in Section 1.1 with a description of the basic genetic programming algorithm. Sections 1.2 and 1.3 contain additional sources of information and public domain software implementations of GP that we hope will be of wide interest. Finally, for all readers, Section 1.4 provides an overview of the remaining chapters of the book that we hope will encourage the simply curious reader to browse creatively and the more deliberate reader to immediately find sought-after material.

---

[1]The address for the list is `genetic-programming@cs.stanford.edu`. To subscribe send an e-mail message with the body "subscribe genetic-programming *your@email.address*" to `genetic-programming-request@cs.stanford.edu`.

1.1   A brief overview of genetic programming

This section treats GP as a specialization of the genetic algorithm (GA) technique [Holland, 1975]. This is complementary to the perspective in *Advances II*, which showed how GP relates to Evolutionary Programming [Angeline, 1996]. The basic procedure of a GA can be abbreviated as follows:

1. Create an initial population of random individuals.

2. Test the "fitness" of each individual.

3. If an individual is sufficiently good then stop and report success.

4. Otherwise create a new population from the more fit individuals, using "genetic operators" such as reproduction, mutation, and crossover.

5. Replace the old population with the new population and return to Step 2.

This algorithm characterizes GAs in general, and one can view GP as a specialization of GA for the evolution of executable programs. The primary differences between GP systems and other GA systems are:

• In a GP system individuals are generally executable structures such as computer programs, while in other GA systems individuals take various forms (typically bit or character strings).

• In a GP system fitness is normally assessed by *executing* the individuals, while in other GA systems fitness is assessed in ways that depend on the structure of individuals and the problem being solved.

To apply GP to a particular problem one must first specify a set of primitive elements, called *functions* and *terminals*, out of which candidate and complete solutions may be constructed. In the simplest case one chooses these elements in a way that ensures that every possible combination of elements will execute without generating an error condition, typically by restricting all values to be of a single data type. One must then provide a *fitness function* that assesses the quality of individuals in the population, and set values for a range of parameters covering details of structure representation, selection method, initialization procedures, genetic operators, and so on. Once these preparatory steps are taken one can run the genetic programming system to start the algorithm outlined above, producing, in the best case, a program that accomplishes the required task in a short amount of time. Variations are possible and in many cases advantageous; many of these are described in detail in this and earlier volumes of this series [Kinnear, Jr., 1994; Angeline and Kinnear, Jr., 1996].

1.2 Other GP Resources

More detail on the basic GP technique, its relation to other work in machine learning and treatment of advanced topics in GP can be found in several sources. [Banzhaf et al., 1998a] is particularly recommended for newcomers to the field as it contains clear introductory examples and also extensive references to the GP literature.

- Books and Journals

– *Genetic Programming: On the Programming of Computers by Means of Natural Selection,* along with followup volumes 2 and 3 (forthcoming) [Koza, 1992; Koza, 1994; Koza et al., 1999].

– *Genetic Programming, An Introduction* [Banzhaf et al., 1998a].

– The first two volumes of *Advances in Genetic Programming* [Kinnear, Jr., 1994; Angeline and Kinnear, Jr., 1996] and (of course) this volume, III.

– *Genetic Programming and Data Structures* [Langdon, 1998]

– *Evolutionary Induction of Binary Machine Code* [Nordin, 1997]

– *Journal of Genetic Programming and Evolvable Machines,* Kluwer (forthcoming)

- Proceedings

– *Genetic Programming '96, '97, '98* [Koza et al., 1996; Koza et al., 1997; Koza et al., 1998], and late breaking papers collections [Koza, 1996; Koza, 1997; Koza, 1998]

– *EuroGP '98, '99* [Banzhaf et al., 1998b; Poli et al., 1999], late breaking papers [Poli et al., 1998]

Many other conference and workshop proceedings have GP related papers. Some examples are the International Conference on Genetic Algorithms (ICGA), Foundations of Genetic Algorithms (FOGA), Parallel Problem Solving from Nature (PPSN), International Conference on Evolutionary Computation (ICEC), Artificial Life (ALife), and European Conference on Artificial Life (ECAL). A good way to find a specific paper or conference volume is to use the GP bibliography (see below).

- [Langdon, 1996] contains a GP bibliography organised by subject. A non indexed (but current) version is available at http://www.cs.bham.ac.uk/~wbl/biblio/gp-bibliography.html

- Mailing lists

* GPlist – *the* GP discussion list. Subscribe by sending email to genetic-program ming-REQUEST@cs.stanford.edu with a single line subscribe in the body of

the message. Beware the FAQ (Frequently Asked Questions) is seriously out of date, especially ftp addresses. A nearly complete archive of previous messages can be found at `http://adept.cs.twsu.edu/~thomas/gpmail.html`

* GA Digest – Moderated list on Genetic Algorithms, approximately monthly bulletins. Subscribe by sending email to `ga-list-REQUEST@aic.nrl.navy.mil` An archive of previous messages, etc. is located at `http://www.aic.nrl.navy.mil/galist`

- WWW and FTP sites

* Many of our authors have extensive Internet World Wide Web (www) pages. For example, John Koza's www pages include information on teaching, publications, GP, www links, etc. See `http://smi-web.stanford.edu/people/koza`. Information about conferences on GP, and on evolutionary computation in general, plus general information on GP can also be found at `http://www.genetic-programming.org`

* GP ftp site, code and early papers `ftp://ftp.mad-scientist.com/pub/genetic-programming`

* GP Notebook — multiple sites e.g. `http://www.geneticprogramming.com`

* ENCORE — The Hitch-Hiker's guide to evolutionary computation — multiple sites, e.g. `ftp://ftp.de.uu.net/pub/research/softcomp/EC`

* Bias within GP tutorial, GP98, `http://www.cs.rochester.edu/u/rosca/GPTutorialPage.html`

* Additional internet resources are documented in [Tufts, 1996].

1.3 Public Domain GP Implementations (unsupported)

C/C++

lilgp — Douglas Zonger, Michigan State University, GARAGe, Genetic ALgorithm Research and Application Group `http://garage.cse.msu.edu/software/software-index.html` 325kb

DGPC — Dave's [Andre] Genetic Programming code in C, (only 2 bytes per tree node) `http://www.cs.berkeley.edu/~dandre/gp.tar.gz` 211kb

GPQUICK/GPdata — Andy Singleton/W. B. Langdon, C++ (only 1 byte per tree node) `http://www.cs.bham.ac.uk/~wbl/ftp/gp-code` 172kb

SGPC — Simple GP in C, Walter Tackett and gpc++ — C++, by Adam Fraser may be found at `ftp://ftp.mad-scientist.com/pub/genetic-programming/code`

Lisp

Lisp code for [Koza, 1992] and [Koza, 1994] is also stored in `ftp://ftp.mad-scient ist.com/pub/genetic-programming/code`

Java

GPsys — Adil Qureshi `http://www.cs.ucl.ac.uk/staff/A.Qureshi`

GP across the Internet — Chong `ftp://ftp.cs.bham.ac.uk/pub/authors/ W.B.Langdon/gp-code/DGP`

Others

Implementations in other languages, for example SmallTalk, Mathematica and Prolog can also be found at `ftp://ftp.mad-scientist.com/pub/genetic-programm ing/code`

1.4   The work in this volume

1.4.1   Part I: Applications

Perhaps the most dramatic change in the field since the previous volumes of *Advances* has been the growth in the number of real-world applications. This is an important sign of the maturity of the field; early GP work included many applications, but many of these were simple and it was rare that the applied work solved hard problems that workers in the application areas really needed to have solved. In several recent cases, however, GP researchers have teamed up with engineers or researchers in other fields and the resulting teams have applied GP tools to significant real-world problems. In other cases the transition to real-world applications has been made without the aid of GP specialists, a sign that GP technology is ready for more widespread use. We chose to start this volume with the applications in part because we would like to show those outside GP that it is feasible to apply it to outstanding problems in their fields. We also feel that GP researchers working on theoretical issues or on extensions to GP technique should keep one eye trained on the real-world uses of GP.

Chapter 2, "An Automatic Software Re-Engineering Tool based on Genetic Programming" by Conor Ryan and Laur Ivan, attacks the difficult and commercially important problem of automatically transforming serial programs into functionally identical parallel programs written in a C-like syntax. The authors argue that their Paragen system extracts parallelism at least as well as human experts in much less time, and that it serves an important need as no other fully automatic parallelization techniques are currently available. They also argue that GP is particularly well-suited to this application area because it is not only able to spot and exploit code patterns but also to explore the possibilities of moving and transforming code in ways that humans would not.

In Chapter 3, "CAD Surface Reconstruction from Digitized 3D Point Data with a Genetic Programming/Evolution Strategy Hybrid" by Robert E. Keller, Wolfgang Banzhaf, Jörn Mehnen and Klaus Weinert, we see GP applied in another commercially important area. In many modern manufacturing processes, after development, prototypical physical workpieces are digitized to obtain their descriptions. Unfortunately, a digitized representation is not sufficient as a computer-aided design object and it is necessary to derive from it an appropriate construction-oriented CAD surface representation before it can be provided as input to rapid-prototype systems or used in other design or construction processes. The authors present a system, SURREAL, that uses a hybrid of GP and Evolution Strategies [Rechenberg, 1994] to perform the requisite "surface reconstruction" task. SURREAL simultaneously performs pattern recognition and structure evolution. It exploits the variable-length representation of genetic programming to explore search spaces without pre-defined dimensionality. The authors note that SURREAL has potential uses beyond the obvious manufacturing applications; for example, it should perform better than existing reconstruction approaches for highly irregular surfaces such as human faces, with possible applications in cosmetics, medicine, entertainment, and person identification.

Carolyn Penstein Rosé provides a promising new GP-based approach to a classical artificial intelligence problem in Chapter 4, "A Genetic Programming Approach for Robust Language Interpretation." The problem of robust language interpretation is to construct a representation of the meaning of a sentence which is independent of its words by using a predefined set of meaning-encoded primitives in relation to each other. A parsing grammar first handles the task, but, because it is necessarily incomplete, it fails on *extra-grammatical* sentences that fall outside its domain producing only partially-parsed sub-expressions. ROSE uses genetic programming to search the space of possible relationships between the meaning representation of these grammatical sub-expressions in order to construct an accurate and complete representation of the entire sentence. The ROSE system depends on GP to be efficient. Using GP obviates the need for an expensive, maximally flexible parser and, as a repair strategy, it avoids the need for hand-coded repair rules. Overall, the author states that ROSE "yields a significantly better time/quality trade-off than previous non-GP approaches".

In Chapter 5, "Time Series Modeling Using Genetic Programming: An Application to Rainfall-runoff Models," P. A. Whigham and P. F. Crapper apply a novel grammar-based variant of GP to a hydrological modeling problem. Their system discovers rainfall-runoff relationships for two different catchments on different continents and with different climates. They show it is more robust than previous methods when rainfall-runoff correlation are poor and when the assumptions built into other methods do not hold. The authors also note that while other machine learning techniques have been applied to rainfall-runoff modeling, their GP-based system produces models that are more readily interpretable in terms of processes and behaviors used in the application area.

In Chapter 6, "Automatic Synthesis, Placement, and Routing of Electrical Circuits, by Means of Genetic Programming," John R. Koza and Forrest H Bennett III present the latest enhancements to their work on GP applications to electrical circuit design. In this chapter they demonstrate for the first time how a single GP process can automatically create the topology, component sizing, placement, and routing of analog electrical circuits, a process that normally requires several human engineers with specialized design skills. In addition to a general description of their technique they provide a detailed example of the evolution of an analog low pass filter. They also point out that GP has now produced many results that are competitive with human-produced results, including many for which patents have previously been awarded, and they discuss GP as an "invention machine".

Chapter 7, "Quantum Computing Applications of Genetic Programming" by Lee Spector, Howard Barnum, Herbert J. Bernstein and Nikhil Swamy, presents work on applying GP to computers that don't yet exist—"quantum computers" that will manipulate the states of atomic-scale objects to gain efficiencies not achievable with digital computers based on classical physics. Even though large-scale quantum computers do not yet exist GP can be used in conjunction with a simulated quantum computer both to discover new quantum computer algorithms and to help explore the the potential power of quantum computing. The authors demonstrate the evolution of several better-than-classical quantum algorithms including both previously discovered and new examples.

1.4.2 Part II: Theory

As the applications of GP have expanded it has become more urgent that we understand how and why the process works when it does, and how and why it fails when it fails. Only on the basis of a solid theoretical understanding of these issues can we intelligently apply or enhance the technique. Early theoretical approaches, based for example on the schema theorem from traditional genetic algorithms, made little progress because of several factors including GP's richer representations, variable length genotypes, and execution semantics for individuals. Neither have attempts to avoid theory, relying for example on blind faith in the power of recombination and natural selection, produced sufficiently satisfying answers to questions about how and why GP works or doesn't work.

Chapter 8, "The Evolution of Size and Shape" by W. B. Langdon, Terry Soule, Riccardo Poli and James A. Foster investigates the phenomenon of growth in program size in GP populations. This has been known for some time but previous explanations have not been completely satisfactory. The authors start from the basics — What is the nature of the search space upon which GP operates? That is, what are program search spaces like? How big are they, i.e. how many possible programs are there? What shapes can they have? How are program shapes (particularly tree shapes) distributed in the search space? How is program performance (i.e. fitness) distributed in the space? They present a maximum likelihood (maximal entropy) model of bloat, which simply suggests programs evolve towards the part of the search space containing the most programs of the current best fitness level. This not only explains the evolution of program length but also program shape (which had not previously been considered). The chapter also considers various GP specific mechanisms in bloat and proposes two new genetic operators which considerably reduce bloat. The keenly interested reader should also read Chapter 11 where Rosca and Ballard also propose a bloat-reducing genetic operator which is derived from an analysis with a different perspective. As well, in Chapter 16, Ito, Iba and Sato propose new genetic operators that foster the protection and growth of building blocks. Their evaluation shows that their self-tuning mechanism also can address bloat.

Chapter 9, "Fitness Distributions: Tools for Designing Efficient Evolutionary Computations" by Christian Igel and Kumar Chellapilla, is an important landmark in the theoretical analysis of subtree mutation operators. Recently there has been impressive experimental work on mutation-only GP [Chellapilla, 1997], and in this chapter the authors start to lay theoretical ground work for this work by analysing the effectiveness of a total of 11 different subtree operators within evolving populations on a total of four benchmark problems. Their analysis yields important conclusions about these operators and recommendations for their future use.

Chapter 10, "Analysis of Single-Node (Building) Blocks in Genetic Programming" by Jason M. Daida, Robert R. Bertram, John A. Polito 2, and Stephen A. Stanhope, addresses the crux of the crossover versus mutation debate in automatic program generation (cf. Chapter 9). That is the question of "building blocks". Do they exist in program parse trees? If so, are the current mechanisms effective in finding them and building complete solutions from them? If not, can more effective mechanisms be devised? The authors empirically analyze the evolutionary process as it combines and exploits the most primitive potential building block in GP — terminals which are ephemeral random constants. Their investigation provides qualified support for the notion of simple building blocks within the current GP framework, but they warn that GP dynamics are complex. They further suggest that the notions of genotype and phenotype need careful rethinking when used in the context of GP.

Chapter 11, "Rooted-Tree Schemata in Genetic Programming" by Justinian P. Rosca and Dana H. Ballard, turns GP on its head. Instead of viewing the GP process as forming solutions in a "bottom up" fashion it suggests GP solutions evolve from the root down in a "top down" fashion. They present detailed quantitative analysis of several important aspects of the dynamics of GP. Following a review of work on Genetic Algorithms (GAs) population dynamics in terms of the schema theorem and Price's Theorem they present a GP schema theorem based on rooted-tree schema. They then extend this to consider the phenomenon of increase in program size in GP and a common response to it, adding a parsimony bias to the fitness function. Their theoretical analysis suggests values for the strength of the parsimony bias which they experimentally verify using the parity and Pac-Man problems. In addition, further analysis indicates that schema growth needs to be controlled so that the size of a program does not influence the likelihood of a tree-schema's survival during crossover. Two methods of exercising this control are delineated and one, which adapts the probability of disruption of a tree as a function of its size, is shown to be effective on the parity and Pac-Man problems.

1.4.3   Part III: Extensions

The final part of the book contains eight chapters that push the genetic programming framework in new directions, either to allow for new classes of applications or to produce qualitative improvements in performance.

Chapter 12, "Efficient Evolution of Machine Code for CISC Architectures using Instruction Blocks and Homologous Crossover" by Peter Nordin, Wolfgang Banzhaf and Frank D. Francone, describes two major advances for the world of linear machine code GP. Both are aimed at significantly extending their commercial GP system Discipulus. The first advance enables machine code GP to evolve machine code for complex instruction set computers (CISC, such as INTEL X86 chips used in most personal computers PCs, JAVA and many embedded processors) whilst retaining the speed and performance advantages of machine code evolution available up to now on reduced instruction set computers (RISC) such as the SUN-Sparc. The second advance is a description of homologous crossover in machine code GP. By ensuring that like parts of programs are crossed over the authors are able to produce a more productive crossover operator in which the offspring are more related to their parent programs. Chapter 12 also contains comparisons between tree and machine code GP and discussions of future applications of machine code GP.

Modern computers typically act on 32 or 64 bits simultaneously. Chapter 13, "Sub-machine-code Genetic Programming" by R. Poli and W. B. Langdon, describes several ways in which GP can exploit this internal parallelism. Their technique is described and demonstrated via several Boolean problems and an optical character recognition (OCR) problem. The technique is easy to implement (pointers to publicly available code are included) and can readily speed up any existing GP implementation dramatically (one to nearly two orders of magnitude).

Astro Teller describes in Chapter 14, "The Internal Reinforcement of Evolving Algorithms", a new approach in which the behaviour of a parent program is used to create a credit-blame map locating the useful and not-so-useful parts within it. The credit-blame map is used to guide the location of crossover points so that the useful parts of the program are more likely to preserved in its offspring. Each program is represented as a directed graph with similarities to artificial neural networks and data flow machines with indexed memory. PADO evolves programs which correctly classify their input into classes. The new system of internal reinforcement, which is demonstrated within PADO on problems of classifying complex real images and sounds, is shown to improve performance.

Chapter 15, "Inductive Genetic Programming with Immune Network Dynamics" by Nikolay I. Nikolaev, Hitoshi Iba and Vanio Slavov, describes a major advance in which previously unconnected streams of GP research (Stroganoff and Immune Genetic Programming) are brought together and shown to be highly effective for example on time-series prediction problems using small populations. Immune Genetic Programming is presented using an analogy of an immune system (GP) evolving to overcome a disease by binding to a number of disease causing antigens (the test cases). Perhaps one of the most important aspects of the new approach is that it provides a principled mechanism for dynamically changing the fitness function (i.e. the active test cases) which improves GP learning efficiency.

Chapter 16, "A Self-Tuning Mechanism for Depth-Dependent Crossover" by Takuya Ito, Hitoshi Iba and Satoshi Sato, proposes an improved crossover operator for tree based GP. They note that traditional crossover tends to swap relatively small subtrees and, while in some problems exchanging larger subtrees appears to improve performance, this is not always the case. Therefore they propose a new operator which takes into account this problem dependency and learns, via a self-tuning mechanism, the best size to use for crossover as the GP run proceeds. The mechanism depends on the assumption that, if depth selection probability is efficiently assigned to a tree, the fitness of the structure's offspring will improve and the depth selection probability will be inherited by subsequent generations. That is, their subtree crossover operator coevolves with the GP population and so can adapt to the problem and achieve improved results. They also note a reduction in population "bloat".

Chapter 17, "Genetic Recursive Regression for Modeling and Forecasting Real-World Chaotic Time Series" by Geum Yong Lee, presents several improved techniques whereby GP can evolve non-linear models of time-varying statistics based upon a history of several GP runs. The improvements are demonstrated on a wide range of different time series data and evolve improved models with small populations and therefore low computational effort.

Chapter 18, "Coevolutionary Fitness Switching: Learning Complex Collective Behaviors Using Genetic Programming" by Byoung-Tak Zhang and Dong-Yeon Cho, tackles one of the important unsolved problems: how to get multiple independent programs/agents/robots to learn to co-operate together to solve complex problems. They present improved learning based upon coevolution and demonstrate it on Robot Soccer games. These games are known for their difficulty and the manual coding of winning teams is far from trivial.

Our final chapter, Chapter 19, "Evolving Multiple Agents by GP" by Hitoshi Iba, continues the multi-agent theme. Here Iba uses the difficult robot navigation problem to demonstrate a new multi-agent learning scheme in which the agents learn to communicate with each other. He compares this with more traditional Q-learning approaches (which scale badly). However the chapter also describes efficient means of combining GP and Q-learning.

Bibliography

Angeline, P. J. (1996), "Genetic programming's continued evolution," in *Advances in Genetic Programming 2*, P. J. Angeline and K. E. Kinnear, Jr. (Eds.), Chapter 1, pp 1–20, Cambridge, MA, USA: MIT Press.

Angeline, P. J. and Kinnear, Jr., K. E. (1996), *Advances in Genetic Programming 2*, Cambridge, MA, USA: MIT Press.

Banzhaf, W., Nordin, P., Keller, R. E., and Francone, F. D. (1998a), *Genetic Programming – An Introduction; On the Automatic Evolution of Computer Programs and its Applications*, Morgan Kaufmann, dpunkt.verlag.

Banzhaf, W., Poli, R., Schoenauer, M., and Fogarty, T. C. (1998b), *Genetic Programming*, volume 1391 of *LNCS*, Paris: Springer-Verlag.

Chellapilla, K. (1997), "Evolving computer programs without subtree crossover," *IEEE Transactions on Evolutionary Computation*, 1(3):209–216.

Holland, J. H. (1975), *Adaptation in natural artificial systems*, Ann Arbor: University of Michigan Press.

Kinnear, Jr., K. E. (1994), *Advances in Genetic Programming*, Cambridge, MA: MIT Press.

Koza, J. R. (1992), *Genetic Programming: On the Programming of Computers by Means of Natural Selection*, Cambridge, MA, USA: MIT Press.

Koza, J. R. (1994), *Genetic Programming II: Automatic Discovery of Reusable Programs*, Cambridge Massachusetts: MIT Press.

Koza, J. R. (1996), *Late Breaking Papers at the Genetic Programming 1996 Conference Stanford University July 28-31, 1996*, Stanford University, CA, USA: Stanford Bookstore.

Koza, J. R. (1997), *Late Breaking Papers at the 1997 Genetic Programming Conference*, Stanford University, CA, USA: Stanford Bookstore.

Koza, J. R. (1998), *Late Breaking Papers at the 1998 Genetic Programming Conference*, University of Wisconsin, Madison, WI, USA: Omni Press.

Koza, J. R., Banzhaf, W., Chellapilla, K., Deb, K., Dorigo, M., Fogel, D. B., Garzon, M. H., Goldberg, D. E., Iba, H., and Riolo, R. (1998), *Genetic Programming 1998: Proceedings of the Third Annual Conference*, University of Wisconsin, Madison, WI, USA: Morgan Kaufmann.

Koza, J. R., David Andre, Bennett III, F. H., and Keane, M. (1999), *Genetic Programming 3*, Morgan Kaufman, Forthcoming.

Koza, J. R., Deb, K., Dorigo, M., Fogel, D. B., Garzon, M., Iba, H., and Riolo, R. L. (1997), *Genetic Programming 1997: Proceedings of the Second Annual Conference*, Stanford University, CA, USA: Morgan Kaufmann.

Koza, J. R., Goldberg, D. E., Fogel, D. B., and Riolo, R. L. (1996), *Genetic Programming 1996: Proceedings of the First Annual Conference*, Stanford University, CA, USA: MIT Press.

Langdon, W. B. (1996), "A bibliography for genetic programming," in *Advances in Genetic Programming 2*, P. J. Angeline and K. E. Kinnear, Jr. (Eds.), Appendix B, pp 507–532, Cambridge, MA, USA: MIT Press.

Langdon, W. B. (1998), *Data Structures and Genetic Programming: Genetic Programming + Data Structures = Automatic Programming!*, Boston: Kluwer.

Nordin, P. (1997), *Evolutionary Program Induction of Binary Machine Code and its Applications*, PhD thesis, der Universitat Dortmund am Fachereich Informatik.

Poli, R., Langdon, W. B., Schoenauer, M., Fogarty, T., and Banzhaf, W. (1998), *Late Breaking Papers at EuroGP'98: the First European Workshop on Genetic Programming*.

Poli, R., Nordin, P., Langdon, W. B., and Fogarty, T. C. (1999), *Genetic Programming, Proceedings of EuroGP'99*, LNCS, Goteborg, Sweden: Springer-Verlag, forthcoming.

Rechenberg, I. (1994), *Evolutionsstrategie'94*, volume 1 of *Werkstatt Bionik und Evolutionstechnik*, Stuttgart: Friedrich Frommann Verlag (Günther Holzboog KG).

Tufts, P. (1996), "Genetic programming resources on the world-wide web," in *Advances in Genetic Programming 2*, P. J. Angeline and K. E. Kinnear, Jr. (Eds.), Appendix A, pp 499–506, Cambridge, MA, USA: MIT Press.

I APPLICATIONS

2 An Automatic Software Re-Engineering Tool Based on Genetic Programming

Conor Ryan and Laur Ivan

This chapter describes a Genetic Programming system, Paragen, which transforms serial programs into functionally identical parallel programs. Unlike most other GP systems, it is possible to prove that the programs generated by the system are functionally identical. The ability to prove that the output of a GP run is correct has greatly improved the chances of GP being used in a commercial situation.

2.1 Introduction

Until recently, parallel programming tended to be restricted to either purely academic activities or to exotic super computer systems which were normally the preserve of wealthy institutions. The advent of systems such as PVM[Geist, 1993] (Parallel Virtual Machine)/ MPI (Message Passing Interface) and Linda[Gelernter, 1985] have changed this, however, by treating a network of (possibly heterogeneous) computers as though each were a node in a parallel computer.

The performance and practicality of these systems has further improved with the use of Beowulf systems, which are generally groups of Intel or Alpha-based machines on a fast (100MBit or greater) local network running a version of PVM or MPI. These systems have all the characteristics of the PVM type systems mentioned above, with the added advantage of extremely fast communication, thus allowing the possibility of increasingly fine grains of execution.

Parallel processing is becoming increasingly important as more and more sophisticated techniques are being developed for areas such as simulations, engineering applications or graphics rendering.

2.1.1 Software Re-engineering

Despite the apparent ease with which one can adopt parallel architectures, they have yet to enjoy widespread use. One important reason for this is that the kind of users who stand to benefit most from parallel processing tend to have large legacy systems running on serial machines. Re-writing this legacy code can represent an enormous cost.

Software re-engineering, the re-writing of code in a different form while retaining its functionality, represents a significant investment, as demonstrated by the existence of re-engineering companies the sole service of whom is to provide Year 2000 solutions[Piercom]. The most successful re-engineering companies are those that have developed tools that automate, or at the very least, semi-automate, the re-engineering process. In general, the greater the level of automation, the greater the success rate and thus, the less testing required.

Due to the difficulties associated with re-writing existing serial code, many organizations are not in a position to take advantage of these attractive new architectures. Many organizations have neither the resources nor expertise required to produce parallel code, and often, those that do, are faced with the problem that the quality of the code is directly related to the expertise of the programmer involved.

There are currently no automatic parallelization tools available. Parallel compilers such as HPF, KAP Fortran etc. can generate parallel code, and, in some cases, (KAP Fortran) identify standard simple transformations, they were designed to take advantage of code that was written with the intention of being executed in parallel, rather than to convert serial code.

Difficulties with the production of good parallel code are not restricted to re-writing, however. The generation of parallel code is an arduous task that requires a substantial mind-shift and no small amount of training, particularly if the code is to be optimized. Persons or institutions wishing to produce parallel code would stand to benefit from a tool that would allow them to develop their code in a traditional manner, and subsequently convert it to parallel code. Of course, programmers who take this route would, by neccesity, demand proof that the newly converted code is equivalent to their original code.

We have developed a software re-engineering tool, Paragen, that adheres to the above demand, to the extent that both re-engineering and testing are fully automated. We have found that GP has proved particularly suitable for the generation of parallel code, because it eagerly embraces the maze of transformations required for re-engineering. Furthermore, the often lateral approach required for parallel program design, while an athema to many programmers raised on imperative mind-set, is tailor made for the bottom up approach GP takes.

2.2 Parallel Problems

Current techniques for auto-parallelization rely heavily on data dependency analysis techniques. This consists of analyzing the statements of a program to determine if there is any data dependency between them. If there is no chain of dependence between two statements then they can execute in parallel. For example, to analyze whether two statements S1 and S2 are independent then the set of used variables S1.U and S2.U, and the set of modified variables S1.M and S2.M must be determined. Then, if

$$S1.M \cap S2.U = \epsilon$$

and

$$S1.U \cap S2.M = \epsilon$$

and

$$S1.M \cap S2.M = \epsilon$$

then statements S1 and S2 are independent[Braunl, 1993]. These data dependencies are known as flow dependencies, anti-dependencies and output dependencies respectively. Note that it is possible for $S1.U \cap S2.U \neq \epsilon$ to hold, but this is reflective of the case where both instructions read the same variable, and as neither modifies it, there is no dependency.

With current auto-parallelization techniques these dependencies must be determined before the correct transformation can be carried out. With Paragen, however, these dependencies can be automatically determined, and subsequently punished, by the fitness function.

2.2.1 Problems with Data Dependency Analysis

Auto-parallelization techniques that rely on data dependency analysis as outlined above have limitations due to both the complexity of discovering which data dependency rules can be used. Further limitations are caused by the difficulty associated with the subsequent determination of the order in which to apply those transformations [Lewis, 1992]. In general, if analysis shows that n transformations can be applied to a program, $n!$ different programs can result, depending on the order in which the transformations are applied. Finding the most suitable order of application is, as yet, an unsolved problem.

This problem, however, is particularly suitable for GP, as it can be used to find at least a near optimal order for these transformations. Moreover, not only can GP discover the order, it can also be used to determine which transformations may be legally applied.

Generally, when parallelizing a program, transformations are performed according to a set of rules, of the form

$$SEQ(A, B) = PAR(A, B)$$

if all the dependency rules from above hold. These rules are associative, so

$$SEQ(A, B, C) = SEQ(A, SEQ(B, C))$$

Clearly, if there are no dependencies between the instructions B and C, but if there were some dependency between A and B, then one could say

$$SEQ(B, C) = PAR(B, C)$$

By substitution we get

$$SEQ(A, B, C) = SEQ(A, PAR(B, C))$$

There are two main difficulties associated with data dependency analysis, the identification of which transformation rules can be applied legally, and the order in which to apply them[Lewis, 1992]. If a system could discover the rules and the order of application, it would not only be able to parallelize a program, but also record exactly how the program was parallelized. Proof of equivalence of such a program would then be a simple matter, as the rules prescribe which statements can be analyzed for dependency.

Paragen significantly reduces the complexities associated with data dependency analysis by utilizing the power of Genetic Programming to direct the programmer to areas of the program that are most likely to benefit from analysis.

2.3   Genetic Structure

Unlike most applications employing GP, Paragen doesn't evolve programs, rather it evolves sequences of *transformations*. The system can be viewed as an *embryonic* one, in that one starts with a serial program, and progressive application of the transformations modify it, until eventually the system produces a parallel version of the program. It is only after this embryonic stage that an individual is tested.

All the transformations employed are standard, and syntax preserving with one caveat; that is, that the area of the program which a transformation affects does not contain any data dependencies. If a transformation violates that condition while being applied it may change the semantics, and any transformation that runs this risk causes an individual's fitness to be reduced.

When calculating an individual's fitness, all the transformations are examined to test if they have caused any dependency clashes. The speed of the program produced by an individual is also calculated, which is simply the number of time-steps it takes to run the program.

The first class of transformation are designed to cater for blocks of sequential code, and are based on standard Occam-like transformation rules. These are rules of the form

$$SEQ(A\,B) = PAR(A\,B)$$

which state that two instructions, A and B, can be executed in parallel if there are no dependencies between them.

However, by far the greatest parallelism can be extracted from loops, as it tends to be within these that the largest amount of processing is carried out. Again, there are a large amount of standard transformations, such as loop skewing, fusion etc.

To reflect the dual nature of the transformations, individuals must be capable of employing both, and applying the appropriate type depending on the nature of the code encountered in the embryonic stage. Each type of transformation is stored separately, the *atom* type, which affect single instructions, are manipulated by standard tree structures in a similar fashion to standard GP. The second type of transformation, the *loop* type are stored in a linear genome.

The reason for the different type of representation can be seen from the example below. An individual is evaluated in "atom mode", that is, the tree is traversed in the normal manner, with the transformations being applied to the serial program. However, if a loop structure is encountered, the system enters "loop mode" and a transformation is instead read from the linear part of the genome, which is then applied. After this, the system returns to atom mode and applies the next available transformation to the code within the loops, thus, not only is it possible to parallelize the loop itself, but also the code contained within the loop.

Separate genomes are required because the loop transformations may only be applied to loops, and a linear genome holds these transformations as all that is required is a sequential list to determine the order in which the transformations should be applied. However, due to the nature of some of the loop transformations which give the property that several transformations may be applied to the same loop (or group of loops) the genome is divided into several sections, each containing a number of possible transformations for each loop.

To permit the system to change seamlessly between the two modes, we view the entire program as atoms. Ordinary instructions are atoms in the normal sense, in that they cannot be broken down further, while loops are known as *Meta-loop* atoms, which consist of one or more adjacent loops.

2.3.1 Atom Mode

Unlike all other implementations of GP, individuals in Paragen are evaluated in normal order[Peyton-Jones, 1992], that is, individuals are evaluated from the outermost level. Usually, GP systems employ applicative order, where individuals are evaluated from the inside out, or, in terms of trees, from the bottom up.

Normal order, also known as *lazy evaluation* or *call by need*, attempts to delay the evaluation of arguments to a function by evaluating the function before the arguments. The arguments are evaluated only if strictly necessary.

Consider the rather unlikely situation

$$(\lambda x.\ 1) < bomb >$$

An applicative order GP will first evaluate the argument, i.e. $< bomb >$. In the case where $< bomb >$ leads to a non-terminating state, e.g. infinite recursion, disaster will follow. However, normal order will not evaluate $< bomb >$ until it is needed, and elegantly avoids any catastrophe because the expression does not examine its argument, instead returning the value 1, regardless of what it is called with.

Consider the expression (using lambda calculus for clarity)

$$(\lambda\ xy.(+\ 3(*\ x\ x)))(+\ 4\ 5)(*\ 3\ 2)$$

This situation is similar to an expressions $(+\ 4\ 5)$ and $(*\ 3\ 2)$ being passed to an ADF $(\lambda(xy)...)$. Using applicative order as is the norm for GP, the following execution sequence results:

$$(\lambda \; xy.(+ \; 3(* \; x \; x)))9 \; (* \; 3 \; 2)$$

$$(\lambda \; xy.(+ \; 3(* \; x \; x)))9 \; 6$$

$$(+ \; 3 \; (* \; 9 \; 9))$$

$$(+ \; 3 \; 81)$$

Notice how the $(*3 \; 2)$ is evaluated regardless of the fact that the lambda expression doesn't actually need it. The sequence would be quite different for normal order:

$$(\lambda \; xy.(+ \; 3 \; (* \; x \; x)))(+ \; 4 \; 5)(* \; 3 \; 2)$$

$$(+ \; 3(* \; (+ \; 4 \; 5)(+ \; 4 \; 5)))$$

The next step would be to apply the outer $+$, but this is a strict function which must have both of its arguments evaluated, so instead the $*$ operator is applied. Again, this is a strict function, so only now are the two $(+ \; 4 \; 5)$ evaluated.

In this case $(+ \; 4 \; 5)$ is evaluated twice, while $(* \; 3 \; 2)$ is not evaluated because it is not needed. Normal order is often used to reduce the number of evaluations, but, as this example demonstrates, is not always successful because the number of evaluations is zero *or more*. Paragen is not concerned with reducing evaluations, rather it exploits the order in which operators are applied when employing normal order.

The simplest transformations in Paragen perform a transformation on the current state of the program, and then execute their argument which is passed the modified state of the program. These functions are described further on.

However, there are other instructions, namely P50 and S50, which take two arguments. These functions divide the program into two separate parts, and apply one argument to each half. Consider the individual in figure 2.1, the P50 divides the program segment P into two parts P' and P''. The lower levels of the tree, A and B are applied to P' and P'' respectively, *after* their parent node has been applied.

These transformations effectively fork the execution of an individual, permitting it to reflect the parallel nature of the program it is modifying.

Each transformation in atom mode operates on the current *program segment*. Typically, a transformation schedules one or more atoms relative to the rest of the program segment, before passing the rest of the segment onto the next transformation(s). The segments get

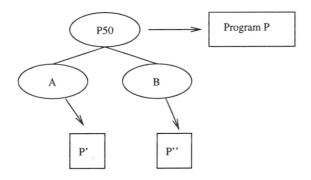

Figure 2.1
An example of normal order evaluation in Paragen. The transformation P50 is applied to all the program, but A and B are only applied to P' and P'' respectively.

increasingly smaller until there are either no atoms left, or all the transformations for a particular segment are exhausted.

The crucial result of using Normal order is that the tree structure of individuals indicates which transformations should be applied to various parts of a program, and, moreover, chains of transformations can be built up, performing all manner of modifications to a program.

2.3.2   Atom Mode Transformations.

All atom mode transformations operate in the same manner. Before any application, the systems checks to see if the first atom in the current program segment is a meta-loop atom. If so, the system enters loop mode, otherwise the transformation is applied to the segment.

There are four categories of atom mode specific transformations defined:

1. *Pxx/Sxx*,

2. *Fxxx/Lxxx*,

3. *SHIFT*,

4. *NULL/PARNULL*.

2.3.2.1   P and S
The Pxx/Sxx transformations are the most general of the transformations. These break the current program segment into two new segments, by putting a certain number of the atoms into each segment. The proportion of atoms that go into each segment is determined by the 'xx' part, which is a percentage. Table 2.1 and figure 2.2 show an example of P20 being applied to [ABCDE].

Table 2.1
The operation of the P20 transformation

Operation	Input chain	Output
P20	[ABCDE]	[A]
		[BCDE]

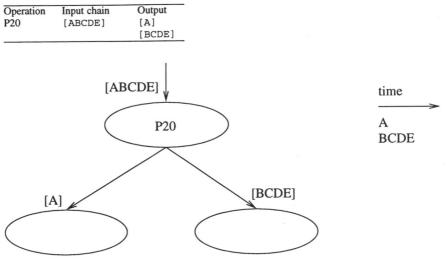

Figure 2.2
A fork of execution caused by the application of the P20 transformation.

The [A] and [BCDE] will be executed in parallel and [A] will be passed on to the left subtree and [BCDE] to the right subtree. When called, the fitness function will determine if there is a data dependency between [A] and [BCDE]. If there is no data dependency between the sequences, then both will be executed in parallel. Otherwise, the information will be used by the fitness function as described later on. Notice that there are now two program segments, one corresponding to each of the two groups of atoms generated by the transformation.

Consider the 'Sxx' operator, with xx=60. This causes the two new segments to be executed in sequence, an operation which preserves their original order. However, this can be of use if some parallelism can be extracted from a smaller segment.

Again, the transformation generates two program segments, each of which can have more transformations applied to them. However, the order specified by the first transformation will always be adhered to, because all scheduling of atoms is done relative to other atoms

Table 2.2
The operation of the S60 transformation

Operation	Input section (program)	Output (result)
S60	[ABCDE]	[ABC] [DE]

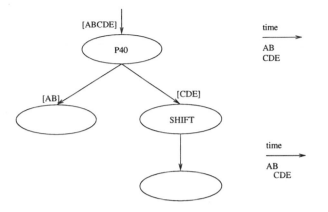

Figure 2.3
The application of SHIFT operator to a program segment, the execution of the entire segment is delayed by one
time-step.

in the current program segment.

2.3.2.2   F and L

These classes can be looked upon as extreme cases of the Pxx/Sxx transformations. The
difference in this case is that only a single (either First or Last) instruction is scheduled,
which is quite helpful when the system needs to trim down a program segment. A consequence of there only being a single instruction scheduled is an increase in the fineness of
the granularity of the code.

Each class has two transformations, namely FPAR/LPAR and FSEQ/LSEQ, all of which
remove one statement from the current program segment and passes the remainder of the
segment onto the next transformation.

The *F* transformations remove the first atom, executing the remainder in either parallel
or in sequence, while the *L* transformations remove the final atom. Again, this atom is
either executed in parallel or in sequence, depending on the nature of the transformation.

2.3.2.3   SHIFT

SHIFT is a simple transformation which doesn't alter the order of a program segment, but
delays the execution of all the atoms it contains by one time step.

If there are other atoms to be executed (in sequence) after the segment shifted, then they
too, are shifted, otherwise a data dependency clash could be introduced, which would be
very difficult to detect.

Shift is necessary as it helps other transformations fine tune their effects. For example, if
P40 was the only operator, and there is a data dependency between A and C, the individual

would be penalized when evaluating the fitness, because P40 states that A and C are to be executed in the same time.

However, if the right branch of P40 contains a SHIFT operator as in figure 2.3 , then the execution of the [CDE] sequence is delayed with one time step. This means C will start to be executed once A is finished. The result is equivalent to:

$$SEQ([A],PAR([B],[CDE])) \qquad (2.1)$$

With this addition, the individual will not be penalized anymore for the A-C data dependency, because A will be executed before C.

2.3.2.4 NULL/PARNULL

The final class of transformations do not take any arguments, and are used to terminate a tree. **NULL** causes all remaining instructions in the current program segment to be executed in their original, sequential order, while **PARNULL** causes any remaining instructions to be executed in parallel.

NULL and PARNULL always appear on the leaves of an individual as they do not take any arguments.

2.3.3 Atom Mode Fitness

The most important factor to be considered for the fitness function is the *correctness of the program*. Clearly, Paragen would quite happily generate massively parallel programs which could run in times as quick as one time step at the cost of correctness.

Only transformations which alter the order of atoms, i.e. FPAR, LPAR, Pxx, need be tested, as it is in these cases that dependency clashes may appear.

Each (parallel) transformation rule is responsible for ensuring that the modifications it makes to the program do not violate any data dependencies. Starting with the most deeply nested rule, each performs any necessary checking on the current program segment. After each is finished checking, it recursively passes the current segment back to the previous rule. Below are detailed algorithms for the checking required by some of the parallel transformations. In all cases, A represents the instruction(s) affected by the operations, and B the instructions remaining in the program segment. We denote the original time step of execution(T_i) of instruction n of group A as A_{ni} and the new time step as A_{nj}. In some cases there will only be one instruction in group A, but for consistency the same notation will be used throughout.

2.3.3.1 Directed Analysis for FPAR

FPAR takes the statement that was originally first in the segment and executes it in parallel with the segment (after the segment has been modified by zero or more subsequent operations). A possible data dependency violation can occur if the first statement is being executed at the same time step as a statement that must occur after it. This is detected by testing all possibilities of a violation:

For all instructions B_i in B

If $A_{0j} == B_{nj}$

check A_0 and B_i for dependency.

If there is a dependency, the individual is punished, but the checking continues.

2.3.3.2 Directed Analysis for LPAR

LPAR takes the statement that was originally last in the segment and executes it in parallel with the segment, again, the remainder of the segment may be modified. There is far more scope of dependency violation in this case, as LPAR is effectively bringing the execution time of the statement forward. In this case, all other statements are examined, as they will all be executed either at the same time or after the statement that was moved.

2.3.3.3 Directed Analysis for Pxx

Pxx divides a segment in two, and executes the result of each segment in parallel. In this case, the execution time setup of several statements are effectively changed, so this operation requires the most analysis. Similar to FPAR above, each statement in the *group* A, is compared with each statement in the group B. Any change in the order of execution of two statements is then examined for dependency violations.

For each statement x in group A

For each statement y in group B

If $((A_{xi} < B_{xi}) \&\& (A_{xj} >= B_{xj}))$

Check

2.3.3.4 Directed Analysis

As can be seen from the above sections, the directed analysis section requires information about when all the instructions are going to be executed. However, when evaluating an individual in normal order, this information isn't yet available, because subsequent transformations are likely to change some of the execution times.

To avoid any incorrect information being passed to the analysis stage, we wait until the entire individual has been evaluated, and then evaluate it a second time, this evaluation uses bottom up, applicative order as normally employed in Genetic Programming.

The bottom up approach of the second evaluation permits us to examine the simplest transformations (i.e. those involving the fewest instructions) first, and pass any information about dependency clashes back up the tree. An example of this is given in section 2.4.

2.3.4 Loop Mode

Paragen remains in atom mode until it encounters a program segment which starts with a meta-loop, whereupon it switches into loop mode. While in loop mode, Paragen reads from the linear genome, which contains one gene for each loop encountered while parsing the original program. Each gene is made up of one or more loop transformations, all of which are applied to the meta-loop.

It is important to have a number of transformations for each meta-loop, as some transformations, e.g. Loop Fusion in section 2.3.4.1 have certain requirements that must be fulfilled before they can be applied. In order to fulfill these requirements it is often necessary to "massage" other loops around, or to ensure that the loops contained within the meta-loop are already parallel.

Loop optimization is crucial for auto-parallelization as the greatest amount of processing tends to be executed within these structures. The body of loops are subject to the same dependencies as other code, but also suffer from the possibility of *cross-iteration* dependencies. These are dependencies which cross over two or more iterations:

```
a[i]=x;
y=a[i-1];
```

Fortunately, there are all manner of modifications and alterations which can be carried out on loops to encourage greater parallelism. We have identified a number of these from which we have generated transformations which are made available to Paragen. Below are a representative sample of some of the more interesting ones.

2.3.4.1 Loop Fusion
Loop Fusion is a loop specific transformation which selectively merges two loops into a single loop [Lewis, 1992]. We use the term "selectively" because two requirements must be filled before loop fusion can be applied, they are that both loops must be already parallelized, and that both loops must contain the same number of iterations.

Consider the following loops:

```
PAR-FOR statement1; END
PAR-FOR statement2; END
```

After applying the Loop fusion operator, the result is:

```
PAR-FOR statement1; statement2; END
```

However, it is relatively unusual for two consecutive loops in a program to meet the two above criteria. If either or both of the loops is not already parallel, Paragen will attempt to parallelize them first. A success in this endeavor will permit the transformation to continue.

Another situation is both loops are of the same type, but the iteration domains are different. There are two ways to approach this:

- if one number of iterations is multiple of the other number, e.g.

```
PAR-FOR i=1 TO 100 statement1; END
PAR-FOR i=1 TO  10 statement2; END
```

then there are several options:

- generate an inner loop

```
PAR-FOR j=1 TO 10
  PAR-FOR k=1 TO 10 statement1(k+10*j); END
  statement2(j);
END
```

- conditioning statement 2 execution within an *if*

```
PAR-FOR j=1 TO 100 statement1;
  IF((j MOD 10)==0)
    //j  is divisible by 10
  statement2(j/10);
END
```

- unrolling the bigger loop

```
PAR-FOR j=1 TO 10
  statement1(0+10*j);   statement1(1+10*j);
  statement1(2+10*j);   statement1(3+10*j);
  statement1(4+10*j);   statement1(5+10*j);
  statement1(6+10*j);   statement1(7+10*j);
  statement1(8+10*j);   statement1(9+10*j);
  statement2(j);
END
```

Notice that the instructions that are created as a result of the loop being unrolled can be further parallelized.

- for un-normalized loops (and indefinite number of iterations)

```
PAR-FOR i=alpha TO beta statement1; END
PAR-FOR i=gamma TO delta statement2; END
```

the solution is:

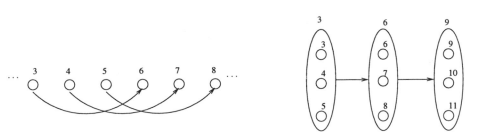

Figure 2.4
The operation of the Shrink transformation. Instructions between the cross-iteration dependencies are grouped together, ensuring that communication only takes place after all instructions in a group are executed.

```
lim1=MAX(alpha,gamma)
lim2=MIN(beta,delta)
PAR-FOR i=alpha TO lim1 statement1; END
PAR-FOR i=gamma TO lim1 statement2; END
PAR-FOR i=lim1 TO lim2 statement2; END
PAR-FOR i=lim2 TO beta statement2; END
PAR-FOR i=lim2 TO delta statement2; END
```

Notice that the two initial loops can be normalized in order to have the same start index or the same end index. Also, note that from the previous statement, one of the first two loops will not be executed. If *lim1 = alpha* then the first loop will not be executed. Otherwise the second loop will not be executed. The same reasoning is applied for the last two loops. In the end, there will be maximum of three loops, and two if we can shift the domain for one of them.

This transformation is quite representative of some of the more elaborate loop transformations in Paragen's repertoire, in that it relies on other transformations to be applied first. Several of Paragen's transformations behave in this way, and it is for this reason that each meta-loop can have several transformations applied to it.

2.3.4.2 Loop Shrinking
Loop Shrinking is a transformation for parallelizing interlaced cross-iteration data dependency loops.

When all dependences in a cycle are flow dependent, there are no direct transformations for obtaining a good result. However, depending on the distance of each dependence, parts of the loops can be parallelized using loop shrinking [Lewis, 1992].

Figure 2.4 presents the input and the result after applying the shrinking operator.

Given the source:

Table 2.3
The view of the program at the start of the evaluation of an individual.

Instruction No.	1	2	3	4-12	13	14-18	19	20
Atom Name	A	B	C	D	E	F	G	H
Pseudo timestep	0	1	2	3	4	5	6	7

```
FOR i=4 TO n  a[i]=a[i-3]+x[i]; END
```

then the operator transforms it in:

```
FOR i=4 TO n STEP 3
  PAR-FOR j=i TO i+2 a[j]=a[j-3]+x[j]; END
END
```

Note that, at the end, the inner loop is already parallelized, not "waiting to be parallelized". The drawback of this operator is that if there is no possible parallelization, then the individual will be penalized. If the loop is already parallel, it will still try to generate a nested loop based on the parallel source, and the individual will not be penalized.

2.4   Example Individual

We now examine an the execution of an example individual taken from a population. The code we are concerned with is illustrated in figure 2.5, and consists of twenty lines of code, containing four loops.

Notice how the loops are divided into two groups, one of three loops and the other containing two (nested) loops. This division is governed by the adjacency of the loops, i.e. the loops containing instructions 4 - 12 are contiguous, and are thus treated as a single meta-loop. This gives eight distinct sections to this program, namely, instructions 1,2,3,4-12, 13, 14-18, 19 and 20.

Furthermore, as we are currently concerned with the execution of these instructions *relative* to each other, we give each statement a *pseudo-timestep*. Clearly, this abstraction will have to be addressed by a scheduler after the experiment if the code is to be optimized, but it is necessary at this stage to ensure that the correct data dependency analysis is performed.

The individual is described in figure 2.4, and consists of a tree with seven nodes. Three of these are atom transformations, while the remaining four are the NULL transformation, used to terminate atom mode.

Before a Paragen run, the program is parsed to extract certain information, namely the set of variables modified and used (read) by each statement. Thus, a table similar to figure 8 is constructed.

This table will subsequently be used to test the transformations for any data dependency clashes. As stated earlier, the individual is executed in normal order, so the first transformation to be applied is the S63, which is applied to the entire program. The only test

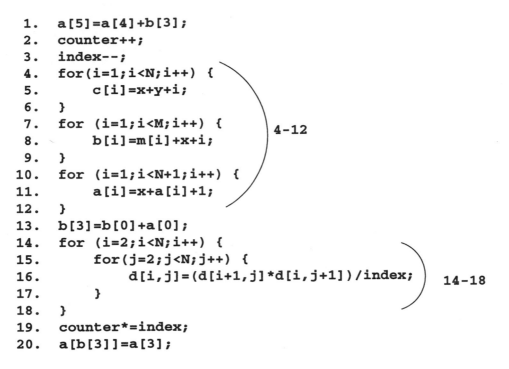

```
 1.   a[5]=a[4]+b[3];
 2.   counter++;
 3.   index--;
 4.   for(i=1;i<N;i++) {
 5.        c[i]=x+y+i;
 6.   }
 7.   for (i=1;i<M;i++) {            4-12
 8.        b[i]=m[i]+x+i;
 9.   }
10.   for (i=1;i<N+1;i++) {
11.        a[i]=x+a[i]+1;
12.   }
13.   b[3]=b[0]+a[0];
14.   for (i=2;i<N;i++) {
15.        for(j=2;j<N;j++) {
16.             d[i,j]=(d[i+1,j]*d[i,j+1])/index;   14-18
17.        }
18.   }
19.   counter*=index;
20.   a[b[3]]=a[3];
```

Figure 2.5
Serial code to be modified, notice how adjacent loops are treated as a single metaloop atom.

carried out at this stage is to see if the first block of code is a loop or atom. In this case, it is an atom, so the transformation can successfully be applied. S63 states that the first 63% of instructions must be executed before the remaining 37%. Clearly, this is an order preserving transformation which will not require any dependency checking. Execution of the individual is now forked, with instructions A-E being passed to the left hand subtree, while instructions F-H are catered for by the right subtree. Regardless of what transformations are subsequently applied, the first five groups will always execute before the remaining three.

The next transformation is P60, which executes the first 60% of its group of instructions in parallel with the remaining 40%, giving a situation as in figure 2.9. In this case, there are two major changes to the program. The group [D E] is now being executed at time step 0, while the group [F G H] is to be executed at time step 3, which is still after the original [A B C D E F] group. In a similar manner to S63, the first half of the group is sent to the left transformation, while the second goes to the right hand one.

The left hand subtree contains the NULL transformation, which merely examines the

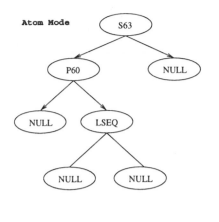

Loop Mode | SWAP | FUSE | SKIP | PAR | PAR | | SKEW | SKIP | SKIP | SKIP | SKIP | | RWND | PAR | PAR | ... |

Figure 2.6
An example individual from Paragen. The familiar tree structure is used for processing atomic instructions, while there is also a set of linear genes, one for each metaloop.

	Modified	Used
1.	a	a
2.	counter	counter
3.	index	index
4-12.	a, b	m, x, a, y
13	b	b, a
15-18.	c	c, index
19.	counter	counter, index
20.	a	b, a

Figure 2.7
The sets of used and modified variables, notice how the loops are treated as compound statements.

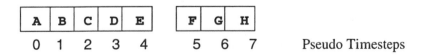

Pseudo Timesteps

Figure 2.8
The state of the program after applying the S63 transformation.

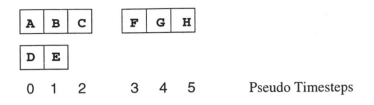

Pseudo Timesteps

Figure 2.9
The state of the program after applying the P60 transformation.

group to test if it begins with a loop. In this case it doesn't, so there will be no further transformations applied to [A B C]. The right hand LSEQ transformation, however, does encounter a loop, and causes Paragen to enter loop mode.

Once Paragen exits loop mode, LSEQ is applied to that program segment, and causes the final atom to be executed after the meta-loop atom.

2.4.1 Loop Mode

Once into loop mode, Paragen is only concerned with the first instruction in the current segment, which will always be a meta-loop. The meta-loop is expanded, in this case into three separate loops, which we denote X, Y and Z:

```
X :for  (i=1;i<N;i++)
        { c[i]=x+y+i; }
Y: for  (i=1;i<M;i++)
        { b[i]=m[i]+x+i; }
Z: for  (i=1;i<N+1;i++)
        { a[i]=x+a[i]+1;  }
```

The first (loop-specific) transformation to be applied to this new [X Y Z] segment is SWAP, which inverts the first two loops, yielding [Y X Z]. The second transformation is FUSE which, as described in section 4.4.1 joins the common parts of X and Z together, giving a program segment which we can describe as [Y XZ z'], where z' is the part of the Z loop which is exceeds the index of the loop in X.

Notice that the loop transformations do not reduce the size of the program segment. Rather they are progressively applied to the loops within the segment. Thus, if there are more transformations left after we have gone through all the loops, we wrap the program segment and continue, which means that each loop can have one or more transformations applied to it. In this case, however, there is a new loop, z', to which the next transformation, SKIP, is applied. SKIP is analogous to the NULL transformation for atom mode, and does not modify a loop.

Since the loops in the segment are exhausted, we wrap it, and continue with the application of our transformations, starting with Y. This transformation is PAR which simply converts the loop into a PAR-FOR, which maps the loop across up to the index number of processors. The final transformation is also a PAR-FOR, and is applied to the newly created XZ loop. At this stage, the transformations are exhausted, so the system reverts to atom mode.

2.4.2 Resumption of Atom Mode

When all the transformations are exhausted, Paragen returns to atom mode. As the next transformation is a NULL, there is no more to be done with this part of the tree, so execution continues with the right hand side of the tree. Eventually, the program below is generated.

```
PAR
  BEGIN
    a[5]=a[4]+b[3];
    counter++;
    index--;
  END
  BEGIN
    PAR-FOR (i=1;i<M;i++) {
        b[i]=m[i]+x+i;}
    PAR-FOR (i=1;i<N;i++) {
        c[i]=x+y+i;
        a[i]=x+a[i]+1; }
    for (i=N;i<N+1;i++) {
        a[i]=x+a[i]+1;}
    b[3]=b[0]+a[0];
  END
END-PAR
PAR-FOR (i=2;i<N;i++) {
  for (j=i+2;j<=i+N-1;j++) {
    d[i,j-1]=(d[i+1,j-i]*d[i,j-i])/index; }
    }
counter*=index;
a[b[3]]=a[3];
```

Testing the speed of this program is a trivial task, however, testing the correctness of the program is another matter, and requires analysis of all the transformations which modified the order of the atoms of the program. Notice that in this particular example, there still exist some areas in which parallelism can be extracted, most notably the first three statements, which are all independent of each other.

2.4.3   Directed Data Dependency Analysis

The final step in Paragen is to determine the number (if any) of data dependency clashes in the parallel program. To do this, the individual is evaluated a second time, this time in the traditional GP manner, from the bottom up. Starting with the most deeply nested transformation, the program segments associated with each of the leaves is examined for possible clashes, checked, and the result passed back up the tree.

The program segment associated with the deepest transformation, i.e. the NULL on the left of LSEQ, is first examined. This consists of just the atom D, a metaloop atom, which may have been subject to some transformation. However, all the system was forced into loop mode by the LSEQ transformation, and not the NULL, so the analysis is delayed until that node in the tree is reached.

After this test, the system examines the right hand side of the LSEQ. This program segment contains a single atom, which is not a loop, and thus requires no further analysis. LSEQ itself is an order preserving transformation, so the atoms D and E can be reassembled without further checking.

Once this program segment ([D E]) exists again, it is checked to see if it begins with a meta-loop, which it does. This causes the metaloop gene to be called a second time, and on this occasion it checks for any dependency clashes that may have occurred. This checking is relatively straightforward, as all the transformations are standard, taken in the most part from sources such as [Burns, 1988] and [Lewis, 1992]. Furthermore, once a particular transformation has been applied to a particular loop, the question of whether or not any dependency clashes have been introduced can be answered immediately if required by any subsequent individuals.

Working back up the tree, we now examine the leaves of P60 transformation, starting with the left subtree which was applied to [A B C]. When the NULL of P60 is applied to that segment, there was no further transformation, as the first atom, namely A is not a meta-loop.

The right hand side has already been checked, as this was a level deeper. Therefore, we now check the effect of P60 itself, and, as none of the first three atoms employ any variables used by the second two, both segments can successfully be executed in parallel.

Taking another step back up the tree, we encounter S63, another order preserving transformation. In this case, it doesn't matter if the segments it created are dependent, because they don't interfere with each other. However, a check is still made on the NULL in its right hand subtree, to investigate the possibility of the presence of a meta-loop atom.

Investigation reveals that there is indeed a meta-loop atom at the head of that program segment, and so the requisite analysis is performed on that atom. Again, as this is a standard transformation, the analysis is quite straightforward.

2.4.4   Experimental Results

Paragen is currently being tested on benchmark code to get an idea of how well it performs relative to other techniques. So far, the code has always performed at least as well as human experts at extracting parallelism, and always does so much more quickly. Furthermore, to our knowledge there are no other fully automatic parallelization techniques available.

The speed up obtained from code depends on the code itself, and there is no simple rule of thumb for determining the level of parallelization likely to be extracted. Code that contains no dependencies, clearly, can achieve greater than code with heavily dependent instructions. Furthermore, code that contains several loops offers a much greater pay-back than code that is simply made up of atomic instructions.

Systems such as High Performance Fortran etc. are unlikely to extract too much parallelism from most code that was written with sequential execution in mind. If such compilers do detect parallelism, it simply good fortune, as they are designed for programs written specifically for parallel architectures. Paragen, on the other hand, actively seeks out possible transformations, and even takes adjacent instructions into account.

Consider the code below :

```
0 : a=1;
1 : for (int i=0;i<100;i++)
        b[i]=a;
2 : a=10;
3 : for (int i=0;i<100;i++)
        c[i]=a;
4 : for (int i=0;i<200;i++)
        d[i]=a;
5 : a=100;
6 : f=a;
7 : b=a;
```

This yields seven atoms, although at first glance it may appear as though there are eight. This is not the case because items #3 and #4 are a metaloop, and are thus treated as a single item. Paragen was applied to this problem using a population for 1000 for 50 generations, and generated the following *best-of-run* individual:

There are just five atom transformations applied, with two sets of metaloop genes. Two sets were chosen as that is the number of meta-loops in the original program. In this heavily data dependent case, all dependencies are preserved, with only a single pair of atoms being executed in parallel. However, a huge speed up is achieved by virtue of the transformation of the loops. The original program took 405 time-steps to execute, and now takes just six.

Notice for the first loop, the **Replace** transformation creates a parallel loop, while the **Skip** transformation is essentially a blank transformation, and doesn't cause any further modification. With the second metaloop, the loops will be fused if possible. As there are a

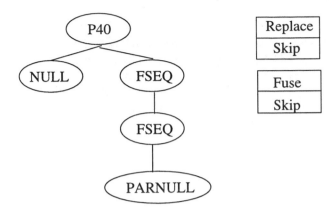

Figure 2.10
Best of run individual that produces the parallel code below. Notice how there is a set of linear genes for each metaloop.

number of ways in which this can be done, Paragen calculates the most useful, and applies that. This set of transformations is again terminated by a **Skip**, as no further modification is required.

The resulting parallel program is as follows:

```
0 : a=1;
1 : par-for (int i=0;i<100;i++)
       b[i]=a;
2 : a=10;
3 : par-for (int i=0;i<100;i++)
       {
       par-for(int j=0;j<2;j++)
         {
         d[i*j]=a;
         }
       d[i]=a;
       }
5 : a=100;
    par-begin
6 : f=a;
7 : b=a;
    par-end
```

As Paragen does not take communication into consideration however, it is unlikely that the program will remain at just six time steps. Another consideration is the number of pro-

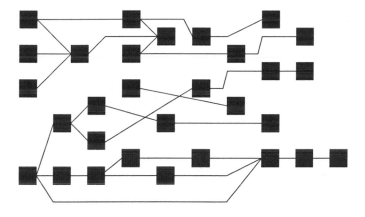

Figure 2.11
A parallel program viewed as a graph. The nodes represent instructions and the edges communication. Unlike many graphs, crossing edges do not cause any difficulties.

cessors available. At its optimal rate, the program is executing 300 instructions in parallel, this means that when it is running on actual hardware, it will run *up to* 300 instructions at the same time, depending on the number of processors available.

2.4.5 Scheduling

One abstraction made at the start of the work was the assumption that all atoms require one time step, which makes it easier for Paragen to schedule atoms relative to one another. However, Paragen does not take into account atoms which require longer execution times, nor does it concern itself with communication costs.

As in the best spirit of computer science, the question of communication is catered for by a separate process. The code produced by Paragen assumes infinite processors, and so must be modified to run on specific machines. This is achieved by drawing a graph of the parallel program, and modifying the layout to reflect the number of processors involved in the runtime execution. Graph layout algorithms such as the Coffman-Graham[Coffman et al, 1972], Branch and Cut Approach[Junger et al, 1997] or Sugiuama[Sugiyama, 1981] can be used to reduce the number of crossings and adjacent, inter-column edges, which represent inter-processor communication. Figure 2.11 shows the sample output of a Paragen run, each node representing an instruction and each edge communication. Essentially, Paragen discovers *when* all instructions should be executed, while not making any comment as to *where* they should go. This must be dictated by the target architecture, taking into consideration both the number of processors and the speed of interprocess communication.

By using simple graph partitioning algorithms[Gerasoulis, 1990] we divide the instructions into tasks, which can then be mapped onto the parallel processors. Ideally, there will be much communication within these tasks, and inter-process communication will be reduced by ensuring that inter-dependent tasks reside on the same processor.

2.5   Conclusion

We have described an automatic software re-engineering tool which uses a modified version of Genetic Programming to evolve sequences of transformations which, when applied to a parallel program, generate a functionally equivalent parallel program.

GP is suitable for a task such as this because when one attempts to understand the logic of a program and then to convert that logic to an equivalent parallel form, the complexity grows enormously as the program increases in size. However, as GP applies its transformations without any understanding of the logic of the program which it is modifying, it scales far more graciously than other methods.

Moreover, while human programmers may have the advantage of being able to take a more holistic view of a program, GP is not only able to spot and exploit any patterns in the code, but also to take advantage of its bottom up approach. By this we mean it can move statements around, swap the location of loops and even join previously transformed loops together, in ways that human programmers are unlikely to think of.

Due to the arbitrary way in which GP cuts up and divides the code, and in particular, the loops, one can make no guarantee as to the readability of the modified code. In general, though, people are no more concerned about this than they are about being able to interpret the object code files from a compiler, so it is not a problem. There may be cases, however, where the end user of the code will want to be able to read it, e.g. if the programmer wished to add some extra, hardware-specific optimizations to the code. If this is strictly necessary, we can direct the loop transformations to insert comments where ever a loop is modified, thus providing an automatically documented piece of code.

Bibliography

Gerasoulis, A. (1990),"Dominant Sequence clustering Heuristic Algorithm for Multiprocessors", Tech Report Rutgers University, NJ.

Burns, A. (1988), *Programming Occam 2*, Prentice-Hall.

Braunl, T. (1993), *Automatic Parallelization and Vectorization, Parallel Programming : An Introduction*, Prentice Hall.

Coffman et al (1972), "Optimal Scheduling for two processor systems", Acta Informatica, 1, 200-213.

Davis, L.V. (1991), *Handbook of Genetic Algorithms*, Van Nostrand Reinhold.

Geist, G (1993), "PVM 3 Beyond Network Computing," in *Lecture Notes in Computer Science 734, 2nd Int. Conf. of the Austrian Center for Parallel Computation* pp. 194-203, Gmunden, Austria : Springer Verlag.

Gelerneter, D. (1985), "Parallel Programming in Linda", Technical Report 359, Yale University Department of Computer Science

Junger, M. and Mutzel, P.(1997) "2-layer straightline crossing minimisation : Performance of exact and heuristic algorithms" in *Journal of Graph Algorithms and Applications*, 1, 11-25.

Lewis, T. (1992), *Introduction to Parallel Computing*, Prentice Hall.

Piercom Ltd. http://www.piercom.ie

Peyton-Jones, S. (1992), *Functional Programming Languages*, Prentice-Hall.

Ryan, C. and Walsh, P. (1997), "The Evolution of Provable Parallel Programs". In *Genetic Programming 1997*, J. Koza et al (Eds.) pp295-302, Stanford, CA, USA : MIT Press.

Ryan, C. and Walsh, P. (1996), "Paragen: A novel technique of the Autoparallelization of Sequential Programs using GP". In *Genetic Programming 1996*, J. Koza et al (Eds.) pp197-204, Stanford, CA, USA : MIT Press.

Ryan, C. and Walsh, P. (1995): "Automatic conversion of programs from serial to parallel using genetic programming", in *Proceedings of Parallel Computing*, V Neagoe et al(Eds.), Gent, Belgium:Springer-Verlag.

Sugiyama, K. et al. (1981), "Methods for visual understanding of hierarchical system structures," IEEE Transactions on Systems, Man and Cybernetics, 11(2).

3 CAD Surface Reconstruction from Digitized 3D Point Data with a Genetic Programming/Evolution Strategy Hybrid

Robert E. Keller, Wolfgang Banzhaf, Jörn Mehnen and Klaus Weinert

Surface reconstruction is a hard key problem in the industrial core domain of computer-aided design (CAD) applications. A workpiece must be represented in some standard CAD object description format such that its representation can be efficiently used in a CAD process like redesign. To that end, a digitizing process represents the object surface as a weakly-structured discrete and digitized set of 3D points. Surface reconstruction attempts to transform this representation into an efficient CAD representation. Certain classic approaches produce inefficient reconstructions of surface areas that do not correspond to construction logic. Here, a new reconstruction principle along with empiric results is presented which yields logical and efficient representations. This principle is implemented as a Genetic-Programming/Evolution-Strategy-based software system.

3.1 Introduction

Genetic programming (GP) [Banzhaf et al., 1998] is an evolutionary search process that generates structures of arbitrary shape and size. The most prominent special case of such a structure is the representation of an algorithm, for instance, as a computer program in a common language like C. The present contribution, however, focuses on GP as an apt tool for the evolution of representations of three-dimensional objects.

The aim of advanced **surface reconstruction (SR)** is the transformation of a physical object into a data representation that meets the high technological requirements of a construction engineer. Such a physical object may be a hand-modeled prototype of a machine part to be produced, and the corresponding data representation may be a computer-aided design (CAD) 3D representation. As an essential part of the associated production process, the engineer modifies this representation with a CAD system so that the resulting representation can be used to produce the corresponding physical object. A CAD system is typically used in mechanical engineering where a physical object, like a prototype of a forging die, often does not have a CAD representation. Especially, the physical object often lacks an exact geometrical representation as a CAD object. This is either because a corresponding CAD data base does not exist, or because the physical object has been changed manually in the course of the production process.

In order to obtain a CAD object, optical or tactile digitizing hardware can be used. For instance, a tactile sensor may systematically scan the physical object's surface. For a practically relevant physical object, a digitizing process generates several megabytes of weakly-structured discrete 3D point data at least. "Weakly-structured" means the 3D point data set does not allow for a trivial recognition of the represented physical object by an automated process.

Modern rapid-prototyping production processes, like high-speed cutting or stereotype lithography, accept surface- or volume-oriented CAD objects and manufacture the corresponding physical object. A surface-oriented CAD object is constructed by combining

CAD surfaces, like a saddle surface, while a volume-oriented object is constructed by combining CAD volumes, like a sphere. Accordingly, there are surface- or volume-oriented CAD systems and hybrid systems used by a construction engineer for operating on such CAD objects. Many CAD objects mainly consist of primitive CAD objects like spheres, cylinders, cuboids or tori. Thus, a CAD system provides corresponding object libraries and supports the manipulation of such objects.

A prominent class of volume-oriented CAD systems employs **constructive solid geometry (CSG)**. The CSG principle is to construct complex CAD objects from primitive objects. The resulting CSG objects represent physical, that is solid, objects. Curved surfaces, like certain parts of car bodies, are typically represented by triangulations, that is a surface approximation by plane triangles. Another well-known representation uses non-uniform rational B-splines (NURBS), which are especially apt for the construction of a smooth curved surface by smoothly joining curved surfaces [Piegl and Tiller, 1997]. NURBS have become the *de facto* standard for smooth-surface representations in the CAD world. They are a powerful tool for geometric design tasks, because they are fast to calculate, numerically stable and allow a rather intuitive use.

Surface reconstruction, that is the automatic construction of a CAD object from data, is a hard and industrially relevant problem. The task being considered in this chapter is the reconstruction from a given 3D point data set. The problem core is that, in $\mathbb{R}^3$, any given set represents infinitely many different *geometrical* surfaces, that is those and only those surfaces that have the set in common. However, the data set represents only one *physical* surface, which is the surface of that physical object from which a digitizing process generated the data set.

Thus, a surface-reconstruction system must reconstruct a CAD object that approximates the physical object. This corresponds to the task of recognizing a physical object in a 3D point set, which is a special case of pattern recognition. The system must perform this task such that a construction engineer can start working with the resulting CAD object without being forced to introduce an expensive manual modification to the representation. Pattern recognition problems are classically covered by artificial intelligence and machine learning. Here, a new and evolutionary approach using a genetic programming/evolution strategy (ES) hybrid is used to reconstruct a CSG object from a non-empty discrete 3D point data set. The approach is represented as the software system SURREAL (Surface Reconstruction by Evolutionary Algorithms).

3.2 Classic context

3.2.1 Digitizing and preprocessing

A digitizing process generates a point-data set, which can be imagined as a point cloud, from a physical-object surface for use by a CAD system. Usually, such a cloud has too many points and is too weakly topologically structured for efficient handling by a CAD system. Thus, preprocessing, like data reduction by chordal deviation [Friedhoff, 1996], depth-pass filtering [Müller and Mencl, 1997], or mesh optimization [Hoppe et al., 1993], is needed. The preprocessed point cloud represents an *approximated* physical-object surface. Preprocessing generates topological information relevant to surface reconstruction. This information has to be calculated only once due to the static nature of the point cloud. Topological information includes normal vectors and Gaussian curvatures which will be explained in section 3.2.2.

Surface reconstruction consists of two key tasks. The first task is to obtain topological information from the preprocessed point cloud by analytic methods. The second task is to construct an *approximating* geometrical surface, that is a surface that approximates the physical surface, from this point cloud by use of the topological information. Typically, a surface-reconstruction method assumes digitizing and preprocessing are topology-preserving, that is the approximated physical surface has a topology close to that of the physical surface. Note that, subsequently, the approximated physical surface will be identified with the physical surface since the former is the best available computer-accessible representation of the latter.

3.2.2   Gridded representation and topological information

A classic surface-reconstruction method uses the idea of constructing an approximating surface with a usually very large number of plane pieces. Triangulation, for instance, yields an approximating surface consisting of triangles as plane pieces. In this context, an intuitive idea of smoothness of the approximating surface is used: the surface is considered "smooth" in a certain area if the angles between the area's plane pieces are not "too wide". The formalized search for a smooth triangulation of a point cloud is hard. Different methods yielding smooth triangulations can be found in [Müller and Mencl, 1997; Weinert et al., 1997a; Schumaker, 1993; Weinert et al., 1997b].

There are several topological properties of a surface that may be used by an advanced classic surface-reconstruction method. In order to determine the peculiar properties of a given surface, a gridded triangulation may be calculated from a smooth triangulation. A triangulation is called "gridded" if and only if the triangle corners are in the normal vectors of the points of a uniform 2D grid. An instance of a gridded triangulation is shown in figure 3.1.

The grid represents a physical plane area on which the physical object rests during the digitizing process. A grid point represents a point that is aimed at by a sensor, like a pin of a tactile digitizing hardware. The sensor aims at this grid point along a vector that is orthogonal to the plane area. For a gridded triangulation, the indicated topological properties can be easier determined than for a non-gridded triangulation. Two examples of such properties are a "normal vector" and "Gaussian curvature".

A *normal vector* in a surface point is orthogonal to the surface. Since the approximating

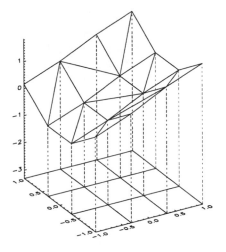

Figure 3.1
Gridded triangulation of a curved surface. Dotted lines represent normal vectors from uniform grid cross points to corresponding triangle corner points.

geometrical surface differs from the approximated physical surface, the normal vector in a point of the approximating geometrical surface must be approximated itself. This approximation can be done, for instance, by help of differential geometrical considerations [Suk and Bhandarkar, 1992] or simulation [Weinert et al., 1998].

The *Gaussian curvature* $K(p) \in \mathbb{R}$ at any point p on a surface S classifies the curvature of S in p [Gray, 1993]. Put vividly, the value says how strong the curvature is and whether it is convex, concave or saddle-like. $K(p)$ is the product of the smallest and largest normal curvatures in point p. In order to calculate the normal curvatures in p, S is intersected by the normal planes in p. The situation is shown in figure 3.2. One instance e of the infinitely many normal planes in p is given. The curvature of the 2D curve resulting from the intersection is called "normal curvature in p". The product of the smallest and the largest normal curvature in p can be positive (convex or concave surface), negative (saddle surface), or zero (plane surface).

Thus, considering an $n \times m$ grid, the result of the first key task can be represented as an $n \times m$ matrix of vectors $s_{n.m} \in \mathbb{R}^{3+3+1}$. $s_{n.m}$ consists of three subvectors: the coordinate vector $c \in \mathbb{R}^3$ of $p_{n.m}$ which represents a physical surface point over the grid point $n.m$; the normal vector $n \in \mathbb{R}^3$ in $p_{n.m}$; the physical-object surface's Gaussian curvature in $p_{n.m}$.

The topological information is used by a typical classic surface-reconstruction method. It is also used by the evolutionary approach that will be presented next.

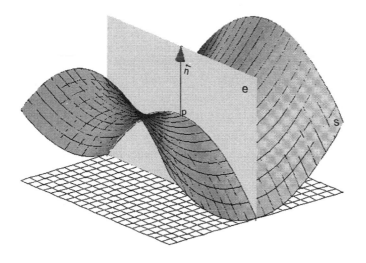

Figure 3.2
A normal plane e with normal vector n intersects saddle surface S, given by function $f(x,y) = x^2 - y^2$, at $p = (0,0,0)$.

3.3 SURREAL– a Genetic programming/Evolution strategy hybrid

An *evolution strategy* is an evolutionary algorithm introduced by Rechenberg and Schwefel in the 1960s [Rechenberg, 1994; Schwefel, 1995]. Its original form and modern variants are powerful tools for solving hard parameter optimization problems as they are ubiquitous in engineering domains.

3.3.1 The approach

A CAD system supports one or more internationally standardized formats for CAD-data exchange, like STEP, VDA-FS, or IGES [Reed et al., 1991]. A geometrical surface can be represented as a *CAD expression* that obeys one of these formats, while the expression represents an algorithm that constructs the surface. The basic idea of SURREAL is to have genetic programming evolve a CAD expression for a given preprocessed point cloud such that the expression represents the physical surface that underlies the cloud. A significant advantage over classic approaches is that curved physical-surface parts can be approximated by curved geometrical surface parts instead of plane geometrical surface pieces like triangles. This is an important feature since a curved physical-surface part, like the surface of a tube, is frequently used in an industrial production process. Approximating such a part by plane pieces is very inefficient in terms of computing resources. Also, approximating curved physical parts by curved geometrical parts may yield a better approximation. Finally, the resulting approximation looks more natural than a plane-piece approximation that often has a "jagged" appearance.

3.3.2   Overview

When designing an evolutionary algorithm, the following major issues must be dealt with:

- algorithmic structure (generational vs. steady-state model, etc.)

- a problem-specific genetic representation of an individual

- a quality measure, implemented as a fitness function, applicable to each evolvable individual

- a search operator set including creation operator(s) and variation operators like mutation and recombination

- a selection of individuals as operands for the genetic operators

- a selection of individuals as members of the next generation

- parameters like maximal run time, maximal leaf number, population size, operator execution probabilities, etc.

These issues will be discussed subsequently with respect to SURREAL. Especially, parameters will be introduced along with the description of the SURREAL parts they control.

3.3.3   Algorithmic structure

The algorithmic structure is a GP/ES hybrid. After creation of a population with fixed population size $\mu > 0$, a generational-cycle model takes over. A parental generation is transformed into an offspring generation of λ individuals by application of variation and reproduction. After the generation of an offspring generation has been completed, a selection method selects μ individuals from the offspring generation into the next parental generation. Then, the cycle restarts and continues until a user-defined fitness value is scored by an individual or the user terminates the run.

Mutation and recombination are tagged with particular execution probabilities m, r by the user, so that, for instance, recombination will be applied with 0.3 probability as next variation. The sum of all execution probabilities must equal 1, so that the reproduction-execution probability is computed by SURREAL as $1 - m - r$.

3.3.4 Genetic representation

3.3.4.1 Constructive solid geometry

The CAD construction of an object is realized either via line- or surface- or volume-oriented (3D) construction methods. A 3D-CAD system has some advantages in comparison to a surface-oriented CAD system. For instance, a 3D-CAD system gives a realistic visual representation of a physical object, which is a major reason why an increasing acceptance of 3D-CAD systems can be expected. *Constructive solid geometry* (CSG) is a prominent object-construction method used by several 3D-CAD systems. A *CSG object* is either a *CSG primitive*, like a cube, or it is a *CSG complex* which is represented as a *CSG sequence* of *construction operators* and CSG objects. Addition, subtraction, and intersection of CSG objects are typical construction operators. A CSG primitive is characterized by its parameters like size, position, and orientation.

A CSG sequence is a word from a context-free language. For instance, the simplified CSG sequence "sphere ∪ sphere" represents the left CSG complex in figure 3.3, obtained by joining spheres. Actually, a real-world CSG sequence as it is used by a CAD system contains parameters like the sphere's radius and center position. A CSG sequence can be represented as a hierarchical structure, that is a CSG tree, which corresponds to an infix expression. For instance, the infix expression "cube ∪ sphere" can be represented as a tree with a ∪-labeled root node that has one cube-labeled and one sphere-labeled child node.

Note that, for each CSG object, there is an infinite number of representing CSG trees, which means the CSG-object representation is not unique. For instance, a sphere can be represented as "sphere", "sphere ∪ sphere", "sphere ∪ sphere ∪ sphere", etc., with all spheres having the same radius and position.

3.3.4.2 Terminal and function set

SURREAL's terminal set contains the CSG primitives "box", "sphere" and "quadric". A quadric is a generic geometric object that can be instantiated as, for instance, a cone or a cylinder. As a special case of a finite quadric, the terminal set contains a cylinder. Other stereometrical primitives like a torus, an obelisc, barrel-shaped bodies, and primitives with non-trivial topologies can be included into the terminal set, if desired. The function set contains the binary construction operators "union", "subtraction", and "intersection".

An example of three CSG complexes can be seen in figure 3.3.

3.3.4.3 Search space

Due to the genetic representation, the search space is the set of all CSG trees with a user-defined maximal leaf number c. SURREAL does not evolve trees with more leaves, that is CSG primitives. The user must set c such that a SURREAL run does not exhaust the available memory.

Note that the CSG-based genetic representation ensures that each CSG object can be represented as an individual. This again ensures that almost any practically relevant physical

Figure 3.3
Union, intersection, and subtraction of two spheres

object can be represented as an individual, since CSG has been designed for the representation of such physical objects. Note also that an arbitrary search space point (a CSG tree) can be generated by an apt sequence of variation operators. This ensures that, in principle, every potential solution can be found by the search process, no matter where in space the search starts. Finally, the genetic representation of an individual can be transformed by a tree traversal into a CSG sequence which can be directly processed by a corresponding CAD system.

3.3.5   Quality measure

Surface reconstruction is an instance of a multi-criterion optimization problem. In the context of surface reconstruction, one obvious optimization criterion is the quality of the approximation of a physical object by a corresponding CSG object resulting from the reconstruction. Another criterion is the parsimony of the CSG tree that represents the approximating CSG object. Since the CSG-object representation is not unique, CSG trees of vastly different sizes represent the same CSG object. In order to save CAD system resources, the representing CSG tree should be small.

Further optimization criteria are related to topological properties of the CSG object and will be explained next. The quality measure is a combination of all optimization criteria, and it is used to assess the overall quality of an individual. It is implemented as a fitness function used by SURREAL. An instance of such a function is shown in section 3.4.2.

3.3.5.1   Distance criterion DELTA
This criterion represents the idea that a well-approximating CSG-object surface should contain the points from the preprocessed point cloud. Subsequently, a *z-value* of a cloud point is the point's height over the corresponding grid point. If this value is greater or equal to a digitizing-hardware-dependent $\epsilon > 0$, this means the digitizing process detected

a physical-object surface over that grid point. A *vanishing z-value* $0 \leq z < \epsilon$ means the digitizing process detected no physical-object surface over that point.

The concept of a vanishing value must be introduced due to the unavoidable imprecision of the physical measuring a digitizing process must perform. For instance, the surface of the table on which a physical object rests during digitizing may have a small unevenness. If this unevenness is digitized, the resulting 3D point data represent noise since the unevenness is not part of the physical object. However, if one sets ϵ high enough with respect to table imperfections and low enough with respect to the physical object, only the physical object will be digitized.

The distance criterion is realized via the sum σ over all grid points of the differences between a physical-object surface point's z-value and the corresponding CSG-object-surface point's z-value. Thus, the time complexity of the computation of DELTA is linear in the number of all $n \cdot m$ grid points. The result is normalized to the interval $0 < x <= 1$ by use of

$$DELTA := (\sigma + 1)^{-1}.$$

Thus, a perfect CSG object results in $DELTA = 1$ since, in this case, σ equals zero.

Note two special cases that come into existence because not each grid point is necessarily covered by a CSG-object. A grid point with no corresponding CSG-object surface point and a vanishing z-value means SURREAL models the situation in this grid point correctly: no physical-object surface – no CSG-object surface. A grid point with a non-vanishing z-value and no corresponding CSG-object surface point means the situation has not yet been modeled correctly: a physical-object surface – no CSG-object surface. Thus, the error in this grid point, represented as an addend of σ, equals the z-value.

3.3.5.2 Angle criterion ABN

This criterion represents the idea that the CSG-object surface should have the same spatial orientation as the physical-object surface. It is realized by taking into consideration the normal vectors of the CSG-object surface points and of the physical-object surface points over all grid points. The physical-object normal vectors have to be computed only once at the beginning of a SURREAL run since the physical-object representation (the preprocessed point cloud) is constant. The criterion is realized as a normalized sum over all grid points. The time complexity of the computation of ABN is linear in the number of all $n \cdot m$ grid points.

An addend of the normalized sum is the absolute cosine value of the angle α_i between the CSG-object normal vector and the physical-object normal vector over the same grid point.

$$ABN = \frac{1}{n \cdot m} \sum_{i=1}^{n \cdot m} |cos \, \alpha_i|.$$

The cosine for each normal-vector pair yields "one" for parallel normal vectors and zero for orthogonal normal vectors, which implies that ABN is in $[0, 1]$ and a perfect CSG object has ABN value "one".

3.3.5.3 Curvature-type criterion CTYPE

A Gaussian curvature type (section 3.2.2) classifies a surface point as belonging to a plane, convex, concave or saddle surface. The curvature types are calculated by preprocessing (section 3.2.1) before the evolutionary algorithm starts. The CTYPE criterion represents the idea that, in corresponding points, the CSG-object surface should have the same curvature type as the physical-object surface.

The purpose of CTYPE is to guide the selection of an apt CSG-primitive for the approximation of a certain physical-object surface area such that primitive and area have identical curvature types. CTYPE is defined as the sum over all grid points of type matches, rated as "one", and mismatches, rated as "zero", divided by the number of grid points. Thus, CTYPE is in $[0, 1]$, and a perfect CSG object has CTYPE value "one", since each grid point represents a type match. The time complexity of the computation of CTYPE is linear in the number of all $n \cdot m$ grid points.

3.3.5.4 Primitive-number criterion PRIM

Evolution may lead to the generation of a CSG object that consists of a huge number of primitives ϕ. Such an object is inefficient in terms of computing resources, since each data representation of a primitive must be stored. Moreover, a CAD system must draw each primitive when drawing the CSG object, and redraw whenever the construction engineer moves or rotates the object on-screen. The more realistic a CSG object appears on screen by application of visual rendering algorithms, like ray tracing, and the higher ϕ is, the more CPU intense the redrawing gets. Even with powerful graphics hardware support, the delay due to redrawing may become annoyingly long.

Thus, the parsimony criterion PRIM is needed in order to guide the search process to small individuals. PRIM is defined as

$$PRIM := 1 - \frac{\phi}{c},$$

where $\phi \leq c \leq n \cdot m, c \in \mathbb{N}$. c has been introduced in section 3.3.4.3. $0 \leq PRIM \leq 1 - 1/c$ holds, and a perfect CSG object has $1 - 1/c$ as PRIM value. c should be set as high as the maximum number of leaves expected necessary to build an acceptable CSG object.

3.3.6 Variation

3.3.6.1 Mutation

A single mutation of an individual has exactly one of the following types:

- **primitive** It random-selects a CSG primitive (CSG tree leaf) and then randomly modifies one parameter, that is either position or size or orientation, with normal distribution for small modifications. Its objective is to tune the evolved geometric surface with many smaller and few bigger changes.

- **construction** It replaces a random-selected construction operator (inner node of a CSG tree), like intersection, by another random-selected construction operator. This mutation type usually introduces a major phenotypic change as can be seen in figure 3.3. The objective is to introduce several topologically qualitatively different phenotypes by repeated application to different individuals in the course of evolution. This, hopefully, generates a phenotype that captures the characteristics of the physical object to be approximated, so that the corresponding genotype may then be tuned.

- **replacing** It replaces a random-selected CSG primitive by another random-selected primitive. Its objective is to tune the evolved geometric surface by exchanging subareas. The parameter settings of the introduced primitives are defined by standard settings.

- **insertion** It replaces a randomly selected CSG primitive by a randomly generated CSG tree which consists of two nodes at least. Its objective is to introduce a significant change of the phenotypic shape. Especially, this operator is imperative for introducing CSG complexes into the population, since creation, as will be discussed later, only generates primitives.

- **deletion** It deletes a random-selected non-trivial subtree that is not the entire individual. Its objective is identical to the insertion objective and it counteracts the genotypic size increase introduced by insertion, thus supporting the evolution of parsimonious individuals.

The mutation-execution probability is controlled by use of an adjustment function that exponentially decreases the user-defined initial value over run time. The decreasing occurs in order to have the search process "home in" on an acceptable local optimum. If mutation is to be the next variation, one of the five presented mutation types is selected for execution. The respective five execution probabilities are user-defined. If "primitive" is selected for execution, one of the parameters (position, size, orientation) is selected for mutation. The respective three selection probabilities are user-defined.

3.3.6.2 Recombination

Recombination is defined as an exchange of two CSG subtrees between two parents. The root nodes of these subtrees are being random-selected such that each node in a parent has equal probability of being selected. This way, every combination of subtrees to be exchanged has the same probability of occurring. Thus, the phenotypic difference between parents and offspring covers the full range from almost identical to very different in shape and size. This implies that recombination, like mutation, generates and maintains genetic diversity in the population. As usual with evolutionary algorithms, genetic diversity is important for preventing SURREAL from premature convergence. Especially, diversity supports the evolution of an ideal phenotype, which is as complex as necessary with respect to approximation quality and as parsimonious as possible.

Furthermore, recombination is expected to be useful since it can construct a complex surface structure (CSG tree) from previously evolved substructures (subtrees).

3.3.7 Creation

A creation operator generates a user-defined number of individuals each of which being a randomly chosen CSG primitive with random parameter settings. This ensures, a reasonably large population size assumed, the occurrence of all primitive types in the initial population. This type diversity is helpful for the synthesis of complex topologies as they are ubiquitous in practically relevant physical objects. Note that structural diversity does not have to be introduced by creation. Instead, the insertion operator described in section 3.3.6.1 quickly introduces diversity into the initial population. Thus, the implementation and application of one or more relatively sophisticated tree creation operators like those described in [Koza, 1992] are unnecessary.

3.3.8 Selection for variation

Once creation or previous evolution have produced a generation of individuals, variation in form of recombination and mutation takes place.

In order to perform recombination, two different parents are selected from the population at random with equal probability. This fitness-independent selection mechanism guarantees that recombination is likely to access also those good substructures that are contained in mediocre or bad individuals. This purely random-based selection mechanism would result in a Monte-Carlo-like search process if it was the only such mechanism present in the system. However, in order to determine the individuals to be subjected to mutation, SURREAL offers four fitness-based selection mechanisms to the user who chooses one that will be used during a run:

- elitist selection

- ranking selection under an exponential distribution

- 2-tournament selection

- fitness-proportional selection

Elitist selection chooses the n best individuals for mutation. Ranking selection under an exponential distribution chooses individuals with an exponentially distributed probability that depends on the fitness rank of an individual within the population. The dependency is such that the lower the rank is, the exponentially lower is the probability of selecting the individual for mutation. 2-tournament selection chooses two individuals from the population at random with an equally distributed probability. The better individual will be mutated. Fitness-proportional selection chooses an individual for mutation with a probability proportional to its fitness.

3.3.9   Selection for the next generation

Once variation has taken place, selection of individuals to be contained in the next generation occurs. Here, SURREAL follows the evolution strategy. The classic evolution strategy introduces a selection pressure on the genotypes via using the plus selection and the comma selection. These selection methods *deterministically* select the μ best individuals for the next generation. Plus-selection selects from $(\mu + \lambda)$ parental and offspring individuals, and comma selection selects only from $\lambda \geq \mu$ offspring individuals. Thus, in order for the comma selection to work, the genetic operators must generate $\lambda \geq \mu$ offspring from μ parents.

SURREAL offers the use of either the plus-selection or the comma-selection in a run. Let us call a SURREAL run a $(\mu + \lambda)$ run when it employs a plus-selection.

An evolutionary algorithm using these selection methods allows for a simple and effective tuning of the selection pressure by adjusting the μ/λ ratio: the larger the ratio, the higher the selection pressure. A high selection pressure yields fast but unsafe search process convergence to an acceptable genotype. A low pressure leads to the opposite: a Monte-Carlo-like slow search process featuring safe convergence when being given very much run time. A theory yielding a good choice for the selection pressure is currently unknown. A good rule of thumb is to choose a ratio of $5/7$ with $\lambda >> 50$ for difficult problems.

Note that, simultaneously, there is beneficial and detrimental potential in both selection methods. Plus-selection may result in a very long existence of a good but still not acceptable individual. This may lead to a critical and fast collapse of genotypic diversity via iterated reproduction of this individual. However, it may also lead to an increase of hi-fitness genetic information which finally may result in the evolution of an acceptable genotype. Comma-selection may result in the situation that the best genotype of the next parental generation is worse than that of the previous one. However, the risk of a population takeover by a good but not acceptable individual is lower than with plus-selection [Bäck, 1994].

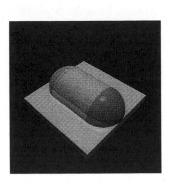

Figure 3.4
Manually constructed CSG object representing a dowel. The plane surface represents the digitizing table.

3.4 Results

3.4.1 Problem: dowel reconstruction

Subsequently, SURREAL will be applied to the surface reconstruction of a simple but practically relevant physical object: a dowel, which is a ubiquitous part in mechanical engineering. Figure 3.4 shows a manually constructed CSG object representing a dowel. The CSG object can be constructed from a cylinder and a half-sphere at each cylinder end.

There are infinitely many CSG trees representing a dowel. A parsimonious one consists of 5 nodes: three leaves for the primitives "left half-sphere", "right half-sphere", "cylinder", and two inner nodes for the construction operators "join".

3.4.2 Parameters

The required grid dimension, that is resolution, depends on the structural complexity of the physical object to be reconstructed. If the resolution is too low, a critical physical surface area may not be digitized. If the resolution is too high, redundant data is being generated during the digitizing process. This redundancy is detrimental, since it results in an unnecessary use of the limited computing resources. For the problem of the dowel reconstruction, a grid dimension of 20×20, which appears to be beneficial to the search process, has been found experimentally.

The structural complexity of the physical object influences the maximum number of leaves a CSG tree should have in order to allow for a successful evolution. A number c, as introduced for the PRIM definition, of 220 is used for the problem. This value has been found empirically like the grid dimension.

The fitness function f is defined as

$$f = 1.5 \cdot CTYPE + 0.5 \cdot ABN + 0.5 \cdot DELTA + 0.5 \cdot PRIM.$$

Thus, an f value is in $0 < f \leq 3 - 0.5/c$, and a perfect CSG object scores the upper-interval-limit value. Judging by the results of numerous trials, the constants used in the fitness function improve convergence speed and reliability of the search process.

Experiments with $(50 + 50)$, $(100 + 300)$, and $(500 + 800)$ runs all resulted in elitist strategies yielding best solutions, shortly followed by tournament selection strategies. Fitness-proportional selection and ranking selection schemes did not perform well which endorses results reported in [Project team SURREAL, 1998].

Each selected individual is either mutated or recombined with 0.5 probability. Thus, in the beginning of a run, the reproduction-execution probability equals zero. This leads to an initially strong generation of genetic diversity, since reproduction cannot yet lead to a premature population take-over by relatively good individuals. Gradually, reproduction starts taking effect, when the mutation-execution probability is decreased by use of the adjustment function.

The mutation-execution probabilities (section 3.3.6.1) of primitive, construction, replacing, insertion and deletion are 0.09, 0.01, 0.1, 0.5 and 0.3 respectively. Construction mutation usually introduces vast phenotypic changes, so that its low execution probability is needed to home in slowly on a local optimum in order not to lose track of it. The probabilities for selecting position, size or orientation during a primitive mutation are 1/3 each.

3.4.3 Discussion

3.4.3.1 Incremental optimization
Note that, in the fitness function, CTYPE clearly has the largest weight, which is due to the experience that an adequate amplification of the curvature-type weight usually yields better results. This high weight forces an early optimization of the CSG-object shape and size, while orientation, evaluated by ABN, and position, evaluated by DELTA, are targets for final tuning. Accordingly, when watching an animated picture sequence assembled from the best-in-generation phenotypes from the first to the last generation of a typical run, one often sees a corresponding structural evolution. This change is reflected by the genotypic size progression, which can be seen in figure 3.5.

One can interpret the sequence of the best-in-generation phenotypes from the first to the last generation of a run as a series of snapshots taken of the structural and spatial evolution of a *meta-individual*. Initially, this individual assumes the topology of the physical object. During this period, the genotypic size increases rapidly, while the surface of the physical object is being approximated roughly by a set of primitives. These primitives have coarse curvature-type relations with physical-surface areas. In this phase, the CTYPE criterion

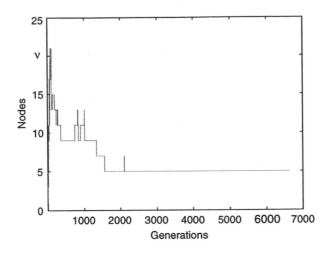

Figure 3.5
Progression of the genotypic size of the best-in-generation genotypes during dowel reconstruction. Genotypic size measured in number ν of CSG tree nodes.

implies topology optimization of the CSG object. Then, the meta-individual rotates into the orientation the physical object had when it was scanned. Due to the PRIM criterion, the number of primitives is being reduced rapidly while the structure of the CSG object is being refined. In this phase, the ABN criterion implies orientation optimization of the CSG object. Finally, after the structure of the physical object has been recognized, the CSG object floats into the position the physical object had relative to the grid. The distance criterion DELTA implies position optimization.

A typical structure evolution of a meta-individual, evolved during a $(50 + 50)$ run with elitist selection, can be seen in figure 3.6.

This type of structure evolution is an instance of incremental optimization, which is a powerful approach to many multi-criteria optimization problems. The idea is to water down the difficulty of the entire task by sequentially solving subproblems. This is effected by a quality measure that is composed of differently weighted elements. We return to this issue below in the context of fitness progression.

3.4.3.2   Fitness progression

The following discussion is concerned with an experiment that consists of 10 $(50 + 50)$ runs with elitist selection, initialized with different randomizer seeds. Each run lasted for, at least, $3,000$ generations and found a perfect CSG object. Fig. 3.7 shows the result of a representative run that was terminated after $6,600$ generations.

Visually, no differences between the physical object and the CSG object can be detected. Especially, SURREAL has recognized the construction logic of a dowel and implemented

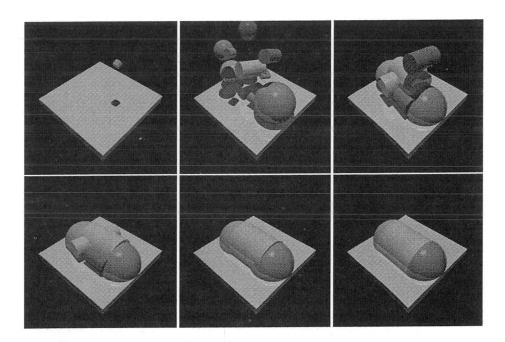

Figure 3.6
One can interpret the sequence of the best-in-generation phenotypes from the first to the last generation of a run as a series of snapshots taken of the structural and spatial evolution of a *meta-individual*. From upper left to lower right: snapshots of meta-individual taken in generations 1, 200, 500, 800, 1100, 1872 of a $(50 + 50)$ run with elitist selection. The plane areas represent the digitizing table. Note: in the bottom right picture, the dowel seems to rest on top of another dowel, which would be a bad reconstruction. Actually, however, the alleged lower dowel is a mirror image produced by the visual rendering algorithm that assumes the digitizing table to reflect light. Thus, the bottom right picture shows a perfect reconstruction. An animation of this reconstruction resides at http://ls11-www.informatik.uni-dortmund.de/people/keller/surreal.html.

Figure 3.7
Perfect SURREAL reconstruction of a dowel in generation 5,159 of a $(50 + 50)$ run with elitist selection. The plane under the dowel represents the table of a digitizing unit where an object is placed for scanning.

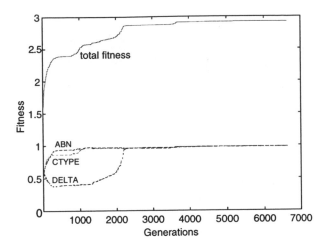

Figure 3.8
Single-criterion-value progressions and the total-fitness progression of the best individual in each generation, taken from the reconstruction of the dowel shown in figure 3.7

it in the evolved CSG object: a half-cylinder, closed by quarter-spheres. The good visual impression is endorsed by the single-criterion-value progressions and the total-fitness progression of the best individual in each generation with the final best values 0.979363 (DELTA), 0.980912 (ABN), and 0.982 (CTYPE). The progressions are displayed in figure 3.8.

Initially, rapidly increasing values of CTYPE and ABN reflect the structure evolution of the meta-individual during an exploring phase of the search process. Then, after the difficult topology and orientation optimization has been more or less completed, the easier position optimization is being dealt with, mirrored by the late start of the DELTA value increase.

3.4.3.3   Population size and convergence
Progressions of the best-individual-in-generation fitness of a representative $(100 + 300)$- and $(500 + 800)$ run using elitist selection are displayed in figure 3.9 on a logarithmic generations scale.

The progressions endorse the rule of thumb that larger populations strongly enhance convergence speed. Both runs evolve the same genotypic optimum, but the $(500 + 800)$ run uses only 35% run time of the time consumed by the $(100 + 300)$ run.

3.4.3.4   Interactive evolution
In the presented runs, SURREAL found the solution without human interaction. Since interactive evolution [Banzhaf, 1997] may be desired by a user in order to support the search

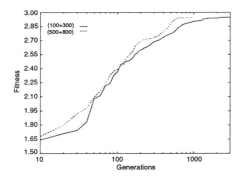

Figure 3.9
Progressions of the best-individual-in-generation fitness of a representative $(100 + 300)$ and $(500 + 800)$ dowel-reconstruction run with elitist selection on a logarithmic generations scale.

process by introducing human knowledge, the system offers a corresponding user interface with several features:

• **Genotypic redesign**   The user may interrupt a run, select an evolved genotype, and order the visual rendering of the corresponding phenotype. The user may then redesign the genotype during a modification/rendering cycle until the redesigned phenotype has satisfactory quality. He or she may finally introduce the redesigned genotype to the current population and restart the halted run. Note that this feature has not been used during the reconstruction runs presented in this chapter.

• **Parameter setting**   The result-enhancing setting of the run parameters, like the population size, is a difficult task for the user, requiring much experience. Successful parameter settings depend on the structural complexity of the object. Inadequate settings yield CSG objects with too many primitives that approximate the physical object only poorly. A TCL/TK interface provides a comfortable way to set, change, and save parameter settings for analysis. Especially, a setting may be changed during a run.

• **On-line visualization**   The system can generate on-line pictures in TGA (Truevision Targa Image File Format) to give an on-the-fly impression of the search progress. For instance, the image sequence shown in figure 3.6 has been generated by use of the on-line visualization.

3.4.4   Problem: cross-structure reconstruction

As another problem, the reconstruction of a cross structure shown in figure 3.10 shall be presented.

Cross structures are frequently needed components of automatic-transmission control units. The structure at hand is a part of a transmission case. The most parsimonious CSG

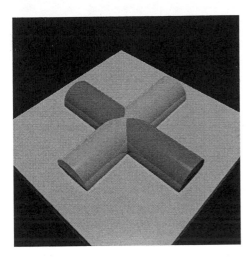

Figure 3.10
Cross structure

tree consists of 3 nodes: two leaves for the primitives "half-cylinder" and an inner node for the construction operator "union".

Especially, $(100 + 300)$ runs are performed. The mutation probability is set to 0.01 only, while the recombination probability is set to 0.5. Thus, recombination and reproduction are the most frequently used operators. The mutation-execution probabilities (section 3.3.6.1) of primitive, construction, replacing, insertion and deletion are 0.2, 0.05, 0.1, 0.5 and 0.3 respectively. The probabilities for selecting position, size or orientation during a primitive mutation are 1/3 each. Subsequently, the results of a particular run are presented. The genotypic size progression can be seen in figure 3.11.

The according structure evolution of the meta-individual can be seen in figure 3.12.

The progressions of the total fitness of the best individual and of the average total fitness are shown in figure 3.13.

The small difference between both values per generation is due to the high reproduction probability compared to the very low mutation probability. Thus, a good individual quickly takes over the population, rising the average fitness. The close linkage of best and average fitness values is also present in the single criterion value progressions as can be seen in figure 3.14. At generation 10 000, the top, middle and bottom double curves show the CTYPE, DELTA, and ABN progressions, respectively.

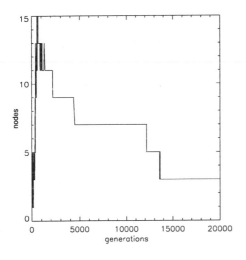

Figure 3.11
Progression of the genotypic size of the best-in-generation individuals during cross structure reconstruction with a $(100 + 300)$ run.

3.5 Conclusion and future work

It has been shown that surface reconstruction by means of Genetic Programming is possible. With the software system SURREAL, a Genetic Programming/Evolution Strategy surface reconstruction approach has been introduced for the first time. SURREAL transforms a weakly-structured digitized 3D representation of a physical object into an efficient and construction-logical standard CAD-object representation. The presented approach simultaneously performs pattern recognition and structure evolution. Genetic Programming is especially apt for such tasks since it can operate in search spaces with *a priori* unknown dimensionality. Especially, the evolution of CSG trees of arbitrary size and shape is possible. Accordingly, the reconstruction of more complex objects is the major target of future work.

Connected with this primary objective, the following issues are identified:

- **Alternative genetic representations**   In order to use the synergy of surface- and volume-based CAD representations for the reconstruction of arbitrary surfaces, further representations like NURBS (see section 3.1) should be evolvable, too.

- **Knowledge-based search operators** Complex objects, consisting of many small objects, dramatically increase the search-space size. A possible answer to this challenge is to supply the search process with "intelligent" search operators that use domain-specific knowledge when being applied. For instance, simple rules to be observed by an operator

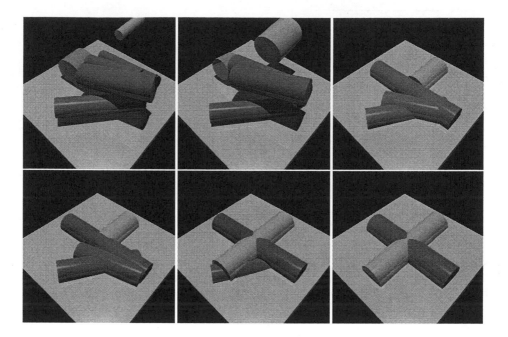

Figure 3.12
One can interpret the sequence of the best-in-generation phenotypes from the first to the last generation of a run as a series of snapshots taken of the structural and spatial evolution of a *meta-individual*. From upper left to lower right: snapshots of meta-individual taken from 6 generations. Last generation: $14,400$

are "each part of a generated object must be connected to at least one other part of this object", "an object must not be completely contained within another object" and "the object to be reconstructed has a maximal height H over the grid".

- **Duplication** Many practically relevant physical objects have symmetric or fractal partial topologies. Duplication, as an additional mutation type, of an existing genotypic part should be beneficial to the evolutionary reconstruction of such objects.

Note that SURREAL could reconstruct arbitrary, also non-artifact, physical objects like human body parts, especially faces. The reconstruction of these objects represents a difficult problem for classic reconstruction approaches due to their highly irregular surface topology. Applications in, for instance, cosmetics, medicine, entertainment, and person identification are conceivable.

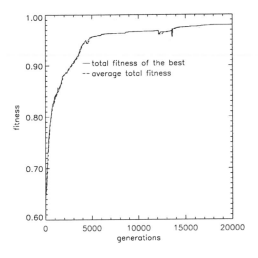

Figure 3.13
Fitness progressions of cross-structure reconstruction. The average-total-fitness curve runs close below the best-total-fitness curve.

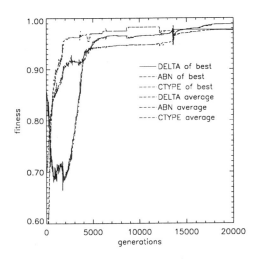

Figure 3.14
Single criterion value progressions of cross-structure reconstruction. Each average-value curve of a criterion runs close below the best-value curve of the same criterion. At generation 10 000, the top, middle and bottom double curves show the CTYPE, DELTA, and ABN progressions, respectively.

Acknowledgments

This research was supported by the Deutsche Forschungsgemeinschaft as part of the Collaborative Research Center "Computational Intelligence" (SFB 531) projects C4 and B2. Special thanks go to the students' project team SURREAL, whose members have implemented the system under the guidance of the authors.

Bibliography

Bäck, T. (1994), "Selective pressure in evolutionary algorithms: A characterization of selection mechanisms," in *Proceedings of the First IEEE Conference on Evolutionary Computation*, IEEE Press.

Banzhaf, W. (1997), "Interactive evolution," in *Handbook of Evolutionary Computation*, Z. M. T. Bäck, D. Fogel (Ed.), pp C2.9,1–7, Oxford University Press.

Banzhaf, W., Nordin, P., Keller, R., and Francone, F. (1998), *Genetic Programming - An Introduction; On the Automatic Evolution of Computer Programs and Its Application*, dpunkt-Verlag, Heidelberg. Morgan Kaufmann, San Francisco.

Friedhoff, J. (1996), *Aufbereitung von 3D-Digitalisierdaten für den Werkzeug-, Formen- und Modellbau*, Essen: Vulkan Verlag.

Gray, A. (1993), "The gaussian and mean curvatures," *Modern Differential Geometry of Curves and Surfaces, Boca Raton, FL: CRC Press*, pp 279–285.

Hoppe, H., DeRose, T., and Duchamp, T. (1993), "Mesh optimization," in *Computer Graphics Proceedings, Annual Conference Series*, pp 21–26, New York: ACM Siggraph. Proceedings of Siggraph '93.

Koza, J. (1992), *Genetic Programming, On the Programming of Computers by Means of Natural Selection*, The MIT Press, Cambridge, Massachusetts.

Müller, H. and Mencl, R. (1997), *Interpolation and Approximation of Surfaces from Three-Dimensional Scattered Data Points*, Dortmund: University of Dortmund, Research Report, No. 662.

Piegl, L. and Tiller, W. (1997), *The NURBS Book*, Springer.

Project team SURREAL (1998), "Flächenrekonstruktion mit Genetischem Programmieren," Technical report, University of Dortmund, Computer Science Department, Dortmund, Germany.

I. Rechenberg (Ed.) (1994), *Evolutionsstrategie '94*, volume 1 of *Werkstatt Bionik und Evolutionstechnik*, Stuttgart, Frommann-Holzboog.

Reed, K., Kelly, J. C., Harrod, D., and Conroy, W. (1991), *The Initial Graphics Exchange Specification (IGES) Version 5.1.*, Fairfax, VA: National Computer Graphics Assoc., Administrator-IGES/PDES Organization.

Schumaker, L. (1993), "Computational triangulation using simulated annealing," *In: Computer Aided Geometry Design*, 10:329–345.

Schwefel, H.-P. (1995), *Evolution and optimum seeking*, Wiley Interscience.

Suk, M. and Bhandarkar, S. (1992), *Three Dimensional Object Recognition from Range Images*, Berlin: Springer.

Weinert, K., Mehnen, J., Albersmann, F., and Drerup, P. (1997a), *New Solutions for Surface Reconstructions from Discrete Point Data by means of Computational Intelligence*, Dortmund: University of Dortmund, Technical Report, CI-22/98, SFB 531 (Collaborative Research Center "Computational Intelligence"), ISSN 1433-3325.

Weinert, K., Mehnen, J., and Prestifilippo, G. (1997b), *Optimal Surface Reconstruction from Digitized Point Data using CI Methods*, Dortmund: University of Dortmund, Technical Report, CI-5/97, SFB 531 (Collaborative Research Center "Computational Intelligence"), ISSN 1433-3325.

Weinert, K., Müller, H., Albersmann, F., and Mehnen, J. (1998), "Efficient Rasterized Offset Computation from Tactile Digitization," in *Proceedings of the ISMTII'98, Sep. 2nd to 4th 1998*, pp 258–264, Miskolc, Hungary: University of Miskolc.

4   A Genetic Programming Approach for Robust Language Interpretation

Carolyn Penstein Rosé

This chapter discusses the application of genetic programming (GP) to the problem of robust language understanding in the context of a large scale multi-lingual speech-to-speech translation system. Efficiently and effectively processing sentences outside of the coverage of a system's linguistic knowledge sources is still an open problem in computational linguistics, a problem that must be faced if natural language interfaces will ever be practical. In this chapter, the GP based ROSE approach to robust language understanding is demonstrated to yield a significantly better time/quality trade-off than previous non-GP approaches. GP is used to search for the optimal way to assemble fragments of a meaning representation. The ROSE approach is the first application of a program induction technique to a problem of this type.

4.1   Introduction

This chapter introduces a new application of genetic programming (GP) to the problem of robust language interpretation and argues that GP is well suited to solve this problem efficiently and effectively. Specifically, GP is used for the purpose of allowing a language understanding system to recover in cases where a parser fails. An empirical evaluation demonstrates that the GP approach yields a significantly better time/quality trade-off than previous non-GP approaches. The ROSE system, RObustness with Structural Evolution, which is described in this chapter, serves as one example of how GP can be used to solve this problem, opening a new area of application for the GP community.

The theory of language understanding underlying the work described in this chapter has its roots in Conceptual Dependency Theory [Schank, 1975]. The basic tenets of this theory state that the purpose of language understanding is for the listener to construct a representation of the meaning of the input sentence. The representation of the meaning is independent of the actual words used to communicate that meaning. Meaning representations are built from a predefined set of primitives where meaning is encoded in the primitives themselves as well as in the relationships represented between those primitives in the structure resulting from the understanding process. However, unlike in Conceptual Dependency Theory, the work described here does not advocate a specific set of primitives. Instead, it can be used with whatever set of primitives are deemed useful for a particular domain.

A language understanding process constructs a meaning for a sentence by matching a set of grammar rules against the sentence that describe possible relationships between words and how these relationships are encoded in meaning representation structures. The impossibility of exhaustively enumerating the patterns of encoded relationships that are found in spontaneous spoken language make the problem of robust language interpretation particularly challenging. Sentences whose structure cannot be completely described by the set of rules in the system's parsing grammar are a common occurrence in naturally occurring language. Since parsing grammars in real systems generally only cover a subset of English or whatever language it is built for, its parser may fail even on sentences that are technically grammatical. These sentences are called extra-grammatical sentences since they are technically not ungrammatical but are nevertheless outside of the coverage of the system's grammar rules. Although the rules that are used to analyze sentences do not cover an entire extra-grammatical expression, often they are at least sufficient for covering its important sub-expressions. It is therefore possible to recover the majority of the meaning of the whole expression if the relationships between the meanings of the analyzed sub-expressions can be determined. Thus, the problem of robust interpretation can be thought of as the process of extracting the meaning of the sub-expressions within an extra-grammatical expression and then determining the relationships between those sub-expressions.

The ROSE approach to the problem of extra-grammaticality is to use a robust parser [Lavie, 1995] to extract the meaning of sub-expressions inside of an extra-grammatical expression. It then uses genetic programming to search the space of possible relationships between the meaning representation structures of those grammatical sub-expressions in order to build a representation of the whole sentence [Rosé, 1997]. Thus, genetic programming is used for the purpose of repair. The ROSE system was developed and evaluated in the context of the large-scale JANUS multi-lingual machine translation project [Lavie et al., 1996; Woszcyna et al., 1993; Woszcyna et al., 1994]. The JANUS project deals with the scheduling domain where two speakers attempt to schedule a meeting together over the phone. It is evaluated on spoken input that has been transcribed by a human. Thus, it contains all of the ungrammaticalities and disfluencies of spoken language without the additional complication of speech recognition errors.

It is ROSE's application of GP that makes it possible for it to operate efficiently. First, because the genetic search can do the work of assembling the meaning representation structures for the analyzed sub-expressions, the ROSE system avoids the overwhelming overhead of maximally flexible parsing approaches such as the Minimum Distance Parsing approach [Lehman, 1989; Hipp, 1992] that attempt to perform the whole task of sentence level interpretation at parse time. ROSE's two stage approach allows it to use a more restrictive, and thus more efficient, partial parser, and to use extra resources (i.e., the GP based repair stage) only in cases where repair is both necessary and possible. Furthermore, since the GP based combination algorithm constructs a ranked set of near-optimal or optimal hypotheses about the meaning of the sentences by searching the space of possible combinations of sub-expressions, it avoids the need for hand-coded repair rules that are featured in otherwise similar approaches [van Noord, 1996; Danieli and Gerbino, 1995].

4.2   Abstraction on the Problem of Parse Repair

The goal of ROSE's genetic search is to construct a meaning representation for an expression from the meaning representations of its sub-expressions. This approach assumes that meanings of sentences can largely be represented compositionally. In other words, the meaning of an expression can be represented in terms of the relationships between the meanings of its immediate sub-expressions. For example, consider the sentence "The cat chases the dog." This sentence describes an action with two participants, one of whom is doing the action, and one to whom the action is being done. The meaning of "the cat" is a representation of the animal that the expression refers to. Likewise, "the dog" has as its meaning the animal that it refers to. "Chases" refers to the action of an actor running after the actee. It is not enough to know the meanings of these sub-expressions, however. In order to understand this sentence, it is necessary to recognize the relationships between these sub-expressions. In other words, it is necessary to realize that it is the cat that is doing the action of chasing and the dog to whom the action of chasing is being done. Although the assumption of compositionality [Gamut, 1991] has some notable exceptions [van den Berg et al., 1994], it has been demonstrated to be a useful simplifying assumption for the purpose of robust semantic interpretation in other recent work [Bod and Kaplan, 1998; Bod, 1998].

This section describes an abstraction of the problem in order to illustrate its scope and lay the foundation for the application of genetic programming to solve it.

4.2.1   The Basic Problem

Each primitive representing a unit of meaning can be thought of as an object with a hook at the top and some number of holes at the bottom. These primitives can then be linked by inserting the hook from the top of one corresponding object in one of the holes at the bottom of another. Each hole represents a relationship between two units of meaning, i.e., the one corresponding to the object with the hole and the one corresponding to the object with the hook. The act of linking these objects together by inserting hooks into holes is analogous to constructing the meaning of an expression from the meanings of its sub-expressions.

Figure 4.1 illustrates how different ways of linking the same three objects results in different meanings. Notice that each hole at the bottom of each primitive is labeled with a role. This role indicates the relationship that is denoted by inserting the hook from one object into the corresponding hole. For example, if the object corresponding to the CAT primitive is inserted into the *actor* hole in the object corresponding to the CHASE primitive, it denotes that the cat is the one who is doing the chasing. Likewise, if the CAT primitive is inserted into the *actee* hole in the CHASE primitive, it denotes that the cat is the one being chased. Furthermore, if the CHASE primitive is inserted into the *behavior* hole in the CAT primitive, it denotes that the chasing is something that the cat in question does. Thus, searching the space of meanings composed of the same primitives is analogous to searching the space of configurations of corresponding objects.

The number of possible configurations grows quickly as the number of objects increases. It is impossible to precisely compute the number of possible configurations for a general set of n objects since the actual number of holes in an object varies from corresponding primitive to corresponding primitive. But it can be computed if one makes the simplifying assumption that holes do not carry meaning so that the effective number of holes per object

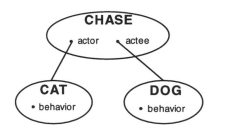

The cat chases the dog.

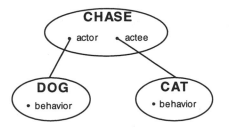

The dog chases the cat.

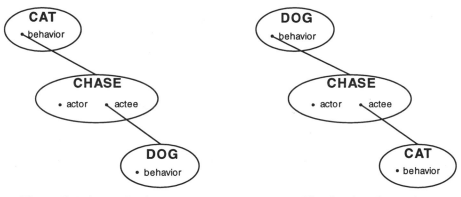

The cat that chases the dog   The dog that chases the cat

Figure 4.1
Here we see how a number of different meanings can be constructed from the same set of semantic primitives. The act of linking primitive units of meaning together is analogous to constructing the meaning of an expression from the meanings of its subexpressions.

Table 4.1
The number of possible configurations grows quickly as the number of objects increases. This table reports a lower bound on the number of possible configurations per number of objects.

Number of Objects	Search Space Size
1	1
2	4
3	18
4	116
5	1120
6	13782
7	212800
8	3801800

becomes one. Table 4.1 illustrates how the number of possible configurations grows quickly as the number of objects increases even with this simplifying assumption. The average number of objects produced by the parser for each example in the evaluation presented in Section 4.5 was 5.66. Since, as demonstrated in Figure 4.1, one hole is not equivalent to another hole in meaning, the actual search space size grows much faster than indicated in Table 4.1. Nevertheless, $S(n)$ provides a lower bound. It was computed using Equation 4.1.

$$S(n) = \sum_{i=1}^{n} \binom{n}{i} \binom{i}{1} \sum_{j=1}^{i-1} T(i-1,j) \tag{4.1}$$

The target configuration may be composed of any subset of the original set of n objects. Thus, the lower bound search space size with n objects is the sum of the number of ways to construct a configuration from every subset of the full set of n objects. The number of configurations with exactly i objects is the number of ways to select one of those objects as the root times the number of ways to divide the remaining objects into subsets and then construct a configuration from each subset. $T(i-1,j)$ is the number of ways to divide $i-1$ objects into j subsets and then construct a configuration from each subset. To compute the actual search space size, instead of the lower bound, T(i-1,j) would be multiplied by the number of ways to insert the resulting j objects into the number of holes in the selected root object.

4.2.2 Program Induction as a Solution

The problem of searching for the correct configuration of objects is easily cast as a program induction problem because of its recursive nature. Composite objects are assembled by inserting hooks from sub-objects into a root sub-object. These sub-objects may themselves be composed of other sub-objects, and so on. If one assumes the existence of a function called COMBINE that can insert the hook from the object that is its second argument into a hole in another object that is its first argument, one can write a program to construct any single configuration of objects. Thus, the target configuration can always be constructed by a program consisting only of instances of the subset of objects needed to construct the target configuration and instances of the COMBINE function.

Figure 4.2.2 shows how instances of COMBINE can be composed in order to construct a configuration. Notice how OBJECT3 is first inserted into OBJECT2. Next, OBJECT4 is inserted into OBJECT2. The composite object with OBJECT2 as its root is then inserted into OBJECT1. Finally, OBJECT5 is inserted into OBJECT1.

Although every target configuration can be constructed using instances of COMBINE and instances of the subset of objects needed for that configuration, not every program consisting only of instances of those objects and instances of COMBINE produces a legal configuration. In particular, more than one instance of the same object may not legally ap-

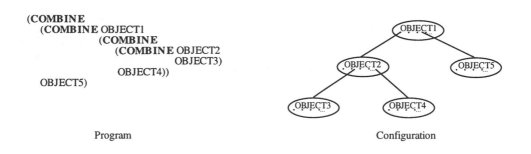

Program   Configuration

Figure 4.2
Here we see the result of evaluating a program consisting of the COMBINE function and primitive semantic objects. OBJECT3 is first inserted into OBJECT2. Next OBJECT4 is inserted into OBJECT2. Then the composite object with OBJECT2 as its root is inserted into OBJECT1. Finally, OBJECT5 is inserted into OBJECT1. The resulting configuration is displayed on the right.

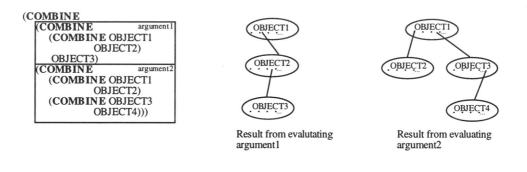

Result from evalutating   Result from evaluating
argument1   argument2

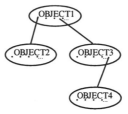

Final result

Figure 4.3
Here we see an example of how COMBINE avoids inserting multiple instances of the same object within a configuration. If the two objects passed in as arguments overlap with one another, the largest of the two is returned as the result.

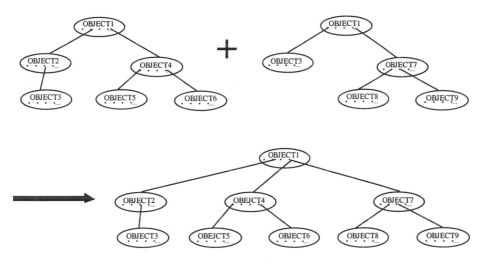

Figure 4.4
If the objects passed into COMBINE can not be combined by inserting the second one into the first one and they have the same root primitive object, they can be combined by merging. Here we see how merging produces a more complete resulting configuration.

pear within the same configuration. So with the most straightforward version of COMBINE, every program that contains more than one instance of the same object produces a result that is not a legal configuration. In order to ensure that every possible program produces a legal configuration, COMBINE must be altered in such a way as to prevent more than one instance of the same object from appearing within the same result. Thus, it inspects its two arguments to test whether they are composed of instances of any of the same objects. If they are, rather than inserting the second object into the first object, it returns the one composed of the largest number of primitive objects. See Figure 4.2.2 for an example of this. The instance of COMBINE at the top level, once its arguments are evaluated, is presented with two composite objects as arguments. Its first argument is composed of objects one through three. Its second argument is composed of objects one through four. Since there is overlap between the two arguments, they cannot be combined into a single legal configuration by inserting one into the other. Instead, the one composed of the largest number of primitive objects is returned. Thus, in this case, the one composed of objects one through four is returned as the result.

As discussed in Section 4.2, each hole on an object corresponds to a relationship that may hold between the associated object and another object. To precisely specify how to construct a configuration, a decision must be made within the COMBINE function of which hole to insert the second object into on the first object. Each hole has restrictions on it about what types of objects may be inserted into it. For example, it does not make sense for an inanimate object to be the actor of an action. A rock cannot chase a mouse. These restrictions are specified in a meaning representation specification that lists the full set of possible primitives, which relationships are associated with each primitive, and what types of objects can be inserted into holes corresponding to those relationships. The COMBINE function makes reference to this specification so that it can ensure that every object it inserts into a hole in another object is appropriate for the specified relationship. In some cases, there will not be an appropriate hole in one object to insert the other object into. In that case, as in the case above, the largest of the two objects will be returned as the result.

In some cases, as in Figure 4.2.2, it is not possible to insert the second object into the first object, but the two objects can be combined by merging instead. Objects that have the same root can be merged into a single, possibly more complete, object. Merging takes place by first pruning the programs that generated the two arguments that were input to COMBINE. This pruning is done such that the only instances of COMBINE in the program that remain are those that when evaluated made insertions that contributed to the construction of those arguments. The remaining instances of COMBINE from the two programs are then combined into a single set. The largest subset of the cumulative set of instances of COMBINE is then extracted such that when they are composed into a single program, every COMBINE will be able to make an insertion when it is evaluated. Whenever it is possible to merge, it is preferable over simply returning the largest argument since it has the potential for returning a result that is more complete. Thus, whenever it is not possible to insert, but it is possible to merge, COMBINE will merge rather than return one or the other argument. In Figure 4.2.2 we see configurations resulting from two programs that can be merged as well as the configuration resulting from the merged program.

It would be possible to have a separate MERGE function in the function set, but it makes sense to keep both actions within the same function. The cases in which it is possible to insert and when it is possible to merge are almost always mutually exclusive in practice, and where they are not, inserting is almost always preferable to merging. Thus, it is possible to get by with a single function that can accommodate each of the three possible cases. This is preferable to having two separate functions since it avoids the case where one or the other function is assigned inappropriately. Note that this is also a reason why GP is more appropriate for this application than GA with configurations as its data structure [Michalewicz, 1994]. Although it would be possible to do almost the equivalent of ROSE's application of GP by using GA with a configuration data structure, typed crossover, and a merge operator, the algorithm would lose control over which specific cases the merge operator is applied to.

Figure 4.2.2 contains the definition of the COMBINE function as it is used in ROSE. It takes two possible composite objects as arguments. If it can insert the second object into a hole in the first object, it selects a hole and then does the insertion. If it is not possible to do an insertion, it tests whether it is possible to merge the two chunks. If this is not possible either, it returns the object composed of the largest number of primitive objects. With this COMBINE function it is true both that every target configuration can be built by a

COMBINE takes as input two objects
    If the two objects do no overlap with one another
    and there is a hole in the first object in which to
    insert the second object
        Select a hole
        Insert the second object into the selected hole in the first object
    Otherwise if both objects have the same primitive root object
        Merge the two objects
    Otherwise return the most comprehensive object

Figure 4.5
Working definition of COMBINE

program with only COMBINE in its function set and that every possible program consisting
of instances of primitive objects and instances of COMBINE produces a legal configuration.

4.3 ROSE's Application of GP

ROSE operates in two stages: partial parsing and combination, each of which are described
in this section. The focus of this chapter is the GP based combination stage. However,
since the output of the partial parsing stage provides the input to the combination stage, it
is necessary to describe both.

4.3.1 The Partial Parsing Stage

The robust parser used in ROSE is Lavie's GLR* parser [Lavie, 1995] modified to produce
analyses for contiguous portions of a sentence. The partial parsing stage is described in
depth in [Rosé, 1997]. In this chapter it is described only briefly.

    The goal of the partial parsing stage is to obtain an analysis for islands of the speaker's
sentence if it is not possible to obtain an analysis for the whole sentence. In Figure 4.6
we see an abstract representation of the parser output for "What did you say about what
was your schedule for Thursday?" The parser produced seven partial analyses covering
different parts of the sentence. The details of the underlying representation are not shown,
but note that it is such that partial analyses can be assembled into configurations in the same
way that primitive objects were in Section 4.2. The one difference between the objects
constructed by the parser and those described in Section 4.2 is that some of these objects
could be said to overlap with one another because they cover overlapping parts of the same
sentence. For example, the object corresponding to "have scheduled for Thursday" and
the object corresponding to "have scheduled" both cover the word "schedule" from the
original sentence. Therefore, these two objects can not both appear together in a legal
configuration. Likewise, the "you" object overlaps with the "what was your" and "was

Sentence: What did you say about what was your schedule for Thursday?

Partial Parse:

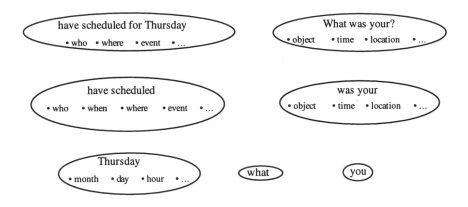

Thursday
• month   • day   • hour   • ...

what   you

Ideal Configuration:

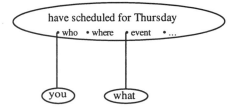

Figure 4.6
Here we see a representation of the objects produced by the partial parser for the sentence "What did you say about what was your schedule for Thursday." The ideal configuration is displayed at the bottom.

Table 4.2
This tableau describes how GP is set up for the Combination problem.

Objective:	Find the program that generates the target configuration
Terminal Set:	Objects produced by the partial parser
Function Set:	COMBINE
Raw Fitness:	Evaluated by an indirect measure. See section 4.3.2.2.
Standardized Fitness:	Same as raw fitness
Hits:	None. Since the target configuration is not known, it is impossible to have absolute certainty that you have a hit
Wrapper:	None.
Parameters:	Population Size = 32, Generations = 4
Success Predicate:	None.

your" objects. Thus, the test for overlap in COMBINE must ensure not only that the same parser object appear at most once in the resulting configuration, but also that the same part of the sentence only be represented once in a resulting configuration.

Because in the parser's output "schedule" is misanalyzed as an action rather than as an object, there is no way to assemble a configuration to represent the exact meaning of this sentence with the available objects. The configuration with the closest meaning to the original sentence that can be constructed from the available objects represents the meaning "What do you have scheduled for Thursday?"

Notice that the ideal configuration does not include both of the objects covering the largest portions of the sentence. Instead, it includes one of them along with the two smallest objects. Thus, the task of selecting the ideal subset of objects produced by the parser to include in the output configuration is not a trivial task. It cannot be predicted with a straightforward metric such as picking the subset that includes the largest non-overlapping objects.

4.3.2   The Combination Stage

The combination stage takes as input the objects returned by the parser. The goal is to evolve a program that builds the ideal configuration out of these objects.

4.3.2.1   Applying Genetic Programming

The GP based combination algorithm used in ROSE is Koza's lisp kernel [Koza, 1992]. The goal of this combination algorithm is to evolve a program that when executed constructs the ideal configuration from the objects returned by the parser. Notice that in Figure 4.6, the ideal configuration is composed of a subset of the full set of objects returned by the parser. Thus, two things are accomplished in parallel by this application of GP. The correct subset of objects is selected, and at the same time, the correct way to assemble them is determined.

The terminal set for the combination problem is the set of objects returned by the parser. The function set contains only the COMBINE function. The initial random population of programs is generated with the ramped half and half method with a maximum depth of 5. Rather than selecting terminal symbols with a uniform distribution, each object is selected with a frequency proportionate to the percentage of the sentence it covers. These large objects are not guaranteed to be the more appropriate objects in the set for building the correct configuration, but in practice they tend to be better than the other smaller objects. By selecting objects as terminal symbols in this way, the most comprehensive objects appear more frequently in the population. Thus, it is more likely for a larger object to appear in a configuration produced by an individual, but it is not impossible for a smaller object to appear.

Once a population of individuals is generated, the fitness of each individual program is computed. The fitness of each individual is calculated using the function described in Section 4.3.2.2 that combines multiple goodness indicators. Each instance of COMBINE has a static local variable that keeps track of which hole in the parent object was selected for inserting the child object. In this way, it can be ensured that each time the program is evaluated, the same result will be produced. The fitness function is trained in such a way that the fitness score assigned to each individual program is indicative of the goodness of the resulting configuration.

Once the fitness for each individual is computed, subsequent generations are computed using fitness proportionate reproduction. The fitness proportionate reproduction fraction was set to 10%, mutation 10%, and crossover 80%, with 75% of crossovers constrained to occur at function points. Since every program composed of instances of the objects produced by the parser and instances of COMBINE is guaranteed to produce a legal configuration, straightforward versions of crossover and mutation can be used. Crossover in ROSE's combination algorithm simply selects a sub-program from each parent program and swaps them. The maximum depth for individuals after crossover is set to 15. Generally, a depth of 15 is far larger than necessary for including the steps necessary for constructing the target configuration. However, since it is common for portions of the evolved program to have no effect on the resulting configuration as discussed in Section 4.2.2, it is necessary to allow larger programs to be evolved. With a larger population and larger number of generations, programs with a smaller depth and equivalent performance could be evolved. However, in order to force the combination algorithm to perform as efficiently as possible, it is allowed here to produce sloppier programs.

When the resulting programs are evaluated, wherever configurations resulting from the execution of sub-programs are no longer appropriate for inserting into the hole where they were previously inserted, a new hole is selected. Similarly, mutation takes place by constructing a random subprogram in the same way that the initial population was generated and inserting it in place of a randomly selected sub-program in the parent program. The maximum depth for randomly generated sub-programs is 4.

4.3.2.2   Fitness Evaluation for the Combination Problem

The programs created by the GP based combination algorithm can be thought of as repair hypotheses. Once a population of hypotheses is generated, each individual in the population is evaluated for its fitness. Evaluating the fitness of repair hypotheses is the most difficult part of applying genetic programming to repair. The ROSE approach to fitness evaluation of repair hypotheses is one of the aspects that makes this application of genetic programming unique. An ideal fitness function for repair would rank hypotheses that generate structures closer to the target structure better than those that are more different. In comparing relative goodness of alternative repair hypotheses, the repair module must consider not only which subset of objects returned by the parser to include in the final result, but also how to put them together. However, it does not know what the ideal configuration is. Since the repair module does not have access to this information, it must rely upon indirect evidence for determining which hypotheses are better than others. A fitness function is trained to use this indirect evidence for the purpose of ranking repair hypotheses in a useful manner.

Four pieces of indirect evidence about the relative goodness of repair hypotheses can be computed for each repair hypothesis: the number of primitive objects in the resulting structure (NUM_CONCEPTS), the number of insertions involved (NUM_STEPS), a statistical score reflecting the goodness of insertions (STAT_SCORE), and the percentage of the sentence that is covered by the resulting configuration (PERCENT_COV). These parameters are generally useful in ranking hypotheses. Both NUM_CONCEPTS and PERCENT_COV provide an estimate of the completeness of solutions. NUM_STEPS provides an estimate of the simplicity of the program. And as much as the statistical goodness score gives a reliable indication of goodness of fit between objects and relationships and quality of parser produced objects, repair hypotheses with better than average statistical score are more likely to be better hypotheses. The statistical score of a hypothesis is calculated by averaging the statistical scores for each repair action, where the statistical score of each included object is the statistical score assigned by the parser to the analysis of that object, and the statistical score of inserting an object into a hole in another object is defined by the information gain between the hole and the type of the inserted object. The information gain between the hole and the type of the inserted object is a measure of how strongly the hole predicts which type of object will fill it.

Intuitively, one would prefer more complete hypotheses over less complete ones. And following the principle of Occam's razor, other things being equal, one would prefer simpler solutions over more complex ones. Since simpler solutions may be less complete, and more complete hypotheses might be more complex, the trained fitness function must learn how to balance these two competing qualities. A fitness function trained with GP was used to combine these four pieces of information in order to rank alternative repair hypotheses.

The fitness function was trained over a corpus of 48 randomly selected sentences from a separate corpus from that used in the evaluation discussed in Section 4.5. Each of these 48 sentences were such that repair was required for constructing a reasonable interpretation. In this corpus each sentence was coupled with its corresponding ideal meaning representation structure. To generate training data for training the repair fitness function, the repair module was run using an ideal fitness function that evaluated the goodness of hypotheses by comparing the meaning representation structure produced by the hypothesis with the ideal structure. It assigned a fitness score to the hypothesis equal to the number of primitive objects in the largest substructure shared by the produced configuration and the ideal configuration. The four scores that serve as input to the trained fitness function were extracted from each of the hypotheses constructed in each generation after the programs were ranked by the ideal fitness function. The resulting ranked lists of sets of scores were used to train a fitness function that can order the sets of scores the same way that the ideal fitness function ranked the associated hypotheses. Thus, although there were only 48 sentences in the training set, there were four times that many training cases. While this is still a relatively small number of training cases, no over fitting effects were observed.

The genetic programming algorithm used to train the repair fitness function took as terminals the four scores plus a random real number function. The function set included addition, subtraction, multiplication, and division. The fitness of alternative proposed fitness functions generated during the genetic search was computed by first ordering the set of scores in each training example using the hypothesized function. The length of the greatest common subsequence between the ideal ordering and the generated ordering was then computed. The greatest common subsequence was computed using Dijkstra's well known algorithm [Cormen et al., 1989]. The fitness of each hypothesized repair fitness function was the average greatest common subsequence score over the entire training corpus of 48 sentences. A single run with a population size of 1000 was used, and the training process continued for approximately 2000 generations, until subsequent generations didn't produce a function with performance better than the previous generation.

4.4   Why GP?

Repairing extra-grammatical sentences is an unusual application for GP in that it requires a relatively small population size and number of generations. In practice, a population size of 32 and 4 generations has been determined to be adequate for repairing extra-grammatical sentences in the scheduling domain.

Although it may appear on the surface that a simpler control structure such as a priority queue would suffice, such an approach would require the system to decide which set of repairs to start with and then which alternative hypotheses logically follow in an ordered manner. However, since the goodness of hypotheses is determined by factors that make competing predictions (completeness versus simplicity), no such prioritization can effectively be determined a priori. Likewise, what distinguishes hypotheses from one another is both which subset of objects is included in the hypotheses and how the objects are composed. It is not clear what principle should be used in generating successive hypotheses to test - whether it is better to change the subset of objects included in the hypothesis or

Sentence: What did you say about what was your schedule for Thursday?

Locally Optimal:

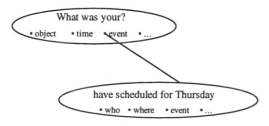

Less Complete but More Correct:

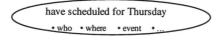

Ideal Configuration:

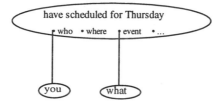

Figure 4.7
Here we see an example of a locally optimal solution for the example in Figure 4.6. It contains the two largest objects returned by the parser. No single operation on this configuration can improve the quality of the solution since removing the suboptimal object results in a solution that is more correct, but less complete.

simply to change the way they are assembled. Finally, it is not clear what stopping criteria one would use for an application of the priority queue method, or how one would avoid locally optimal solutions.

The problem of locally optimal solutions is a big one in this application. A locally optimal solution from the example in Figure 4.6 is found in Figure 4.4. The locally optimal solution is composed of the two largest objects produced by the parser. It can not be made to cover any more of the sentence by inserting any additional objects since every other object in the set returned by the parser overlaps with one of the objects already included in the configuration. However, the object covering "what" and "you" included in that solution corresponds to a suboptimal analysis of that portion of the sentence. Before the best configuration can be built, the object corresponding to "What was your?" must be removed, resulting in a configuration that covers less of the sentence than the suboptimal solution, but not containing the suboptimal analysis. The optimal configuration can then be constructed by inserting the objects corresponding to "what" and "you" separately into the object corresponding to "have scheduled for Thursday". Thus, the result must temporarily be made less complete in order to be made both correct and complete.

Thus, GP's opportunistic search method is very sensible in this case, although the appropriateness of GP-like approaches such as SIHC [O'Reilly and Oppacher, 1995] have yet to be tested as alternatives for this application. GP first samples its search space widely and shallowly and then narrows in on the regions surrounding the most promising looking points. It has the ability to search a large space efficiently. As described in Section 4.2.1, the number of alternative configurations grows quickly as the number of objects produced by the parser increases. The number of alternative individuals evaluated by the genetic programming algorithm can be fixed ahead of time by setting the population size and the maximum number of generations. By limiting the population size to 32 and the number of generations to 4, the repair module is constrained to search only 128 alternatives. Thus, if the number of objects produced by the parser is any more than four, the GP approach searches only 11% or less of the lower bound estimate on the number of alternative hypotheses. If the number of objects produced by the parser is exactly four, the number of alternatives explored is similar. The average number of objects produced by the parser in the evaluation presented in Section 4.5 was 5.66. In 55.7% of the cases, the parser produced more than four objects. Thus, the GP approach yields a significant savings in time in more than half of the cases where repair is used. The great success with examining such a small portion of the search space is perhaps due to the statistical bias within the COMBINE function.

4.5 Evaluation

ROSE's performance was evaluated in terms of efficiency and effectiveness in comparison with the two main competing approaches to robust interpretation, namely the maximally

Table 4.3
This table reports the percentage of sentences for the alternative interpretation strategies that either produced a nil result or were assigned a grade of Bad, Partial, Okay, or Perfect by an impartial human judge.

	NIL	Bad	Partial	Okay	Perfect	Total Acceptable
MDP 1	21.4%	3.4%	3.4%	18.4%	53.4%	71.8%
MDP 3	16.2%	4.2%	5.0%	19.6%	55.0%	74.6%
MDP 5	8.4%	8.2%	6.0%	21.0%	56.4%	77.4%
GLR with Restarts	9.2%	6.4%	12.8%	19.4%	52.2%	71.6%
GLR with Restarts + Repair	0.4%	9.6%	11.8%	23.4%	54.8%	78.2%
GLR*	2.2%	8.8%	11.6%	21.4%	56.0%	77.4%
GLR* + Repair	0.6%	8.8%	10.6%	23.6%	56.4%	80.0%

flexible parsing approach [Lehman, 1989; Hipp, 1992] and the restrictive partial parsing approach [Lavie, 1995; Abney, 1996; Ehrlich and Hanrieder, 1996; Srinivas et al., 1996; Federici et al., 1996; Jensen and Heidorn, 1993; Hayes and Mouradain, 1981; Kwasny and Sondheimer, 1981; Lang, 1989]. The purpose of this evaluation was to demonstrate the appropriateness of employing GP for the purpose of repairing extra-grammatical sentences. ROSE's two stage approach, employing a GP based combination algorithm, is demonstrated here to achieve a better effectiveness/efficiency trade-off than either of the above mentioned single stage approaches.

In order to compare the alternative approaches keeping as many factors constant as possible, the same parser was used in each case, parameterized to control the flexibility of the algorithm. The GLR* parser [Lavie, 1995; Lavie and Tomita, 1993] is used in five different parameter settings described in depth in [Rosé, 1997], Chapter 10, Section 3. The most restrictive version, GLR w/restarts, constructs analyses for contiguous portions of the input text. The less restrictive GLR* setting allows the parser to skip over words in order to construct analyses for non-contiguous portions of the input. The more flexible MDP 1, MDP 3, and MDP 5 settings allow the parser to either insert or delete up to 1, 3, or 5 words respectively in order to search for an analysis for each extra-grammatical sentence. GLR w/restarts and GLR* serve as representatives of the restrictive partial parsing approach. MDP 1, MDP 3, and MDP 5 serve as representatives of the maximally flexible parser approach. ROSE is evaluated using each of the restrictive partial parsers, referred to as GLR w/restarts + repair and GLR* + repair respectively. Thus, seven different specific approaches are evaluated in the experiments described here. Each approach was evaluated using the same semantic grammar with approximately 1000 rules, with the same lexicon of approximately 3000 lexical items, on the same previously unseen test corpus of 500 sentences.

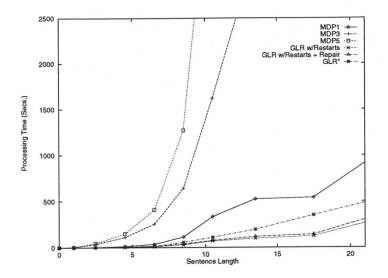

Figure 4.8
This diagram displays mean run times for six alternative interpretation strategies as it varies for different sentence lengths. Notice that the three **MDP** approaches are far slower than the other approaches with or without the GP based repair stage.

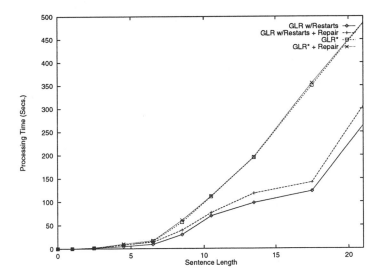

Figure 4.9
Here we see mean processing time for two alternative partial parsers, namely **GLR w/restarts** and **GLR***, with and without repair. Notice that the GP based repair stage does not dramatically increase the practical run time of the parsers.

For each sentence, the meaning representation structure returned by the alternative interpretation processes was passed to a generation component that generates a sentence in English. This text was then graded by a human judge as Bad, Partial, Okay, or Perfect in terms of interpretation quality. The human judge was a staff person on the JANUS project experienced in grading interpretation quality but not having been involved in the development of any portion of the system being evaluated. The judge was not aware of which approach produced each result. A grade of "Partial" indicates that the result communicated part of the content of the original sentence while not containing any incorrect information. "Okay" indicates that the generated sentence communicated all of the relevant information in the original sentence but not in a perfectly fluent way. "Perfect" indicates both that the result communicated the relevant information and that it did so in a smooth, high quality manner.

Run times for all seven approaches are found in figures 4.8 and 4.9. Notice that all of the MDP approaches are significantly slower than the other approaches. Also notice that the partial parsing approaches with repair are not significantly slower than their corresponding partial parsing approaches without repair. In particular, in Figure 4.9 we see that run times for GLR* and GLR* + repair are barely distinguishable. This small difference in run times between the versions with repair and without are accounted for by the fact that the repair stage is not time consuming (taking 30 seconds on average) and is only used when both necessary and possible.

By comparing the run times for the alternative conditions in Figures 4.8 and 4.9 with the interpretation quality scores found in Table 4.3, it becomes evident that the two-stage ROSE approach achieves a better effectiveness/efficiency trade-off than either the maximally flexible parsing approach or the restrictive partial parsing approach. Predictably, MDP 5 shows an improvement over MDP 1, with an associated significant cost in run time. Also, not surprisingly, the very restrictive GLR w/restarts, while it is fastest, has a correspondingly lower associated interpretation quality. However, GLR w/restarts + repair outperforms all of the single stage approaches, second only to GLR* + repair, which is slightly slower although still faster than MDP 1. Though these results demonstrate certain trends in the performance of the alternative approaches, the differences in interpretation quality overall are very small. Nevertheless, the very significant difference in runtime performance demonstrates that the two-stage ROSE approach is a clear winner.

The contribution made by ROSE's GP based Combination stage is more evident when considering the maximum potential repair that is possible using chunks produced by the parser. For example, with GLR w/restarts + repair, the percentage of sentences in the test corpus where it was true both that repair was necessary and that the parser produced sufficient chunks for actually constructing an acceptable hypothesis was only 8.6%. Therefore, the 6.6% of additional acceptable hypotheses produced by ROSE constitutes 76.7% of the maximum potential improvement. Though this still leaves room for further work, it demonstrates that a significant percentage of the maximum improvement that is possible to achieve with repair was indeed realized by ROSE's application of GP.

4.6 Challenges

This chapter describes ROSE, RObustness with Structural Evolution, an application of GP to the problem of robust interpretation of extra-grammatical sentences. The genetic programming algorithm searches for the near-optimal or optimal ways to assemble analyses for fragments of an extra-grammatical sentence into a single meaning representation structure. ROSE is demonstrated here to achieve a better effectiveness/efficiency trade-off than either the restrictive partial parsing approach or the maximally flexible parsing approach.

These promising results point the way towards a number of avenues for future exploration of GP applied to the problem of robust interpretation. For example, since each individual generated by ROSE is a program that constructs a single meaning representation structure, it works best only in cases where an utterance contains a single sentence. For processing multi-sentence utterances, the GP algorithm would have to be able to construct individuals composed of multiple programs each assembling a subset of the chunks produced by the parser. Not only would the genetic search be responsible for determining which chunks to include in the final analysis, but it would also have to decide how to partition this set into subsets each representing a single sentence, and then how to compose the chunks for each sentence into a single meaning representation structure.

Secondly, since ROSE works by assembling the chunks returned by the parser, the resulting meaning representation structure can only represent the portions of the sentence that the parser is able to construct a partial analysis for. One can imagine that something similar to the Random Constant used in many numerical GP applications could be used to make guesses about the missing portions (perhaps statistically). The genetic search would then be responsible for determining when it was the case that an essential part of the analysis was missing and what was likely to be missing.

Finally, just as ROSE is used for determining how sub-sentence units of meaning relate to one another, one can imagine GP being used to determine how the meanings for individual sentences fit together into a larger discourse structure. [Mason and Rosé, 1998] reports on some preliminary work in this area, specifically in evolving constraint functions for operators to function within a plan-based discourse processor [Rosé et al., 1995].

Acknowledgements

The work described in this chapter is part of the author's dissertation research. Lori Levin, Barbara Di Eugenio, Jaime Carbonell, Alon Lavie, Johanna Moore, and Sandra Carberry served on the committee that advised this research and all deserve recognition for the valuable contribution they made in countless direct and indirect ways. In particular, Lori Levin, who served as the author's thesis advisor, tirelessly read and commented on numerous drafts of this work and kept the author focused and on track throughout her journey towards the completion of her PhD. Alon Lavie more than anyone else acted as a partner in this research, collaborating on its evaluation, but even more importantly providing critical feedback on many of its core underlying ideas. Most of all, Eric Rosé deserves the author's deepest gratitude for originally introducing her to genetic programming, but most of all for providing constant support, encouragement, and companionship without which this work would have been impossible. This chapter is dedicated to the author's precious baby daughter Rachel, the apple of her mother's eye.

This continuing research is partly supported by the Office of Naval Research, Cognitive and Neural Sciences Division (Grant #N00014-93-I-0812).

Bibliography

Abney, S. (1996), "Partial parsing via finite-state cascades," in *Proceedings of the Eighth European Summer School In Logic, Language and Information, Prague, Czech Republic*.

Bod, R. (1998), "Spoken dialogue interpretation with the dop model," in *Proceedings of COLING-ACL '98*.

Bod, R. and Kaplan, R. (1998), "A probabilistic corpus-driven model for lexical-functional analysis," in *Proceedings of COLING-ACL '98*.

Cormen, T. H., Leiserson, C. E., and Rivest, R. L. (1989), *Introduction to Algorithms (Ch 25)*, The MIT Press.

Danieli, M. and Gerbino, E. (1995), "Metrics for evaluating dialogue strategies in a spoken language system," in *Working Notes of the AAAI Spring Symposium on Empirical Methods in Discourse Interpretation and Generation*.

Ehrlich, U. and Hanrieder, G. (1996), "Robust speech parsing," in *Proceedings of the Eighth European Summer School In Logic, Language and Information, Prague, Czech Republic*.

Federici, S., Montemagni, S., and Pirrelli, V. (1996), "Shallow parsing and text chunking: a view on underspecification in syntax," in *Proceedings of the Eighth European Summer School In Logic, Language and Information, Prague, Czech Republic*.

Gamut, L. T. F. (1991), *Logic, Language, and Meaning Volume 2: Intensional Logic and Logical Grammar*, University of Chicago Press.

Hayes, D. and Mouradain, G. V. (1981), "Flexible parsing," *Computational Linguistics*, 7(4).

Hipp, D. R. (1992), *Design and Development of Spoken Natural-Language Dialog Parsing Systems*, PhD thesis, Dept. of Computer Science, Duke University.

Jensen, K. and Heidorn, G. E. (1993), *Parse Fitting and Prose Fixing (Ch 5), In Natural Language Processing: the PLNLP Approach*, Kluwer Academic Publishers.

Koza, J. (1992), *Genetic Programming: On the Programming of Computers by Means of Natural Selection*, MIT Press.

Kwasny, S. and Sondheimer, N. K. (1981), "Relaxation techniques for parsing grammatically ill-formed input in natural language understanding systems," *American Journal of Computational Linguistics*, 7(2).

Lang, B. (1989), "Parsing incomplete sentences," in *Proceedings of the 12th International Conference on Computational Linguistics (COLING 89)*.

Lavie, A. (1995), *A Grammar Based Robust Parser For Spontaneous Speech*, PhD thesis, School of Computer Science, Carnegie Mellon University.

Lavie, A., Gates, D., Gavalda, M., Mayfield, L., and Levin, A. W. L. (1996), "Multi-lingual translation of spontaneously spoken language in a limited domain," in *Proceedings of COLING 96, Kopenhagen*.

Lavie, A. and Tomita, M. (1993), "GLR* - an efficient noise-skipping parsing algorithm for context free grammars.," in *Proceedings of the Third International Workshop on Parsing Technologies*.

Lehman, J. F. (1989), *Adaptive Parsing: Self-Extending Natural Language Interfaces*, PhD thesis, School of Computer Science, Carnegie Mellon University.

Mason, M. and Rosé, C. P. (1998), "Automatically learning constraints for plan-based discourse processors," in *Working Notes for the AAAI Spring Symposium on Machine Learning and Discourse Processing*.

Michalewicz, Z. (1994), *Genetic Algorithms + Data Structures = Evolution Programs*, New York: Springer-Verlag.

O'Reilly, U. and Oppacher, F. (1995), "A comparative analysis of genetic programming," in *Advances in Genetic Programming II*, P. J. Angeline and J. K. Kinnear (Eds.), The MIT Press.

Rosé, C. P. (1997), *Robust Interactive Dialogue Interpretation*, PhD thesis, School of Computer Science, Carnegie Mellon University.

Rosé, C. P., Eugenio, B. D., Levin, L. S., and Ess-Dykema, C. V. (1995), "Discourse processing of dialogues with multiple threads," in *Proceedings of the ACL*.

Schank, R. (1975), *Conceptual information processing*, North Holland, Amsterdam.

Srinivas, B., Doran, C., Hockey, B., and Joshi, A. (1996), "An approach to robust partial parsing and evaluation metrics," in *Proceedings of the Eighth European Summer School In Logic, Language and Information, Prague, Czech Republic*.

van den Berg, M., Bod, R., and Scha, R. (1994), "A corpus based approach to semantic interpretation," in *Proceedings of the Nineth Amsterdam Colloquium*.

van Noord, G. (1996), "Robust parsing with the head-corner parser," in *Proceedings of the Eighth European Summer School In Logic, Language and Information, Prague, Czech Republic*.

Woszcyna, M., Aoki-Waibel, N., Buo, F. D., Coccaro, N., Horiguchi, K., Kemp, T., Lavie, A., McNair, A., Polzin, T., Rogina, I., Rosé, C. P., Schultz, T., Suhm, B., Tomita, M., and Waibel, A. (1994), "JANUS 93: Towards spontaneous speech translation," in *Proceedings of the International Conference on Acoustics, Speech, and Signal Processing*.

Woszcyna, M., Coccaro, N., Eisele, A., Lavie, A., McNair, A., Polzin, T., Rogina, I., Rosé, C. P., Sloboda, T., Tomita, M., Tsutsumi, J., Waibel, N., Waibel, A., and Ward, W. (1993), "Recent advances in JANUS: a speech translation system," in *Proceedings of the ARPA Human Languages Technology Workshop*.

5 Time Series Modeling Using Genetic Programming: An Application to Rainfall-Runoff Models

P. A. Whigham and P. F. Crapper

This chapter describes the application of a grammatically-based Genetic Programming system to discover rainfall-runoff relationships for two vastly different catchments. A context-free grammar is used to define the search space for the mathematical language used to express the evolving programs. A daily time series of rainfall-runoff is used to train the evolving population. A deterministic lumped parameter model, based on the unit hydrograph, is compared with the results of the evolved models on an independent data set. The favourable results of the Genetic Programming approach show that machine learning techniques are potentially a useful tool for developing hydrological models, especially when the relationship between rainfall and runoff is poor.

5.1 Introduction

Many problems of interest to natural resource scientists may be expressed in the form of a time series model. This chapter describes a geographic problem, represented at the catchment scale and daily time scale, which attempts to relate the rainfall incident on a catchment to the stream flow at the exit from the catchment. The produced function has the form $\mathcal{F}(r_1, r_2, .. r_n)$, where $r_1 .. r_n$ are rainfall variables from current and/or previous days. $\mathcal{F}$ represents the current days streamflow. The difficulties involved with producing $\mathcal{F}$ are clear when we consider the numerous complex features that directly and indirectly contribute to the measured behaviour. The response of the catchment (especially Australian catchments) is highly capricious, depending not only on the catchment characteristics (e.g. topography, area), vegetation characteristics and antecedent conditions, but the meteorological conditions (e.g. areal distribution of rainfall) in a highly non-linear and unpredictable fashion. Developing models that describe this relationship help in understanding the overall behaviour of the catchment and support the development of more process-based models and catchment classification schemes. Additionally, many natural resource models use streamflow as an input. Although reliable rainfall records often exist for a catchment, only limited streamflow data is generally available.

This chapter compares the performance of a variant of Genetic Programming (GP) (Koza, 1992) to a traditional hydrological model which predicts the rainfall-runoff relationship for specific catchments. Rainfall-runoff models have been previously developed using other machine learning techniques, such as neural networks (Minns and Hall,1996), however the form of these models was not easily translated into interpretations of catchment process and behaviour. The advantage of using a symbolic learning system, such as GP, is that the resulting model may be interpreted in terms of the process and behaviour of the catchment. This can often help in understanding the underlying processes that drive the catchment response and can be used to classify and generalise differing catchments. GP has been previously applied to time series prediction (Mulloy, Riolo and Savit, 1996) however no previous work, to the authors knowledge, has applied GP to the problem of predicting rainfall-runoff relationships.

5.2 The Genetic Programming System CFG-GP

A variant of genetic programming, context-free grammar GP (CFG-GP), (Whigham, 1996) uses a grammar to define the space of legal sentences that can be explored during evolution. The system allows a transparent definition of language bias by instantiating the way in which terminals of the language may be legally combined.

A formal grammar is a production system which defines how nonterminal symbols may be transformed to create terminal sentences of a language. A grammar is represented by a four-tuple (N, Σ, P, S), where N is the alphabet of nonterminal symbols, Σ is the alphabet of terminal symbols, P is the set of productions and S is the designated start symbol. For example, the following grammar, G_{math}, defines a language for generating all possible mathematical expressions using the operators +, -, *, /, and a set of random real numbers, represented by the symbol, $\Re$.

$G_{math} =$
$\qquad${S,
$\qquad$N = {M},
$\qquad\Sigma$={+,-,*,/,$\Re$},
$\qquad$P =
$\qquad\quad${
$\qquad\quad$ S $\rightarrow$ M
$\qquad\quad$ M $\rightarrow$ + M M | - M M | * M M | / M M | $\Re$
$\qquad\quad$ }
$\qquad$ }

The initial random population is generated using the grammar by selecting random productions which match the current nonterminals in the derivation, starting with S, and limited by some maximum depth of derivation tree. A derivation step represents the application of a production to some string which contains a nonterminal. In general, a series of derivation steps may be represented by a syntax tree or derivation tree. These trees have genetic operators applied to them in a manner similar to normal GP program trees, except that crossover sites between derivation trees must use matching nonterminal sites.

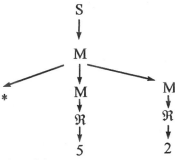

Figure 5.1
A Derivation Tree for the expression * 5 2, generated using the grammar G_{math}. S,M and $\Re$ are nonterminals symbols, while *, 5 and 2 are terminal symbols of the language.

For example, using G_{math}, the expression string * 5 2 could be generated from the following derivation steps:

$$S \Rightarrow M \Rightarrow * M M \Rightarrow * \Re M \Rightarrow * 5 M \Rightarrow * 5 \Re \Rightarrow * 5 2 \qquad \text{Equation 5.1}$$

The corresponding derivation tree for this sequence is shown in Figure 5.1. Crossover and mutation operators are applied directly to these trees.

Two search operators are used to modify the evolving rainfall-runoff model; the crossover operator is used as the search operator for each generation, mixing elements of potentially useful partial solutions in an attempt to build a better solution; a hill-climbing mutation is used as a fine-tuning operator that allows the random constants within the final best solution to be modified in an attempt to move towards a more optimal solution.

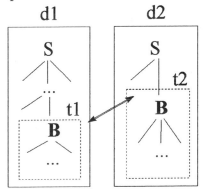

Figure 5.2
Crossover between derivation trees d1 and d2. The subtrees t1 and t2, with root node nonterminal B, are swapped to produce two new derivation trees (i.e. new programs). Crossover always swaps subtrees with the same root nonterminal.

Crossover applies 2 (parent) individuals and creates 2 (offspring) individuals. Each crossover operation is defined by two parameters: the probability of crossover occurring and the nonterminal $B \in N$ where crossover will be applied. Assuming that the crossover operator has been selected, two programs with derivation trees d_1 and d_2 are selected from the current population using a proportional fitness selection. Crossover, as shown in Figure 5.2, is then performed as follows:

1. Randomly select a subtree t1 from d1 with root node B.
2. Randomly select a subtree t2 from d2 with root node B.
3. Swap t1 and t2 thereby creating two new derivation trees d1* and d2*.
4. Insert d1* and d2* into the next-generation population.

If d_1 or d_2 do not contain the nonterminal B then no crossover is possible and the operation is aborted. The benefit of using derivation trees to represent the population now becomes clear; by defining crossover to swap subtrees at the same nonterminal guarantees that the space of possible programs is constrained to be part of the language defined by the grammar.

The rainfall-runoff grammar G_{flow} (see Section 5.4) defines mathematical expressions which are initially seeded with variables relating to current or previous rainfall, and random real numbers. These real numbers are used as constants throughout the evolution, and are combined into the partial solutions that are evolved. A final solution that uses one or more of these constants may be improved (based on the training data) by slight modifications of these constants. The hill climbing mutation applies small random changes to the constants of the best final program (derivation tree) and maintains the new solution only if it improves the final performance based on the training data. This mutation is applied a fixed number of times and may be considered as a fine tuning of the evolved solution.

A proportional fitness measure is used to select programs (i.e. derivation trees) each generation for crossover and reproduction.

5.3 Rainfall Runoff Modelling

One of the traditional approaches to hydrograph modelling (Jakeman, Littlewood, and Whitehead, 1990) is to use the concept of the Instantaneous Unit Hydrograph (IUH). The IUH is defined as the hydrograph produced by the instantaneous application of a unit depth of rainfall to a catchment. The shape of the IUH is similar to a single peak hydrograph with a rapid rise and a slower decay. The fundamental assumption in the IUH model is that the precipitation input is equal to the integrated streamflow output. The non-linear relationship between rainfall and streamflow has led to the development of the concept of *effective rainfall*, which is determined by applying a non-linear filter to the raw rainfall data. This effective rainfall is then equated with the integrated streamflow for the specified catchment.

The IHACRES model applied in this paper is based on IUH principles. The model defines a unit hydrograph for total streamflow by defining separate unit hydrographs for the quickflow and the slowflow components. The model is defined by six parameters, four of which are determined directly from the raw rainfall, streamflow and temperature (or a surrogate), while the other two (the non-linear parameters) are calibrated using a trial and error search procedure, optimising the model to fit the observed rainfall-runoff relationship. The fundamental conceptualisation in the non-linear module of the model is that catchment wetness varies with recent past rainfall and with evapotranspiration. A 'catchment wetness index' is computed for each time step on the basis of recent rainfall and temperature. The percentage of rainfall which becomes effective rainfall in any time step varies linearly between 0% and 100% as the catchment wetness index varies between zero and unity. An alternative conceptualisation of the catchment wetness index is that it represents the proportion of the catchment at a given time step which contributes eventually to streamflow, but it is important not stretch the physical interpretation of catchment wetness index too far. Conceptualisation of spatially distributed processes in both the non-linear and the linear modules is severely restricted by the spatially lumped nature of the model. An advantage of this approach is that the model needs only a small number of parameters. Additional details about the model are contained in (Littlewood and Jakeman, 1994). It is worth noting that this model is considered to be one of the standard approaches to rainfall-runoff modelling, and has been used successfully for a number of years.

5.4 CFG-GP Setup

The grammar, G_{flow}, used by CFG-GP to develop the rainfall-runoff models allowed simple mathematical functions to be evolved, and was defined as follows.

$G_{flow} =$

    {S,
     N = {EQU, NL, EXPN},
     Σ={+,-,*,/,exp,r0,r1,r2,r3,r4,r5,av5,av10,av15,
        av20,av25, av30, av40, av50,av60,av100,$\Re$},
     P =
     {
            S → + EQU NL
            NL → * EQU EXPN
            EXPN → exp EQU
            EQU → + EQU EQU | - EQU EQU
            EQU → * EQU EQU | / EQU EQU
            EQU → exp EQU
            EQU → r0 | r1 | r2 | r3 | r4 | r5
            EQU → av5 | av10 | av15 | av20 | av25
            EQU → av30 | av40 | av50 | av60 | av100
            EQU → $\Re$
     }
    }

The terminal symbols r0,r1,..r5 represent the rainfall for the current day up to the last 5 days rain. The av5, av10, .. av100 terminals are the average rainfall for the last 5, 10, ... 100 days, respectively. The terminal $\Re$ is a random floating point number between -10.0 and 10.0 which is generated for each occurrence of $\Re$ when the initial population is created. These random constants are potentially modified using the hill climbing mutation once the best, final generation, solution has been found using crossover. The exponential function is represented by the terminal string "exp". The grammar has a structural bias to form equations that are composed of a linear component and a non-linear (exponential) component. This is shown by the production S → + EQU NL, which forces all programs to have the minimal structure of A + B * exp(C), where A, B and C are climate variables or a random real number. The production EQU → exp EQU allows the exponential function to be included with any part of the evolved mathematical expression. The language bias merely forces the use of the exponential function at least once in the final solution.

Table 5.1
CFG-GP Parameter Settings used for all experiments.

CFG-GP Parameter	Value
POPULATION SIZE	1000
GENERATIONS	50
GRAMMAR	G_{flow}
MAX. TREE DEPTH	15
CROSSOVER $\otimes$ = {EQU}	90%
HILL CLIMB MUTATION	1000 times
FITNESS MEASURE	Minimise RMSE

Table 5.1 shows the CFG-GP setup parameters which were used to develop both catchment models. The crossover operator is applied only to the nonterminal EQU, with a probability of 90%. Hence approximately 10% of the population is passed unchanged into each subsequent generation. This ensures that good solutions are not prematurely removed from the population and that the building blocks that are useful are maintained. The root mean square error (RMSE) was used as the fitness measure. If P_t is the predicted runoff value at time t, A_t is the actual runoff value at time t, and there are N points in the training data (N > 1), then RMSE is defined as follows (Chatfield, 1984):

$$RMSE = \sqrt{\frac{\sum (P_t - A_t)^2}{N-1}} \qquad \text{Equation 5.2}$$

The CFG-GP system used the same training data as IHACRES to evolve the rainfall-runoff models. For IHACRES, the training data was used to calibrate the constants which appear in the IHACRES conceptual model. In the case of CFG-GP, the training data was used to both evolve suitable constants and to develop the underlying structure of the model itself. Comparison of results will only refer to the simulation (test) runs which use previously unseen data for the same location. The CFG-GP system was run 100 times for each catchment, with the best equation on the training data selected as a candidate for the final solution. The best candidate solution on the unseen data was selected as the resulting equation. The RMSE is used to compare the IHACRES and CFG-GP models for the simulation period. As an additional measure of performance the error in predicted total discharge (i.e. the sum of streamflow) for the simulation period is also calculated. However, this error is not used as part of the CFG-GP fitness function.

5.5 Catchment Descriptions and Results

In order to test the modelling approaches two very different catchments were chosen. The first catchment was the Teifi catchment at Glan Teifi in Wales, United Kingdom. The second catchment was located within the Namoi River catchment in northeastern New South Wales, Australia.

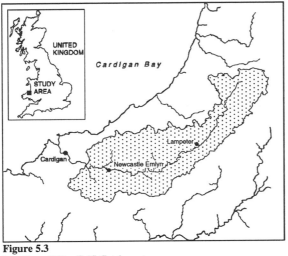

Figure 5.3
Location of Glan Teifi Catchment.

5.5.1 The Glan Teifi Catchment

The Teifi catchment is a rural catchment draining 893.6 km^2 with an average annual rainfall of 1368 mm. This station was maintained and operated by the UK Environment Agency and the data can be obtained from the Institute of Hydrology, Wallingford, Oxon, U.K. Compared with the Namoi catchment, the number of rain days per annum is much greater at Teifi but the maximum daily rainfall is only about half the value for the Namoi. The other major difference between the catchments is that runoff percentages (i.e. total runoff/total rainfall * 100) are very much higher at Glan Teifi. . The calibration run for Teifi was done from 27th July, 1982 to 31st July, 1985 and the simulation run was done from 23rd July, 1979 to the 27th July, 1982. For the calibration period the runoff percentage was 66.7% and for the simulation period the runoff percentage was 74.95%. The measured rainfall and streamflow for the Teifi catchment between July 1979 and July 1982 is shown in Figure 5.4 (rainfall events are shown as black columns). It is worth noting that the Glan Teifi catchment has a strong seasonal signal and that there appears to be a strong relationship between rainfall and runoff.

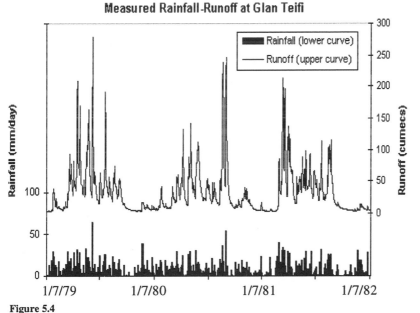

Figure 5.4
Measured Rainfall and Runoff at Glan Teifi.

5.5.2 Results

The simulated streamflows determined by IHACRES and CFG-GP are shown in Figures 5.5 and 5.6. The daily error for each model, calculated as (predicted flow - actual flow), is shown in the right-hand graphs for each figure. A visual comparison with the measured streamflow (Figure 5.4), indicates that both approaches have captured the basic response of the catchment, however IHACRES appears to have better represented the extreme streamflow events. The root mean square error (RMSE) for IHACRES was 0.0139 and for CFG-GP was 0.0142. The total discharge for the simulation period was measured as 35,600 cumecs, with IHACRES predicting 34,776 cumecs (2.3% error) and the evolved CFG-GP solution predicting 33,295 cumecs (6.4% error). The CFG-GP equation which was evolved for the Teifi catchment was defined as follows.

$$+(+(r1,+(av40,*(av10,av100))),*($$
$$*(av5, +(-17.121983,*(av5,av40))),exp(-3.739896))) \qquad \text{Equation 5.3}$$

This may be simplified to give:

$$r1 + av40+ (av10 * av100) +$$
$$(av5 * (-17.121983 + (av5 * av40)))* 0.0237 \qquad \text{Equation 5.4}$$

Equation 5.4 shows that the catchment was influenced by antecedent conditions that could extend for several months into the past (the av100 variable represents the average rainfall for the last 100 days). Note also that the constant exponential expression in Equation 5.3, namely exp(-3.739896), means that the resultant equation for runoff is only a linear function of r1 (previous days rain) ,av5, av10, av40, and av100. There is no non-linear component.

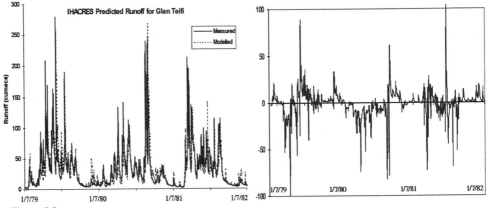

Figure 5.5
IHACRES Modelled Runoff at Glan Teifi for the test (unseen) time period. The Error (Predicted Value - Measured Value) is shown in the right-hand graph.

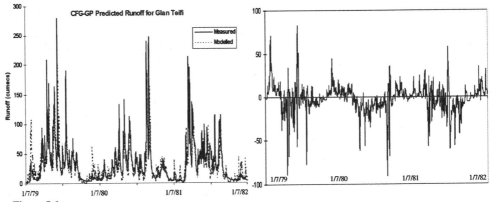
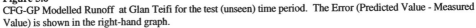

Figure 5.6
CFG-GP Modelled Runoff at Glan Teifi for the test (unseen) time period. The Error (Predicted Value - Measured Value) is shown in the right-hand graph.

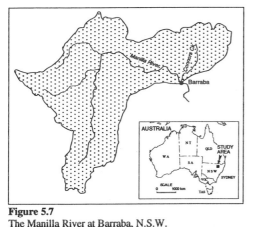

Figure 5.7
The Manilla River at Barraba, N.S.W.

5.5.3 The Namoi River Catchment

The Namoi River catchment (see Figure 5.7) was chosen to be as different as possible from the Teifi catchment. Using the Department of Land and Water Conservation (the gauging authority) naming convention the catchment is referred to as 419030 or the Manilla Rv at Barraba (30° 23' 24" S and 150° 37' 08" E). This catchment is approx. 568 km^2 and drains the southern part of the Nandewar Range. Within the catchment there are three reliable long-term raingauge stations with average annual rainfalls of 686mm, 704mm and 727mm. These stations have a reasonable spread of location and altitude and the average of the three values has been used as the catchment rainfall. More sophisticated techniques do exist for determining catchment rainfall but given that there were only three rainstations such sophisticated approaches are inappropriate. For very large rainfall events (greater than 100mm) there was a strong relationship between rainfall and runoff but as the size of the event decreased the relationship between rainfall and runoff became more random. The rainfall in this part of the country is strongly summer dominated, which influenced the selection of the calibration and simulation periods. The calibration run was done from 13 November 1965 to 10 March 1966 and the simulation run was done from 4 November 1966 to 13 March 1967. This short time period for calibration was necessary because IHACRES could not converge when longer periods were chosen. This was due to the requirement that the start and end points should be selected to be at low flow periods. When the calibration period was chosen with several low flow periods this assumption was violated and meant that the model would not converge. In spite of this catchment having a comparatively high rainfall (by Australian standards at least) and our selection of the high rainfall months, the runoff percentage over the calibration period was only 6.12% and the simulation period was 8.24%.

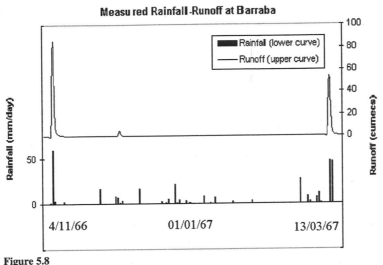

Figure 5.8
Measured Rainfall and Runoff at Barraba.

5.5.4 Results

The measured rainfall and subsequent streamflow for the simulation period in the Barrada catchment is shown in Figure 5.8. As can be seen from this data, for large events there is a strong relationship between rainfall and runoff. For smaller events, however, there is not a significant relationship between the rainfall and runoff.

The simulated streamflows determined by the two approaches are shown in Figures 5.9 and 5.10. The error for each model (predicted value - measured value) is shown in the graphs on the right-hand side of each figure. The RMSE for the IHACRES approach was 0.0474 and for CFG-GP was 0.0439. The total discharge for the simulation period was measured as 187 cumecs, with IHACRES predicting 330 cumecs (76% error) and the evolved CFG-GP solution predicting 99 cumecs (47% error). For the purposes of our comparison (based on RMSE) these results are similar.

The evolved equation found by CFG-GP was:

$$+(/(/(/(/(/(r0,-1.911790),-0.474622),-4.164400),$$
$$-(/(-1.542888,5.944119),-(av10,r0))),$$
$$*(r0,\exp(/(0.251564,av10)))) \qquad \text{Equation 5.5}$$

which may be simplified to

$$(r0/-3.7) -0.26-av10 - r0 - (r0 * \exp(0.251564 / av10)) \qquad \text{Equation 5.6}$$

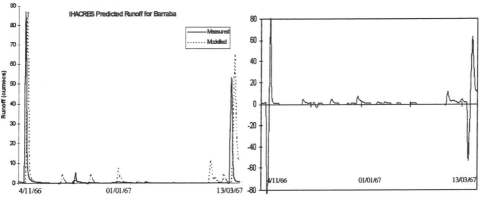

Figure 5.9
IHACRES Modelled Runoff at Barraba for the test (unseen) time period. The Error (Predicted - Measured Value) is shown in the right-hand graph.

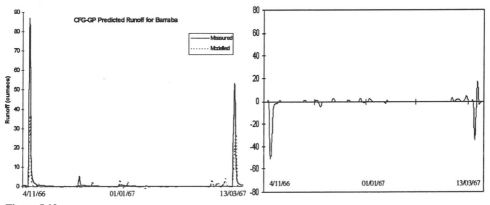

Figure 5.10
CFG-GP Modelled Runoff at Barraba for the test (unseen) time period. The Error (Predicted - Measured Value) is shown in the right-hand graph.

It is worth noting that Equation 5.6 uses the current days rainfall (r0), and the average of the last 10 days rainfall (av10). Additionally, Equation 5.6 has the nonlinear term (exp(/(0.251564,av10))), which is a function of av10. A comparison of equations 5.4 and 5.6 shows that the two catchments have been modelled in very different ways. The Welsh catchment has been modelled using long term averages in a linear combination, whereas the Australian catchment has been modelled using short average times and the current day in a nonlinear fashion. This would suggest that the underlying processes that are driving the water movement throughout both catchments are quite different.

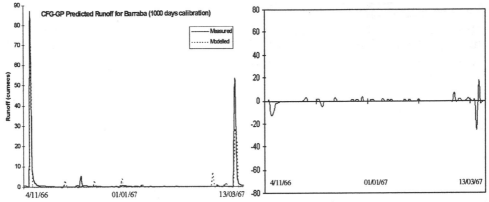

Figure 5.11
CFG-GP Modelled Runoff after using 1000 days of training data, applied to the previous 3 months test (unseen) time period. The Error (Predicted - Measured Value) is shown in the right-hand graph.

When an attempt was made to calibrate over different consecutive seasons for the Barraba data, the IHACRES model was not able to find coefficients to suit all seasons, and therefore could not converge. This accounts for the short calibration and simulation periods of only 4 months that has been used for testing these models. However, the CFG-GP approach, because it makes no assumption about underlying relationships, was able to be calibrated over successive seasons and therefore use more information about the catchment response to rainfall. When CFG-GP was calibrated using a period of 1000 days the resultant model achieved significantly better results on the original simulation data set (RMSE = 0.0237). Additionally, the predicted total discharge changed to 157 cumecs (16% error), which is superior to either previous solution. The response of this modelled streamflow, and the associated errors, are shown in Figure 5.11. The evolved equation was:

$$+(\exp(+(/(\exp(-4.874963),-0.796608),$$
$$/(/(r0,-1.864706),+(-3.018028,-4.418388)$$
$$))),*(-3.240420,\exp(-1.181253)))) \qquad \text{Equation 5.7}$$

which may be simplified to give

$$\exp(0.0096+ (r0/13.35)) - 0.994 \qquad \text{Equation 5.8}$$

The interesting comparison between Equations 5.6 and 5.8 is that using the larger dataset for calibration (training) resulted in a solution that was a nonlinear function solely of (r0), which represents the current days measured rainfall. No average rainfall value was found to be useful. This implies that the Barrada catchment has a very quick response between rainfall and runoff, and no significant seasonal signal.

5.7 Discussion

The previous examples of applying CFG-GP to modelling rainfall-runoff has been encouraging. The use of a simple, non-linear mathematical grammar has allowed the system to produce equations that capture some measure of the underlying response of the catchment. The linear, strongly seasonal model evolved for the Teifi catchment has a natural interpretation with the underlying climatic and topographic characteristics of this catchment. The non-linear, weakly seasonal model evolved for the Namoi catchment also corresponds with the perceived behaviour of this Australian landscape.

The grammar, G_{flow}, had only a weak bias towards forming certain types of mathematical expressions. Future work will involve extending the set of useful mathematical functions (power and logarithmic functions are often used in natural system modelling) and exploring other language forms which may have more direct interpretation with natural processes.

5.8 Conclusion

In the present work we have compared the results obtained with a deterministic lumped parameter model, based on the unit hydrograph approach, with those obtained using a stochastic machine learning model.

For the Welsh catchment the results between the two models were similar. Since rainfall and runoff were highly correlated the deterministic assumption underlying the IHACRES model was satisfied. Therefore IHACRES could achieve a satisfactory correlation between calibration and simulation data. It is also interesting to note that for this catchment the runoff ratio was approximately 70% which suggests that a relationship does indeed exist between the rainfall and runoff. The CFG-GP approach does not require any causal relationships but achieved similar results.

The behaviour of the studied Australian catchment was found to be quite different from the Welsh catchment. The runoff ratio was very low (7%) and hence the *a priori* assumptions of IHACRES (and other deterministic models) were a poor representation of the real world. This was demonstrated by the inability of IHACRES to use more than one seasons data for calibration purposes and only able to use data from a high rainfall period. Since the CFG-GP approach did not make any assumptions about the underlying physical processes, calibration periods over more than one season could be used. These led to significantly improved generalisations for the modelled behaviour of the catchment.

In summary, either approach worked satisfactorily when rainfall and runoff were correlated. However, when this correlation was poor, the CFG-GP had some advantages because it did not assume any underlying relationships. In these circumstances the use of evolutionary algorithms warrants further consideration.

Acknowledgments

The authors would like to thank Heinz Buettikofer of CSIRO Land and Water for producing the artwork for each of the maps. The authors would also like to thank the Institute of Hydrology, Wallingford, Oxon, UK for supplying the spatial and rainfall/runoff data of the Glan Teifi catchment.

References

Chatfield, C. (1984). The Analysis of Time Series: An Introduction. Chapman and Hall, 1984

Jakeman, A. J., Littlewood, I. G. and Whitehead, P.G. (1990). Computation of the instantaneous unit hydrograph and identifiable component flows with application to two small upland catchments. Journal of Hydrology, 117, 275-300, 1990

Koza, J.R. (1992). *Genetic Programming: on the programming of computers by means of natural selection.* A Bradford Book, MIT Press, 1992

Littlewood, I. G. and Jakeman, A. J. (1994) A new method of rainfall-runoff modelling and its applications in catchment hydrology. In: P. Zannetti (ed) Environmental Modelling (Volume II), Computational Mechanics Publications, Southampton, UK, 143-171.

Minns, A W, and Hall, M J, (1996) Artificial neural networks as rainfall-runoff models. Hydrological Sciences Journal,41(3), pp 399-417

Mulloy, B., Riolo, R. and Savit, R. (1996). Dynamics of Genetic Programming and Chaotic Time Series Prediction. In Genetic Programming: proceedings of the first annual conference. J. Koza (ed). Stanford University, CA, USA: MIT Press, July 1996

Whigham, P.A. (1996) Language Bias, Search Bias and Genetic Programming. In Genetic Programming: proceedings of the first annual conference. J. Koza (ed). Stanford University, CA, USA: MIT Press, July 1996

6 Automatic Synthesis, Placement, and Routing of Electrical Circuits by Means of Genetic Programming

John R. Koza and Forrest H Bennett III

The design of an electrical circuit entails creation of the circuit's topology, sizing, placement, and routing. Each of these tasks is either vexatious or computationally intractable. Design engineers typically perform these tasks sequentially– thus forcing the engineer to grapple with one vexatious or intractable problem after another. This chapter describes a holistic approach to the automatic creation of a circuit's topology, sizing, placement, and routing. This approach starts with a high-level statement of the requirements for the desired circuit and uses genetic programming to automatically and simultaneously create the circuit's topology, sizing, placement, and routing. The approach is illustrated with the problem of designing an analog lowpass filter circuit. The fitness measure for a candidate circuit considers the area of the fully laid-out circuit as well as whether the circuit passes or suppresses the appropriate frequencies. Genetic programming requires only about 1 1/2 orders of magnitude more computer time to create the circuit's topology, sizing, placement, and routing than to create the topology and sizing for this illustrative problem.

6.1 Introduction

The design process entails creation of a complex structure to satisfy user-defined requirements. Design is a major activity of practicing engineers. Since the design process typically involves tradeoffs between competing considerations, the end product is usually a satisfactory, as opposed to a perfect, design. The design process is usually viewed as requiring human intelligence. Consequently, the field of design is a source of challenging problems for automated techniques of machine learning and artificial intelligence.

The design process for electrical circuits begins with a high-level description of the circuit's desired behavior and entails creation of the circuit's topology, sizing, placement, and routing. The *topology* of a circuit involves specification of the gross number of components in the circuit, the type of each component (e.g., a capacitor), and a *netlist* specifying where each of a component's leads are to be connected. *Sizing* involves specification of the values (typically numerical) of each component. *Placement* involves the assignment of each of the circuit's components to a particular physical location on a printed circuit board or silicon wafer. *Routing* involves the assignment of a particular physical location to the wires between the leads of the circuit's components.

All four of the above aspects of circuit design (topology, sizing, placement, and routing) are vexatious or computationally intractable for analog electrical circuits.

Specifically, until recently, there has been no general technique for automatically creating the topology and sizing for an entire analog electrical circuit from a high-level statement of the circuit's desired behavior. In describing the process of creating the topology and sizing of an analog circuit, Aaserud and Nielsen [1995] observed,

Analog designers are few and far between. In contrast to digital design, most of the analog circuits are still handcrafted by the experts or so-called 'zahs' of analog design. The design process is characterized by a combination of experience and intuition and requires a thorough knowledge of the process characteristics and the detailed specifications of the actual product.

Analog circuit design is known to be a knowledge-intensive, multiphase, iterative task, which usually stretches over a significant period of time and is performed by designers with a large portfolio of skills. It is therefore considered by many to be a form of art rather than a science.

The placement problem and the routing problem (for both analog and digital circuits) are examples of computationally intractable combinatorial optimization problems that require a computing effort that increases exponentially with problem size [Wong, Leong, and Liu 1988; Garey and Johnson 1979; Ullman 1984]. Since it is considered unlikely that efficient algorithms can be found for such problems, considerable effort has been expended on finding efficient approximate solutions to such problems [Wong, Leong, and Liu 1988; Cohn, Garrod, Rutenbar, and Carley 1994; Maziasz and Hayes 1992; Joobbani 1986; Sechen 1988]. The most important consideration in placement and routing is that there must be a wire connecting 100% of the nodes that must be connected. Wires cannot cross on a particular layer of a silicon chip or on a particular side of a printed circuit board. While it is possible to make connections (called *vias*) from another layer of the silicon chip or printed circuit board, the number of layers that are available and the type of components that can be located on each layer is strictly limited by the particular technology being used. For example, a printed circuit board or silicon chip may consist of one, two, or some other (small) number of layers. However, only one layer of currently used silicon chips can house components other than wires and at most two layers of a printed circuit boards can house anything other than wires. Once an acceptable placement and routing is discovered for a particular circuit, the next most important consideration is usually minimization of the area of the bounding rectangle of the laid-out circuit. Minimization of area has a substantial and direct economic impact in the manufacture of electronic circuitry. In addition, it is often desirable to minimize the length of wires connecting components and to minimize the number of vias.

As shown in figure 6.1, each of the above four vexatious or computationally intractable phases of circuit design (topology, sizing, placement, and routing) are currently tackled more or less sequentially.

The question arises as to whether all four aspects of circuit design can be combined into a unified automatic process. At first glance, it would appear that the four aspects are so different in character that such a combination would be impossible. Or, if such a combination is possible, it would appear that such a combination might require prohibitively large amounts of computer time. This chapter demonstrates that genetic programming can be used to automatically create the topology, sizing, placement, and routing of analog electrical circuits.

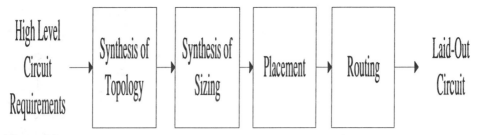

Figure 6.1
The process of designing a circuit includes creation of the circuit's topology, sizing of the circuit's components, placement of the components onto the substrate, and the routing of wires between the components.

Section 6.2 provides background. Section 6.3 presents our method. Section 6.4 describes an illustrative problem of designing an analog lowpass filter circuit. Section 6.5 details the preparatory steps required to apply our method to the illustrative problem. Section 6.6 presents the results. Section 6.7 discusses the amount of computer time required. Section 6.8 speculates on the role of genetic programming as an invention machine.

6.2 Automatic Creation of Circuit Topology and Sizing

There has been extensive previous work on the problem of automating various aspects of the design of electrical circuits using simulated annealing, artificial intelligence, and other optimization techniques (as detailed in Koza, Bennett, Andre, and Keane 1999), including genetic algorithms [Kruiskamp and Leenaerts 1995; Grimbleby 1995; Thompson 1996]. All of the existing techniques are limited to certain highly specialized types of circuits or address only one or two of the four aspects (topology, sizing, placement, and routing) of circuit design. Some of these techniques involve choosing pre-established alternative subcircuits for pre-established places within a pre-established overall circuit design. Many preexisting non-genetic techniques require the user to supply a reasonably good working circuit as a starting point (with the automated technique then merely adjusting the sizing of the components) or require repeated interactive intervention by the user.

Recently, a general technique using genetic programming has emerged for automatically creating the topology and sizing for an analog electrical circuit from a high-level statement of the circuit's desired behavior [Koza, Bennett, Andre, Keane, and Dunlap 1997; Koza, Bennett, Andre, and Keane 1999].

Genetic programming [Koza 1992; Koza and Rice 1992] is an extension of the genetic algorithm [Holland 1975] that automatically creates computer programs to solve problems. Genetic programming is also capable [Koza 1994a, 1994b] of evolving multi-part programs consisting of a main program and one or more reusable, parametrized, hierarchically-called automatically defined functions (subroutines). Architecture-altering operations [Koza 1995; Koza, Bennett, Andre, and Keane 1999] enable genetic programming to automatically determine the number of subroutines, the number of arguments that each possesses, and the nature of the hierarchical references, if any, among such automatically defined functions. They also enable genetic programming to automatically determine whether and how to use internal memory, iterations, and recursion in evolved programs. Additional information on current research in genetic programming can be found in Banzhaf, Nordin, Keller, and Francone 1998; Langdon 1998; Kinnear 1994; Angeline and Kinnear 1996; Koza, Goldberg, Fogel, and Riolo 1996; Koza, Deb, Dorigo, Fogel, Garzon, Iba, and Riolo 1997; Koza, Banzhaf, Chellapilla, Deb, Dorigo, Fogel, Garzon, Goldberg, Iba, and Riolo 1998; and Banzhaf, Poli, Schoenauer, and Fogarty 1998.

Numerous circuits have been designed using genetic programming, including lowpass, highpass, bandpass, bandstop, crossover, multiple bandpass, and asymmetric filters, amplifiers, computational circuits, a temperature-sensing circuit, a voltage reference circuit, a frequency-measuring circuit, and source identification circuits. The circuits evolved using genetic programming include eleven previously patented circuits.

Genetic programming can be applied to circuit design by establishing a mapping between the rooted, point-labeled acyclic graphs (trees) with ordered branches used in genetic programming and the specialized type of cyclic graphs germane to electrical circuits. The creative work of Kitano [1990] on using developmental genetic algorithms to evolve neural networks, the innovative work of Gruau [1992] on using genetic programming to evolve neural networks (cellular encoding), and the principles of developmental biology suggest a method for mapping trees into electrical circuits by means of a growth process that begins with a simple embryo. For electrical circuits, we use an embryo consisting of one (and sometime more) modifiable wires. The embryo is embedded into a test fixture consisting of fixed (hard-wired) components (such as a source resistor and a load resistor) and certain fixed wires that provide connectivity to the circuit's external inputs and outputs and that enable the behavior of the evolving circuitry to be evaluated. Until the modifiable wires are modified by the developmental process, the circuit produces only trivial output. An electrical circuit is developed by progressively applying the functions in a circuit-constructing program tree (in the population being bred by genetic programming) to the modifiable wires of the original embryo and to the modifiable components and modifiable wires created during the developmental process.

An electrical circuit is created by executing the functions in a circuit-constructing program tree. The functions are progressively applied in a developmental process to the embryo and its successors until all of the functions in the program tree are executed. That is, the functions in the circuit-constructing program tree progressively side-effect the embryo and its successors until a fully developed circuit eventually emerges. The functions are applied in a breadth-first order.

The functions in the circuit-constructing program trees are divided into five categories: (1) topology-modifying functions that alter the circuit topology, (2) component-creating functions that insert components into the circuit, (3) development-controlling functions that control the development process by which the embryo and its successors is changed into a fully developed circuit, (4) arithmetic-performing functions that appear in subtrees as argument(s) to the component-creating functions and specify the numerical value of the component, and (5) automatically defined functions that appear in the function-defining branches and potentially enable certain substructures of the circuit to be reused (with parameterization).

Each branch of the program tree is created in accordance with a constrained syntactic structure (strong typing). Each branch is composed of topology-modifying functions, component-creating functions, development-controlling functions, and terminals. Component-creating functions typically have one arithmetic-performing subtree, while topology-modifying functions, and development-controlling functions do not. Component-creating functions and topology-modifying functions are internal points of their branches and possess one or more arguments (construction-continuing subtrees). This constrained syntactic structure is preserved using structure-preserving crossover with point typing. For details, see Koza, Bennett, Andre, and Keane 1999.

The foregoing method for automatically creating circuit topology and sizing does not address the problem of automatically placing and routing of components and wires at particular physical locations on a printed circuit board or silicon wafer.

6.3   Method for Automatic Creation of Circuit Topology, Sizing, Placement, and Routing

This section describes how all four aspects of circuit design (topology, sizing, placement, and routing) can be combined into a unified approach using genetic programming.

6.3.1 The Initial Circuit

An electrical circuit is created in a developmental process by executing a circuit-constructing program tree that contains various component-creating, topology-modifying, and development-controlling functions. The starting point of the developmental process for transforming a program tree in the population into a fully developed electrical circuit is an initial circuit consisting of an embryo and a test fixture.

All the wires and components of the initial circuit are located at specified physical locations on a printed circuit board or silicon wafer. A board or wafer has a limited number of layers that are available for wires and a limited number of layers (usually one for a wafer and one or two for a board) that are available for both wires and components.

The embryo is an electrical substructure consisting of at least one modifiable wire. The test fixture is a substructure composed of nonmodifiable wires and nonmodifiable electrical components. The test fixture provides access to the circuit's external input(s) and permits testing of the circuit's behavior and probing of the circuit's output. An embryo has one or more ports that enable it to be embedded into a test fixture.

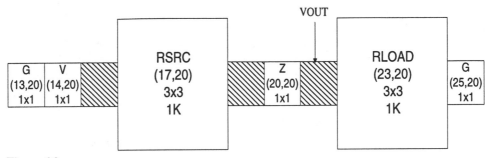

Figure 6.2
One-input, one-output initial circuit consisting of two ground points G, an incoming voltage signal V, a source resistor RSRC, a modifiable wire Z, a load resistor RLOAD, and three pieces of nonmodifiable wire. Each element is of a particular size and is located at a certain location. In addition, the two resistors have components values (1 kΩ each).

Figure 6.2 shows a one-input, one-output initial circuit located on one layer of a silicon wafer or printed circuit board. This initial circuit consists of the ground G (at the far left), the source V for the incoming voltage signal, a piece of nonmodifiable wire (hashed), a fixed 1 kilo-Ohm (kΩ) source resistor RSRC, another piece of nonmodifiable wire, a piece of modifiable wire Z, another piece of nonmodifiable wire, a fixed 1 kΩ load resistor RLOAD, and the ground G (at the far right). The output probe point VOUT is the place where the circuit's output voltage is measured.

Each element of a circuit resides at particular physical location on the circuit's two-dimensional substrate and occupies a particular amount of space. The two resistors each occupy a 3 × 3 area while all the other elements of this initial circuit each occupy a 1 × 1 area. The location of the 1 × 1 ground point G at the far left of the figure is (13, 20); the location of the incoming signal source V is (14,20); the location of the center of the 3 × 3 source resistor RSRC is (17, 20), and the location of the 1 × 1 modifiable wire Z is (20, 20). As will be seen momentarily, circuit elements typically change locations numerous times during the developmental process.

The embryo of this initial circuit consists of the single 1 × 1 piece of modifiable wire Z. All development originates from this embryo. The remaining elements (all fixed) of the initial circuit constitute the test fixture.

6.3.2 Circuit-Constructing Functions

A program tree may contain component-creating functions, topology-modifying functions, and development-controlling functions. Each of these three types of functions is associated with a modifiable wire or modifiable component in the developing circuit. The construction-continuing subtree(s), if any, of these functions point to a successor function or terminal in the circuit-constructing program tree.

A program tree may also contain arithmetic functions and constants. The arithmetic-performing subtree of a component-creating function consists of a composition of arithmetic functions (addition and subtraction) and random constants (in the range -1.0 to +1.0). The arithmetic-performing subtree specifies the numerical value of a component by returning a floating-point value that is interpreted on a logarithmic scale as the value for the component in a range of 10 orders of magnitude (using a unit of measure that is appropriate for the particular type of component). The details of this process are the same as used in Koza, Bennett, Andre, and Keane 1999.

6.3.2.1 Component-Creating Functions

The component-creating functions insert a component into the developing circuit and assign component value(s) to the new component.

The two-argument capacitor-creating LAYOUT-C function inserts a capacitor into a developing circuit in lieu of a modifiable wire (or modifiable component). Figure 6.3 shows a partial circuit containing four capacitors (C2, C3, C4, and C5) and a modifiable wire Z0. Each capacitor occupies a 3×3 area. Each piece of wire occupies a $1 \times n$ or an $n \times 1$ area. The modifiable wire Z0 occupies a 1×1 area and is located at (20, 20).

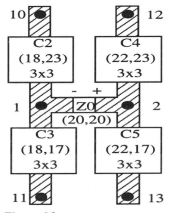

Figure 6.3
Partial circuit with a 1×1 piece of modifiable wire Z0 at location (20, 20) and four capacitors.

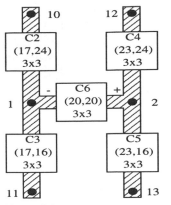

Figure 6.4
The application of the LAYOUT-C function to the modifiable wire Z0 of figure 6.3 causes a 3 × 3 capacitor C6 to be inserted at location (20, 20). The insertion of the new capacitor C6 forces a change in location for the other capacitors in the figure.

Figure 6.4 shows the result of applying the two-argument capacitor-creating LAYOUT-C function to the modifiable wire Z0 of figure 6.3. The newly created capacitor C6 occupies a 3 × 3 area and is centered at location (20, 20). The newly created component is larger in both directions than the 1 × 1 piece of modifiable wire that it replaces. Thus, its insertion affects the locations of all preexisting components in the developing circuit. In particular, preexisting capacitor C2 is pushed north and west by one unit thereby relocating it from (18, 23) to (17, 24). Similarly, preexisting capacitor C5 is pushed south and east by one unit thereby relocating it from (22, 17) to (23, 16). In our actual implementation, all adjustments in location are made after the completion of the entire developmental process; however, we will explain each circuit-constructing function as if the required adjustment is made at the time that the function is executed. The first argument of the capacitor-creating function is an arithmetic-performing subtree that specifies the value of the newly created capacitor in micro-Farads. The second argument of the capacitor-creating function is the construction-continuing subtree. The newly created capacitor C6 remains subject to subsequent modification.

Similarly, the two-argument inductor-creating LAYOUT-L function causes an inductor to be inserted into a developing circuit in lieu of a modifiable wire (or other modifiable component). The inductors in this chapter each occupy a 3 × 3 area; however, different components may, in general, have different dimensions. The value of the new inductor in micro-Henrys is specified by the arithmetic-performing subtree (the function's first argument). The function's second argument is the construction-continuing subtree.

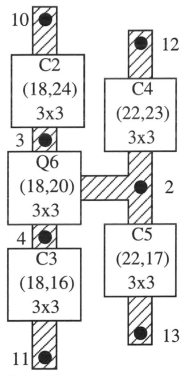

Figure 6.5
The application of LAYOUT-CMOS-TRANSISTOR function to the modifiable wire Z0 of figure 6.3 causes a three-leaded transistor Q6 occupying a 3 × 3 area to be inserted at location (18, 20).

Three-leaded components, such as transistors, may also be inserted into a developing circuit. Figure 5 shows the result of applying the one-argument transistor-creating LAYOUT-CMOS-TRANSISTOR function to the modifiable wire Z0 of figure 3. The newly created transistor Q6 occupies a 3 × 3 area and is located at (18, 20). The newly created component is larger than that which it replaces thereby affecting the locations of two preexisting components (C2 and C3) in the developing circuit. Specifically, preexisting capacitor C2 is pushed north by one unit thereby relocating it from (18, 23) to (18, 24). Similarly, preexisting capacitor C3 is pushed south by one unit thereby relocating it from (18, 17) to (18, 16). The argument of the transistor-creating function is an arithmetic-performing subtree that specifies the transistor's width. The newly created transistor Q6 is not subject to subsequent modification (and hence this function possesses only one argument and takes no construction-continuing subtree).

6.3.2.2 Topology-Modifying Functions

Each topology-modifying function modifies the topology of the developing circuit.

The two-argument SERIES-LAYOUT function creates a series composition consisting of the modifiable wire or modifiable component with which the function is associated and a copy of it. The function also creates two new nodes. Figure 6.6 shows a partial circuit containing six capacitors (C2, C3, C4, C5, C6, and C7). Figure 6.7 shows the result of applying the SERIES-LAYOUT function to modifiable capacitor C6 located at (20, 20) of figure 6.6. The SERIES-LAYOUT function creates a new capacitor C8 occupying a 3 × 3 area. The newly created capacitor C8 has the same values as modifiable capacitor C6. The function does not move the preexisting component (C6). Instead, room is made for the newly created capacitor C8 in the direction of a specified one of the two leads (the positive lead) of the preexisting component. Thus, C8 is located at (22, 20) to the east of C6 in this example. The addition of the four units horizontally to accommodate C8 affects the horizontal (but not vertical) location of the four preexisting capacitors. For example, preexisting capacitor C2 is pushed west by two units thereby relocating it from (17, 24) to (15, 24). Similarly, preexisting capacitor C5 is pushed east by two units thereby relocating it from (23, 16) to (25, 16). The addition of the four units horizontally to accommodate C8 also affects other parts of the developing circuit. For example, the wires to the east and west of preexisting capacitor C7 are lengthened (by two units each) to reflect the addition of the four horizontal units associated with the creation of C8. Both arguments of the SERIES-LAYOUT function are construction-continuing subtrees, so that both C6 and C8 remain subject to subsequent modification. New node 3 is located between preexisting capacitor C6 and new capacitor C8 at the original location(20, 20) of preexisting capacitor C6.

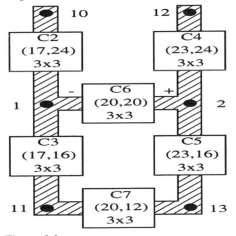

Figure 6.6
Partial circuit with a 3 × 3 modifiable capacitor C6 at location (20, 20) with five nearby capacitors.

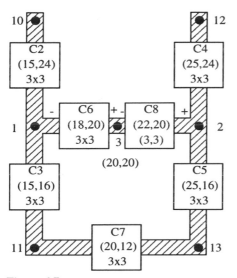

Figure 6.7
The application of the SERIES-LAYOUT function to the modifiable capacitor C6 of figure 6.6 causes a new 3 × 3 capacitor C8 to be inserted at location (22, 20) in series with C6.

Each of the two functions in the PARALLEL-LAYOUT family of four-argument functions creates a parallel composition consisting of two new modifiable wires, the preexisting modifiable wire or modifiable component with which the function is associated, and a copy of the modifiable wire or modifiable component. Each function also creates two new nodes. Figure 6.8 shows the result of applying the PARALLEL-LAYOUT-LEFT function to modifiable capacitor C6 located at (20, 20) of figure 6.4. The function does not change the location of the modifiable component or modifiable wire with which the function is associated. The function creates a new capacitor C7 occupying a 3 × 3 area with the same values as modifiable capacitor C6. The function positions the new capacitor C7 to the left of C6 (looking from the negative to positive lead of the modifiable component or modifiable wire with which the function is associated). The function does not affect the location of preexisting circuitry to the right of C6 (i.e., C3 and C5). The function inserts a new 1 × 1 modifiable wire Z9 at (23, 22) to the left of C6, a new 1 × 1 piece of wire between preexisting node 2 and new modifiable wire Z9, and a new 1 × 1 piece of wire between new node 4 and Z9. The function inserts a new 1 × 1 modifiable wire Z8 at (17, 22) to the left of C6, a new 1 × 1 piece of wire between preexisting node 1 and new modifiable wire Z8, and a new 1 × 1 piece of wire between new node 3 and Z8. The new capacitor C7 is located at (20, 24).

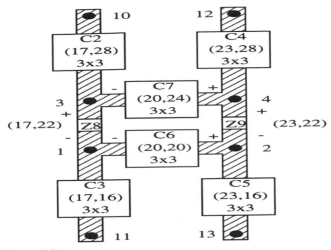

Figure 6.8
The application of the PARALLEL-LAYOUT-LEFT function to the modifiable capacitor C6 of figure 6.4 causes a new 3×3 capacitor C7 to be inserted at location (20, 24) in parallel with C6.

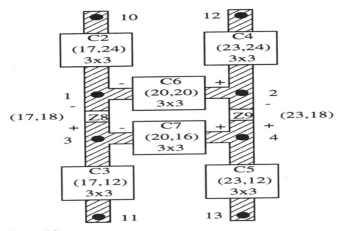

Figure 6.9
The application of the PARALLEL-LAYOUT-RIGHT function to the modifiable capacitor C6 of figure 6.4 causes a new 3×3 capacitor C7 to be inserted at location (20, 16) in parallel with C6.

The function also relocates the preexisting circuitry to the left of C6. Specifically, preexisting capacitor C2 is pushed to the north from (17, 24) to (17, 28) and preexisting capacitor C4 is pushed to the north from (23, 24) to (23, 28).

Figure 6.9 shows the result of applying the PARALLEL-LAYOUT-RIGHT function to modifiable capacitor C6 located at (20, 20) of figure 6.4. This function operates in a manner similar to the PARALLEL-LAYOUT-LEFT function, except that new capacitor C7 is located to the right of C6 and the location of preexisting circuitry to the right of C6 is pushed south.

The one-argument polarity-reversing FLIP function reverses the polarity of the modifiable component or modifiable wire with which the function is associated.

All of the foregoing circuit-constructing functions operate in a plane. However, most practical circuits are not planar. Vias provide a way to connect distant points of a circuit. Each of the four functions in the VIA-TO-GROUND-LAYOUT family of three-argument functions creates a T-shaped composition consisting of the modifiable wire or modifiable component with which the function is associated, a copy of it, two new modifiable wires, and a via to ground. The function also creates two new nodes.

Figure 6.10 shows the result of applying the VIA-TO-GROUND-NEG-LEFT-LAYOUT function to modifiable capacitor C6 located at (20, 20) of figure 6.4. The function creates a new node 3 at the location (20, 20) of the modifiable component or modifiable wire with which the function is associated and also creates a new 2 × 1 area at the negative end of the modifiable component or modifiable wire with which the function is associated and a new 4 × 1 area to the left.

The new 4 × 1 area consists of a new 1 × 1 piece of wire perpendicular and to the left of the modifiable component or modifiable wire with which the function is associated (facing from the negative to positive lead of the modifiable component or modifiable wire with which the function is associated), a new 1 × 1 modifiable wire Z9 at location (20, 22) beyond the new 1 × 1 piece of wire, a new node 4 at (20, 23) beyond Z9 and the new 1 × 1 piece, and a via to ground G at (20, 24) beyond node 4, Z9, and the new 1 × 1 piece.

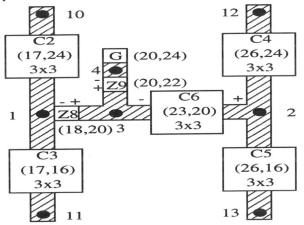

Figure 6.10
The application of the VIA-TO-GROUND-NEG-LEFT-LAYOUT function to the modifiable capacitor C6 of figure 6.4 causes a new 1 × 1 connection to ground G to be inserted at location (20, 24).

The new 2×1 area consists of a new 1×1 piece of wire at (19, 20) at the negative lead of the modifiable component or modifiable wire with which the function is associated and a new modifiable wire Z8 at (18,20). Since the VIA-TO-GROUND-NEG-LEFT-LAYOUT function creates a new 2×1 area at the negative end of preexisting capacitor C6 and a new 1×1 node 3, capacitor C6 is pushed to the east by three units so that C6 becomes centered at (23, 20). Consequently, preexisting capacitor C4 is pushed east from (23, 24) to (26, 24) and preexisting capacitor C5 is pushed east from (23, 16) to (26, 16).

The three other members of this family of functions are named to reflect the fact that they create the new 2×1 area at the positive (instead of negative) end of the modifiable component or modifiable wire with which the function is associated and that they create the new 4×1 area to the right (instead of left).

If desired, similar families of three-argument functions can be defined to allow direct connections to a positive power supply or a negative power supply.

In addition, if desired, numbered vias can be created to provide connectivity between two different parts of a circuit. A distinct four-member family of three-argument functions is used for each via. For example, VIA-2-NEG-LEFT-LAYOUT makes connection with an imaginary layer numbered 2 of the imaginary multi-layered silicon wafer (or multi-layered printed circuit board) on which the circuit resides.

The initial circuit complies with the requirement that wires cannot cross on a particular layer of a silicon chip or on a particular side of a printed circuit board and with the requirement that there must be a wire connecting 100% of the leads. Each of the component-creating and topology-modifying functions preserves compliance with these two mandatory requirements for successful placement and routing, so any sequence of such functions yields a fully laid-out circuit that complies with these two requirements.

6.3.2.3 Development-Controlling Functions

The zero-argument END function makes the modifiable wire or modifiable component with which it is associated into a non-modifiable wire or component (thereby ending a particular developmental path).

The one-argument NOOP ("No Operation") function has no effect on the modifiable wire or modifiable component with which it is associated; however, it has the effect of delaying the developmental process on the particular path on which it appears.

6.3.3 The Developmental Process

An electrical circuit is created by executing the functions in a circuit-constructing program tree. The functions are progressively applied in a developmental process to the embryonic circuit and its successors until all of the functions in the program tree are executed. That is, the functions in the circuit-constructing program tree progressively side-effect the embryonic circuit and its successors until a fully developed circuit eventually emerges. The functions are applied in a breadth-first order.

6.4   Statement of the Illustrative Problem

The method will be illustrated on the problem of creating the topology, sizing, placing, and routing for a lowpass filter. A simple *filter* is a one-input, one-output circuit that passes the frequency components of the incoming signal that lie in a specified range (called the *passband*) while suppressing the frequency components that lie in all other frequency ranges (the *stopband*). The desired lowpass filter is to pass all frequencies below 1,000 Hertz (Hz) and to suppress all frequencies above 2,000 Hz. The circuit is to be constructed on a two-sided printed circuit board whose top side contains discrete components (capacitors and inductors) that are connected by perpendicularly intersecting metallic wires and whose bottom side is devoted to connections to ground.

6.5   Preparatory Steps

Before applying genetic programming to a problem of circuit design, seven major preparatory steps are required: (1) identify the initial circuit, (2) determine the architecture of the circuit-constructing program trees, (3) identify the terminals, (4) identify the primitive functions, (5) create the fitness measure, (6) choose parameters, and (7) determine the termination criterion and method of result designation.

6.5.1 Initial Circuit

The one-input, one-output initial circuit consisting of an embryo with one modifiable wire and a test fixture as shown in figure 6.2 is suitable for this problem.

6.5.2 Program Architecture

Since there is one result-producing branch in the program tree for each modifiable wire in the embryo, the architecture of each circuit-constructing program tree has one result-producing branch. Neither automatically defined functions nor architecture-altering operations are used in this chapter.

6.5.3 Function and Terminal Sets

The function set, $\mathcal{F}_{ccs}$, for each construction-continuing subtree is

$$\mathcal{F}_{ccs} = \{\text{C-LAYOUT, L-LAYOUT, SERIES-LAYOUT, PARALLEL-LAYOUT-LEFT,}$$
$$\text{PARALLEL-LAYOUT-RIGHT, FLIP, NOOP, VIA-TO-GROUND-NEG-LEFT-}$$
$$\text{LAYOUT, VIA-TO-GROUND-NEG-RIGHT-LAYOUT, VIA-TO-GROUND-}$$
$$\text{POS-LEFT-LAYOUT, VIA-TO-GROUND-POS-RIGHT-LAYOUT}\}.$$

These functions possess 2, 2, 1, 4, 4, 1, 1, 3, 3, 3, and 3 arguments, respectively.

The terminal set, $\mathcal{T}_{ccs}$, for each construction-continuing subtree is

$$\mathcal{T}_{ccs} = \{\text{END}\}.$$

The terminal set, $\mathcal{T}_{aps}$, for each arithmetic-performing subtree consists of

$$\mathcal{T}_{aps} = \{\Re\},$$

where $\Re$ represents floating-point random constants from -1.0 to $+1.0$.

The function set, $\mathcal{F}_{aps}$, for each arithmetic-performing subtree is,

$$\mathcal{F}_{aps} = \{+, -\}.$$

6.5.4 Fitness Measure

The high-level statement of requirements for the desired circuit is translated into a well-defined measurable quantity (the fitness measure) that is used by genetic programming to guide the evolutionary search for a satisfactory solution.

The fitness measure for this problem is multiobjective. It is expressed in terms of minimization of area of the bounding rectangle around the fully laid-out circuit, suppression of frequencies in the stopband of the desired filter, and passage at full power of frequencies in the passband of the desired filter.

The evaluation of each individual circuit-constructing program tree in the population begins with its execution. This execution progressively applies the functions in the program tree to the embryo of the circuit, thereby creating a fully developed (and fully laid out) circuit. A netlist is created that identifies each component of the developed circuit, the nodes to which each component is connected, and the value of each component. The netlist becomes the input to our modified version of the SPICE (Simulation Program with Integrated Circuit Emphasis) simulation program [Quarles, Newton, Pederson, and Sangiovanni-Vincentelli 1994]. SPICE is a 217,000-line industrial-strength electrical circuit simulator written over a period of several decades at the University of California at Berkeley. The SPICE simulator (and its many spinoffs) dominates the field of simulation for general-purpose electrical circuits. There are several hundred thousand copies in daily use by practicing electrical engineers throughout the world [Perry 1998]. Our modified version of SPICE (described in Koza, Bennett, Andre, and Keane 1999) then determines the circuit's behavior. Since the high-level statement of the behavior for the desired circuit is expressed (in part) in terms of frequencies, the output voltage VOUT is measured in the frequency domain. SPICE performs an AC small signal analysis and report the circuit's behavior over five decades (between 1 Hz and 100,000 Hz) with each decade being divided into 20 parts (using a logarithmic scale), so that there are a total of 101 fitness cases (sampled frequencies).

Since the developmental process for creating the fully developed circuit in this problem includes the actual physical placement of components and the actual physical routing of wires between the components, the area of the bounding rectangle for the fully developed circuit is easily computed.

The desired lowpass filter has a passband below 1,000 Hz and a stopband above 2,000 Hz. Each circuit is driven by an incoming AC voltage source with a 2 volt amplitude. Each circuit is tested by a test fixture containing a 1 kΩ source (internal) resistor RSRC and a kΩ load resistor RLOAD. There should be a sharp drop-off from 1 to 0 Volts in the transitional ("don't care") region between 1,000 Hz and 2,000 Hz.

The *attenuation* of the filter is defined in terms of the output signal relative to the reference voltage (half of 2 volts here). A *decibel* is a unitless measure of relative voltage that is defined as 20 times the common (base 10) logarithm of the ratio between the voltage at a particular probe point and a reference voltage (1 volt).

In this problem, a voltage in the passband of exactly 1 volt and a voltage in the stopband of exactly 0 volts is regarded as ideal. The (preferably small) variation within the passband is called the *passband ripple*. Similarly, the incoming signal is never fully reduced to zero in the stopband of an actual filer. The (preferably small) variation within the stopband is called the *stopband ripple*. A voltage in the passband of between 970 millivolts and 1 volt (i.e., a passband ripple of 30 millivolts or less) and a voltage in the stopband of between 0 volts and 1 millivolts (i.e., a stopband ripple of 1 millivolts or less) is regarded as acceptable. Any voltage lower than 970 millivolts in the passband and any voltage above 1 millivolts in the stopband is regarded as unacceptable.

A fifth-order *elliptic (Cauer) filter* with a modular angle Θ of 30 degrees (i.e., the arcsin of the ratio of the boundaries of the passband and stopband) and a reflection coefficient ρ of 24.3% can satisfy the above design goals [Williams and Taylor 1995].

Fitness is defined for this problem using one or two of the following terms.

The first term is the sum, over the 101 fitness cases (sampled frequencies), of the absolute weighted deviation between the actual value of the voltage that is produced by the circuit at the probe point VOUT and the target value for voltage (0 or 1 volts). Specifically, this term is

$$F(t) = \sum_{i=0}^{100} (W(d(f_i), f_i) d(f_i))$$

where f_i is the frequency of fitness case i; $d(x)$ is the absolute value of the difference between the target and observed values at frequency x; and $W(y,x)$ is the weighting for difference y at frequency x.

The second term is the area of the bounding rectangle for the fully developed circuit divided by 100,000 square units of area.

The term of the fitness measure involving the filter's frequency response is designed to not penalize ideal voltage values, to slightly penalize every acceptable voltage deviation, and to heavily penalize every unacceptable voltage deviation.

Specifically, the procedure for each of the 61 points in the 3-decade interval between 1 Hz and 1,000 Hz for the intended passband is as follows: If the voltage equals the ideal value of 1.0 volt in this interval, the deviation is 0.0. If the voltage is between 970 millivolts and 1 volt, the absolute value of the deviation from 1 volt is weighted by a factor of 1.0. If the voltage is less than 970 millivolts, the absolute value of the deviation from 1 volt is weighted by a factor of 10.0.

The acceptable and unacceptable deviations for each of the 35 points from 2,000 Hz to 100,000 Hz in the intended stopband are similarly weighed (by 1.0 or 10.0) based on the amount of deviation from the ideal voltage of 0 volts and the acceptable deviation of 1 millivolts. For each of the five "don't care" points between 1,000 and 2,000 Hz, the deviation is deemed to be zero. The number of hits is defined as the number of fitness cases for which the voltage is acceptable or ideal or that lie in the "don't care" band.

The term involving the bounding rectangle is much smaller than the term involving the filter's frequency response until a circuit scores 101 (or near 101) hits. For individuals not scoring the maximum number (101) of hits, fitness is the sum of the two terms. For individuals scoring the maximum number of hits, fitness is only the area-based term. In any event, the smaller the value of fitness, the better. A value of zero is unattainable because no actual circuit occupies zero area and because no actual analog filter can perfectly satisfy the problem's requirements in the frequency domain.

The SPICE simulator is remarkably robust; however, it cannot simulate every conceivable circuit. In particular, many circuits that are randomly created for the initial population of a run of genetic programming and many circuits that are created by the crossover and mutation operations in later generations are so pathological that SPICE cannot simulate them. These circuits receive a high penalty value of fitness (10^8) and become the worst-of-generation programs for each generation.

6.5.5 Control Parameters

The population size, M, is 1,120,000. A maximum size of 600 points (functions and terminals) was established for each circuit-constructing program tree. Our usual control parameters are used [Koza, Bennett, Andre, and Keane 1999, Appendix D].

6.5.6 Termination Criterion and Results Designation

The maximum number of generations, G, is set to an arbitrary large number and the run was manually monitored and manually terminated when the fitness of the best-of-generation individual appeared to have reached a plateau.

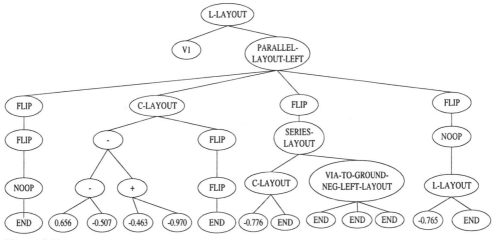

Figure 6.11
Best individual circuit-constructing program tree of generation 0. The program tree is a composition of component-creating, topology-modifying, and development-controlling functions.

6.5.7 Implementation on Parallel Computer

This problem was run on a home-built Beowulf-style [Sterling, Salmon, Becker, and Savarese 1999] parallel cluster computer system consisting of 56 processing nodes (each containing a 533-MHz DEC Alpha microprocessor and 64 megabytes of RAM) arranged in a two-dimensional 7×8 toroidal mesh. The system has a DEC Alpha computer as host. The processing nodes are connected with a 100 megabit-per-second Ethernet. The processing nodes and the host use the Linux operating system. The distributed genetic algorithm with unsynchronized generations and semi-isolated subpopulations [Andre and Koza 1996] was used. There was a subpopulation size of $Q = 20,000$ at each of $D = 56$ demes. On each generation, four boatloads of emigrants, each consisting of $B = 2\%$ (the migration rate) of the node's subpopulation (selected on the basis of fitness) were dispatched to each of the four adjacent processing nodes.

6.6   Results

A run of genetic programming starts with the random creation of an initial population of circuit-constructing program trees composed of the functions and terminals identified in the previous section. The initial random population (generation 0) of a run of genetic programming is a blind random search of the search space of the problem.

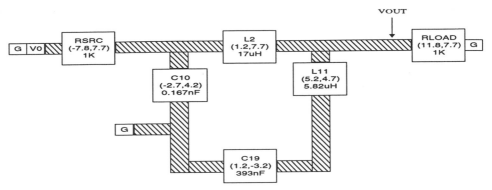

Figure 6.12
Best circuit of generation 0 containing two inductors (L2 and L11) and two capacitors (C10 and C19) in addition to all of the nonmodifiable elements of the original test fixture of the initial circuit of figure 6.2.

Generation 0 provides a baseline for comparing the results of subsequent generations. About a quarter of the circuits in generation 0 are so pathological that the SPICE simulator cannot simulate them (compared to 2% to 5% for later generations). We use the best circuit-constructing program tree (figure 6.11) from generation 0 to illustrate the developmental process used to convert a tree into a fully developed and fully laid-out electrical circuit.

This circuit-constructing program tree is shown below in the style of a LISP S-expression:

```
(L-LAYOUT
  V1
  (PARALLEL-LAYOUT-LEFT
    (FLIP (FLIP (NOOP END)))
    (C-LAYOUT
      (- (- 0.656 -0.507) (+ -0.463 -0.970))
      (FLIP (FLIP END)))
    (FLIP
      (SERIES-LAYOUT
        (C-LAYOUT -0.776 END)
        (VIA-TO-GROUND-NEG-LEFT-LAYOUT END END END)))
    (FLIP
      (NOOP (L-LAYOUT 0.765 END))))))
```

The program begins with a two-argument inductor-creating L-LAYOUT function. The value of the new inductor is established by the first argument of this L-LAYOUT function. Since this particular argument is a large arithmetic-performing subtree composed of addition, subtraction, and floating-point random constants, it is abbreviated and labeled V1 in figure 6.11 and this program. The second argument (construction-continuing subtree) of this L-LAYOUT function is a PARALLEL-LAYOUT-LEFT function.

The first argument of the four-argument PARALLEL-LAYOUT-LEFT function executes two one-argument polarity-reversing FLIP functions and one one-argument NOOP ("No Operation") function before reaching a development-terminating zero-argument END function.

The second argument of the PARALLEL-LAYOUT-LEFT function executes a capacitor-creating two-argument C-LAYOUT function whose value is established by a seven-point arithmetic-performing subtree (shown in its entirety in the figure) and whose construction-continuing subtree contains two polarity-reversing FLIP functions and one NOOP function.

The third argument of the PARALLEL-LAYOUT-LEFT function is a one-argument FLIP function whose construction-continuing subtree consists of a two-argument SERIES-LAYOUT function. The first construction-continuing subtree of the SERIES-LAYOUT function executes a second capacitor-creating C-LAYOUT function. The value of the second capacitor is established (in the manner described earlier) by the one-point arithmetic-performing subtree consisting of the floating-point random constant -0.7763983. The second construction-continuing subtree of the SERIES-LAYOUT function executes a three-argument VIA-TO-GROUND-NEG-LEFT-LAYOUT function.

The fourth argument of the PARALLEL-LAYOUT-LEFT function is a FLIP function whose construction-continuing subtree executes a one-argument NOOP function which, in turn, causes execution of a second two-argument inductor-creating L-LAYOUT function. The value of the second inductor is established by the one-point arithmetic-performing subtree consisting of the floating-point constant 0.7648563.

When this circuit-constructing program tree for the best-of-generation circuit of generation 0 is executed, it yields a fully laid-out circuit (figure 6.12) with two created inductors (L2 and L11) and two created capacitors (C10 and C19). The four components, the connecting wires, the ground points, and the source of the incoming signal are all assigned a precise physical location in this fully laid-out circuit. Notice that all of the nonmodifiable elements of the original test fixture of the initial circuit of figure 6.2 (including, in particular, the incoming signal V, the source resistor RSRC, the load resistor RLOAD) survive in this fully developed and fully laid-out circuit (albeit in different locations). In addition, notice that this fully laid-out circuit complies with the requirement that wires cannot cross on a particular layer of a silicon chip or on a particular side of a printed circuit board and with the requirement that there must be a wire connecting 100% of the leads.

This best-of-generation circuit from generation 0 scores 53 hits and has a fitness of 57.961037. The incoming signal V first passes through source resistor RSRC located at position (-7.8, 7.7) at the top left of the figure. The signal passes into inductor L2 located at position (1.2, 7.7) to load resistor RLOAD located at position (11.8, 7.7) and to ground G (at the top right of the figure). In addition, capacitor C10 located at (-2.7, 4.2) is connected to the ground G (in the middle left of the figure). Also, the series composition of inductor L11 and capacitor C19 is also connected to the same ground point G in the middle left of the figure. The area-based term of the fitness measure is only 0.003710 at this at this early stage of the run.

Figure 6.13 shows the behavior in the frequency domain of the best circuit of generation 0. The horizontal axis represents five decades of frequency on a logarithmic scale. The vertical axis represents voltage linearly. As can be seen, the behavior of this circuit bears very little resemblance to the desired lowpass filter. The circuit delivers a full volt for all frequencies up to about 50 Hz. The output approximates 0 volts only for a few frequencies near 100,000 Hz. There is a very large and leisurely transition region.

Both the average fitness of all individuals in the population and the fitness of the best individual in the population improve over successive generations. The best circuit of generation 8 (figure 6.16) scores 82 hits and has a fitness of 9.731077 (of which only 0.008138 is contributed by the area-based term of the fitness measure). The result-producing branch of its circuit-constructing program tree contains 165 points. The circuit has five inductors and three capacitors. The incoming signal V passes through source resistor RSRC (at the bottom left of the figure) and is fed into a parallel-series composition of inductors L13, L2, and L12 (which are together electrically equivalent to one inductor). In a lowpass filter, the capacitors that are connected to ground are called *shunts* and the inductors positioned in series (along the bottom of this figure) between the source resistor and load resistor are called *series* inductors [Williams and Taylor 1995]. When all the parallel and series compositions of like components are combined, this circuit is equivalent to a first series inductor (the L13, L2, and L12 combination), a first capacitive shunt (C18), a second series inductor (L11), a second capacitive shunt (the C16 and C19 combination), and a third series inductor (L16). The series inductors and capacitive shunts of a lowpass filter are typically drawn on paper to resemble a ladder. The capacitive shunts correspond to the rungs of the ladder. The series inductors correspond to one side of the ladder. The second side of the ladder is a common ground wire to which each capacitive shunt is connected. This circuit is a two-rung ladder. The best-of-run circuit that emerges below in generation 138 is a four-rung ladder.

Figure 6.14 shows the behavior in the frequency domain of the best circuit of generation 8. This circuit contains five inductors and three capacitors. As can be seen, the behavior of this circuit bears some resemblance to the desired lowpass filter. It delivers 1 volt for all frequencies up to about 900 Hz and about 0 volts for all frequencies above 10,000 Hz. However, there is a very leisurely transition from the frequencies that are passed to the frequencies that suppressed.

The first circuit scoring 101 hits (out of 101) appears in generation 25 (figure 6.17). It has a fitness of 0.01775. The result-producing branch of its circuit-constructing program tree contains 548 points. The circuit has five capacitors and 11 inductors. The incoming signal V passes through source resistor RSRC (at the bottom left of the figure) and is fed into a composition of inductors along the straight line connecting the incoming signal V to the load resistor RLOAD (at the bottom right of the figure). Along the way, there is a series composition of L2, L12, the L11/L23 parallel combination, L10, L26, the L9/L33 parallel combination, L32, and L31. There are four shunts to ground G. Three of these shunts consist of one capacitor each (C19, C29, and C40). The fourth shunt consists of inductor L16 and the C17/C19 parallel combination. As can be seen, this figure 6.occupies a considerable area.

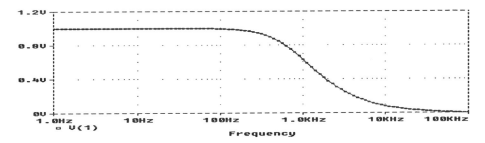

Figure 6.13
Frequency domain behavior of best circuit from generation 0.

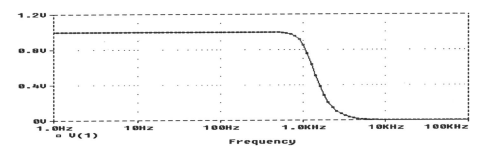

Figure 6.14
Frequency domain behavior of best circuit from generation 8.

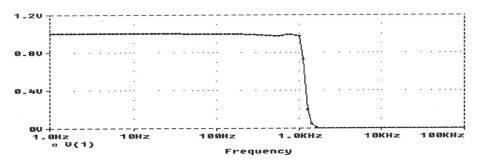

Figure 6.15
Frequency domain behavior of 100%-compliant circuit from generation 25.

Figure 6.15 shows the behavior in the frequency domain of the 100%-compliant 16-component circuit of generation 25. As can be seen, this circuit delivers approximately a full volt for all frequencies up to about 1,000 Hz and about 0 volts for all frequencies above 2,000 Hz. The drop-off in the transition region between the passband

and stopband is far sharper than that of the best-of-generation circuits from generations 0 and 8. This circuit occupies an area of 1775.2. This circuit is indeed a lowpass filter.

In generation 30, the best-of-generation circuit (figure 6.18) has a fitness of 0.00950. It also scores 101 hits. This circuit has 10 inductors and five capacitors. This 100%-compliant 15-component circuit (occupying an area of 950.3) occupies only 54% of the area of the 100%-compliant 16-component circuit from generation 25.

The best-of-run circuit (figure 6.19) appears in generation 138. It has a near-zero fitness of 0.00359 (more than five orders of magnitude better than the fitness of the best circuit of generation 0). The result-producing branch of its circuit-constructing program tree contains 463 points. This circuit has four inductors and four capacitors (half as many components as the best circuit from generation 25). The circuit has a compact layout. There are no series or parallel compositions of capacitors or inductors that redundantly connect the same two points of the circuit. The topology of this best-of-run circuit is a four-rung ladder.

This best-of-run circuit occupies an area of 359.4 (only 20% of the area of the 100%-compliant best circuit from generation 25 in figure 6.17). Note that, for reasons of space, figures 6.17, 6.18, and 6.19 are not drawn to scale.

Table 6.1 shows the number of capacitors, the number of inductors, the number of capacitive or inductive shunts to ground, the area in terms of the number of square units of the bounding rectangle, the frequency-based term of fitness for the 101 fitness cases, and the total fitness for the three best-of-generation circuits (each scoring 101 hits) from generations 25, 30, and 138.

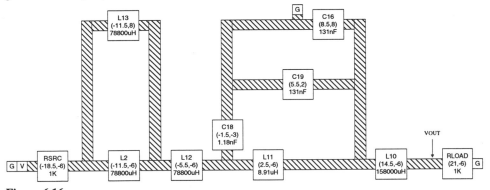

Figure 6.16
Best circuit of generation 8 containing five inductors and three capacitors.

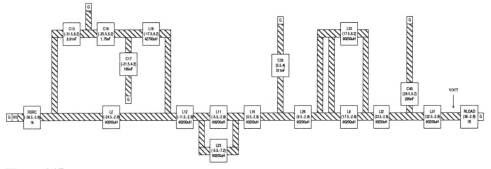

Figure 6.17
100%-compliant best circuit of generation 25 containing five capacitors and 11 inductors (total of 16 components) occupying an area of 1775.2.

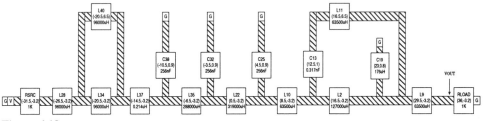

Figure 6.18
100%-compliant best circuit of generation 30 containing 10 inductors and five capacitors (total of 15 components) occupying an area of 950.3.

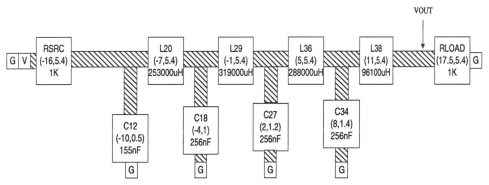

Figure 6.19
100%-compliant best-of-run circuit of generation 138 containing four inductors and four capacitors (total of only eight components) occupying an area of 359.4.

As can be seen in table 6.1, all three of these best-of-generation circuits have the same number (four) of capacitive or inductive shunts to ground. That is, they solve the problem with more or less the same approach. However, the best-of-generation circuits from the two earlier generations (25 and 30) each have a total of 16 inductors and capacitors, while the best-of-run circuit from generation 138 has only eight. Moreover, the best-of-run circuit from generation 138 has only one fifth of the area of the best-of-generation circuit from generation 25. The frequency-based term of the fitness measure (all of which are near zero) is shown for reference only.

Table 6.1
Comparison of three best-of-generation circuits scoring 101 hits.

Generation	Number of Capacitors	Number of Inductors	Number of Shunts	Area	Frequency-Based Term	Fitness
25	5	11	4	1775.2	0.264698	0.01775
30	10	5	4	950.3	0.106199	0.00950
138	4	4	4	359.4	0.193066	0.00359

6.7   Computer Time

This run involving a population of 1,120,000 required 1.55×10^8 fitness evaluations and took 28.4 hours (1.02×10^5) seconds on the 56-node parallel computer system described above. The 56 533-MHz processors operate at an aggregate rate of 2.98×10^{10} Hz, so that the run consumes a total of 3.04×10^{15} computer cycles (about 3 petacycles).

We estimate that about 1 1/2 orders of magnitude more computer time is required by genetic programming to automatically create the circuit's topology, sizing, placement, and routing than is required to merely create the circuit's topology and sizing. The basis for this rough estimate is as follows. In *Genetic Programming III* [Koza, Bennett, Andre, and Keane 1999, section 54.2], genetic programming automatically created the topology and sizing (but not placement and routing) of a lowpass filter circuit with the same specification as used in this chapter. Based on 64 runs of the simpler version of this problem with a population size of 30,000, a computational effort of $E = 4,683,183$ (30,000 × 43 generations × 3.63 runs) was required to yield a solution with 99% probability. When the population size was other than 30,000 for this problem in *Genetic Programming III*, a greater computational effort was found to be necessary to yield a solution to the simpler form of this problem (based on several groups of about 64 runs each). Moreover, none of the numerous additional isolated runs of the simpler form of this problem in *Genetic Programming III* required as few as 4,683,183 fitness evaluations. Although we cannot say with certainty that 30,000 is the optimal population size or that 4,683,183 fitness evaluations is the minimal computation effort required for the simpler form of this problem, we use 4,683,183 fitness evaluations as the best available estimate of the computational effort for the simpler form of this problem.

Each fitness evaluation (in both the simpler form of the problem and the run described in this chapter involving automatic creation of the topology, sizing, placement, and routing) entails a SPICE simulation consuming an average of 2.3×10^7 cycles. Thus, it is reasonable to say that the simpler form of this problem can be solved with a total of 1.08×10^{14} cycles with 99% probability.

Although it is not practical to make 64 28.4-hour runs of the more difficult version of this problem described in this chapter (involving automatic creation of the topology, sizing, placement, and routing) and although we cannot say that 1,120,000 is the optimal population size for this version of this problem, we use 3.04×10^{15} cycles as the best available estimate of the computational effort for the more difficult version of this problem. With these qualifications, we can say that the automatic creation of the topology, sizing, placement, and routing of a lowpass filter takes about 28 times more computer cycles than the automatic creation of merely the circuit's topology and sizing.

There are 14 instances in *Genetic Programming III: Darwinian Invention and Problem Solving* [Koza, Bennett, Andre, and Keane 1999, table 61.1] where genetic programming produced results that are competitive with human-produced results. Eleven of these involve the rediscovery by genetic programming of a previously patented invention. The runs that yielded these 14 instances consumed an average of 1.5×10^{15} computer cycles. Thus, the single run described in this chapter (involving automatic creation of the topology, sizing, placement, and routing of a circuit) took 2.03 times more cycles than the average of the 14 results in *Genetic Programming III*.

6.8   Genetic Programming as an Invention Machine

The best-of-run circuit from generation 138 (figure 6.19) has the recognizable features of the circuit for which George Campbell of American Telephone and Telegraph received U. S. patent 1,227,113 in 1917 [Campbell 1917]. Claim 2 of Campbell's patent covered,

> An electric wave filter consisting of a connecting line of negligible attenuation composed of a plurality of sections, each section including a capacity element and an inductance element, one of said elements of each section being in series with the line and the other in shunt across the line, said capacity and inductance elements having precomputed values dependent upon the upper limiting frequency and the lower limiting frequency of a range of frequencies it is desired to transmit without attenuation, the values of said capacity and inductance elements being so proportioned that the structure transmits with practically negligible attenuation sinusoidal currents of all frequencies lying between said two limiting frequencies, while attenuating and approximately

extinguishing currents of neighboring frequencies lying outside of said limiting frequencies.

An examination of the evolved circuit of figure 6.19 shows that it indeed consists of "a plurality of sections" (specifically, four). Also, as can be seen in the figure, "Each section include[es] a capacity element and an inductance element." Specifically, the first of the four sections consists of inductor L20 and capacitor C12; the second section consists of inductor L29 and capacitor C18; and so forth. Moreover, "one of said elements of each section [is] in series with the line and the other in shunt across the line." As can be seen in the figure, inductor L20 of the first section is indeed "in series with the line" and capacitor C12 is "in shunt across the line." This is also the case for the remaining three sections of the evolved circuit. In addition, the topology of the circuit in figure 6.19 of this chapter exactly matches the topology of the circuit in figure 7 in Campbell's 1917 patent. Finally, this circuit's 100%-compliant frequency domain behavior confirms the fact that the values of the inductors and capacitors are such as to transmit "with practically negligible attenuation sinusoidal currents" of the passband frequencies "while attenuating and approximately extinguishing currents" of the stopband frequencies. In short, the circuit created by genetic programming has all the features contained in claim 2 of Campbell's 1917 patent.

Campbell received a patent for his invention of the ladder filter because it satisfied the legal criteria for obtaining a U. S. patent in that his filter was "new" and "useful" and

. . . the differences between the subject matter sought to be patented and the prior art are such that the subject matter as a whole would [not] have been obvious at the time the invention was made to a person having ordinary skill in the art to which said subject matter pertains. [35 *United States Code* 103a].

The fact that genetic programming rediscovered an electrical circuit that was unobvious "to a person having ordinary skill in the art" establishes that this evolved result satisfies Arthur Samuel's criterion [Samuel 1983] for artificial intelligence and machine learning, namely

The aim [is] ... to get machines to exhibit behavior, which if done by humans, would be assumed to involve the use of intelligence.

Interestingly, the remainder of 35 *United States Code* 103a (quoted in part above) goes on to state,

Patentability shall not be negatived by the manner in which the invention was made.

This wording suggests the permissibility of using genetic programming as an "invention machine" to produce patentable inventions. Unencumbered by preconceptions that may channel human thinking along well-trodden paths, genetic programming starts each run as a new adventure that is free to innovate in any manner that satisfies the requirements of the problem. Genetic programming is a search that is guided by the necessities articulated by the fitness measure of the particular problem at hand. Genetic programming approaches each new problem in terms of "what needs to be done" - not "how to do it."

6.9 Conclusion

This chapter establishes the principle that genetic programming is capable of automatically creating the topology, sizing, placement, and routing of an analog electrical circuit. Specifically, the chapter starts with a high-level statement of the requirements for an analog lowpass filter and creates the topology, sizing, placement, and routing of a satisfactory circuit.

Bibliography

Aaserud, O. and Nielsen, I. R. 1995. Trends in current analog design: A panel debate. *Analog Integrated Circuits and Signal Processing*. 7(1) 5-9.

Andre, David and Koza, John R. 1996. Parallel genetic programming: A scalable implementation using the transputer architecture. In Angeline, P. J. and Kinnear, K. E. Jr. (editors). 1996. *Advances in Genetic Programming 2*. Cambridge, MA: The MIT Press.

Angeline, Peter J. and Kinnear, Kenneth E. Jr. (editors). 1996. *Advances in Genetic Programming 2*. Cambridge, MA: The MIT Press.

Banzhaf, Wolfgang, Nordin, Peter, Keller, Robert E., and Francone, Frank D. 1998. *Genetic Programming – An Introduction*. San Francisco, CA: Morgan Kaufmann and Heidelberg: dpunkt.

Banzhaf, Wolfgang, Poli, Riccardo, Schoenauer, Marc, and Fogarty, Terence C. 1998. *Genetic Programming: First European Workshop. EuroGP'98. Paris, France, April 1998 Proceedings. Paris, France. April l998.* Lecture Notes in Computer Science. Volume 1391. Berlin, Germany: Springer-Verlag.

Campbell, George A. 1917. *Electric Wave Filter*. Filed July 15, 1915. U. S. Patent 1,227,113. Issued May 22, 1917.

Cohn, John M., Garrod, David J., Rutenbar, Rob A., and Carley, L. Richard. 1994. *Analog Device-Level Layout Automation*. Boston: Kluwer.

Grimbleby, J. B. 1995. Automatic analogue network synthesis using genetic algorithms. *Proceedings of the First International Conference on Genetic Algorithms in Engineering Systems: Innovations and Applications*. London: Institution of Electrical Engineers. Pages 53–58.

Garey, Michael R. and Johnson, David S. 1979. *Computers and Intractability: A Guide to the Theory of NP-Completeness*. New York, NY: W. H. Freeman.

Gruau, Frederic. 1992. *Cellular Encoding of Genetic Neural Networks*. Technical report 92-21. Laboratoire de l'Informatique du Parallélisme. Ecole Normale Supérieure de Lyon. May 1992.

Holland, John H. 1975. *Adaptation in Natural and Artificial Systems*. Ann Arbor, MI: University of Michigan Press.

Kinnear, Kenneth E. Jr. (editor). 1994. *Advances in Genetic Programming*. Cambridge, MA: The MIT Press.

Kitano, Hiroaki. 1990. Designing neural networks using genetic algorithms with graph generation system. *Complex Systems*. 4(1990) 461–476.

Koza, John R. 1992. *Genetic Programming: On the Programming of Computers by Means of Natural Selection*. Cambridge, MA: The MIT Press.

Koza, John R. 1994a. *Genetic Programming II: Automatic Discovery of Reusable Programs*. Cambridge, MA: MIT Press.

Koza, John R. 1994b. *Genetic Programming II Videotape: The Next Generation*. Cambridge, MA: The MIT Press.

Koza, John R. 1995. Evolving the architecture of a multi-part program in genetic programming using architecture-altering operations. In McDonnell, John R., Reynolds, Robert G., and Fogel, David B. (editors). 1995. *Evolutionary Programming IV: Proceedings of the Fourth Annual Conference on Evolutionary Programming.* Cambridge, MA: The MIT Press. Pages 695–717.

Koza, John R., Banzhaf, Wolfgang, Chellapilla, Kumar, Deb, Kalyanmoy, Dorigo, Marco, Fogel, David B., Garzon, Max H., Goldberg, David E., Iba, Hitoshi, and Riolo, Rick. (editors). 1998. *Genetic Programming 1998: Proceedings of the Third Annual Conference, July 22-25, 1998, University of Wisconsin.* San Francisco, CA: Morgan Kaufmann.

Koza, John R., Bennett III, Forrest H, Andre, David, and Keane, Martin A. 1999. *Genetic Programming III: Darwinian Invention and Problem Solving.* San Francisco, CA: Morgan Kaufmann.

Koza, John R., Bennett III, Forrest H, Andre, David, Keane, Martin A, and Dunlap, Frank. 1997. Automated synthesis of analog electrical circuits by means of genetic programming. *IEEE Transactions on Evolutionary Computation.* 1(2). Pages 109 – 128.

Koza, John R., Deb, Kalyanmoy, Dorigo, Marco, Fogel, David B., Garzon, Max, Iba, Hitoshi, and Riolo, Rick L. (editors). 1997. *Genetic Programming 1997: Proceedings of the Second Annual Conference.* San Francisco, CA: Morgan Kaufmann.

Koza, John R., Goldberg, David E., Fogel, David B., and Riolo, Rick L. (editors). 1996. *Genetic Programming 1996: Proceedings of the First Annual Conference.* Cambridge, MA: The MIT Press.

Koza, John R., and Rice, James P. 1992. *Genetic Programming: The Movie.* Cambridge, MA: The MIT Press.

Kruiskamp Marinum Wilhelmus and Leenaerts, Domine. 1995. DARWIN: CMOS opamp synthesis by means of a genetic algorithm. *Proceedings of the 32nd Design Automation Conference.* New York, NY: Association for Computing Machinery. Pages 433–438.

Langdon, William B. 1998. *Genetic Programming and Data Structures: Genetic Programming + Data Structures = Automatic Programming!* Amsterdam: Kluwer.

Maziasz, Robert L. and Hayes, John P. 1992. *Layout Minimization of CMOS Cells.* Boston: Kluwer.

Perry, Tekla S. 1998. Donald O. Pederson - The Father of SPICE. *IEEE Spectrum.* 35(6) 22 – 27. June 1998.

Quarles, Thomas, Newton, A. R., Pederson, D. O., and Sangiovanni-Vincentelli, A. 1994. *SPICE 3 Version 3F5 User's Manual.* Department of Electrical Engineering and Computer Science, University of California, Berkeley, CA. March 1994.

Samuel, Arthur L. 1983. AI: Where it has been and where it is going. *Proceedings of the Eighth International Joint Conference on Artificial Intelligence.* Los Altos, CA: Morgan Kaufmann. Pages 1152 – 1157.

Sechen, Carl. 1988. *VLSI Placement and Global Routing using Simulated Annealing.* Boston, MA: Kluwer.

Sterling, Thomas L., Salmon, John, and Becker, Donald J., and Savarese. 1999. *How to Build a Beowulf: A Guide to Implementation and Application of PC Clusters.* Cambridge, MA: The MIT Press.

Thompson, Adrian. 1996. Silicon evolution. In Koza, John R., Goldberg, David E., Fogel, David B., and Riolo, Rick L. (editors). 1996. *Genetic Programming 1996: Proceedings of the First Annual Conference.* Cambridge, MA: The MIT Press.

Thompson, Adrian. 1998. *Hardware Evolution: Automatic Design of Electronic Circuits in Reconfigurable Hardware by Artificial Evolution.* Conference of Professors and Heads of Computing / British Computer Society Distinguished Dissertation series. Berlin: Springer-Verlag.

Ullman, Jeffrey D. 1984. *Computational Aspects of VLSI.* Rockville, MD: Computer Science Press.

Williams, Arthur B. and Taylor, Fred J. 1995. *Electronic Filter Design Handbook.* Third Edition. New York, NY: McGraw-Hill.

Wong, D. F., Leong, H. W., and Liu. C. L. 1988. *Simulated Annealing for VLSI Design.* Boston, MA: Kluwer.

7 Quantum Computing Applications of Genetic Programming

Lee Spector, Howard Barnum, Herbert J. Bernstein, and Nikhil Swamy

Quantum computers are computational devices that use the dynamics of atomic-scale objects to store and manipulate information. Only a few, small-scale quantum computers have been built to date, but quantum computers can in principle outperform all possible classical computers in significant ways. Quantum computation is therefore a subject of considerable theoretical interest that may also have practical applications in the future.

Genetic programming can automatically discover new algorithms for quantum computers [Spector et al., 1998]. We describe how to simulate a quantum computer so that the fitness of a quantum algorithm can be determined on classical hardware. We then describe ways in which three different genetic programming approaches can drive the simulator to evolve new quantum algorithms. The approaches are standard tree-based genetic programming, stack-based linear genome genetic programming, and stackless linear genome genetic programming. We demonstrate the techniques on four different problems: the *two-bit early promise* problem, the *scaling majority-on* problem, the *four-item database search* problem, and the *two-bit and-or* problem. For three of these problems (all but *majority-on*) the automatically discovered algorithms are more efficient than any possible classical algorithms for the same problems. One of the better-than-classical algorithms (for the *two-bit and-or* problem) is in fact more efficient than any previously known quantum algorithm for the same problem, suggesting that genetic programming may be a valuable tool in the future study of quantum programming.

7.1 Quantum Computation

Quantum computers use the dynamics of atomic-scale objects, for example 2-state particles, to store and manipulate information ([Steane, 1998]; see [Braunstein, 1995] for an on-line tutorial; see [Milburn, 1997] for an introduction for the general reader). Devices at this scale are governed by the laws of quantum mechanics rather than by classical physics, and this makes it possible for a quantum computer to do things that a common digital ("classical") computer cannot. In particular, quantum computers can solve certain problems using less time and space resources than classical computers require [Jozsa, 1997]. The physical basis of a real quantum computer might take various forms. Current experimental hardware is based on the use of ion traps, cavity quantum electrodynamics, or nuclear magnetic resonance techniques, all of which appear to have weaknesses [Preskill, 1997], although some physicists are optimistic that new developments will allow for the construction of large-scale quantum computers.

Richard Feynman hinted at the possible power of quantum computation at least as early as 1981 [Milburn, 1997, page 164], but the idea didn't attract widespread attention until a few dramatic examples were discovered more than a decade later. Perhaps the most dramatic was Peter Shor's quantum factoring algorithm, which finds the prime factors of an n-digit number in time $O(n^2 \log(n) \log \log(n))$ [Shor, 1998]. The best currently known classical factoring algorithms require at least time $O(2^{n^{\frac{1}{3}}\log(n)^{\frac{2}{3}}})$, so Shor's algorithm appears to provide a near-exponential speedup [Shor, 1994; Beckman et al., 1996]. This is not certain, however, because a classical lower bound for factoring has not yet been proven. Another intriguing result was provided by Lov Grover, who showed how a quantum computer can find an item in an unsorted list of n items in $O(\sqrt{n})$ steps; classical algorithms clearly require $O(n)$, so this is a case in which quantum computation clearly beats classical computation on a commonly occurring problem [Grover, 1997]. It is not yet clear exactly how powerful quantum computers are relative to classical computers, but this is a subject of active investigation by several research groups.

In the following section we describe how to build a virtual quantum computer to simulate the operation of a quantum computer on ordinary classical computer hardware. We then show how the virtual quantum computer can be used, in conjunction with genetic programming techniques, to evolve new quantum algorithms. This is followed by a presentation of results for four different problems and some concluding remarks.

7.2   A Virtual Quantum Computer

The smallest unit of information in a quantum computer is called a *qubit*, by analogy with the classical *bit*. A classical system of n bits is at any time in one of 2^n states. Quantum mechanics tells us, however, that we must think of a quantum system of n qubits as having a distinct probability of "being in" (that is, "being found in upon measurement") each of the 2^n classical states at any given time. Of course the probabilities must sum to 1—we will always find the system in some particular state when we measure it. The system is said to be in a "superposition" of all states for which there is non-zero probability.

A quantum mechanical system of n qubits can be modeled as a vector of 2^n complex numbers, one *probability amplitude* for each of the 2^n classical states. The probability of finding the system in a particular state is calculated as the square of the modulus of the corresponding amplitude. Computations in the system are modeled as linear transformations, often represented as matrices, applied to the vector of probability amplitudes. Some of these transformations simply move probability from one state to another, in a manner analogous to classical logic gates, but others "spread" or recombine probability between multiple states in more interesting ways (see below). Readers familiar with wave mechanics will recognize these phenomena as instances of quantum interference.

In the following subsections we present some useful notation and then describe the operation of the virtual quantum computer. We also trace the execution of an example quantum algorithm and make some brief observations about the power of quantum computation in light of the simulation.

7.2.1 State Representation and Notation

We represent the state of an n-qubit system as a unit vector of 2^n complex numbers $[\alpha_0, \alpha_1, \alpha_2, \ldots, \alpha_{2^n-1}]$. Each of these numbers can be viewed as paired with one of the system's classical states. The classical states are called the "computational basis vectors" of the system and are labled by n-bit strings, represented as $|b_{n-1}b_{n-2}\ldots b_j \ldots b_0\rangle$ where each b_j is either 0 or 1.[1] The state labels can be abbreviated using the binary number formed by concatenating the bits; that is, we can write $|k\rangle$ in place of $|b_{n-1}b_{n-2}\ldots b_j \ldots b_0\rangle$ where $k = b_0 + 2b_1 + 4b_2 + \ldots + 2^{n-1}b_{n-1}$. For example we can write $|6\rangle$ in place of $|110\rangle$. The modulus squared of each amplitude α (for example $|\alpha_k|^2$) is the probability that measurement of the system will find it in the corresponding classical state ($|k\rangle$).

As an example, the complete state of a two-qubit system is represented in the following form:

$$\alpha_0|00\rangle + \alpha_1|01\rangle + \alpha_2|10\rangle + \alpha_3|11\rangle$$

If we measure the system's state, each of the computational basis vectors is a possible outcome. The probability that the state of the system is $|00\rangle$ is $|\alpha_0|^2$, the probability that we will find the state of the system to be $|01\rangle$ is $|\alpha_1|^2$, etc.

7.2.2 Quantum Gates

The primitive operations supported by a quantum computer are called *quantum logic gates*, by analogy with traditional digital logic gates. Several small sets of quantum logic gates are *universal* for quantum computation in almost the same sense that *NAND* is universal for classical computation; one can implement any quantum algorithm with at most polynomial slowdown using only primitive gates from one of these sets ([Barenco et al., 1995] and references therein). For example, all quantum computations can be implemented using only the U_2 and *CNOT* gates described below.

We will describe and represent quantum gates as matrices that operate on a quantum system via matrix multiplication with the vector of amplitudes. Gates representing physically possible dynamics (time-evolution) of a closed (or isolated) quantum system must be *unitary*—that is, each gate U must satisfy $U^\dagger U = UU^\dagger = 1$, where $U^\dagger$ is the Hermitean adjoint of U, obtained by taking the complex conjugate of each element of U and then transposing the matrix [Löwdin, 1998].

7.2.2.1 Quantum *NOT* and *SQUARE ROOT OF NOT*

A simple example of a quantum gate is the quantum counterpart of classical *NOT*. Classical *NOT* inverts the value of a single bit, changing 0 to 1 and 1 to 0. Quantum *NOT* operates

---

[1] The "$|\ldots\rangle$" notation is for "ket" vectors; this notation is standard in the quantum computation literature and it will be used here even though the "bra-ket" notation system of which it is part is beyond the scope of this chapter (but see [Chester, 1987]).

on a single qubit. In a one-qubit system (which we represent with two amplitudes, one for $|0\rangle$ and one for $|1\rangle$) the quantum *NOT* operation simply swaps the values of the two amplitudes. That is, a single qubit system in the state $\alpha_0|0\rangle + \alpha_1|1\rangle$ will be transformed by quantum *NOT* into $\alpha_1|0\rangle + \alpha_0|1\rangle$. Quantum *NOT* can be represented in matrix form as $\left[\begin{smallmatrix} 0 & 1 \\ 1 & 0 \end{smallmatrix}\right]$, and its operation on a one qubit system $\alpha_0|0\rangle + \alpha_1|1\rangle$, represented as a column vector $\left[\begin{smallmatrix} \alpha_0 \\ \alpha_1 \end{smallmatrix}\right]$, can be shown as:

$$\begin{bmatrix} 0 & 1 \\ 1 & 0 \end{bmatrix} \begin{bmatrix} \alpha_0 \\ \alpha_1 \end{bmatrix} = \begin{bmatrix} \alpha_1 \\ \alpha_0 \end{bmatrix}$$

Another interesting one-qubit gate is the *SQUARE ROOT OF NOT* (*SRN*) gate:

$$\begin{bmatrix} \frac{1}{\sqrt{2}} & -\frac{1}{\sqrt{2}} \\ \frac{1}{\sqrt{2}} & \frac{1}{\sqrt{2}} \end{bmatrix}$$

A single application of *SRN* will in effect randomize the state of a qubit that was previously in a "pure" state of 0 or 1. That is, it will transform a situation in which there is a probability of 1 for reading the state as "0" (or a situation in which there is a probability of 1 for reading the state as "1") into one in which there is a probability of $\frac{1}{2}$ for reading the state as "0" and a probability of $\frac{1}{2}$ for reading the state as "1". But applying this gate twice in succession will produce the same inverting effect as *NOT*, thereby extracting information from the seemingly randomized intermediate state.[2]

7.2.2.2 Applying quantum gates to multi-qubit systems

When applied to qubit j of a multi-qubit system, quantum *NOT* swaps the amplitudes of each pair of basis vectors that differ from one another only in the jth position. For example, in a two-qubit system the application of quantum *NOT* to qubit 0 will swap the amplitude of $|00\rangle$ with that of $|01\rangle$, and the amplitude of $|10\rangle$ with that of $|11\rangle$. This can be represented in matrix form as follows:

$$\begin{bmatrix} 0 & 1 & 0 & 0 \\ 1 & 0 & 0 & 0 \\ 0 & 0 & 0 & 1 \\ 0 & 0 & 1 & 0 \end{bmatrix}$$

One typically describes only the minimal version of a gate, for example the 2×2 matrix for *NOT*, and expands it as needed for application to a larger system. For an n-qubit system the expansion will always be a $2^n \times 2^n$ matrix of complex numbers which, when multiplied

---

[2]The double application of *SRN* is not quite equivalent to *NOT* because there is a change in sign: $\begin{bmatrix} \frac{1}{\sqrt{2}} & -\frac{1}{\sqrt{2}} \\ \frac{1}{\sqrt{2}} & \frac{1}{\sqrt{2}} \end{bmatrix} \begin{bmatrix} \frac{1}{\sqrt{2}} & -\frac{1}{\sqrt{2}} \\ \frac{1}{\sqrt{2}} & \frac{1}{\sqrt{2}} \end{bmatrix} = \begin{bmatrix} 0 & -1 \\ 1 & 0 \end{bmatrix}$. But this change in sign has no immediate effect because we square the amplitudes when reading the state of the system.

by the vector of amplitudes, has the effect of applying the gate to the specified qubit or set of qubits.

To understand how quantum gates are applied in multi-qubit systems one must bear in mind that all amplitudes in the state representation encode part of the value for each qubit. For example, in a two-qubit system the amplitudes for $|00\rangle$ and $|10\rangle$ both contribute to the probability that the right-most qubit (qubit 0) is zero, and the amplitudes for $|01\rangle$ and $|11\rangle$ both contribute to the probability that qubit 0 is one. So a gate applied to a small subset of the qubits of a multi-qubit system may nonetheless change all of the amplitudes in the state representation.

To apply an m-qubit gate to a set Q of m qubits in an n-qubit system ($m \leq n$), one must in general operate on *all* 2^n amplitudes in the system. The $2^n \times 2^n$ matrix that one uses should have the effect of applying the $2^m \times 2^m$ minimal version of the gate to each of 2^{n-m} different column vectors. Each of these column vectors corresponds to a set of basis vectors that varies only with respect to Q and is constant in all other bit positions. For example, consider the 4×4 *NOT* matrix above, which is a *NOT* gate for qubit 0 in a two-qubit system. This 4×4 matrix has the effect of applying the 2×2 *NOT* matrix ($\begin{bmatrix} 0 & 1 \\ 1 & 0 \end{bmatrix}$) to the amplitudes for $|00\rangle$ and $|01\rangle$, that is to $\begin{bmatrix} \alpha_0 \\ \alpha_1 \end{bmatrix}$, to produce new amplitudes for $|00\rangle$ and $|01\rangle$, and also of applying the 2×2 *NOT* matrix to the amplitudes for $|10\rangle$ and $|11\rangle$, that is to $\begin{bmatrix} \alpha_2 \\ \alpha_3 \end{bmatrix}$, to produce new amplitudes for $|10\rangle$ and $|11\rangle$. This can be generalized for any m; one wants the $2^n \times 2^n$ matrix which, for each set of 2^m basis vectors that vary only with respect to Q, multiplies the $2^m \times 2^m$ minimal version of the gate by the corresponding set of amplitudes.

An implementation option is to build up the $2^n \times 2^n$ matrix that has the required effect explicitly, and to multiply this matrix by the vector of amplitudes. Alternatively one can operate on the amplitudes one at a time, dynamically computing for each one the necessary matrix elements. Because the full expanded matrices are large and mostly zero we generally take the latter approach. Note that in any case one must perform an exponentially large amount of work (with respect to n) in order to apply a single gate; this is the source of the exponential slowdown in the simulation of quantum computations.

7.2.2.3 Other Quantum Gates

Another useful quantum gate is *controlled NOT* (or *CNOT*), which takes two qubit indices as arguments; we will call these arguments *control* and *target*. *CNOT* is an identity operation for basis vectors with 0 in the control position, but it acts like quantum *NOT* applied to the target position for basis vectors with 1 in the control position. For the case of a two-qubit system, with qubit 1 as the control and qubit 0 as the target (recall that we start counting with 0 from the rightmost position in the ket vector labels), this can be shown in matrix form as follows:

$$\begin{bmatrix} 1 & 0 & 0 & 0 \\ 0 & 1 & 0 & 0 \\ 0 & 0 & 0 & 1 \\ 0 & 0 & 1 & 0 \end{bmatrix}$$

CNOT flips the state with respect to its target qubit wherever its control qubit is 1. By making the condition on this flipping more complex, using more controlling qubits, we can construct analogous gates for any classical boolean function. For example, consider the classical *NAND* gate which takes two input bits and outputs 0 if both inputs are 1, and 1 otherwise. That is, it has the following truth table:

A	B	A *NAND* B
0	0	1
0	1	1
1	0	1
1	1	0

Such a truth table can be used to form a quantum gate by interpreting a 1 in the output (rightmost) column of a particular row as an instruction to swap amplitudes between each pair of basis vectors that match that row's values for the input qubits and differ only in their values for the output qubit. That is, we can construct a quantum gate, called quantum *NAND*, that takes three qubit indices (these can be thought of as 2 inputs and 1 output[3]) and swaps amplitudes of all pairs of basis vectors that are equivalent with respect to their input qubits but differ in their output qubit, except for those for which both input qubits are 1 (the bottom row of the truth table). For a three-qubit system, with qubits 1 and 2 as inputs and qubit 0 as output, this can be represented in matrix form as follows[4]:

$$\begin{bmatrix} 0 & 1 & 0 & 0 & 0 & 0 & 0 & 0 \\ 1 & 0 & 0 & 0 & 0 & 0 & 0 & 0 \\ 0 & 0 & 0 & 1 & 0 & 0 & 0 & 0 \\ 0 & 0 & 1 & 0 & 0 & 0 & 0 & 0 \\ 0 & 0 & 0 & 0 & 0 & 1 & 0 & 0 \\ 0 & 0 & 0 & 0 & 1 & 0 & 0 & 0 \\ 0 & 0 & 0 & 0 & 0 & 0 & 1 & 0 \\ 0 & 0 & 0 & 0 & 0 & 0 & 0 & 1 \end{bmatrix}$$

---

[3]The designation of quantum gate arguments as "inputs" and "outputs" is convenient but may in some cases be misleading. When applied to certain states quantum *NAND* (and other gates described below) can affect "input" as well as "output" qubits. We retain the "input/output" terminology because it allows for more intuitive explanations.

[4]A reviewer suggested that would normally be called "NOT Controlled-Controlled-NOT" in the quantum computation literature.

The work described in this chapter also uses a *Hadamard* gate which can be used to split the amplitude between opposite values for a single qubit:

$$H = \frac{1}{\sqrt{2}} \begin{bmatrix} 1 & 1 \\ 1 & -1 \end{bmatrix}$$

and simple rotation by an angle θ:

$$U_\theta = \begin{bmatrix} \cos(\theta) & \sin(\theta) \\ -\sin(\theta) & \cos(\theta) \end{bmatrix}$$

and a conditional phase gate that takes a single real parameter α:

$$CPHASE = \begin{bmatrix} 1 & 0 & 0 & 0 \\ 0 & 1 & 0 & 0 \\ 0 & 0 & 0 & e^{i\alpha} \\ 0 & 0 & e^{-i\alpha} & 0 \end{bmatrix}$$

and generalized rotation with four real parameters α, θ, ϕ, and ψ:

$$U_2 = \begin{bmatrix} e^{-i\phi} & 0 \\ 0 & e^{i\phi} \end{bmatrix} \times \begin{bmatrix} \cos(\theta) & \sin(-\theta) \\ \sin(\theta) & \cos(\theta) \end{bmatrix} \times \begin{bmatrix} e^{-i\psi} & 0 \\ 0 & e^{i\psi} \end{bmatrix} \times \begin{bmatrix} e^{i\alpha} & 0 \\ 0 & e^{i\alpha} \end{bmatrix}$$

The U_2 gate can emulate any other single bit gate, at the cost of taking four real-valued parameters. A generalized 2-qubit gate with sixteen real-valued parameters (U_4) also exists, but we did not use this in the work described here.

7.2.3 Running a Quantum Algorithm

A quantum algorithm is run by putting the system into a known initial state, subjecting it to a sequence of gates, and then reading out (i.e., measuring) the final state of the system. The initial state is usually a computational basis vector—that is, a state in which a single amplitude is 1 and all others are 0; in the work reported here the system is always started in state $|00\ldots0\rangle$, meaning that the amplitude for $|00\ldots0\rangle$ is initially 1. The final measurement is usually made in the computational basis, and each gate usually involves no more than a few qubits. These conditions ensure that the number of gates in a quantum circuit is a reasonable measure of its computational complexity. The final state is read by squaring the modulus of each amplitude, summing those that correspond to the same values for the output bits, and reporting the output bit pattern with the highest sum. This is the output that would most likely be produced if the same sequence of operators was run on a real quantum computer. The simulation can also report the actual probability of obtaining this most-likely result; this is just the sum of $|\alpha|^2$ for the states having the most probable output pattern. If the probability for returning the correct answer is less than 1 but greater than $\frac{1}{2}$, the algorithm may nonetheless be useful. This is because one can often show that re-running the algorithm some small number of times will reduce the indeterminacy to any required level. A quantum algorithm is said to compute a function with *2-sided-error* if it always returns an answer which is correct with probability at least p, where $\frac{1}{2} < p < 1$ [Beals et al., 1998]. For algorithms intended to scale to systems of any number of qubits n, p must not depend on n, or at least not decrease too rapidly with n.

7.2.4 Example Execution Trace

To clarify the way in which quantum algorithms are executed we will trace the execution of a simple, arbitrary algorithm in some detail. Consider the following quantum algorithm for a two qubit system:

```
Hadamard qubit:0
Hadamard qubit:1
U-theta qubit:0 theta:pi/5
Controlled-not control:1 target:0
Hadamard qubit:1
```

Execution starts in the state $1|00\rangle + 0|01\rangle + 0|10\rangle + 0|11\rangle$. The *Hadamard* gate on qubit 0 is then applied by means of two matrix multiplications:

• The *Hadamard* matrix is multiplied by a column vector made from the amplitudes for $|00\rangle$ and $|01\rangle$, and the new values for the amplitudes of $|00\rangle$ and $|01\rangle$ are taken from the resulting column vector.

• The *Hadamard* matrix is multiplied by a column vector made from the amplitudes for $|10\rangle$ and $|11\rangle$, and the new values for the amplitudes of $|10\rangle$ and $|11\rangle$ are taken from the resulting column vector.

This transforms the state to $\frac{1}{\sqrt{2}}|00\rangle + \frac{1}{\sqrt{2}}|01\rangle + 0|10\rangle + 0|11\rangle$. At this point there is an equal probability of finding the state $|00\rangle$ or the state $|01\rangle$, but the other states have zero probability. This means that one could find qubit 0 to be 0 or 1 (each with equal probability), but one would definitely find qubit 1 to be 0. The subsequent *Hadamard* gate on qubit 1 transforms the state to $\frac{1}{2}|00\rangle + \frac{1}{2}|01\rangle + \frac{1}{2}|10\rangle + \frac{1}{2}|11\rangle$. At this point all states have the same probability. The U_θ gate rotates qubit 0 by $\frac{\pi}{5}$, using the same procedure as described for the *Hadamard* gates but with a different matrix, producing approximately $0.698|00\rangle + 0.111|01\rangle + 0.698|10\rangle + 0.111|11\rangle$. The subsequent *CNOT* flips qubit 0 for basis vectors in which qubit 1 is "1", producing $0.698|00\rangle + 0.111|01\rangle + 0.111|10\rangle + 0.698|11\rangle$. The final *Hadamard* again manipulates qubit 1, producing a final state of approximately $0.572|00\rangle + 0.572|01\rangle + 0.416|10\rangle - 0.416|11\rangle$. The probabilities of finding the system in each of the possible classical states upon measurement are approximately as follows:

state	probability
$\lvert 00 \rangle$	0.33
$\lvert 01 \rangle$	0.33
$\lvert 10 \rangle$	0.17
$\lvert 11 \rangle$	0.17

We can measure the system and read the output from either or both of the qubits. If we read only qubit 1 there is a probability of $0.33 + 0.33 = 0.66$ that we will find it to be "0" and a probability of $0.17 + 0.17 = 0.34$ that we will find it to be "1". Qubit 0's value will be completely random, with a probability of 0.5 for each state. So the example algorithm takes the state $\lvert 00 \rangle$ to a state with a random value for qubit 0 and a biased value for qubit 1, with probability 0.66 to be "0".

7.2.5   The Power of Quantum Computation

Having examined the mechanics of a virtual quantum computer and traced its execution we may now be in a better position to see the source of the power of quantum computation. The vector of 2^n complex amplitudes clearly contains more information than a classical state of n bits, but it is maintained with only n quantum mechanical bit registers (e.g., n spin-$\frac{1}{2}$ particles). We cannot read the entire state because the measured result is always a single computational basis vector and there will generally be some uncertainty about which computational basis vector we will actually read. Further, measurement interferes with the system so it can only be read once. But the additional information in the state can nonetheless sometimes be extracted and harnessed to perform real computational work. In some cases the extra information can be used to perform computations on several different somewhat probable states simultaneously, and clever manipulations allow us to extract useful information from all of them. Of course we are paying for this in the simulator with exponential resources, so we can only work with relatively small systems. Fortunately, small systems are adequate for the evolution of some new algorithms, including some algorithms that can be scaled up to work on larger problem instances when real quantum computing hardware becomes available.

7.3   Evolving Quantum Algorithms

Given a simulator for a quantum computer, one can use genetic programming techniques to evolve quantum algorithms [Spector et al., 1998]. Genetic programming systems evolve programs (algorithms), and one can use a genetic programming system to evolve quantum algorithms by ensuring that the programs in the population have the proper form and by assessing their fitness on the simulated quantum computer.

Many open questions in quantum computation concern the computational resources required to scale algorithms up to larger problem instances. For this reason it would be most useful if we could evolve *scalable* quantum algorithms that work on problem instances of any size. Scaling is also important because classical simulation of quantum computers consumes an amount of resources that grows exponentially with respect to the number of qubits in the system, and this limits us to simulating quantum algorithms for small systems. But quantum computation is most interesting when applied to much larger problems, for which their exponential savings in resource requirements really pays off. We can ameliorate the problem by using small cases of several sizes for fitness evaluation during evolution. In some cases this will produce algorithms that scale correctly to all sizes; scaled-up versions of these algorithms could be run on much larger problem instances on real quantum computer hardware in the future.

The scaling results reported in this chapter are modest, but the technique that we use was designed to allow for the evolution of scalable algorithms and we show an example of this in section 7.4.2 below. One should also note that new quantum algorithms may be of significant interest even if they do not scale, although it is obviously preferable to find scaling algorithms.

Our technique for finding scalable algorithms involves evolving classical programs that, when executed, construct the actual quantum algorithms. Because the classical programs can include iteration structures and constants related to the size of a particular problem instance, a single evolved program can produce different quantum algorithms for problem instances of different sizes. This technique is related to a theoretical construction used by Peter Shor to define quantum complexity classes [Shor, 1998, pages 473–474]. It is also similar to "second-order encoding" techniques, in which evolved programs must be run to produce the sought-after executable structures, that have previously been used to evolve neural networks and electrical circuits [Gruau, 1994; Koza and Bennett, 1999]. The use of such second-order encodings to provide scaling appears to be novel with this work.

7.3.1 Standard Tree-based Genetic Programming

To evolve quantum algorithms using a standard (weakly typed) tree-based genetic programming engine [Koza, 1992] we start with a set of functions that add gates to an initially empty quantum algorithm. These functions are parameterized by numbers, so the *closure* type for the function set is number (which includes integers, ratios, floating point numbers, and complex numbers). The algorithm-building functions include the following:

H-GATE   Takes 1 argument, which is coerced to a valid qubit index by taking the truncated real part of the argument modulo the number of qubits in the system. (All coercions specified below are performed in a similar way.) A *Hadamard* gate on the given qubit is added to the end (output side) of the quantum algorithm. The function call returns the argument (un-coerced).

U-THETA-GATE Takes 2 arguments, the first of which is coerced to a valid qubit index, and the second of which is interpreted as an angle in radians. A rotation (U_θ) gate is added to the end of the quantum algorithm. The function call returns the first argument.

CNOT-GATE Takes 2 arguments, both of which are coerced to valid qubit indices. A *CNOT* gate is added to the end of the quantum algorithm, using the first argument as the control qubit and the second argument as the target qubit, unless the two qubit indices are the same (in which case no action is taken). The function call returns the first argument.

NAND-GATE Takes 3 arguments, all of which are coerced to valid qubit indices. A *NAND* gate is added to the end of the quantum algorithm, using the first two arguments as inputs and the third argument as output, unless any of the qubit indices are the same (in which case no action is taken). The function call returns the third argument.

Similar functions may be added for the other quantum gates. We also include iteration control structures that help to evolve scalable quantum algorithms:

ITERATE An iteration control structure. Takes 2 arguments, the first of which is coerced to a non-negative integer, and determines the number of iterations that the second argument, a body of code, will be executed. If a (typically very large) bound on the number of iterations is exceeded the calling program immediately halts. The number of iterations is returned as the value of the control structure expression.

IQ An iteration control structure that takes one argument: a body of code. This is equivalent to a call to ITERATE with a first argument equal to the number of qubits in the system.

IVAR Takes one argument, which is coerced to a non-negative integer. (IVAR 0) returns the value of the loop counter of the immediately enclosing iteration structure. (IVAR 1) returns the value of the loop counter for the next iteration structure out, etc. The argument is reduced modulo the number of iteration structures that enclose the call to IVAR. Calls to IVAR outside of all iteration structures return 0.

We also include a collection of arithmetic functions: + (returns the sum of its two arguments), 1+ (returns the sum of its single argument and 1), – (returns the difference of its two arguments), 1– (returns the difference of its single argument and 1), * (returns the product of its two arguments), *2 (returns the product of its single argument and 2), %p (protected division: returns the quotient of its two arguments; returns 1 if its second argument is 0), %2 (returns the quotient of its single argument and 2), 1/x (returns the quotient of 1 and its single argument; returns 1 if its argument is 0).

In the genetic programming terminal set we include `*NUM-QUBITS*` (a constant equal to the number of qubits in the system), `*NUM-INPUT-QUBITS*` (a constant equal to the number of qubits used for input), `*NUM-OUTPUT-QUBITS*` (a constant equal to the number of qubits used for output), and a variety of useful constants, sometimes including 0, 1, 2, π (3.1415...), and i ($\sqrt{-1}$). In some runs we also include an ephemeral random constant specifier [Koza, 1992] that can produce random floating point constants (usually in the range [-10.0 to $+10.0$], although we have experimented with various ranges).

7.3.2 Stack-Based, Linear Genome Genetic Programming

Although standard tree-based genetic programming (*TGP*) can be used to evolve quantum algorithms, other approaches may have certain advantages. The tree structure of *TGP* representations plays several roles; for example it provides an elegant mechanism for adaptive determination of program size and shape [Langdon et al., 1999] and it also allows for natural expression of *functional* programming constructs, in which sub-expressions return values that are used for various purposes in the larger expressions within which they are nested. But the tree representations come at a cost (time, space, complexity), and there is no guarantee that they will be the most appropriate representations for all problems.

Notice that the algorithm-building functions described in the previous section all work by "side effect"; that is, they do their useful work by making changes to the quantum algorithm that is being constructed, and they return uninformative values (copies of their arguments). This suggests that the function set is ill-suited to the functional programming paradigm, and that the tree structure of *TGP* representations will therefore have diminished utility in this domain. It is possible that the tree structure is actually a liability in cases such as this, since a sub-expression's contribution to its enclosing expression (its return value) is related to its function (side effect) in arbitrary ways. One could argue that it would be difficult for evolution to untangle return values and side effects, for example to preserve an important return value while modifying a side effect of the same sub-expression, and that this would put unnecessary burdens on the genetic programming system.

While the reliance on side effects is due in part to our specific design choices, *any* representation of quantum algorithms is likely to have similar features. This is because *measurement* (accessing values of variables) in a quantum system changes the system, which will usually destroy prepared superpositions and ruin the computation. In more concrete terms, we cannot access the amplitudes in our state representation and use the values to influence the choice of future computational steps, because any such access on a real quantum computer would change the system's state. So steps in a quantum algorithm must always be blind, to a certain extent, to the values (amplitudes) produced by earlier steps.

In a stack-based, linear genome genetic programming (*SBGP*) system, programs are represented not as trees but rather as linear sequences of functions that can communicate via a global stack [Perkis, 1994; Stoffel and Spector, 1996]. This eliminates the conflation of return value and side effect, since functions with no meaningful return values can simply be coded not to "return" values onto the stack. It is well suited to the evolution of sequential, side-effect-based programs because the program structure is itself sequential and less biased toward functional (return-value-based) programming style. For example, in SBGP programs a side-effect-producing function can be replaced with another without the danger that a different (possibly arbitrary) return value will change the behavior of an enclosing expression.

SBGP systems offer several other advantages. Their linear program structure simplifies the expression of genetic operators (one can use operators from traditional string-based genetic algorithms), reduces memory requirements (since there are no growing trees—one can use fixed-length programs with non-functional noop operators to allow for shorter programs), and allows for very high performance genetic programming engines [Stoffel and Spector, 1996]. In addition, anecdotal reports suggest that SBGP may require less computational effort than TGP for many problems [Perkis, 1994; Stoffel and Spector, 1996].

We have found SBGP to be preferable to TGB for our quantum algorithm problems, though we have not conducted a careful comparison of the techniques. With SBGP we have low memory requirements per program (allowing for larger populations), we are freed from concerns about tree growth dynamics and return-value/side-effect interactions, and results appear to emerge more quickly than in our prior TGP work. Further research may provide a more scientific comparison of TGB and SBGP for evolution of quantum algorithms.

We used the *MidGP* SBGP system [Spector, 1997], a simple, flexible Lisp-based system derived from HiGP [Stoffel and Spector, 1996]. The translation of quantum algorithm-building and arithmetic functions from TGP to *MidGP* is straightforward, but the translation of the iteration structures can be done in various ways. We have experimented with both structured and unstructured (GOTO-based) iteration mechanisms, and in principle one could use any control structures from other stack-based languages such as FORTH and Postscript. In SBGP one generally also includes a collection of stack-related functions, for example to duplicate (dup) or remove (pop) the top stack element, to swap the top two elements, etc. Because of the ease with which they can be written for *MidGP*, we have also used several new genetic operators in our *MidGP*-based work on quantum algorithms. For example, we have used program rotation operators, crossover operators that concatenate randomly selected chunks from parent programs, and a mutation operator that adds small random floating-point values to numeric constants.

7.3.3 Stackless Linear Genome Genetic Programming

Although the scaling of quantum algorithms is in many cases important, there are other cases for which it suffices to find a single quantum algorithm that works for a single problem size. In these cases there may (depending on the structure of the problem) be no need for iteration in the quantum algorithm-building program, since the primary role of the iteration structures in the function set is to allow for scaling of the quantum algorithms. If, in addition, there is no compelling reason for the gates to be able to share parameter values, then there may be no need for any sort of storage (return values or the stack) at all.

For such cases we have found it useful to use a very simple technique, in which a quantum algorithm is represented as a linear sequence that includes *only* noop functions and *encapsulated gates*. An encapsulated gate is a package that includes, internally, the type of quantum gate and values for all required parameters. The quantum algorithm is run by executing each of the gates in sequence, and no global value stack is required.

We have implemented this approach within *MidGP*, generating all gates and parameters randomly via *MidGP*'s ephemeral random constant mechanism. We use a function set containing only noop and ephemeral-random-quantum-gate; when ephemeral-random-quantum-gate is selected a new encapsulated gate is created with a random choice of gate type and all necessary parameters. It might also be useful to include a mutation operator that manipulates the parameters encapsulated within a gate, but we have not yet found it necessary to do so; our current mutation mechanism simply adds a new random gate (with random parameters) at a random location in the program. Surprisingly, this very simple mechanism suffices to evolve some interesting quantum algorithms, including the algorithm for the *and-or* problem discussed below (Section 7.4.4).

7.3.4   Fitness Function

We use a standardized fitness function (for which lower values mean "more fit") with three components: a *misses* component that records the number of fitness cases for which the program misbehaves, an *error* component that records the total error for all cases in which the program misbehaves, and a *length* component that records the total number of gates in the quantum algorithms built by the program for all fitness cases. A program is said to "misbehave" on a case if the probability that the quantum algorithm it produces will give the correct answer for the case is less than 0.48; this allows for the evolution of non-deterministic algorithms with *2-sided-error* (see section 7.2.3) and is sufficiently far from 0.5 to ensure that errors below the threshold are not due to roundoff errors in the quantum computer simulator.

The three components could be combined in various ways. We recommend a *lexicographic* [Ben-Tal, 1979] ordering, with the components ordered: misses (most significant), error, length (least significant). This means that programs will be compared first with respect to misses, with error being used only to break ties. Length will be used only to break ties between programs with identical misses scores and identical error scores.

The actual fitness function that we used in our runs approximates the lexicographic fitness function described above, but because it was developed and modified in an ad hoc fashion during the course of our work it varies from this fitness function in several minor ways. It is documented in full in [Spector et al., 1998].

7.4   Results

7.4.1   Deutsch's Early Promise Problem

In 1985 David Deutsch presented a problem for which quantum computers can clearly out-perform classical computers. This problem, like many in the quantum computation literature, involves determining properties of an unknown function. We can call the unknown function in programs that we write (or evolve) but we aren't given access to the function's code. For this reason the unknown function is often called a "black box" function or an "oracle."

Suppose you are given an oracle that computes an unknown binary function of n input bits. Suppose further that you are promised that the function is either *uniform*, meaning that it always returns 0 or always returns 1, or that it is *balanced*, meaning that it will return an equal number of 0s and 1s if called on all possible inputs. Deutsch's *early promise problem* is the problem of determining whether such an oracle is uniform or balanced.

It is easy to see that the best deterministic classical algorithm for this problem will in the worst case require $\frac{2^n}{2} + 1$ oracle calls. If the first $\frac{2^n}{2}$ calls all return the same value, then it is still possible that the oracle is either uniform or balanced, but the answer will be known for certain after one more oracle call. A probabilistic classical algorithm can do somewhat better, because it is unlikely that a balanced oracle will produce $\frac{2^n}{2}$ of the same value in sequence. Nonetheless, it is also clear that a *single* call to the oracle on a classical computer produces *no* information that can be helpful in solving the problem, whether deterministically or probabilistically—0 and 1 are both equally likely outputs from such a call whether the oracle is uniform or balanced.

Deutsch showed that quantum computers can do better here [Deutsch, 1985; Deutsch and Jozsa, 1992; Costantini and Smeraldi, 1997]. If the oracle is implemented as an operator on a quantum computer's state, then information useful in solving the problem can be obtained using fewer oracle calls than would be required by any classical algorithm. Note that this does not imply that we must know anything about the implementation of the oracle except that it is a well-behaved quantum mechanical operator.

We used the standard tree-based genetic programming techniques described above (Section 7.3.1) to automatically discover a quantum algorithm that provides information on the two-bit early promise problem using only one oracle call. We evolved quantum algorithms for a three-qubit quantum computer, using two qubits for the oracle's input and one for its output. The qubits are referred to with the indices 0, 1, and 2. For each fitness case the quantum computer was prepared in the initial state of $|000\rangle$, the algorithm was executed, and the result was then read from qubit 2. The algorithms could include H, U_θ, $CNOT$ and $NAND$ gates as described above, along with an $ORACLE$ gate implemented analogously to $NAND$, but with a truth table corresponding to the function that the oracle computes. Each fitness case uses a different oracle function—the goal is to find a single quantum algorithm which puts qubit 2 into the "1" state if the oracle is uniform or into the "0" state if the

Table 7.1
Genetic programming parameters for a run on the two-bit early promise problem.

max number of generations	1,001
size of population	10,000
max depth of new individuals	6
max depth of new subtrees for mutants	4
max depth after crossover	12
reproduction fraction	0.2
crossover at any point fraction	0.1
crossover at function points fraction	0.5
selection method	tournament (size=5)
generation method	ramped half-and-half
function set	+, -, *, %p, sqrt, 1+, 1-, *2, %2, 1/x, iterate, ivar, iq, H-gate, U-theta-gate, CNOT-gate, NAND-gate, ORACLE-gate
terminal set	*num-qubits*, *num-input-qubits*, *num-output-qubits*, $0, 1, 2, \pi, i$

```
(IQ
 (NAND-GATE
  (+ (* (1- 0) (ITERATE PI PI))
     (U-THETA-GATE -1 (*2 *NUM-INPUT-QUBITS*)))
  (%2
   (+ (H-GATE (IQ (IQ (1- PI))))
      (ITERATE
        (1- (SQRT (CNOT-GATE (U-THETA-GATE 1 (IVAR *NUM-QUBITS*))
                             (IVAR (ITERATE PI *NUM-OUTPUT-QUBITS*)))))
       (1/X
        (NAND-GATE
         (* (SQRT -1) (- (%P (IVAR 0) *NUM-QUBITS*) *NUM-INPUT-QUBITS*))
         (1/X *NUM-INPUT-QUBITS*) PI)))))
  (NAND-GATE (IQ (1- (IQ (%2 (%2 (IQ (*2 *NUM-INPUT-QUBITS*)))))))
             (IQ (IVAR PI))
             (SQRT (%2 (1- (ORACLE-GATE)))))))
```

Figure 7.1
An evolved program that produces a quantum algorithm for the two-bit early promise problem.

```
U-theta qubit:2 theta:4
Hadamard qubit:0
U-theta qubit:1 theta:1
Oracle (input-qubits:0,1 output-qubit:2)
NAND input-qubits:2,1 output-qubit: 0
U-theta qubit:2 theta:4
Hadamard qubit:0
U-theta qubit:1 theta:2
Controlled-not control:1 target:2
(read output from qubit 2)
```

Figure 7.2
An quantum algorithm for the two-bit early promise problem, produced by the program in Figure 7.1. The system is initialized to the state $|000\rangle$ and then the algorithm is run, leaving qubit 2 in the "1" state with high probability if the provided oracle is uniform, or in the "0" state with high probability if the provided oracle is balanced. The final *Hadamard* gate on qubit 0 is unnecessary and can be removed.

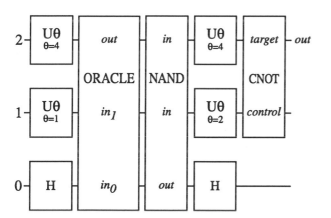

Figure 7.3
A graphic view of the quantum algorithm in Figure 7.2 for the two-bit early promise problem.

oracle is balanced. The oracle was set to use qubits 0 and 1 as inputs and qubit 2 as output, although in other experiments we allowed the oracle indices to evolve.

One run of this system, using Koza's Lisp genetic programming code [Koza, 1992] and the parameters shown in Table 7.1, produced the program shown in Figure 7.1 at generation 46. (The parameters in Table 7.1 were chosen by intuition and have not been optimized.) When executed, this program produces the quantum algorithm shown in Figure 7.2. Using notation similar to that in the quantum computation literature, this can be represented diagrammatically as in Figure 7.3.

The evolved algorithm is not minimal—at least the final H can be removed, although interestingly the *NAND* cannot. This is because of the way in which qubit values are distributed across the vector of amplitudes; it turns out that quantum gates can affect their "inputs" as well as their "outputs." The quantum algorithm in Figure 7.3 solves or provides information useful in solving the two-bit early promise problem for all 8 possible two-bit oracles, using only one call to the oracle in each case. (There are only 8 possible oracles because only 8 of the 16 2-input boolean functions are either balanced or uniform.) The probabilities of error for the 8 cases are (rounded to two decimal places): 0.02, 0.29, 0.23, 0.13, 0.13, 0.23, 0.30, and 0.04.

While this result is not new to the field of quantum computation, it demonstrates that genetic programming can automatically find better-than-classical quantum algorithms.

7.4.2   The Scaling Majority-On Problem

Consider an oracle version of the *majority-on* problem. (Genetic programming is applied to the standard non-oracle version of majority-on by Koza [Koza, 1992]) This problem is the same as the early promise problem, discussed above, except that all binary oracles are allowed (there is no promise that the oracles will be either balanced or uniform) and the program's job is to determine if the majority of the oracle's outputs would be "1" if it were run on all possible inputs. In addition, we seek a single program that will produce correct quantum algorithms for oracles of any size. For example, if we have an oracle that takes 5 bits of input then we'd like the evolved program, when run with `*num-input-qubits*` set to 5 and other variables set appropriately, to produce a quantum algorithm which will reliably tell if the oracle outputs "1" for a majority of the possible inputs or not. Using standard tree-based genetic programming and similar parameters to those described above we evolved a program that produces the following quantum algorithms for this problem:

For one-bit oracles:

```
Hadamard qubit:0
Oracle input-qubit:0 output-qubit:1
(read output from qubit 1)
```

For two-bit oracles:

```
Hadamard qubit:1
Hadamard qubit:0
Oracle input-qubits:0,1 output-qubit:2
(read output from qubit 2)
```

For three-bit oracles:

```
Hadamard qubit:1
Hadamard qubit:2
Hadamard qubit:0
Oracle input-qubits:0,1,2 output-qubit:3
(read output from qubit 3)
```

For four-bit oracles:

```
Hadamard qubit:1
Hadamard qubit:2
Hadamard qubit:3
Hadamard qubit:0
Oracle input-qubits:0,1,2,3 output-qubit:4
(read output from qubit 4)
```

And so on; for each problem size the program produces a quantum algorithm that applies a *Hadamard* gate to each intput qubit and then calls the oracle. The algorithms work by spreading the probability out among all basis vectors and then using a single oracle call, which can be thought of as operating on the superposition of all oracle inputs simultaneously, to compute the output. It works quite well for oracles that produce mostly 1s or mostly 0s, but for exactly balanced oracles (for which the answer should be 0—a majority is not on) the output error will be 0.5. This means that there will be a 50% chance of getting the wrong answer for balanced oracles, but this can be remedied by running the program multiple times; if the answer is 1 50% of the time then we know that the oracle is balanced and that the real answer is therefore 0.

In contrast to the early promise algorithm exhibited above, this majority-on quantum algorithm is not better than classical. A probabilistic classical algorithm for majority-on can simply call the oracle with a random input; if the output is 1 then it should answer 1, otherwise it should answer 0. This too will have a 50% chance of being wrong for balanced oracles (and some smaller chance of being wrong for other oracles), and this too can be remedied with multiple runs. In this case the genetic programming system found a quantum algorithm that works in the same way as a probabilistic classical algorithm, and in fact it does not appear that quantum computation can do any better than classical computation on this problem [Beals et al., 1998].

7.4.3   The Database Search Problem

The problem of searching an unsorted database for an item that it is known to contain (we're looking for its specific address) can also be recast as an oracle problem. We are given an oracle that accesses the database at a particular address and returns 1 if the item we're looking for is at that address, and 0 otherwise. The problem is to determine which address will cause the oracle to return 1.

Consider a four-item database, addressed via two binary inputs. On a deterministic classical machine we would have to query the database three times, in the worst case, to be sure about the location of the item we're looking for. If we haven't found it after three queries then we know that it is in the one location we haven't looked. But after only two luckless queries there would still be a 50% chance of error for any choice we could make.

Lov Grover showed that this is a problem for which quantum computers can beat classical computers. Grover's algorithm finds an item in an unsorted list of n items in $O(\sqrt{n})$ steps, while classical algorithms require $O(n)$. We initially thought this meant that the four-item database problem could be solved using two as opposed to the three classically-required database queries, and we conducted genetic programming runs to search for such a solution. We were happily surprised when the genetic programming system found a solution that uses only *one* database call and is nearly deterministic. Further examination revealed that Grover's algorithm also finds the item in one query, and that the solution found by genetic programming is in fact almost identical to Grover's algorithm.

We used stack-based, linear genome genetic programming (*MidGP*) with the parameters shown in Table 7.2, attempting to solve the four-item database problem with a five qubit system. The DB-gate function listed in Table 7.2 is analogous to the ORACLE-gate function from Section 7.4.1; it adds a call to the database lookup function (oracle) to the end of the quantum algorithm. The goal was to evolve a single quantum algorithm which, given a database containing a 1 only in position k (for k in $\{0, 1, 2, 3\}$), leaves qubits 3 and 4 in states q_3 and q_4 such that $2q_4 + q_3 = 3 - k$.[5]

Figure 7.4 lists the quantum algorithm produced by the best-of-run program. Notice that only four qubits are mentioned in the algorithm. In addition, both gates using qubit 1 can be eliminated without changing the behavior of the algorithm, so it requires only three qubits. The algorithm may be further simplified by omitting the 0-angle rotation along with the first *CPHASE* and the first *CNOT* (which are controlled by qubits in state $|0\rangle$, and hence act as the identity). The final *CPHASE* can be replaced with a *CNOT* because it has $\alpha = 1$. If we also combine the successive rotations on qubit 4 and change the resulting rotation angle in the fourth decimal place (to exactly $-\frac{\pi}{4}$; this eliminates an error probability of approximately 10^{-6}) then we get the quantum algorithm diagrammed in Figure 7.5. This algorithm acts just like a single iteration of Grover's algorithm except that it gives phases of -1 to some of the computational basis states, which has no effect on the final probabilities.

---

[5] It would have been more standard to use $2q_4 + q_3 = k$.

Table 7.2
MidGP parameters for a run on the four-item database search problem.

max number of generations	1,001
size of population	1,000
max program length	256
reproduction fraction	0.5
crossover fraction	0.1
mutation fraction	0.4
max mutation points	127
selection method	tournament (size=5)
function/terminal set	noop, +, -, *, %p, DB-gate, H-gate, U-theta-gate, CNOT-gate, CPHASE-gate, U2-gate, 0, 1, 2, 3, 4, π, ephemeral-random-constant, pop

```
U2 qubit:4 phi:0 theta:3 psi:3.14159 alpha:0.25908
Controlled-phase control-qubit:3 target-qubit:4, alpha:39.54646
Controlled-not control-qubit:0 target-qubit:3
U-theta qubit:0 theta:0.02934
Hadamard qubit:3
U-theta qubit:4 theta:3.14159
Hadamard qubit:0
Controlled-not control-qubit:1 target-qubit:3
U-theta qubit:4 theta:-4.06820
U-theta qubit:0 theta:-7.82538
Database-lookup input-qubits:4,3 output-qubit:0
Hadamard qubit:4
U-theta qubit:1 theta:4
U-theta qubit:3 theta:0
Controlled-phase control-qubit:3 target-qubit:4, alpha:0
Hadamard qubit:3
(read output from qubits 3 and 4)
```

Figure 7.4
Evolved quantum algorithm for the four-item database search problem on a five-qubit system. The system is initialized to the state $|00000\rangle$ and then the algorithm is run, leaving qubits 3 and 4 in states that indicate the position k of the single "1" in the database according to the formula $2q_4 + q_3 = 3 - k$.

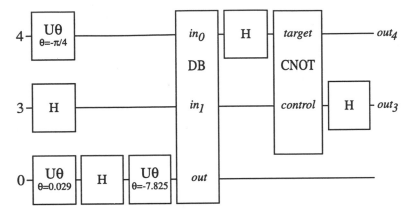

Figure 7.5
Diagram of the quantum algorithm for the four-item database search problem in Figure 7.4, reduced to use only the three essential qubits. This diagram also omits gates that have no effect, combines the rotations on qubit 4, and adjusts the combined rotation in the fourth decimal place to eliminate an error of 10^{-6}.

7.4.4 The And-Or Query Problem

The "and-or query problem" is the problem of determining whether a specific boolean function evaluates to true or false when applied to the values returned by a given oracle. The boolean function is an and-or binary tree with "AND" ($\land$) at the root, alternating layers of "OR" and "AND" ($\lor$) below, and the values of the oracle function, in order, at the leaves. For a one-bit oracle f, which has just the two values $f(0)$ and $f(1)$, the problem is to determine whether the expression "$f(0) \land f(1)$" is true or false. For a two-bit oracle f, with values $f(0), f(1), f(2)$, and $f(3)$, the problem is to determine whether the expression "$(f(0) \lor f(1)) \land (f(2) \lor f(3))$)" is true or false. For a three-bit oracle the expression is "$((f(0) \land f(1)) \lor (f(2) \land f(3)) \land ((f(4) \land f(5)) \lor (f(6) \land f(7)))$". And so on.

We chose to work on the two-bit oracle version of this problem because its quantum complexity is not yet completely understood and because we hoped that genetic programming could provide new information. Ronald de Wolf, a researcher who has worked on the quantum complexity of boolean functions [Beals et al., 1998], suggested this as an open problem and remarked that it would be "surprising" if there was a 2-sided-error solution that uses only one call to the oracle [de Wolf, personal communication]. Our genetic programming system found this "surprising" result.

We used stackless linear genome genetic programming (described above) with the parameters listed in Table 7.3. In generation 212 a program was evolved that produces the quantum algorithm in Figure 7.6. This algorithm works for all possible two-bit oracle functions, with all errors less than 0.41, using only a single call to the oracle function. We were able to analyze this algorithm and to improve and simplify it by hand, producing the al-

Table 7.3
MidGP MidGP parameters for a run on the two-bit and-or query problem.

max number of generations	1,000
size of population	100
max program length	32
reproduction fraction	0.2
crossover fraction	0.4
mutation fraction	0.4
max mutation points	8
selection method	tournament (size=7)
function/terminal set	`noop`, `ephemeral-random-quantum-gate`

gorithm in Figure 7.7. This algorithm's error is zero for the all-zero oracle function, $\frac{3}{8}$ for all other cases for which the correct answer is 0, and $\frac{1}{4}$ for the cases in which the correct answer is 1.

Notice that the quantum algorithm is better than the following classical probabilistic algorithm [Meyer, personal communication]:

1. Query the function for a random value of the input.

2. If the oracle returns 0, guess FALSE; else, guess TRUE.

Averaged over all inputs, this classical algorithm is correct $\frac{11}{16}$ of the time. Viewed in this way the quantum algorithm in Figure 7.6 is better but only slightly; it is correct $\frac{23}{32}$ of the time. On the other hand, the quantum algorithm is much better if one is considering only a single random input. In this case the classical algorithm will have an error probability of $\frac{1}{2}$ for six cases; that is, it is no better than guessing, even if run repeatedly. The quantum algorithm has a worst-case error probability of $\frac{3}{8}$, so it provides information about the correct answer that increeases with repetition.

One way to explain how this algorithm works is to use wave-mechanical descriptions of the quantum system. (Readers unfamiliar with wave mechanics may wish to skip the remainder of this paragraph.) To compute the OR function we use interference between the input states to the database gate. The purpose of this interference is to reinforce the amplitudes for bit values equal to "1" and to destructively interfere those for bit values equal to "0." The AND function at the root of the tree must simply effect an 'addition' of the 1 amplitudes with which it is provided. The algorithm achieves this task as follows: Remember that the database gate outputs the negation of the query result when bit 2 has initial value "1" and the result itself when that value is "0." Before querying the database the U_θ and *Hadamard* transform the state to a superposition with very unequal weight for states with bit-2 values "1" and "0." Following the database query, amplitudes for the two output values are mixed through a second rotation. Combined with the CNOT gate, which entangles the zeroth bit with the output register, this allows for interference *only* between the leaves of each of the OR nodes in the tree. The specific angle arguments of the gates ensure that the necessary amplitude pattern obtains.

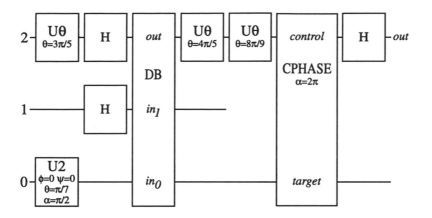

Figure 7.6
Evolved quantum algorithm for the two-bit and-or query problem. The system is initialized to the state $|000\rangle$ and then the algorithm is run, leaving qubit 2 in the "1" state with high probability if the "and-or" query is true for the provided oracle, or in the "0" state with high probability otherwise.

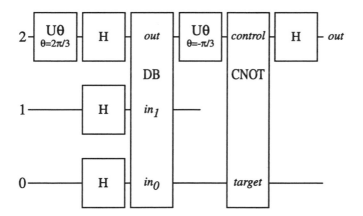

Figure 7.7
Hand-simplified and improved version of the quantum algorithm in Figure 7.6.

7.5 Conclusions

Genetic programming has been used to automatically discover new quantum algorithms, several of which are more efficient that any possible classical algorithms for the same problems, and one of which is more efficient than any previously known quantum algorithm for the same problem (Section 7.4.4). It has also been used to evolve quantum algorithms that can be scaled to work on problem instances of different sizes (Section 7.4.2).

Genetic programming appears to be a useful tool for exploring the power of quantum computation, and perhaps for developing software for the quantum computers of the future. Although we presented three different genetic programming approaches for quantum computation, we have not yet performed careful comparisons between these techniques or developed a theory about how genetic programming can best be applied in this area; this is a topic for future research. Other avenues for further investigation include:

- Application of the same techniques to other problems with incompletely understood quantum complexity.

- Modification of the techniques to support hybrid quantum/classical algorithms and quantum algorithms that include intermediate measurements.

- Genetic programming *on* quantum computers, using better-than-classical search algorithms that are already in the literature (such as Grover's) and other quantum computing efficiencies to speed up the genetic programming process.

Acknowledgements

Supported in part by the John D. and Catherine T. MacArthur Foundation's MacArthur Chair program at Hampshire College, by National Science Foundation grant #PHY-9722614, and by a grant from the Institute for Scientific Interchange (ISI), Turin. Some work reported here was performed at the Institute's 1998 Research Conference on Quantum Computation, supported by ISI and the ELSAG-Bailey corporation. Ronald de Wolf provided valuable information on the and-or query problem and its complexity, and David Meyer and Bill Langdon provided essential reviewer's comments. Special thanks to Rebecca S. Neimark for assistance with the figures.

Bibliography

Barenco, A., Bennett, C. H., Cleve, R., DiVincenzo, D. P., Margolus, N., Shor, P., Sleator, T., Smolin, J. A., and Weinfurter, H. (1995), "Elementary gates for quantum computation," *Physical Review A*, 52:3457–3467.

Beals, R., Buhrman, H., Cleve, R., Mosca, M., and de Wolf, R. (1998), "Tight quantum bounds by polynomials," in *Proceedings of the Thirty-ninth Annual Symposium on Foundations of Computer Science (FOCS)*, To appear. Preliminary version available from http://xxx.lanl.gov/abs/quant-ph/9802049.

Beckman, D., Chari, A. N., Devabhaktuni, S., and Preskill, J. (1996), "Efficient networks for quantum factoring," Technical Report CALT-68-2021, California Institute of Technology, http://xxx.lanl.gov/abs/quant-ph/9602016.

Ben-Tal, A. (1979), "Characterization of pareto and lexicographic optimal solutions," in *Multiple Criteria Decision Making Theory and Application*, Fandel and Gal (Eds.), pp 1–11, Springer-Verlag.

Braunstein, S. L. (1995), "Quantum computation: a tutorial," Available only electronically, on-line at URL http://chemphys.weizmann.ac.il/~schmuel/comp/comp.html.

Chester, M. (1987), *Primer of Quantum Mechanics*, John Wiley & Sons, Inc.

Costantini, G. and Smeraldi, F. (1997), "A generalization of Deutsch's example," Los Alamos National Laboratory Quantum Physics E-print Archive, http://xxx.lanl.gov/abs/quant-ph/9702020.

Deutsch, D. (1985), "Quantum theory, the Church-Turing principle and the universal quantum computer," in *Proceedings of the Royal Society of London A 400*, pp 97–117.

Deutsch, D. and Jozsa, R. (1992), "Rapid solution of problems by quantum computation," in *Proceedings of the Royal Society of London A 439*, pp 553–558.

Grover, L. K. (1997), "Quantum mechanics helps in searching for a needle in a haystack," *Physical Review Letters*, pp 325–328.

Gruau, F. (1994), "Genetic micro programming of neural networks," in *Advances in Genetic Programming*, K. E. Kinnear Jr. (Ed.), pp 495–518, MIT Press.

Jozsa, R. (1997), "Entanglement and quantum computation," in *Geometric Issues in the Foundations of Science*, S. Huggett, L. Mason, K. P. Tod, S. T. Tsou, and N. M. J. Woodhouse (Eds.), Oxford University Press, http://xxx.lanl.gov/abs/quant-ph/9707034.

Koza, J. R. (1992), *Genetic Programming: On the Programming of Computers by Means of Natural Selection*, MIT Press.

Koza, J. R. and Bennett, III, F. H. (1999), "Automatic synthesis, placement, and routing of electrical circuits by means of genetic programming," in *Advances in Genetic Programming 3*, Spector, Langdon, O'Reilly, and Angeline (Eds.), MIT Press.

Langdon, W. B., Soule, T., Poli, R., and Foster, J. A. (1999), "The evolution of size and shape," in *Advances in Genetic Programming 3*, L. Spector, W. B. Langdon, U.-M. O'Reilly, and P. J. Angeline (Eds.), MIT Press.

Löwdin, P. (1998), *Linear Algebra for Quantum Theory*, John Wiley and Sons, Inc.

Milburn, G. J. (1997), *Schrödinger's Machines: The Quantum Technology Reshaping Everyday Life*, W. H. Freeman & Co.

Perkis, T. (1994), "Stack-based genetic programming," in *Proceedings of the 1994 IEEE World Congress on Computational Intelligence*, pp 148–153, IEEE Press.

Preskill, J. (1997), "Quantum computing: Pro and con," Technical Report CALT-68-2113, California Institute of Technology, http://xxx.lanl.gov/abs/quant-ph/9705032.

Shor, P. W. (1994), "Algorithms for quantum computation: Discrete logarithms and factoring," in *Proceedings of the 35th Annual Symposium on Foundations of Computer Science*, S. Goldwasser (Ed.), IEEE Computer Society Press.

Shor, P. W. (1998), "Quantum computing," *Documenta Mathematica*, Extra Volume ICM:467–486, http://east.camel.math.ca/EMIS/journals/DMJDMV/xvol-icm/00/Shor.MAN.ps.gz.

Spector, L. (1997), "MidGP, a Common Lisp stack-based genetic programming engine similar to HiGP," http://hampshire.edu/lspector/midgp1.5.lisp.

Spector, L., Barnum, H., and Bernstein, H. J. (1998), "Genetic programming for quantum computers," in *Genetic Programming 1998: Proceedings of the Third Annual Conference*, J. R. Koza, W. Banzhaf, K. Chellapilla, K. Deb, M. Dorigo, D. B. Fogel, M. H. Garzon, D. E. Goldberg, H. Iba, and R. L. Riolo (Eds.), pp 365–374, Morgan Kaufmann.

Steane, A. (1998), "Quantum computing," *Reports on Progress in Physics*, 61:117–173, http://xxx.lanl.gov/abs/quant-ph/9708022.

Stoffel, K. and Spector, L. (1996), "High-performance, parallel, stack-based genetic programming," in *Genetic Programming 1996: Proceedings of the First Annual Conference*, J. R. Koza, D. E. Goldberg, D. B. Fogel, and R. L. Riolo (Eds.), pp 224–229, MIT Press.

II THEORY

8 The Evolution of Size and Shape

W. B. Langdon, T. Soule, R. Poli and J. A. Foster

The phenomenon of growth in program size in genetic programming populations has been widely reported. In a variety of experiments and static analysis we test the standard protective code explanation and find it to be incomplete. We suggest bloat is primarily due to distribution of fitness in the space of possible programs and because of this, in the absence of bias, it is in general inherent in any search technique using a variable length representation.

We investigate the fitness landscape produced by program tree-based genetic operators when acting upon points in the search space. We show bloat in common operators is primarily due to the exponential shape of the underlying search space. Nevertheless we demonstrate new operators with considerably reduced bloating characteristics. We also describe mechanisms whereby bloat arises and relate these back to the shape of the search space. Finally we show our simple random walk entropy increasing model is able to predict the shape of evolved programs.

8.1 Introduction

The rapid growth of programs produced by genetic programming (GP) is a well documented phenomenon [Koza, 1992; Blickle and Thiele, 1994; Nordin and Banzhaf, 1995; McPhee and Miller, 1995; Soule et al., 1996; Greeff and Aldrich, 1997; Soule, 1998]. This growth, often referred to as "code bloat", need not be correlated with increases in the fitness of the evolving programs and consists primarily of code which does not change the semantics of the evolving program. The rate of growth appears to vary depending upon the particular genetic programming paradigm being used, but exponential rates of growth have been documented [Nordin and Banzhaf, 1995].

Code bloat occurs in both tree based and linear genomes [Nordin, 1997; Nordin and Banzhaf, 1995; Nordin et al., 1997] and with automatically defined functions [Langdon, 1995]. Recent research suggests that code bloat will occur in most fitness based search techniques which allow variable length solutions [Langdon, 1998b; Langdon and Poli, 1997b].

Clearly, an exponential rate of growth precludes the extended use of GP or any other search technique which suffers from code bloat. Even linear growth seriously hampers an extended search. This alone is reason to be concerned about code growth. However, the rapid increase in solution size can also decrease the likelihood of finding improved solutions. Since no clear benefits offset these detrimental effects, practical solutions to the code bloat phenomenon are necessary to make GP and related search techniques feasible for real-world applications.

Many techniques exist for limiting code bloat [Koza, 1992; Iba et al., 1994; Zhang and Mühlenbein, 1995; Blickle, 1996; Rosca, 1997; Nordin et al., 1996; Soule and Foster, 1997; Hooper et al., 1997]. However, without definitive knowledge regarding the causes of code bloat, any solution is likely to have serious shortcomings or undesirable side effects. A robust solution to code bloat should follow from, not precede, knowledge of what actually causes the phenomenon in the first place.

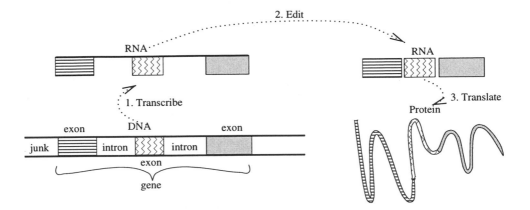

Figure 8.1
How cells express DNA: 1. Transcribe DNA to RNA; 2. Remove introns; 3. Translate to proteins (not to scale).

We present the latest research into the causes of code bloat. This research clearly demonstrates that there are several distinct causes of code bloat. Each of these causes appears to operate in both GP and other, related, search techniques. Thus, any general strategy for countering code bloat should address all of these causes.

This research promises to do more than merely lead to more feasible controls for code bloat. It also sheds some much needed light on the process of evolution, or, at least, artificial evolution. Code bloat research helps identify more of the many, often conflicting, forces which influence an evolving population.

In the next section we describe the historical background to bloat including previous work on it. In Section 8.3 we suggest program spaces may be to a large extent independent of program length, in that over a wide range of program lengths the distribution of fitness values does not change dramatically. Section 8.4 reconciles this with bloat and indeed suggests bloat, in the absence of bias, is general. Sections 8.5 to 8.7 experimentally test these theories. The experiments are followed by a discussion of their significance and of bloat more generally in Section 8.8 and conclusions in Section 8.9. Finally we give some suggestions for future work.

8.2 Background

In living organisms, molecules transcribe the DNA in each gene into RNA, edit out portions of the RNA, and then translate the remaining RNA into a protein. *Exons* are gene segments which produce protein building blocks, and *introns* are the non-expressed segments. See Figure 8.1.

Many natural genomes contain both *genic* DNA, which encodes the genes, and *non-genic* (sometimes called "junk") DNA. Many genomes are predominantly non-genic. For example, human DNA is approximately 95% non-genic. There is no correlation between genome size and the ratio of genic to non-genic DNA, the complexity of the organism, or the ancestry of the organism [Cavalier-Smith, 1985; Li and Graur, 1991].

There are many distinctions between introns and non-genic DNA. Introns provide vital functions for the organism and perhaps even for evolution itself [Mattick, 1994; Li and Graur, 1991]. Non-genic DNA apparently contributes little to an organism's fitness, though it may serve some structural role or provide an environment for genetic parasites [Li and Graur, 1991]. The origins of both non-genic DNA and introns are unclear. However, organisms with selective pressure toward streamlined genomes, such as bacteria and viruses, have little non-genic DNA and few, if any, introns. In some cases, such as ΦX-174 (a virus which lives in *E. coli*) [Kornberg, 1982] or some genes coding for human mitochondrial RNA [Anderson et al., 1981], a single sequence of DNA codes simultaneously for more than one protein—a kind of natural data compression.

In GP fitness neutral sections of code are commonly referred to as introns, whereas sections of code which effect fitness are called exons. There are several problems with the intron/exon distinction as it is used in GP. First, these terms are often used without precise definitions. The formal definitions which have been published are not always compatible. Perhaps more importantly the terms intron and exon have quite different meanings in the biological community. The lack of a transcription process in typical GP makes it impossible to reasonably associate biological introns and exons with types of GP code. Thus, the terms intron and exon can make communication with biologists difficult. Finally, in many cases dividing GP code into more than two categories is necessary to understand the evolution of bloat. For these reasons we chose to introduce two entirely new terms: operative and viable.

Definition 1 *A node* n *in a program's syntax tree is* operative *if the removal of the subtree rooted at that node (and replacing it with a null operation) will change the program's output. Conversely a node is* inoperative *if it is not operative.*

Definition 2 *A node* n *in a program's syntax tree is* viable *if there exists a subtree such that replacing the subtree rooted at node* n *with the new subtree will change the program's output on some input. Conversely a node is* inviable *if it is not viable.*

Although we chose to define these terms for tree based genomes, modifying these definitions to apply to other genomes is not difficult. For example if a linear genome was used the definition would need to refer to linear subsections of code rather than subtrees.

Notice that with these definitions inviable code is a subset of inoperative code. Thus any program will have at least as much inoperative code as it has inviable code.

As an example consider two code fragments:

$$\frac{X+(1-(4-3))}{Y+(0*Z)} \text{ and}$$

where X, Y, and Z are additional sections of code. In each fragment the underlined section contributes nothing and could be removed without affecting the output or fitness of the individual containing this code. Thus, both underlined sections are inoperative. In addition, assuming there are no side-effects, fragment Z is inviable since no replacement for fragment Z will affect performance. While the fragment (1-(4-3)) is viable, because changes to this fragment could change performance. Quite often inviable code is code which does not get executed, such as code following an if(false) statement.

In roughly equivalent theories, [Nordin and Banzhaf, 1995], [McPhee and Miller, 1995] and [Blickle and Thiele, 1994] have argued that code growth occurs to protect programs against the destructive effects of crossover and similar operators. Clearly any operator which only affects inviable code cannot be destructive (or beneficial) and any operator affecting only inoperative code is less likely to be destructive because the code which is being changed doesn't contribute to the fitness. Thus individuals which contain large amounts of inviable or inoperative code and relatively small amounts of operative code are less likely to have damaged offspring, and therefore enjoy an evolutionary advantage. Inviable and inoperative code have a protective role against the effects of crossover and similar operators.

[McPhee and Miller, 1995] argue more generally that evolution favors programs which replicate with semantic accuracy, i.e. that there is a Replication Accuracy Force acting on the population. This is a general force which should respond to replication inaccuracies caused by crossover, mutation or any other primarily destructive operator. This force also favors maximizing total code while minimizing viable code.

Although code bloat apparently serves a protective function, this does not mean that it is necessarily beneficial in producing improved solutions. These hypotheses suggest that code bloat performs a purely conservative role. Code bloat preserves existing solutions, but makes it difficult to modify, and thereby improve upon, those solutions. Thus code bloat is a serious problem for sustained learning.

It has also been argued that code bloat could act as a storehouse for subroutines which may be used later [Angeline, 1994]. However, there is no clear experimental evidence that this generally occurs.

Several techniques for limiting code bloat have been proposed. One of the first and most widely used is to set a fixed limit on the size or depth of the programs [Koza, 1992]. Programs exceeding the limit are discarded and a parent is kept instead. This technique is effective at limiting code bloat but has certain drawbacks. Some prior domain knowledge is necessary to choose a reasonable limit and code bloat occurs fairly rapidly until the average program approaches the limit. Recent research also suggests that a limit can interfere with searches once the average program size approaches the size limit [Gathercole and Ross, 1996; Langdon and Poli, 1997a].

Parsimony pressure attempts to use the evolutionary process to evolve both suitable and small solutions. A term is added to the fitness function which penalizes larger programs, thereby encouraging the evolution of smaller solutions. Commonly the penalty is a simple linear function of the solution size, but other more, and less, subtle approaches have been used. Of these, variable penalty functions, which respond to the fitness and size of individuals within the population appear to be the most robust [Iba et al., 1994; Zhang and Mühlenbein, 1995; Blickle, 1996]. Other studies have shown a degradation in performance when parsimony pressure is used [Koza, 1992; Nordin and Banzhaf, 1995]. Recent research suggests that the effect of parsimony pressure depends on the magnitude of the parsimony function relative to the size-fitness distribution of the population [Soule, 1998]. Populations with a stronger correlation between high fitness and large size are less likely to be negatively affected by parsimony pressure. When the correlation is low, smaller programs are heavily favored and the population tends towards minimal individuals, which seriously hampers further exploration.

Another approach to reducing code bloat has been to modify the basic operators. Notable operator modification approaches include varying the rate of crossover (and mutation) to counter the evolutionary pressure towards protective code [Rosca, 1997], varying the selection probability of crossover points by using explicitly defined introns [Nordin et al., 1996], and negating destructive crossover events (a form of hill climbing) [Soule and Foster, 1997; O'Reilly and Oppacher, 1995; Hooper et al., 1997]. Each of these approaches has the goal of reducing the evolutionary importance of inviable and inoperative code. Although each has shown some promise none of them appear to be universally successful.

8.3 Program Search Spaces

The problem of automatically producing programs can be thought of as the problem of searching for and finding a suitable program in the space of all possible programs. The first requirement is that we choose a search space which does contain suitable programs. In GP this means that the function and terminal sets are suffiently powerful to be able to express a solution. We must also ensure that limits on the size of programs don't exclude solutions. Given finite terminal and function sets and a bound on the size or depth of programs we have a finite number of possible programs, i.e. a finite search space. However even in simple GP problems, the size of the search spaces are huge, typically growing approximately exponentially with the size of the largest program allowed.

Like the number of different programs of a given size, the number of different tree shapes of a given size also grows approximately exponentially with size. For binary trees of length l (i.e. comprised of $l/2$ internal nodes and $(l + 1)/2$ external nodes or leafs) the shortest or most compact tree has a depth of $\lceil \log_2 l + 1 \rceil$ and the tallest $(l + 1)/2$. The most popular height lies between these extremes (for reasonable programs sizes it is near $l^{0.63}$, while the average height converges slowly to $2\sqrt{\pi(l-1)/2} + O(l^{1/4})$ as l increases [Flajolet and Oldyzko, 1982, page 200]) and almost all programs have a maximum height near this peak (see Figure 8.9).

It is often assumed that we know almost nothing about the distribution of solutions within these vast search spaces, that they are neither continuous nor differentiable and so classical search techniques will be incapable of solving our problems and so we have to use stochastic search techniques, such as genetic programming. However random sampling of a range of simple GP benchmark problems suggests a common features of program search spaces is that over a wide range of program lengths the distribution of fitness does not vary greatly with program length [Langdon and Poli, 1998d; Langdon and Poli, 1998a; Langdon and Poli, 1998e]. These results suggest in general longer programs are on average the same fitness as shorter ones. I.e. there is no intrinsic advantage in searching programs longer than some problem dependent threshold. Of course, in general, we will not know in advance where the threshold is. Also it may be that some search techniques perform better with longer programs, perhaps because together they encourage the formation of smoother more correlated or easier to search fitness landscapes [Poli and Langdon, 1998a]. However in practice searching at longer lengths is liable to be more expensive both in terms of memory and also time (since commonly the CPU time to perform each fitness evaluation rises in proportion to program size). Given this why should progressive search techniques which decide where to explore next based on knowledge gained so far, such as genetic programming, encounter bloat?

8.4 Bloat Inherent in Variable Length Representations

In general with variable length discrete representations there are multiple ways of representing a given behaviour. If the evaluation function is static and concerned only with the quality of each trial solution and not with its representation then all these representations have equal worth. If the search strategy were unbiased, each of these would be equally likely to be found. In general there are many more long ways to represent a specific behaviour than short representations of the same behaviour. For example in the sextic polynomial problem, Section 8.5, there are about 3,500 times as many high scoring programs of length $n + 2$ as there are with the same score and a length of n. Thus, assuming an unbiased search strategy, we would expect a predominance of long representations.

Practical search techniques are biased. There are two common forms of bias when using variable length representations. Firstly search techniques often commence with simple (i.e. short) representations, i.e. they have an in built bias in favour of short representations. Secondly they have a bias in favour of continuing the search from previously discovered high fitness representations and retaining them as points for future search. I.e. there is a bias in favour of representations that do at least as well as their initiating point(s).

On problems of interest, finding improved solutions is relatively easy initially but becomes increasingly more difficult. In these circumstances, especially with a discrete fitness function, there is little chance of finding a representation that does better than the representation(s) from which it was created. (Cf. "death of crossover" [Langdon, 1998a,

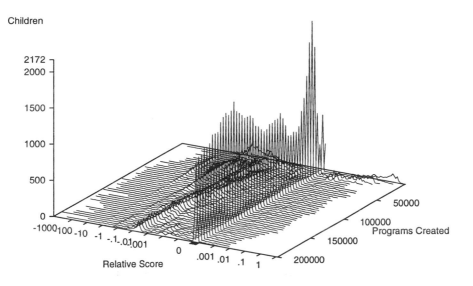

Figure 8.2
Fitness relative to first parent. First GP run of sextic polynomial problem. Peak at no change in fitness has zero width in the initial generation. In later generations the peak widens and by the end of the run 15% of children have a fitness different from their first parent but the difference is less than 10^{-5}.

page 206]). So the selection bias favours representations which have the same fitness as those from which they were created.

For example in our experiments with the artificial ant problem by the end of 50 runs crossover made no improvements at all in any of them [Langdon and Poli, 1997b, Figure 9]. Similarly in continuous problems most crossovers do not improve programs. Figure 8.2 shows while about 50% of crossovers in the sextic polynomial problem (see Section 8.5) did not change the measured fitness of the programs or changed it by less than 10^{-5}, in the last generation of the run only 3% of crossovers produced children fitter than their first parent.

In general the easiest way to create one representation from another and retain the same fitness is for the new representation to represent identical behaviour. Thus, in the absence of improved solutions, the search may become a random search for new representations of the best solution found so far. As we said above, there are many more long representations than short ones for the same solution, so such a random search (other things being equal) will find more long representations than short ones. In Section 8.7 we show another aspect of this random expansion towards the parts of the search space containing most programs; the search drifts towards the most popular program shapes.

Bloat can be likened to diffusion where there is a macroscopic change which appears to be directed but it is in fact the effect of many microscopic random fluctuations which cause the physical system to move from an initial highly unlikely (low entropy) state to a more likely one (high entropy). In the same way the initial GP population is usually constrained to be in one of a relatively small number of states (as the programs in it start relatively short). Over time the effect of the many random changes made by crossover, mutation and selection cause the population to evolve towards the part of the search space containing the most programs simply because this means there are many more states the population can be in. I.e. if we choose a state uniformly at random is likely to be one in which the population contains long programs as there are many more long programs than short ones. The law of exponential growth in number of programs gives a very strong bloat pressure which is difficult for random fluctuations produced by mutation and crossover to ignore. However in Section 8.5.3 we describe a mutation operator which does have much reduced bloating characteristics.

While most previous attempts to explain bloat during evolution have concentrated upon inoperative or inviable code in genetic programming the above explanation is more general in two important ways. Firstly it predicts code growth is general and is expected in all un-biased search techniques with variable length representations. In Section 8.5 we investigate bloat in continuous domain non-GP search. [Langdon, 1998b] showed bloat in a discrete problem under a range of non-GP search techniques. Secondly it is able to explain the evolution of program shapes as well as sizes. That is not to say the other approaches are wrong, only that we suggest they are less general.

Like physical entropy, this explanation only says the direction in which change will occur but nothing about the speed of the change. Price's Covariance and Selection Theorem [Price, 1970] from population genetics can be applied to GP populations [Langdon, 1998a; Langdon and Poli, 1997a]. In particular it can be applied to program size. Provided the genetic operators are random and unbiased, given the covariance between program's length and the number of children they have (which is given by their fitness and the selection technique), Price's theorem says what the expected mean change in length will be between this generation and the next. The increase is proportional to the covariance. So the greater the correlation between size and fitness the faster bloat will be. In practice most of the covariance, and hence most of the bloat, is due not to long children being better than their parents but due relatively short ones being worse than average. (See, for example, Section 8.5.4).

Essentially Price's theorem gives a quantitative measurement of the way genetic algorithms (GAs) search. If some aspect of the genetic material is positively correlated with fitness then, other things being equal, the next generation's population will on average contain more of it. If it is negative, then the GA will tend to reduce it in the next generation.

Table 8.1
GP Parameters for the Sextic Polynomial Problem

Objective:	Find a program that produces the given value of the sextic polynomial $x^6 - 2x^4 + x^2$ as its output when given the value of the one independent variable, x, as input
Terminal set:	x and 250 floating point constants chosen at random from 2001 numbers between -1.000 and +1.000
Functions set:	$+ - \times \%$ (protected division)
Fitness cases:	50 random values of x from the range -1 ... 1
Fitness:	The mean, over the 50 fitness cases, of the absolute value of the difference between the value returned by the program and $x^6 - 2x^4 + x^2$.
Hits:	The number of fitness cases (between 0 and 50) for which the error is less than 0.01
Selection:	Tournament group size of 7, non-elitist, generational
Wrapper:	none
Population Size:	4000
Max program:	8000 program nodes (however no run was effected by this limit)
Initial population:	Created using "ramped half-and-half" with a maximum depth of 6 (no uniqueness requirement)
Parameters:	90% one child crossover, no mutation. 90% of crossover points selected at functions, remaining 10% selected uniformly between all nodes.
Termination:	Maximum number of generations G = 50

8.5 Sextic Polynomial

In studies of a number of benchmark GP problems which have discrete representations and simple static fitness functions we tested the predictions of Section 8.4 and show they essentially hold (see [Langdon and Poli, 1997b; Langdon and Poli, 1998b; Langdon, 1998b] and Section 8.6). In this and the following sections we extend this to a continuous problem which uses floating point operations and has a continuous fitness function, i.e. it has an effectively unlimited number of fitness value. We use the sextic polynomial $x^6 - 2x^4 + x^2$ regression problem [Koza, 1994, pages 110–122]. The fitness of each program is given by its error averaged over all 50 test cases (as given in Table 8.1). We used two ways to test the generality of the evolved solutions. Either using 51 test points chosen to lie in the interval -1 to +1 at random points between the 50 fitness test case points or we used 2001 points sampling every 0.001 between -1 and +1.

8.5.1 GP Runs

In 46 out of 50 runs bloat occurs (see Figure 8.3). In the remaining 4 runs, the GP population remains stuck with the best of generation individual yielding a constant value with mean error of 0.043511. In these four runs the lengths of programs within the population converge towards that of the best individual and no bloat occurs. In 45 of the remaining 46 runs there was a progressive improvement in the fitness of the best of generation individual. In one run the population bloated and there was no improvement in fitness. In some runs the generalised performance of the best of population individual (calculated from 2001 test points) improves steadily with the measured fitness. In other runs generalised perfor-

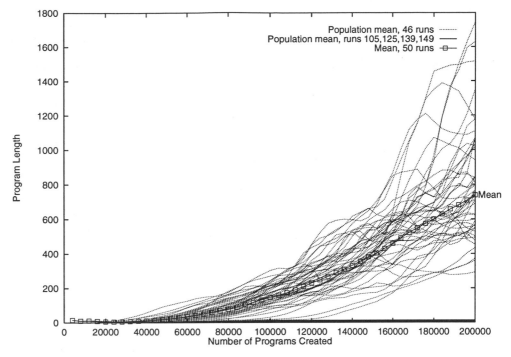

Figure 8.3
Evolution of population mean program length. 50 GP runs of sextic polynomial problem.

mance varies widely and may be exceedingly poor, even for apparently very fit programs. Figure 8.4 plots the fitness and generality for three representative runs.

Figure 8.5 shows the evolution of the behaviour of the best of generation individual in the first run. This shows the typical behaviour that the best of the initial random population is a constant. After a few generations typically the GP finds more complex behaviours which better match the fitness test cases. Later more complex behaviours often "misbehave" between points where the fitness test cases test the programs behaviour. In fact the behaviour of the best of generation individual (including its misbehaviour) is remarkably stable. Note this is the behaviour of single individuals not an average over the whole population. We might expect more stability from an average. This stability stresses GP is an evolutionary process, making progressive improvements on what it has already been learnt.

8.5.2 Non GP Search Strategies

In Section 8.4 we predicted bloat in non-GP search. In this section we repeat experiments conducted on discrete benchmark problems but on a continuous domain problem using four non-GP search techniques.

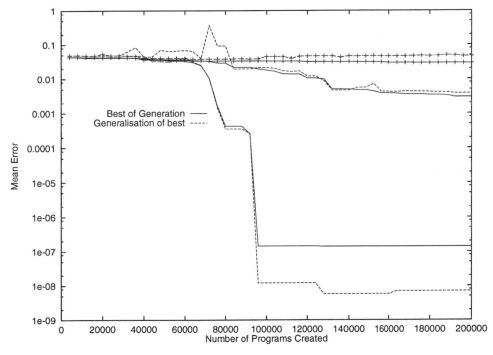

Figure 8.4
Evolution of fitness and generalisation of best individual in population. Best of 50 GP runs, first successful run and first unsuccessful run on sextic polynomial problem.

In Simulated Annealing (SA) an initial random individual is created using the ramped "half and half" method. Each new trial program is created using the mutation operator. It is then evaluated. If its score is better or the same as that of the current one, it replaces the current one. If it is worse then its chance of replacing the current one is $\exp(-\Delta \text{fitness}/T)$. Where T is the current *temperature*. In these experiments the temperature falls exponentially from 0.1 to 10^{-5} after 200,000 trial programs have been created. Whichever program does not become the current one is discarded. A run is deemed successful if at any point it finds a program which scores 50 hits.

Hill climbing (HC) can be thought of as simulated annealing with a zero temperature, i.e. a worse program is never accepted. The runs do not restart (except in the sense that mutation at the root replaces the whole program with a new randomly created one). Strict hill climbing (SHC) is like normal hill climbing except the new program must be better than the current one in order to replace it. Finally population search is a mutation only genetic algorithm with 91% of each generation being created by performing one mutation on a parent in the previous generation and 9% being direct copies of parents in the previous generation. Tournaments of 7 were used to select parents in both cases.

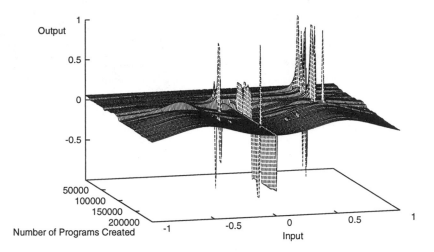

Figure 8.5
Evolution of phenotype. Value returned by the "best" program in the population. First of 50 GP runs of the sextic polynomial problem.

The parameters used are substantially the same as were used in [Langdon, 1998b] on the artificial ant problem. The mutation runs described in these sections use the same parameters as in the GP runs in Section 8.5.1, however a smaller population of 500 rather than 4,000 was used. Also the maximum program size was 2,000 rather than 8,000, see Table 8.2.

Table 8.2
Parameters used on the Sextic Polynomial mutation runs.

Objective etc:	as Table 8.1
Selection:	SA, HC, SHC or Tournament group size of 7, non-elitist, generational
Population Size:	1 or 500
Max program size:	2,000
Initial trial:	Created using ramped "half and half" with a maximum depth of 6
Parameters:	Initial temp 0.1, final 10^{-5} exponential cooling; max inserted mutation subtree 30; mutation points chosen uniformly
Termination:	Maximum number of trials 200,000

8.5.3   New Tree Mutation Operators

For these experiments it is important to be clear about the causes of bloat and so it is more important that the mutation operator should not introduce either a parsimony bias or a tendency to increase program size. Accordingly we introduced a new mutation operator which generates random trees with a specific distribution of sizes, choosing this distribution so on average the new subtree is the same size as the one it replaces. (The algorithm used to create random trees is substantially the same as that given in [Langdon, 1997, Appendix A]. C++ code can be found at `ftp://ftp.cs.bham.ac.uk/pub/authors/W.B.Langdon/gp-code/rand_tree.cc`).

In the first method the size of the replacement subtree is chosen uniformly in the range $l \pm l/2$ (where l is the size of the subtree selected to be deleted). We refer to this as 50%–150% fair mutation. Thus on average the new subtree is the same size as the subtree it is to replace. Should it be impossible to generate a tree of the chosen size or $l + l/2$ exceeds 30 a new mutation point is selected and another attempt to create a new random tree is made. This loop continues until a successful mutation has been performed. Note 50%–150% fair mutation samples programs near their parent uniformly according to their length. Thus neighbouring programs which have the same length as many other neighbouring programs are less likely to be sampled than neighbouring programs which have the same length as few others. As there are many more long programs than short ones each long one is relatively less likely to be sampled compared to a shorter one. That is the 50%–150% size distribution has an implicit parsimony bias.

In the second method the size of the replacement subtree is the size of a second subtree chosen at random within the same individual. We call this subtree fair mutation. Since this uses the same mechanism as that used to select the subtree to replace, the new subtree is on average the same size as the subtree it replaces. It should always be possible to generate a tree of the chosen size, however a limit of 30 was imposed to keep certain tables within reasonable bounds.

8.5.3.1   50–150% Fair Mutation Runs

In simulated annealing runs at initial high temperatures fitness and length vary rapidly but as the temperature falls the variability of program fitness also falls. In contrast the size of the current program continues to vary rapidly as it appears to execute a random walk. However on average program size shows little variation after an initial rise.

In runs using 50–150% mutation with both hill climbing and strict hill climbing there is very little variation in either length or fitness. Indeed 50–150% mutation hill climbing finds it difficult to progress past the best constant value. Few runs are successful but bloat does not happen.

When 50–150% mutation is used in a population it is easier to pass the false peak associated with returning constant value and more runs are successful (albeit only 6 out of 50, see Table 8.3). There is limited growth in program size in the first few generations (as-

Table 8.3
Sextic Polynomial and Artificial Ant: Means at the end of 50 runs. The number of Sextic Polynomial runs which found a program which scored 50 hits, the number where a best of generation individual scored 2001 hits on the generalisation test and the mean length of programs in the final population. The number of Ant runs where a program was able to complete the Santa Fe trail (89 hits) within 600 time steps and the the mean length of programs in the final population.

| | Sextic Polynomial | | | | | | Artificial Ant, 25,000 trials | | | |
| | 50%–150% | | | Subtree-sized | | | 50%–150% | | Subtree-sized | |
	50 hits	2001	Size	50 hits	2001	Size	89	Size	89	Size
Simulated Annealing	6	0	217	32	4	1347	4	95	2	1186
Hill Climbing	1	1	21	15	0	1838	3	41	2	1074
Strict Hill Climbing	2	1	22	16	0	1517	8	32	3	78
Population	6	2	32	28	0	553	12	40	6	127
Population after 10^6 and 10^5 trials							19	287	6	329

sociated with improvement in the population fitness) followed by a long period where the population size average size is almost constant. As in the artificial ant problem [Langdon, 1998b], very slight growth in the programs within the population can be observed.

8.5.3.2 Subtree Fair Mutation Runs

At the start of simulated annealing runs while the temperature is relatively high the fitness of the current program fluctuates rapidly. As does its size. If we look at the average behaviour less fluctuation is seen, with mean error falling to a low value but on average programs grow rapidly to about half the available space (2,000 nodes) see Table 8.3. On average this slows further growths. However there is still considerable fluctuation in program size in individual runs.

Similar behaviour is seen when using hill climbing or strict hill climbing. Subtree Sized strict hill climbing runs either bloat very rapidly or get trapped at very small (3 or 5 node) programs. In ten of 50 runs programs of fitness 0.043511 were rapidly found but no improvements were found and no bloat occurred. While initially the same happens in the hill climbing runs, eventually in all 50 runs the hill climber was able to move past 0.043511 and rapid bloat follows. With both search techniques average program length grows rapidly towards the maximum size allowed.

When subtree sized fair mutation is used in a population there is a steady, almost linear, increase in program length. This is in contrast to the initial fall and subsequent rapid non-linear growth when using crossover (albeit with a different population size, see Figure 8.3).

The right hand side of Table 8.3 summarises our results when using the same mutation operators and search strategies on the artificial ant problem [Langdon, 1998b]. Comparing program sizes for the sextic polynomial and the artificial ant we essentially see the same bloating characteristics (except in one case).

In the sextic polynomial problem using subtree sized fair mutation and strict hill climbing bloat occurs whereas it did not in the artificial ant problem. We suspect this is simply due to the continuous nature of the problem's fitness function. With gaps between fitness values, strict hill climbing imposes a barrier protecting the current point on the search. This barrier is lowered when the fitness function is continuous and any improvement in performance (no matter how small) can now displace the current program. Thus there is little difference between hill climbing and strict hill climbing.

Very slow bloat is observed in the sextic polynomial when 50–150% fair mutation is used in a population, as was bloat on the ant problem. The rate is even slower in the sextic polynomial at about 0.009 nodes per generation, compared to 0.13. Studying individual runs indicate the populations converge towards the size of the best individual in the population. While the fitness of this program may vary a little from generation to generation it does not show steady improvement and the search remains trapped, often only marginally better than the best fitness a constant can achieve. The slower bloat may indicate it is more difficult for small Sextic Polynomial programs to contain inviable code than it is for small artificial ant programs.

The difference in the performance of the two mutation operators may indicate 50-150% mutation is searching programs that are too short. Certainly the shortest solutions found by the 50 GP runs (at 67 nodes) were bigger than almost all the programs tested by 50-150% mutation. Unfortunately the low density of solutions means that we have not been able to explore the search space using random search to plot the density of solutions w.r.t. length. It would be nice to repeat these experiments using bigger initial programs, i.e. in the neighbourhood of 67 nodes.

8.5.4   Direct Measurement of Genetic Operators Effects on Performance

In this section we isolate the effect different genetic operators have from other influences (e.g. selection, noise, population size) by performing all possible variations of each genetic operation on representative programs and measuring the change in fitness and change in size. We used the 223 best of generation programs from our 50 GP runs which are between 101 and 201 nodes in length and with a fitness no better than 0.02. We know due to convergence of the GP populations these and their descendents are responsible for bloat.

8.5.4.1   Self Crossover

A new program was created by crossing over each program with itself at each possible pair of crossover points As expected most crossovers produce very small changes in both size and fitness. The effects of self crossover are asymmetric. In almost all cases on average children which do worse than their parents are smaller than them. While in about half the cases on average children which have the same fitness as their parent are nearly the same length, the remainder are on average at least one node longer. In most cases it is possible for self crossover to find improvements. In all but 16 of 233 cases these improved children are on average at least one node longer than their parents.

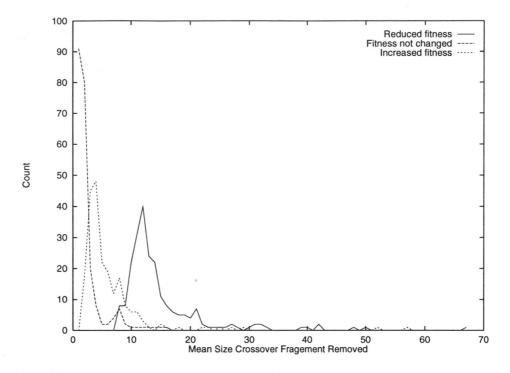

Figure 8.6
Effect of self crossover on best of generation individuals in the Sextic Polynomial problem. For all possible
children of the 223 programs the plots show the mean size of the subtree removed by self crossover averaged over
those with improved, same and worse measured fitness. "Removal bias" is indicated as worse children have more
code removed.

By considering the sizes of the subtree removed from the parent and the size of that
inserted we can discover the cause of this asymmetry. Figure 8.6 shows the size of the code
removed by self crossover in most cases is on average bigger when the children perform
worse than when either they perform the same or perform better. Figure 8.6 offers clear
evidence of "removal bias" (as discussed in Section 8.6.2). In contrast the size of new
inserted code is not particularly asymmetric.

8.5.4.2   Mutation Operators
As expected 50–150% Fair Mutation is nearly symmetric. In all cases the mean change
in length of worse children is within -0.5 and +0.5. The mean change in length for better
children and children with the same fitness are also almost symmetric.

The affects of subtree sized fair mutation are similar to those of self crossover, especially
w.r.t. the asymmetry of change in fitness and change in size.

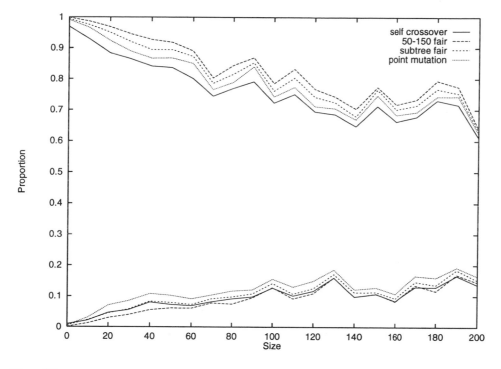

Figure 8.7
Effect of mutations on best of generation individuals in the Sextic Polynomial problem. (Means of data grouped into bins of size 10). The protective effect of inviable code is shown in the general trend for longer programs to be less likely to be disrupted.

Figure 8.7 shows the proportion of single point changes that increase fitness and those that make it worse. Initially programs are short but increase as the population evolves, so a similar plot is obtained if we replace size as the horizontal axis by generations. As expected initially all high fitness individuals are fragile and over 95% of point mutation reduce fitness. As programs grow, the chance of a single point mutation reducing fitness decreases (and the chance of it improving fitness grows). This is entirely as expected and corresponds to larger programs containing more inviable code. The proportion of worse, same and better programs produced by self crossover, 50–150% fair mutation and subtree sized fair mutation are essentially the same as that of point mutation. This indicates the chance the offspring has a changed behaviour depends mainly on the point in the program which is changed (particularly whether it is viable or not) rather than how it is changed.

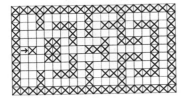

Figure 8.8
The maze used for the maze navigation problem. Walls are indicated by crosses and the start by the arrow.

Table 8.4
Summary of the maze navigation and even 7 Parity problems

Objective:	To navigate a simple maze	To find parity of 7 boolean inputs
Terminal set:	forward, back, left, right, no_op, wall_ahead, no_wall_ahead	The 7 input values
Function set:	if_then_else, while, prog2	AND, NAND, OR, XOR
Restrictions:	Programs were halted after 3000 instructions to avoid infinite loops	
Fitness:	Distance traveled from left wall (0 to 18)	Number of correct cases (of $2^N = 127$)
Selection:	stochastic remainder	
Population size:	500	
Initial population:	random trees	
Parameters:	66.6% crossover, no mutation, results averaged over fifty trials	
Termination:	fixed number of generations	
# of Trials:	50	

8.6 Bloat in Discrete Problems

8.6.1 Code Bloat as Protection

This series of experiments tests the hypothesis that code bloat is a mechanism to protect existing solutions from the destructive effects of crossover and similar code modifying operations. This hypothesis was described in detail in Section 8.2. We began by using a non-destructive (hill-climbing) version of crossover. In the modified operation the fitness of an offspring produced with crossover is compared to the fitness of the parent which supplied the offspring's root node. The offspring replaces the parent only if the offspring's fitness equals or exceeds the parent's fitness, otherwise the parent remains in the population and the offspring is discarded. Thus, survival does not depend on avoiding the destructive effects of crossover and the presumed evolutionary benefit of code bloat is removed.

These experiments were performed on two test problems: a simple maze navigation problem, and the even 7 parity problem. These two problems are summarized in Table 8.4. The maze used with the maze navigation problem is shown in Figure 8.8.

Table 8.5
Code size and fitness at generation 75 with normal or non-destructive crossover.

	Size		Fitness	
	Maze navigation	Even 7 parity	Maze navigation	Even 7 parity
Normal Crossover	590.58	542.81	15.23	91.39
Non-destructive Crossover	185.67	158.64	16.68	99.24

Table 8.5 compares the size and performance of programs evolved using normal and non-destructive crossover. The trials with normal crossover show obvious bloat, in contrast with non-destructive crossover the program sizes are much smaller. The use of non-destructive crossover significantly lowers the amount of code growth observed but there is no significant change in fitness by the end of the runs. These results agree with other results using non-destructive crossover [O'Reilly and Oppacher, 1995; Hooper et al., 1997; Soule and Foster, 1997] This is very strong evidence that code growth occurs, at least partially, as a protective mechanism against the destructive effects of crossover.

If code bloat is a protective, conservative mechanism it should occur to protect against other, primarily destructive, operations. We tested this possibility by looking at the rates of code growth when mutation was used in addition to crossover.

If mutation is applied at a constant rate per node then the probability of a mutation occurring at a given, viable, node is not diminished by the presence of inviable nodes and there is no evolutionary advantage to excess inviable code. Therefore mutation at a *constant rate per node* should not produce code growth.

To test if inviable code is advantageous we used a modified mutation rate. A program was selected for mutation with probability p_m. Once a program was selected for mutation the program's size was used to fix the mutation rate so that an average of N_m nodes would be mutated (i.e. $mutation rate = N_m/program size$). We refer to this form of mutation as *constant number* mutation. Because the average number of mutated nodes is constant, a larger number of inviable nodes makes it less likely that viable code is affected, presumably producing an evolutionary advantage in favor of code bloat.

For these experiments $p_m = 0.3$ and $N_m = 4$. It is important to note that a single tree node is mutated. Thus, this mutation operation does not change the size of the program. Because code size is not directly affected by the inclusion of mutations any changes in code bloat must be an evolutionary effect. The rate of crossover was reduced from 0.667 to 0.333. This decreases the total amount of bloat making the effects of mutation on size, if any, easier to observe. Crossover was applied, with offspring replacing their parents, to produce a new population. Then mutation was applied to that population.

We also applied mutation at a constant rate per node. The probability of a node mutating was 0.02. In this case additional bloat cannot protect against the destructive effects of mutation and additional bloat is not expected.

Table 8.6
The effects of mutations on code bloat in the maze navigation and even 7 parity problems. The data are averaged over 50 trials and taken after generation 50.

	Size		Fitness	
	Maze navigation	Even 7 parity	Maze navigation	Even 7 parity
No mutations	245.6	240.6	14.3	90.4
Constant Rate	206.4	285.8	10.8	85.9
Constant Number	363.5	420.3	13.0	95.7

Table 8.7
Code size and fitness at generation 75 with normal, non-destructive, or rigorous non-destructive crossover.

	Size		Fitness	
	Maze	Even 7 parity	Maze	Even 7 parity
Normal Crossover	590.58	542.81	15.23	91.39
Non-destructive Crossover	185.67	158.64	16.68	99.24
Rigorous Non-destructive Crossover	69.68	66.93	16.03	92.49

Table 8.6 shows the effects of mutation for the maze navigation and even 7 parity problems at generation 50. As expected the baseline rate of code bloat is lower for these data because of the decreased crossover rate. It is clear from these results that constant number mutations cause a dramatic, significant increase in code bloat whereas constant rate mutations have a much smaller, more ambiguous effect.

These results make it clear that, at least in part, code bloat is a protective mechanism against the destructive effects of code modifying operations. When the possibility of damage from an operator is removed, in this case with non-destructive crossover, the amount of code bloat decreases. When the probability of damage increases, in this case with the addition of mutation, the amount of code bloat increases. Further, code bloat only increases if inviable code can play a protective role. When mutations were applied at a constant rate per node additional viable code could not shield viable code and no additional growth was observed.

8.6.2   Code bloat due to "Removal Bias"

In this section we suggest "Removal Bias" is a second cause of bloat and conduct dynamic experiments to show its effects in evolving GP populations. We use two different types of non-destructive crossover. The first version is identical to the non-destructive crossover described previously. While the second is a more rigorous form in which an offspring replaces its parent only if its fitness *exceeds* its parent's fitness. Table 8.7 shows rigorous non-destructive crossover produces significantly less bloat.

The only difference between the two forms of crossover is that the non-rigorous form allows offspring of equal fitness to be preserved. Thus, the change in code bloat indicates that the offspring of equal fitness are, on average, larger than their parents. Larger, equivalent solutions are more plentiful and, thus, easier to find than smaller, equivalent solutions. This produces a general increases in size even though fitness may not be improving. However, when rigorous non-destructive crossover is used, the larger equivalent programs are no longer kept and most of the bloat vanishes.

Equivalently we can view this in terms of the program landscapes of the three crossover operators. Subtree crossover densely links the search space allowing ready access to the neighbouring programs. Most of these with similar fitness are bigger than the start point and bloat follows. With non-destructive crossover all the links to worse programs are replaced with links back to the current program. This reduces the rate of bloat because the chance of moving away from the current program is significantly reduced. Strict non-destructive crossover replaces all the links to programs of the same fitness by links back to self. This leaves only links to better programs connected but naturally these are few in number and although they on average lead to bigger programs (because there are more bigger programs) there is much less chance of any movement at all through the program landscape, so bloat is dramatically reduced. In continuous fitness problems there are many links to programs with better fitness (albeit the improvement may be tiny) so we would expect non-destructive crossover not to be so effective in such cases.

In addition, we can hypothesize a particular mechanism which produces these larger, equivalent programs. The instructions in a program syntax tree are distributed in such a way that inviable instructions cluster near the branch tips except in extremely pathological trees [Soule and Foster, 1998]. This means that removing a relatively small branch during crossover will decrease the probability of affecting viable code, whereas removing a larger branch increases the probability of affecting viable code. Thus, removing a small branch is less likely to be damaging, because any random change to viable code is more likely to be harmful than to be beneficial. In contrast the size of a replacement branch is not connected to changes in fitness. Thus, there is an overall bias in favor of offspring which only had a small branch removed during crossover.

This "removal bias" leads to steady growth. At each generation the offspring which grew during crossover, because a smaller than average branch was removed, will be favored.

The total average size change during crossover is zero, as every branch removed from one individual is added to another individual and vice versa. However measurements shows that offspring which are at least as fit as their parent are on average slightly bigger, exactly as predicted by the notion of removal bias. Initially the percentage increase is large but within 10–20 generations these transients vanish and steady growth from parent to offspring of the order of 5% is observed. Although the change in size is relatively small it is compounded at each generation and, over many generations, it leads to exponential growth. Thus, this apparently minor bias can have a significant effect on code size.

Removal bias is not limited to crossover. In most versions of subtree mutation a randomly selected subtree is removed and replaced by a randomly generated one. The previous argument regarding the size of the removed and replacement branches applies equally well to this type of subtree mutation. However, removal bias can only occur when the size of the removed branch and the replacement branch are independent. Thus, with the 50%–150% fair mutation used earlier removal bias is not expected to occur, whereas with subtree-sized fair mutation removal bias should take place. This agrees with the results presented previously.

These results make it clear that code bloat has at least two causes. Code bloat occurs as a protective mechanism which minimizes the destructive affects of code modifying operations. Code bloat also occurs because the search space is more heavily weighted towards larger solutions. These solutions are easily found because of the bias in the removal stage of crossover or subtree mutation.

8.7 Evolution of Program Shapes

In addition to changing size, programs with a tree structured genome can also change shape, becoming bushier or sparser as they evolve. In this section we consider the size and depth of the trees. While the density of trees affects the size of changes made by subtree crossover and many mutation operators [Rosca, 1997; Soule and Foster, 1997] our experiments show bloating populations evolve towards shapes that are of intermediate density. As Figure 8.9 shows this can be explained as simple random drift towards the most popular program shapes. In the case of three radically different problems the populations evolve in very similar ways. We suggest this is because all three contain only binary functions and so while the number of different programs in the three cases are very different, the location of the most common shape is the same. For problems with functions with more than two arguments or mixtures of numbers of arguments the exact distribution of depth v. size in the search space will be different but will have the same general characteristics.

Experiments where maze navigation populations were initialised as either all full trees or as all minimal trees of the same size (31 nodes) show in both cases the population evolves away from full trees or minimal trees towards the most common tree shape. However they don't appear to converge (within 75 generations) to the peak, i.e. most common, tree shape. This may be because, as the 5% and 95% lines in Figure 8.9 show, there is a wide spread of probable sizes around the peak.

While we have not yet completed a mathematical analysis of the rate of tree growth with crossover between random trees, such analysis may be tractable. Figure 8.10 gives a strong indication that the average depth of binary trees in a population grows linearly at about one level per generation. Using the relationships between size and depth for random binary trees given in Section 8.3, this corresponds to growth in size of $O(\text{generations}^{1.6})$ for reasonable size programs rising to a limit $O(\text{generations}^2)$ for programs of programs of more than 32,000 nodes. Note this indicates quadratic or sub-quadratic growth rather than exponential growth. Also the actual program sizes will depend upon their depth when the linear growth begins and so will be problem dependent.

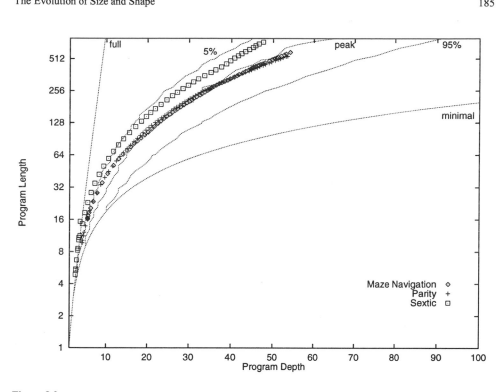

Figure 8.9
Evolution of program tree shapes for the maze navigation, even parity, and sextic polynomial problems. Each point represents the mean size and mean depth of trees in a single generation. Means of 50 GP runs on each problem. For comparison full and minimal trees are plotted with dotted lines, as are the most popular shapes and the boundary of the region containing 5% and 95% of trees of a given length. Note log scale.

This analysis and these data only looked at tree based genomes. It is clear that shape considerations will not apply to linear genomes. However, it is possible that the linear distribution of viable and inviable nodes are subject to some similar considerations. For example, a very even distribution of viable nodes in a linear genome may make it more likely that at least a few viable nodes will be affected by most operations. In which case an even distribution of viable nodes is unlikely to be favored evolutionarily. More complex genomes, such as graph structures, do have shapes and it seems likely that they are also subject to the evolutionary pressures discussed here.

8.8 Discussion

As programs become longer it becomes easier to find neighbouring programs with the same performance. Indeed in our continuous problem it became easier to find neighbours

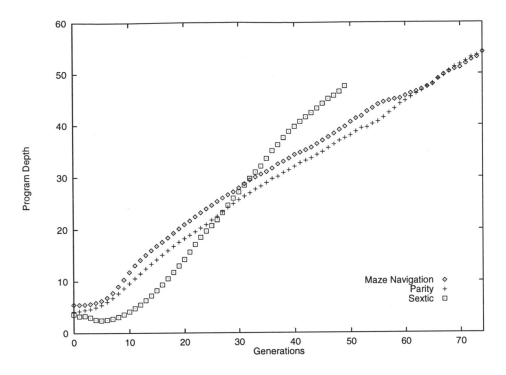

Figure 8.10
Evolution of program tree depth for the maze navigation, even parity, and sextic polynomial problems. Means of 50 GP runs on each problem. Note apparently linear growth in tree depth.

of slightly better fitness. I.e. the fitness landscape becomes smoother for long programs. Alternatively we may view this as it becomes more difficult to make large moves as programs get bigger. Figure 8.5 shows GP is an evolutionary process with stable populations evolving only gradually. From an optimisation point of view this is of course very vexing since it means the stable GP population is not learning. This problem that evolution isn't an optimisation process has been faced before in Genetic Algorithms [De Jong, 1992].

The exponential growth in the number of programs is a very strong driving factor. It may be the cause of bloat even if the fitness function changes rapidly [Langdon and Poli, 1998c]. If we conduct the reverse experiment to Section 8.6 and instead of rewarding programs with the same fitness we penalise them we may still get bloat [Langdon and Poli, 1998c]. Effectively instead of replacing links to worse programs with links back to the current point we remove links to programs of equal fitness. This increases the chance of moving to either better or worse programs but there are still remain overwhelmingly more links to longer programs. So the population still bloats even though inviable code would appear to be a liability.

In Section 8.5.4.2 we showed 50–150% fair mutation removes the large correlation between offspring size and change in fitness seen in other genetic operators. This indicates that by carefully controlling the size of the new code we can avoid "removal bias" as a cause of bloat.

In these experiments it appears that there is faster bloat with subtree crossover than common mutation operators firstly because it does not have an implicit size bias and secondly because it allows larger size changes in a single operation. We can also speculate that random code generated by mutation is less likely to contain inviable code than code swapped by crossover. This potential cause of bloat, if it exists, would be specific to crossover.

8.9   Conclusions

Code growth is a general phenomenon of variable length representations. It is not just a feature of GP. While it is not possible to show it occurs in every case, in Section 8.4 we have argued it is can be expected where there isn't a parsimony bias and we have shown here and elsewhere [Langdon, 1998b] that code growth happens in a variety of popular stochastic search techniques on a number of problems.

Code bloat is such an insidious process because in variable length representations there are simply more longer programs than short ones. It appears to be common for the proportion of programs of a given fitness to be more-or-less independent of program size. In the absence of length bias, the effect of fitness selection on the neighbourhoods of common genetic operators is to prefer programs which act like their parents but exponentially more of these are long than are short. Therefore code growth can be explained as the population evolving in a random diffusive way towards the part of the search space where most of the programs are to be found. Another aspect of this is the shape of trees within the population also evolves towards the more common shapes.

Our research shows that code bloat arises in at least two separate points in the evolutionary process.

1. The mechanics of crossover and subtree mutation typically involve the removal and replacement of a subtree. Often comparatively small changes are more likely not to reduce performance (meaning successful offspring differ little from their primary parent). If the size of the inserted code is independent of that removed this means the added code in successful children is on average bigger than that removed. Thus offspring are more likely to maintain their parent's fitness if the net effect of crossover or subtree mutation is to increase their size. We have called this *removal bias*.

2. It appears to be common that larger programs are on average more likely to produce offspring which retain their parents fitness and thus are more likely to survive. Thus being larger is an evolutionary benefit because a larger program is more likely to have equally fit offspring. This evolutionary benefit arises because the extra code in a larger program has

a protective effect. This makes it less likely that the program's offspring will be damaged during crossover or mutation, regardless of whether the offspring increased or decreased in size.

We have shown in one problem that the proportions of worse, better and unchanged programs are similar for a range of genetic operators. This is consistent with the view that the primary reason for offspring to behave as their parent is that their parent contained inviable code which makes no difference to the program when it is modified. We also show the proportion of inviable code grows with parent size.

In the sextic polynomial problem these proportions are much the same as those of randomly chosen programs of similar fitness suggesting similar behaviour may be expected in large parts of the search space. The implication of this is GP is mainly sampling "typical" programs. We of course want it to find solutions, i.e. to sample extraordinary programs.

We have proposed a number of new genetic operators. Two of these show promise in controlling bloat. 50–150% fair mutation is carefully constructed to avoid bloat due to the exponential nature of tree search spaces. In discrete problems, non-destructive crossover may limit code growth due to the evolutionary advantage of inviable code.

8.10 Future Work

The success of 50-150% fair mutation at controlling bloat suggests it is worth investigating size fair crossover operators. Such new operators might not only control the size of the replacement subtree but also additional benefits might be found by controlling more tightly from where in the other parent the replacement subtree is taken. One point [Poli and Langdon, 1998b] and uniform crossover [Poli and Langdon, 1998a] and Nordin's homologous crossover (Chapter 12) suggest this later step might improve the crossover operator in other ways as well as controlling bloat.

Acknowledgments

This research was partially funded by the Defence Research Agency in Malvern. I would like to thank Lee Spector, Paul Vitanyi and Martijn Bot for helpful suggestions and criticism.

Bibliography

Anderson, S., Bankier, A. T., Barrell, B. G., de Bruijn, M. H. L., Coulson, A. R., Drouin, J., Eperon, I. C., Nierlich, D. P., Roe, B. A., Sanger, F., Schreier, P. H., Smith, A. J. H., Staden, R., and Young, I. G. (1981), "Sequence and organization of the human mitochondrial genome," *Nature*, 290:457–464.

Angeline, P. J. (1994), "Genetic programming and emergent intelligence," in *Advances in Genetic Programming*, K. E. Kinnear, Jr. (Ed.), Chapter 4, pp 75–98, MIT Press.

Blickle, T. (1996), "Evolving compact solutions in genetic programming: A case study," in *Parallel Problem Solving From Nature IV. Proceedings of the International Conference on Evolutionary Computation*, H.-M. Voigt, W. Ebeling, I. Rechenberg, and H.-P. Schwefel (Eds.), volume 1141 of *LNCS*, pp 564–573, Berlin, Germany: Springer-Verlag.

Blickle, T. and Thiele, L. (1994), "Genetic programming and redundancy," in *Genetic Algorithms within the Framework of Evolutionary Computation (Workshop at KI-94, Saarbrücken)*, J. Hopf (Ed.), pp 33–38, Im Stadtwald, Building 44, D-66123 Saarbrücken, Germany: Max-Planck-Institut für Informatik (MPI-I-94-241).

Cavalier-Smith, T. (1985), *The Evolution of Genome Size*, John Wiley & Sons.

De Jong, K. A. (1992), "Are genetic algorithms function optimisers?," in *Parallel Problem Solving from Nature 2*, R. Manner and B. Manderick (Eds.), pp 3–13, Brussels, Belgium: Elsevier Science.

Flajolet, P. and Oldyzko, A. (1982), "The average height of binary trees and other simple trees," *Journal of Computer and System Sciences*, 25:171–213.

Gathercole, C. and Ross, P. (1996), "An adverse interaction between crossover and restricted tree depth in genetic programming," in *Genetic Programming 1996: Proceedings of the First Annual Conference*, J. R. Koza, D. E. Goldberg, D. B. Fogel, and R. L. Riolo (Eds.), pp 291–296, Stanford University, CA, USA: MIT Press.

Greeff, D. J. and Aldrich, C. (1997), "Evolution of empirical models for metallurgical process systems," in *Genetic Programming 1997: Proceedings of the Second Annual Conference*, J. R. Koza, K. Deb, M. Dorigo, D. B. Fogel, M. Garzon, H. Iba, and R. L. Riolo (Eds.), p 138, Stanford University, CA, USA: Morgan Kaufmann.

Hooper, D. C., Flann, N. S., and Fuller, S. R. (1997), "Recombinative hill-climbing: A stronger search method for genetic programming," in *Genetic Programming 1997: Proceedings of the Second Annual Conference*, J. R. Koza, K. Deb, M. Dorigo, D. B. Fogel, M. Garzon, H. Iba, and R. L. Riolo (Eds.), pp 174–179, Stanford University, CA, USA: Morgan Kaufmann.

Iba, H., de Garis, H., and Sato, T. (1994), "Genetic programming using a minimum description length principle," in *Advances in Genetic Programming*, K. E. Kinnear, Jr. (Ed.), Chapter 12, pp 265–284, MIT Press.

Kornberg, A. (1982), *Supplement to DNA Replication*, Freeman.

Koza, J. R. (1992), *Genetic Programming: On the Programming of Computers by Natural Selection*, Cambridge, MA, USA: MIT Press.

Koza, J. R. (1994), *Genetic Programming II: Automatic Discovery of Reusable Programs*, Cambridge Massachusetts: MIT Press.

Langdon, W. B. (1995), "Evolving data structures using genetic programming," in *Genetic Algorithms: Proceedings of the Sixth International Conference (ICGA95)*, L. Eshelman (Ed.), pp 295–302, Pittsburgh, PA, USA: Morgan Kaufmann.

Langdon, W. B. (1997), "Fitness causes bloat: Simulated annealing, hill climbing and populations," Technical Report CSRP-97-22, University of Birmingham, School of Computer Science.

Langdon, W. B. (1998a), *Data Structures and Genetic Programming: Genetic Programming + Data Structures = Automatic Programming!*, Boston: Kluwer.

Langdon, W. B. (1998b), "The evolution of size in variable length representations," in *1998 IEEE International Conference on Evolutionary Computation*, pp 633–638, Anchorage, Alaska, USA: IEEE Press.

Langdon, W. B. and Poli, R. (1997a), "An analysis of the MAX problem in genetic programming," in *Genetic Programming 1997: Proceedings of the Second Annual Conference*, J. R. Koza, K. Deb, M. Dorigo, D. B. Fogel, M. Garzon, H. Iba, and R. L. Riolo (Eds.), pp 222–230, Stanford University, CA, USA: Morgan Kaufmann.

Langdon, W. B. and Poli, R. (1997b), "Fitness causes bloat," in *Soft Computing in Engineering Design and Manufacturing*, P. K. Chawdhry, R. Roy, and R. K. Pant (Eds.), pp 13–22, Springer-Verlag London.

Langdon, W. B. and Poli, R. (1998a), "Boolean functions fitness spaces," in *Late Breaking Papers at the Genetic Programming 1998 Conference*, J. R. Koza (Ed.), University of Wisconsin, Madison, Wisconsin, USA: Stanford University Bookstore.

Langdon, W. B. and Poli, R. (1998b), "Fitness causes bloat: Mutation," in *Proceedings of the First European Workshop on Genetic Programming*, W. Banzhaf, R. Poli, M. Schoenauer, and T. C. Fogarty (Eds.), volume 1391 of *LNCS*, pp 37–48, Paris: Springer-Verlag.

Langdon, W. B. and Poli, R. (1998c), "Genetic programming bloat with dynamic fitness," in *Proceedings of the First European Workshop on Genetic Programming*, W. Banzhaf, R. Poli, M. Schoenauer, and T. C. Fogarty (Eds.), volume 1391 of *LNCS*, pp 96–112, Paris: Springer-Verlag.

Langdon, W. B. and Poli, R. (1998d), "Why ants are hard," in *Genetic Programming 1998: Proceedings of the Third Annual Conference*, J. R. Koza, W. Banzhaf, K. Chellapilla, K. Deb, M. Dorigo, D. B. Fogel, M. H. Garzon, D. E. Goldberg, H. Iba, and R. Riolo (Eds.), pp 193–201, University of Wisconsin, Madison, Wisconsin, USA: Morgan Kaufmann.

Langdon, W. B. and Poli, R. (1998e), "Why "building blocks" don't work on parity problems," Technical Report CSRP-98-17, University of Birmingham, School of Computer Science.

Li, W.-H. and Graur, D. (1991), *Fundamentals of Molecular Evolution*, Sinauer.

Mattick, J. S. (1994), "Introns - evolution and function," *Current Opinions in Genetic Development*, pp 1–15.

McPhee, N. F. and Miller, J. D. (1995), "Accurate replication in genetic programming," in *Genetic Algorithms: Proceedings of the Sixth International Conference (ICGA95)*, L. Eshelman (Ed.), pp 303–309, Pittsburgh, PA, USA: Morgan Kaufmann.

Nordin, P. (1997), *Evolutionary Program Induction of Binary Machine Code and its Applications*, PhD thesis, der Universitat Dortmund am Fachereich Informatik.

Nordin, P. and Banzhaf, W. (1995), "Complexity compression and evolution," in *Genetic Algorithms: Proceedings of the Sixth International Conference (ICGA95)*, L. Eshelman (Ed.), pp 310–317, Pittsburgh, PA, USA: Morgan Kaufmann.

Nordin, P., Banzhaf, W., and Francone, F. D. (1997), "Introns in nature and in simulated structure evolution," in *Bio-Computation and Emergent Computation*, D. Lundh, B. Olsson, and A. Narayanan (Eds.), Skovde, Sweeden: World Scientific Publishing.

Nordin, P., Francone, F., and Banzhaf, W. (1996), "Explicitly defined introns and destructive crossover in genetic programming," in *Advances in Genetic Programming 2*, P. J. Angeline and K. E. Kinnear, Jr. (Eds.), Chapter 6, pp 111–134, Cambridge, MA, USA: MIT Press.

O'Reilly, U.-M. and Oppacher, F. (1995), "Hybridized crossover-based search techniques for program discovery," in *Proceedings of the 1995 World Conference on Evolutionary Computation*, volume 2, p 573, Perth, Australia: IEEE Press.

Poli, R. and Langdon, W. B. (1998a), "On the search properties of different crossover operators in genetic programming," in *Genetic Programming 1998: Proceedings of the Third Annual Conference*, J. R. Koza, W. Banzhaf, K. Chellapilla, K. Deb, M. Dorigo, D. B. Fogel, M. H. Garzon, D. E. Goldberg, H. Iba, and R. Riolo (Eds.), pp 293–301, University of Wisconsin, Madison, Wisconsin, USA: Morgan Kaufmann.

Poli, R. and Langdon, W. B. (1998b), "Schema theory for genetic programming with one-point crossover and point mutation," *Evolutionary Computation*, 6(3):231–252.

Price, G. R. (1970), "Selection and covariance," *Nature*, 227, August 1:520–521.

Rosca, J. P. (1997), "Analysis of complexity drift in genetic programming," in *Genetic Programming 1997: Proceedings of the Second Annual Conference*, J. R. Koza, K. Deb, M. Dorigo, D. B. Fogel, M. Garzon, H. Iba, and R. L. Riolo (Eds.), pp 286–294, Stanford University, CA, USA: Morgan Kaufmann.

Soule, T. (1998), *Code Growth in Genetic Programming*, PhD thesis, University of Idaho, Moscow, Idaho, USA.

Soule, T. and Foster, J. A. (1997), "Code size and depth flows in genetic programming," in *Genetic Programming 1997: Proceedings of the Second Annual Conference*, J. R. Koza, K. Deb, M. Dorigo, D. B. Fogel, M. Garzon, H. Iba, and R. L. Riolo (Eds.), pp 313–320, Stanford University, CA, USA: Morgan Kaufmann.

Soule, T. and Foster, J. A. (1998), "Removal bias: a new cause of code growth in tree based evolutionary programming," in *1998 IEEE International Conference on Evolutionary Computation*, pp 781–186, Anchorage, Alaska, USA: IEEE Press.

Soule, T., Foster, J. A., and Dickinson, J. (1996), "Code growth in genetic programming," in *Genetic Programming 1996: Proceedings of the First Annual Conference*, J. R. Koza, D. E. Goldberg, D. B. Fogel, and R. L. Riolo (Eds.), pp 215–223, Stanford University, CA, USA: MIT Press.

Zhang, B.-T. and Mühlenbein, H. (1995), "Balancing accuracy and parsimony in genetic programming," *Evolutionary Computation*, 3(1):17–38.

9 Fitness Distributions: Tools for Designing Efficient Evolutionary Computations

Christian Igel and Kumar Chellapilla

Fitness distributions are employed as tools for understanding the effects of variation operators in Genetic Programming. Eleven operators are analyzed on four common benchmark problems by estimating generation dependent features of the fitness distributions, e.g. the probability of improvement and the expected average fitness change.

9.1 Introduction

Evolutionary optimization methods can be described as computation procedures that operate on a population of candidate solutions through an iterated process of variation and selection. Different paradigms for evolutionary algorithms (EAs), such as evolutionary programming (EP), evolution strategies (ES), genetic algorithms (GAs), and genetic programming (GP), differ in their representation of solutions in the population, the selection scheme and the representation specific variation operators.

There exists a variety of possible operators that could be used to generate offspring given a representation of the solutions in the population. Operators that provide good rates of finding acceptable solutions through efficient search are desired. From the theoretical point of view, the operators in conjunction with the applied selection scheme should guarantee convergence to the global optimum with probability one at least for finite search spaces [Rudolph, 1997]. The choice of suitable operators has traditionally relied on theoretical models of the dynamics induced by these operators under selection or heuristic information regarding the desired parent-offspring fitness changes [Rechenberg, 1994; Rosca and Ballard, 1994; Utecht and Trint, 1994; Rosca and Ballard, 1995]. In practice, multi-parent multi-offspring self-adaptive EAs on multi-modal objective functions are used to solve problems. For the sake of mathematical tractability and ease of analysis, most theoretical models work with simplified versions of EAs and simple objective functions and the applicability of the following result, in light of the simplifying assumptions used to obtain the result, becomes questionable. Hence, as long as the used EAs cannot be analyzed analytically, heuristic design methodologies have to be applied. However, general heuristic design methodologies such as the principle of strong causality [Rechenberg, 1994] may be difficult to apply to discrete and discontinuous search spaces without an empirical analysis of the interaction of the variation operator under consideration and the problem representation [Rosca and Ballard, 1995; Sendhoff et al., 1997; Igel, 1998]. In GP we are in general concerned with such search spaces and confronted with several variation operators whose effects are far from being understood completely.

In this investigation, we utilize the concept of fitness distribution analysis as a tool for characterizing the behavior of variation operators in GP; a method that may lead to a better understanding of the search process and to simple design heuristics that improve the evolutionary computation.

9.2   Background

Variation operators may be broadly classified into two groups, namely exploratory (or global) search operators and exploitative (or local) search operators. Global optimization requires operators of both types. While local search operators are needed for gradually approaching optima, global search operators are needed for identifying basins of attraction of various optima and also escaping local optima. Exploration and exploitation may be incorporated into an evolutionary scheme in different ways. The same operator may be used to probabilistically act both as a local (exploitative) and global (exploratory) search operator, e.g. Gaussian mutations for real-valued parameter optimization, wherein changes of varying degrees are probabilistically generated even when the variances are fixed. Small changes are generated more often and result in local search whereas large step sizes occur less frequently and constitute a more global search.

Furthermore, the explorative or exploitative nature of an operator may be controlled by parameters like the variances in case of Gaussian mutation. Variation may also be conducted through the use of a set of operators, some of which are tuned to perform local search, while others perform global search. Examples of such a strategy include the use of multiple variation operators for the evolution of the structure and parameters of finite state machines [Chellapilla and Fogel, 1998], neural networks [Yao and Liu, 1996], and parse trees [O'Reilly, 1995; Angeline, 1996; Chellapilla, 1998].

Fitness landscape analysis has been proposed as a tool for analyzing evolutionary computations, see [Macken and Stadler, 1993] for an overview. The fitness landscape is determined by the fitness function and a distance measure on the genotype space, i.e., mathematically it is defined as a map from a (finite) metric space into the real numbers. The results obtained using fitness landscape analysis only hold for the distance measure used. Therefore, the analysis of an evolutionary algorithm based on the fitness landscapes approach requires a metric that is defined with regard to the genetic operators. Examples of such metrics include the Hamming distance for point mutations when using binary representations and the tree edit distance for program spaces [O'Reilly, 1997]. Instead of a standard metric when given a representation, the metric should be defined in terms of the variation operators themselves, with each application of a variation operator generating a unit change in distance. However, the calculation of such a distance measure can be very complex and computationally expensive. Further, if an operator depends on the composition of the current population, as does crossover, the distance measure is different every generation and the distance computations become hard to handle. Kinnear examined the fitness landscapes on which GP operates by comparing the autocorrelation functions of random walks and analyzing adaptive walks with respect to the problem difficulty. The "unusually low" autocorrelations appeared to be "not a particularly good way" to indicate the difficulty of the test problems [Kinnear, Jr., 1994].

The fitness correlation coefficient (FCC) has been proposed as a means for the analysis of variation operators in EAs [Manderick et al., 1991]. The FCC of an operator v is defined as

$$\mathrm{FCC}_v = \frac{\mathrm{cov}(F_{\overline{p}}, F_o)}{\sigma_{F_{\overline{p}}} \sigma_{F_o}} \quad , \tag{9.1}$$

where $\sigma_{F_{\overline{p}}}$ and σ_{F_o} represent the standard deviations of the mean parent fitness and offspring fitness, respectively, and cov represents the covariance function. An absolute FCC value of one indicates a linear dependency between parent and offspring fitness and a value of zero indicates linear independence. An FCC close to zero is regarded as an indicator of a rugged landscape and therefore of weak performance of an EA based on the operator in question. However, instructive counter examples exist that show that the fitness correlation coefficient does not necessarily reflect evolvability [Altenberg, 1995; Fogel and Ghozeil, 1996], one of the main properties determining the quality of evolutionary search. Evolvability means the ability of a parent population to produce variants fitter than any yet existing [Altenberg, 1994].

9.3 Fitness distributions

Fitness distributions (FDs) have been proposed as a means of experimentally estimating the true nature of variation operators on different performance or objective functions. The FD of an operator was described in [Grefenstette, 1995] as the distribution of the offspring fitness given the mean parent fitness. For a variation operator v that produces an offspring from one or more parents the fitness distribution FD_v was defined by the conditional probability

$$\mathrm{FD}_v(F_{\overline{p}}) = P(F_o|F_{\overline{p}}) \quad , \tag{9.2}$$

where the random variables $F_{\overline{p}}$ and F_o denote the mean fitness of the parents used by v to generate the offspring, o, and the resulting offspring fitness, respectively. More generally, the FD_v can depend on all the individual parent fitnesses. Mathematically,

$$\mathrm{FD}_v(F_{\{p\}}) = P(F_o|F_{\{p\}}) \quad , \tag{9.3}$$

where $F_{\{p\}}$ depends on the set of fitness values of all parents that produced the offspring.

The FD_v is generally quite complex and difficult to compute. However, it is usually sufficient to be able to focus on estimating important features of the FD [Grefenstette, 1995; Fogel and Ghozeil, 1996]. In the remainder of this section, we introduce such features of the FD.

Adaptation does not only depend on how often offspring better than their parents are produced, but also on how much better they are [Altenberg, 1994]. Both aspects of the offspring FD must be considered while investigating the properties of variation operators. Therefore, the probability of improvement and expected improvement have been proposed as tools for designing efficient evolutionary computations. Improvement has been defined in different ways. Firstly, improvement can be regarded as the distance covered *on the gradient path* towards the (known) optimum [Rechenberg, 1994]. Secondly, it can be defined as the distance covered to the optimum [Schwefel, 1995]. Thirdly, improvement can simply be defined as the increase in fitness. The first two definitions measure improvement in the search space. An explicit metric on the search space is needed and the optima have to be known. For our purpose, the analysis of GP operators, these definitions (that were designed for real-valued parameter optimization) would not work, so we define improvement in the fitness space. The expected improvement EI_v of an operator is therefore defined as the expectation of the fitness difference between parent(s) and offspring [Fogel and Ghozeil, 1996]. A positive EI indicates that on average the offspring fitness is greater than the parent fitness and a negative EI indicates that the mean offspring fitness is lower than the mean parent fitness. An alternative way to define the expected improvement is to calculate the average change in fitness only when an offspring was fitter than its parent(s), i.e. mathematically the expected improvement is given by $\mathcal{E}(\max\{0, F_o - F_{\{p\}}\})$, where $\mathcal{E}(.)$ denotes the expectation. In this case, the expected improvement is always non-negative [Tuson and Ross, 1998; Fogel and Ghozeil, 1996].

The probability of improvement of a variation operator v, IP_v, is defined as the fraction of the generated offspring that is better than their parents. While an IP value close to one indicates that on average fitter offspring are generated through the use of the operator, an IP value close to zero indicates that on average offspring worse than their parents are generated.

The IP and EI values can be computed analytically for very simple objective functions, e.g. IP and EI for Gaussian mutations using real-valued representation [Rechenberg, 1994] or IP for point mutations using binary representation [Bäck, 1996]. In general, these FD features have to be estimated numerically through Monte-Carlo methods. This has been done for real-valued representation and Gaussian mutations in [Fogel and Ghozeil, 1996].

If the computational effort to produce an offspring is different for the used operators, then the features of the FD should be normalized by the needed effort for comparison.

Unlike with most fitness landscape analysis approaches, the analysis of evolutionary computations using dynamic FD features does not need a specific metric on the search space.

The features of the FD are not static but change with the problem at hand and also during the evolutionary process (e.g. it gets progressively more difficult to create a fitter offspring). In view of this, dynamic (i.e. generation dependent) FD measures are presented that better capture the properties of variation operators during different phases of evolution. In [Nordin and Banzhaf, 1995] the change in fitness (measured in percent) using crossover was calculated in a generation dependent manner for a symbolic regression problem in GP.

Here we estimate seven different features of the FD for investigating the effects of eleven different variation operators for four common test problems in GP. These features are the

Table 9.1
Summary of the investigated features of the fitness distributions, $F_{\{p\}}$ and F_o depend on the fitness of the parent(s) and the corresponding offspring, respectively, $\sigma_{F_{\{p\}}}$ and σ_{F_o} denote the standard deviations, F_b stands for the fitness of the current best individual and $\mathcal{E}(.)$ denotes the expectation

AC	average change	$\mathcal{E}(\lvert F_o - F_{\{p\}} \rvert)$
EI	expected improvement	$\mathcal{E}(F_o - F_{\{p\}})$
IP	improvement probability	$P(F_o > F_{\{p\}})$
WP	worsening probability	$P(F_o < F_{\{p\}})$
SVP	silent variations probability	$P(F_o = F_{\{p\}})$
IP*	probability of being better than the best	$P(F_o > F_b)$
FCC	fitness correlation coefficient	$\dfrac{\operatorname{cov}(F_{\{p\}}, F_o)}{\sigma_{F_{\{p\}}} \sigma_{F_o}}$

expected absolute fitness change (AC), the expected improvement (EI), probability of improvement (IP), the probability of silent variation (SVP), the worsening probability (WP), the fitness correlation coefficient (FCC), and the probability of global improvement (IP*).

- The absolute change in fitness, AC_v, of an operator v is defined as the expectation of the absolute change in fitness between the parent and offspring caused by the application of operator v. The AC_v can be used as an indicator of local (small AC values) and global search (large AC values). This feature can be coupled with other information such as the region of application of the variation operator (such as the depth of the node in the parse tree that was used as the crossover point) to determine the sensitivity of different parts of the genotype to the application of the operator.

- In this investigation, the expected improvement, EI_v, is defined as the average change in fitness between the parent and offspring caused by the application of operator v.

- The probability of improvement, IP_v, of an operator v is defined as the fraction of successful applications of the operator, where an application of the operator v is considered successful if it generates an offspring that is better than its parent.

- The probability of worsening is denoted by WP_v and defined as the fraction of unsuccessful applications of the operator.

- The probability of silent variations, SVP_v, measures the fraction of the application of the operator v that produce no change in fitness.

- The global improvement probability IP_v^* is defined as the frequency with which offspring fitter than any existing parent in the population are produced by the operator. This FD feature describes the evolvability.

- The fitness correlation coefficient, FCC_v, see Eq. (9.1).

The mathematical definitions of these FD features are summarized in Table 9.1.

In the current study, the FD features are viewed as dynamic variables that change during evolution. Their definitions are extended to make them functions of the generation. For example, $AC_v(t)$ is defined as the average absolute change in fitness between the offspring and their corresponding parent(s) at generation t. These generation dependent FD properties for any problem may be conveniently estimated using a set of independent Monte-Carlo trials.

When using multi-parent operators, only the fitness of the *first* parent is used for the calculation of the FD features, i.e., $F_{\{p\}} = F_{p_1}$, see next section. Therefore, since the application of an operator v either increases, decreases, or does not change fitness, we have $IP_v(t) + WP_v(t) + SVP_v(t) = 1$. Using the fitness of the first parent as the reference fitness may not be the best choice for all investigations, e.g. the fitness of the best parent involved may be used instead.

The FD values are amenable to statistical tests. In this investigation, the EI and AC differences were validated using t-tests, the IP, WP, SVP and IP* differences were validated using a χ^2-test, and the FCC differences were tested using a t-test after a z-transformation [Press et al., 1994].

9.4 Evolving computer programs using evolutionary programming

Experiments were conducted by varying the operator(s) used to generate offspring in an evolutionary programming framework. Computer programs were represented as parse trees whose structure and elements were to be evolved. A population of trial computer programs was maintained, variation operators produced changes in these programs, and selection was used to determine which programs were to survive to the next generation and which programs were to be culled from the pool of trials.

9.4.1 Initialization

There are several methods for generating subtrees which can be used to initialize the population. The *full, grow* and *ramped half-and-half* methods of subtree generation were introduced in [Koza, 1992] and are based on tree depth. The ramped half-and-half method is the most commonly used method of generating random parse trees because of its relatively higher probability of generating subtrees of varying depth and size [Koza, 1992; Banzhaf et al., 1998]. However, these methods do not produce a uniform sampling of the search space [Iba, 1996]. The subtree generation method used here was based on the length of the subtree, rather than the depth. First the length of the program was randomly selected to be between 3 and L_{max}. A random program was generated with approximately that length to initialize the parent. Suppose a tree of length 24 was to be generated. In the beginning, as the tree was constructed, nodes and leaves were selected with a 50% probability. No discrimination was made between which nodes and leaves were to be added to the tree. As the length of the tree came close to 24, the selection of functions and terminals was restricted to only those that would make the length of the program exactly 24 (cf. [Chellapilla, 1998]). In this study, each of the simulations were carried out with a set of 500 parents, as e.g. in [Koza, 1992]. Each initial tree was randomly generated using the above subtree generation method with a length between 3 and 50.

9.4.2   Offspring generation through variation

A set of eleven variation operators $V_{all} = \{OneNode, AllNodes, Swap, Grow, Trunc, OneC, AllC, Macro, CrossU, CrossSHC, CrossWHC\}$ was employed to generate offspring from the parents. From the various GP variation operators introduced so far, we chose operators based on [Angeline, 1997a; Chellapilla, 1998] for our investigation.

In the EP framework presented here, each parent generated a single offspring through an application of one randomly selected operator with uniform probability from V_{all}. The operators are described as operating on a single parent, say p_1, to generate a single offspring. The two-parent variation operators operated on the parent p_1, and a mating parent, say p_2, that was either randomly selected from the population or randomly generated. If the offspring genotype did not differ from the parent p_1, this offspring was discarded and a new offspring was generated using p_1.

• *OneNode* randomly selected a node in the program and replaced it with another node of the same arity. *AllNodes* selected each and every node in the program and replaced it with a random node of the same arity.

• *Swap* selected a node that took more than one argument, randomly selected two of its arguments and swapped them.

• *Grow* selected a random leaf in the program and replaced it with a newly generated subtree.

• *Trunc* randomly selected a function node in the program and replaced it with a terminal, thus effectively clipping the tree at that node.

• The *OneC* operator was the same as Gaussian mutation [Chellapilla, 1998] and was applied only to those terminal nodes in the tree that were numeric constants. It perturbed a randomly selected numeric constant by a Gaussian random number with zero mean and a standard deviation of 0.1.

• The *AllC* operator perturbed every numeric constant with independent and identically distributed Gaussian random numbers with mean zero and standard deviation of 0.1.

• The *Macro* operator [Chellapilla, 1998] applied a sequence of simple mutation operators to generate an offspring from a parent using the following steps:

1. A Poisson random number N, with mean λ, was generated.

2. N random variation operators were uniformly selected with replacement from the set of variation operators, $V_{Macro} = \{OneNode, AllNodes, Swap, Grow, Trunc, OneC, AllC\}$. If there were no numeric constants in the terminal set for the problem, then *OneC* and *AllC* operators were excluded from the set.

3. These N mutation operators were applied in sequence one after the other to the parent to generate the offspring. As an example, if the value N were 2 and the operators selected were *OneNode* and *Grow*, then the offspring would be given by

$$\text{Offspring} = Grow(OneNode(\text{Parent}))$$

For the experiments in this study, the mean value λ was selected to be 4.

• The *CrossU* operator was a modified version of the subtree crossover operator defined in [Koza, 1992]. When a parent, p_1, had to be varied using *CrossU*, a mate, p_2, was selected uniformly at random from the existing population at that generation. Randomly selected subtrees were swapped between p_1 and p_2 to generate two intermediate offspring, say o_1 and o_2. Both crossover points are selected in an unbiased manner, i.e., there was no bias towards selecting function nodes more often than terminal nodes as in [Koza, 1992]. If either of the two intermediate offspring violated the size constraint $L_{\max} = 50$ it was considered infeasible. If only one intermediate offspring was feasible, it became p_1's offspring. If both the intermediate offspring were feasible, then one was selected at random to become the offspring. An equal probability of selecting functions and terminal nodes for crossover coupled with an upper limit of $L_{\max}$ nodes provided a parsimony bias to the crossover operator.

• The strong and weak versions of the random mate crossover, *CrossSHC* and *CrossWHC*, were inspired by the headless-chicken crossover operators in [Angeline, 1997a; Angeline, 1997b]. These operators exchanged randomly selected subtrees between the parent, p_1, and a randomly generated mate, p_2, to obtain two intermediate offspring, say o_1 and o_2. The randomly generated mate, p_2, comprised a randomly selected parent, say p', from the population that was subsequently modified through the application of *AllNodes*. Thus, p_2, had the structure of the parent p' but any "content information" was completely randomized. *CrossSHC* returned the intermediate offspring that had the same root node as p_1 whereas *CrossWHC* returned one of the two intermediate offspring at random. If the intermediate offspring to be returned by *CrossWHC* violated the size constraint, then the other offspring which would definitely be feasible was returned. On the other hand, if the offspring to be returned by *CrossSHC* violated the size constraint, the process was repeated by regenerating a new set of intermediate offspring through the selection of different crossover points.

9.4.3 Parent selection

EP-style tournament selection [Fogel, 1995] with ten opponents was applied to select the parents for the next generation: Every program in the population was compared with ten randomly selected opponents out of the population. For each comparison in which the program's fitness was better or equal, it received a win. The better half of the population with the largest number of wins became the parents for the next generation. This process of variation and selection was repeated every generation for a predefined number of generations, $k_{\max}$.

9.4.4 Test problems

Our experiments were conducted on a suite of four problems: the 6-bit multiplexer problem, the artificial ant problem (Santa Fe trail), the cart centering problem, and the sunspot modeling problem. Brief descriptions of these problems follow. For a more detailed description the reader is referred to [Koza, 1992] and [Angeline, 1996].

The goal of the 6-multiplexer [Koza, 1992] problem is to find a computer program consisting of primitive Boolean functions, namely not, and, or, and if, that computes the output of a four-input two-select multiplexer. The fitness of an individual is the number of correct outputs that the program generates when tested on all the 64 possible inputs. A successful program correctly maps all 64 inputs to their corresponding outputs.

In the artificial ant problem, the goal is to evolve a computer program that would act as a move generating rule for guiding an ant to find all food packets lying on an irregular trail. The "Santa Fe trail" [Koza, 1992] containing 89 food items was used. The function and terminal sets were {left, right, move} and {If-food-ahead, Prog2, Prog3}, respectively. A move rule was considered to be successful if it could guide the ant to collect all 89 food packets on the trail.

The cart centering problem requires the discovery of a control law that centers a cart that is free to move to the left or right on a frictionless surface. The terminal set consisted of the two state variables of the system (the position x and the velocity $\dot{x}$) whereas the function set was $\{+, -, *, \%, \text{abs}, \text{gt}\}$. At any given time, the control law determined the direction of a force (of 1.0 N) to be applied. The total time needed to center the cart from a set of twenty initial states $(x, \dot{x})$ selected uniformly at random from $[-0.75, 0.75]^2$ were used to compute the quality of the control law in centering the cart. The set of initial states was kept fixed during evolution. A trial was considered to be successful if a control law was found that could center the cart with a total time that was within 1% of the total time taken by the mathematically solution that is optimal over $[-\infty, \infty]^2$. The cart was considered to be centered when $\sqrt{x^2 + \dot{x}^2} < 0.1$. Each controller was given a maximum of 10 seconds (500 steps of 0.02 seconds each) to center the cart. Any control law that failed to center the cart within this time was given a time score of 10 seconds.

Table 9.2
Computational effort results for the artificial ant, 6-bit multiplexer, cart centering, and sunspot modeling problems using all variations operators, V_{all}. Computation effort analysis indicates that $R(z)$ number of independent trials, each lasting N generations, need to be conducted with a population size of $M(= 500)$, to achieve a success probability of $z = 0.99$, resulting in a total of $I(M, N, z)$ number of individuals being processed (see [Koza, 1992] for further details). (∗) indicates that all trials were successful and the results correspond to $z = 1.0$. The first two columns give the mean fitness and the corresponding standard deviation of the fitness at generation 200.

	Mean	sd	N	$R(z)$	$I(M, N, z)$
Artificial Ant	89	0	143	1	72,000*
6-bit Multiplexer	64	0	104	1	52,500*
Cart Centering	38.990	5.012	155	1	78,000*
Sunspot Modeling	2991.03	384.82			——

The goal of the sunspot series modeling problem is to compute the average number of sunspots observed in year y using the average number of sunspots observed in the years $y - 1$, $y - 2$, $y - 4$, and $y - 8$, denoted by S_{y-1}, S_{y-2}, S_{y-4}, S_{y-8}, respectively. Sunspot data from the years 1700 to 1989 containing 290 samples were used as the training set. The terminal set was $\{S_{y-1}, S_{y-2}, S_{y-4}, S_{y-8}$, numeric constants$\}$. The functions set was $\{+, -, *, \%, \sin, \cos\}$. The mean square error over the 290 samples in the training set was taken to be the error score of the individual. The ability of the solutions to generalize was not considered: We only judged how well the solutions fitted the data set and not, as should be done in real world application, how well the solution really modeled the time series.

9.4.5 Experiments

Parent and offspring fitness data were collected in every generation, for each application of every operator, on each of the four problems, over 50 independent trials of the above described algorithm. Each trial used a population size of 500 and evolution lasted for $k_{max} = 200$ generations. The collected data were used to estimate the FD features in Table 9.1 of the eleven different operators.

9.5 Results

All 50 artificial ant and 6-bit multiplexer trials were successful by generations 143 and 104, respectively. The sum squared error on the sunspot modeling problem quickly decreases in the first 75 generations. Even at generation 200, when the trials were terminated, the sum squared error continues to decrease as models and parameters that better fit the training data are found. This does not necessarily imply that the found solutions are better models of the time series, because they may overfit the training data (the same holds for the cart centering results). At the end of 200 generations, the mean best sum squared error (over all 50 trials) was 2991.03 with a standard deviation of 384.82. It appears that models with higher fitness

Table 9.3
Mean cumulative FD features (averaged over all generations and 50 independent trials) on the 6-bit multiplexer problem for the different variation operators used to generate offspring in an evolutionary programming procedure for evolving computer programs. These seven fitness distribution features are absolute change in fitness (AC), expected improvement (EI), improvement probability (IP), silent variation probability (SVP), worsening probability (WP), fitness correlation coefficient (FCC), and global improvement probability (IP*). The values in parentheses indicate the rank of the operator in terms of the FD feature. Smaller ranks imply a larger FD feature value. All differences in feature values were statistically significant ($p < 0.05$) except for those marked by daggers: (†) indicates that the difference between the table entry and the next higher ranking entry in the same column were not statistically significant.

	AC	EI	IP	SVP	WP	FCC	IP*/10^{-3}
OneNode	$4.32^{(7)}$	$-4.25^{(3)}$	$0.013^{(3)}$	$0.371^{(2)}$	$0.616^{(8)}$	$0.759^{(2)}$	$0.126^{(3)†}$
AllNodes	$24.53^{(1)}$	$-24.48^{(9)}$	$0.005^{(8)}$	$0.007^{(9)}$	$0.988^{(1)}$	$0.045^{(9)}$	$0.022^{(9)}$
Swap	$3.75^{(9)}$	$-3.73^{(1)}$	$0.004^{(9)}$	$0.678^{(1)}$	$0.319^{(9)}$	$0.596^{(3)}$	$0.037^{(8)†}$
Grow	$4.28^{(8)}$	$-4.16^{(2)}$	$0.023^{(2)}$	$0.341^{(3)}$	$0.636^{(7)}$	$0.855^{(1)}$	$0.168^{(2)†}$
Trunc	$7.55^{(4)}$	$-7.48^{(6)}$	$0.012^{(5)}$	$0.287^{(6)}$	$0.701^{(4)}$	$0.495^{(6)}$	$0.098^{(5)†}$
Macro	$18.74^{(2)}$	$-18.68^{(8)}$	$0.008^{(7)}$	$0.098^{(8)}$	$0.894^{(2)}$	$0.174^{(8)}$	$0.038^{(7)†}$
CrossU	$6.77^{(5)}$	$-6.62^{(5)}$	$0.027^{(1)}$	$0.328^{(5)}$	$0.645^{(6)}$	$0.513^{(5)}$	$0.176^{(1)†}$
CrossWHC	$15.98^{(3)}$	$-15.92^{(7)}$	$0.009^{(6)}$	$0.154^{(7)}$	$0.837^{(3)}$	$0.216^{(7)}$	$0.078^{(6)}$
CrossSHC	$6.06^{(6)}$	$-5.99^{(4)}$	$0.013^{(3)}$	$0.333^{(4)}$	$0.654^{(5)}$	$0.583^{(4)}$	$0.110^{(4)†}$

Table 9.4
Mean cumulative fitness distribution features on the artificial ant problem

	AC	EI	IP	SVP	WP	FCC	IP*/10^{-3}
OneNode	$37.09^{(6)}$	$-36.99^{(4)}$	$0.009^{(3)}$	$0.423^{(2)}$	$0.569^{(7)}$	$0.325^{(4)}$	$2.154^{(2)†}$
AllNodes	$74.04^{(1)}$	$-73.99^{(9)}$	$0.006^{(9)}$	$0.003^{(9)}$	$0.991^{(1)}$	$-0.012^{(9)}$	$2.005^{(6)†}$
Swap	$39.74^{(4)}$	$-39.66^{(6)}$	$0.008^{(5)}$	$0.405^{(4)}$	$0.587^{(5)}$	$0.295^{(6)}$	$1.898^{(8)}$
Grow	$35.95^{(8)†}$	$-35.80^{(2)}$	$0.016^{(2)}$	$0.405^{(4)}$	$0.579^{(6)}$	$0.363^{(1)}$	$4.668^{(1)}$
Trunc	$39.25^{(5)}$	$-39.16^{(5)}$	$0.008^{(5)}$	$0.392^{(6)}$	$0.600^{(4)}$	$0.308^{(5)}$	$1.655^{(9)}$
Macro	$66.07^{(2)}$	$-66.01^{(8)}$	$0.007^{(7)}$	$0.087^{(8)}$	$0.906^{(2)}$	$0.115^{(8)}$	$2.048^{(3)†}$
CrossU	$35.81^{(9)}$	$-35.35^{(1)}$	$0.028^{(1)}$	$0.412^{(3)}$	$0.560^{(9)}$	$0.329^{(2)†}$	$2.045^{(4)†}$
CrossWHC	$57.42^{(3)}$	$-57.35^{(7)}$	$0.007^{(7)}$	$0.193^{(7)}$	$0.801^{(3)}$	$0.178^{(7)}$	$1.909^{(7)†}$
CrossSHC	$36.75^{(7)}$	$-36.65^{(3)}$	$0.009^{(3)}$	$0.429^{(1)}$	$0.562^{(8)}$	$0.327^{(3)†}$	$2.032^{(5)†}$

Table 9.5
Mean cumulative FD features on the cart centering problem

	AC	EI	IP	SVP	WP	FCC	IP*/10^{-3}
OneNode	$39.46^{(7)}$	$-39.19^{(3)}$	$0.012^{(3)}$	$0.274^{(3)}$	$0.714^{(7)}$	$0.309^{(3)}$	$0.185^{(4)}$
AllNodes	$137.10^{(1)}$	$-136.90^{(9)}$	$0.004^{(8)}$	$0.007^{(9)}$	$0.988^{(1)}$	$0.063^{(9)}$	$0.027^{(9)}$
Swap	$26.25^{(9)}$	$-26.14^{(1)}$	$0.004^{(8)}$	$0.712^{(1)}$	$0.285^{(9)}$	$0.354^{(2)}$	$0.031^{(8)†}$
Grow	$37.12^{(8)}$	$-36.38^{(2)}$	$0.027^{(2)}$	$0.277^{(2)}$	$0.696^{(8)}$	$0.484^{(1)}$	$0.523^{(1)}$
Trunc	$49.85^{(4)}$	$-49.61^{(6)}$	$0.010^{(5)}$	$0.193^{(6)}$	$0.797^{(4)}$	$0.270^{(6)}$	$0.128^{(5)†}$
Macro	$93.69^{(3)}$	$-93.48^{(7)}$	$0.006^{(7)}$	$0.167^{(7)}$	$0.826^{(3)}$	$0.145^{(7)}$	$0.087^{(7)}$
CrossU	$45.46^{(5)}$	$-44.77^{(5)}$	$0.034^{(1)}$	$0.200^{(5)}$	$0.766^{(5)}$	$0.280^{(5)}$	$0.292^{(2)†}$
CrossWHC	$94.43^{(2)}$	$-94.19^{(8)}$	$0.008^{(6)}$	$0.103^{(8)}$	$0.889^{(2)}$	$0.142^{(8)}$	$0.099^{(6)†}$
CrossSHC	$43.40^{(6)}$	$-43.13^{(4)}$	$0.012^{(3)}$	$0.228^{(4)}$	$0.760^{(6)}$	$0.301^{(4)}$	$0.234^{(3)†}$

Table 9.6
Mean cumulative FD features on the sunspot modeling problem

	$AC/10^4$	EI	IP	SVP	WP	FCC	$IP^*/10^{-3}$
OneNode	$10.90^{(5)}$	$-109000.0^{(7)}$	$0.137^{(5)}$	$0.029^{(4)}$	$0.834^{(7)}$	$0.066^{(6)}$†	$0.990^{(4)}$†
OneC	$0.00432^{(11)}$	$-30.13^{(1)}$	$0.340^{(1)}$	$0.149^{(2)}$	$0.511^{(10)}$	$0.998^{(1)}$	$1.676^{(2)}$
AllC	$0.01091^{(10)}$	$-70.85^{(2)}$	$0.300^{(2)}$	$0.032^{(3)}$	$0.667^{(9)}$	$0.984^{(2)}$	$2.126^{(1)}$
AllNodes	$52.25^{(1)}$	$-521400.0^{(11)}$	$0.009^{(11)}$	$0.000^{(11)}$	$0.991^{(1)}$	$-0.066^{(11)}$	$0.006^{(11)}$
Swap	$3.42^{(9)}$	$-33970.0^{(3)}$	$0.033^{(10)}$	$0.554^{(1)}$	$0.412^{(11)}$	$0.175^{(3)}$	$0.144^{(10)}$
Grow	$11.96^{(4)}$	$-119000.0^{(8)}$	$0.149^{(3)}$	$0.023^{(8)}$	$0.828^{(8)}$	$0.086^{(5)}$	$0.859^{(6)}$†
Trunc	$6.55^{(8)}$	$-64810.0^{(4)}$	$0.110^{(7)}$	$0.026^{(5)}$	$0.864^{(4)}$	$0.093^{(4)}$†	$0.683^{(7)}$
Macro	$28.62^{(3)}$	$-285400.0^{(9)}$	$0.062^{(9)}$	$0.026^{(5)}$	$0.912^{(3)}$	$-0.009^{(9)}$†	$0.431^{(9)}$
CrossU	$8.01^{(7)}$	$-78760.0^{(5)}$	$0.141^{(4)}$	$0.013^{(9)}$	$0.846^{(6)}$	$0.041^{(8)}$	$1.062^{(3)}$†
CrossWHC	$29.53^{(2)}$	$-294300.0^{(10)}$	$0.063^{(8)}$†	$0.012^{(10)}$	$0.925^{(2)}$	$-0.012^{(10)}$	$0.490^{(8)}$†
CrossSHC	$10.09^{(6)}$	$-100500.0^{(6)}$	$0.125^{(6)}$	$0.025^{(7)}$†	$0.850^{(5)}$	$0.061^{(7)}$	$0.960^{(5)}$†

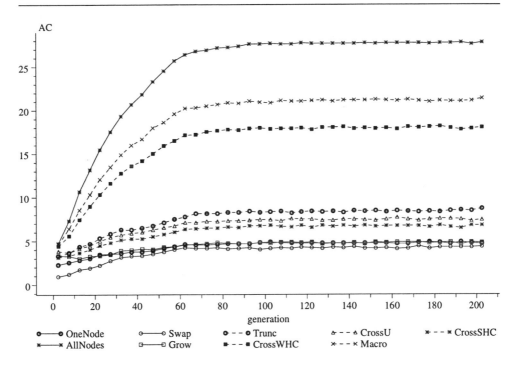

Figure 9.1
Expected absolute change, $AC_v(t)$, on the 6-bit multiplexer problem. As evolution progresses, the amount of change generated by an operator increases. In view of the fact that the maximum fitness is 64 and that randomly selected individuals in the search space have a mean fitness around 32, the *AllNodes* operator almost completely degenerates the solutions to random samples from the search space. The AC values for *AllNodes* are followed by those of *Macro*, *CrossWHC*, *Trunc*, *CrossU*, *CrossSHC*, *CrossSHC*, *Grow*, *OneNode*, and *Swap*. The lowest AC values for Swap were generated due to a large percentage of silent variations (see Figure 9.6).

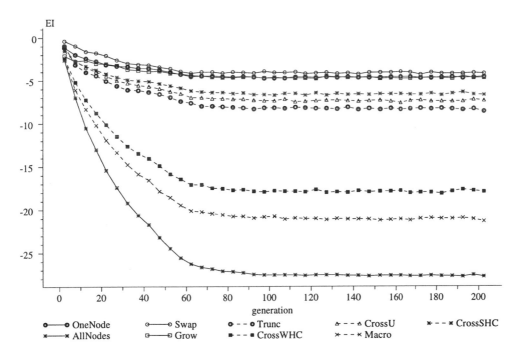

Figure 9.2
Expected improvement, $EI_v(t)$, on the 6-bit multiplexer problem. The EI ranking of the operators are exactly opposite to the AC ranking indicating that on the multiplexer problem small changes in fitness were likely to lead to greater improvement, i.e. in this case lesser degradation.

are likely to be found if evolution were continued beyond 200 generations. In the cart centering problem, the mathematically optimal rule centered the cart in roughly 2.0088 seconds [Chellapilla, 1997]. We observe that our algorithm consistently found solutions that were better than the optimal solution. The reason for this was that the mathematically optimal solution is optimal over initial states $(x, \dot{x})$ in $[-\infty, \infty]^2$ and not over the subset $[0.75, 0.75]^2$. Detailed analysis of the cart centering problem may be found in [Chellapilla, 1997]. By generation 155, all 50 cart centering trials were successful. The computational effort results of the four test problems are presented in Table 9.2.

Figures 9.1–9.7 graph the binned, generation dependent values of the seven features of the FD for the 6-bit multiplexer problem. The corresponding graphs for the artificial ant problem were very similar. The curves for the cart centering and sunspot modeling problems were similar to each other but differed from those for discrete problems. Where necessary, some figures for the sunspot modeling problem have been included.

In order to obtain smoother graphs that were easier to interpret, these feature values were distributed into consecutive bins five generations wide and the mean value in each bin was

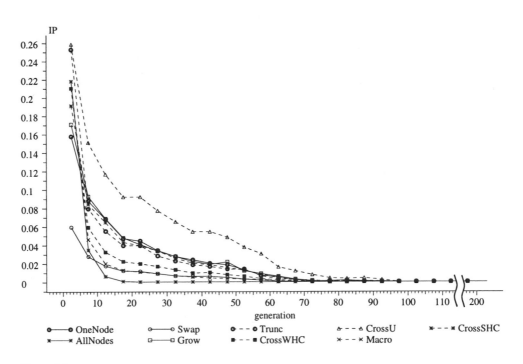

Figure 9.3
Probability of improvement, $IP_v(t)$, on the 6-bit multiplexer problem. Among the operators investigated, the *CrossU* operator produces significantly higher IP values and is followed by the *Grow* operator.

plotted as a function of the middle generation of the bin. It is interesting to note that all the smoothened FD curves, with the exception of the IP* and some FCC curves, for the various operators maintain a relatively consistent ranking throughout evolution indicating that the FD features were identifying properties intrinsic to these variation operators. Operators that generated relatively large values of these features during initial phases of evolution continued to do so till the end of the evolutionary process. The relative ranking of these operators on different problems also appears to be similar.

The AC curves (Figure 9.1) start out small during the first few generations and gradually increase and attain their highest values towards the end of the trial. Similarly, the EI curves start out high and progressively drop down to low values (see Figure 9.2). Further, the expected improvement was always negative for all four problems. In comparison with the EI results on optimization problems in the continuous domain [Fogel and Ghozeil, 1996] where positive EI values are common, program evolution problems appear to be much more difficult.

Figure 9.8 shows the IP graph for the sunspot modeling problem. Similar to the EI values in the first few generations the IP values (Figures 9.3 and 9.8) start out high and quickly

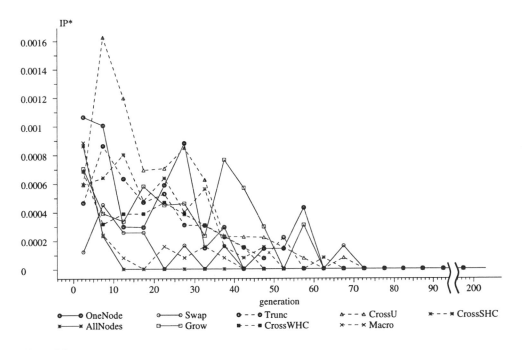

Figure 9.4
Global improvement probability, IP$_v^*(t)$, on the 6-bit multiplexer problem. *CrossU*, *OneNode*, and *Grow* appear to produce the most global improvements, while *AllNodes* and *Macro* generate the lowest number of global improvements.

decrease. The initial IP values were relatively lower on the discrete problems (ant, mux) than those for continuous the problems (cart, sunspot). The rate of decrease was also much higher on discrete problems than on the continuous problems. On continuous optimization problems gradual changes in fitness values are possible. This gradual change in fitness and error scores allows evolutionary search to generate frequent enhancements resulting in higher IP values.

The WP curves were completely determined by the IP and SVP curves. When the IP values were low and the SVP values were high (e.g. on the ant, mux, and cart problems) the WP curves were inverted versions of the SVP curves, whereas when the IP values were high and the SVP values were low (e.g. on the sunspot problem) the WP curves were inverted versions of the IP curves.

On all four problems, every operator generated global improvements in at least one generation. Of all the features, the IP* was directly related to the rate of finding good solutions of the algorithm especially when the range of the objective function is discrete and bounded. For example, on the 6-bit multiplexer problem, there are just 64 possible test

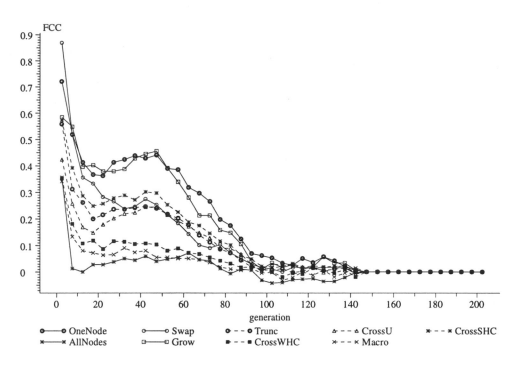

Figure 9.5
Fitness correlation coefficient, $FCC_v(t)$, on the 6-bit multiplexer problem. The FCC values decrease because it becomes progressively difficult to generate offspring that have a fitness close to the parents fitness as the parent fitness increases.

cases that determine the fitness and the minimum improvement in fitness is one point. This implies that at most 64 global improvements per individual can be generated before finding an optimal solution.

The IP* graphs for the sunspot problem are shown in Figure 9.9. On continuous problems high IP* values should also occur with high EI values. Unfortunately, global improvements occur very rarely, the IP* probabilities are orders of magnitude lower than corresponding IP values. Hence, it is difficult to obtain significant results and therefore it is problematic to rely on IP* as a measure for estimating operator usefulness.

On finding the global best solution all IP* values fall to zero. As a result, the IP* curves for the mux and ant problems reached zero at generations 104 and 143, respectively. The IP* curves for the cart centering and sunspot modeling problems show persistent changes even at the end of the trials, indicating that if evolution is continued further solutions with higher fitness will be obtained.

On the discrete problems (ant and mux) the FCC curves (Figure 9.5) started out high, rapidly fell in the first ten generations, then increased, peaked, and finally gradually de-

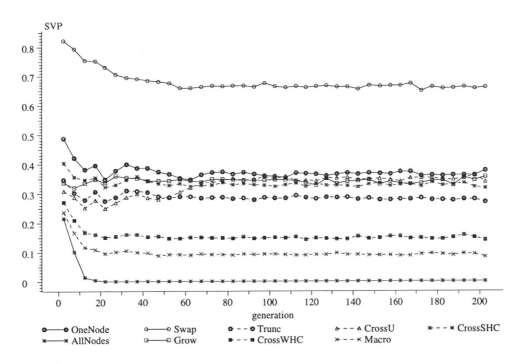

Figure 9.6
Probability of silent variations, $SVP_v(t)$, on the 6-bit multiplexer problem. The high SVP values for the *Swap* operator were caused by the commutative boolean functions (and, or). *AllNodes* had the lowest SVP values followed by *Macro* (which probabilistically uses *AllNodes*) and *CrossWHC*. After the first 15 generations the SVP values undergo little change.

creased resulting in a hump during generations 10–70. Towards the end of the runs the FCC values became very small and reached zero. On the continuous problems (cart and sunspot) the FCC curves for all operators, with the exception of those for the *OneC* and *AllC*, rapidly fell down to very low (< 0.15) values indicating that there was no correlation between the parent and offspring fitnesses and the relative ranking of the various operators juggled rapidly. This lack of correlation appears to be caused by large changes in fitness and error scores between the parent and offspring. On the contrary, the *OneC* and *AllC* operators used in the sunspot modeling problem, produced small changes in the sum squared error and consequently exhibited large FCC values close to one. Overall, we did not find that the FCC predicted interesting characteristics of the operators that were not already captured by the other FD features.

For all operators with the exception of *CrossU*, the SVP values showed a slight decrease in the initial stages of evolution and remained nearly constant in subsequent generations, see Figure 9.6. For *CrossU* we measured a slight increase in later generations. Not surpris-

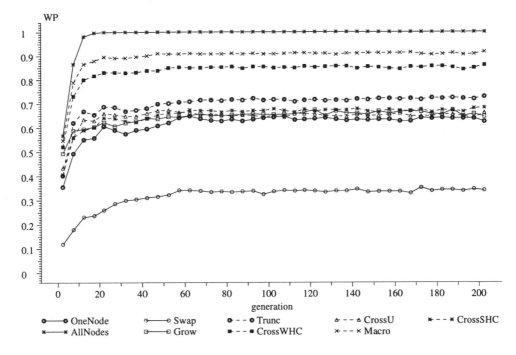

Figure 9.7
Probability of worsening, $WP_v(t)$, on the 6-bit multiplexer problem. The WP was lowest for the *Swap* operator to due the large number of silent variations it generates (see Figure 9.6). On the other hand, the WP for *AllNodes* reaches 1.0 after generation 25 and stays there throughout evolution, depicting its extremely destructive nature. The high WP values for *AllNodes* are followed by those for *Macro* (which probabilistically uses *AllNodes*) and *CrossWHC*. For most of the operators, due to the really low IP values (see Figure 9.3), the WP curves are simply the inverted version of the $SVP_v(t)$ curves in Figure 9.6.

ingly, the *Swap* operator generated really high (SVP > 0.65) rates of silent variations when commutative functions were present in the function set. *AllNodes* did not generate any silent variations after generation 20 in any of the four problems studied here. *Macro* and *CrossSHC* generated very few silent variations. All remaining operators generated silent variations in one out of every three times they were applied when numeric constants were not included in the terminal set. However, when numeric constants were included in the terminal set, the rate of silent variations for these operators were considerably lower (< 0.1). In symbolic regression problems, when numeric constants are also evolved, the range space typically spans the whole real line or a dense subset of the real line. The likelihood of these remaining operators generating changes to the symbolic expression that produce no change in the fitness falls and silent variations become less probable, especially in the absence of conditionals such as if.

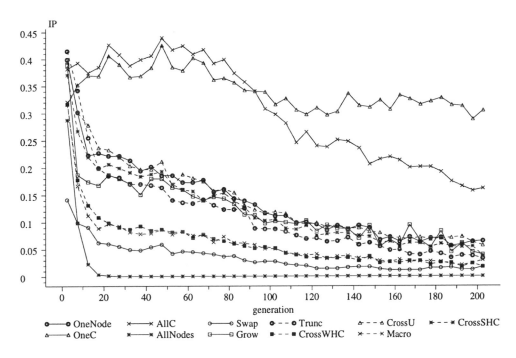

Figure 9.8
Probability of improvement, IP$_v(t)$, on the sunspot problem. In the first 100 generations *AllC* generates the highest IP values and is closely followed by *OneC*. However, during the later stages of evolution, as would be expected *OneC* generates larger IP, values indicating that smaller changes are preferable in the later stages of evolution. *OneNode* and *CrossU* also produce relatively high IP$_v(t)$ values and are closely followed by the *Grow* operator.

As expected, all the FD features indicate that as evolution progresses it becomes increasingly difficult to find better solutions.

As the relative ranking of the operators varied only very slightly on all four problems during evolution, the cumulative FD features, averaged over all generations and all trials, can be used as a concise and useful measure for analyzing the properties of the examined variation operators. These cumulative FD features for the eleven variation operators on the four test problems are presented in Tables 9.3, 9.4, 9.5, and 9.6, respectively. The relative ranking of each operator on each cumulative feature is also presented in these tables. For all FD features, lower ranks imply a larger feature value.

Most differences in AC, EI, IP, SVP, WP, and FCC were statistically significant. The number of global improvements were very few in comparison with the number of samples collected over all 50 trials and as a result the IP* differences were mostly statistically not significant.

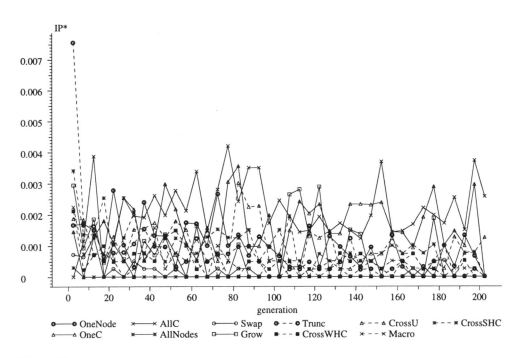

Figure 9.9
Global improvement probability, $IP_v^*(t)$, on the sunspot modeling problem. *OneC* and *AllC* generated far higher global improvements indicating importance of evolving appropriate constants during evolution. *OneNode*, *Grow*, and *CrossU* also appear to generate relatively large IP* values. Because global improvements occur rarely, the generation dependent IP* plots are very noisy and not very informative.

In the experiments without numeric constants, *OneNode* performs the smallest structural change in the genotype with respect to the tree edit distance [O'Reilly, 1997]. In view of this, it was considered to be a rather local search operator with most applications of the operator resulting in small changes in fitness and error scores, i.e. small AC values. However, the results show that it ranked higher (with larger AC values) than *Swap* and *Grow* operators on three of the four problems, and occasionally ranked higher than *CrossU*, *CrossSHC*, and *Trunc*. Thus, contrary to what was initially expected, the changes in the fitness space produced by *OneNode* were not small. Furthermore, it consistently ranked third in terms of IP and between second and fourth in terms of IP*.

The *AllNodes* operator had the lowest rate of silent mutations and the highest probability of worsening in all test problems. It generated a less fit offspring nearly every time it was applied with cumulative WP values of 0.998, 0.991, 0.988 and 0.991 on the four problems. It almost never generated silent variations with cumulative SVP values of 0.007, 0.003, 0.007 and zero on the four problems. Additionally, *AllNodes* had the lowest EI values on all four problems. The FCC scores close to zero indicate that there was no linear correlation between parental and offspring fitness when *AllNodes* was used to generate offspring. The only similarity between the offspring generated using *AllNodes* and the corresponding parent is the shape of the parse tree. The *AllNodes* results indicate that the spatial structure, i.e. the shape of the parse tree without its labels, carries negligible information about the quality of the computer program. *AllNodes* rarely generated any offspring that were better than the best parent in that generation and as a result ranked last (mux, cart, sunspot) or third last (artificial ant) in terms of IP*. On all four problems after the first 30 generations the *AllNodes* operator never generated any global enhancements. Similarly, after 30 generations, on the mux, ant, and cart centering problems, the *AllNodes* operator never generated any improvements or silent variations, i.e., the IP, SVP, and WP values were zero, zero, and one.

The *Swap* operator had the highest number of silent variations on the mux, cart centering, and sunspot modeling problems. This was caused by the function sets for these problems containing commutative functions such as and, or (mux), $+$, and $*$ (cart and sunspot), wherein swapping the order of the arguments did not produce any change in the behavior and the corresponding fitness of the program. As a result, in two out of three applications, the *Swap* operator generated no change in fitness. For the same reason, on these problems, *Swap* ranked last in terms of WP, and had poor IP values. However, as would be expected, the corresponding EI values that were negative moved closer to zero resulting in the *Swap* operator ranking highest on the EI curves. On the artificial ant problem, none of the functions in the function set, $\{$If-food-ahead, Prog2, Prog3$\}$, were commutative and as a result, *Swap* ranked fourth in terms of silent variations, and fifth in terms of IP and WP (smaller ranks imply larger feature values). Over all four problems, the *Swap* operator rarely produced offspring that did better than the population-best at that generation and ranked next to *AllNodes* in terms of IP*.

The *Grow* operator had the highest FCC score on the ant, mux, and cart problems. On these problems, it ranked first (ant and cart) or second (mux) in generating offspring that were better than the best parent at that generation (i.e. in terms of IP*). *Grow* consistently ranked second in terms of the IP and EI. Thus, on the first three problems, the *Grow* operator appears to be very efficient in generating better solutions. On the sunspot problem, the performance of *Grow* in terms of IP*, IP, and EI was average. Except for the sunspot problem, *Grow* ranked eighth in terms of AC, i.e. led to small changes in the fitness space most of the time. Taking into consideration that *Grow* is the only structure changing operator in our investigation that is solely applied to the leaves of the trees, these results coincide with the hypothesis in [Rosca and Ballard, 1995] that the longer the path from the application point of a variation to the root node the less is the probability of large changes in the fitness. The *Grow* operator, i.e. adding code at the leaves of a tree, showed a comparatively low probability of worsening. The effect that on average growing is less destructive than pruning is one reason for the observed code growth in GP.

In the sunspot series modeling problem, the *OneC* and *AllC* operators ranked highest in terms of the IP, EI, FCC, and IP* features. As would be expected *OneC* generated changes that were more local than those generated using *AllC*. As a result, *OneC* ranked higher than *AllC* in terms of the IP, EI and FCC, whereas *AllC* ranked better in terms of IP*. The results show that on symbolic regression problems that involve numeric constants, most of the global improvements are generated by operators used to evolve constants. Structure optimization is obviously harder than parameter adaptation.

It is very important to have operators that can efficiently evolve not only the structure of the symbolic expression but also the right set of constants in the solution. The *OneC* and *AllC* operators appear to be well suited for optimizing such constants during evolution. Most of the changes generated by *OneC* and *AllC*, as depicted by their AC values, were orders of magnitude lower than those generated by all other operators. In the first 100 generations *AllC* generated the highest IP values and was closely followed by *OneC*. However, during the later stages of evolution, as would be expected *OneC* generates larger IP values indicating that smaller changes were preferred in the later stages of evolution.

The *CrossU* operator had the highest IP values on the ant, mux, and cart problems and the differences between the IP values for *CrossU* and the other operators on these problems were statistically significant. In terms of IP*, it ranked first on the artificial ant and mux problems, second on the cart centering, and third on the sunspot problems. Moreover, *CrossU* had the highest expected improvement on the ant problem, and ranked fifth in terms of EI, on the mux, cart, and sunspot problems. The large IP* and IP values indicate that the *CrossU* operator is well suited for generating, with a high probability, offspring, that are better both than their parents and the population-best parent. Consequently *CrossU* appears to be a useful operator on the four problems tested here. Encouraged by the good results, we ran the algorithm described in Section 9.4 with *CrossU* as the only operator used for variation. Again, 50 runs were conducted per test problem. The results are shown in Table 9.7. As the good FD values indicated, the algorithm showed very good performance, not only compared to the results in Table 9.2. Although *CrossU* can be used as the only search operator, this setting does not fulfill the conditions necessary for the theoretical convergence property briefly mentioned in the introduction.

The *CrossSHC* showed consistent above average FD results (this coincides with the good performance shown in [Angeline, 1997a; Angeline, 1997b] and in own experiments) and the *Trunc* operator ranked below average on most features while the *Macro* and *CrossWHC* operators performed poorly on all four problems, but were always better than *AllNodes*. This poor performance of *Macro* which probabilistically uses *AllNodes* appears to be caused by the extremely destructive nature of *AllNodes*.

Most of the differences between the FD features of the headless-chicken operators, i.e. *CrossSHC* and *CrossWHC*, and *CrossU*, were statistically significant. This indicates different dynamics of these closely related operators.

Table 9.7
Computational effort results for the artificial ant, 6-bit multiplexer and cart centering problem using only crossover. The population size was 500 in all the trials. The computational effort corresponds to $z = .99$ except for the multiplexer problem where all runs were successful by generation 56 and the result corresponds to $z = 1.0$. Two of the artificial ant runs failed to find an optimal solution by generation 200 and only 41 of the 50 cart centering trials were successful by generation 200. The reason why not all of the ant and cart centering trials were successful may be premature convergence due to the exclusion of mutation.

	Mean	sd	N	R(z)	I(M, N, z)
Artificial Ant	88.4	3.71	59	2	60,000
6-bit Multiplexer	64	0	56	1	28,500*
Cart Centering	38.00	4.91	1	19	19,000
Sunspot Modeling	2987.5	431.57		———	

9.6 Discussion

When evolutionary search is conducted through the use of a set of variation operators, in the most general case, the performance of the algorithm is determined not only by the effects generated by each operator but also by the interactions between these constituent operators. Operators that perform well when used alone might not work constructively when used together. On the other hand, certain operators might synergistically interact with other operators resulting in enhanced performance.

Some operators may not be able to traverse the whole search space of desired computer programs. For example, among the operators investigated, the *OneNode*, *AllNodes*, *Swap*, *Grow*, *Trunc*, *OneC*, and *AllC*, are not capable of searching the entire program tree space when used alone. In such cases there is a need for the design of suites of operators that can traverse the whole program space.

As it is desirable to find as good a solution as possible in reasonable time, operators that simultaneously generate large IP, EI, and IP* values over successive generations are needed. Operators such as *AllNodes* that rarely or never generate offspring better than their parents and the population-best parent may be excluded from the set of operators. However, these FD features do not describe all necessary properties of an EA. For example, operators that show good rates of improvement may increase the speed of the search process but on the other hand may decrease the solution quality due to the loss of diversity in the population which might lead to premature convergence when using certain operators.

Operators such as *Swap* that mostly generate silent variations may be acting as catalysts enhancing the performance of other operators. It might therefore be more appropriate to use them with a lower probability than completely excluding them. Furthermore, efficient evolutionary computations may be designed by varying the probabilities of using various operators such that small changes in fitness are produced more often and large changes are produced less often.

The above analysis of the fitness distributions features indicates that *CrossU*, *Grow*, and *CrossSHC* possess a high probability of generating beneficial variations and variation may be generated by selecting these operators more often. The performance of the *Macro* operator may be enhanced by (a) dropping *AllNodes* form the set of operators used during an application of the *Macro* operator (V_{Macro}), and (b) decreasing the probability of using *Swap*. The *CrossWHC* operator is better suited for exploration and its probability of application may be decreased.

Results from the FD analysis may enable us to tune the evolutionary search, e.g. to make it more exploitative or exploratory. The off-line results of the FD analysis can be used to improve the performance of an EA for program induction, as shown briefly by improving the search performance of the used algorithm by using just one operator that showed over average good FD values. However, the FD of an operator may potentially vary with the set of variation operators being used with it. Additionally, it may depend on the composition of the population (as in the case of crossover).

Instead of an iterated procedure of off-line FD analysis followed by a subsequent change in design of the evolutionary algorithm and further experimentation, the FD analysis may be used on-line. In such an approach the FD results from the previous generation(s) would guide the usage of various operators in subsequent generation(s). Overviews of operator adaptation in GAs can be found in [Tuson and Ross, 1998; Smith and Fogarty, 1997]. The design of such on-line FD analysis tools and procedures in GP remains an area of further research.

9.7 Conclusion

Fitness distributions (FDs) have been utilized as tools for understanding the behavior and dynamics of variation operators when evolving computer programs represented as parse trees. A set of seven dynamic FD features has been proposed that describes the effects of variation operators during evolution. Using these FD features, the behavior of eleven different single- and multi-parent operators has been analyzed on four common benchmark problems. Results indicate that these FD features help us to empirically investigate the dynamic behavior of various operators and contribute to a better understanding of how these variation operators work. Instructive examples were found that show that certain assumptions, such as that *OneNode* generates small changes most of the time or *AllNodes* is useful for search, may not hold. Such enhanced understanding of operator effects may enable us to choose (problem dependent) the appropriate evolutionary algorithm to obtain better solutions and reduce computation time. Future work will be directed towards designing both off-line and on-line methods of incorporating the knowledge obtained from FD analysis for the design of more efficient evolutionary computations.

Acknowledgments

The authors would like to thank M. Kreutz, B. Sendhoff, and P. Stagge for their stimulating discussions and D. B. Fogel for his valuable comments on the work. Christian Igel would like to acknowledge support from the BMBF under grant SONN II 01IB701A0.

Bibliography

Altenberg, L. (1994), "The evolution of evolvability in genetic programming," in *Advances in Genetic Programming*, K. E. Kinnear, Jr. (Ed.), Chapter 3, pp 47–74, MIT Press.

Altenberg, L. (1995), "The Schema Theorem and Price's Theorem," in *Foundations of Genetic Algorithms 3*, L. D. Whitley and M. D. Vose (Eds.), pp 23–49, Estes Park, Colorado: Morgan Kaufmann.

Angeline, P. J. (1996), "An investigation into the sensitivity of genetic programming to the frequency of leaf selection during subtree crossover," in *Genetic Programming 1996: Proceedings of the First Annual Conference*, J. R. Koza, D. E. Goldberg, D. B. Fogel, and R. L. Riolo (Eds.), pp 21–29, Stanford University, CA: MIT Press.

Angeline, P. J. (1997a), "Comparing subtree crossover with macromutation," in *The Sixth Conference on Evolutionary Programming*, P. Angeline, R. Reynolds, J. McDonnel, and R. Eberhart (Eds.), pp 101–111, Indianapolis, Indiana: Springer-Verlag.

Angeline, P. J. (1997b), "Subtree crossover: Building block engine or macromutation?," in *Genetic Programming 1997: Proceedings of the Second Annual Conference*, J. R. Koza, K. Deb, M. Dorigo, D. B. Fogel, M. Garzon, H. Iba, and R. L. Riolo (Eds.), pp 9–17, Stanford University, CA: Morgan Kaufmann.

Bäck, T. (1996), *Evolutionary Algorithms in Theory and Practice*, Oxford University Press.

Banzhaf, W., Nordin, P., Keller, R. E., and Francone, F. D. (1998), *Genetic Programming – An Introduction; On the Automatic Evolution of Computer Programs and its Applications*, Morgan Kaufmann, dpunkt.verlag.

Chellapilla, K. (1997), "Evolutionary programming with tree mutations: Evolving computer programs without crossover," in *Genetic Programming 1997: Proceedings of the Second Annual Conference*, J. R. Koza, K. Deb, M. Dorigo, D. B. Fogel, M. Garzon, H. Iba, and R. L. Riolo (Eds.), pp 431–438, Stanford University, CA: Morgan Kaufmann.

Chellapilla, K. (1998), "Evolving computer programs without subtree crossover," *IEEE Transactions on Evolutionary Computation*, 1(3):209–216.

Chellapilla, K. and Fogel, D. B. (1998), "Revisiting evolutionary programming," in *Proceedings of the SPIE: Application and Science of Computational Intelligence*, volume 3390, pp 2–11, Orlando, Florida: SPIE – The International Society for Optical Engineering.

Fogel, D. B. (1995), *Evolutionary Computation: Toward a New Philosophy of Machine Intelligence*, IEEE Press.

Fogel, D. B. and Ghozeil, A. (1996), "Using fitness distributions to design more efficient evolutionary computations," in *Proceedings of 1996 IEEE Conference on Evolutionary Computation*, pp 11–19, Nagoya: IEEE Press.

Grefenstette, J. J. (1995), "Predictive models using fitness distributions of genetic operators," in *Foundations of Genetic Algorithms 3*, L. D. Whitley and M. D. Vose (Eds.), pp 139–161, Estes Park, Colorado: Morgan Kaufmann.

Iba, H. (1996), "Random tree generation for genetic programming," in *Parallel Problem Solving from Nature IV, Proceedings of the International Conference on Evolutionary Computation*, H.-M. Voigt, W. Ebeling, I. Rechenberg, and H.-P. Schwefel (Eds.), pp 144–153, Berlin: Springer-Verlag.

Igel, C. (1998), "Causality of hierarchical variable length representations," in *Proceedings of the 1998 IEEE International Conference on Evolutionary Computation*, pp 324–329, Anchorage, Alaska: IEEE Press.

Kinnear, Jr., K. E. (1994), "Fitness landscapes and difficulty in genetic programming," in *Proceedings of the 1994 IEEE World Conference on Computational Intelligence*, Z. Michalewicz, J. D. Schaffer, H.-P. Schwefel, D. B. Fogel, and H. Kitano (Eds.), volume 1, pp 142–147, Orlando, Florida: IEEE Press.

Koza, J. R. (1992), *Genetic Programming: On the Programming of Computers by Means of Natural Selection*, Cambridge, MA: MIT Press.

Macken, C. A. and Stadler, P. F. (1993), "Evolution on fitness landscapes," in *Lectures in Complex Systems*, L. Nadel and D. L. Stein (Eds.), Santa Fe Institute Studies in the Science of Complexity, pp 43–86, Addison-Wesley.

Manderick, B., d. Weger, M., and Spiessens, P. (1991), "The genetic algorithm and the structure of the fitness landscape," in *Proceedings of the Fourth International Conference on Genetic Algorithms*, R. K. Belew and L. B. Booker (Eds.), pp 143–150, UCSD, La Jolla, CA: Morgan Kaufmann.

Nordin, P. and Banzhaf, W. (1995), "Complexity compression and evolution," in *Proceedings of the Sixth International Conference on Genetic Algorithms*, L. J. Eshelman (Ed.), pp 310–317, Pittsburgh, PA: Morgan Kaufmann.

O'Reilly, U.-M. (1995), *An Analysis of Genetic Programming*, PhD thesis, Carleton University, Ottawa-Carleton Institute for Computer Science, Ottawa, Ontario, Canada.

O'Reilly, U.-M. (1997), "Using a distance metric on genetic programs to understand genet ic operators," in *Late Breaking Papers at the Genetic Programming 1997 Conference*, J. R. Koza (Ed.), pp 188–198, Stanford University, CA: Stanford University Bookstore.

Press, W., Teukolsky, S., Vetterling, W., and Flannery, B. (1994), *Numerical Recipes in C*, Cambridge University Press, 2nd edition.

Rechenberg, I. (1994), *Evolutionsstrategie '94*, Werkstatt Bionik und Evolutionstechnik, Stuttgart: Frommann-Holzboog.

Rosca, J. P. and Ballard, D. H. (1994), "Hierarchical self-organization in genetic programming," in *Proceedings of the Eleventh International Conference on Machine Learning*, pp 251–258, New Brunswick, NJ: Morgan Kaufmann.

Rosca, J. P. and Ballard, D. H. (1995), "Causality in genetic programming," in *Proceedings of the Sixth International Conference on Genetic Algorithms*, L. J. Eshelman (Ed.), pp 256–263, Pittsburgh, PA: Morgan Kaufmann.

Rudolph, G. (1997), *Convergence Properties of Evolutionary Algorithms*, Hamburg: Kovač.

Schwefel, H. (1995), *Evolution and Optimum Seeking*, New York: John Wiley & sons.

Sendhoff, B., Kreutz, M., and von Seelen, W. (1997), "A condition for the genotype-phenotype mapping: Causality," in *Proceedings of the Seventh International Conference on Genetic Algorithms*, T. Bäck (Ed.), pp 73–80, MSU, East Lansing, MI: Morgan Kaufmann.

Smith, J. E. and Fogarty, T. C. (1997), "Operator and parameter adaptation in genetic algorithms," *Soft Computing*, 1(2):81–87.

Tuson, A. and Ross, P. (1998), "Adapting operator settings in genetic algorithms," *Evolutionary Computation*, 6(2):161–184.

Utecht, U. and Trint, K. (1994), "Mutation operators for structure evolution of neural networks," in *Parallel Problem Solving from Nature III*, Y. Davidor, H.-P. Schwefel, and R. Männer (Eds.), pp 492–501, Jerusalem: Springer-Verlag.

Yao, X. and Liu, Y. (1996), "Fast evolutionary programming," in *Evolutionary Programming V: Proceedings of the Fifth Annual Conference on Evolutionary Programming*, L. J. Fogel, P. J. Angeline, and T. Baeck (Eds.), pp 451–460, San Diego, CA: MIT Press.

10 Analysis of Single-Node (Building) Blocks in Genetic Programming

Jason M. Daida, Robert R. Bertram, John A. Polito 2, and Stephen A. Stanhope

This chapter addresses the question "what is a building block in genetic programming?" by examining the smallest subtree possible—a single leaf node. The analysis of these subtrees indicates a considerably more complex portrait of what exactly is meant by a building block in GP than what has traditionally been considered.

10.1 Introduction

What is a building block in genetic programming (GP)? Intuitively, we might answer simple pieces of code, subprograms, that GP uses to build more complex programs. Intuitively, too, that idea resonates with some theoretical developments in genetic algorithms. Some have taken building blocks as a given and have built algorithms and systems to enhance their production (e.g., [Iba and de Garis 1996; Rosca and Ballard 1996; Ito et al. 1998]). However, one would be hard pressed to describe exactly what constitutes a building block. One would be even harder pressed to show what they are analytically (i.e., what are the salient mechanisms, processes, and mathematics that describe the creation, propagation, and use of a building block). Answers to those questions would likely be found at the core of understanding the dynamics associated with GP. Unfortunately, as researchers have found, such answers have not been easily forthcoming.

Towards this end, an increasing amount of basic research has focused on addressing the question "what is a building block?" This includes work in GP theory, including [Altenberg 1994; O'Reilly and Oppacher 1995; Whigham 1995; Poli and Langdon 1997; Rosca 1997; Banzhaf et al. 1998]. Of these, [O'Reilly and Oppacher 1995] stands out because they were one of the first who applied the corresponding theory from genetic algorithms to genetic programs. They found that the resulting building block definition was insufficient in describing the kind of dynamics that occur in GP. There is also work, mostly empirical, that either focuses or speculates on the nature of building blocks. These include [Koza 1992; Angeline 1994; Haynes 1997; Poli and Langdon 1997; Langdon and Poli 1998; Luke and Spector 1998; Poli et al. 1998]. Alternatives to what conventional wisdom would dictate about building blocks also appear in [Tackett 1994; Mulloy et al. 1996; Punch et al. 1996; Soule et al. 1996; Angeline 1997; Fuchs 1998].

10.1.1 Current Usages and Definitions

At face-value, the term *building blocks* refers to a conceptually simple definition: simple components out of which more complex things can be made. In evolutionary computation, the term first gained widespread usage in describing the dynamics that underlie genetic algorithms (e.g., see [Holland 1975,1992; Goldberg 1989).[1] At the outset of GP, Koza (1992) suggested that GP uses building blocks in a similar fashion. Early anecdotal information seemed to bear this out, as a few have reported seeing repeated code in their results that have been highly suggestive of building blocks (e.g., [Tackett 1993]).

However, subsequent research has yielded several meanings of the term *building block,* if only to rigorously define it. A building block of a GP tree has been defined to be a subtree of a solution tree [Iba and de Garis 1996; Ito et al. 1998]; blocks of code [Altenberg 1994]; and a rooted subtree [Rosca 1997]. The dynamics of building blocks, especially concerning how they are created and propagated, has been a subject of contention [Altenberg 1994; O'Reilly and Oppacher 1995; Rosca and Ballard 1996; Haynes 1997; Poli and Langdon 1997]. Part of this contention, however, is driven by what exactly constitutes a building block. We would also maintain that what exactly constitutes a building block has been driven, in part, by the metaphors that have been applied to explain it.

Of these metaphors, two stand out: genotype and phenotype. Many in the field would agree that there is a distinction between the two and that both have origins in the biological sciences. However, what exactly in evolutionary computation maps to genotype and phenotype is open to debate.

Genotype is often equated with structures. Depending on one's point of view, genotype is akin to information carried within bit strings or parse trees. Alternatively, genotype is that which underlies a single trait or a set of traits [Bäck and Fogel 1997]. There is probably little disagreement that the computational genotype is analogous to a biological genotype.

What is meant by phenotype is less than clear. A common definition is that a phenotype is the behavioral expression of the genotype in a specific environment [Bäck and Fogel 1997]. Some researchers simply define phenotype as observed behaviors [Fogel 1992]. Some have gone so far as to define the phenotype as equivalent to vector values, as in those used for fitness scoring [Altenberg 1994]. Others have opted for a more abstract definition by equating phenotype with semantics [Haynes 1997].

The relationships between building blocks, genotype, and phenotype have also been open to debate. The prevailing view is that building blocks are genotypes (structures) and that the mathematical formalism of a building block is a schema. Schemata have long been regarded as similarity templates [Holland 1975, 1992; Goldberg 1989]. With regard to GP,

---

[1]Recently, [Macready and Wolpert 1998] challenges the prevailing formalization of building blocks in genetic algorithms [Holland 1973]. If that paper does hold true, it means that the prevailing formalization may not represent an accurate description of building blocks in genetic algorithms. The outcome is not clear-cut, since genetic algorithms were developed independently from the formalization (i.e., see [Goldberg 1989]). It could mean, for example, that the phenomena of building blocks exists in genetic algorithms, but just not in the way described by the Schema Theorem. The implications of [Macready and Wolpert 1998] are even less clear for GP, since GP theory is not necessarily contingent on theoretical findings in genetic algorithms.

schemata have been further formalized as tree fragments that represent multiple subexpressions (e.g., [O'Reilly and Oppacher 1995; Poli and Langdon 1997]). Schemata have also been formalized to represent single subexpressions (e.g., [Whigham 1995]). Some have formalized schemata as rooted tree fragments (e.g., [Rosca and Ballard 1996]). One alternative view holds that for GP, the genotype and the phenotype are one and the same (i.e., [Nordin et al. 1996]). Another alternative view is that building blocks in GP exist in both the genotype and the phenotype (e.g., [Haynes 1997]).

10.1.2 Objectives

The goal of this chapter is to query the nature of a GP building block by observing single-node subtrees from a fitness-enhancing perspective and a population-building-blocks-dynamics perspective. We have sought to push the extent of what has generally been considered a GP building block—a subtree—by considering the smallest possible subtree—a single leaf node (i.e., a terminal). Of interest to us is how GP discovers and exploits *existing* subtrees. Our interest differs from previous work, which have examined how GP creates and discovers *new* subtrees, then exploits them for solution building. By considering single-node units, we have simplified analysis by setting aside the effects that have been associated with crossover within a building block. As this chapter demonstrates, even if building blocks were somehow indivisible (as are single-node subtrees or automatically defined functions (ADFs)), the dynamics associated with such blocks are far from simple.

While there are a large number of contexts among which to examine a single-node subtree, we have chosen to focus on the contexts concerning whether a single-node subtree is functionally expressed in a GP individual. In our case, this means considering at least a second type of subtree that can control the functional expression of single-node subtrees. For us, this interaction is significant because it addresses the issues of genotype and phenotype.

The crux of this chapter lies in determining whether these single-node subtrees are, in fact, building blocks. Using a simple, conceptual sense of the term, we would say yes, this chapter supports that. On the other hand, the analysis of these subtrees suggests a considerably more complex portrait of what exactly is meant by a building block in GP than what has traditionally been considered.

This chapter consists of six other sections. Section 10.2 discusses the setup and methods covered in this chapter. Sections 10.3 and 10.4 describe the experiments, while Section 10.5 discusses the results of these experiments in the context of the question "what is a building block?" Section 10.6 summarizes our conclusions. The three appendices augment our reasoning behind the case-study selection and type of analyses employed.

10.2 Case Study Description

For our case study, we used an example from symbolic regression and had GP solve for the problem $f(x) = (x + 1)^3$. We analyze the propagation and use of ephemeral random constants (ERCs), a specific type of single-node subtree. The following subsections highlight our reasoning for featuring this problem and describe the setup used in our experiments.

10.2.1 Motivations

One of the earliest, intuitive applications of GP has involved data modeling under the label of symbolic regression (i.e., [Koza 1989]). In [Koza 1992], symbolic regression has been synonymous with function identification, which involves finding a mathematical model that fits a given data set. Closely linked problems have included sequence induction, Boolean concept learning, empirical discovery, and forecasting. Typically, practitioners use GP and symbolic regression in several ways: as a benchmark problem to test GP systems, as a software demonstration or tutorial, and as a means of generating mathematical models for real-world data sets. The latter area includes examples in control systems, bioengineering, biochemistry, and finance.

We specifically chose $f(x) = (x + 1)^3$, in part because there are a few *thousand* approaches to obtain a solution and, in part, because there exist several opportunities in which subsolutions can be reused. This problem has well-known mathematical properties that can be exploited for analysis. For example, GP solutions can be constructed from several different coefficients, two of which can be reused: i.e., "1," "2," and "3." These coefficients appear in the following solutions: $(x + 1)^3$, $(1 + 2x + x^2)(x + 1)$, and $(1 + 3x + 3x^2 + x^3)$. Equivalent solutions can also be constructed with other permutations of addition, subtraction, multiplication, and division. Approximate solutions can also be obtained with rational polynomials. See Appendix A.10.1.

We chose to generate fitness cases on the interval $[-1, 0)$ to introduce some ambiguity to the problem, since that interval exists on just one side of that function's only inflection point. Consequently, both even and odd polynomials could, in theory, be used to approximate a solution.

We had three major reasons to use ERCs to setup GP to solve this problem. First and foremost, ERCs are individually traceable throughout the course of a GP trial (also called a GP *run*; we use the words *run* and *trial* interchangeably). The term *ephemeral* random constant is somewhat of a misnomer, at least for some implementations of GP. In the implementation of GP that we used, an ERC is created just once at population initialization. All ERCs remain—values unchanging—in the population for as long as they are used by at least one individual. We have specified that at the outset of a GP trial, that ERCs have a uniform probability density function (PDF) (i.e., uniformly distributed between specified values). In this way, usage of certain values, if any, are noted by changes in the probability density function of ERC values. Also at the outset of a GP trial, there are large numbers of ERCs that are generated and used in a population. In our case, this amounts to several thousand unique ERC values (floating point, double precision) being used by every trial— enough to generate ERC statistics at the level of a generation within a GP run.

Second, ERCs have variable worth with respect to solving for $f(x) = (x + 1)^3$. For instance, an ERC can either be "noise" or be a "contributing" value. In effect, GP has to solve not one, but two problems. One problem involves creating a mathematical model such that this model fits the supplied data points. This problem is the one a user specifies. The other problem involves creating error-correcting mechanisms to deal with errant ERC values, as we show in Appendix A.10.2. This other problem is an emergent one that GP needs to address in order to solve for $f(x)$. We can illustrate the latter, emergent problem with the following scenario. Let $f'(x)$ be an individual in a GP population. Furthermore let $f'(x) = f(x) + r$, where r is an ERC with a value of 5. GP can obtain the desired solution $f(x)$ in the next generation by *eliminating* r, i.e., by exchanging r with a subtree that evaluates to zero. GP might also be able to *absorb* r by multiplying that ERC with a subtree that evaluates to zero. In this scenario, either elimination or absorption represent error-correcting mechanisms that deal with errant ERC values.

Third, the valuation of an ERC at any given generation may not be well correlated with the larger context for solving for $f(x)$. Just as GP would need to eliminate "extraneous" ERCs, ERCs on the whole would be propagating and increasing in number. Furthermore, this propagation and increase in number would occur in spite of the different approaches to solving for $f(x)$. What we would need to do in order to demonstrate this is measure the change in ERC PDFs. In a sense, ERC implicit fitness would be measured by counting the total number of ERCs in a population and noting what ERC values were used. If there exists an implicit fitness for ERCs, there would likely exist a pattern in ERC PDFs that would transcend the approaches used by GP to solve for $f(x) = (x + 1)^3$. In Appendix A.10.3, we present a derivation supporting this conjecture.

10.2.2 Method

We have listed three reasons for using ERCs, with the latter two suggesting the following questions:

1. How does GP solve for the data model that fits data points generated by the equation $f(x) = (x + 1)^3$, given that ERCs may both aid or interfere with this process?

2. How do ERCs remain in a population in spite of some ERCs having questionable worth with respect to solving $f(x)$?

These questions suggest two different viewpoints for analysis. One viewpoint is fitness-centric and focuses on how ERCs are used by GP to solve for $f(x)$. The other viewpoint is ERC-centric and focuses on how ERCs are maintained in a population. We examine each of these viewpoints by conducting an experiment. For either viewpoint, we emphasize that we are looking at the same phenomena.

Those phenomena are described by the following experimental setup. Fitness cases were 50 equidistant points generated from the equation $f(x) = (x + 1)^3$ over the interval $[-1, 0)$. Raw fitness score was the sum of absolute error. A hit was defined as being within 0.01 in ordinate of a fitness case: 50 hits total. The stop criterion was when an individual in a population scored 50 hits. Adjusted fitness was the reciprocal of the quantity one plus the raw fitness score.

The terminal set consisted of $\{X, \mathcal{R}\}$. ERCs in $\mathcal{R}$ were generated with a uniform distribution over a specified interval of the form $[-a_\mathcal{R}, a_\mathcal{R}]$, where $a_\mathcal{R}$ is a real number that specifies the range for the ERCs. The function set consisted of $\{+, -, \times, \div\}$, where $\div$ is the protected division operator that returns one if the denominator is exactly zero.

We used lilgp to generate the data.[2] Most of the GP parameters were identical to those mentioned in Chapter 7 [Koza 1992]. Population size = 500; crossover rate = 0.9; replication rate = 0.1; population initialization with ramped half-and-half; initialization depth of 2–6 levels; and fitness-proportionate selection. Other parameter values were maximum generations = 200 and maximum tree depth = 26. (Note: these last two parameters differ from those presented in [Koza 1992], which specifies a maximum number of generations = 51 and a maximum depth = 17. Part of the reason we extended these parameters was to avoid possible effects that occur when GP processes individuals at these limits.)

---

[2]We used a patched version of lilgp v.1.02 [Zongker and Punch 1995], a C implementation of GP that is in use in the research community. The patches came from three sources: Luke, Andersen, and Daida. Luke's patches consist of memory leak fixes, multi-threading bug fixes. His enhancements also include provisions for strong-typing (which we did not use) and population initialization. Andersen's fixes included patches to Luke's population initialization routine, so that population initialization could include integer-valued ERCs. Our patches include modifications to the population initialization routine, so that population initialization could include real-valued ERCs.

Our patches also include a different random number generator (RNG). The effect of an RNG on empirical results has been noted in [Koza 1992; Daida, Ross et al. 1997]. Of concern has been that the empirical results obtained are possibly biased: differences between theoretical and empirical results could exist not because of genuine discrepancies between either, but because of idiosyncrasies corresponding to a particular random number generator. Because of concerns with the generator used in lilgp (see [Daida, Ross et al. 1997]), we used the Mersenne Twister [Matsumoto and Nishimura 1997; Matsumoto and Nishimura 1998], a recent variant of TT800. This particular generator is fast, has immense periodicity ($2^{19.937}$ -1, as opposed to 2^{31} -2 for some generators), and has excellent theoretical support for its use. We note, too, that we used lilgp in single-thread mode (as opposed to using multi-thread) because of possible concerns in parallelizing RNGs. (See [Hellekalek 1997; Hellekalek 1998] for recent accounts on choosing and using an appropriate RNG.) *cont.*

10.3 Fitness-Centric Experiment

The first experiment addressed the following question: how does GP solve for the data model that fits data points generated by the equation $f(x) = (x + 1)^3$, given that ERCs may both aid or interfere with this process?

To understand ERCs from this fitness-centric viewpoint, we changed the range $a_\mathfrak{R}$ of the ERCs. We used three values of $a_\mathfrak{R}$: 1, 10, 100. We also ran one control with no ERCs. Four data sets were collected: Control (no ERCs), Unity (ERC: [-1, 1]); Ten (ERC: [-10, 10]); Hundred (ERC: [-100, 100]). Each data set consisted of 600 trials for a total of 2400 runs for this experiment. (We note that increasing $a_\mathfrak{R}$ does *not* increase the size of the combinatorial search space for GP. While it is true that increasing $a_\mathfrak{R}$ is likely to increase the absolute value apportioned to each ERC, the total number of ERCs observed in any given population remains statistically constant. See Appendix A.10.3.)

What we were looking for was the effect of varying ERC content on GP's ability to solve for $f(x)$. If ERCs are building blocks (which presupposes "useful" content), we should note an effect by changing ERC values. Towards this end, we were interested in the gross characteristics of the best-of-trial individuals: e.g., size (number of nodes), generation in which a best-of-trial individual is found, depth, and adjusted fitness.

10.3.1 Fitness-Centric Results

Figure 10.1 summarizes and discusses the results from the following data sets: Control, Unity, Ten, and Hundred. Each plot shows 600 points, with each point corresponding to a best-of-trial individual. Columns are arranged by data set.

In creating the plots for the second and third rows, we added a small amount of uniform random noise to both (x, y) coordinates of each point. We did this for visualization only. The quantities corresponding to node count, depth, and generation are integer values—because of this, a single dot could correspond to many data points. The noise was added to displace points visually away from each other. That technique was not repeated for the first row, if only because adjusted fitness is a real-, not integer-valued quantity.

Footnote 2 cont. We also installed non-invasive data taps to collect population snapshots of a run. One of these taps is a modified version of a checkpoint file, which saves the entire state of a GP system at some intermediate step. This tap allows for capturing populations at some arbitrary interval prior to the specified last generation. These population dump files contain only an ERC listing, plus a human-readable version of every individual in that population. This tap also allows for us to capture the initial population, which lilgp does not do when checkpointing.

This patched version of lilgp v.1.02 served as the system for most of the trials that we discuss in this chapter. For the remaining runs, we generated one additional version (called version No-Null). In this version, we installed a problem specific patch in the population generation portion of lilgp. In Section 10.4, we note that a prevalent and pivotal structure was a null of the form (- x x). This patch was designed to knock out that null by replacing the last x in this structure with an ERC.

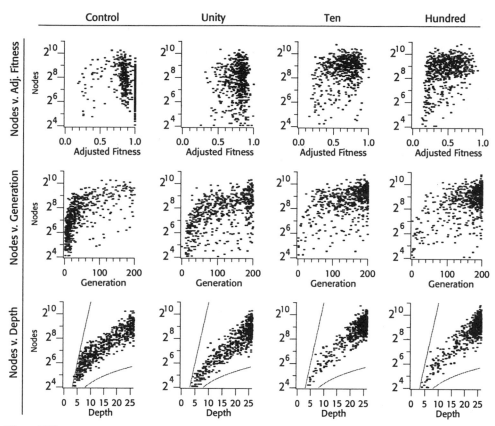

Figure 10.1
Best-of-trial results of fitness-centric experiment. Each column summarizes a data set, where each data set consisted of 600 trials. This figure shows the effect of increasing ERC values on the size and shape of best-of-trial individuals.

Figure 10.1 First Row shows the effect of ERC range on node count versus adjusted fitness. There are what appear to be four groupings. These groupings are indicated roughly as follows: a line interval between 2^5 and 2^9 nodes with adjusted fitness 1.0; a vertical cloud that exists in the interval between 2^5 and 2^{10} nodes with an adjusted fitness of nominally 0.85; a horizontal cloud that exists in the interval of 0.2 and 0.9 in adjusted fitness with a node count of nominally 2^9; and a steeply inclined cloud in the interval between 2^4 and 2^{10} nodes with adjusted fitness of nominally 0.15.

Figure 10.1 Second Row shows the effect of ERC range on node count versus the generation in which the best-of-trial individual was identified. Note that individuals that occur near generation 0 are concise and have likely required less computational effort to generate than those solutions that occur near generation 200. The distribution suggests two group-ings, one near generation 0 and another near the maximum number of generations (200).

Figure 10.1 Third Row shows the effect of ERC range on node count versus the depth of the best-of-trial individuals. The lines indicate the upper and lower bounds for the num-ber of nodes that can be present in a tree for a certain depth.[3] There appears to have been only one grouping that occurs near the maximum depth specification.

10.3.2 Fitness-Centric Discussion

ERCs can have a significant effect on whether GP can solve for $f(x)$. Essentially, the greater the ERC range beyond $a_{\Re} = 1$, the more difficulty GP encountered. The easiest task for GP was the Control case (no usage of ERCs), with 283 individuals (out of 600 possible) having perfect 1.0 adjusted fitness scores. The next easiest was the Unity case, except there was only one individual having a perfect adjusted fitness score.[4]

The overall effect of increasing the range of ERCs used in our problem was detrimental. The detrimental effect increased with increasing $a_{\Re}$, even though there were no statistical differences in the total number of ERCs that were initially allocated.

The idea of increasing difficulty with increasing $a_{\Re}$ is not altogether surprising. We note, however, that the reason for these phenomena was *not* because there were many more ERCs from which to choose. Rather, the phenomena of increasing difficulty may have occurred because there can be an increase in fitness penalty for choosing an increasingly "wrong" ERC. As an illustration, let r be an ERC value in a GP individual of the form $(x + r)^3$. The consequences for having r picked from the interval [-1, 1] differ markedly for having r picked from the interval [-100, 100]: on the whole, fitness scores would be lower for [-100, 100]. (Alternately, the phenomena of increasing difficulty may have also occurred because there are fewer numbers of potentially useful ERCs from which to use.) For that reason, a significant fraction of ERCs in Ten and Hundred would likely be "noise." On the other hand, ERCs in Unity could serve either as "noise" or as "contributing" value. A manual examination of 50-hit individuals in Unity (numbering 219 best-of-trial individuals) veri-fied that many of those individuals had ERCs integrated into the solutions represented by those individuals.

---

[3]The upper bound represents trees that are completely filled (i.e., binary trees with no vacancies). The lower bound represents sparse trees, where for the most part, each depth consists of one operator and one terminal.

[4]Adjusted fitness and hits served two different purposes in our experiments. Adjusted fitness was used in determining fitness-proportionate selection. Hits were used as a rough indicator of solution quality—50-hits means that an individual has met this indicator perfectly. Note that a 50-hits individual does not necessarily correspond to a perfect-adjusted-score individual, which is $f(x)$ exactly and has an adjusted score of exactly 1.0. A 50-hits indi-vidual generally had an adjusted score in the range of 0.8 – 1.0. Consequently, although there was only one perfect-adjusted-score individual in Unity, it turned out that 219 trials (out of 600) had 50-hits (i.e., a third of the trials produced a "reasonable" individual). Likewise for Control, there were 502 trials (out of 600) with 50-hits.

We selected the Unity data set for further examination, in part because the effect of ERCs for that data set was *both* deleterious and positive. We also note that in terms of the groupings shown in Figure 10.1, the Unity data set seemed to represent a transitional "snapshot" between Control and the remaining data sets.[5]

10.4 ERC-Centric Experiment

The second experiment addressed the following question: how do ERCs remain in a population in spite of some ERCs having questionable worth with respect to solving $f(x)$?

To understand ERCs from this ERC-centric viewpoint, we manipulated the contexts in which ERCs can appear. (This is in contrast to the fitness-centric experiment, which involved manipulating ERC *contents*, not their *contexts*.) As we mentioned earlier, while there are a large number of contexts among which to examine ERCs, we have chosen to focus on just a few. In particular, we have been interested in whether an ERC is expressed in a GP individual. Towards that end, we have identified a key structure as $(- X X)$, which we have called the null structure.

We note that there are many other null structures that are possible (i.e., those that map to exactly zero everywhere in x) in the course of a GP run. However, it is $(- X X)$ that represents the highest probability structure to occur either at population initialization or later. (Note that this even exceeds the probability of obtaining an ERC value of an exact zero by several orders of magnitude.) See Appendix A.10.2. For that reason, we use the terms *null*, *null structure*, and $(- X X)$ interchangeably in subsequent sections of this chapter. Note that a null structure is similar to an approximate zero because it can be used to zero out other subtrees (when used with multiplication or division). A null structure is distinguished from an approximate zero because only it can be used with protected division to create an exact one, which happens to be a coefficient for $f(x) = (x + 1)^3$.

Null structures introduce the most pronounced context shift possible for an ERC. Depending on where an ERC occurs with respect to a null structure, an ERC may ultimately be incorporated to form a solution coefficient or it may ultimately be voided.

We subsequently generated a companion data set, Unity No-Null, with a No-Null version of the kernel. In this version of kernel, all occurrences of the null structure $(- X X)$ were removed at population initialization and replaced with $(- X r)$, where $r \in \mathcal{R}$. Unity

---

[5]Of particular concern has been the groupings near limits of specification (e.g., maximum generations = 200 or maximum depth of trees = 26). These groupings are essentially artifacts. However, other works (e.g., [McPhee and Miller 1995; Banzhaf, Nordin et al. 1998]) suggest that different processes (e.g., compression) may predominate in regions suggested by these groupings. For instance, Banzhaf, Nordin et al. (1998) would contend that dynamics that describe GP at the beginning of a run would differ from the dynamics when GP operates on individuals that are near the specifications for the maximum size.

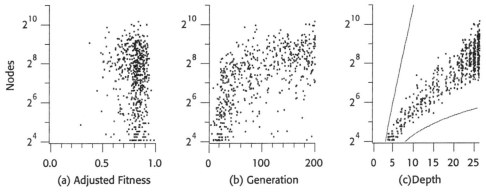

Figure 10.2
Best-of-trial results of ERC-centric experiment. These three scatterplots depict results from Unity No-Null, the companion data set to Unity (shown in the second column in Figure 10.1). This figure shows the effect of removing (-X X) from population initialization.

No-Null consisted of 600 trials and ERCs in the range of [-1, 1]. Furthermore, we reran both the Unity and Unity No-Null data sets and took a snapshot of both the initial population and the population in which the best individual was found. The specific interval of which to take these snapshots was subsequently determined *a posteriori*.

Of interest are the gross statistical characteristics concerning ERCs. In particular, if building blocks do exist among ERCs, we should eventually find evidence for that in a nonuniform statistical distribution of ERCs. Furthermore, if the contexts in which ERCs appear are significantly altered, we should find a corresponding change in statistical distribution between Unity and Unity No-Null.

10.4.1 ERC-Centric Results

The results in this section have been divided into two parts. The first-half results overlap Section 10.3 by examining a few fitness-centric characteristics of the Unity No-Null data set, the companion to Unity. We expect differences between Unity and Unity No-Null, if only because we have altered the contexts in which ERCs appear in GP individuals. These differences should subsequently appear at the level of individual.

Figure 10.2 summarizes part of the Unity No-Null data set, the companion to Unity. Figure 10.2a depicts a slight but noticeable fraction of points that have been affected by removing the null structure. The shift in pattern is downwards: in comparison to Unity, the Unity No-Null results show an enhancement in the region from 2^4 to 2^6 nodes and a shift of the cloud from 0.5 to 0.7 in adjusted fitness. Figures 10.2b and 10.2c show slight shifts towards the origin in comparison to their Unity counterparts in Figure 10.1.

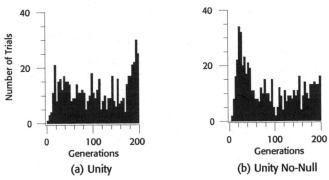

Figure 10.3
Comparison of histogram distributions of generation in which a best-of-trial individual was found. Removing
(- X X) reduced the computational effort required to produce a best-of-trial individual.

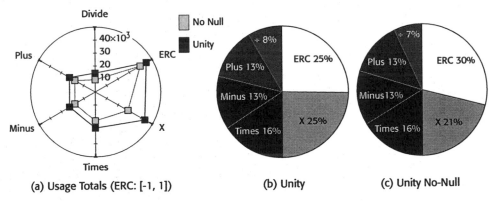

Figure 10.4
Comparison of node-type distributions for best-of-trial individuals from Unity and Unity No-Null data sets. This
figure shows the effect of removing (- X X) on components that made up best-of-trial individuals.

Figure 10.3 compares histograms from Unity and Unity No-Null. Each histogram depicts the frequency of trials versus the generation in which a best-of-trial individual was
identified. This figure shows a slight but noticeable fraction of trials that shifted away from
the maximum generation possible (200) in the Unity data set to the peak at 30 generations in
the Unity No-Null data set.

In the second-half results, we distinguish between node types and focus the remaining
analysis on ERC distributions.

Figure 10.4 shows distributions of all node types for the best-of-trial individuals in both
Unity and Unity No-Null data sets. The spider plot at left compares the raw counts of terminals and functions that were used in constructing best-of-trial individuals for Unity and

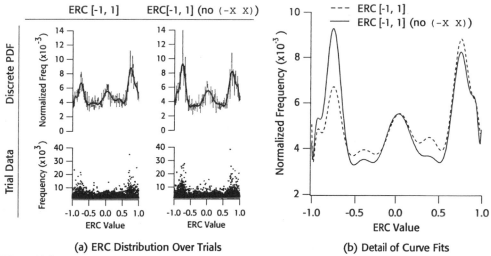

Figure 10.5
Comparison of ERC distributions. This figure shows that ERCs were nonuniformly distributed by the times the best-of-trial individuals were identified. The statistics shown in this figure are for all ERCs in all individuals in every population that a best-of-trial individual was identified (600 populations total). Figure 10.5a shows the intermediate steps taken to generate Figure 10.5b.

Unity No-Null. The hull pattern described by Unity No-Null is not affine with respect to the corresponding pattern for Unity. The pie charts at middle and right have the raw counts normalized. The pie charts in Figure 10.4 show that the ratio of ERCs to X in Unity is lower than the corresponding ratio for Unity No-Null.

Figure 10.5 shows the statistics corresponding to ERC distribution. The left-hand side illustrates our process of data reduction. The bottom row corresponds to the raw data collected from Unity and Unity No-Null. As mentioned in Section 10.2.1, we needed to look at frequencies of ERC values in a population, and not just for best-of-trial individuals. Consequently, each point in the bottom row corresponds to the frequency count of an ERC value as it occurs in a population for a single trial. Each scatterplot subsequently depicts the ERC node counts from 30,000 individuals (500 individuals per population per trial, 600 trials total). The scatterplot for Unity, then, is a summary of 26.0 million ERCs; for Unity No-Null, 23.2 million.

Since scatterplots represent only the ensemble of histogrammic data per trial, we needed to integrate the trial data over all trials to create a normalized distribution: a numerical PDF with discretized bins in 0.01 intervals. The staircase plots in the upper row just above the scatterplots show the numerical PDFs corresponding to Unity and Unity No-Null. To indicate general trends, we overlaid a 20th-order polynomial fit (dark line) on each staircase plot (gray line). The right-hand side of Figure 10.5 is a comparison of those general trends.

10.4.2 ERC-Centric Discussion

The first-half results showed that by altering the low-level contexts in which ERCs appear in GP individuals, we can induce changes at the higher level of individual.

By removing the null structure (- X X) from the initial population, we have essentially removed a means by which ERCs can "hide" in the introns (i.e., unexpressed code) of an individual (i.e., either through multiplication or protected division of ERC-bearing subtrees with the null structure). We suspect that these otherwise hidden ERC values would then appear as "contributing" values, which would subsequently affect the fitness of any given GP individual.

Larger individuals would have correspondingly larger numbers of expressed ERCs, which may increase the likelihood that ERCs might negatively affect the fitness of an individual. Figure 10.2 supports the notion that for the fraction of larger individuals that were affected by this altered context, these individuals were selected against (i.e., as depicted in shifts toward smaller individuals). Smaller individuals are more likely to occur near the outset of a GP run, as shown in Figure 10.3.

The second-half results showed that ERCs exhibit a nonuniform distribution and that those distributions are also affected by altering the low-level contexts in which ERCs appear. Furthermore, the nonuniform distributions are not well correlated with what one would intuit in solving for $f(x) = (x + 1)^3$. (In particular, we would reasonably expect values -1, 1, and maybe 0.)

We start this part of the discussion by comparing ERCs with other node types. On one hand, in comparison with these other types, ERCs do not appear remarkably different. Figure 10.4 shows that ERCs constitute roughly half of all the terminals used in the best of trial individuals for either Unity or Unity No-Null. On the other hand, the gross differences in the Figure 10.4 spider plot supports the earlier observation that Unity No-Null individuals are, on the whole, smaller than their Unity counterparts.

The smaller differences suggest that altering contexts also changes the way in which ERCs are maintained in GP individuals. Not only are the Unity No-Null individuals smaller, but the constituent node types are apportioned differently from their counterparts in Unity. In particular, the ratio of ERCs to X in Unity is 1:1; the corresponding ratio in Unity No-Null is 3:2. Figure 10.4 indirectly suggests that the underlying ERC PDFs would also differ.

We do offer a caveat in interpreting the ERC distributions between Unity and Unity No-Null. We noted earlier that at population initialization, the No-Null kernel replaces the second X in (- X X) with r. Although we felt that this replacement was minimally invasive, the replacement not transparent and increased the ratio of ERCs to X on the order of 5–6%. In Figure 10.4, we show comparative differences on that order. We emphasize, however, that the replacement strategy used in the No-Null kernel occurred only at population initialization; the plots shown in Figure 10.4 (as well as Figure 10.5) were taken from results sometime after GP had run for several generations. We do not have, as of this writing, a full explanation of why these differences at population initialization were maintained, if in fact "maintenance" is what actually happened.[6]

Indeed, the term *maintenance* does not easily convey the GP dynamics that transform a uniformly distributed set of ERCs to the results shown in Figure 10.5. To appreciate the amount of transformation that occurs, one needs only to examine the trial data. As we mentioned earlier, each point represents the frequency (number of times) that *one* ERC value occurs in the best-of-trial population for a particular GP run. Typical values range from 1,000 to 10,000 counts. Those figures by themselves do not seem remarkable, unless one takes into account *that each of those figures arose from just one instance of that ERC value* at start. Amplifications for single ERC values usually meant amplification for ERCs as a whole in a given GP run, albeit not as dramatically; often just a fraction of the initial ERC values persisted until the best-of-trial generation. Nevertheless, the total number of ERCs in a best-of-trial population can easily be an order of magnitude more than at start.[7]

Not all ERC values were of equal worth. Figure 10.5b generally depicts what we would expect if ERCs were used as building blocks: enhanced distribution in the intervals of "useful" ERC values and diminished distribution in the intervals of "less-than-useful" ERC values. Noteworthy is that this pattern transcends approaches for solving for $f(x)$. In other words, this pattern occurred across Unity and Unity No-Null data sets, across the 600 populations represented by each data set, across the 30,000 individuals represented by those populations, and across the few thousand different approaches represented by those individuals. That the pattern exists is not in question, but what exactly determined ERC valuations of use?

It is not a given that ERCs are valued at all, since in Section 10.3 we established that GP can build solutions without ERCs. However from Figure 10.5b, we can surmise that at least part of ERC valuation comes from solving for $f(x)$. Note that in that figure, both Unity and Unity No-Null have similar, but not identical, distributions. We contend that these differences in distribution occurred largely because in Unity No-Null, we have essentially removed a means by which ERCs can hide in the introns of an individual. One consequence we mentioned in the discussion of the first-half results was that individuals were smaller in

---

[6]Note that population initialization does not account for the differences in the ratio of function types. At population initialization for both Unity and Unity No-Null, there were roughly equal amounts of each function type allocated at generation 0. In the best-of-trial individuals, that ratio changed substantially.

[7]Typically, about 4,500 to 5,000 ERCs are generated at population initialization using the GP parameters described in Section 10.2.2.

Unity No-Null than in Unity. Figure 10.5b supports another consequence: that more ERCs in Unity No-Null individuals were expressed than in Unity individuals. More ERCs expressed means that more ERCs contributed in solving for $f(x)$, which further implies that ERCs with greater worth in solving for $f(x)$ were selected for (and the corollary that ERCs with less worth were selected against). In terms of an ERC distribution, then, we would expect two key differences. First, we would expect Unity No-Null to have exhibited greater enhancements over those ERC values most used in solving for $f(x)$ than Unity would exhibit. Second, we would also expect Unity No-Null to have exhibited lower distributions over those ERC values least used in solving for $f(x)$ than Unity would exhibit. Figure 10.5b shows most of these two key differences in distributions between Unity No-Null and Unity—we consequently surmise that part of the ERC valuation came from solving for $f(x)$.

We would also contend, however, that ERC valuation was not well correlated with the task of solving for $f(x)$. The most useful ERC distributions in solving for $f(x)$ involve narrow peaks around ± 1, and maybe a peak at 0. In fact, Figure 10.5b shows a peak at 0 (for both Unity and Unity No-Null), but also shows peaks at roughly ± 0.75. It is not obvious why peaks exist at ± 0.75. The evidence suggests that these peaks were not statistical aberrations: both curves represent over fifty million ERCs. The evidence also suggests that these peaks were not artifacts from processing or smoothing: these peaks can also be found in the raw trial data and the numerical PDFs in Figure 10.5a. The data strongly suggests that the values around ± 0.75 have worth—the peaks are highly pronounced—but to what can that worth be ascribed?

In Section 10.2.1 and Appendix A.10.3, we mentioned that we might expect this type of behavior from ERCs. Namely, we might obtain a pattern in distribution that would transcend the approaches used to solve for $f(x)$ and that would also not be well correlated with the larger context for solving for that problem. Although there is not yet a formal analysis as of this writing, the derivation that led to this speculation in the first place may shed some insight on the direction such an analysis might take.

Our derivation, simply put, involved arbitrarily designating the GP Control case configuration (no ERCs) as host and ERCs as symbionts (parasites in this case).[8] The experiment configuration subsequently represented a symbiosis of host and parasites. The goal of the host was solve for $f(x)$. The goal of the parasites was to increase their progeny. If we were to extend this frame further, we could expect the following. The host attempts to shed its parasites, but does not have sufficient mechanisms by which to do so. Parasites attempt to infiltrate the host, but do so at the host's expense. An evolutionary stable strategy be-

---

[8]We defer to the original definition of symbiosis—*Zusammenleben ungleichnamiger Organismen* [de Bary 1879], relationships that are constant and intimate between dissimilar species. Under Anton de Bary's definition, symbiosis subsumes all systems of dissimilar species that live in this type of relationship, whether that system is characterized as mutualistic, commensal, or parasitic.

tween host and parasites is represented by the scenario whereby the host manages to fill its own niche while carrying as many parasites as is possible to survive in that niche.

Given this frame, it may well be that the peaks around ±0.75 occurred not because those were the values most needed to solve for $f(x)$, but because those were the values that enabled the most numbers of ERCs to persist *in spite of* GP solving for $f(x)$. We leave exploring this conjecture to further work.

10.5 Implications for Building Blocks

Are ERCs building blocks?

In the intuitive sense of the term *building blocks* (i.e., simple components out of which more complex things can be made), our response would be a qualified yes, ERCs are building blocks. We have observed that GP assembled individuals that solved for $f(x)$ by using multiple instances of particular ERC values within an individual. This chapter has further shown that multiple instances of particular ERC values are distributed throughout a population.

We would not contend, however, that ERCs correspond to the view of building blocks as *context-free* structural schemata—the evidence did not totally support that. Context mattered. We showed that altering contexts changed the ability of GP to solve for $f(x)$ and modified the distribution of ERCs within a population. ERCs manifested themselves in different contexts throughout the course of a GP run—say, as "contributing value" (when creating numerical constants required by an individual) or as "don't care" (when appearing in an intron). At best, we would say that ERCs are structural schemata, which are sometimes used to build a solution.

Even the notion that ERCs are structural schemata may be open to debate. The prevailing view of structural schemata as genotype is questionable, as far as ERCs are concerned. The evidence in this chapter suggests that ERCs may be simultaneously both genotype (i.e., heritable information) and phenotype (i.e., behavior weakly coupled to solving for $f(x)$). It has not escaped our attention that our treatment of ERCs in this chapter does not preclude extension to other single-node subtree types (e.g., other terminals) or even encapsulated code (such as ADFs).

For that reason, we would contend that the assumption of a GP parse tree as a biological analog for real-world DNA may be tenuous. Goldberg and O'Reilly's comment in [Goldberg and O'Reilly 1998] was particularly insightful. The question, they claimed, is not so much what is a building block, but what is a gene. In biology, a gene maps to a particular physical structure. Heritable information and physical DNA structure are bijective quantities: a polypeptide generally maps to a particular gene, which is equivalent to saying that a polypeptide maps to a particular structure in DNA. As the results suggest, subtrees do not behave in this manner because of content and context dependency. In particular, we have demonstrated that an ERC can have germane information or can mean nothing at all depending on the particular location, content, context, and approach being employed in a given run. The mathematical structure that underlies a parse tree is fundamentally different from that of its biological counterpart—structure and heritable information in GP are not bijective. In the history of genetics, a gene was the heritable unit of information of which little was known. It just so happened that a biological gene maps bijectively to a DNA structure. In GP this is not the case. Consequently, to treat structures, whether single-node or multiple-node subtrees, as a biological gene is at best tenuous, and at worst, fallacious. We would say that usual metaphors of genotype and phenotype break down at this level of description. We subsequently argue that we would need to revisit the metaphors of genotype and phenotype.

We conjecture that unlike biology, building blocks in GP are ephemeral, just as the informational worth of an ERC changes over the course of a GP run. Building blocks are ephemeral because the projection of a parse tree into the space of worthwhile information would result in blocks that alternately appear and disappear.[9] Unlike the other implied metaphor of real building blocks, GP building blocks apparently phase in and out of worth. It isn't children's blocks that GP "plays" with—that scenario implies the existence of simple components to be available for use during the entire playing time. It's more like a cosmic game of Tetris, where one tries to solve a two-dimensional problem with N-dimensional blocks—so that now a block can seemly disappear at one moment and maybe reappear at another moment at another location with another shape.

10.6 Conclusions

This chapter has described the analysis of single-node subtrees, ephemeral random constants (ERCs), for a simple symbolic regression problem, which has as its target solution $f(x) = (x + 1)^3$. We have shown that in the intuitive sense of the term *building blocks* (i.e., simple components out of which more complex things can be made), our response would be a qualified yes, such single-node subtrees are building blocks.

We have demonstrated that we can manipulate the efficacy of GP to solve for $f(x)$ by adjusting the *contents* within the bounds of the allocated type corresponding to these single-node subtrees (as opposed to changing the structural complexity of an ERC or by increasing combinatorial search space). By so doing, we have demonstrated that these single-node

---

[9]This work supports O'Reilly and Oppacher's (1995) speculation on the idea of building blocks disappearing and reappearing, even though their discussion centered on building block disruption.

building blocks are significant to understanding the dynamics of GP for more than just their structural (single-node) aspect. Their intrinsic content mattered to the degree that different content resulted in different individual program sizes and depths.

We have also demonstrated that we can manipulate the efficacy of GP to solve for $f(x)$ by adjusting the *contexts* surrounding these single-node subtrees. By altering ERC contexts, we have shown that ERCs exhibit a pattern of distribution that transcends the many approaches that GP can use to solve for $f(x)$. We have also shown that this ERC distribution was not well correlated with the larger context of solving for $f(x)$ and have suggested an alternative frame based on a metaphor of symbiosis to account for this behavior. Using this frame, we have indicated that ERCs may be maintained in GP individuals not because they are useful in solving for $f(x)$, but because GP individuals allow for their existence. In other words, we have suggested that ERCs may exhibit dynamics that are only somewhat related to the selection pressure indicated by solving for $f(x)$.

Finally, we have discussed various implications of the results from this study in understanding what is a building block. As we have indicated, a building block in GP appears to be quite different from what we would expect to find in their biological counterpart. We contended that the assumption of a GP parse tree as a biological analog for real-world DNA may be tenuous. We subsequently argued that we would need to revisit the metaphors of genotype and phenotype with respect to their current usage in defining a GP building block.

For more information (other papers and code), please see our research group's site at http://www.sprl.umich.edu/acers.

Acknowledgments

The authors thank the editors L. Spector, W. Langdon, U.-M. O'Reilly, and P. Angeline for their kind invitation and support; W. Langdon and U.-M. O'Reilly, for their reviews, D. Ampy and S. Chang, for analysis tool support; D. Zongker and W. Punch for lilgp, S. Luke and P. Andersen for their patches to lilgp; M. Matsumoto and T. Nishimura for mt19937.c, their C implementation of the Mersenne Twister; and the original Challenges team of S. Ross, J. McClain, D. Ampy, and M. Holczer for doing early unpublished work on the empirical case study. We thank R. Riolo for his critique on an early draft of this chapter, A. Armstrong for allowing us to give a seminar on this chapter, as well as the following who gave additional reviews: S. Chaudhary, O. Chaudhri, G. Eickhoff, J. Khoo, H. Li, P. Litvak, M. Ratanasavetavadhana, and S. Yalcin. This chapter has benefited from our informal conversations with P. Angeline, W. Banzhaf, T. Bersano-Begey, D. Fogel, J. Foster, D. Goldberg, T. Haynes, W. Langdon, U.-M. O'Reilly, J. Rice, R. Poli, and J. Rosca. This research was partially supported through grants from U-M CoE, SPRL, NSF, OVPR, and UROP. We thank J. Vesecky, S. Gregerman, T. Killeen, and M. Combi for their continued support. The first author acknowledges I. Kristo and S. Daida. In memory of T. Daida, A. Bertram, F. Polito, and K. Daida.

Appendix A.10.1 Approaches to Solving $f(x)$

Although identifying the $f(x) = (x + 1)^3$ from 50 equidistant points distributed on the interval [-1,0) might seem straightforward, the means by which GP could obtain a solution—either perfect or approximate—are not. Some solutions are concise, but that is more the exception than the rule. The ability to analyze the mappings between a solution and parse tree structure is not trivial, even given our problem. One can begin to appreciate the difficulty of this task by realizing that one approach (an approximate solution valid only on the given interval) consists of building a rational polynomial of order 50.

Of perfect solutions, there exist several approaches. A few of these approaches can be categorized as $(x + 1)^3$, $(1 + 2x + x^2)(x + 1)$, and $(1 + 3x + 3x^2 + x^3)$. (See Table 10.1.) For the purposes of this paper, we call these categories *transitive equivalence classes*. We define an equivalence class as a mathematical abstraction of structures that evaluates individuals to a particular expression. An equivalence class is not assumed to have the properties of closure, transitivity, associativity, and is not assumed to be distributive. However, in our case, we are not concerned about the ordering of factors (e.g., $(1 + 2x + x^2)(x + 1) = (x + 1)(1 + 2x + x^2)$ and $(1 + 3x + 3x^2 + x^3) = (x \times 3 + 1 + x^3 + 3x^2)$), so we use the term transitive equivalence class. For the remainder of this appendix, then, we assume that transitive equivalence and equivalence to mean the same, even though, technically speaking, they are somewhat different.

To illustrate the difficulty of exhaustively enumerating all GP approaches to solving for $f(x)$, we describe the approaches that can be taken with just those shown in Table 10.1. Note that each approach subsumes three different primary components: I, II, and III. Out of these primary components, come 56 total component variations, which includes both the primary components and close approximates. A close approximate is defined as a component that has parameter values that are within a specified tolerance of those in the corresponding primary component. Note, too, that we distinguish between implicit and explicit parameters. Terms like $1x$ and x are subsequently different, if only because the explicit parameter "1" maps to particular structures and the implicit "1" usually refers to an absence of associated structure. Note that Table 10.1 does not include the approaches that are purely approximate, which include solutions of more than three zeros and rational polynomials.

For the sake of completeness, there are nine other equivalence classes, in addition to the three shown in Table 1, that are based on addition and multiplication. These classes include the following: $(x + 1)(1 + x + x + x^2)$, $(1 + x + x + x + x^2 + x^2 + x^2 + x^3)$, $(1 + 2x + x + x^2 + x^2 + x^2 + x^3)$, $(1 + 3x + x^2 + x^2 + x^2 + x^3)$, $(1 + x + x + x + 2x^2 + x^2 + x^3)$, $(1 + x + x + x + 3x^2 + x^3)$, $(1 + 2x + x + 2x^2 + x^2 + x^3)$, $(1 + 2x + x + 3x^2 + x^3)$, $(1 + 3x + 2x^2 + x^2 + x^3)$. There are also further equivalence classes based on other permutations of subtraction, division, multiplication, and addition.

An equivalence class in GP is rarely bijective with an associated parse tree structure. As demonstrated in our particular problem, multiple structures can be mapped to a single equivalence class. For example, the equivalence class that corresponds to the value "1" subsumes structures like $(\div\ \mathtt{X}\ \mathtt{X})$, $(\div\ \mathtt{X}\ \mathtt{0})$, $(\div\ \mathtt{r}\ \mathtt{0})$. It is also true that multiple equivalence classes can be mapped to a single structure. For example, the structure $(\div\ \mathtt{X}\ \mathtt{X})$ belongs as a partial solution to equivalence classes "3," "2," "1," and even "0." We defer to [Koza 1992] for further discussion of the building of numerical constants with GP.

As mentioned previously, each equivalence class presumes a different approach and different blocks for solution generation. That roots form a basis for solutions for many of these approaches is not surprising: root finding is a well established numerical technique. Finding roots is also a rapid way to come close to a target function, since a factor intersects with at least part of the target solution. Consequently, finding roots is one way to establish part of the "shape" of a solution.

Note that this analysis has been extended just to perfect solutions and their close approximates. It does not include any other types of approximations with, say, those that are purely approximate, which include solutions of more than three roots and rational polynomials. Purely approximate polynomials can be used to fit the fitness cases of 50 equidistant points on the interval $[-1, 0)$ within a given tolerance bound, but not necessarily to fit any other points taken from $f(x)$. A common rational polynomial approach has been to place poles in the intervals outside of $[-1, 0)$, although some approaches feature poles inside the interval $[-1, 0)$ and between points from the fitness case. A conservative estimate on the number of equivalence classes with approximate approaches, including rational polynomials, is on the order of a few thousand.

Appendix A.10.2 Known ERC Strategies

From a listing of equivalence classes, one could infer that there are only a few low-level strategies that are required to solve the problem of ERCs: incorporation, elimination, and absorption. An ERC can be *incorporated* into an individual by serving as a component parameter. For example, an ERC with value 0.99 could find use wherever a unity value is required. An ERC can be *eliminated* from an individual via crossover. An ERC can also be eliminated from further consideration (i.e., a population) if individuals bearing this ERC neither reproduce nor replicate

Table 10.1
Detail of perfect and close approximate approaches using addition and multiplication.

	Class		
	$(x+1)^3$	$(x+1)(x^2+2x+1)$	(x^3+3x^2+3x+1)
Primary Component	I	I, II	III
Variants	$I^{-,1}$, $I^{1,1}$, $I^{\gamma_1,1}$, I^{-,γ_1}, I^{1,γ_1}, I^{γ_1,γ_1}, I^{γ_1,γ_2}	$I^{-,1}$, $I^{1,1}$, $I^{\gamma_1,1}$, I^{-,γ_1}, I^{1,γ_1}, I^{γ_1,γ_1}, I^{γ_1,γ_2} $II^{-,a,1}$, $II^{1,a,1}$, $II^{\gamma_1,a,1}$, II^{-,a,γ_1}, II^{1,a,γ_1}, II^{γ_1,a,γ_1}, II^{γ_1,a,γ_2}, where $a \in \{2, \lambda\}$	$III^{-,a,b,1}$, $III^{1,a,b,1}$, $III^{\gamma_1,a,b,1}$, III^{-,a,b,γ_1}, III^{1,a,b,γ_1}, $III^{\gamma_1,a,b,\gamma_1}$, $III^{\gamma_1,a,b,\gamma_2}$, where $a \in \{3, \eta_1\}$ and $b \in \{3, \eta_1\}$ $III^{-,\eta_1,\eta_2,1}$, $III^{1,\eta_1,\eta_2,1}$, $III^{\gamma_1,\eta_1,\eta_2,1}$, $III^{-,\eta_1,\eta_2,\gamma_1}$, $III^{1,\eta_1,\eta_2,\gamma_1}$, $III^{\gamma_1,\eta_1,\eta_2,\gamma_1}$, $III^{\gamma_1,\eta_1,\eta_2,\gamma_2}$
Number Variants	I(7)	I(7), II(14)	III (35)
Root Factors	3	1	0
Parameter Values	1	1,2	1,3

for the next generation. An ERC can be *absorbed* by being part of a structure that is, for all practical purposes, not expressed. For example, an ERC could be multiplied by the null structure (- X X) so that the overall subtree evaluates to null. In GP jargon, structures that do not directly affect a solution's fitness are called introns (after [Angeline 1994]). (Both theoretical and empirical evidences support the notion that introns emerge because genetic operators can result in decreased fitness [Nordin and Banzhaf 1995; Rosca and Ballard 1995; Nordin et al. 1996; Soule et al. 1996; Banzhaf et al. 1998]. Introns tend to grow exponentially in numbers. Introns may have differing effects before and after exponential growth of introns begins [McPhee and Miller 1995; Banzhaf et al. 1998]. Opinion on whether introns benefit or hinder GP is moot, since supportive research can be found on either side of the subject, (e.g., [Andre and Teller 1996] versus [Nordin et al. 1996]).)

There are 12 different ways to construct either an approximate zero or a null structure, for trees up to depth 2 and for $r \cong 0$ (where $r \in \Re$) using a tolerance of 0.01. Note that the most likely structure (- X X) to appear out of these ways also represents the only structure that evaluates to a perfect null: probability P(structure|depth) = 6.25% for (- X X), in comparison to the next highest probability structure, an approximate zero, which has a P(structure|depth) = 1.36%. The remaining approximate zero structures have P(structure|depth) no greater than 0.5%.

Note that by multiplying a subexpression with a perfect null, any number of ERCs can be absorbed. In contrast, an approximate null has only a limited ability to absorb ERC values through multiplication. By dividing a subexpression with a perfect null, again any number of ERCs can be absorbed, but with the added benefit that protected division returns unity. (The value "1" can subsequently be used as a component parameter in variants of I, II, or III.) Dividing a subexpression with an approximate null would likely result in anything but unity.

Appendix A.10.3 Alternative Frame for Analyzing GP and ERCs

Conventional wisdom concerning ERCs would suggest that ERCs are but another software component in GP from which to build solutions. Upon second look, though, we found GP using ERCs as reminiscent of a class of hybrid systems that we had been studying for several years [Daida et al. 1995; Daida et al. 1996] and have developed several systems around the concept. Although we used the concept for synthesis, it occurred to us that we could use the associated theoretical concepts developed in [Daida et al. 1995] as an alternative frame for this chapter's analysis.

Our theoretical framework has used biological symbiosis—relationships that are constant and intimate between dissimilar species—as a metaphor. In [Daida et al. 1995], we define a symbiotic system as follows:

Let system $\mathcal{S}$ represent a set of adaptive systems

$$\mathcal{S} = \bigcup_{\forall i \in \Sigma} \left\{ \mathcal{S}^i : \mathcal{S}^i = \left(\mathcal{a}^i, \Omega^i, \tau^i, \mathcal{B}^i, \Omega_{\mathcal{B}}^i, \tau_{\mathcal{B}}^i, I^i \right) \right\},$$

where Σ is an index set corresponding to elements in $\mathcal{S}$, $\mathcal{a}$ is the set of attainable structure and is the domain of action for the adaptive plan, Ω is the set of operators for modifying structures $\mathcal{a}$, τ is the adaptive plan that determines what operator is to be applied, $\mathcal{B}$ is the set of attainable artifacts generated by the adaptive system. $\Omega_{\mathcal{B}}$ is the set of operators for modifying artifacts, $\tau_{\mathcal{B}}$ is the adaptive plan that determines what operator is to be applied to $\mathcal{B}$, and I is the set of possible inputs to the system from the environment. System $\mathcal{S}$ is symbiotic if and only if there exists an instance where

$$B^i \supset I^j, \exists_i : i \neq j, \forall_{i,j \in \Sigma} : i \neq j, \text{ and } \bigcup_{\forall k \in \Sigma} B^k \neq \varnothing.$$

A symbiotic system $\mathcal{S}$ is considered minimal if and only if only one element $\mathcal{S}^i$ describes an adaptive system.

We use the concept of a minimal symbiotic system to create our alternative frame of analysis. To do so, we arbitrarily define a minimal symbiotic system $\mathcal{S}$ that consists of two component systems $\mathcal{S}^1$ and $\mathcal{S}^2$. In our case we designate $\mathcal{S}^1$ as the adaptive system and $\mathcal{S}^2$ as the non-adaptive one. We let $\mathcal{S}^1$ be a GP system (adaptive) with the terminal set = $\{x, \Gamma\}$, where Γ is a set of indexed terminal placeholders. We further let $\mathcal{S}^2$ be an ERC generator (non-adaptive) that outputs $\{\rho\}$, where ρ is an indexed set of random number values that are uniformly distributed in the interval $[-a_{\mathcal{R}}, a_{\mathcal{R}}]$. Under this definition, we share the set of indices that point to Γ and ρ such that indexes in Γ serve as input to ρ and indexes in ρ serve as input to Γ. We let indexes in Γ serve as pointers, and indexes in ρ serve as addresses. In a sense, the shared indices serve as simple tags, numerical labels that formed the interface between the two systems.

Framing the GP system (and ERC generator) in this way has been helpful because it is similar to one we studied in [Daida et al. 1995]. That system $\mathcal{S}$ also had two component systems $\mathcal{S}^1$ and $\mathcal{S}^2$, where $\mathcal{S}^1$ was a genetic algorithm and $\mathcal{S}^2$ an arbitrary, but fixed heuristic. Both component systems interacted via numerical tags. For instance, for $\mathcal{S}^2$, the numerical tags served as "locks," while for $\mathcal{S}^1$, numerical tags served as "keys." Locks and keys were independently generated by either system. Behind every lock was a vector that was generated by the fixed heuristic. Behind every key was a function that used elements from an indexed vector (like one generated by the fixed heuristic). Although matching lock and key sets could be rapidly determined, the task of discovering "useful" content was left to $\mathcal{S}^1$. We showed in that experiment that the selection of locks and keys was not deterministic, was subject to positive feedback, and was opportunistic. The pattern of which heuristics were chosen also seemed probabilistic— $\mathcal{S}^1$ would build a solution around a vector by choosing a vector first, rather finding the best attainable solution and then finding the heuristic that would make further refinements. Given that type of behavior, we were able to demonstrate a few ways to manipulate the search dynamics of $\mathcal{S}^1$ through tags.

In the GP system that we used, keys would be the kernel's pointers to ERCs; locks would be the hash table associated with ERC values. ERC values are generated once at population initialization. Unlike the system described in [Daida et al. 1995], each GP individual that uses ERCs uses not one, but a set of keys. Our hypothesis, however, was that we would find a similar type of behavior.

Bibliography

Altenberg, L. (1994). The Evolution of Evolvability in Genetic Programming. In K. E. Kinnear, Jr. (Ed.), *Advances in Genetic Programming* (pp. 47–74). Cambridge: The MIT Press.

Andre, D. and A. Teller (1996). A Study in Program Response and the Negative Effects of Introns in Genetic Programming. In J. R. Koza, D. E. Goldberg, D. B. Fogel, and R. L. Riolo (Eds.), *Genetic Programming 1996: Proceedings of the First Annual Conference: July 28–31, 1996, Stanford University* (pp. 12–20). Cambridge: The MIT Press.

Angeline, P. (1994). Genetic Programming and Emergent Intelligence. In K.E. Kinnear, Jr. (Ed.), *Advances in Genetic Programming* (pp. 75–97). Cambridge: The MIT Press.

Angeline, P. J. (1997). Subtree Crossover: Building Block Engine or Macromutation? In J. R. Koza, K. Deb, M. Dorigo, D. B. Fogel, M. Garzon, H. Iba, and R. L. Riolo (Eds.), *Genetic Programming 1997: Proceedings of the Second Annual Conference, July 13-16, 1997, Stanford University* (pp. 9–17). San Francisco: Morgan Kaufmann Publishers, Inc.

Bäck, T. and D. B. Fogel (1997). Glossary. In T. Bäck, D. B. Fogel, and Z. Michalewicz (Eds.), *Handbook of Evolutionary Computation* (pp. Glos:1–Glos:10). Bristol: Institute of Physics Publishing.

Banzhaf, W., P. Nordin, R. E. Keller, and F. D. Francone (1998). *Genetic Programming: An Introduction: On the Automatic Evolution of Computer Programs and Its Applications*. San Francisco, Morgan Kaufmann Publishers, Inc.

Daida, J. M., C. S. Grasso, S. A. Stanhope, and S. J. Ross (1996). Symbionticism and Complex Adaptive Systems I: Implications of Having Symbiosis Occur in Nature. In L. J. Fogel, P. J. Angeline and T. Bäck (Eds.), *Evolutionary Programming V: Proceedings of the Fifth Annual Conference on Evolutionary Programming* (pp. 177–86). Cambridge: The MIT Press.

Daida, J. M., S. J. Ross, and B. C. Hannan (1995). Biological Symbiosis as a Metaphor for Computational Hybridization. In L. J. Eshelman (Ed.), *Proceedings of the Sixth International Conference on Genetic Algorithms* (pp. 328–35). San Francisco: Morgan Kaufmann Publishers, Inc.

Daida, J. M., S. J. Ross, J. J. McClain, D. S. Ampy, and M. Holczer (1997). Challenges with Verification, Repeatability, and Meaningful Comparisons in Genetic Programming. In J. R. Koza, K. Deb, M. Dorigo, D. B. Fogel, M. Garzon, H. Iba, and R. L. Riolo (Eds.), *Genetic Programming 1997: Proceedings of the Second Annual Conference, July 13-16, 1997, Stanford University* (pp. 64–9). San Francisco: Morgan Kaufmann Publishers, Inc.

de Bary, A. (1879). *Die Erscheinung der Symbiose. Vortrag, Gehalten auf der Versammlung Deutscher Naturforscher und Aerzte zu Cassel*. Strassburg: R.J. Trübner.

Fogel, D. B. (1992). A Brief History of Simulated Evolution. In *The First Annual Conference on Evolutionary Programming* (pp. 1–16). San Diego: Evolutionary Programming Society.

Fuchs, M. (1998). Crossover versus Mutation: An Empirical and Theoretical Case Study. In J. R. Koza, W. Banzhaf, K. Chellapilla, et al. (Eds.), *Genetic Programming 1998: Proceedings of the Third Annual Conference, July 22–25, 1998, University of Wisconsin, Madison* (pp. 78–85). San Francisco: Morgan Kaufmann Publishers, Inc.

Goldberg, D. E. (1989). *Genetic Algorithms in Search, Optimization, and Machine Learning*. Reading, Addison-Wesley Publishing Company, Inc.

Goldberg, D. E. and U.-M. O'Reilly (1998). Where Does the Good Stuff Go, and Why? In W. Banzhaf, R. Poli, M. Schoenauer, and T. C. Fogarty (Eds.), *Proceedings of the First European Conference on Genetic Programming, Paris, France*. Berlin: Springer-Verlag.

Haynes, T. (1997). Phenotypical Building Blocks for Genetic Programming. In T. Bäck (Ed.), *Proceedings of the Seventh International Conference on Genetic Algorithms* (pp. 26–33). San Francisco: Morgan Kauffmann Publishers.

Hellekalek, P. (1997). A Note on Pseudorandom Number Generators. *Simulation Practice and Theory* 5(6): 6–8.

Hellekalek, P. (1998). Good Random Number Generators Are (Not So) Easy to Find. *Mathematics and Computers in Simulation* 46(5–6): 487–507.

Holland, J. H. (1973). Genetic Algorithms and the Optimal Allocation of Trials. *SIAM Journal on Computing* 2(2): 88–105.

Holland, J. H. (1975). *Adaptation in Natural and Artificial Systems*. Ann Arbor, University of Michigan Press.

Holland, J. H. (1992). *Adaptation in Natural and Artificial Systems: An Introductory Analysis with Applications to Biology, Control, and Artificial Intelligence*. Cambridge, The MIT Press.

Iba, H. and H. de Garis (1996). Extending Genetic Programming with Recombinative Guidance. In P. J. Angeline and K.E. Kinnear, Jr. (Eds.), *Advances in Genetic Programming* (pp. 69–88). Cambridge: The MIT Press.

Ito, T., H. Iba, and S. Sato (1998). Depth-Dependent Crossover for Genetic Programming. In *The 1998 IEEE International Conference on Evolutionary Computation Proceedings: IEEE World Congress on Computational Intelligence* (pp. 775–80). Piscataway: IEEE Press.

Koza, J. R. (1989). Hierarchical Genetic Algorithms Operating on Populations of Computer Programs. In N. S. Sridharan (Ed.), *Proceedings of the Eleventh International Joint Conference on Artificial Intelligence* (pp. 768–74). San Francisco: Morgan Kaufmann.

Koza, J. R. (1992). *Genetic Programming: On the Programming of Computers by Means of Natural Selection*. Cambridge, The MIT Press.

Langdon, W. B. and R. Poli (1998). Why Ants Are Hard. In J. R. Koza, W. Banzhaf, K. Chellapilla, K. Deb, M. Dorigo, D. B. Fogel, M. H. Garzon, D. E. Goldberg, H. Iba, and R. L. Riolo (Eds.), *Genetic Programming 1998: Proceedings of the Third Annual Conference, July 22–25, 1998, University of Wisconsin, Madison* (pp. 193–201). San Francisco: Morgan Kaufmann Publishers, Inc.

Luke, S. and L. Spector (1998). A Revised Comparison of Crossover and Mutation in Genetic Programming. In J. R. Koza, W. Banzhaf, K. Chellapilla, et al (Eds.), *Genetic Programming 1998: Proceedings of the Third Annual Conference, July 22–25, 1998, University of Wisconsin, Madison* (pp. 208–13). San Francisco: Morgan Kaufmann Publishers, Inc.

Macready, W. G. and D. H. Wolpert (1998). Bandit Problems and the Exploration/Exploitation Tradeoff. *IEEE Transactions on Evolutionary Computation* 2(2): 2–22.

Matsumoto, M. and T. Nishimura (1997). *mt19937.c*. Keio, Department of Mathematics, Keio University. http://www.math.keio.ac.jp/~matumoto/emt.html.

Matsumoto, M. and T. Nishimura (1998). Mersenne Twister: A 623-Dimensionally Equidistributed Uniform Pseudorandom Number Generator. *ACM Transactions on Modeling and Computer Simulation* 8(1): 3–30.

McPhee, N. F. and J. D. Miller (1995). Accurate Replication in Genetic Programming. In L. J. Eshelman (Ed.), *Proceedings of the Sixth International Conference on Genetic Algorithms* (pp. 303–309). San Francisco: Morgan Kaufmann Publishers, Inc.

Mulloy, B. S., R. L. Riolo, and R. S. Savit (1996). Dynamics of Genetic Programming and Chaotic Time Series Prediction. In J. R. Koza, D. E. Goldberg, D. B. Fogel and R. L. Riolo (Eds.), *Genetic Programming 1996: Proceedings of the First Annual Conference: July 28–31, 1996, Stanford University* (pp. 166–74). Cambridge: The MIT Press.

Nordin, P. and W. Banzhaf (1995). Complexity Compression and Evolution. In L. J. Eshelman (Ed.), *Proceedings of the Sixth International Conference on Genetic Algorithms* (pp. 310–17). San Francisco: Morgan Kaufmann Publishers, Inc.

Nordin, P., F. Francone, et al. (1996). Explicitly Defined Introns and Destructive Crossover in Genetic Programming. In P. J. Angeline and K.E. Kinnear, Jr. (Eds.), *Advances in Genetic Programming* (pp. 111–34). Cambridge: The MIT Press.

O'Reilly, U.-M. and F. Oppacher (1995). The Troubling Aspects of a Building Block Hypothesis for Genetic Programming. In L. D. Whitley and M. D. Vose (Eds.), *Foundations of Genetic Algorithms 3* (pp. 73–88). San Francisco: Morgan Kaufmann Publishers, Inc.

Poli, R. and W. B. Langdon (1997). An Experimental Analysis of Schema Creation, Propagation and Disruption in Genetic Programming. In T. Bäck (Ed.), *Proceedings of the Seventh International Conference on Genetic Algorithms* (pp. 18–25). San Francisco: Morgan Kauffmann Publishers, Inc.

Poli, R. and W. B. Langdon (1997). A New Schema Theory for Genetic Programming with One-Point Crossover and Point Mutation. In J. R. Koza, K. Deb, M. Dorigo, D. B. Fogel, M. Garzon, H. Iba, and R. L. Riolo (Eds.), *Genetic Programming 1997: Proceedings of the Second Annual Conference, July 13-16, 1997, Stanford University* (pp. 279–85). San Francisco: Morgan Kaufmann Publishers, Inc.

Poli, R., W. B. Langdon, and U.-M. O'Reilly (1998). Analysis of Schema Variance and Short Term Extinction Likelihoods. In J. R. Koza, W. Banzhaf, K. Chellapilla, K. Deb, M. Dorigo, D.B. Fogel, M. H. Garzon, D. E. Goldberg, H. Iba, and R. L. Riolo (Eds.), *Genetic Programming 1998: Proceedings of the Third Annual Conference, July 22–25, 1998, University of Wisconsin, Madison* (pp. 284–92). San Francisco: Morgan Kaufmann Publishers, Inc.

Punch, W., D. Zongker, and E. Goodman (1996). The Royal Tree Problem, A Benchmark for Single and Multiple Population Genetic Programming. In P. J. Angeline and K.E. Kinnear, Jr. (Eds.), *Advances in Genetic Programming* (pp. 299–316). Cambridge: The MIT Press.

Rosca, J. P. (1997). Analysis of Complexity Drift in Genetic Programming. In J. R. Koza, K. Deb, M. Dorigo, D. B. Fogel, M. Garzon, H. Iba, and R. L. Riolo (Eds.), *Genetic Programming 1997: Proceedings of the Second Annual Conference, July 13-16, 1997, Stanford University* (pp. 286–94). San Francisco: Morgan Kaufmann Publishers, Inc.

Rosca, J. P. and D. H. Ballard (1995). Causality in Genetic Programming. In L. J. Eshelman (Ed.), *Proceedings of the Sixth International Conference on Genetic Algorithms* (pp. 256–63). San Francisco: Morgan Kaufmann Publishers, Inc.

Rosca, J. P. and D. H. Ballard (1996). Discovery of Subroutines in Genetic Programming. In P. J. Angeline and K.E. Kinnear, Jr. (Eds.), *Advances in Genetic Programming* (pp. 177–201). Cambridge: The MIT Press.

Soule, T., J. A. Foster, and J. Dickinson (1996). Code Growth in Genetic Programming. In J. R. Koza, D. E. Goldberg, D. B. Fogel, and R. L. Riolo (Eds.), *Genetic Programming 1996: Proceedings of the First Annual Conference: July 28–31, 1996, Stanford University* (pp. 215–23). Cambridge: The MIT Press.

Soule, T., J. A. Foster, and J. Dickinson (1996). Using Genetic Programming to Approximate Maximum Clique. In J. R. Koza, D. E. Goldberg, D. B. Fogel, and R. L. Riolo (Eds.), *Genetic Programming 1996: Proceedings of the First Annual Conference: July 28–31, 1996, Stanford University* (pp. 400–405). Cambridge: The MIT Press.

Tackett, W. A. (1993). Genetic Programming for Feature Discovery and Image Discrimination. In S. F. Forrest (Ed.), *Proceedings of the Fifth International Conference on Genetic Algorithms* (pp. 303–309). San Mateo: Morgan Kaufmann Publishers, Inc.

Tackett, W. A. (1994). *Recombination, Selection and the Genetic Construction of Computer Programs*. Ph.D. Thesis, Electrical Engineering. Los Angeles, University of Southern California.

Whigham, P. (1995). A Schema Theorem for Context-Free Grammars. In *The 1995 IEEE Conference on Evolutionary Computation* (pp. 178–81). Piscataway: IEEE Press.

Zongker, D. and W. Punch (1995). *lilgp*. Lansing, Michigan State University, Genetic Algorithms Research and Applications Group. http://garage.cps.msu.edu/software/software-index.html.

11 Rooted-Tree Schemata in Genetic Programming

Justinian P. Rosca and Dana H. Ballard

In this chapter we present a novel way of addressing the issue of variable complexity of evolved solutions and a revised interpretation of how Genetic Programming (GP) constructs solutions, based on the rooted-tree schema concept.

A rooted-tree schema is a simple relation on the space of tree-shaped structures which provides a quantifiable partitioning of the search space. Formal manipulation of rooted-tree schemata allows: (1) The role of the size in the selection and survival of evolved expressions to be made explicit; (2) The interrelationship between parsimony penalty, size, and fitness of evolved expressions to be clarified and better understood; (3) The introduction of alternative approaches to evolving parsimonious solutions by preventing rooted-tree schema from bloating.

The rooted-tree schema concept provides a top-down perspective of how program expressions are evolved, contrary to the common belief that small pieces of code, or building blocks, are gradually assembled to create solutions. Analysis shows that GP, while it improves solutions, combines both bottom-up and top-down refinement strategies.

11.1 Introduction

Complexity (or the size or length) of evolved structures is a non-issue in most of the recent evolutionary computation (EC) literature. EC techniques such as genetic algorithms (GAs) [Holland, 1992], evolutionary programming (EP) [Fogel et al., 1966; Fogel, 1995], and evolution strategies (ES) [Bäck et al., 1991] use mostly fixed length encodings for the structures to be evolved. This design decision seriously limits their applicability solely to the domain of parametric problems. Many applications could benefit enormously from simulated evolution that is open-ended with respect to the complexity of evolved solutions, i.e. when no particular structure is assumed *a priori*. This would be particularly the case with complex design or control problems where the structure of a satisfactory solution is unknown in advance.

Genetic programming (GP) uses open-ended complexity representations that have flexible semantics [Koza, 1992]. GP evolves a population of programs in some problem dependent language in the form of tree expressions of variable length (complexity) and shape that encode solutions to the problem. A program can be used to generate practically any computation such as classification, regression, prediction, or control, side effect, or create a secondary structure representing the learned model. For example, the program can construct the architecture and the corresponding number of parameters of a model such as a belief network or a neural network. Thus, evolved programs are very general non-parametric encodings, in the sense that the number of parameters can be very large and their role is very flexible.

The behavior of GP is extremely hard to characterize formally. Yet expanding the range of applications to new problems and domains requires a qualitative understanding of its behavior. This goal can be furthered by a careful analysis of the characteristics and limitations of the search process. In this contribution we focus on the specific characteristics and limitations of GP with variable complexity representations.

GP searches the space of programs. At every search step, the GP engine ranks the population of program expressions according to a problem dependent measure, the fitness function. Then it applies fitness proportionate selection and random variation of expressions in the population in order to generate a next step population. The complexity of evolved expressions can drastically vary over the span of the search.

One serious problem of standard GP is that evolved expressions appear to drift towards larger forms that take longer to evaluate on average. This threatens to limit the performance of the GP engine because prespecified threshold parameters such as the total size or depth of manipulated expressions are met [Sims, 1991; Tackett, 1994; Angeline, 1994; Nordin et al., 1995; Rosca, 1996; Soule et al., 1996; Langdon and Poli, 1998; Langdon and Poli, 1997]. Performance near the edge of these parameters is not desirable. The simple-minded solution is to monitor when such non-desirable operating conditions are reached and to increase the values of the relevant parameters to avoid such conditions. The GP run could be continued if resources still allow. Another solution to control size growth is to include a parsimony penalty component into the fitness function in order to limit the growing size of expressions [Iba et al., 1994; Rosca and Ballard, 1994; Zhang and Muhlenbein, 1995]. However, the penalty component changes the fitness landscape. How heavily should the parsimony penalty be weighted or how should it be adapted in order to not affect the underlying optimization process?

This chapter presents a novel view on the role played by size growth in evolutionary computation. It discusses a particular property of GP representations that sheds light on the role of variable complexity of evolved structures. The property of interest is the *rooted-tree schema* relation on the space of tree-shaped structures which provides a quantifiable partitioning of the search space. The analysis answers questions such as: What role does variable complexity play in the selection and survival of structures? What is the influence of parsimony pressure on selection and survival of structures? What is the role played by the weighting factor of the complexity term? Are there alternative approaches to imposing parsimony pressure that do not result in a change of the fitness landscape? The paper provides theoretical answers to these questions, interpretation of these results and an experimental perspective. Answers to such questions are considered critical in the challenging attempt of understanding and controlling the behavior of evolutionary computation algorithms operating with variable complexity representations and on future work in EC.

The structure of the chapter is as follows. Section 11.2 overviews schema theory [Holland, 1992] and attempts to define the notion of GP schema. Section 11.3 defines the rooted-tree schema relation. It then develops a theoretical analysis of the role played by the variable complexity of evolved representations and discusses interpretations of the theory. Next, Section 11.4 analyzes the effect of parsimony penalty on selection and in the tree-schema growth formulae. Section 11.5 discusses two alternative ways for controlling schema growth. An alternative based on dynamic adaptation of mutation and crossover probabilities will be experimentally examined in the following section. Section 11.6 discusses results of simulations of the standard GP algorithm with and without a parsimony penalty and presents an adaptive algorithm for controlling complexity. Based on the rooted-tree schema theory, Section 11.7 further discusses how the ideas of competing schemata and refinement of schemata suggest a top-down theory of solution acquisition. Section 11.8 reviews related work from the machine learning perspective, in general, and the EC perspective, in particular. Finally, section 11.9 summarizes this work.

11.2   Schema Theory

11.2.1   Schemata in genetic algorithms

Of all theoretical studies on the dynamics of a simple genetic algorithm, *schema theory* and the *building block hypothesis* have been the most controversial. In this section we review schema theory and its extension to GP, in order to contrast the new approach to be described later.

The concept of *schema* was introduced by Holland in order to characterize the informal notion of "building block." It was intuitively thought that GAs work by recombining building blocks. For linear binary representation of fixed length L, a schema is defined by a string of length L over the binary alphabet extended with a *don't care* symbol. A schema is interpreted as a template string whose 0 and 1 bits represent a fragment, or block of a chromosome.

The Schema Theorem gives an estimate of the change in the frequency of a schema in the population as a result of fitness-proportionate reproduction, crossover, and mutation ([Holland, 1992], see also [Goldberg, 1989]). We will restate it below.

Let $\mathcal{H}$ be a fixed schema of defining length $\delta(\mathcal{H})$ and $m(\mathcal{H}, t)$ be the number of copies of $\mathcal{H}$ in the population at time (generation) t. Let $f_{\mathcal{H}}$ be the average fitness of all strings in the population matching $\mathcal{H}$ and f be the average fitness of the population. Consider a simple GA using fitness proportionate selection for reproduction. Offspring are created through copying or single-point crossover, and additional variation through mutation. The probabilities for crossover and mutation are respectively p_c and p_m. Then, a lower bound on the number of copies of $\mathcal{H}$ in the next generation is given by [Goldberg, 1989]:

$$m(\mathcal{H}, t+1) \geq m(\mathcal{H}, t) \cdot \frac{f_{\mathcal{H}}}{f} \left(1 - p_c \frac{\delta(\mathcal{H})}{L-1}\right) (1 - p_m)^{o(\mathcal{H})} \qquad (11.1)$$

The coefficient of $m(\mathcal{H}, t)$ on the right hand side of relation (11.1) represents an approximation of the growth factor of schema $\mathcal{H}$. The constructive effect of variation operations was not considered. A super-unitary growth factor indicates that the next generation will contain more samples of the schema.

The theorem has been interpreted as showing that schemata with fitness values above population average, of low order and short length – all intuitive conditions for a super-unitary growth factor – will receive an exponentially increasing number of samples in the next generations. Such schemata are *building blocks*. Good individuals tend to be made up of good schemata, i.e. building blocks. The GA discovers and recombines such building blocks in parallel to create solutions. This is the essence of the Building Block Hypothesis as presented in [Goldberg, 1989]. Moreover, Holland argued that the search for an optimal string combines exploitation (preservation of schemata) and exploration (creation of new schemata) in close to an optimal proportion. The argument relied on the analogy between the allocation of samples to schemata in the GA with the allocation of effort in the Two-Armed-Bandit problem [Holland, 1992].

Schema theory has been criticized for not reflecting the processing done by a GA and not being really informative. One such critique is that GA allocates trials to schemata very differently from the optimal allocation given by the Two-Armed-Bandit solution. This was shown on contrived examples [Grefenstette and Baker, 1989; Mühlenbein, 1991]. Some of the discussions of schema theory caveats, such as that schema frequency variation is in disharmony with the Schema Theorem, are summarized in [Mitchell, 1996]. The problem with current interpretations is that they do not take into account what are independent schemata. Schema interdependence is due to inclusion relationships and epistasis. A formal notion of schema independence should take into account such effects. Independence can be defined relative to fitness contribution. Analysis and interpretations should therefore focus on the relevant entities, i.e. the independent competing schemata.

Another critique is that schemata do not necessarily capture relationships among meaningful properties that determine fitness [Altenberg, 1995]. Generalized schemata can be defined by partitioning the space of structures with many other relations. Such attempts have been presented in the GA literature [Vose and Liepins, 1991; Radcliffe, 1991]. Relations analogous to the schema theorem will hold for other representations as well [Radcliffe, 1992]. Indeed, schema theory explains the proliferation of substructures through selection. However, such properties can rather be used to refute a schema hypothesis. An argument for this remark is the intended use of Price's covariance and selection theorem [Price, 1970]. Price's theorem states that the variation in the frequency of a gene between the offspring and the parent population is proportional to the covariance between the frequency of the gene in an individual and the number of offspring of that individual over the parent population. Price outlined that his theorem helps in constructing hypotheses about selection, such as whether a certain behavioral feature is advantageous:

> Recognition of covariance is of no advantage for numerical calculation, but of much advantage for evolutionary reasoning and mathematical model building [Price, 1970, page 521].

Altenberg [Altenberg, 1995] brought attention on Price's theory and its general implications in GA theory. Although he dismissed the merit of current interpretations of the schema theory in explaining GA performance, he pointed out that the Schema Theorem is a particular case of Price's covariance theorem.[1] Altenberg further generalized the view of Price's theorem by considering *measurements* other than the frequency of a gene (schema).

Both schema theory and Price's theorem explain the variation in the frequency of a schema (Holland) or a group of genes (Price) over successive generations, but they rely on different arguments. Holland concentrates on the effects of selection, reproduction, crossover and mutation, so that his derivation explicitly incorporates fitness due to its role in selection. Price's analysis relies, more generally, on the correlation between the number of offspring produced from parents and the frequency of a certain gene in the parent population. Also, both theorems can be used to construct hypothesis about the evolutionary process, rather than fully explain its dynamics.

In Section 11.3 we introduce a new relation on the space of programs that allows us to focus on the interaction between fitness and complexity in variable complexity representations. Our measurement is the frequency of individuals in the population satisfying the relation. Before that, we critically examine approaches to extend the schema notion to GP.

11.2.2 Schemata in genetic programming

GA schemata have been interpreted from two interchangeable perspectives. The first perspective focuses on what genome parts can remain unchanged after repeated crossover operations and how these parts are assembled through recombination. The building block hypothesis shares this view. The second perspective interprets a schema as the set of individuals sharing common constraints (the defined elements) on their structure. By creating schemata with more defined elements, i.e. of higher order, the GA focuses search on smaller regions of the space.

It is not at all obvious how the GA schemata interpretations can be transferred to the variable length structures manipulated by GP. What property of variable length representations would be useful to observe or analyze in order to explain changes in structure or fitness and predict the dynamics of GP?

Again one can take two different perspectives of a GP schemata. The first focuses on the structural variation through crossover and mutation while the second focuses on subsets of the search space. In GA schema theory the two views were just the two sides of the same coin. In GP each of the two interpretations leads to different definitions and suggests different insights. Next we will review two definitions that take the first perspective and then present a new approach, the rooted-tree schema theory, that takes the second perspective.

GP searches the space of trees constrained by a maximum size or depth of trees. The tree representation can be also viewed as a string made of function and terminal symbols. The GP string has a default parenthesized structure imposed by the original hierarchical

---

[1] To see how an approximation of the Schema Theorem can be derived from Price's theorem, take into account that in a GA the number of offspring containing a gene (and its correspondent, a schema) is correlated with the deviation of fitness from the average population fitness for fitness proportional selection.

shape. Although the GA schema concept cannot be directly applied to the parenthesized string, it is helpful to think of GA schema as sets of fixed-length bit strings that have a number of features (bits) in common and then extend the definition to GP by considering sets of programs that have features in common. The question that remains is what kind of features would be most informative. Koza's schema definition focuses on subtrees as features. Programs in a GP schema set have in common one or more specified subtrees:

> A schema in genetic programming is the set of all individual trees from the
> population that contain, as subtrees, one or more specified trees. A schema is
> a set of LISP S-expressions sharing common features [Koza, 1992, page 117].

While a GA schema implicitly specifies through bit positions how two low order schemata are to be combined, this GP schema definition does not. Subtrees defining a schema can appear anywhere within the structure of an individual that belongs to the schema, provided that the entire structure obeys a maximum size or depth constraint.

The definition above suggests the intuitive idea that subtrees may play the role of functional features and that good features may be functionally combined to create good representations [Rosca and Ballard, 1996a].

Another, more general, GP schema definition is provided in [O'Reilly and Oppacher, 1995]. The previous definition allows for trees to be combined only as subtrees in larger structures. This second definition makes explicit how schema components can be combined in larger structures in analogy to a GA schema by using wildcards.

> A GP-schema H is a set of pairs. Each pair is a unique S-expression tree or
> fragment (i.e. incomplete S-expression tree with some leaves as wildcards) and
> a corresponding integer that specifies how many instances of the S-expression
> tree or fragment comprise H. [[O'Reilly and Oppacher, 1995], page 77]

While the Koza definition considers only the type of component manipulated by the crossover operation, this definition allows for the incomplete specification of fragments of a tree "corresponding to what is left intact by repeated crossovers." The extension allows a schema such as one or more contiguous fragments of a tree, where each tree fragment may have wildcards at its root or on its leaves.[2] Additionally, a duplication factor is considered for each fragment. In contrast to a GA schema, there is no predetermined way to combine the fragments.

Both definitions support the intuition that subtrees may be building blocks. However, the problem with both definitions is that they only implicitly specify a subset of the space of all tree structures with trees that match the schema. This makes it extremely difficult to characterize how GP allocates trials to regions of the space of program trees. The difficulty

---

[2] The root and leaf tree fragment wildcards have slightly different meanings. A root wildcard indicates that the fragment can be embedded in some higher level subtree, while a leaf wildcard indicates possible refinement with any subtree (fragment), possibly a terminal.

is reflected in the inconclusive attempt for deriving a GP Schema Theorem based on the second schema definition presented above [O'Reilly and Oppacher, 1995].

Other definitions of GP schemata, not discussed here, also take a structural perspective and only implicitly specify what a schema stands for. The resulting theories account for GP with special operators (such as one-point crossover and mutation, see [Poli and Langdon, 1997]) or more general representations (program derivation trees, see [Whigham, 1995]).

11.3 Portraying Variable Complexity Representations

In contrast to fixed length GA representations, each member x of the GP population has a variable size s_x. The goal of this section is to define a property, the rooted-tree schema property, that makes it possible to estimate the growth in the number of individuals satisfying the property as a function of the complexity of evolved individuals, in analogy to Equation (11.1). This analysis will represent the foundation for theoretical developments, interpretations, and experiments along the following lines:

- Role of variable complexity during evolution

- Influence of parsimony penalty

- Balance between fitness/error and complexity penalty

- Alternative approaches for imposing parsimony pressure

11.3.1 The rooted-tree schema property

Generalized schemata can be defined by partitioning the space of structures with other relations. Such attempts have been presented in the GA literature [Vose and Liepins, 1991; Radcliffe, 1991]. Next we propose a simple structural property that defines a different type of partitioning of the space of programs. The space of programs will be partitioned based on the topmost structure of trees. We will call the relation induced by this property a *rooted-tree schema* or *tree-schema*.

Definition. *A* rooted-tree schema *or* tree-schema *of order k is a rooted and contiguous tree fragment specified by k function and terminal labels,* see Figure 11.1.

The definition takes advantage of the hierarchical nature of program representations. It constructively specifies the correspondence between the tree-schema representation and the subset of programs defined by the tree-schema. One can easily check if a tree belongs to a given tree-schema. The definition will allow us to capture a different view of how the space of trees is searched. It is important to note that all tree-schema of a fixed shape and order are independent and are theoretically competing for a share of the search effort.

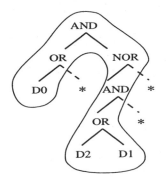

Figure 11.1
A rooted-tree fragment is the property of interest in analyzing the dynamics of GP. This example represents a tree-schema of order eight in the language used for inducing parity Boolean functions.

Figure 11.2
Three different tree structures defined by the same rooted-tree schema.

Note that we have dropped the implicit wild card on top of a fragment used in the previous GP schema definitions. The rooted-tree fragment can be instantiated only by refining the wild cards downwards to terminals. A rooted fragment precisely specifies, in a structural manner, the region in the space of programs to which all its instantiations will belong. It may also specify, through its composition, a collection of subtrees that are of particular importance (such as $(OR\ D_2\ D_1)$ in Figure 11.1) and how the trees are functionally combined.

There are more ways to build a tree "top," in analogy to the 2^k instantiations of k fixed bits of a GA-schema of order k. All the possible labelings of a fixed shape of the root fragment correspond to one *tree-schema class*. For any given class, the class tree-schemata compete for existence in the GP population. The larger the root fragment, the greater the number of competing tree-schemata. However, only a small fraction of them would be present in the population at any given time.

Now we can easily translate GA considerations similar to the schemata theorem or Price's theorem to GP. The distinguishing element is the variable length of chromosomes.

11.3.2   Growth of rooted-tree schemata

Consider a tree-schema $\mathcal{H}$ and the subpopulation that matches $\mathcal{H}$ (see an example in Figure 11.2.) Let $\|\mathcal{H}\|$ be the schema order[3] and $m(\mathcal{H}, t)$ be the number of copies of $\mathcal{H}$ in the population at time (generation) t. Let $f_{\mathcal{H}}$ be the average fitness of all trees matching $\mathcal{H}$ in the population and f be the average fitness of the population.[4] Consider the standard GP procedure, as defined in [Koza, 1992], that uses fitness proportionate selection for reproduction. Offspring are created through copying, tree crossover, and mutation. The probabilities for crossover and mutation are respectively p_c and p_m. Let also $p_d = p_c + p_m$.

In a population of size M, the expected number of offspring of individual $x \in \mathcal{H}$ is proportional with its fitness:

$$\frac{f_x}{\sum_{y=1}^{M} f_y} \cdot M = \frac{f_x}{f} \tag{11.2}$$

The probability of destruction for instances of individual $x \in \mathcal{H}$ is

$$p_d \cdot \frac{\|\mathcal{H}\|}{s_x} \tag{11.3}$$

By combining relations (11.2) and (11.3) we obtain a lower bound on the expected number of instances of $\mathcal{H}$ that results from offspring generated by x

$$\frac{f_x}{f} - p_d \cdot \frac{\|\mathcal{H}\|}{s_x} \cdot \frac{f_x}{f} \tag{11.4}$$

To obtain a lower bound on the expected number of copies of $\mathcal{H}$ in the next generation, we sum relations (11.4) for all trees $x \in \mathcal{H}$

$$m(\mathcal{H}, t+1) \geq \left(\sum_{x \in \mathcal{H}} \frac{f_x}{f} \right) - p_d \cdot \frac{\|\mathcal{H}\|}{f} \cdot \left(\sum_{x \in \mathcal{H}} \frac{f_x}{s_x} \right) \tag{11.5}$$

This is equivalent to

$$m(\mathcal{H}, t+1) \geq \left(\sum_{x \in \mathcal{H}} \frac{f_x}{f} \right) \left[1 - p_d \cdot \frac{\sum_{x \in \mathcal{H}} \frac{f_x}{s_x}}{\sum_{x \in \mathcal{H}} \frac{f_x}{\|\mathcal{H}\|}} \right]$$

or, taking into account that $m(\mathcal{H}, t) = \frac{1}{f_{\mathcal{H}}} \cdot \sum_{x \in \mathcal{H}} f_x$, we get

---

[3] The order and the defining complexity of a tree-schema schema $\mathcal{H}$ are identically defined as the number of nodes in $\mathcal{H}$, $o(\mathcal{H}) = \delta(\mathcal{H}) = \|\mathcal{H}\|$.

[4] From now on we will denote the average of quantity q over set $\mathcal{A}$ by $q_{\mathcal{A}}$ or $(q)_{\mathcal{A}}$. We also drop the index altogether when the set is the entire population. For example $s_{\mathcal{H}}$ is the average complexity of tree structures over tree-schema $\mathcal{H}$ and $\left(\frac{f}{s} \right)_{\mathcal{H}}$ is the average of ratios $\frac{f}{s}$ over $\mathcal{H}$. Similarly s is the average complexity over the entire population.

$$m(\mathcal{H}, t+1) \geq m(\mathcal{H}, t) \cdot \frac{f_{\mathcal{H}}}{f} \cdot \left[1 - p_d \cdot \underbrace{\frac{\sum_{x \in \mathcal{H}} \frac{f_x}{s_x}}{\sum_{x \in \mathcal{H}} \frac{f_x}{\|\mathcal{H}\|}}}_{a} \right] \qquad (11.6)$$

Equation 11.6 accounts for the variation in the number of individuals matching tree-schema $\mathcal{H}$ due to selection and the destructive effects of crossover and mutation.[5] Let us denote as a the coefficient of p_d on the right-hand side above. It is obvious that the variation of tree-schemata is also a function of the evolved size s_x of individuals $x \in \mathcal{H}$. If all trees had the same size S ($s_x = S$, $\forall x \in \mathcal{H}$) then a would reduce to $\frac{\|\mathcal{H}\|}{S}$ which is analogous to the term combining the destructive effect of crossover and mutation in the Schema Theorem (see relation 11.1). Here, the order of the tree plays the role of defining length. When a has a very small value it does not influence the growth of above average fitness tree-schemata. A bigger value of a dampens this growth. Next we analyze in detail this dependence of the right-hand side of 11.6 on size.

11.3.3 The role of variable size during evolution

Relation 11.6 can be also written as

$$m(\mathcal{H}, t+1) \geq R_1 \cdot m(\mathcal{H}, t) \cdot \left(1 - \frac{R_2}{m(\mathcal{H}, t)} \right) \qquad (11.7)$$

where R_1 and R_2 are defined as

$$R_1 = \frac{f_{\mathcal{H}}}{f}$$

$$R_2 = p_d \cdot \|\mathcal{H}\| \cdot \frac{\left(\frac{f}{s} \right)_{\mathcal{H}}}{f_{\mathcal{H}}}$$

For above average fitness tree-schemata

$$f_{\mathcal{H}} \geq f \qquad (11.8)$$

i.e. $R_1 \geq 1$. We are interested in conditions under which the right-hand side of 11.7 is greater ($\geq$) or much greater ($\gg$) than $m(\mathcal{H}, t)$. Under the respective conditions, by the transitivity of $\geq$ or $\gg$, it would follow that

$$m(\mathcal{H}, t+1) \geq m(\mathcal{H}, t) \text{ or } m(\mathcal{H}, t+1) \gg m(\mathcal{H}, t) \qquad (11.9)$$

---

[5]Fitness and complexity are time dependent too. Notations hide this time dependence for simplicity.

To determine such conditions, under which 11.9 is true, we substitute the right-hand side of equation 11.7 for $m(\mathcal{H}, t+1)$ in the first part of relation 11.9 and take into account inequality 11.8. We get

$$m(\mathcal{H}, t+1) \geq m(\mathcal{H}, t) \text{ if } m(\mathcal{H}, t) \geq \frac{R_1 R_2}{R_1 - 1} \tag{11.10}$$

After substituting R_1 and R_2, this implication can be written as

$$m(\mathcal{H}, t+1) \geq m(\mathcal{H}, t) \text{ if } m(\mathcal{H}, t) \geq \theta(\mathcal{H}, f, t) \tag{11.11}$$

where $\theta(\mathcal{H}, f, t)$ is defined as

$$\theta(\mathcal{H}, f, t) = \left(\frac{f}{s}\right)_{\mathcal{H}} \cdot \frac{1}{f_{\mathcal{H}}} \cdot \left(1 + \frac{1}{\frac{f_{\mathcal{H}}}{f} - 1}\right) \cdot p_d \cdot \|\mathcal{H}\| \tag{11.12}$$

Note that $\left(\frac{f}{s}\right)_{\mathcal{H}}$ is the average of $\frac{f}{s}$ values over the set of individuals $\mathcal{H}$. We have proved the following property:

Theorem 1. *For a given schema $\mathcal{H}$ ($\|\mathcal{H}\|$=fixed and p_d = constant), the number of instances of tree-schema $\mathcal{H}$ increases if $m(\mathcal{H}, t)$ exceeds a threshold value $\theta = \theta(\mathcal{H}, f, t)$ (see relations 11.11 and 11.12).*

The interpretation is that an individual $x \in \mathcal{H}$ can increase the survival rate of $\mathcal{H}$ by decreasing the threshold factor θ in one of the following two ways (see relation 11.12):

- By increasing its fitness f_x. This would determine an increase of $f_{\mathcal{H}}$ bigger than an increase in f.

- By increasing its complexity s_x. This would determine a decrease of $\left(\frac{f}{s}\right)_{\mathcal{H}}$.

Relation 11.11 can be further analyzed as follows. The expression for $\theta = \theta(\mathcal{H}, f, t)$ can be rewritten by grouping terms that are interpretable using Chebyshev's monotonic inequality[6]

$$m(\mathcal{H}, t+1) \geq m(\mathcal{H}, t) \text{ if } m(\mathcal{H}, t) \geq \underbrace{\left(\frac{f}{s}\right)_{\mathcal{H}} \cdot \frac{s_{\mathcal{H}}}{f_{\mathcal{H}}}}_{b} \cdot \underbrace{\left(1 + \frac{1}{\frac{f_{\mathcal{H}}}{f} - 1}\right)}_{c} \cdot p_d \cdot \frac{\|\mathcal{H}\|}{s_H} \tag{11.13}$$

---

[6]Chebyshev's monotonic inequality states that if $a_1 \leq a_2 \leq \ldots \leq a_n$ and $b_1 \leq b_2 \leq \ldots \leq b_n$ then $(\frac{1}{n}\sum_{i=1}^{n} a_i) \cdot (\frac{1}{n}\sum_{i=1}^{n} b_i) \leq \frac{1}{n}\sum_{i=1}^{n} a_i b_i$. Also, the sense of the inequality is reversed if $b_1 \geq b_2 \geq \ldots \geq b_n$, [Graham et al., 1994].

Relation 11.13 is an equivalent form of relation 11.11 and can be interpreted as follows. Assume that $s_{\mathcal{H}} = $ constant over time steps t and $t + 1$. Then the right-hand side of 11.13 depends on factors b and c. An increased value of the product $b \cdot c$ results in an increased threshold value in equation 11.13. The b factor captures the interaction between fitness and size within tree-schema $\mathcal{H}$. Let the members of $\mathcal{H}$ be indexed by $1, 2, ..., k$. If they can be ordered such that

$$s_1 \leq s_2 ... \leq s_k$$

and

$$\frac{f_1}{s_1} \leq \frac{f_2}{s_2} \leq \frac{f_k}{s_k}$$

i.e. they can be ordered such that increases in size are overcompensated by increases in fitness within $\mathcal{H}$, then by Chebyshev's inequality it would follow that $b \leq 1$. The smaller b, the smaller the threshold θ. Under the above conditions, the growth of schema $\mathcal{H}$ is favored as compared to another schema that has the same average fitness but does not satisfy the conditions. On the contrary, if fitness increases undercompensate the increases in complexity, the b component has a value bigger than 1. This determines a higher threshold value and implies that the growth of schema $\mathcal{H}$ is not equally favored.

In conclusion, this section has provided a sufficient condition for the increase in the number of instances of a tree-schema (relation 11.11) which outlines the role of variable complexity of evolved structures. By increasing in complexity but not in fitness, an individual determines a decrease in the threshold θ used in relation 11.11. If coupled with no other innovations in the population, this facilitates the increase of the individual's survival rate. For strict fitness to be dominant, fitness increases should overcompensate increases in complexity.

The increase in the survival rate of an individual solely through an increase in complexity is not a desirable tendency. Can such an effect generalize to the entire population? Section 11.6 will present simulations to answer this question. A "yes" answer is plausible, and it would indicate that the performance of GP search can be seriously degraded. The next section extends the present analysis when adding parsimony pressure during selection in order to confine the expected survival of individuals of ever increasing complexity.

11.4 Adding Parsimony

Parsimony pressure is given by an additive component $p(s_x)$ in the fitness function. Its coefficient, or weighting factor, is negative in order to penalize a size increase. With parsimony, the raw fitness function f_x is replaced by f_x^p

$$f_x^p = f_x + p(s_x) \tag{11.14}$$

A commonly used parsimony measure is linearly dependent on size

$$p(s_x) = -\sigma s_x \qquad (11.15)$$

In GP practice, the choice of the weighting factor σ is very much an art. Intuitively, small positive values should be used, so that the $p(s_x)$ component is negligible compared to f_x. This can be achieved by choosing σ as follows:

$$\sigma \ll inf_x \left[\frac{f_x}{s_x} \right] \qquad (11.16)$$

where infimum is taken over a set of best solutions evolved with no parsimony pressure.

For inductive problems, we can define a fitness function that trades error and complexity. Both error and complexity are measured in information bits that have to be transmitted over a line in order to be able to recreate the original data at the other end of the line. By applying the minimum description length principle similarly to [Quinlan and Rivest, 1989], we obtain the following definition of the parsimony component:

$$p(s_x) = -k_1 s_x \log s_x - k_2 s_x \qquad (11.17)$$

where k_1 depends on the inverse of the log of the number of fitness cases and k_2 is proportional to the number of bits needed to encode all symbols and inversely proportional to the log of the number of fitness cases [Rosca and Ballard, 1994].

In the rest of the article we will use a linear parsimony component.

11.4.1   Selection with a parsimonious fitness function

We compare the selection pressure in the following two cases: (1) when using a linear parsimony component (as defined in relations 11.14 and 11.15), and (2) when using "plain" fitness. The result is synthesized by the following theorem:

Theorem 2. *With linear parsimony penalty, individuals x with a fitness-complexity ratio greater than the ratio of population averages f and s:*

$$\frac{f_x}{s_x} \geq \frac{f}{s} \qquad (11.18)$$

have greater selection likelihood. This property is true regardless of the value of σ.

Proof: The role of parsimony can be formally analyzed by comparing the expected number of offspring of an individual x in the two cases above ("∨" below means "versus"):

$$\frac{f_x - \sigma s_x}{\sum_y (f_y - \sigma s_y)} \cdot M \vee \frac{f_x}{\sum_y f_y} \cdot M \qquad (11.19)$$

Relation 11.18 is obtained after truth preserving simplifications in 11.19. □

Theorem 2 allows one to interpret whether selection is stronger with or without parsimony. With parsimony, individuals x with a fitness-complexity ratio greater than the ratio of population averages f and s have greater selection likelihood. Although σ is factored out relation 11.18, it influences how much bigger the selection pressure is and what gets selected. A stronger selection pressure towards more effective individuals is useful in early stages of evolution and may be undesirable in later stages due to the decreased population diversity and thus stronger convergence tendency towards a local optimum.

11.4.2 Growth of rooted-tree schemata with parsimony

When a parsimonious fitness function is used, f is replaced by f^p, which is defined here according to relations 11.14 and 11.15.[7] Let θ^p be the value of θ obtained by substituting f^p for f in equation 11.12. The survival rates of a schema in the two cases can be compared by comparing the value of θ^p with θ.

The direct comparison $\theta \vee \theta^p$ can be written as

$$\left(\frac{f}{s}\right)_{\mathcal{H}} \cdot \frac{1}{f_{\mathcal{H}} - f} \vee \left(\frac{f - \sigma s}{s}\right)_{\mathcal{H}} \cdot \frac{1}{(f - \sigma s)_{\mathcal{H}} - (f - \sigma s)} \qquad (11.20)$$

The average operator over $\mathcal{H}$, implicit in the average notation $(\cdot)_{\mathcal{H}}$, has the following properties that are used to simplify equation 11.20:

$$\left(\frac{f - \sigma s}{s}\right)_{\mathcal{H}} = \left(\frac{f}{s}\right)_{\mathcal{H}} - \sigma$$

$$(f - \sigma s)_{\mathcal{H}} = f_{\mathcal{H}} - \sigma s_{\mathcal{H}}$$

After simplifications, $\theta \vee \theta^p$ becomes equivalent to

$$\left(\frac{f}{s}\right)_{\mathcal{H}} \cdot \frac{1}{f_{\mathcal{H}} - f} \vee \left[\left(\frac{f}{s}\right)_{\mathcal{H}} - \sigma\right] \cdot \frac{1}{(f_{\mathcal{H}} - f) - \sigma(s_{\mathcal{H}} - s)} \qquad (11.21)$$

When complexity $s_{\mathcal{H}}$ increases the left-hand side of 11.21 decreases. However, this is not necessarily true with the right-hand side, where the term

$$\frac{1}{(f_{\mathcal{H}} - f) - \sigma(s_{\mathcal{H}} - s)}$$

increases with $s_{\mathcal{H}}$. As expected, this shows that size plays a different role in the dynamics of GP with parsimony pressure. In this case it is obvious that selection will favor the smaller of two evolved structures of equal raw fitness

$$s_{x_1} \leq s_{x_2} \Leftrightarrow f^p_{x_1} \leq f^p_{x_2} \qquad (11.22)$$

---

[7] So far we have bypassed details about the nature of f, such as whether f is raw fitness or normalized fitness (see [Koza, 1992]), and rather considered that the fitness function f supplies values used during the selection phase of the GP algorithm.

This implies size decreases over periods of time when fitness does not improve.

When $\mathcal{H}$ identifies a worthy individual x just discovered, relation 11.20 can be simplified. The worthy structure is propagated throughout the population at a higher rate if the threshold θ is much lower than the threshold with parsimony θ^p. This is true if and only if the right hand side below holds

$$\theta \gg \theta^p \Leftrightarrow \frac{f_x}{s_x} \gg \frac{f}{s} \tag{11.23}$$

The following theorem covers the general case:

Theorem 3. *For an above average schema $\mathcal{H}$, if σ is chosen as in relation 11.16 and the relative increase in schema fitness is bigger than the relative increase in schema size times the average of ratios $\left(\frac{f}{s}\right)_{\mathcal{H}}$, then a better than average schema has better chances of surviving and propagating in the population. More precisely*

$$\theta \gg \theta^p \Leftrightarrow (f_{\mathcal{H}} - f) \gg \left(\frac{f}{s}\right)_{\mathcal{H}} \cdot (s_{\mathcal{H}} - s) \tag{11.24}$$

The above conclusions are consistent with the analysis of the role of size in selection and can be particularized for the case $\mathcal{H} = \{x\}$ to reach the same conclusion as in 11.23.

The size increase tendency is deamplified, as expected, when a parsimonious fitness function is considered versus the case of the tree-schema growth in equation 11.11. However in demarcation situations, such as the discovery and proliferation of a fit structure, size influences its rate of survival as shown in relation 11.23. In section 11.6 we will explore the role of size in GP simulations where a parsimonious fitness function is considered.

11.5   Controlling Schema Growth

The probability of destruction of instances of individual $x \in \mathcal{H}$ depends on the complexity s_x (see equation 11.3). In one likely scenario the complexity of the current best programs tends to increase. Also, the proportion of the more complex of these programs in the population increases although they do not improve in raw performance. This would make GP prone to local minima and result in a waste of computational effort. The result is comprised in the growth of tree-schemata in relation 11.11 and the interpretation of Theorem 1. GP search is unjustifiably biased towards exploring structures of higher and higher complexity independently of raw fitness.

On the contrary, when using parsimony the above problem is apparently accounted for. This is done at the price of modifying the fitness function to penalize for increases in complexity. However, search optima with the new fitness function are not necessarily search optima with the original fitness function. In other words, the fitness "landscape" changes.

It would be desirable to inhibit the propagation of structures that increase in complexity without improving in fitness. The remedy to this problem is to control tree schema growth so that the complexity of structures does not influence the probability of tree-schema destruction. In other words, GP should not allow overall size growth to "protect" a rooted-tree schema from disruption. This can be achieved in two ways.

First, such an effect could be approximately obtained by predefining a probability mass function for choosing crossover and mutation points within tree structures, which would assign most of the probability mass to the higher tree levels, i.e. to nodes closer to the root. Figure 11.3 gives an example of the desired shape of the probability mass function, which is chosen to be the Pascal (negative binomial) distribution. The depth of the point of variation is chosen based on this probability mass function, and the node itself is chosen uniformly among all nodes of the same depth. If a depth is not represented in some tree structure, that structure is copied unchanged. A tree structure grows downwards, so that the cumulative probability of disrupting a given number of the high layers in the tree becomes independent of the tree size. Therefore, this method achieves the goal of disrupting a tree-schema with constant, complexity independent, probability. Unfortunately, the method introduces the parameters of the probability mass function that would have to be eventually adjusted (see Figure 11.3). Another practical disadvantage is the intricacy of any method for determining the actual crossover/mutation point.

Second, we could directly affect the probabilities of crossover and mutation, i.e. make them adapt, so that disruption of tree-schemata occurs with probability independent of complexity. The basic idea is to redefine the probability of disruption of structure x to be a function of s_x

$$p'_d = \begin{cases} p_d & \text{if } s_x < s_0 \\ \min\{1, p_d \cdot \frac{s_x}{s_0}\} & \text{if } s_x \geq s_0 \end{cases} \tag{11.25}$$

where s_0 is a predefined parameter playing the role of a threshold complexity value (see Figure 11.4). With this change, disruption of schema $\mathcal{H}$ occurs with constant probability when $s_x \geq s_0$

$$p'_d \cdot \frac{\|\mathcal{H}\|}{s_x} = p_d \cdot \frac{\|\mathcal{H}\|}{s_0} = \text{constant} \tag{11.26}$$

If s_x increases then the probability of destruction of x remains constant. The number of instances of x in the next generation will be exclusively influenced by its fitness and the appearance in the population of better individuals.

11.6 Experimental Results

This section presents experiments aimed at reinforcing conclusions that have been suggested by the previous theoretical analysis.

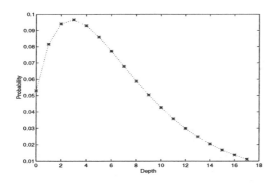

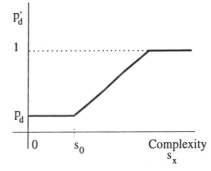

Figure 11.3

Depth of variation points is chosen using a negative binomial distribution with $r = 2$ and $p = 0.23$. The cumulative distribution up to a depth of trees of 17 is 0.999.

Figure 11.4

Rule for the automatic adaptation of the probability of disruption p'_d. Probabilities p_m and p_c can be updated proportionately so that their sum is p'_d.

One cannot know in advance what particular schema is to be preferred by the evolutionary process in a run of GP. Moreover, it is extremely hard to trace a schema property for all competing tree-schemata of any given shape and size. However, one can examine relevant properties globally, for the entire population, and narrowly, for the best individual in the population. The experiments below provide a consistent view of GP dynamics by looking at a common set of measures over three types of runs of the standard GP engine. The measures are quantities that have appeared throughout our derivations and have been used to qualitatively explain results. They are the averages over the population (f, s, $\frac{f}{s}$) and the best individual in a generation f_{best}, s_{best}, or $\left(\frac{f}{s}\right)_{best}$. The types of runs performed are:

1. Standard GP with raw fitness being only a measure of performance.

2. Standard GP with parsimony pressure. The fitness function combines raw fitness and a linear parsimony component to penalize a size increase.

3. GP with adaptive probabilities of crossover and mutation. These probabilities are updated dynamically as in Figure 11.4 in order to impose a constant parsimony pressure on competing tree-schemata regardless of the complexity of evolved structures.

Two test problems are used. The first problem is the induction of a Boolean formula (circuit) that computes parity on a set of bits [Koza, 1994]. The raw fitness function has access to fitness cases that show the parity value for all inputs, and counts the number of correct parity computations. These experiments use the following parameters: population size $M = 4000$, number of generations $N = 50$, crossover rate $p_c = 89\%$ (20% on leaf nodes), mutation rate $p_m = 1\%$, reproduction rate $p_r = 10\%$, number of fitness cases = 2^n where n is the order of the parity problem. The second problem is the induction of a controller for a robotic agent in a dynamic and nondeterministic environment, as in the Pac-Man game [Koza, 1992; Rosca and Ballard, 1996a]. Raw fitness here is computed from the performance of evolved controllers over a number of simulations. The parameters for these runs are $M = 500$, $N = 150$, $p_c = 89\%$, $p_m = 1\%$, $p_r = 10\%$, with three simulations determining the individual fitness. Also, $s_0 = 100$.

Each of Figures 11.5-11.7 contains three plots: (a) Variation of average complexity s and the complexity of the best-of-generation individual s_{best} (top); (b) Variation of the ratio of averages $\frac{f}{s}$ and of $\left(\frac{f}{s}\right)_{best}$ (middle); (c) The fitness learning curve f_{best} and variation of average fitness f (bottom).

11.6.1   Fitness based on pure performance

Over the time span of evolution in a GP run, often there are long periods of time when no fitness improvements are noticed. Section 11.3.2 has proved that an increase of the individual's survival rate can be accomplished by the increase in its complexity, but not in its fitness. Can this effect generalize to the entire population? We suggested that a "yes" answer is plausible, which indicates that the performance of the GP engine can be seriously degraded. Here we present experimental evidence.

The variation in the complexity of evolved structures can be seen in plots correlating the learning curves and complexity curves for the two test problems. When fitness remains constant, both the best of generation complexity s_{best} and the average complexity s indeed increase over time. Plateaus of f_{best} can be observed in Figure 11.5(c) (left) between generations 33 and 59, or Figure 11.5(c) (right) between generations 15 and 47, or 53 and 101. During the corresponding time intervals, size almost doubles in Figure 11.5(a) (left) and significantly increases in Figure 11.5(a) (right) while average fitness also increases. The increase in average size is explained by the predominant increase in survival rate of above average individuals of increased size in the absence of any fitness improvements.

11.6.2   Parsimonious fitness

Next we present experiments where parsimony pressure is applied during selection in order to confine the survival of individuals of ever increasing complexity and thus to guard against the apparent loss of efficiency of GP search. An important question is whether parsimony would deter GP search from finding fit solutions at the expense of finding parsimonious solutions. This could happen because of the artificial distortion in fitness created by the parsimony component.

We expect to see a decrease in size over spans of time with no improvement in fitness. Three such intervals can be noticed in Figure 11.6(a) and (c) (left): generations 18 to

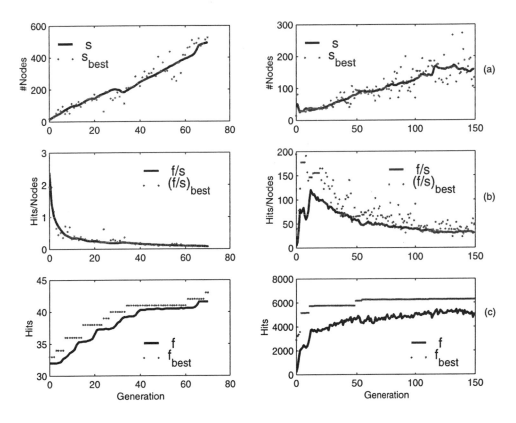

Figure 11.5
Average and best-of-generation variation in (a) size, (b) fitness-size ratio, and (c) fitness in a run of GP without parsimony pressure: Parity (left) and Pac-Man (right).

57, 58 to 72, and 73 to 99. The GP algorithm discovers a new best solution, having a complexity higher than every other previous individual at the beginning of each of these intervals. Following the complexity curves towards the end of the intervals, we note a gradual decrease in s_{best}. The same tendency is conspicuous in the average complexity plot s, which has a shape similar to s_{best} and is delayed with about four to five generations. The delay period is the time needed by selection to pick up on the opportunities created at the beginning of the above intervals.

One remarkable feature of the f plot in Figure 11.6(c) is that average fitness decrease is correlated with average size decrease s. The explanation is that parsimony pressure induces a decrease in complexity, which makes mutation and crossover operations more disruptive. This generates a decrease in average fitness over the population. The effect is even clearer when the value of the weighting factor σ increases (see Figure 11.6) (right).

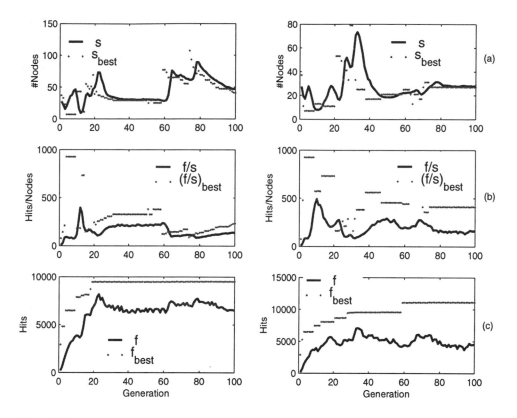

Figure 11.6
Average and best-of-generation variation in (a) size, (b) fitness-size ratio, and (c) fitness in a run of GP with
parsimony pressure $\sigma = 0.1$ (left) and $\sigma = 1.0$ (right) for the Pac-Man problem.

Note also the rapid increases in fitness in early generations in Figure 11.6(b) (left) and
(right). They show that the following relation holds in very early generations in contrast to
Figure 11.5(b) (left) and (right).

$$\frac{f_{best}}{s_{best}} \gg \frac{f}{s}$$

i.e. the stronger selection pressure towards more effective individuals due to parsimony
is useful to rapidly focus search towards good structures (as in the discussion of equations
11.18 and 11.23). The ability of the GP engine to find fit solutions appears to have improved
considerably when using a parsimonious fitness function.

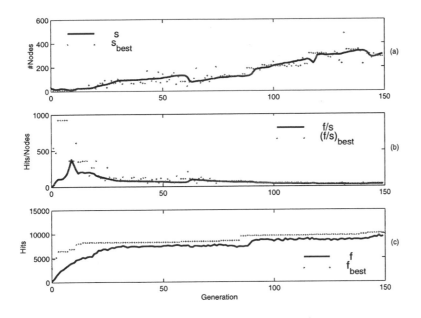

Figure 11.7
Average and best-of-generation variation in (a) size, (b) fitness-size ratio, and (c) fitness in a Pac-Man run of GP with autoadaptive crossover, mutation, and reproduction rates.

11.6.3 Adaptive probability of destruction

In this third experiment we modify the standard GP engine to consider an adaptive probability of disruption of an expression (mutation and crossover) dependent on the size of the expression, as in equation 11.25. The standard GP procedure varies selected subexpressions in proportion to p_c and p_m and keeps around (in next generation) surviving selected structures in proportion to $p_r = 1 - p_c - p_m$. This is done globally in the sense that a p_c fraction of the next generation is obtained through crossover on selected structures, etc. In contrast, the size-adaptive procedure decides what genetic operation to apply for each selected individual. In this way, the complexity of the individual can be used in taking the decision of mutation, crossover or survival. The procedure records the proportions of the next generation obtained with each genetic operation.

An example is given in Figure 11.8 where one can see the variations in the probability of crossover (the only type of variation used). The changes in p_c can be correlated with the changes in the average complexity s (Figure 11.7). Although size increases over time, the higher destruction appears to limit the size increase without disrupting the search process.

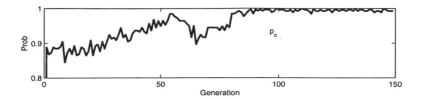

Figure 11.8
Adaptation in the probability of crossover for the run in Figure 11.7.

11.6.4 Summary of experiments

The experiments above have attained three main goals in relation with the theoretical analysis of tree-schema growth:

• Traced the GP-specific variable complexity during evolution and interpreted its variations from the perspective of the size-dependent growth formula 11.11. Complexity increases can derail the search effort of the GP engine. This is showed by the long stable periods with no improvements in the most fit structures.

• Traced the influence of an additive parsimony component to fitness. Experiments show a considerable increase in efficiency and offer insight into the choice for the value of σ, the weighting factor of the parsimony component.

• Observed at work the second proposed alternative to imposing parsimony pressure. By increasing the probability of variation while the size of expressions increases, we preserve the exploration ability of GP in the space of expressions. More experiments are needed to assess the advantage of this adaptive method.

11.7 Solution Acquisition in GP

It is important to understand how partial solutions are refined, knowing that GP does not merely guess solutions. Such an understanding would facilitate the design of tools to make the evolutionary process more transparent and moreover to control it. Efforts along this line have been recently reported in [Goldberg and O'Reilly, 1998; O'Reilly and Goldberg, 1998], who looked at how independent sub-solutions are acquired as a function of their fitness contributions. Here, we are rather interested in the structural aspect of solution construction, when it is unknown what constitutes a subsolution.

The classical view, in line with the building block hypothesis in GA/GP, is that GP solutions are refined *bottom-up*, i.e. by starting with small pieces of useful code and then by combining them to compose higher and higher order components. Such pieces of code should be protected from crossover and other disruptive genetic operators [Banzhaf et al., 1998]. There is little evidence of what building blocks actually are in this case.

The GP representation using Automatically Defined Functions [Koza, 1992] makes unambiguous what could possibly be building blocks, namely subroutines. Subroutines can be hierarchically invoked in order to build solutions, and are also subject to genetic variations. The bottom-up view appears justified when using subroutines. ADFs or subroutines should be *stable* building blocks. Experimental evidence that they are indeed refined bottom-up was presented in [Rosca, 1995]. [Rosca, 1995] considered representations with three components: two subroutines and the main program body. It computed the percentage of genetic changes in a component, taken over all programs in the genealogic tree of a solution created by GP, as a function of generation. The analysis showed that the percentage of changes in a component (such as an ADF) achieves a maximum at times directly proportional to the place of the component in the component hierarchy. Thus, components at the bottom of the hierarchy (such as ADF_0) are learned first, and are subsequently used to define higher level components.

The rooted-three schema theory suggests a radically different view, namely that solutions are refined *top-down*, starting with the root of the tree and specializing the problem decomposition in a top-down manner. Indeed, a small number of independent rooted-tree schemata compete for existence in the population at any given time. A rooted-tree schema that wins the competition is further refined downwards (i.e top-down). Equivalently, the competition within a certain schema order ends (with one rooted-tree schema being a winner). It gradually transforms into a competition among independent rooted-tree schemata descendents (of the winning schema) having higher order. Two rooted-tree schemata are different if and only if they diverge in shape or, if they have the same shape, they have at least one different point. Different rooted-tree schemata are independent, i.e. they refer to (syntactically) disjoint regions of the search space (as opposed to GA schemata, which may not be independent even when they are different).

The top-down refinement hypothesis advanced here is consistent with the observation that crossover acts as a "macromutation." In other words, simply using a mutation operator that replaces a randomly chosen subtree with a new randomly created subtree results in at least similar performance to GP with crossover [Angeline, 1997].

Although the top-down and bottom-up views are radically different, they are not mutually exclusive. Top-down refinement may lead to program components that are effective and essential in any fitness computation. Such components are still evolved bottom-up, nonetheless the overall process of solution refinement is top-down, as evidenced in the experiments from[Rosca, 1995] (see a detailed account in [Rosca, 1997]). A related idea informally states that "two types of building blocks are used to construct solutions" [Poli and Langdon, 1997, page 284]. These would correspond to rooted-tree fragments and subtree fragments.

11.8 Related Work

The GP literature is rich in deliberations on the bloat phenomenon (size increase), and bloat control schemes. Herein, we recapitulate a few and place them in a broader perspective.

Early, [Tackett, 1994] pointed out that bloating cannot be selection-neutral. He presented experiments suggesting that average growth in size is proportional to the selection pressure. In our analysis, selection pressure itself is complexity dependent. Tackett also suggested that the larger programs selected by GP contain expressions which are inert overall (introns), but contain useful subexpressions, thus correlating bloating with hitchhiking.

Related to the size problem, GP research has focused on the analysis of introns. *Introns* are pieces of code with no effect on the output. An analysis of introns goes hand in hand with an analysis of bloating. [Nordin et al., 1995] tracked introns in an assembly language GP system based on a linear but variable length program representation. The analysis suggested that the increase in size is a "defense against crossover." A similar conclusion is reached here in Theorem 1 (Section 11.11). In the linear representation, the noticed increase in the size of programs was attributed to introns. Based on experiments with controlled crossover or mutation rate within intron fragments, [Nordin et al., 1995] suggested that a representation which generates introns leads to better search effectiveness. Thus, introns may have a positive role in GP search protecting against destructive genetic operations. For hierarchical GP representations [Rosca, 1996] showed that much of the size increase is due to ineffective code too. However, the role of introns has been disputed in the case of GP using tree representations [Andre and Teller, 1996]. For one thing, the overhead introduced by exponentially increasing tree sizes may offset any protective effects of introns.

More recently, the GP literature contains several puzzlingly simple and informal attempts to explaining the bloat phenomenon. [Langdon and Poli, 1997] claims that larger, semantically equivalent programs are more abundant, therefore they are more likely to be found by GP search. However, non-equivalent larger programs are much more abundant. Therefore, it is unclear whether the proportion of semantically equivalent larger programs increases with the depth or size of programs. [Soule and Foster, 1998] outlines a processing bias called "removal bias" of standard GP operators. The replacement of small subtrees with bigger ones is more likely not to affect offspring, therefore size tends to increase. This explanation agrees with the increase in survivability of offspring predicted by rooted-tree schemata.

A diversity of bloat control schemes have been proposed in the literature. These vary from complexity bounds and penalties, to submodule reuse, biased genetic operations to counteract the bloat bias, and multi-objective or co-evolving fitness.

The problem of learning a non-parametric model without biasing for particular structures has been addressed in the area of nonparametric statistical inference. In statistical terms this is the problem of learning with low bias or tabula-rasa learning. However, low bias in the choice of models is paid for by a high variance (see [Geman et al., 1992] for an excellent introduction to the bias/variance dilemma). Methods for balancing bias and variance include techniques that rely on a complexity penalty function which is added to the error term in order to promote parsimonious solutions. The basic idea is to trade the complexity of the model for its accuracy. This idea resonates with one of the fundamental principles in inductive learning represented by Ockham's razor principle, which is interpreted as: "Among the several theories that are consistent with the observed phenomena, one should pick the simplest theory" [Li and Vitanyi, 1992]. What is simple often turns out to be more general.

One common approach to dealing with a variable complexity model within the Bayesian estimation framework is Rissanen's minimum description length (MDL) principle [Li and Vitanyi, 1993]. The MDL principle trades off the model code length, i.e. the complexity term, against the error code length, i.e. the data not explained by the model or error term. Complexity is naturally expressed as the size of code or data in bits of information.

Informed approaches to including a parsimony component, such as the MDL principle, implicitly expect that the capability of the learned model is a smooth function of its complexity, i.e. as a solution grows it is fitter. This is not true for Genetic Programming, which furthermore cannot afford to exploit a large number of training examples and use infinite populations in order to overcome the problem. A small change in a program can entirely destroy its performance. The capability of a model specified with a program is not a smooth function of its complexity. Nonetheless GP manages to sample the space of programs and to discover automatically satisfiable models of variable complexity.

The MDL principle has been also applied in GP to extend the fitness function of hybrid classification models [Iba et al., 1993; Iba et al., 1994]. For example [Iba et al., 1994] applied the MDL principle in the learning rule of a GP-regression tree hybrid. [Zhang and Muhlenbein, 1995] used an adaptive parsimony strategy in a GP-neural net hybrid. In both cases GP manipulates tree structures corresponding to a hierarchical multiple regression model of variable complexity, decision trees, or sigma-pi neural networks, rather than programs. MDL-based fitness functions have been unsuccessful in the case of GP evolving pure program structures. Iba outlined that the MDL-based fitness measure can be applied problems satisfying the "size-based performance" criterion [Iba et al., 1994], where the more the tree structure grows the better its performance becomes.[Rosca and Ballard, 1994] has used the MDL principle to assess the suitability of an extension of GP with subroutines called adaptive representation (AR).

The most common approach to circumvent complexity-induced limitations in GP has been the use of a parsimonious fitness function. Parsimony imposes constraints on the complexity of learned solutions. However the effects of such constraints in GP have not been elucidated. Parsimony pressure clearly improves efficiency of search and understandability of solutions if well designed. The quality and, in particular, the generality of solutions may also be improved in inductive problems.

However, adding the right parsimony pressure has been more of an art. One example of avoiding this decision by means of an ad-hoc algorithm is "disassortative mating" [Ryan,

1994]. This GP algorithm selects parents for crossover from two different lists of individuals. One list of individuals is ranked based on fitness while the other is ranked based on the sum of size and weighted fitness. The goal is to evolve solutions of minimal size that solve the problem. However, it was recognized that by directly using the size constraint the GP algorithm is prevented from finding solutions. The disassortative mating algorithm is reported to improve convergence to a better optimum while maintaining speed.

Another suggestion for limiting the increase in complexity is to employ modular GP extensions such as algorithms based on the evolution of the architecture [Koza, 1994], module acquisition [Angeline, 1993], heuristic extensions for the discovery of subroutines [Rosca and Ballard, 1994; Rosca and Ballard, 1996a], or GP with architecture modifying operation using code duplication [Koza, 1995]. Evolved modular programs theoretically have a lower descriptional complexity [Rosca and Ballard, 1994] and also appear to present better generality [Rosca, 1996; Rosca and Ballard, 1996b].

The problem that evolved expressions tend to drift towards large and slow forms without necessarily improving the results was recognized in some excellent early work in GP applied to the simulation of textures for use in computer graphics [Sims, 1991]. The solution devised was heuristic. Mutation frequencies were tailored so that a decrease in complexity was slightly more probable than an increase. This did not prevent increases towards larger complexity but more complex solutions were due to the selection of improvements. It is not apparent how this was accomplished precisely. Interestingly, the solution to controlling complexity presented in section 11.5 achieves exactly this effect and is theoretically founded.

An alternative approach to program induction based on different search principles is taken in ADATE [Olsson, 1995]. ADATE essentially performs iterative deepening, exhaustive search in the space of program constructs, and it proves quite successful for small target programs. Interestingly enough from the perspective of how GP assembles solutions, ADATE refines solutions in a top-down manner by design.

11.9   Conclusion

Researchers from machine learning in general and evolutionary computation in particular have long debated the utility of the schema theory originated by Holland in the mid-seventies as a mathematical tool for characterizing the mechanism of a genetic algorithm. This chapter addressed the issue of finding a relevant property of GP evolved structures whose analysis, inspired in the GA schema theory, could provide insight into how GP works and reveal possible search limitations caused to the standard GP engine by the variable complexity of evolved structures.

The property of interest, called *rooted-tree schema*, is defined as a relation on the space of program structures. Rooted-tree schemata provide a partitioning of the GP search space and show how GP allocates effort to *independent* regions of the search space described by independent competing rooted-tree schemata. The analysis of rooted-tree schemata is remarkably simple and powerful.

Formal analysis of rooted-tree schemata makes it possible to understand the role played by variable complexity of evolved structures. The analysis showed the influence of a parsimony component and discussed choices on the complexity weighting factor values. Alternative approaches to parsimony pressure were proposed, based on the idea of varying the probability of destructive genetic operations proportionally to the complexity of structures. Last but not least, the rooted-tree schema theory suggests a radically different view of program refinement in GP, namely that solutions are refined top-down starting with the root of the tree. This observation is important from the perspective of defining more powerful genetic operators and second tier control heuristics of the GP system itself. Theoretical results were also interpreted and discussed from an experimental perspective.

The rooted-tree schema analysis reveals insights about the mechanisms at work in GP, and should be of interest to a machine learning audience eager to find formal arguments in addition to pure experimental evidence from the field of genetic programming.

Acknowledgements

Una-May deserves sincere thanks for her careful reading and excellent suggestions for improving this chapter. Bill deserves many thanks for being such a terrific colleague.

Bibliography

Altenberg, L. (1995), "The schema theorem and Price's theorem," in *Foundations of Genetic Algorithms 3*, L. D. Whitley and M. D. Vose (Eds.), pp 23–49, San Mateo, CA, USA: Morgan Kaufmann.

Andre, D. and Teller, A. (1996), "A study in program response and the negative effects of introns in genetic programming," in *Genetic Programming 1996: Proceedings of the First Annual Conference*, J. R. Koza, D. E. Goldberg, D. B. Fogel, and R. L. Riolo (Eds.), pp 12–20, The MIT Press.

Angeline, P. J. (1993), *Evolutionary Algorithms and Emergent Intelligence*, PhD thesis, Ohio State University.

Angeline, P. J. (1994), "Genetic programming and emergent intelligence," in *Advances in Genetic Programming*, K. E. Kinnear, Jr. (Ed.), Chapter 4, pp 75–98, Cambridge, MA, USA: MIT Press.

Angeline, P. J. (1997), "Subtree crossover: Building block engine or macromutation?," in *Genetic Programming 1997: Proceedings of the Second Annual Conference*, J. R. Koza, K. Deb, M. Dorigo, D. B. Fogel, M. Garzon, H. Iba, and R. L. Riolo (Eds.), pp 9–17, Stanford University, CA, USA: Morgan Kaufmann.

Bäck, T., Hoffmeister, F., and Schwefel, H.-P. (1991), "A survey of evolutionary strategies," in *Proceedings of the Fourth International Conference on Genetic Algorithms*, Morgan Kaufmann Publishers, Inc.

Banzhaf, W., Nordin, P., Keller, R. E., and Francone, F. D. (1998), *Genetic programming: An Introduction*, Morgan Kaufmann and dpunkt.

Fogel, D. B. (1995), *Evolutionary computation : toward a new philosophy of machine intelligence*, IEEE Press.

Fogel, L. J., Owens, A. J., and Walsh, M. J. (1966), *Artificial intelligence through simulated evolution*, Wiley.

Geman, S., Bienenstock, E., and Doursat, R. (1992), "Neural networks and the bias/variance dilemma," *Neural Computation*, (4):1–58.

Goldberg, D. and O'Reilly, U.-M. (1998), "Where Does the Good Stuff Go, and Why? How contextual semantics influences program structure in simple genetic programming," in *Proceedings of the First European Workshop on Genetic Programming*, W. Banzhaf, R. Poli, M. Schoenauer, and T. C. Fogarty (Eds.), volume 1391 of *LNCS*, Paris: Springer-Verlag.

Goldberg, D. E. (1989), *Genetic Algorithms in Search, Optimization, and Machine Learning*, Addison-Wesley.

Graham, R. L., Knuth, D. E., and Patashnik, O. (1994), *Concrete mathematics : a foundation for computer science*, Addison-Wesley, 2nd edition.

Grefenstette, J. and Baker, J. (1989), "How genetic algorithms work: a critical look at implicit parallelism," in *Proceedings of the 3rd International Conference on Genetic Algorithms*, J. Schaffer (Ed.), Morgan Kaufmann.

Holland, J. H. (1992), *Adaptation in Natural and Artificial Systems, An Introductory Analysis with Applications to Biology, Control and Artificial Intelligence*, Cambridge, MA: MIT Press, Second edition (First edition, 1975).

Iba, H., de Garis, H., and Sato, T. (1994), "Genetic programming using a minimum description length principle," in *Advances in Genetic Programming*, K. Kinnear Jr. (Ed.), MIT Press.

Iba, H., Kurita, T., de Garis, H., and Sato, T. (1993), "System identification using structured genetic algorithms," in *Proceedings of the Fifth International Conference on Genetic Algorithms*, Pittsburg, PA, USA: Morgan Kaufmann Publishers, Inc.

Koza, J. R. (1992), *Genetic Programming: On the Programming of Computers by Means of Natural Selection*, MIT Press.

Koza, J. R. (1994), *Genetic Programming II*, MIT Press.

Koza, J. R. (1995), "Gene duplication to enable genetic programming to concurrently evolve both the architecture and work-performing steps of a computer program," in *IJCAI*, C. S. Mellish (Ed.), volume 1, pp 734–740, Morgan Kaufmann.

Langdon, W. B. and Poli, R. (1997), "Fitness causes bloat," in *Second On-line World Conference on Soft Computing in Engineering Design and Manufacturing*.

Langdon, W. B. and Poli, R. (1998), "Fitness causes bloat: Mutation," in *Proceedings of the First European Workshop on Genetic Programming*, W. Banzhaf, R. Poli, M. Schoenauer, and T. C. Fogarty (Eds.), volume 1391 of *LNCS*, pp 37–48.

Li, M. and Vitanyi, P. (1993), *An Introduction to Kolmogorov Complexity and its Applications*, Springer-Verlag.

Li, M. and Vitanyi, P. M. B. (1992), "Inductive reasonong and kolmogorov complexity," *Journal of Computer and Systems Sciences*, 44:343–384.

Mühlenbein, H. (1991), "Evolution in time and space – the parallel genetic algorithm," in *Foundations of Genetic Algorithms 1*, G. J. Rawlins (Ed.), pp 316–337, Morgan Kaufmann.

Mitchell, M. (1996), *An Introduction To Genetic Algorithms*, MIT Press.

Nordin, P., Francone, F., and Banzhaf, W. (1995), "Explicitly defined introns and destructive crossover in genetic programming," in *Proceedings of the ICML Workshop on Genetic Programming: From Theory to Real-World Applications (NRL TR 95.2)*, J. P. Rosca (Ed.), pp 6–22, University of Rochester.

Olsson, R. (1995), "Inductive functional programming using incremental program transformation," *Artificial Intelligence*, 74:55–81.

O'Reilly, U.-M. and Goldberg, D. (1998), "How fitness structure affects subsolution acquisition in genetic programming," in *Proceedings of the Third Annual Genetic Programming Conference*, J. R. Koza, W. Banzhaf, K. Chellapilla, K. Deb, M. Dorigo, D. B. Fogel, M. H. Garzon, D. E. Goldberg, H. Iba, and R. L. Riolo (Eds.), Madison, WI, USA: Morgan Kaufmann.

O'Reilly, U.-M. and Oppacher, F. (1995), "The troubling aspects of a building block hypothesis for genetic programming," in *Foundations of Genetic Algorithms 3*, L. D. Whitley and M. D. Vose (Eds.), pp 73–88, San Mateo, CA, USA: Morgan Kaufmann.

Poli, R. and Langdon, W. B. (1997), "A new schema theory for GP with one-point crossover and point mutation," in *Genetic Programming 1997: Proceedings of the Second Annual Conference*, J. R. Koza, K. Deb, M. Dorigo, D. B. Fogel, M. Garzon, H. Iba, and R. L. Riolo (Eds.), pp 278–285, Stanford University, CA, USA: Morgan Kaufmann.

Price (1970), "Selection and covariance," *Nature*, 227:520–521.

Quinlan, J. R. and Rivest, R. L. (1989), "Inferring decision trees using the minimum description length principle," *Information and Computation*, pp 227–248.

Radcliffe, N. J. (1991), "Equivalence class analysis of genetic algorithms," *Complex Systems 5*, (2):183–205.

Radcliffe, N. J. (1992), "Non-linear genetics representations," in *Parallel Problem Solving from Nature, 2*, R. Männer and B. Manderick (Eds.), Elsevier Science Publishers.

Rosca, J. P. (1995), "Genetic programming exploratory power and the discovery of functions," in *Evolutionary Programming IV Proceedings of the Fourth Annual Conference on Evolutionary Programming*, J. R. McDonnell, R. G. Reynolds, and D. B. Fogel (Eds.), pp 719–736, San Diego, CA, USA: MIT Press.

Rosca, J. P. (1996), "Generality versus size in genetic programming," in *Genetic Programming 1996: Proceedings of the First Annual Conference*, J. R. Koza, D. E. Goldberg, D. B. Fogel, and R. L. Riolo (Eds.), pp 381–387, Cambridge, MA: The MIT Press.

Rosca, J. P. (1997), *Hierarchical Learning with Procedural Abstraction Mechanisms*, PhD thesis, University of Rochester, Rochester, NY 14627.

Rosca, J. P. and Ballard, D. H. (1994), "Hierarchical self-organization in genetic programming," in *11th International Conference on Machine Learning*, pp 251–258, Morgan Kaufmann.

Rosca, J. P. and Ballard, D. H. (1996a), "Discovery of subroutines in genetic programming," in *Advances in Genetic Programming 2*, P. Angeline and K. E. Kinnear, Jr. (Eds.), Chapter 9, Cambridge, MA, USA: MIT Press.

Rosca, J. P. and Ballard, D. H. (1996b), "Evolution-based discovery of hierarchical behaviors," in *Proc. of the Thirteenth National Conference on Artificial Intelligence (AAAI-96)*, pp 888–894, AAAI Press/The MIT Press.

Ryan, C. O. (1994), "Pygmies and civil servants," in *Advances in Genetic Programming*, K. E. Kinnear, Jr. (Ed.), MIT Press.

Sims, K. (1991), "Artificial evolution for computer graphics," *Computer Graphics*, 25(4):319–328.

Soule, T. and Foster, J. A. (1998), "Removal bias: a new cause of code growth in tree based evolutionary programming," in *1998 IEEE International Conference on Evolutionary Computation*.

Soule, T., Foster, J. A., and Dickinson, J. (1996), "Code growth in genetic programming," in *Genetic Programming 1996: Proceedings of the First Annual Conference*, J. R. Koza, D. E. Goldberg, D. B. Fogel, and R. L. Riolo (Eds.), pp 215–223, Stanford University, CA, USA: MIT Press.

Tackett, W. A. (1994), *Recombination, Selection and the Genetic Construction of Computer Programs*, PhD thesis, University of Southern California.

Vose, M. D. and Liepins, G. (1991), "Punctuated equilibria in genetic search," *Complex Systems*, (5):31–44.

Whigham, P. A. (1995), "A schema theorem for context-free grammars," in *1995 IEEE Conference on Evolutionary Computation*, volume 1, pp 178–181, Perth, Australia: IEEE Press.

Zhang, B.-T. and Muhlenbein, H. (1995), "Balancing accuracy and parsimony in genetic programming," *Evolutionary Computation*, 3(1):17–38.

III   EXTENSIONS

12 Efficient Evolution of Machine Code for CISC Architectures Using Instruction Blocks and Homologous Crossover

Peter Nordin, Wolfgang Banzhaf and Frank D. Francone

Evolutionary program induction using binary machine code is the fastest known Genetic Programming method. It is, in addition, the most well studied Genetic Programming system that uses a linear genome. This chapter describes recent advances in genetic programming of machine code. Evolutionary program induction using binary machine code was originally referred to as *Compiling Genetic Programming System* (CGPS). For clarity, the name was changed in early 1998 to *Automatic Induction of Machine Code—Genetic Programming* (AIM-GP). AIM-GP stores evolved programs as linear strings of native binary machine code, which are directly executed by the processor. The absence of an interpreter and complex memory handling increases the speed of AIM-GP by about two orders of magnitude. AIM-GP has so far been applied to processors with a fixed instruction length (RISC) using integer and floating-point arithmetic. We also describe several recent advances in the AIM-GP technology. Such advances include enabling the induction of code for CISC processors such as the INTEL x86 as well as JAVA and many embedded processors. The new techniques also make AIM-GP more portable in general and simplify the adaptation to any processor architecture. Other additions include the use of floating point instructions, control flow instructions, ADFs and new genetic operators e.g. aligned homologous crossover. This chapter also discusses the benefits and drawbacks of register machine GP versus tree-based GP. This chapter is directed towards the practitioner, who wants to extend AIM-GP to new architectures and application domains.

12.1 Introduction

In less than a generation, the performance of computing devices has improved by several orders of magnitude. At the same time, their price has dropped dramatically. Today, a complete one-chip computer may be purchased for less than the price of one hour of work.

But the cost of software has not kept pace with falling hardware prices. From 1955 to the early 1990's, the proportion of system development costs attributable to software rose from 10% to 90%. Today, the demand for software greatly exceeds supply. Studies show that demand may outstrip supply by as much as three-to-one. This mismatch is sometimes referred to as a *software crisis*.

The reasons for this software crisis are not difficult to fathom. Hardware is mass-produced; the economies of scale and mass production exert constant downward pressure on hardware prices. Falling hardware prices have driven a rapid growth of demand for software.

But software is not mass-produced. It is still hand-crafted by a limited supply of programmers. While programming advances like structured programming, object-oriented programming, rapid application development and CASE tools have increased programming productivity to some extent, 99% of available CPU cycles are not used.

Further increases in hardware speed and capacity will lower the cost of system development to some extent. But it is likely that much of any such increase will result only in more unused CPU cycles. Serious reductions in system development costs in the future will likely focus on the largest remaining cost component of system development, software.

One possible approach to the software crisis is to have computers write computer programs, in other words, *automatic programming*. Such an ambitious goal would have been regarded as science fiction as recently as fifteen years ago. But today, there are a number of different approaches to automatic programming extant: Genetic Programming [Koza, 1992; Banzhaf et al., 1998], ADATE [Olsson, 1997], PIPE [Salustowicz et al., 1997] and others. All of these approaches generate computer programs by using CPU cycles instead of human programmers. In a real sense, automatic programming holds the promise that computer programs, like computer hardware, may someday be mass-produced.

But mass-production of computer programs faces significant obstacles. One of the most formidable is, ironically, limitations on available CPU time. Put simply, Genetic Programming and other automatic programming techniques are *very* computationally expensive. AIM-GP (Automatic Induction of Machine Code) addresses this obstacle by evolving programs using direct manipulation of native machine code. This results in a speedup of almost two orders of magnitude over other automatic programming systems.

AIM-GP has been the subject of extensive research and development for several years at the University of Dortmund in Germany and, during that time, has been the subject of many published articles. Originally limited to RISC chips and to a small number of inputs, AIM-GP has recently been extended to CISC environments such as the WINTEL (MS-Windows on Intel) platform and Java byte code. Today, AIM-GP is available on WINTEL machines in the commercial software package, Discipulus^{TM}, and in an academic research version for Java byte code.

AIM-GP has also been extended to include many new features such as floating-point arithmetic, greatly expanded input capabilities, conditional branching, flexible control over the function and terminal set, and an important new genetic operator, Homologous Crossover. These advances make AIM-GP more flexible and portable in general and simplify its adaptation to any processor architecture.

While such additional capabilities are simple to add in a typical Genetic Programming system, they pose a considerably greater challenge in AIM-GP, where all evolved programs must be made up of synctactically correct native machine code. The purpose of this chapter is to report the new techniques that made possible the recent advances in AIM-GP.

12.2   Why Evolve Machine Code?

All commercial computers are built around a CPU that executes native machine code. In fact, every task computers perform, including genetic programming, will in the end be executed as machine code.

It is, of course, possible to perform genetic programming using high-level data structures that represent computer programs. Most Genetic Programming systems, including all tree-based systems, represent evolving programs in this manner [Banzhaf et al. 1998, pages

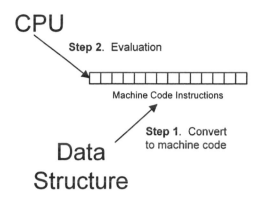

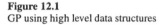

Figure 12.1
GP using high level data structures

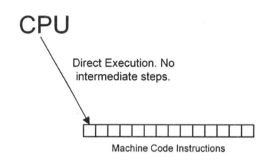

Figure 12.2
AIM-GP using direct binary manipulation

309-338;Koza 1992; Keith and Martin, 1994]. Figure 12.1 demonstrates this approach.
In such systems, high-level data structures that represent programs are converted into machine code at runtime (Step 1). Then, the resulting native machine code is evaluated for fitness (Step 2) This approach provides flexibility. The trade-off is that Step 1 is *very* computationally intensive.

But it is often advantageous evolve machine code directly in Genetic Programming. Figure 12.2 demonstrates the AIM-GP approach. In the direct binary approach of AIM-GP, there is no conversion step. The population of evolving programs is maintained, transformed, and evaluated in native machine code.

12.2.1   Advantages of Evolving Machine Code

In general the reasons for evolving machine code, rather than higher level languages, are similar to the reasons for programming by hand in machine code or assembler. The most important reason for using the direct machine code approach is speed. There are, however, other reasons also to evolve machine code directly:

1. The most efficient optimization is done at the machine code level. This is the lowest level for optimization of a program and it is also where the highest gains are possible. The optimization could be for speed, space or both. Genetic programming could be used to evolve short machine code subroutines with complex dependencies between registers, stack and memory.

2. High level tools could simply be missing for the target processor. This is sometimes the case for processors used for embedded control systems.

3. Machine code is hard to learn, program and master. This may be a matter of taste but it may be easier to let the computer itself evolve small machine code programs rather than writing machine code by hand.

4. Machine code genetic programming is inherently *linear*. That is, both the genome and the phenome are linear. Another reason to use a linear approach is that there is some evidence that the linear structure with side effects may yield a more efficient search for some applications, see section 12.7.

Some of these benefits may be achieved with a traditional tree-based Genetic Programming system evolving using a constrained crossover operator. However, there are additional reasons, in addition to speed, for working with binary machine code:

• A binary machine code system is usually memory efficient compared to a traditional Genetic Programming system. This is partly because knowledge of the program encoding is supplied by the CPU designer in hardware. Hence there is no need to define the language and its interpretation. In addition, the system manipulates the individual as a linear array of op-codes, which is more efficient than the more complex symbolic tree structures used in traditional Genetic Programming systems. Finally, CPU manufacturers have spent thousands of man-years to ensure that machine instruction codes are efficient and compact. Genetic Programming systems that use machine code instructions benefit directly from the manufacturers' optimization efforts.

• Memory consumption is usually more stable during evolution with less need for garbage collection etc. This could be an important property in real time applications.

• The use of machine code ensures that the behavior of the machine is correctly modeled since the same machine is used during fitness evaluation and in the target application.

On a more abstract level, machine code is the "natural" language of all computers. Higher level languages such as C, Pascal, LISP and even Assembler are all attempts to make it easier for humans to think about programming without having to deal with the complexity of machine code. Traditional genetic programming systems "think" about programming in a manner analogous to higher level computer languages. It may well be that these high-level, human techniques of thinking about programming are completely unnecessary when a computer is doing the programming. In fact, such higher level constructs may prevent the computer from programming as efficiently as it might.

12.3 Why is Binary Manipulation so Fast?

The approach of direct binary manipulation is between sixty and two-hundred times faster than comparable tree based interpreting systems. A partial explanation for its speed may be found in how an interpreter works.

To evaluate the expression $x = y + z$ in an interpreting system would normally require at least five different steps:

1. Load operand y from memory (e.g. stack)

2. Load operand z from memory

3. Look up symbol "+" in memory and get a function pointer

4. Call and execute the addition function

5. Store the resulting value (x) somewhere in memory

It is not difficult to calculate the best performance possible from an interpreting system for this evaluation. A memory operation normally takes at least three clock cycles for the CPU, even when there is a *cache hit*. The three memory operations listed above will, therefore, take nine clock cycles at best. Looking up the function pointer requires another memory access in an ideal hash table which means three additional clock cycles. Calling and executing a function usually takes from six to fifteen additional clock cycles depending on compiler conventions and type of function. All in all, this means that the best performance from an interpreting system for this simple function is about twenty clock cycles.

By way of contrast, Genetic Programming systems that work directly on the binary machine code execute the $x = y + z$ expression as a single instruction in one (1) clock cycle. AIM-GP should therefore be at least twenty times faster than an interpreting system. In fact, the speedup is by somewhat more than a factor of twenty. The remaining difference in performance is probably due to cache issues. All timing issues on modern CPUs are very sensitive to cache dependencies. Thus, any analysis that assumes cache hits must be viewed as the minimum speedup possible from the AIM-GP approach.

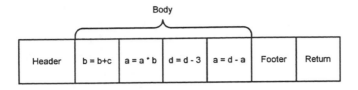

Figure 12.3
Structure of a program individual

12.4 Overview of AIM-GP

AIM-GP was formerly known as *Compiling Genetic Programming Systems* or *CGPS*. While AIM-GP is the best known system that works in a machine code type environment, there are others such systems. All such systems use a linear representation of the genome in contrast to the common tree-based Genetic Programming representation.

Genetic Programming systems that operate in a machine-code type environment may, in principle, be classified into three categories:

1. Approaches that evolve programs with a small virtual (toy) machine for research purposes [Cramer, 1985][Huelsberger, 1996].

2. Approaches that evolve programs using a simulation of a real machine or with a virtual machine designed for real applications [Crepeau, 1995].

3. Approaches that manipulate the native machine code of a real processor such AIM-GP. This third approach is, of course, the focus of the remainder of this chapter.

AIM-GP may be regarded as a large alphabet genetic algorithm operating on a variable-length, linear string of machine code instructions. Each individual consists of a header, body, footer, return instruction, and buffer. Figure 12.3 shows the structure of an evolved program in AIM-GP: The body contains machine code instructions contained in the terminal set of an AIM-GP run. All genetic operators are applied to the *body* of evolved programs in AIM-GP. For basic details regarding AIM-GP see [Nordin, 1997, Banzhaf et. al., 1998, Section 11.6.2-11.6.3].

AIM-GP evolves *imperative* programs. Imperative programs consist of instructions affecting a *state*. For example, instructions that assign values to variables or operating on the values contained in CPU registers are imperative instructions. Most commercial programming languages, such as C++, Pascal and Fortran, are imperative languages.

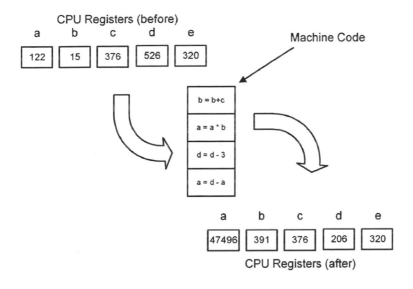

Figure 12.4
State transformations in CPU registers caused by AIM-GP program

Figure 12.4 is an example of how a sequence of AIM-GP instructions might transform the state of the registers of a hypothetical CPU. By way of contrast, traditional tree based Genetic Programming approaches are often inspired by *functional* programming approaches [Koza 1992]. More recently, there has been a trend in tree based Genetic Programming to view the tree more like a list of imperative instructions operating on state, than a function tree. This includes approaches using memory and *cellular encoding* [Gruau, 1995].

AIM-GP systems are now running on several different platforms and architectures. So far implementations exist for the following platforms using five different processor families:

- SUN-SPARC

- MOTOROLA POWER-PC

- INTEL 80X86

- Sony PlayStation

- Java Bytecode

The POWER-PC, Sony PlayStation and SPARC are all RISC architectures while INTEL 80X86 is a CISC architecture. The POWER-PC version works both on the Macintosh architecture and in a PARSYTEC parallel machine.

Java byte code occupies a spot by itself. It has a handful of instructions longer than a byte. So it could be seen as a CISC architecture even though it is possible to implement powerful systems using only the instructions of the fixed one-byte size. Furthermore, when running on the Java Virtual Machine, Java byte code is not precisely native machine code although it bears many similarities.

12.5   Making Machine Code Genetic Programming Work on CISC Processors

Many of the additions to AIM-GP reported here are the result of porting AIM-GP to CISC architectures. In particular, Instruction Blocks and Instruction Annotation made the transition straightforward and flexible.

12.5.1   The Importance of Extending AIM-GP to CISC Processors

The first AIM-GP systems was only able to evolve programs for *reduced instruction set computer* (RISC) architectures. A RISC processor has instructions of *equal length* and a relatively simple instruction grammar. By way of contrast, a CISC (Complex Instruction Set Computer) has instructions of varying length and, for lack of a better term, a messier instruction syntax.

The *PC de-facto-standard* is built on CISC and so are also many computers used for embedded applications. Other commonly-used computer architectures operate with variable length instructions, for example, the Motorola 68XXX and to some extent Java byte code. Being able to handle CISC processors is important for any Genetic Programming paradigm.

In addition to making AIM-GP work on the most common computer architectures, CISC processors also have large instruction sets with many special instructions. These special instructions are very useful in extending the capabilities of binary machine code induction systems like AIM-GP. For example, the INTEL X86 has a set of powerful string and loop instructions, which are never found on RISC machines:

• CMPS/CMPSB/CMPSW/CMPSD–Compare String Operands. These instructions can be used to compare strings for example in text search applications.

• STOS/STOSB/STOSW/STOSD Store String, LODS/LODSB/LODSW/LODSD Load String and MOVS/MOVSB/MOVSW/MOVSD–Move Data from String to String. Can be used when copying strings for instance in text data mining.

• LOOP/LOOP cc–Loop instructions allows for very compact and efficient loop constructs.

These single, powerful instructions, available only in CISC architectures, are important because such single instructions, when included in the function set, perform the same role as an external function call in a less complex and much faster manner.

12.5.2   Challenges in Moving AIM-GP to CISC Processors

Moving AIM-GP to CISC processors posed some real technical problems. Most approaches to AIM-GP perform crossover and mutation directly on the native machine code. It is easy to find where you are in RISC machine code since all instructions are the same length. Thus, if you know where the evolved program begins, you can easily find the instruction boundaries during crossover and mutation. For example, where all instructions are 32 bits long, the programmer always knows that a new instruction begins every 4 bytes.

CISC instructions are completely different. One encounters instructions that are 8 bits, 16 bits, 24 bits, 32 bits and more in length. Finding the instruction boundaries requires the programmer either to parse the entire evolved program to locate the instruction boundaries or to maintain information about program structure. Discipulus^{TM} (the commercial version of AIM-GP) maintains that information both implicitly (with Instruction Blocks) and explicitly (with Instruction Annotations). The next two sections of this chapter describe these innovations.

12.5.3   Instruction Blocks

To perform crossover and mutation in AIM-GP, we must know where the boundaries between instructions reside. Locating these boundaries can be difficult in CISC programs because of the variable instruction lengths. Figure 12.5 represents an evolved program comprised of variable length CISC instructions:

In Discipulus^{TM}, we imposed order on this scheme by combining one or more variable length instructions into fixed length *Instruction Blocks*. For example, in one scheme, we might fix the Instruction Block length at 32 bits. Each Instruction Block may contain any combination of instructions that are, taken together, 32 bits in length. Various examples of four different ways to put together an Instruction Block are illustrated in Figure 12.5. The Instruction Blocks may also contain NOPs (No Operation Instructions).

After grouping CISC instructions into Instruction Blocks, an Evolved program may be represented as in Figure 12.7:

Crossover With Instruction Blocks

The fixed length Instruction Blocks shown in Figure 12.7 simplify the crossover operator and memory management. They also make it straightforward to use new crossover methods such as aligned (homologous) crossover, as seen below Section 12.6.3.

Crossover with fixed length Instruction Blocks works only on the boundaries of the instruction blocks. This allows crossover to calculate and access each crossover point directly as shown in Figure 12.8. The size of the Instruction Blocks may be a settable parameter. In that case, the block size must be set so that the largest instruction used will fit in the block. However it should be small enough to allow the crossover operator to do useful recombination.

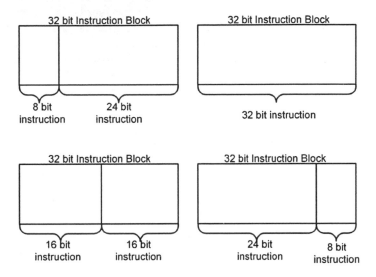

Figure 12.5
Four different 32 bit Instruction Blocks

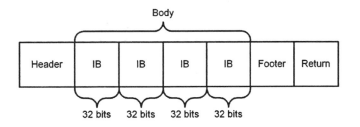

Figure 12.6
CISC AIM-GP evolved program

PARENT PROGAMS

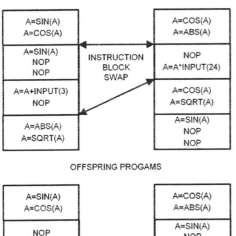

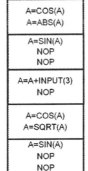

OFFSPRING PROGAMS

Figure 12.7
The Crossover Operator Using Instruction

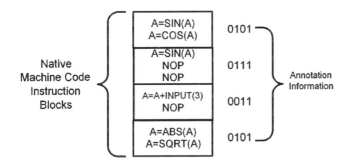

Figure 12.8
Blocks CISC AIM-GP evolved program with Instruction Blocks (*IB*)

Mutation With Instruction Blocks

As noted above, the crossover operator works blindly *in between* the blocks. On the other hand, mutation operates inside the Instruction Blocks. Discipulus^{TM} implements three different types of mutation:

- *Block Mutation* replaces an existing Instruction Block with a new, randomly-generated Instruction Block.

- *Instruction Mutation* replaces a single instruction (inside of an Instruction Block) with a new, randomly-generated instruction.

- *Data Mutation* replaces one of the operands of a single instruction with another, randomly-generated operand.

12.5.4   Instruction Annotations

To perform Instruction Mutation or Data Mutation, AIM-GP operates inside the Instruction Blocks. Because there may be more than one instruction within an Instruction Block, the mutation operator needs to know where the boundaries of instructions reside. There are two ways to do this:

- The point where one instruction finishes and another one begins may be determined by *decompiling* the binary code and determining the length of each instruction from a lookup table.

- The simpler way is to add extra information to each instruction in a separate array. This *annotation array* gives information about the position of instruction boundaries within an Instruction Block. The annotation information is a short binary string. Each binary digit corresponds to a *byte* in the block. If the binary digit is a 1 then a new instruction starts in this byte. If the binary digit is 0 then the previous instruction continues in this byte, see Figure 12.9.

When evolving Java byte code, annotation information is very useful. The Java virtual machine is a stack machine. *Current stack depth* is an example of annotation information kept with every instruction in our Java AIM-GP approach. We have also used annotation information to keep track of jump offsets in the Java system.

   A word of caution is in order. If too much annotation information is used then the system probably contains a *compiler* translating annotation information into an executable. If this is the case then manipulating binary code might not be worth the extra complexity. So, there is a trade-off between annotation information, expressiveness and efficiency.

PARENT PROGAMS

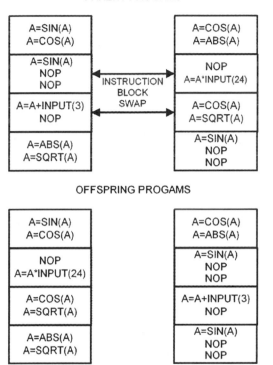

OFFSPRING PROGAMS

Figure 12.9
The homologous crossover operator with blocks

12.5.5   The Benefits of "Glue"

Both Instruction Blocks and Instruction Annotations are different ways to *glue* multiple
instructions together into functional groupings. Instruction Blocks comprise implicit *glue*
because their constant length is recognized by the crossover operator. Instruction Annotations may be used as explicit *glue*, delineating the start of compound instructions. Such
glued instructions are very useful since they can be seen as small and very efficient user-
defined functions. Compound instructions are also useful for special tricks such as ADFs,
jumps and string manipulation.

Glued instructions also have benefits for applications on RISC architectures. In particular, the ability to glue instructions together can yield more efficient constructs than using
functions calls for the same feature. Previously, special *leaf functions calls* in assembler,
were used for user-defined-functions, ADFs, and protected functions [Nordin 1997]. How-

ever, a good deal of overhead is involved in a function call and it is also a more complex solution. A glued block does the same job and is usually more efficient than using function calls.

Finally, glued instructions held together in Instruction Blocks also appear to assist the Genetic Programming algorithm by making it easy to protect real *building blocks* against crossover. One building block observed by the authors that evolves repeatedly is a block comprised of an absolute value instruction followed by a square root instruction. Of course, the absolute value ensures that the square root function (which only accepts positive numbers) will return a number and not an error symbol. A block consisting of these two instructions is nothing but a protected function that evolves spontaneously through mutation over-and-over in AIM-GP runs that have Instruction Blocks.

12.6   Other AIM-GP Innovations

A number of other additions to the AIM-GP architecture are of note and are detailed in this section.

12.6.1   Memory Access and Large Input Sets

A CISC processor usually has fewer registers than a RISC processor. The CPU compensates for this by more efficient instructions for mixing values in memory with register operations. Such operations can be especially efficient if the *cache* is aligned. In that case, these operations are almost as fast as a register-to-register operation.

Previously, with the RISC approach, the maximum number of inputs available in AIM-GP systems was around fourteen variables. The fast and convenient memory access available on CISC machines makes it easy to expand the number of inputs efficiently. Currently Discipulus^{TM} may use up to sixty-four inputs although that number may be easily increased.

AIM-GP has with this version been used for data mining applications with wide input sets consisting of 40 columns or more. In such applications Genetic Programming seems to work well without any specific external *variable selection algorithm*. Instead Genetic Programming does an excellent job selecting relevant input columns and omitting irrelevant inputs from the resulting program.

12.6.2   Decompilation

Evolved machine code can be disassembled into compilable C-code. Decompilation is very useful for platform portability of the evolved programs. In Discipulus^{TM} we decompile to ANSI C programs. As a result, the decompiled programs may be compiled directly to most processors for which a C compiler is available.

The example below is a decompiled evolved program from Disciplus^{TM}. Even though this programs was evolved on a Pentium machine, the decompilation converts register and memory references in the machine code into values that may be used by most processors.

It this example, the f array in the program below, stands for the eight FPU registers available in the Pentium FPU while the v array represents the array of input values. Thus, the instruction $f[0]* = v[27]$ means that register 0 should be assigned the value of input number 27 multiplied by the preexisting value in register 0.

```
#define LOG2(x)  ((float) (log(x)/log(2)))
#define LOG10(x) ((float) log10(x))
#define LOG_E(x) ((float) log(x))
#define PI 3.14159265359
#define E  2.718281828459

float DiscipulusCFunction(float v[])
{
  double f[8];
  double tmp = 0;

  f[1]=f[2]=f[3]=f[4]=f[5]=f[6]=f[7]=0;
  f[0]=v[0];

  l0: f[0]-=f[0];
  f[0]*=f[0];
  l1: f[0]-=0.5;
  l2: tmp=f[1]; f[1]=f[0]; f[0]=tmp;
  f[0]-=f[0];
  l3: f[0]*=f[0];
  l4: f[0]+=f[0];
  f[0]=fabs(f[0]);
  l5: tmp=f[0]; f[0]=f[0]; f[0]=tmp;
  f[0]*=f[0];
  l6: f[0]*=0;
  l7: f[0]-=0.5;
  l8: f[0]*=v[27];
  l9: f[0]*=f[0];
  l10: f[0]*=v[32];
  l11: f[0]*=v[4];
  l12: f[0]+=f[1];
  l13: f[0]+=f[0];
  f[0]=fabs(f[0]);
  l14: f[0]-=f[1];
  f[0]+=f[1];
  l15: f[0]*=v[61];
  l16:
```

12.6.3 Homologous Crossover

One of the principal criticisms of standard Genetic Programming is that the crossover operator is too *brutal*. It performs crossover by exchanging any sub-tree regardless of the context in which the sub-tree operated. The standard crossover operator exchanges subtrees with such little selectivity that crossover could be argued to be more of a mutation operator and Genetic Programming more like a hill-climbing algorithm with a population than a system working with recombination [Banzhaf et al. 1998, pages 143-173]. The same argument can be made regarding the usual two-point string crossover in AIM-GP [Nordin 1997].

Natural crossover does not usually exchange *apples* and *pies*. Foot-genes are rarely crossed-over with nose-genes. In natural crossover, the DNA of the parents are aligned before a crossover takes place. This makes it likely that genes describing similar features will be exchanged during sexual recombination. Thus, biological crossover is *homologous* [Banzhaf et al., 1998, pages 48-54].

In nature, most crossover events are successful. That is, they result in viable offspring. This is in sharp contrast to Genetic Programming crossover, where 75% of the crossover events are what would be termed in biology *lethal*.

Homologous Crossover Mechanism. AIM-GP now contains a mechanism for crossover that fits the medium of Genetic Programming and that may achieve results similar to homologous crossover in nature. In nature, homologous crossover works as follows:

- Two parents have a child that combines some of the genomes of each parent.

- The natural exchange is strongly biased toward experimenting with features exchanging very similar chunks of the genome, specific genes performing specific functions, that have *small* variations among them, e.g., red eyes would be exchanged against green eyes, but not against a poor immune system.

Homologous crossover exchanges blocks at the same position in the genome allowing certain meaning to be developed at certain loci in the genome. Homologous crossover can be seen as an emergent implicit grammar where each position, *loci*, represents a certain *type of feature* in many ways similar to how *grammar based GP* systems work [Banzhaf et. al. 1997]. *Homologous Crossover Effects.* The authors have noted several effects of making the homologous crossover operator the dominant crossover operator. They are:

- Significant and consistent improvement in search performance.

- Less *bloat* or code growth. This makes sense if bloat is partly seen as a defense against the destructive effects of crossover. A reasonable hypothesis is that the homologous crossover exchanging blocks at the same position will be less destructive after some initial stabilizing of features at loci.

- Implementation efficiency. The execution of the evolved programs is so fast in AIM-GP that even the time to perform crossover becomes significant (20%). Homologous crossover is faster than standard crossover since it exchanges segments with the same size. Therefore, no blocks of machine code need to be shifted forward or back.

Tree Based Homologous Crossover. Homologous crossover is easy to formulate and implement in a linear imperative system such as AIM-GP since two evolved programs can be aligned in a manner analogous to DNA crossover in nature. With tree based systems it is not as easy to find a natural way to align the two parents. However, so-called *one-point crossover* is a very interesting development in tree-based Genetic Programming that, we speculate, may act in a manner similar to linear homologous crossover [Poli and Langdon, 1998]. In one-point crossover, the nodes of the two parents are traversed to identify nodes with the same position and shape (arity). In this way, the trees can be partly aligned.

Such a tree based system has an interesting property in that it allows the insertion of a sub-trees of any size without violating alignment. This is not as easy in a linear system such as DNA or AIM-GP. The only way to achieve the same effect in AIM-GP is to use *ADFs*. Using ADFs allows the homologous insertion of a block calling an ADF with arbitrary size, see Section 12.6.5. A mechanism like this is important since a new individual with very different alignment will have severe difficulties surviving in a population with a majority of differently aligned individuals. In this way alignment can be seen as a kind of speciation.

12.6.4   Floating Point Arithmetic

Many conventional Genetic Programming systems operate with floating-point arithmetic. Until recently, AIM-GP has used the ALU (Integer and Logic Unit). However, floating-point arithmetic has many benefits. One of them is access to efficient hardware, which implements common mathematical functions such as SIN, COS, TAN, ATN, SQRT, LN, LOG, ABS, EXP etc. as single machine code instructions. There are also a dozen well-used constants, such as PI, available.

Another substantial benefit of floating-point representations is portability of evolved code. All floating-point units adhere to a common standard about how to represent numbers and how certain functions (such as rounding) should be performed. The standard also describes what to do with exceptions (e.g. division by zero). All floating-point exceptions are well-defined and result in an error symbol (for instance INF) being placed into the result register. This causes fewer problems with protected functions because execution continues with the symbol in the register. When the function returns the symbol, this can be detected outside the evolved program and punished by a poor fitness evaluation.

Processor manufacturers have recently discovered the benefits of *conditional loads* in the FPU. Such instructions loads a value into a register if a certain condition holds. The calculation following the conditional load can then take very different paths depending on if the value was loaded or not. This way the instruction works as an efficient single instruction *if-statement*.

Even if floating point processors have many powerful new instructions, it is still important to select instructions with care. For instance the FPU of the INTEL processor has eight registers organized as a stack. But stack type instructions cause some problems in evolution. Best results in evolution have to date been obtained by omitting instructions that push or pop the stack. Instead it is more efficient to use the FPU registers as normal registers machine registers and load input directly into them.

Constants are more difficult to implement in AIM-GP floating point systems than in integer based systems. In integer systems there are *immediate data* available as part of the instructions. These immediate data may be used as constants in the individual and mutated to explore the search space of integer constants during evolution. In the floating-point instruction set, there are no constants in the instruction format. Instead constants must be initialized at the beginning of a run and then, during the run, loaded from memory much like the input variables.

Another possible feature when using CISC processors and floating-point units is the ability to use multiple outputs. The transfer of a function's result on a CISC floating-point application is communicated through memory. This technique enables the use of multiple outputs by assignment of memory in the individual. In principle there is no limit on the number of items in the output vector. A multiple output system is important in for instance control applications where it is desirable to control for instance several motors and servos.

12.6.5 Automatically Defined Functions

Even though the value of ADFs has been questioned in a register machine approach such as AIM-GP (see Section 12.7 below), it may have benefits in connection with homologous crossover. Previously ADFs have been implemented by calling a special subfunction, a *leaf function*, which then in turn calls one of a fixed number of ADFs in the individual, see Figure 12.10. The reason for having an extra function in-between is that necessary boundary checks can be made in the leaf functions. Calling a function represents a considerable overhead. ADFs can be implemented more elegantly with blocks.

We need two blocks to realize ADFs. One block containing a *call* and one containing a *return* instructions. These blocks are then arbitrarily inserted into the individual. To work properly during evolution there must be control instructions in these blocks that check that there is no stack underflow or stack overflow. (The allowed calling depth need only be a few levels.) The blocks are initialised to call forward 5 or 10 blocks. A second check (also within the instruction blocks) is therefore needed to make sure that no call is made past the boundary of the individual. In this way no special ADF structure in the individual is necessary. Instead the subroutines are chaotically intermixed in a single individual. The benefits are a larger freedom for the system to control how many ADF's will be used and in what way. The block approach is also faster since multiple function calls are eliminated.

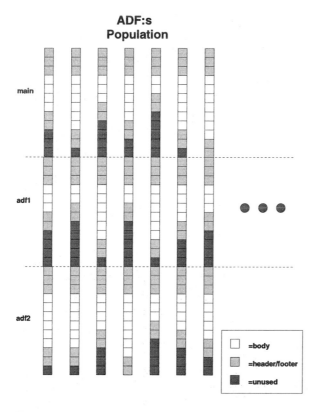

ADF:s
Population

main

adf1

adf2

□ =body
▨ =header/footer
■ =unused

Figure 12.10
The structure of a population consisting of individuals with two ADF parts and a main part in AIM-GP

12.7   AIM-GP and Tree–Based GP

The greatest advantage of AIM-GP is the considerable speed enhancement compared to an interpreting system, as discussed above. An interesting question is whether the performance of the register machine system is comparable on a *per-generation or per-evaluation basis*.

AIM-GP has possible advantages over Tree based Genetic Programming other than speed. Consider that a four line program in machine language may look like this:

```
(1)     x=x-1
(2)     y=x*x
(3)     x=x*y
(4)     y=x+y
```

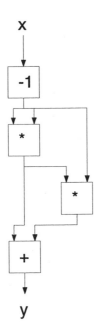

Figure 12.11
The dataflow graph of the $(x-1)^2 + (x-1)^3$ polynomial

The program uses two registers, x, y, to represent the function. In this case the polynomial is:

$$g(x) = (x-1)^2 + (x-1)^3 \tag{12.1}$$

The input to the function is placed in register x and the output is what is left in register y after all four instructions have been executed. Register y is initially zero. Note that the registers are variables that could be assigned at any point in the program. Register y, for example, is used as temporary storage in instruction number two ($y = x * x$) before its final value is assigned in the last instruction ($y = x + y$). The program has more of a graph structure than a tree structure, where the register assignments represent edges in the graph. Figure 12.11 shows a dataflow graph of the $(x-1)^2 + (x-1)^3$ computation. In that figure, the machine code program closely corresponds to this graph. Compare this to an equivalent individual in a tree–based Genetic Programming system as in figure 12.12. It has been argued that the more general graph representation of the register machine is an advantage compared to the tree representation of traditional GP. For this reason there is less need to use an explicit ADF feature in AIM-GP

In fact, the temporary storage of values in registers may be seen as a "poor man's ADF" The reuse of calculated values can, in some cases, replace the need to divide the programs

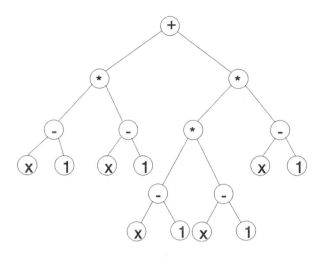

Figure 12.12
The representation of $(x - 1)^2 + (x - 1)^3$ in a tree–based genome

into subroutines or subfunctions. Reuse of useful instruction sequences is repeatedly observed in evolved AIM-GP programs.

To determine if this theoretical advantage of AIM-GP over tree-based Genetic Programming has any empirical support, we carefully tuned two Genetic Programming systems, one standard tree–based as well as one register based and evaluated their performance on a real world test problem. This problem is from the speech recognition domain and has been used previously as a benchmark problem in the machine learning community, with connectionist approaches. The problem consists of pre-processed speech segments, which should be classified according to type of phoneme.

The PHONEME recognition data set contains two classes of data: nasal vowels (Class 0) and oral vowels (Class 1) from isolated syllables spoken by different speakers. This database is composed of two classes in 5 dimensions [ELENA, 1995]. The classification problem is cast into a symbolic regression problem where the members of class zero have an ideal value of zero while the ideal output value of class one is 100.

The function set consisted, in both cases, of the arithmetic operator times, subtract, plus and the logical shift left (SLL) and logical shift right (SRL) operators. The selection method used was a steady state tournament of size four. Homologous crossover was not used. The population size was chosen to 3000 individuals and each experiment was run for 1000 generation equivalents.

Each system performed 10 runs on the problem and the average of the 10 runs was plotted. Figure 12.13 shows the average over 10 runs of the best individual fitness for the two systems.

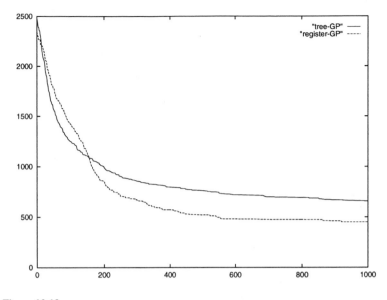

Figure 12.13
Comparison of fitness of the best individual with a tree and register based Genetic Programming system over 1000 generation equivalents

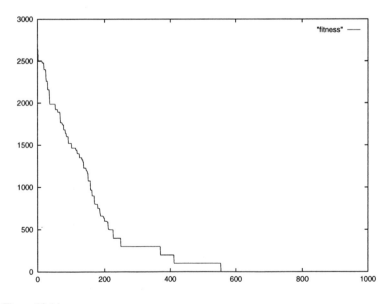

Figure 12.14
Evolution of best fitness over 1000 generation equivalents

The tree–based system starts out with a sharper drop in fitness but at generation 180 the register based system has a better fitness. The average of best fitness at termination after 1000 generation equivalents is 657.9 for the tree–based Genetic Programming and 450.9 for register based GP. This means that the average fitness advantage is 31% in favor of the register based system.

The results show that the register machine system, on this problem, converges to an equal or better fitness value than the tree–based system. These results suggest that AIM-GP could have advantages in addition to its superior speed.

12.8 Future Work

Many of the AIM-GP techniques currently in use are proven in practical applications. More thorough evaluations are planned. New additions to the system have opened-up completely new possibilities in several application areas:

• The introduction of blocks improves portability and we plan to exploit this by porting the system to embedded processors. Programming very complex tasks e.g. speech recognition is difficult to do in machine code with limited hardware resources. While AIM-GP has proven that it can evolve efficient solutions (as efficient short machine code programs) to such hard problems [Conrads et al., 1998]. Applied in an inexpensive embedded processor such as the PIC, it could have many commercially applications.

• AIM-GP has previously been used in control domains such as on-line control on autonomous robots. We have begun work which will extend this domain to more complex walking robots. Autonomous robots need high processing capabilities in compact memory space and AIM-GP is therefore well suited for on-board learning.

• Genetic Programming differs from other evolutionary techniques and other *soft computing* techniques in that it produces symbolic information (e.g. computer programs) as output. It can also process symbolic information as input very efficiently. Despite this unique strength genetic programming has so far been applied mostly in numerical or Boolean problem domains. We plan to evaluate the use of machine code evolution for text data mining of e.g. the Internet.

Other potential applications for AIM-GP are in special processors, such as:

• Video processing chips, compression, decompression (e.g. MPEG), blitter chips

• Signal processors

• Processors for special languages, for example, LISP-processors and data flow processors

• New processor architectures with very large instruction sizes

- Parallel vector processors

- Low power processors for example 4-bit processors in watches and cameras

- Special hardware, e.g. in network switching

12.9   Summary and Conclusion

We have presented additions to the AIM-GP making the approach more portable and enabling its use with CISC processors. Additions consist of blocks and annotations which enable safe use of genetic operators despite varying length instructions. Benefits of the CISC architecture are the large number of instructions in the instruction set, increasing the likelihood that the instructions needed for a specific application can be found. Complex instructions include LOOP instructions and special instructions for string manipulation. The use of the FPU further expands the directly possible instruction set by inclusion of important mathematical functions such as $SIN, COS, TAN, ATN, SQRT, LN, LOG, ABS, EXP$ etc. All these additions are important for the practical applicability of one of the fastest methods for Genetic Programming.

Acknowledgments

Peter Nordin gratefully acknowledges support from the Swedish Research Council for Engineering Sciences.

Bibliography

Banzhaf, W., Nordin, P. Keller, R. E., and Francone, F. D. (1998) Genetic Programming – An Introduction. On The Automatic Evolution Of Computer Programs And Its Applications. Morgan Kaufmann, San Francisco, USA and dpunkt, Heidelberg, Germany.

Conrads, M., Nordin P. and Banzhaf W. (1998) Speech Recognition using Genetic Programming. In Proceedings of the First European Workshop on Genetic Programming. W. Banzhaf, R. Poli, M. Schoenauer and T. Fogarty (eds.). ,Paris, LNCS Volume 1391, Springer, Berlin and New York.

Cramer, N.L. (1985) A Representation For Adaptive Generation Of Simple Sequential Programs. In Proceedings of the 1st International Conference on Genetic Algorithms and Their Applications, J. Grefenstette (ed.), p.183-187.

Crepeau, R.L. (1995) Genetic Evolution of Machine Language Software, In Proceeding of the Genetic Programming workshop at Machine Learning 95, Tahoe City, CA, J. Rosca(ed.), University of Rochester Technical Report 95.2, Rochester, NY, p. 6-22.

ELENA partners (1995) Esprit Basic Research Project Number 6891, Jutten C., Project Coordinator. Document Number R3-B1-P.

Gruau, f. (1993) Automatic Definition Of Modular Neural Networks. Adaptive Behaviour, 3(2):151-183.

Huelsberger L. (1996) Simulated Evolution of Machine Language Iteration. In Proceedings of the first International Conference on Genetic Programming, Stanford, USA. J. Koza (ed.), Morgan Kaufmann, San Francisco, USA.

Koza, J. R. (1992) Genetic Programming: On the Programming of Computers by Means of Natural Selection. MIT Press, Cambridge, MA, USA.

Nordin, J.P. (1997) Evolutionary Program Induction of Binary Machine Code and its Application. Krehl Verlag, Muenster, Germany.

Olsson, J. (1998) The Art of Writing Specifications for the ADATE Automatic Programming System. In Proceedings of the Third International Conference on Genetic Programming. Morgan Kaufmann, San Francisco, USA.

Poli, R. and Langdon, W. B. (1998) On the Search Properties of Different Crossover Operators in Genetic Programming. In Proceedings of the Third International Conference on Genetic Progarmming. Morgan Kaufmann, Wisconsin, USA.

Salustowicz, R. and Schmidhuber J. (1997) Probabilistic Incremental Program Evolution. In Evolutionary Computation 5(2):123-141.

13 Sub-machine-code Genetic Programming

Riccardo Poli and William B. Langdon

CPUs are often seen as sequential, however they have a high degree of internal parallelism, typically operating on 32 or 64 bits simultaneously. This chapter explores the idea of exploiting this internal parallelism to extend the scope of genetic programming (GP) and improve its efficiency. We call the resulting form of GP *sub-machine-code GP*. The differences between sub-machine-code GP and the usual form of GP are purely semantic and largely language independent, i.e. any GP system can potentially be used to do sub-machine code GP. In this chapter this form of GP and some of its applications are presented. The speed up obtained with this technique on Boolean classification problems is nearly 2 orders of magnitude.

13.1 Introduction

Genetic Programming (GP) [Koza, 1992; Koza, 1994; Banzhaf et al., 1998] is usually seen as quite demanding from the computation load and memory use point of view. So, over the years a number of ideas on how to improve GP performance have been proposed in the literature. We recall the main speedup techniques published to date in Section 13.2.

Some of these techniques are now used in many GP implementations. Thanks to this and to the fact that the power of our workstations is increasing exponentially (today's CPUs are now more than 10 times faster than those used in early GP work), nowadays we can run 50 generations a typical GP benchmark problem with a population of 500 individuals in perhaps ten seconds on a normal workstation. Nonetheless, the demand for more and more efficient implementations has not stopped. This is because extensive experimental GP studies (like [Langdon and Poli, 1998] or [Luke and Spector, 1998]) and complex applications (like [Poli, 1996] or [Luke, 1998]) may still require from days to months of CPU time to complete.

Most computer users consider the machines on their desks as sequential computers. However, at a lower level of abstraction CPUs are really made up of parallel components. In this sense the CPU can be seen as a Single Instruction Multiple Data (SIMD) processor. In this chapter we present a novel way of doing GP which exploits this form of parallelism to improve the efficiency and the range of applications of genetic programming. We term this form of GP *sub-machine-code GP*.

Sub-machine-code GP which extends the scope of GP to the evolution of *parallel programs running on sequential computers*. These programs are faster as, thanks to the parallelism of the CPU, they perform multiple calculations during a single program evaluation. Since these programs may be very difficult to find for human programmers and are certainly beyond the scope of current optimising compilers, this is an important new extension.

In addition, in some domains, sub-machine-code GP can be used to speed up the evaluation of sequential and parallel programs very effectively. In the chapter we show that nearly 2 orders of magnitude speedups can be achieved by any standard GP system, independently of the implementation language used, with minimal changes.

The chapter is organised as follows. After describing earlier work on speed up techniques for GP (Section 13.2), in Section 13.3 we start exploring the idea of using modern CPUs at their very lowest level of computational resolution to do genetic programming. In Section 13.4 we describe applications of sub-machine-code GP to problems where different components of the CPU perform different calculations concurrently. We illustrate how to achieve substantial speedups in the evaluation of sequential programs using sub-machine-code GP in Section 13.5. We give some indications of possible extensions of this idea and we draw conclusions in Section 13.6.

13.2 Background

John Koza's first book [Koza, 1992] included a number of tricks to speed up his Lisp GP implementation. However, soon people started trying to go beyond the inefficiencies of the Lisp language, and some GP implementations in C and C++ appeared (see for example [Singleton, 1994]). These can be several times faster than the equivalent Lisp implementations. So, they spread very quickly in the community and nowadays many researchers use some sort of C or C++ GP system. To go beyond the speedup provided by the language, some drastic changes are required.

Some speed up techniques rely on a better representation for the trees in the population. An example is the idea, firstly proposed by Handley [Handley, 1994], of storing the population of trees as a single directed acyclic graph, rather than as a forest of trees. This leads to considerable savings of memory (structurally identical subtrees are not duplicated) and computation (the value computed by each subtree for each fitness case can be cached). Another idea is to evolve graph-like programs, rather than tree like ones. For example, the grid-based representation used in Parallel Distributed Genetic Programming (PDGP) [Poli, 1997] has been used to evolve very efficient graph-like programs. In PDGP the speedup derives from the fact that, on problems with a high degree of regularity, partial results can be reused by multiple parts of a program without having to be recomputed.

Other techniques are based on trying to speed up as much as possible the execution of programs. For example, recently techniques have been proposed which are based on the idea of compiling GP programs either into some lower level, more efficient, virtual-machine code or even into machine code. For example, in [Fukunaga et al., 1998] a genome compiler has been proposed which transforms standard GP trees into machine code before evaluation. The possibilities offered by the Java virtual machine are also currently being explored [Klahold et al., 1998; Lukschandl et al., 1998a; Lukschandl et al., 1998b]. Well before these recent efforts, since programs are ultimately executed by the CPU, other researchers proposed removing completely the inefficiency in program execution inherent in interpreting trees and directly evolve programs in machine code form [Nordin, 1994; Nordin and Banzhaf, 1995; Nordin, 1997; Nordin, 1998]. This idea has recently led to a commercial GP system called Discipulus (Register Machine Learning Technologies, Inc.) which is claimed to be at least one order of magnitude faster than any GP system based on higher-level languages.

Since the evaluation of the fitness of programs often involves their execution on many different fitness cases, some researchers have proposed speeding up fitness evaluation by reducing the number of fitness cases. For example, this can be done by identifying the hardest fitness cases for a population in one generation and evaluating the programs in the following generation only using such fitness cases [Gathercole and Ross, 1997]. Alternatively, the evaluation of fitness cases can be stopped as soon as the destiny of a particular program (e.g. whether the program will be selected to be a parent or not and, if so, how many times) is known with a big enough probability [Teller and Andre, 1997; Langdon, 1998]. A related idea is to reduce the computation load associated with program execution by avoiding the re-evaluation of parts of programs. This can be done, for example, by caching the results produced by ADFs the first time they are run with a certain set of arguments, and using the stored results thereafter [Langdon, 1998].

Finally, some research has been devoted to parallel and distributed implementations of GP (see for example [Andre and Koza, 1996; Stoffel and Spector, 1996; Juille and Pollack, 1996; Sian, 1998]). These are usually based on the idea of distributing a population across multiple machines with some form of communication between them to exchange useful genetic material. A similar, but more basic, speed up technique is to perform independent multiple runs of a same problem on different machines. It should be noted that in a sense these are not really speed up techniques, since the amount of CPU time per individual is not affected by them.[1]

13.3 Sub-machine-code GP

As indicated in the introduction CPUs can be seen as made up of a set of interacting SIMD 1-bit processors. In a CPU some instructions, such as all Boolean operations, are performed in parallel and independently for all the bits in the operands. For example, the bitwise AND operation (see Figure 13.1(a)) is performed internally by the CPU by concurrently activating a group of AND gates within the arithmetic logic unit as indicated in Figure 13.1(b). In other instructions the CPU 1-bit processors can be imagined to interact through communication channels. For example, in a shift left operation each processor will send data

---

[1] It has been reported in [Andre and Koza, 1996] that the use of subpopulations and a network of transputers delivered a super-linear speed-up in terms of the ability of the algorithm to solve a problem. So, the amount of CPU time per individual was reduced. This happened because partitioning the population was beneficial for the particular problem being solved. The same benefits could be obtained by evolving multiple communicating populations on a single computer.

to its left neighbour while in an add operation some 1-bit processors will send a carry bit to one of their neighbouring processors. Other operations might involve more complicated patterns of communication.

Some operations (like Boolean operations or shifts) can be imagined to be executed synchronously by all 1-bit processors at the same time. Others, like addition, require some different form of synchronisation (e.g. in some CPUs carry bits are only available after the corresponding 1-bit processors have performed their bit-addition). Nonetheless, as far as the user of a CPU is concerned the CPU 1-bit processors run in parallel, since the results of the operation of all processors become available at the same time.

If we see the CPU as a SIMD computer, then we could imagine that each of its 1-bit processors will be able to produce a result after each instruction. Most CPUs do not allow handling single bits directly. Instead all the values to be loaded into the CPU and the results produced by the CPU are packed into bit vectors, which are normally interpreted as as integers in most programming languages.[2] For example, in many programming languages the user will see a bitwise AND operation as a function which receives two integers and returns an integer, as indicated in Figure 13.1(c).

All this powerful parallelism inside our CPUs has been ignored by the GP community so far, perhaps because many of us are not used to think in term of bits, nibbles, carries, registers, etc. For example, to the best of our knowledge, in every implementation operations like the logical AND shown in Figure 13.2(a) are executed sequentially. This exercises only one of the 1-bit processors within the CPU as indicated in Figure 13.2(b).

The simplest ways to exploit the CPU's parallelism to do GP is to make it execute the same program on different data in parallel and independently. This can be done as follows:

• The function set should include operations which exploit the parallelism of the CPU, e.g. bitwise Boolean operations.

• The terminal set should include integer input variables and constants, which should be interpreted as bit vectors where each bit represents the input to a different 1-bit processor. For example, the integer constant 21, whose binary representation is 00010101 (assuming an 8-bit CPU), would be see as 1 by the 1-bit processors processing bits 1, 3 and 5. It would be seen as 0 by all other 1-bit processors.

• The result produced by the evaluation of a program should be interpreted as a bit vector, too. Each bit of this vector represents the result of a different 1-bit processor. E.g. if the output of a GP program is the integer 13, this should be converted into binary (obtaining 00001101) and decomposed to obtain 8 binary results (assuming an 8-bit CPU).

---

[2] Often bit vectors of different sizes are allowed (e.g. bytes, words, double words), but this is irrelevant for the present discussion.

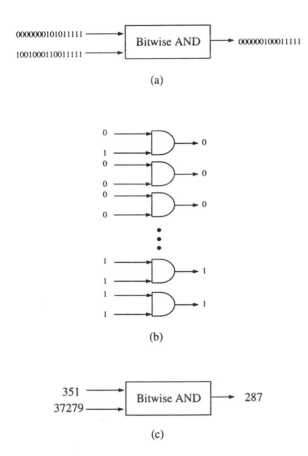

Figure 13.1
Three different ways of looking at a bitwise AND operation as performed by a 16-bit CPU: (a) bitwise AND between binary numbers, (b) implementation of the operation in (a) within the CPU, and (c) the same bitwise AND as seen by a CPU's user as an operation between integers.

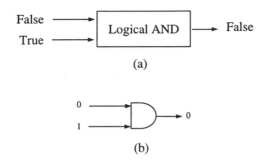

Figure 13.2
A logical AND (a), and its equivalent using AND gates (b).

To exploit the parallelism of the CPU it is not necessary to manipulate machine code directly. In fact, most high level languages include some operations which the compiler converts directly into the corresponding machine code operations. E.g. integer arithmetic operations (multiplication, addition, subtraction, division), bitwise logical operations (AND, OR, NOT), bit shift and rotate operations. By using such high level instructions in the function set of GP, it is possible to exploit the parallel nature of the CPU in most high level languages. Since the other differences w.r.t. the usual form of GP are related only to the interpretation of the inputs and outputs of each program, *any GP system can potentially be used to do sub-machine code GP.*

An ideal application for this paradigm is to evaluate multiple fitness cases in parallel. Boolean induction problems lend themselves to this use of sub-machine-code GP, leading to 1.5 to 1.8 orders of magnitude speedups (for 32 and 64 bit machines, respectively). We describe this in detail in Section 13.5.

More complex applications of this idea can be envisaged in which the CPU 1-bit processors, although executing the same program, can still perform different computations. Obviously, this could be done by re-wiring a CPU so as to do something it has not being designed to do (except when the CPU's microcode is stored in rewritable memory, which is not the case for the CPUs in standard workstations). However, it is possible to do it by passing different data to different processors thus making them behave differently. This can be done either by feeding different data in the various bits of the input variables, or by using constants with different bits set. For example, let us consider a 2-bit CPU which is computing a bitwise XOR between a variable x and a constant $c = 2$ (which is the binary 10), and suppose that x is either 0 (binary 00) or 3 (binary 11). In these conditions, the first 1-bit processor will perform (XOR x 1) and will therefore return the negation of the corresponding bit in x, i.e. it will compute the function (NOT x). The second 1-bit processor will instead compute (XOR x 0) and so will simply copy the corresponding bit in x, i.e. it will compute the identity function.

13.4   Examples

In this section we will describe a few sample applications of sub-machine-code GP. The runs described in the section were performed with our own GP implementation in Pop-11. The results presented in Section 13.5 were instead obtained with a C implementation. Reimplementing these examples within GP systems written in other languages is trivial.

13.4.1   1-bit and 2-bit Adder Problems

Let us consider the problem of evolving a 1-bit adder program based on Boolean operations. The adder has two inputs a and b and two outputs sum and carry. The truth table for the adder is:

a	b	sum	carry
0	0	0	0
1	0	1	0
0	1	1	0
1	1	0	1

Each row in this table can be used as a fitness case.

This problem would be extremely easy to solve by hand if one could use two separate program trees to express the solution. In that case it would be sufficient to use (XOR a b) to compute sum and (AND a b) to compute carry. However, by exploiting the parallelism in the CPU it is possible to perform both computations at the same time. This could be done by slicing the output of a *single* program into its component bits and interpreting one of them as sum and one as carry. Of course to do this it would be necessary to include in the program some appropriate constants which would excite differently different parallel components of the CPU.

This version of the problem is much harder to solve for humans, but can be easily solved by evolution using sub-machine-code GP. To do that and to keep the example simple we decided to use only the bit-0 and bit-1 processors within the CPU since there are only two outputs in this problem. The function set was {AND, OR, NOT, XOR}, where all functions where implemented using bitwise operations on integers. The terminal set was {x1, x2, 1, 2}. The constants 1 and 2 where selected since they have the binary representation 01 and 10 which allows GP to modify selectively the behaviour of different parts of the program for different 1-bit processors.

For each of the four fitness cases, the variable x1 took the value 3 (which corresponds to the binary number 11) when the corresponding entry in column a of the truth table above was 1, the value 0 (i.e. the binary number 00) otherwise. Likewise, x2 took the value 3 when b was 1, 0 otherwise. This was done to provide the same inputs both to the bit-0 processor and to the bit-1 processor of the CPU.

Each program in the population was run with each of the four possible settings for the variables x1 and x2. The two least significant bits of the integer produced as output in each fitness case were compared with the target values for sum and carry indicated in the previous table. The fitness function was the sum of the number of matches between such bits, i.e. a perfect program had a fitness of 8, 4 for sum and 4 for carry.

Except for the fitness function, no change of our standard-GP system was necessary to run sub-machine-code GP. As far as GP was concerned it was solving, using bitwise primitives, a symbolic regression problem with fitness cases:

x1	x2	target
0	0	0
3	0	2
0	3	2
3	3	1

rather than the 1-bit adder problem. Under this interpretation, in the fitness function the program outputs and the target outputs were compared to produce a fitness measure in a way quite unusual for symbolic regression problems. For example, if in one fitness case the program output was 2 (binary 10) and the target was 1 (01) that gave a contribution of 0 to the total fitness, while if the program output was 3 (11) the fitness contribution of the fitness case was 1!

In our runs we used a population of 1000 individuals, up to 100 generations, standard subtree crossover (with uniform probability of selection of the crossover points) with crossover probability 0.7, no mutation and tournament selection with tournament size 7. The random initialisation of the population was performed so as to obtain a uniform distribution of program sizes between 1 and 50 nodes.

Figure 13.3(a) shows a solution to this problem discovered by GP at generation 3 of a run. As far as the bit-0 processor of the CPU (the one which computes sum) is concerned this program is equivalent to the one shown on the left of Figure 13.3(b). This version of the program has been obtained by replacing the constants in Figure 13.3(a) with the LSB of their binary representation (i.e. 1 (binary 01) is replaced with 1 and 2 (binary 10) with 0). As shown on the right of the same figure, as expected this program is equivalent to the XOR function. Figure 13.3(c) shows the program as seen by the bit-1 processor (the one which computes carry), which is equivalent to the AND function.

In another run we solved also the two-bit adder (without carry) problem which requires the use of four input variables: x1, x2 which represent the least significant bit and the most significant bit of the first operand, respectively, and x3 and x4 to represent the second operand. All the other parameters were the same as in the 1-bit adder problem except that we included also the constants 0 and 3 in the terminal set and that the output bits are interpreted as sum1 and sum2 rather than sum and carry. Figure 13.4 shows a solution found by sub-machine-code GP at generation 11.

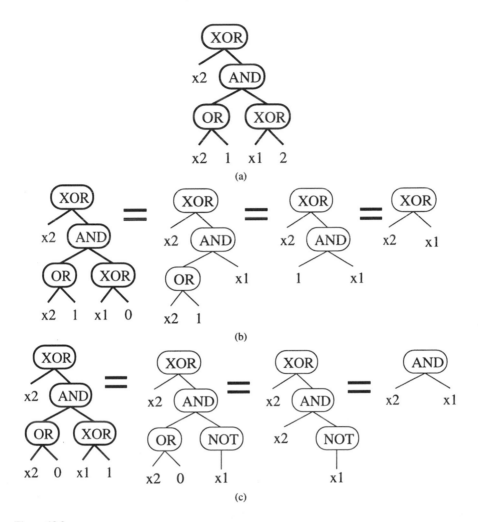

Figure 13.3
(a) Program evolved using sub-machine-code GP to solve the 1-bit adder problem, (b) the same program as seen by the bit-0 processor within the CPU (in thick line) and some of its simpler equivalents (in thin line), and (c) the corresponding program executed by the bit-1 processor and its simplifications.

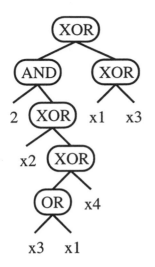

Figure 13.4
Program evolved using sub-machine-code GP to solve the 2-bit adder problem without carry.

By slightly modifying the setup of the experiments described above we were also able to evolve a solution to the two-bit adder problem where the carry bit is also computed. This problem has three output bits and so requires using three 1-bit processors. So, the inputs variables x1, x2, x3 and x4 (which have the same meaning as in the previous paragraph) took the values 0 and 7 (i.e. binary 111) depending on whether the corresponding bit of the 2-bit adder truth table was 0 or 1. The constants 0, 1, 2, 3, 4, 5, 6 and 7 were included in the terminal set. The fitness function was the sum (over all the 16 possible combinations of inputs) of the number of matches between the actual output of each program (i.e. sum1, sum2 and carry) and the desired output (maximum score 48) decreased by 0.001 times the number of nodes in a program. This was done to promote parsimonious solutions. All the other parameters were as in the previous experiments. A solution to this problem was found by GP at generation 27 of a run. The solution included 80 nodes. By allowing the run to continue, by generation 69 GP had simplified this solutions down to 29 nodes. The simplified solution is shown in Figure 13.5.

13.4.2 Character Recognition Problem

In the adder problems the 1-bit processors used to perform the task did not communicate in any way. However, in some problems, like the character recognition problem described below, adding some form of communication between processors can be useful.

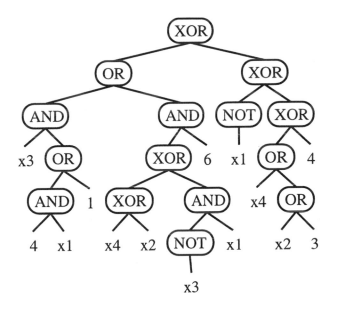

Figure 13.5
Program evolved using sub-machine-code GP to solve the 2-bit adder problem with carry.

The character recognition problem we considered to illustrate this idea included only three input patters, an A, a B and a C, represented by the 5×5 bitmaps shown in Figure 13.6. The black squares represent 1's and white ones represent 0's of the corresponding bit map (the additional role of the squares with gray borders is explained below). Each character represented one fitness case. The objective was to evolve a program capable of identifying the three characters.

Each character in Figure 13.6 was represented by a 25-bit binary string by reading the bits from each bit map from left to right and top to bottom. This produces the strings A=0010001010100011111110001, B=1111010001111101000111110 and C=0111010001100001000101110. So we decided to use 25 1-bit processors. The terminal set included only one variable, x, and random integer constants between 0 and 33554431 (which corresponds to the binary number 1111111111111111111111111). The variable x takes the values 4540401, 32045630 or 15254062 which are the decimal equivalents of the bit-strings representing the characters A, B and C, respectively. In order to determine which character was present in input we designated the bit-11, bit-12 and bit-13 processors as result returning processors (i.e. all the bits of the integer resulting from the evaluation of each program were ignored except bits 11, 12 and 13). When an A was presented in input, the target output was the pattern 100. When a B was presented the target was 010. The

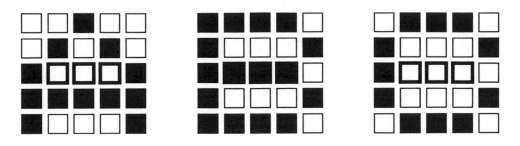

Figure 13.6
A, B and C bitmaps used in the character recognition problem.

target was 001 when C was the input. The fitness function was the sum (over the 3 possible inputs, A, B and C) of the number of matches between the actual output and the desired output for bits 11, 12, and 13 (maximum score 9) decreased by 0.001 times the number of nodes in a program.

Bits 11, 12 and 13 were chosen as outputs since the characters A and C cannot be differentiated just by looking at bits 11, 12 and 13 of their binary representations as it can be easily inferred by comparing the patterns in the squares with gray borders in Figure 13.6. Therefore, this problem could not be solved without allowing some form of communication between processors. To keep things as simple as possible we decided to try using simple bit shift operations to start with. So, we used the function set {NOT, OR, AND, XOR, SL, SR}, where SR (SL) is an arity-1 function which performs a 1-bit shift to the right (left) of the bit pattern representing its integer argument.

Expecting this problem to be much harder than the previous ones we used a population of 10,000 individuals in our runs. The other parameters where as in the 2-bit adder with carry problem. However, the problem was in fact quite easy to solve: a solution was found at generation 0 of each of the five runs we performed. In one run the generation-0 solution included 31 nodes, but by allowing the run to continue for 7 more generations we obtained the simplified 8-node solution shown in Figure 13.7.

This solution is quite clever. It uses communication to create two modified (shifted) versions of the input bit pattern. In the first version the characters B and C can be differentiated from A by looking at bits 11, 12 and 13. In the second version A and C can be differentiated from B. Then by combining such modified bit patters with an XOR not only the three characters can be properly differentiated, but the desired encoding for the result is also achieved. The steps performed by the program when A, B or C are presented in input are shown in Table 13.1.

The only changes necessary to solve this problem with our GP implementation in Pop-11 were within the fitness function. To clarify how little effort these required we report in Figure 13.8 the actual implementation of the fitness function used in the character recognition experiments.

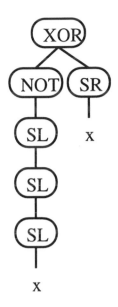

Figure 13.7
Program evolved using sub-machine-code GP to solve the character recognition problem.

13.4.3 Discussion

The evolution of the programs described in the previous subsections was very quick except for the 2-bit adder with carry, which was solved only in 2 runs out of 10. At this stage we cannot say whether evolving one program that does more than one job using sub-machine-code GP *always* requires less effort than evolving separate programs in independent runs. It is entirely possible that the constraints imposed by the SIMD nature of the CPU will make the search harder when one wants to use several 1-bit processors to do totally unrelated tasks. In this case, it would be possible that the advantage in terms of evaluation time offered by sub-machine-code GP programs would be outweighed by an increased number of evaluations required to solve the problem.

Given the relative difficulty with which the 2-bit adder with carry was solved, we expected that this would happen in the character recognition problem where we used 25 processors. However, evolution seemed to be greatly facilitated by the representation adopted. So, clearly there are domains where sub-machine-code GP can exploit the CPU parallelism fully. Even if there are cases where finding a parallel program with sub-machine-code GP is hard, if one is able to find one such program, then execution of it will presumably still be much faster than if using multiple standard sequential programs. This advantage may

Table 13.1
Steps in the execution of the program in Figure 13.7. The bits read as the output of the program are shown in bold.

	Input pattern		
Subexpression	A	B	C
x	00100	11110	01110
	01010	10001	10001
	10001	**11110**	**10000**
	11111	10001	10001
	10001	11110	01110
(SL (SL (SL x)))	00010	10100	10100
	10100	01111	01100
	01111	**10100**	**00100**
	11100	01111	01011
	01000	10000	10000
(NOT (SL (SL (SL x))))	11101	01011	01011
	01011	10000	10011
	10000	**01011**	**11011**
	00011	10000	10100
	10111	01111	01111
(SR x)	00010	01111	00111
	00101	01000	01000
	01000	**11111**	**11000**
	11111	01000	01000
	11000	11111	10111
(XOR (NOT (SL (SL (SL x)))) (SR x))	11111	00100	01100
	01110	11000	11011
	11000	**10100**	**00011**
	11100	11000	11100
	01111	10000	11000

become prevalent over the search effort, whenever the programs are used in applications where they are run repeatedly and frequently for an extended period of time.

CPUs are not the only computational devices available within modern workstations. For example, devices like graphic accelerators can also perform certain forms of computation in parallel on huge quantities of data very efficiently. For example, most graphic cards are able to shift and to perform bitwise operations on large portions of their video memory in microseconds using specialised, very high speed processors. Good graphics libraries will exploit such operations. Sub-machine-code GP could be run on a video card, rather than on the CPU, with minimum effort (perhaps one day we will even have sub-machine-code GP screen savers!). Some CPUs also include similar specialised high-throughput graphics operations (like the MMX extensions on Pentium processors) which could be exploited to do GP.

```
define char_rec_fitness_function( prog );
    vars match_count = 0, target, output, x, i;

    fast_for x, target in_vectorclass      ;;; This FOR loop binds X and
                                           ;;; TARGET simultaneously

            {2:001000101010001111111110001 ;;; Inputs A, B, C
             2:111101000111110100011110    ;;; (2:XXXX = XXXX in base 2)
             2:011101000110000100101110},

            {2:00000000000010000000000000 ;;; Desired outputs for A, B, C
             2:00000000000001000000000000 ;;; (all bits ignored except 11,
             2:00000000000000100000000000};;; 12 and 13)
            do

                eval( prog ) -> output;    ;;; Run evolved program

                for i from 11 to 13 do
                    if getbit(i,output) == getbit(i,target) then
                        1 + match_count -> match_count;
                    endif;
                endfor;
    endfor;
    match_count - 0.001 * nodes( prog ) -> fitness( prog );
enddefine;
```

Figure 13.8
Pop-11 implementation of the character recognition problem fitness function.

13.5   Fast Parallel Evaluation of Fitness Cases

As indicated in the previous sections, sub-machine-code GP offers many advantages. However, given the SIMD nature of the CPU, it might also require an increased number of evaluations to solve problems where the 1-bit processors of a CPU are required to perform unrelated tasks in parallel. These additional search costs disappear when using the CPU processors to do exactly the *same* task but on different input data.

One such cases is the use of sub-machine-code GP to evaluate multiple fitness cases in parallel. This can be done very easily in Boolean classification problems. The approach used is a simple modification of the approach used in the examples in the previous sections. The only differences with respect to standard GP are: independently. This can be done as follows:

• Bitwise Boolean functions are used.

• Before each program execution the input variables need to initialised so as to pass a different fitness case to each of the different 1-bit processors of the CPU.

- The output integers produced by a program need to be unpacked since each of their bits has to be interpreted as the output for a different fitness case.

In the Appendix we provide a simple C implementation of this idea which demonstrates the changes necessary to do sub-machine-code GP when solving the even-5 and even-10 parity problems.

In practical terms this evaluation strategy means that all the fitness cases associated with the problem of inducing a Boolean function of n arguments can be evaluated with a *single program execution* for $n \leq 5$ on 32 bit machines, and $n \leq 6$ on 64 bit machines. Since this can be done with any programming language, this technique could lead to speedups of up to 1.5 or 1.8 orders of magnitude.

Because of the overheads associated to the packing of the bits to be assigned to the input variables and the unpacking of the result the speedup factors achieved in practice are to be expected to be slightly lower than 32 or 64. However, these overheads can be very small. For example, it is possible to pre-pack the values for the input variables and store them in a table (this has been done only in part in the code in the Appendix). If also the targets are precomputed (we did not do that in our implementation), in many problems the only computation required with the output returned by a program would be the calculation of the Hamming distance between two integers.

The implementation in the Appendix (with a slightly different main function) was used to perform an evaluation of the overheads in sub-machine-code GP. We ran our tests on an Sun Ultra-10 300MHz workstation using a 32-bit compiler. In the tests we first evaluate 1,000,000 times the 20-node program (NOT (XOR (X1 (XOR (X2 (XOR (X3 (XOR (X4 (XOR X5 (XOR X6 (XOR X7 (XOR X8 (XOR X9 X10))....)))) using the even-10 parity function which involves 1024 test cases. This required 134 seconds of CPU time. Running the one-node program x1 required 38 seconds. The difference between the two, 96 seconds, indicates that our implementation is able to evaluate

$$\underbrace{(20-1)}_{\text{nodes}} \times \underbrace{1,000,000}_{\text{evaluations}} \times (\ \underbrace{1024}_{\text{fitness cases}}\ /\ \underbrace{32}_{\text{CPU bits}}\ )\ /\ \underbrace{96}_{\text{CPU time}}\ \approx 6,300,000$$

primitives per second. However, there are 38 seconds of overheads (evaluating the target, unpacking, etc.), which reduce the actual number of primitives per second to around 4,800,000 (i.e. $20 \times 1,000,000 \times (1024/32)/134$). So, rather than a 32-fold speed up we obtain a speed up of approximately 24 times for programs of 20 nodes. However, the speed up is better for longer programs. For example, for a program including 200 nodes the actual number of primitives per second is around 6,100,000 with a 31-fold speedup. To match this with standard GP one would have to find a computer capable of evaluating around 190 million primitives per second (in C): not an easy task. For larger programs the speed up can be even better. For 64 bit machines these performance figures can be substantially improved. Indeed we found speedups exceeding 60-fold.

In a typical run of our C implementation of sub-machine-code GP on the even-10 parity problem, a DEC Alpha 500 workstation with a 400MHz 64-bit CPU can evolve a population of 1000 individuals for 100 generations in 140.6 seconds. The number of nodes evaluated by the system in this time is more than 1.2 billion (10^9) which is approximately 8,600,000 nodes per second. This figure needs to be multiplied by 64 to obtain the number of primitives per second. The result is above 550 millions, which is bigger than the clock speed of the machine (400MHz). Sub-machine-code GP executes 1.3 operations per clock tick. Since this is more than any other GP implementation (where at most one instruction per clock tick is executed), the claim that on 64-bit machines our GP implementation is the fastest in the world would seem justifiable.

Together with other new techniques, sub-machine-code GP has allowed us to solve very high-order parity problems without ADFs (manuscript in preparation).

Finally, it should be noted that the technique described in this section and those used in the previous section can be combined. For example, if for a particular problem only a small number of 1-bit processors is necessary, it is then possible to evaluate multiple fitness cases of the same problem using the remaining processors.

13.6 Conclusions

In this chapter we have presented a GP technique which exploits the internal parallelism of CPUs, either to evolve efficient programs which solve multiple problems in parallel, or to compute multiple fitness cases in parallel during a single execution of a program. We call this form of genetic programming sub-machine-code GP. We have demonstrated remarkable speedups and presented examples where we have evolved parallel programs which can be executed directly and efficiently on standard computer hardware.

Sub-machine-code GP has a considerable potential which we will continue to explore in future research. One particularly interesting issue is whether it is possible to use this form of GP to solve efficiently also problems which require primitives with side effects. Another issue is to see on which classes of problems the bias imposed by the SIMD nature of the CPU is not a limit but an advantage for sub-machine-code GP.

The potential of sub-machine-code GP is real and already available. This is demonstrated by the 24- to 60-fold speedups it can achieve in Boolean classification problems without requiring any significant change to the GP system used and independently of the language it is implemented in. On a 64-bit machine, with this technique GP is able to evaluate 64 fitness cases with a single program evaluation. This means that the fitness function for a problem like the even-10 parity problem, which has never been solved with standard GP without ADFs or recursion, now has about the same computation load as the fitness function of an even-4 parity problem.

On Boolean classification problems, the speedup achieved by sub-machine-code GP makes our 64-bit C implementation of the fastest GP system in the world. If we believe

Moore's law (which predicts a doubling in speed of computers every 1.5 years), the speed up obtained is equivalent to the one we should expect to obtain in approximately 10 years using standard GP.

13.A   Appendix: Implementation

This appendix describes a simple C program which illustrates the ideas behind the fast parallel evaluation of fitness cases with sub-machine-code GP. The code has been only partly optimised. No optimisation has been performed in the packing of program inputs, in the target output determination, and in the comparison between actual and target output.

13.A.1   Description

The program includes the following functions:

`run()` is a simple interpreter capable of handling variables and a small number of Boolean functions. The interpreter executes the program stored in prefix notation as a vector of bytes in the global variable `program`. The interpreter returns an unsigned long integer which is used for fitness evaluation.

`e5parity()` computes the target output in the even-5 parity problem for a group of 32 fitness cases.

`e10parity()` does the same but in the even-10 parity problem.

`even5_fitness_function( char *Prog )` given a vector of characters representing a program, executes it and returns the number of entries of the even-5 parity truth table correctly predicted by the program.

`even10_fitness_function( char *Prog )` does the same for the even-10 parity problem. In this case the program is executed 32 times (instead of 1024), once of each iterations of the five `for` loops. These loops are used to make the interpreter evaluate the program on a different part of the truth table of the even-10 parity function. This is why the variables `x1` to `x5` initialised in the loops take the binary values 000...000 or 111...111 (i.e. FFFFFFFF in hexadecimal).

`main()` runs the even-5 parity fitness function on two programs: a non-solution, `(XOR X1 X2)`, and a solution, `(NOT (XOR (X1 (XOR (X2 (XOR (X3 (XOR (X4 (X5))))))))))`. It then does the same for the even-10 parity fitness function with the programs `(XOR X1 X2)` (a non-solution) and `(NOT (XOR (X1 (XOR (X2 (XOR (X3 (XOR (X4 (XOR X5 (XOR X6 (XOR X7 (XOR X8 (XOR X9 X10)))))))))))))` (a solution).

13.A.2 Code

```c
#include <stdio.h>

enum {X1, X2, X3, X4, X5, X6, X7, X8, X9, X10, NOT, AND, OR, XOR};

unsigned long x1, x2, x3, x4, x5, x6, x7, x8, x9, x10;
char *program;

unsigned long run() /* Interpreter */
{
  switch ( *program++ )
    {
    case X1  : return( x1 );
    case X2  : return( x2 );
    case X3  : return( x3 );
    case X4  : return( x4 );
    case X5  : return( x5 );
    case X6  : return( x6 );
    case X7  : return( x7 );
    case X8  : return( x8 );
    case X9  : return( x9 );
    case X10 : return( x10 );
    case NOT : return( ~run() );           /* Bitwise NOT */
    case AND : return( run() & run() );  /* Bitwise AND */
    case OR  : return( run() | run() );  /* Bitwise OR  */
    case XOR : return( run() ^ run() );  /* Bitwise XOR */
    }
}

unsigned long e5parity()  /* Bitwise Even-5 parity function */
{
  return(~(x1^x2^x3^x4^x5)); /* (NOT (XOR x1 (XOR x2 (XOR x3 (XOR x4 x5))))) */
}

int even5_fitness_function( char *Prog ) /* Even-5 parity fitness function */
{
  char i;
  int fit = 0;
  unsigned long result, target, matches, filter;

  x1 = 0x0000ffff;  /* x1 = 00000000000000001111111111111111 */
  x2 = 0x00ff00ff;  /* x2 = 00000000111111110000000011111111 */
  x3 = 0x0f0f0f0f;  /* x3 = 00001111000011110000111100001111 */
  x4 = 0x33333333;  /* x4 = 00110011001100110011001100110011 */
  x5 = 0xaaaaaaaa;  /* x5 = 01010101010101010101010101010101 */

  program = Prog;
  result = run();

  target = e5parity();
  matches = ~(result ^ target); /* Find bits where TARGET = RESULT */
  filter = 1;
  for( i = 0; i < 32; i ++ )    /* Count bits set in MATCHES */
    {
      if( matches & filter  ) fit ++;
      filter <<= 1;
    }

  return( fit );
}
```

```
unsigned long e10parity() /* Bitwise Even-10 parity function */
{
  return(~(x1^x2^x3^x4^x5^x6^x7^x8^x9^x10));
}

int even10_fitness_function( char *Prog ) /* Even-10 parity fitness function */
{
  char cx1, cx2, cx3, cx4, cx5, i;
  int fit = 0;
  unsigned long result, target, matches, filter;

  for( cx1 = 0; cx1 < 2; cx1 ++ ) /* Set x1, ..., x5 to 000...000 and 111....111 */
    {
      x1 = cx1 ? 0 : 0xffffffff;
      for( cx2 = 0; cx2 < 2; cx2 ++ )
        {
          x2 = cx2 ? 0 : 0xffffffff;
          for( cx3 = 0; cx3 < 2; cx3 ++ )
            {
              x3 = cx3 ? 0 : 0xffffffff;
              for( cx4 = 0; cx4 < 2; cx4 ++ )
                {
                  x4 = cx4 ? 0 : 0xffffffff;
                  for( cx5 = 0; cx5 < 2; cx5 ++ )
                    {
                      x5 = cx5 ? 0 : 0xffffffff;
                      x6 = 0x0000ffff;  /*  x6 = 00000000000000001111111111111111 */
                      x7 = 0x00ff00ff;  /*  x7 = 00000000111111110000000011111111 */
                      x8 = 0x0f0f0f0f;  /*  x8 = 00001111000011110000111100001111 */
                      x9 = 0x33333333;  /*  x9 = 00110011001100110011001100110011 */
                      x10 = 0xaaaaaaaa; /* x10 = 01010101010101010101010101010101 */

                      program = Prog;
                      result = run();

                      target = e10parity();
                      matches = ~(result ^ target); /* Bits where TARGET = RESULT */
                      filter = 1;
                      for( i = 0; i < 32; i ++ )    /* Count bits set in MATCHES */
                        {
                          if(  matches & filter  ) fit ++;
                          filter <<= 1;
                        }
                    }
                }
            }
        }
    }

  return( fit );
}
```

```
void main()
{
  /* Incorrect solution */
  char s1[] = {XOR, X1, X2};

        /* Even-5 parity solution */
  char s2[] = {NOT, XOR, X1, XOR, X2, XOR, X3, XOR, X4, X5};

  /* Even-10 parity solution */
  char s3[] = {NOT, XOR, X1, XOR, X2, XOR, X3, XOR, X4, XOR, X5,
               XOR, X6, XOR, X7, XOR, X8, XOR, X9, X10};

  printf("Even-5 Problem\n"
         "Testing (XOR X1 X2)\n"
         "Score %d\n\n", even5_fitness_function( s1 ) );

  printf("Even-5 Problem\n"
         "Testing (NOT (XOR (X1 (XOR (X2 (XOR (X3 (XOR (X4 (X5)))))))))\n"
         "Score %d\n\n", even5_fitness_function( s2 ) );

  printf("Even-10 Problem\n"
         "Testing (XOR X1 X2)\n"
         "Score %d\n\n", even10_fitness_function( s1 ) );

  printf("Even-10 Problem\n"
         "Testing (NOT (XOR (X1 (XOR (X2 (XOR (X3 (XOR (X4 \n"
         "(XOR X5 (XOR X6 (XOR X7 (XOR X8 (XOR X9 X10)))))))))))))\n"
         "Score %d\n\n", even10_fitness_function( s3 ) );
}

/* This file is also available at:
   ftp://ftp.cs.bham.ac.uk/pub/authors/R.Poli/code/smc_gp.c */
```

Acknowledgements

The authors wish to thank the members of the Evolutionary and Emergent Behaviour Intelligence and Computation (EEBIC) group at Birmingham for useful comments and discussion.

Bibliography

Andre, D. and Koza, J. R. (1996), "Parallel genetic programming: A scalable implementation using the transputer network architecture," in *Advances in Genetic Programming 2*, P. J. Angeline and K. E. Kinnear, Jr. (Eds.), Chapter 16, pp 317–338, Cambridge, MA, USA: MIT Press.

Banzhaf, W., Nordin, P., Keller, R. E., and Francone, F. D. (1998), *Genetic Programming – An Introduction; On the Automatic Evolution of Computer Programs and its Applications*, Morgan Kaufmann, dpunkt.verlag.

Fukunaga, A., Stechert, A., and Mutz, D. (1998), "A genome compiler for high performance genetic programming," in *Genetic Programming 1998: Proceedings of the Third Annual Conference*, J. R. Koza, W. Banzhaf, K. Chellapilla, K. Deb, M. Dorigo, D. B. Fogel, M. H. Garzon, D. E. Goldberg, H. Iba, and R. Riolo (Eds.), pp 86–94, University of Wisconsin, Madison, Wisconsin, USA: Morgan Kaufmann.

Gathercole, C. and Ross, P. (1997), "Tackling the boolean even N parity problem with genetic programming and limited-error fitness," in *Genetic Programming 1997: Proceedings of the Second Annual Conference*, J. R. Koza, K. Deb, M. Dorigo, D. B. Fogel, M. Garzon, H. Iba, and R. L. Riolo (Eds.), pp 119–127, Stanford University, CA, USA: Morgan Kaufmann.

Handley, S. (1994), "On the use of a directed acyclic graph to represent a population of computer programs," in *Proceedings of the 1994 IEEE World Congress on Computational Intelligence*, pp 154–159, Orlando, Florida, USA: IEEE Press.

Juille, H. and Pollack, J. B. (1996), "Massively parallel genetic programming," in *Advances in Genetic Programming 2*, P. J. Angeline and K. E. Kinnear, Jr. (Eds.), Chapter 17, pp 339–358, Cambridge, MA, USA: MIT Press.

Klahold, S., Frank, S., Keller, R. E., and Banzhaf, W. (1998), "Exploring the possibilites and restrictions of genetic programming in Java bytecode," in *Late Breaking Papers at the Genetic Programming 1998 Conference*, J. R. Koza (Ed.), University of Wisconsin, Madison, Wisconsin, USA: Stanford University Bookstore.

Koza, J. R. (1992), *Genetic Programming: On the Programming of Computers by Means of Natural Selection*, MIT Press.

Koza, J. R. (1994), *Genetic Programming II: Automatic Discovery of Reusable Programs*, Cambridge, Massachusetts: MIT Press.

Langdon, W. B. (1998), *Data Structures and Genetic Programming: Genetic Programming + Data Structures = Automatic Programming!*, Boston: Kluwer.

Langdon, W. B. and Poli, R. (1998), "Why ants are hard," in *Genetic Programming 1998: Proceedings of the Third Annual Conference*, J. R. Koza, W. Banzhaf, K. Chellapilla, K. Deb, M. Dorigo, D. B. Fogel, M. H. Garzon, D. E. Goldberg, H. Iba, and R. Riolo (Eds.), pp 193–201, University of Wisconsin, Madison, Wisconsin, USA: Morgan Kaufmann.

Luke, S. (1998), "Genetic programming produced competitive soccer softbot teams for robocup97," in *Genetic Programming 1998: Proceedings of the Third Annual Conference*, J. R. Koza, W. Banzhaf, K. Chellapilla, K. Deb, M. Dorigo, D. B. Fogel, M. H. Garzon, D. E. Goldberg, H. Iba, and R. Riolo (Eds.), pp 214–222, University of Wisconsin, Madison, Wisconsin, USA: Morgan Kaufmann.

Luke, S. and Spector, L. (1998), "A revised comparison of crossover and mutation in genetic programming," in *Genetic Programming 1998: Proceedings of the Third Annual Conference*, J. R. Koza, W. Banzhaf, K. Chellapilla, K. Deb, M. Dorigo, D. B. Fogel, M. H. Garzon, D. E. Goldberg, H. Iba, and R. Riolo (Eds.), pp 208–213, University of Wisconsin, Madison, Wisconsin, USA: Morgan Kaufmann.

Lukschandl, E., Holmlund, M., and Moden, E. (1998a), "Automatic evolution of Java bytecode: First experience with the Java virtual machine," in *Late Breaking Papers at EuroGP'98: the First European Workshop on Genetic Programming*, R. Poli, W. B. Langdon, M. Schoenauer, T. Fogarty, and W. Banzhaf (Eds.), pp 14–16, Paris, France: CSRP-98-10, The University of Birmingham, UK.

Lukschandl, E., Holmlund, M., Moden, E., Nordahl, M., and Nordin, P. (1998b), "Induction of Java bytecode with genetic programming," in *Late Breaking Papers at the Genetic Programming 1998 Conference*, J. R. Koza (Ed.), University of Wisconsin, Madison, Wisconsin, USA: Stanford University Bookstore.

Nordin, P. (1994), "A compiling genetic programming system that directly manipulates the machine code," in *Advances in Genetic Programming*, K. E. Kinnear, Jr. (Ed.), Chapter 14, pp 311–331, MIT Press.

Nordin, P. (1997), *Evolutionary Program Induction of Binary Machine Code and its Applications*, PhD thesis, der Universitat Dortmund am Fachereich Informatik.

Nordin, P. (1998), "AIMGP: A formal description," in *Late Breaking Papers at the Genetic Programming 1998 Conference*, J. R. Koza (Ed.), University of Wisconsin, Madison, Wisconsin, USA: Stanford University Bookstore.

Nordin, P. and Banzhaf, W. (1995), "Evolving turing-complete programs for a register machine with self-modifying code," in *Genetic Algorithms: Proceedings of the Sixth International Conference (ICGA95)*, L. Eshelman (Ed.), pp 318–325, Pittsburgh, PA, USA: Morgan Kaufmann.

Poli, R. (1996), "Genetic programming for image analysis," in *Genetic Programming 1996: Proceedings of the First Annual Conference*, J. R. Koza, D. E. Goldberg, D. B. Fogel, and R. L. Riolo (Eds.), pp 363–368, Stanford University, CA, USA: MIT Press.

Poli, R. (1997), "Evolution of graph-like programs with parallel distributed genetic programming," in *Genetic Algorithms: Proceedings of the Seventh International Conference*, T. Back (Ed.), pp 346–353, Michigan State University, East Lansing, MI, USA: Morgan Kaufmann.

Sian, C. F. (1998), "A java based distributed approach to genetic programming on the internet," Master's thesis, Computer Science, University of Birmingham.

Singleton, A. (1994), "Genetic programming with C++," *BYTE*, pp 171–176.

Stoffel, K. and Spector, L. (1996), "High-performance, parallel, stack-based genetic programming," in *Genetic Programming 1996: Proceedings of the First Annual Conference*, J. R. Koza, D. E. Goldberg, D. B. Fogel, and R. L. Riolo (Eds.), pp 224–229, Stanford University, CA, USA: MIT Press.

Teller, A. and Andre, D. (1997), "Automatically choosing the number of fitness cases: The rational allocation of trials," in *Genetic Programming 1997: Proceedings of the Second Annual Conference*, J. R. Koza, K. Deb, M. Dorigo, D. B. Fogel, M. Garzon, H. Iba, and R. L. Riolo (Eds.), pp 321–328, Stanford University, CA, USA: Morgan Kaufmann.

14 The Internal Reinforcement of Evolving Algorithms

Astro Teller

There is a fundamental problem with genetic programming as it is currently practiced, the genetic recombination operators that drive the learning process act at random, without regard to how the internal components of the programs to be recombined behaved during training. This research introduces a method of program transformations that is principled, based on the program's *internal behavior*, and significantly more likely than random local sampling to improve the transformed programs' fitness values. The contribution of our research is a detailed approach by which principled credit-blame assignment can be brought to GP and that credit-blame assignment can be focused to improve that same evolutionary process. This principled credit-blame assignment is done through a new program representation called *neural programming* and applied through a set of principled processes called, collectively, *internal reinforcement in neural programming*. This *internal reinforcement* of evolving programs is presented here as a first step toward the desired gradient descent in program space.

14.1 Introduction

There is a fundamental problem with evolutionary computation, and particularly with genetic programming, as it is currently practiced. The problem is that in the space of programs, even if it has been carefully defined so that most or all examined programs are legal, the density of functions that do something "interesting" is very low. This is increasingly the case as the expressiveness of the language in which the programs are written moves up the ladder from regular languages to Turing machines. For example, in the space of Turing machines, the density of programs that act for multiple steps and then halt is conjectured to be set of measure zero [Hopcroft and Ullman, 1979].

This low density of computationally non-trivial programs, combined with the random recombination that still characterizes genetic programming, has marginalized GP, an exciting and valuable subfield of machine learning. GP needs search operators that tend to focus on good solutions and GP search operators are currently not focused, but instead altered by random transformations.

We develop a novel solution to this problem. As part of the evolutionary process, we introduce a method of program transformations that is principled, based on the program's behavior, and significantly more likely to create new programs that are worth searching than random local sampling. The contribution of our research is the identification of this problem in genetic programming and a detailed approach, both comprehensive and analytical, on how to address it. The main algorithmic innovation of this research is the process by which principled credit-blame assignment can be brought to evolution of algorithms and that credit-blame assignment can be used to improve that same evolutionary process. This principled credit-blame assignment is done through a new program representation called *neural programming* (NP) and applied through a set of principled processes called, collectively, *internal reinforcement in neural programming* (IRNP). This *internal reinforcement* of evolving programs is presented in this chapter as a first step toward the desired gradient descent in program space.

Genetic programming is a successful representative of the machine learning practice of *empirical credit assignment* [Angeline, 1993]. Empirical credit assignment allows the dynamics of the system to implicitly determine credit and blame. Evolution does just this [Altenberg, 1994]. Machine learning also has successful representatives (e.g., ANNs) of the practice of *explicit credit assignment*. In explicit credit assignment machine learning techniques, the models to be learned are constructed so that why a particular model is imperfect, what part of that model needs to be changed, and how to change the model can all be described analytically with at least locally optimal (i.e., greedy) results. To be clear, this work on *internal reinforcement* is not only an attempt to approach gradient descent in program space. Internal Reinforcement is also designed to bridge this credit-blame assignment gap by finding ways in which explicit and empirical credit assignment can find mutual benefit in a single machine learning technique. In summary, the main question that our research addresses is:

> Can the evolution of algorithms be extended in a domain-independent way to incorporate accurate credit-blame assignment of each program's internal structure and behavior in such a way that focused, principled reinforcement information improves the evolutionary process?

14.2   Neural Programming

Genetic programming is a successful machine learning technique that provides powerful parameterized primitive constructs and uses evolution as its search mechanism. However, unlike some machine learning techniques, such as Artificial Neural Networks (ANNs), GP does not have a principled procedure for changing parts of a learned structure based on that structure's past performance. GP is missing a clear, locally optimal update procedure, the equivalent of gradient-descent backpropagation for ANNs. Why adapt GP instead of simply using a machine learning technique like ANNs? In general, it is not possible to give an ANN an input for every possible parameterization of each user defined primitive function that a GP program can be given. And it is far from obvious how to work complex functions into the middle of an otherwise homogeneous network of simple non-linear functions. Yet gradient-descent learning procedures, like backpropagation in ANNs, are an extremely powerful idea. Backpropagation is not only a kind of local performance guarantee, it is a kind of performance explanation. It is to achieve this kind of dual benefit that the research this chapter reports on was undertaken.

This chapter shows how to accumulate explicit credit-blame assignment information in the Neural Programming representation. These values are collectively referred to as the *Credit-Blame map*. By organizing the GP programs into a network of heterogeneous nodes and replacing program *flow of control* with *flow of data*, we can use the Credit-Blame map to propagate punishment and reward through each evolving program.

The goal of *internal reinforcement* is to provide a reasoned method to guide search in the field of program induction. Hill-climbing in a space means sampling local points and then choosing the best of those to continue from. When the gradient is available, however, it is always better (locally at least) to move in the direction of the gradient. Program evolution can work with random samplings of nearby point in program space, but can work much more effectively with *internal reinforcement*. We introduce internal reinforcement as a program evolution approximation to the gradient function in program fitness space. Said another way, it would be desirable to be able, in GP, to have reinforcement of programs be more specific (directed towards particular parts or aspects of a program) and more appropriate (telling the system *how* to change those specific parts). As will become clear later in this chapter, internal reinforcement is a partial, not complete solution to this problem.

In Section 14.3, we describe how this representation can be used to deliver explicit, useful, internal reinforcement to the evolving programs to help guide the learning search process. And in Section 14.4, we demonstrate the effectiveness of both the representation and its associated internal reinforcement strategy through an experiment on an illustrative signal classification problem.

14.2.1 The Neural Programming Representation

The essence of a programming language is a set of basic constructs and a set of legal ways of combining those constructs. A measure of the extensibility of a language is the ease with which new constructs or new construct combinations can be add to the language. It is the high degree of extensibility in GP that we want to wed to the focused update policies possible in other machine learning techniques.

The Neural Programming representation consists of a graph of nodes and arcs that support a **flow of data**, rather than the flow of control typical in programming languages. The nodes in a neural program compute arbitrary functions of the inputs. So a node can be the sum of inputs to the node and a sigmoid threshold. But it can also use other functions such as MULT, READ, WRITE, IF-THEN-ELSE, and, most importantly, potentially complex user defined functions for examining the input data. Examples NP programs are given later in this chapter. Figure 14.1 contains the important characteristics of the NP representation.

Throughout this chapter, the characteristics of NP will be used and discussed in greater detail. Let us here highlight a few aspects of NP. A parameterized signal primitive (PSP)

- An NP program is a general graph of nodes and arcs.
- Each NP node executes one of a set of functions (e.g., Read-Memory, Write-Memory, Multiply, Parameterized-Signal-Primitive-3, etc.) or zero-arity functions (e.g., constants, *Clock*, etc.).
- An arc from node x to node y (notated (x, y)) indicates that the output of x flows to y as an available input.
- On **each** time step t $(0 < t < T)$, **every** node takes some of its inputs, according to the arity of its function, computes that function, and outputs that value on *all* of its output arcs. *Data flow, not control flow.*
- One type of node function is "Output." Output nodes collect their inputs and create the program response through a function *OUT* of those values. In this chapter *OUT* is a simple weighted average. Each value is weighted by the timestep it appears on.

Figure 14.1
The critical characteristics of the NP representation.

is a piece of code, written by a user that expresses a way of extracting information of the input signal in a parameterized form. An example PSP might return the AVERAGE or VARIANCE of values in a range of the input data as specified by the inputs to that node. This kind of embedding of complex (often co-evolved) components as primitives in the evolving GP system has repeatedly been shown to be effective (e.g., [Koza, 1994]). Furthermore, these powerful parameterized-signal-primitives, as part of the learning process, can be used in place of brittle (fixed/static) preprocessing. As has been discussed already, the salient distinction here is the parameterization of input "features."

Each NP node may have many output arcs. See Figure 14.3 for a simple example. The multiple forked distribution of good values from any point in the program is a valuable aspect of the NP representation. Seen from a GP vantage, this is similar to a kind of highly flexible automatically defined functions (ADF) [Koza, 1994] mechanism. The idea is that once a "valuable" piece of information has been created, it can be sent to different parts of the NP program to be used further in a variety of different ways. This fan-out is an advantage of connectionist representations from which GP program representations can profit by incorporating (see [Nordin, 1997] for an alternate method).

A timestep threshold T (see Figure 14.1) is imposed on the evolving programs (in order to avoid having to solve the Halting problem). Given such a threshold, a reasonable question to ask is, "How much of a burden is this threshold?" or alternately "Can the evolving programs take advantage of additional time in which to examine an input signal?" The answers is to these questions are provided in Section 14.4.4.

There are two dominant forms of change that evolving programs typically undergo: crossover and mutation.

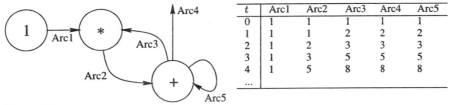

t	Arc1	Arc2	Arc3	Arc4	Arc5
0	1	1	1	1	1
1	1	1	2	2	2
2	1	2	3	3	3
3	1	3	5	5	5
4	1	5	8	8	8
...					

Figure 14.2
A simple NP program that computes the successive elements of the Fibonacci series. All input/arc values are 1 on the first time step. On the right, progression of arc values over time.

While NP programs look more like recurrent ANNs than traditional tree-structured GP programs, NP programs are changed, not by adjusting arc weights (NP arcs have no weights), but by changing both what is inside each node as well as the topology and size of the program.

14.2.2 Illustrative Examples

NP programs are evolved and explanations using evolved examples are not practical because the evolved examples are not concise. Instead we illustrate the NP representation through a set of constructed examples. Of course, any of the following example programs and program fragments could have been the result of evolution.

14.2.2.1 Example 1: The Fibonacci Series
Figure 14.2 shows an extremely simple NP program. This program computes the Fibonacci series, sending successive elements out on Arc4. The Fibonacci series is defined to be $\text{Fib}(n) = \text{Fib}(n-1) + \text{Fib}(n-2)$ with $\text{Fib}(0)=\text{Fib}(1)=1$.

There is only one initialization necessary for the correct operation of NP programs: "what input values should all nodes use on their very first computation?" Since NP programs are data flow machines, each arc is a potential input value and so there must be some initial state to the program. For this example, let us initialize each program so that all arcs have the value 1 when a program starts up. Figure 14.2 also shows how the values of the arcs change over time.

14.2.2.2 Example 2: The Golden Mean
Let us now change slightly the computation of the simple NP program from example 1. Instead of producing a list of exponentially increasing values (as in the program shown in Figure 14.2) let us design an NP program that approximates the "Golden Mean" ($\frac{\text{fib}(i)}{\text{fib}(i-1)} = 1.618034$) through its OUTPUT node. To do this, all we need to do is to add an extra node that does Division (DIV) and pass it as its two parameters (i.e., its two input arcs) fib(i) and

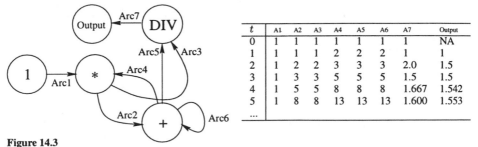

Figure 14.3
A simple Neural Program that iteratively improves an approximation to the golden mean. This program assumes that all input values are 1 on the first time step. On right, progression of arc values over time.

t	A1	A2	A3	A4	A5	A6	A7	Output
0	1	1	1	1	1	1	1	NA
1	1	1	1	2	2	2	1	1
2	1	2	2	3	3	3	2.0	1.5
3	1	3	3	5	5	5	1.5	1.5
4	1	5	5	8	8	8	1.667	1.542
5	1	8	8	13	13	13	1.600	1.553
...								

fib($i - 1$) as they are computed (shown in Figure 14.3). Figure 14.3 also shows how this computation plays out through the arcs as the timesteps pass.

14.2.2.3   Example 3: Foveation

Foveation is the process changing focus of attention in response to previous perceptions. For example, this iterative process of foveation is what gives us the illusion of seeing with high-resolution across our field of vision when, in fact, our fovea (the high resolution area of the retina) fills less than 5% of our field of view.

The Fibonacci examples illustrate how the flow of data works and how the fan out of values can significantly reduce the size of a solution expression. In this example we illuminate another important feature of NP programs: the ability to foveate. NP programs have the ability to use the results of an examination of the input signal to *guide* the next part of that examination. NP programs view their inputs (called *signals* when appropriate to avoid confusion with "inputs" to a node) through *Parameterized Signal Primitives* (PSP), variable argument functions defined by the NP user.

Let us assume that this NP program is examining signals that are video images. PSP-Variance is a function that takes four arguments, a_0 through a_3, (interpreted as the rectangular region with upper-left corner (a_0, a_1) and lower-right corner (a_2, a_3)) as input and returns the variance of the pixel intensity in that region. Figure 14.4 shows what could be part of a larger NP program. The node indicated with a double circle computes the function PSP-Variance.

To simplify the explanation, this particular NP program fragment delivers static values for three of those four inputs. The fourth input indicated by a dashed circle, changes as the program proceeds. That means that PSP-Variance, at each time step, computes its function over the region $(50,17,104,a_3)$. The simplest way to explain this mechanism is to give the pseudo-code to which it is equivalent (see Figure 14.4). Assuming again that all arcs are initialized to 1, this program finds a one-sided local minimum of PSP-Variance with respect

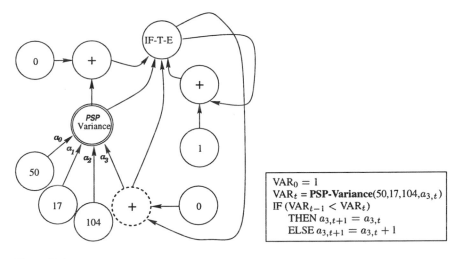

Figure 14.4
A simple NP program fragment. The output value from the dashed circle node is being iteratively refined to minimize the value returned by the PSP-Variance node. On right, pseudo-code for the behavior of this NP program fragment. VAR_t denotes the value of VAR at time t and $a_{3,t}$ denotes the value of argument a_3 at time t.

to its fourth parameter. In general, the program fragment increments the fourth parameter only if $(PSP\text{-}Variance(50,17,104,a_{3,t}) < PSP\text{-}Variance(50,17,104,a_{3,t-1}))$ (where $a_{3,t}$ is a_3 on timestep t). This is a concise example of an NP program foveating: using the values the program receives through it's PSPs to focus further examination of the input signal.

14.3 Internal Reinforcement in NP

Evolution is a learning process. In NP (or GP for that matter) programs are tested for fitness, preferred according to those fitness tests, and then changed. These program transformations have a specific goal, to produce programs that are better, which is to say score higher on the fitness evaluations, than their ancestors. Much of the time this will not happen, but the success of evolution as a learning process is directly linked to how often a novel program is really more valuable than the parent it came from. Currently, program transformations are usually random in GP. Even when they are not random, they do not transform the programs based on how those programs have behaved in the past. If we could only look into a program and see which parts of it are "good" and which parts "bad," we could write transformation rules that were much more effective, which is to say, we could dramatically improve the action of evolution. That is the motivation for the principled update procedure at the heart of this research: *internal reinforcement*.

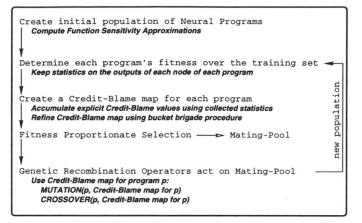

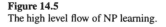

IRNP additions to EC

Figure 14.5
The high level flow of NP learning.

Now that we have introduced the neural programming representation, we can describe a mechanism to accomplish *internal reinforcement*. In Internal Reinforcement of Neural Programs (IRNP), there are two main stages. The first stage is to classify each node and arc of a program with its perceived contribution to the program's output. This set of labels is collectively referred to as the *Credit-Blame map* for that program. The second stage is to use this Credit-Blame map to change that program in ways that are likely to improve its performance.

Our ongoing research includes investigation into which methods to use to best accomplish the goals of internal reinforcement. We have identified several methods for accomplishing each of the two stages. This chapter focuses on one technique for each of the two stages.

Figure 14.5 shows the evolutionary learning process for NP and how IRNP fits into that picture. One Credit-Blame map is created *for each population program* and when the time comes to perform genetic recombination on a particular program, the Credit-Blame map for that particular program is used.

14.3.1 Creating a Credit-Blame Map

Without loss of generality, we can assume that the evolving NP programs are trying to solve a target value prediction problem. This is so because classification problems (a non-ordered set of output symbols to be learned) can be decomposed into target value prediction problems (an ordered set of output symbols to be learned). This decomposition takes the general form of mapping 1 C-way classification problem of the form "To which of C classes does this input belong" into C different binary classification problems of the form "Does this input belong to class i ($1 \leq i \leq C$) or not?" (see [Teller, 1998] for details). Therefore, let us consider an abstract input to output mapping to be learned by the neural programs.

14.3.1.1 Accumulation of Explicit Credit Scores

For each program p, for each node x in p, over all time steps on a particular training example S_i, we compress (combine) all the values node x outputs into a single value H_x^i. The compression function used in this chapter is the *mean*. Let the correct answer (the correct target value) for training instance S_i be L_i. In other words, L_i is the desired output for program p on training instance S_i.

We now have two vectors for all $|S|$ training instances: $\vec{L} = [L_1..L_i..L_{|S|}]$ and $\vec{H}_x = [H_x^1..H_x^i..H_x^{|S|}]$. We can compute the statistical correlation between them. We call the absolute value of this correlation the explicitly computed **Credit Score** for node x, notated as $\mathbf{CS}_x$. This computation is shown in Equation 14.1 (in which E is the *expected value*).

$$
\mathbf{CS}_x = \left| \frac{E(\vec{H}_x - \mu_{\vec{H}_x}) * E(\vec{L} - \mu_{\vec{L}})}{\sigma_{\vec{H}_x} \times \sigma_{\vec{L}}} \right| \tag{14.1}
$$

This credit score for each node is an indication of how valuable that node is to the program. It is the case that nodes with low credit scores at this stage may still be critical to the program in question, but it is also certainly the case that nodes with high credit scores could be very valuable to the program, even if they are currently unutilized. Note that an NP program is, by definition, 100% correct if it has a node with a credit score of 1 and that node is the only node with an outgoing arc that terminates in an OUTPUT node. This *explicit* credit score can also be thought of as the *individual* credit score for the node. That is, the explicit credit score takes into account only how the node acts as an individual, not how it acts as part of a group of tightly coupled nodes (i.e., the program it is a part of).

The set of explicit credit scores for all nodes provides a Credit-Blame map for the program: a value associated with each node in the program that indicates its individual contribution to the program. However, we want the Credit-Blame map to capture not only a node's immediate (individual) usefulness, but also it's usefulness in the context of the program topology. The following example highlights why the explicit credit scores do not, by themselves, capture this information.

In this example, nodes x and y produce values and node z computes an XOR of these two values. In this case, even if z has a high credit score, x and y may not (e.g. $\mathbf{CS}_z = 0.97, \mathbf{CS}_x = 0.14, \mathbf{CS}_y = 0.07$). There is nothing provably wrong with this situation but clearly, the topological notion of usefulness has not been captured in these explicit credit scores. This can be seen because the nodes x and y in this example are partly responsible for node z's success (and are therefore useful) but still have low credit scores.

The Credit-Blame map can be refined to attend to this type of indebtedness relationships by passing credit and blame back through the NP programs along the arcs. The statistical correlation between $\vec{L}$ and $\vec{H}_x$ constitutes a first approximation to the credit score for node x. Because nodes are connected to each other and only a few are directly connected to the OUTPUT node, and because each node performs a specific function, the Credit-Blame map needs to be further refined. This process of refining the Credit-Blame map to take advantage of the topology of the program is described in Section 14.3.1.3.

14.3.1.2 Function Sensitivity Approximation

To pass back credit and blame through the neural program topology, we must first answer an important question: "How does each node act as a function of its inputs?" In other words, "What is the responsibility of each input parameter for the output value produced by each atomic function used in evolution?" This problem is very difficult for arbitrary functions, which is one of the main reasons why ANN backpropagation requires differentiable functions (e.g., the sigmoid or the Gaussian). Unfortunately, we can not always differentiate the functions used in NP programs as they may not always be differentiable (e.g. If-Then-Else).

In our work, we introduce *Function Sensitivity Approximation*, a method for "differentiating" an arbitrary function that can be treated as a black box. The main question that function sensitivity approximation answers about a black box function's relation to its inputs is "For argument a_i of function f, what is the likelihood that f's output will change *at all* when the value of a_i is changed to a new *random value* selected uniformly from the legal range of values?" This discovered sensitivity is a substitute to the function's derivative. This sensitivity is written as $S_{f,A,i}$, the sensitivity of a particular parameter a_i for some function f that is given a parameter vector with A elements. [Teller, 1998] contains details on how such values are automatically calculated. It should also be noted that the $S_{f,A,i}$ values are computed under the assumption that each node computes a function with no side effects. [Teller, 1998] also describes NP's robustness in spite of this simplification.

14.3.1.3 Refining the Credit-Blame Map

We can now combine the topology of the NP program, the explicit credit score for each node, and the sensitivity values of each primitive function in a bucket-brigade style backward propagation. This bucket-brigade refines the credit scores at each node following the procedure presented in Figure 14.6. The credit scores are refined according to the network topology and sensitivity of the node functions. To understand why a bucket-brigade backward propagation of credit is critical, refer back to the XOR example in Section 14.3.1.1.

> **Until no further changes**
>   **For each node x in the program**
>   **For each output arc (x, y) of that node**
> y is, by definition, the destination node of (x, y)
>   Let f_y be y's node function
>   Let A_y be the number of inputs y has
>   Let i be such that (x, y) provides a_i to y
>   Let $\mathcal{S}_{f_y, A_y, i}$ = Sensitivity of f_y (relative to A_y and i)
> $\mathbf{CS}_x = \mathbf{MAX}(\mathbf{CS}_x, \mathcal{S}_{f_y, A_y, i} * \mathbf{CS}_y)$

Figure 14.6
The bucket brigade refinement of Credit Scores (CS) throughout an NP program.

The high level structure of the procedure presented in Figure 14.6 is as follows. For each node, for each output arc from that node, the node's credit-score is updated to be the maximum of the credit-score it already has and the credit-score of the node pointed to by that output arc multiplied by the sensitivity of that destination node to that particular output arc. We explain this process in detail through a series of questions and answers.

A good first question for this particular method of spreading credit and blame out more appropriately over each neural program is, "does this process always converge?" The answer is that as long as the definition of "no further changes" is more specifically "no node changed its CS value by more than ϵ" ($\epsilon > 0$) then the process always halts[1] and typically in only a few passes. Because of the way $\mathcal{S}_{f,A,i}$ is defined and implemented it is, in practice, always less than 1.0, contributing to the small number of passes required for the Credit-Blame map to reach quiescence. This answer to the convergence question is also the answer to the question, "why do not you use a discount factor (γ)? Is not that usual in various forms of bucket brigade?" Using a discount factor is a common way to insure convergence, but as just noted, it is empirically unnecessary.

In this context, in which we make clear the use of a sensitivity value for each function, we can now ask "why define sensitivity in that way?" Remember that we said that the sensitivity of function f_y with arity A to input a_i is the likelihood that the output will change *at all* when the value of a_i is changed to a new *random value* selected uniformly from the legal range of values. There is no reason to believe that, in a complex system such as an evolving NP program, a node that outputs O_1 will always have a similar effect to a node that outputs O_2, no matter how close O_1 and O_2 are on the number line. For example,

---

[1] Proof: If the halt criteria isn't satisfied after a pass, then at least one node credit score has increased by at least ϵ and no credit score has decreased in value (by construction, see Figure 14.6). The total value in the Credit-Blame map for program p can be at most N_p (the number of nodes in p), so the total number of loops can be no more than $\frac{N_p}{\epsilon}$.

consider the function READ-MEMORY(O_1) that returns the value stored in the program's memory array index O_1. Out of context of a particular program, READ-MEMORY(5) and READ-MEMORY(6) have as much semantic similarity as READ-MEMORY(5) and READ-MEMORY(77). For this reason, sensitivity in NP is a percentage of how often the output value of a function is changed at all, not by how much that output changes.

There is also little reason to believe that in a complex system such as an evolving NP program, any particular set of numbers is more or less likely than any other to occur as inputs to a node. The sensitivity discovery process could, for example, change a_i to $(a_i \pm \Delta)$. Then $\mathcal{S}_{f,A,i}$ would measure the likelihood that the output will change when small changes are made to the input a_i. But since, unlike explicit credit-blame assignment systems (e.g., ANNs), NP cannot enforce these small changes throughout the program, it is better to have a measure of sensitivity that matches how the inputs are likely to change: to first approximation, *uniform randomness*.

Finally, consider the equation for refining the credit scores: $\mathrm{CS}_x = \mathrm{MAX}(\mathrm{CS}_x, \mathcal{S}_{f_y,A_y,i} * \mathrm{CS}_y)$. "Why should CS_x be set to the maximum of itself and $\mathcal{S}_{f_y,A_y,i} * \mathrm{CS}_y$?" We first address the function MAX as an appropriate operator and then examine the appropriateness of the second operand. In an NP program it is the norm for a single node's output to be used in a number of different contexts. We would not want to penalize a node for creating an output that is very useful in one part of the program, but is not taken advantage of in another part of the program. If even one of the outputs of a node is "taken advantage of" (in the sense defined by the explicit credit score measure), then it is clear that the blame for not taking advantage of that output elsewhere in the program is a problem with that other part of the program, not the node in question. This means that a node's credit score should be a maximum of some function of the credit scores of the nodes to which it outputs.

Further, consider the case in which node x has an explicitly computed credit score of CS_x. Even if none of x's children (i.e., nodes that take x's output as input) has a credit score as high as CS_x, if we believe that the explicit credit score measure is a good first approximation to the usefulness of a node in a program, then we should insure that CS_x is never less than its original value. Thus, we introduce $\mathrm{CS}_x = \mathrm{MAX}(\mathrm{CS}_x, F_r(\mathrm{CS}_y))$ where F_r is some function to be determined. Now we need to pick some reasonable function F_r to apply to the credit scores of the children of node x.

The introduced sensitivity analysis of Section 14.3.1.2. can now be used. We already have a value that expresses the sensitivity of a node y to an input a_i as a function of how many inputs y has and the particular function that y happens to compute. But that's exactly what we want! The amount of reward (think CS_x) a node x that points to a node y deserves for that "reference," is exactly how good node y is, CS_y, scaled by (i.e., times) how responsive (i.e., sensitive) y is to changes in the values that x is passing it. So we have our function $F_r(\mathrm{CS}_y)$; it is $\mathcal{S}_{f_y,A_y,i} * \mathrm{CS}_y$.

This discussion highlighted the characteristics of our reinforcement procedure. So in summary, the refinement of credit scores in the Credit-Blame map is derived from the initial credit scores, the program's topology, and the discovered sensitivity of each possible node function.

14.3.1.4 Credit Scoring the NP arcs

NP program transformations operators (e.g., crossover and mutation) also affect NP program arcs. So far, the discussion of the Credit-Blame map has entirely focused on assigning credit and blame to the nodes. The topology of the NP programs, that is the program nodes and arcs, is used heavily in making this map, but the resulting map assigns one floating point number to each node and no number to the arcs.

The explanation for this discrepancy is that arcs are even more context dependent than the nodes that define them. For example, when considering whether to delete a particular arc (x, y), CS_y is a relevant value, but the value of CS_x is much less so. This is so because deleting one of node x's output arcs doesn't affect the other arcs from x, but deleting an input arc potentially changes what node y outputs on all it's output arcs. When, on the other hand, considering whether to reroute arc (x, y) to some other node z (i.e., $arc(x, y) \to arc(x, z)$) the current values CS_x, CS_y, and CS_z are all relevant. As is detailed in the next section, the Credit-Blame map has a great impact on the arcs during the IRNP process, but only indirectly through the credit scores of the nodes in the program to be recombined.

14.3.2 Exploration vs. Exploitation Within a Program

A tension exists between exploration (try out something new) and exploitation (stick with the best you've seen) within the recombination of a single program. IRNP could leave alone the "best" parts of the program and focus its changes on the "worse" program aspects. There are, however, two problems with this view. The first is that a "bad" part of the program must be more carefully defined. There are program nodes that have very low scores in the program's Credit-Blame map and **do** affect the values flowing into the OUTPUT nodes and there are low score nodes that **do not** affect the values flowing into the program OUTPUT nodes. This is the *node participation* problem. To be most effective, IRNP should change the first type of low score nodes, but not the second. This is so because, for example, changing what function a particular node computes is a piece of wasted search if that node's old function had no effect on any of the program's OUTPUT nodes (under the assumption that none of the functions have side-effects).

There is a second problem with seeing IRNP's job as simply focusing on the "bad" parts of a program. Occasionally, the best way to improve a program is to make the right change to an aspect of the program that is already working well. It is easy to imagine a program in

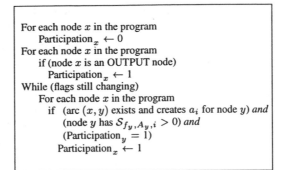

For each node x in the program
    Participation$_x \leftarrow 0$
For each node x in the program
    if (node x is an OUTPUT node)
        Participation$_x \leftarrow 1$
While (flags still changing)
    For each node x in the program
        if (arc (x, y) exists and creates a_i for node y) *and*
            (node y has $S_{f_y, A_y, i} > 0$) *and*
            (Participation$_y = 1$)
        Participation$_x \leftarrow 1$

Figure 14.7
The procedure for assigning the *participation flags* to nodes in each program's Credit-Blame map.

which node y computes $a_0 + a_1$ is almost right, but the program would work even better if that node computed $a_0 * a_1$ instead.

IRNP does address both of these issues. With regards to the second problem, IRNP does occasionally change high credit-score aspects of a program. It is partly for this very reason that the mutation operators only look at a fraction of the nodes in a program before picking one to change. This means that with low probability, the "worst" program aspect seen by a particular mutation operator, will still be one of the high credit-score nodes for that program. An interesting piece of future work for IRNP is the following. Instead simply restricting how often the recombination operators change high credit-score aspects of a program, how these aspects are changed could be different. In other words, for example, mutation could be further refined so that it did "less damaging" mutations when a high credit-score node was chosen to be changed (e.g., ADD $\rightarrow$ MULT is "less damaging" than ADD $\rightarrow$ If-Then-Else).

IRNP also addresses the node participation problem. Credit-Blame map includes a *participation* flag for each program node. IRNP takes advantage of these flags by augmenting the mutation and crossover policies described in Sections 14.3.3.1 and 14.3.3.2. These participation flags are set using the process shown in Figure 14.7.

14.3.3 Using a Credit-Blame Map

The second phase of the internal reinforcement is the use of the created Credit-Blame map to increase the probability that the genetic operators lead either to a better solution or to a similar solution in less time. There are two basic ways that the Credit-Blame map can be used to do this enhancement: through improvement of either the mutation or crossover operators.

The possibility of using internal reinforcement (explicit credit-blame assignment) not only for mutation (which has analogies to the world of ANNs) but for crossover as well is important. Traditional GP uses random crossover and relies entirely on the mechanism of empirical credit-blame assignment. Work has been done to boot-strap this mechanism by using the evolutionary process itself to evolve improved crossover procedures (e.g. [Angeline, 1996b; Teller, 1996]). This work has reaped some success, but because of the co-evolutionary nature of the work, it has not yielded deep insights into the basic mechanism of crossover. IRNP has the future potential not only to improve on the existing GP mechanism, but also to help study the central mystery of GP, namely crossover.

14.3.3.1 Mutation: Applying a Credit-Blame Map

Mutation can take a variety of forms in NP. These various mutations are: add an arc, delete an arc, swap two arcs, change a node function, add a node, delete a node. Notice that change a node function and swap two arcs are not atomic, but have been included as examples of non-atomic, but basic mutation types. In the experiments shown in the next section, each of these mutations took place with equal likelihood in both the random and internal reinforcement recombination cases. For example, to add an arc under random mutation to an NP program, we simply pick a source and destination node at random from the program to be mutated and add the arc between the nodes.

Internal reinforcement can have a positive effect on this recombination procedure. For each recombination type, we pick a node or arc (depending on the mutation type) that has maximal or minimal credit score as appropriate. For example, when deleting a program node, we can delete the node with the lowest credit score instead of just deleting a randomly selected node.

Below are the IRNP procedures for each of the six mutation types. Notice that when the terms "large" and "low" are used (as opposed to the unambiguous terms "highest" and "lowest"), this indicates that the largest or least credit score is selected from among a *sampled subset* of nodes or arcs, depending on the context.

Add an Arc : First, pick a node x with a large credit score. Then pick a node y with a low credit score **and Participation$_y$** $= 1$ and A inputs such that y would still be sensitive to input a_{A+1}. Finally, add an arc (x, y).

Delete an Arc : First, pick a node y with a low credit score such that y would still be sensitive to its inputs if one were removed **and Participation$_y$** $= 1$. Then pick a node x with a low credit score such that there exists an arc (x, y). Finally, delete arc (x, y).

Swap Two Arcs : First, let x be the node with highest CS_x. Then let (x, y) be the output arc of x to a node y that minimizes CS_y. Then, for all arcs (u, v) such that v is an OUTPUT node, pick the arc (u, v) that minimizes CS_u. Finally, delete arcs (x, y) and (u, v) and create arcs (x, v) and (u, y).

Change a Node Function : First, pick a node x that has a low credit score and such that (x, y) exists and creates input a_i for node y and $\mathcal{S}_{f_y, A_y, i} > 0$ **and Participation**$_y = 1$. Then change the function that x computes to another function of similar or lower arity.

Add a Node : First, create a new node z with f_z, a randomly selected function. Then let A be the arity of f_z and let O_z be the number of output arcs from z. Then find high credit score nodes $x_1, ...x_A$ and create the arcs (x_1, z) ... (x_A, z). Then find low credit score nodes $y_1, ... y_{O_z}$ such that $\mathcal{S}_{f_{y_i}, A_{y_i}+1, A_{y_i}+1} > 0$ **and Participation**$_{y_i} = 1$ for all i in $[1..O_z]$. Finally, create the arcs (z, y_1) ... (z, y_{O_z})

Delete a Node : First, pick a low credit score node x **with Participation**$_x = 1$. Then, remove x and arcs (x, y) and (z, x) for all nodes y and all nodes z in the program.

For each of the procedures, the alternative to IRNP is the equivalent of the traditional recombination strategy in GP. This less focused strategy in NP is simply to chose randomly among all syntactically legal options (i.e., no program-behavior based bias in the recombination). Equivalently, this "vanilla" method for recombination can be thought of as IRNP with random values in the Credit-Blame map.

14.3.3.2 Crossover: Applying a Credit-Blame Map

In the random version of crossover, one simply picks a "cut" from each graph (i.e., a subset of the program nodes) at random and then exchanges and reconnects them. Figure 14.8 pictures this division of a program into two pieces. Details on how this fragment exchange can be accomplished so as to minimize the disruption to the two programs can be seen in [Teller, 1996]. In summary, sewing two fragments back together so as to minimize disruption is largely a matter of satisfying as far as possible the criteria that each "dangling" output arc is connected to an node that lost an input arc when its program was fragmented.

We keep this underlying mechanism and present an IRNP procedure that selects "good" program fragments to exchange. This means that IRNP has, as its only job to choose the fragments to be exchanged, but the way in which program fragments are exchanged and reconnected is unaffected by IRNP. There is much to be gained by taking advantage of the Credit-Blame map during this fragment exchange and reconstitution phase, but to focus the research work and contributions, this aspect of the use of credit-blame assignment has been left as future work.

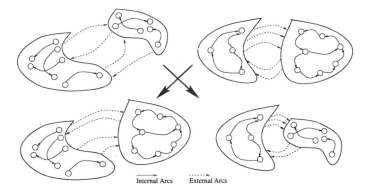

Internal Arcs   External Arcs

Figure 14.8
Crossover in NP: A single graph of nodes and arcs is fragmented with a cut into two fragments such that every
node in the original graph is now either in Fragment₁ or Fragment₂ and every arc is either an *internal* or *external*
arc.

Given that we separate a program into two fragments before crossover, let us define
CutCost to be the sum of all credit scores of *inter*-fragment arcs, and *InternalCost* to be the
sum of all credit scores of *intra*-fragment arcs in the program to be crossed-over.

NP program arcs have a shifting meaning and so their credit score must be interpreted
within the context of the search operator being used. For crossover we take the credit
score of an arc to be the credit score of its destination node. This is done because, as was
described in Section 14.3.1.4, the disruption of an arc affects the destination node more so
than the source node.

Now we say that the cost of a particular fragmentation of a program is equal to *Cut-
Cost/InternalCost*. If we try to minimize this value for both of the program fragments we
choose, we are much less likely to disrupt a crucial part of either program during crossover.
Figure 14.9 outlines this IRNP crossover procedure.

14.3.4   The Credit-Blame Map Before/After Refinement

This chapter has explained exactly how IRNP is carried out and the impact that it has on
the evolution of the programs involved. It was claimed that the bucket brigade algorithm
described in Section 14.3.1.3 actually does spread the credit score values out to aspects of
the program that previously were not rewarded. This section illustrates this value spreading
using a real snap-shot during the IRNP in a normal run. Table 14.1 shows a typical (though
small) NP program (without the arcs) from generation 8 of a run learning to classify signals
from a manufactured signal domain.

The first set of numbers in Table 14.1 shows the Credit Scores for each node at an inter-

```
Pick k random cuts of prog p (Fragment₁, Fragment₂)
For candidate cut i
  For each arc(x, y) in p
    Let CS_arc(x,y) = CS_y
    if (x and y are in the same Fragment_j) (j∈{1,2})
       InternalCost = InternalCost + CS_arc(x,y)
    else
       CutCost = CutCost + CS_y
    CutRanking_i = CutCost / InternalCost
  Choose the cut that produced the LOWEST CutRanking with
  at least one participating node on each side of the cut
```

Figure 14.9
The IRNP process for choosing a "good" fragment of a program to exchange through crossover.

mediate stage in the credit-blame assignment process as described in this chapter. Namely, the credit scores shown in Table 14.1 have undergone the process of Section 14.3.1.1, but not the process of detailed in Section 14.3.1.3. The second set of numbers in Table 14.1 shows this same NP program after the bucket brigade refinement process has taken place.

The bold faced credit scores in Table 14.1 are those values that changed during the bucket brigade credit score refinement process. Notice that more than half of the credit scores changed values during this process, many of them dramatically. The number of credit scores at 0.0 dropped from 52.17% to 17.39% due to the refinement process. Notice also that even the OUTPUT nodes have their credit scores changed during this process since the output from an OUTPUT node may be very useful, even if it is not, itself, the highest correlation node in the program.

14.3.5 IRNP Discussion

It should have been made clear by this point in this chapter that NP programs are "nearly" Turing complete in that they have a sufficiently complex function set, memory, and iteration. The topology and execution of NP programs provides iteration. Technically, a Turing complete program must have access to arbitrarily extendible memory, though in practice this is never actually provided. In NP, the form of memory that has been described, and that will be used throughout the rest of this chapter, is the data-flow memory of a program. A program with, for example, 312 arcs has a memory capacity of 312 distinct values and many billions of states even for a restricted value range. This is *implicit memory use* (i.e., memory use through the representation itself) rather than *explicit memory use*.

Table 14.1
A sample NP program (without the arcs) at the end of generation 8 **after** the Credit Scores have been assigned, shown both **before** and **after** the bucket brigade refinement of this Credit-Blame map has taken place. # indicates the node number. *The bold values highlight Credit Score values that changed during the refinement process.*

Credit-Blame map **before** Refinement. (Explicit Credit Scores)

#	$CS_\#$	Function	#	$CS_\#$	Function	#	$CS_\#$	Function	#	$CS_\#$	Function
0	0.0000	060	1	0.0000	Clock	2	0.0000	144	3	0.0000	Clock
4	0.0000	211	5	0.0000	Clock	6	0.0000	094	7	0.0000	182
8	0.0000	145	9	0.0000	165	10	0.0000	182	11	0.0000	045
12	0.0000	036	13	0.2069	Output	14	0.2562	PSP-Pnt	15	0.0000	Divide
16	0.6973	Output	17	0.1301	Add	18	0.1963	PSP-Max	19	0.3576	Add
20	0.0000	Multiply	21	0.3315	Output	22	0.2254	PSP-Pnt	23	0.0391	Multiply
24	0.3143	Subtract	25	0.0000	If-T-E	26	0.2254	Multiply	27	0.2380	If-T-E
28	0.0000	Split	29	0.0915	PSP-Max	30	0.7351	Split	31	0.4334	Subtract
32	0.1208	Add	33	0.0000	Subtract	34	0.4335	PSP-Pnt	35	0.0046	Add
36	0.0000	Multiply	37	0.0000	Add	38	0.2822	PSP-Max	39	0.2254	Multiply
40	0.0000	If-T-E	41	0.0162	Add	42	0.6992	Output	43	0.3315	Subtract
44	0.0000	Add	45	0.0000	Add	46	0.0000	Add			

Credit-Blame map **after** Refinement.

#	$CS_\#$	Function	#	$CS_\#$	Function	#	$CS_\#$	Function	#	$CS_\#$	Function
0	0.0000	060	1	0.0000	Clock	2	0.0000	144	3	**0.6681**	Clock
4	0.0000	211	5	**0.1185**	Clock	6	**0.4326**	094	7	**0.0854**	182
8	**0.0011**	145	9	**0.0858**	165	10	**0.1665**	182	11	**0.6942**	045
12	**0.1629**	036	13	**0.2538**	Output	14	0.2562	PSP-Pnt	15	**0.0398**	Divide
16	0.6973	Output	17	**0.6406**	Add	18	**0.6857**	PSP-Max	19	0.3576	Add
20	0.0000	Multiply	21	**0.6811**	Output	22	**0.6675**	PSP-Pnt	23	0.0391	Multiply
24	**0.6858**	Subtract	25	0.0000	If-T-E	26	**0.2502**	Multiply	27	0.2380	If-T-E
28	**0.4254**	Split	29	0.0915	PSP-Max	30	0.7351	Split	31	0.4334	Subtract
32	0.1208	Add	33	0.0000	Subtract	34	**0.4335**	PSP-Pnt	35	0.0046	Add
36	**0.2637**	Multiply	37	**0.6854**	Add	38	0.2822	PSP-Max	39	**0.6697**	Multiply
40	0.0000	If-T-E	41	**0.6550**	Add	42	0.6992	Output	43	**0.6834**	Subtract
44	**0.6437**	Add	45	**0.6714**	Add	46	**0.0001**	Add			

Indexed Memory [Teller, 1994] is an example of *explicit memory use* in GP. In Indexed Memory, the evolving program is given access to an array of memory cells through the two functions READ(O_0), and WRITE(O_0,O_1). READ(O_0) returns the value stored in MEMORY[O_0]. WRITE(O_0,O_1) returns the value stored in MEMORY[O_0] and has the side-effect of updating MEMORY[O_0] to it's new value: O_1. Indexed Memory has been extensively studied in GP (e.g., [Teller, 1994; Andre, 1995; Langdon, 1995; Langdon, 1996; Spector and Luke, 1996]) and has demonstrated itself to be a valuable form of memory use for evolving programs. [Teller, 1998] reports on positive results on the use of indexed memory in NP learning.

NP and IRNP were designed simultaneously to add computational expressiveness to algorithm evolution (NP vs. traditional tree-GP) and to solve some of the learning difficulties this new level of computational expressiveness introduced (IRNP vs. unguided genetic operators). This does not mean, however, that IRNP only applies to NP. The concept of internal reinforcement is very general and can be illustrated in other representations. The single most popular representation for algorithm evolution is the tree representation (S-expression) of traditional GP. [Teller, 1998] describes in detail how to implement IRNP in tree-based GP.

14.4   Experimental Results

Because the following experiments were run in the context of the PADO learning system, a few words must be given as explanation. PADO is a learning environment that decomposes classification problems into discrimination problems, evolves sub-solutions to these discrimination problems, and then orchestrates these sub-solutions into an overall solution to the original classification problem. The evolution that takes place inside PADO can be of any type and in the context of this chapter that evolution is the evolution of NP programs with and without IRNP for the purposes of comparison. Significant detail about PADO can be found in [Teller and Veloso, 1995; Teller and Veloso, 1997; Teller, 1998].

14.4.1   Experimental Overview

The purpose of any set of experiments is to test a set of hypotheses. The goal of the experiments shown in this chapter are to demonstrate two general attributes of the NP and IRNP approaches. The first is that the NP representation successfully applies to a wide variety of signal domains. The second is that the IRNP procedure does substantially improve learning across a variety of signal domains.

Table 14.2 gives the values for the most important parameters and Table 14.3 gives the fixed set of program primitives used in all the experiments. [Teller, 1998] addresses the issue of IRNP's sensitivity to the parameters shown in Table 14.2, and shows in an experiment that IRNP works at least as well when crossover is the dominant recombination strategy (instead of mutation as shown in Table 14.2).

Experiments are run on two dissimilar domains and in both, the PADO approach does quite well. The experiments show both that NP programs can be usefully evolved and that in all those cases PADO does noticeably better when IRNP is active as part of the learning process. Notice in particular that, empirically, the harder the problem, the greater the efficiency gain provided by IRNP.

Table 14.2
Fixed experimental values for the most important PADO parameters.

Crossover Percent Chance	36
Mutation Percent Chance	60
Population Size	(250× Number of Classes)
Maximum Number Nodes	80
Minimum Number Nodes	10
Number In Tournament	5
Number Time Steps To Run	10
Maximum Generations	80
Maximum Number Outputs	5
Maximum Number Inputs	4

Table 14.3
PADO program primitives used

Manipulation type					
Continuous	Add	Sub	Mult	Div	OUTPUT
Choice	If-Then-Else	Split			
Signal	$SignalPrimitive_0$	...	...	...	$SignalPrimitive_i$
Zero-Arity	0..MaxValue	Clock			

A word of description about the method of presentation before we launch into the experiments. Each point on each graph is the mean performance level achieved on over many independent runs, meaning that the results presented are not the best NP has ever done on a particular domain, but a report of the kind of performance you can expect from during an average run.

14.4.2 Natural Images

There are seven classes in the domain used in the following experiments. Figure 14.10 shows one randomly selected video image from each of the seven classes in both the training and testing sets. This particular domain was created as a domain for machine learning and computer vision [Thrun and Mitchell, 1994]. Each element is a 150x124 video image with 256 level of grey. Originally, these images were color images, but the color was later removed from the images to make the problem sufficiently difficult to be interesting [Teller and Veloso, 1997].

The seven classes in this domain are: Book, Bottle, Cap, Coke Can, Glasses, Hammer, and Shoe. The lighting, position and rotation of the objects varies widely. The floor and the wall behind and underneath the objects are constant. Nothing else except the object is in the image. However, the distance from the object to the camera ranges from 1.5 to 4 feet and there is often severe foreshortening and even deformation of the objects in the image.

TRAIN

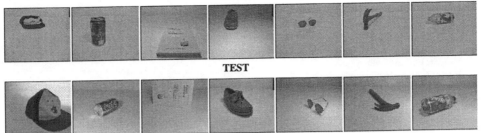

Figure 14.10
A random training and testing signal from each of the 7 classes in this classification problem.

14.4.2.1   Setting PADO up to Solve the Problem

In the experiment in this section, the total population size was 1750 (i.e., $250 * 7$). Each point on each graph is an average of at least 60 independent runs. A total of 350 (50 from each of 7 classes) images were used for training and a separate set of 350 (50 from each of 7 classes) images were withheld for testing afterwards.

The Parameterized Signal Primitives (PSPs) used in this experiment were as follows: *PSP-Point*(a_0, a_1) returns the pixel intensity at the pixel/point (a_0, a_1). *PSP-Average* (a_0, a_1, a_2, a_3) returns the *average* pixel intensity in the image region specified by the rectangle with upper left corner (a_0, a_1) and lower right corner (a_2, a_3). *PSP-Variance* (a_0, a_1, a_2, a_3) returns the *variance* of the of the pixel intensities in image region specified by the rectangle with upper left corner (a_0, a_1) and lower right corner (a_2, a_3). *PSP-Min*(a_0, a_1, a_2, a_3) returns the *lowest* pixel intensity value in the image region specified by the rectangle with upper left corner (a_0, a_1) and lower right corner (a_2, a_3). *PSP-Max*(a_0, a_1, a_2, a_3) returns the *largest* pixel intensity value in the image region specified by the rectangle with upper left corner (a_0, a_1) and lower right corner (a_2, a_3). *PSP-Diff*(a_0, a_1, a_2, a_3) returns the absolute different between the *average* pixel intensity above and below the diagonal line (a_0, a_1) to (a_2, a_3) inside the bounding rectangle with opposite corners (a_0, a_1) and (a_2, a_3). In all of these cases, if the dimension is negative (e.g., $a_2 < a_0$) the two values are interchanged.

14.4.2.2   The Results

During each run, the generalization performance on a separate set of testing images was recorded and Figure 14.11 plots the *mean* of each of these values. Figure 14.11 shows the computational effort in generations required to reach a particular level of test-set generalization performance for NP learning with and without IRNP.

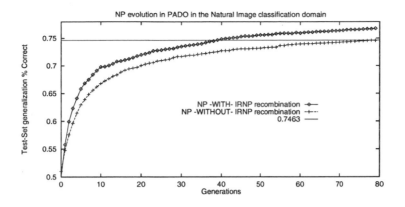

Figure 14.11
NP learning with and without IRNP (Natural Images Domain).

The most important feature of Figure 14.11 is that NP learns more than twice as fast when IRNP is applied to the recombination during evolution. That is, NP arrives at the same level of generalization performance in less than half as many generations when learning with IRNP as compared to learning without it. Also notice that NP learns quite well on this difficult image classification problem. Random guessing in this domain would achieve only about 14.28% correct generalization performance.

It is worth noting that the performance that achieved on any domain is related to the particular orchestration strategy chosen. NP has, on this particular domain, achieved generalization performance rates as high as **86%**.

14.4.3 Acoustic Signals

The database used in this experiment contains 525 three second sound samples. These are the raw wave forms at 20K Hertz with 8 bits per sample (about 500,000 bits per sample). These sounds were taken from the SPIB ftp site at Rice University (anonymous ftp to spib.rice.edu). This database has an appealing seven way clustering (70 from each class): *the sound of a Buccanneer jet engine, the sound of a firing machine gun, the sound of an M109 tank engine, the sound on the floor of a car factory, the sound in a car production hall, the sound of a Volvo engine,* and *the sound of babble in an army mess hall.* There are many possible ways of subdividing this sound database; the classes chosen for these experiments are typical of the sort of distinctions that might be of use in real applications.

14.4.3.1 Setting PADO up to Solve the Problem

In the experiment in this section, the total population size was 1750 (i.e., $250 * 7$). Each point on each graph is an average of at least 55 independent runs. A total of 245 (35 from each of 7 classes) images were used for training and a separate set of 245 (35 from each of 7 classes) images were withheld for testing afterwards.

The PSPs used in this experiment were as follows: *PSP-Point*(a_0, a_1) returns the wave height at the moment in time specified by $(a_0*256+a_1)$. *PSP-Average*(a_0, a_1, a_2, a_3) returns the *average* wave height in the sound starting at time $(a_0 * 256 + a_1)$ and ending at time $(a_2 * 256 + a_3)$. This PSP is useless for long time intervals. *PSP-Variance*(a_0, a_1, a_2, a_3) returns the *variance* of the wave height in the sound starting at time $(a_0*256+a_1)$ and ending at time $(a_2 * 256 + a_3)$. *PSP-Min*(a_0, a_1, a_2, a_3) returns the *lowest* wave height in the sound starting at time $(a_0 * 256 + a_1)$ and ending at time $(a_2 * 256 + a_3)$. *PSP-Max*(a_0, a_1, a_2, a_3) returns the *largest* wave height in the sound starting at time $(a_0 * 256 + a_1)$ and ending at time $(a_2 * 256 + a_3)$. *PSP-Diff*(a_0, a_1, a_2, a_3) is equivalent to ABS(PSP-Average$(a_0, a_1, a_{0'}, a_{1'})$ − PSP-Average$(a_{0'}, a_{1'}, a_2, a_3)$) where $(a_{0'}, a_{1'})$ is the time midpoint between (a_0, a_1) and (a_2, a_3).

Notice that, other than minor adjustments necessary to reflect the change in signal type, these parameterized signal primitives are exactly the same as the PSPs used in the visual classification experiment discussed in Section 14.4.2. This was not done to demonstrate the generality of these PSPs. Quite the contrary, this similarity in the experimental procedure was done to highlight how little was done to tune NP in order to achieve the reported results. NP, using IRNP, is able to make good use of these very simple PSPs that are not well focused to solving either of the domains in which they were applied.

The fitness used for evolutionary learning (training of the NP programs) was based upon distance from returned confidence to the correct confidence for each training example. Given this model of one class chosen per sound, if the NP program just guessed randomly, it could achieve an generalization performance of $1/7$ (14%) correct.

14.4.3.2 The Results

Figure 14.12 shows the generalization percent correct NP reaches on average on each generation, with and without IRNP.

Notice that in these experiments, for both orchestration strategies, IRNP learning is almost three times as efficient as learning without it. That is, NP arrives at the same level of test set generalization performance in about one third as many generations when learning with IRNP as compared to learning without it.

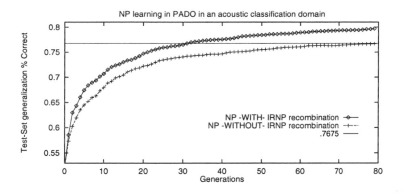

Figure 14.12
NP learning with and without IRNP (Acoustic Signals Domain).

14.4.4 Acoustic Signals Revisited

One of the most important implied aspects of this chapter is that, given more time to examine each signal the NP programs will be able to improve their evolved performance. If NP programs are really looping and foveating on the input signals, increasing the amount of time (i.e., maximum timestep threshold, T) should increase the evolved program performance. Therefore, let us revisit the acoustic signal classification problem described in the previous section. As in the rest of this chapter, the experimental results in the previous section were achieved with an NP timestep threshold of 10 timesteps. In this section, we will double this value to a timestep threshold of $T = 20$ timesteps to see how that change affects both the efficiency and, more importantly, the effectiveness of NP learning within PADO.

Since this chapter has claimed that there is an advantage to be gained from the addition of iteration and/or recursion, a demonstration that increasing the time available to each program (without increasing the number of degrees of freedom in the model being learned) will strengthen this argument. The NP programs evolving in this section have the exact same number of degrees of freedom (independently adjustable learning "parameters") as in the previous section. Programs in all ways similar to those in the previous section are simply allowed to "think longer" about the input signal. Therefore, improved performance in this experiment demonstrates that NP programs are making use of the looping/foveating aspects of the NP representation.

The domain and problem for this set of experiments is in every detail identical to the domain and problem described in the previous section.

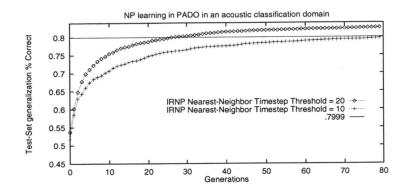

Figure 14.13
NP learning with IRNP and Timestep Threshold = 10 *and* 20 (Acoustic Signals Domain).

14.4.4.1   Setting PADO up to Solve the Problem

In setting up PADO to solve this acoustic signal classification problem, every aspects was left exactly as in the previous section with a single exception. This exception was that the timestep threshold (that maximum number of timesteps after which the response is extracted from each NP program) was increased from 10 to 20.

14.4.4.2   The Results

Each point in Figure 14.13 is an average over at least 60 independent trials. Notice that it takes more time to compute the fitness of each particular program on each particular signal, the same amount of learning is done with two different timestep thresholds. Said in another way, the additional computation time is spent because the fitness takes twice as long to measure, not because twice as many decisions are made with the same information. This is significant by itself, but more significant still when we remember that learning to take advantage of this additional time available to each NP program must be done using the same amount of learning (i.e., the same number of search steps). This means, that in some sense, this test would have been more fair if more learning (and therefore more computation time) had been given for the experiments in this section, not less computation time as the computation time note in the previous paragraph seems to suggest.

Figure 14.13 shows the generalization percent correct PADO reaches on average on each generation with IRNP using this enlarged timestep threshold. The results of this experiment are quite exciting. IRNP learning with a timestep threshold of $T = 20$ is three times as efficient as learning under the same conditions with $T = 10$. Notice that this means that IRNP learning with $T = 20$ actually accomplished the same amount of learning as do NP learning without IRNP using $T = 10$ using only about 13% of the effort.

14.5 Related Work

The main areas of work related to the topic of this chapter are: algorithm evolution applied to signal understanding, the learning of recurrent networks, and particularly, other attempts to improve the effectiveness of the search operators in GP.

In the area of evolution applied to signal understanding past work has included bitmap understanding (e.g., [Andre, 1994; Koza, 1994]), signal understanding aids (e.g., [Nguyen and Huang, 1994; Tackett, 1993; Daida, 1996; Poli, 1996b]), time series prediction (e.g, [Angeline, 1996a]), and speech discrimination (e.g., [Conrads et al., 1998; Nordin and Banzhaf, 1996].

In an important related area, considerable work has been done on the complex memory structure and use (e.g., [Langdon, 1995; Andre, 1995; Andre and Teller, 1996; Brave, 1996a; Langdon, 1996; Spector and Luke, 1996]). Some research has been done on recursion and looping in GP (e.g., [Kinnear, Jr., 1993; Brave, 1996b; Langdon, 1995]), but how to tractably evolve complex programs with these elements is still an open question.

Both because of its representational similarities and because of its computational class equivalence (i.e., both are Turing complete representations), recurrent ANNs (e.g., [Rumelhart et al., 1986]) are also of relevance to the NP and IRNP research. In ANNs, the focus on improving the power of the technique has not been on changing what is inside an "artificial neuron." Works like [Dellaert and Beer., 1994; Sharman et al., 1995] have, however, investigated the possible additional benefit of complicating and un-homogenizing artificial neurons. Though its similarity to NP is in representation, not in use or objectives (i.e., IRNP), [Poli, 1996a] is an interesting example of the evolution of graph structured programs as is [Angeline, 1997]. For a survey on data flow machine, see [Treleaven et al., 1982].

One of the best descriptions of and attacks on the lack of a clear, locally optimal update procedure is [O'Reilly, 1995]. In her thesis, O'Reilly gives good evidence for this as an important flaw in the GP paradigm and introduces a locally optimal hill-climbing variant as a recombination element within GP. [Olsson, 1995] uses a form of iterative deepening done on minimum description length codes with ML-specific program transformations. [Angeline, 1996b] and [Fogel et al., 1995] describe possible approaches for allowing the mechanism of evolution to provide self-adaptation all the way down to the single node level. Another take on guided crossover can be seen in [Langdon, 1996].

The bucket-brigade algorithm is one of the oldest versions of credit assignment discussed as an explicit mechanism by Holland [Holland, 1975] or as an implicit mechanism in works such as [Wilson, 1987]. The variant of a *profit-sharing plan* was introduced in [Holland and Reitman, 1978]. The bucket-brigade algorithm is just a special case of the general temporal difference methods (TDM) [Sutton, 1988] like Q-learning [Watkins, 1989].

14.6   Conclusions

This research has contributed a new representation for learning complex programs. This new connectionist program language, *Neural Programming*, has been developed with the goal of enabling a principled update policy for algorithm evolution called *Internal Reinforcement*. This is the first such principled update policy created for the field of genetic programming. Neural Programming enables the construction of a *Credit-Blame map* for each evolving program. Sensitivity-based bucket-brigade for refining each program's Credit-Blame map leads to a credit assignment of sufficient detail to allow internal reinforcement to perform focused, beneficial search operations during the algorithm evolution. We illustrated these techniques with experiments that showed that internal reinforcement improves the speed and accuracy of Neural Programming learning. These same experiments also demonstrated that Neural Programming can successfully learn to correctly classify large signals from many classes in real world domains.

The goal of this chapter has been to communicate the exciting result that, through the exploration of new program representations, we have captured the explanation and principled update power of explicit credit-assignment with the flexibility and generality of genetic programming.

Acknowledgements

This work has been funded through the generosity of the Fannie and John Hertz Foundation.

Bibliography

Altenberg, L. (1994), "The evolution of evolvability in genetic programming," in *Advances In Genetic Programming*, K. E. Kinnear, Jr. (Ed.), pp 47–74, MIT Press.

Andre, D. (1994), "Automatically defined features: The simultaneous evolution of 2-dimensional feature detectors and an algorithm for using them," in *Advances In Genetic Programming*, K. E. Kinnear, Jr. (Ed.), pp 477–494, MIT Press.

Andre, D. (1995), "The evolution of agents that build mental models and create simple plans using genetic programming," in *Genetic Algorithms: Proceedings of the Sixth International Conference (ICGA95)*, L. Eshelman (Ed.), pp 248–255, Pittsburgh, PA, USA: Morgan Kaufmann.

Andre, D. and Teller, A. (1996), "A study in program response and the negative effects of introns in genetic programming," in *Genetic Programming 1996: Proceedings of the First Annual Conference*, J. R. Koza, D. E. Goldberg, D. B. Fogel, and R. L. Riolo (Eds.), pp 12–19, Stanford University, CA, USA: MIT Press.

Angeline, P. J. (1993), *Evolutionary Algorithms and Emergent Intelligence*, PhD thesis, Ohio State University, Computer Science Department.

Angeline, P. J. (1996a), "An investigation into the sensitivity of genetic programming to the frequency of leaf selection during subtree crossover," in *Genetic Programming 1996: Proceedings of the First Annual Conference*, J. R. Koza, D. E. Goldberg, D. B. Fogel, and R. L. Riolo (Eds.), pp 21–29, Stanford University, CA, USA: MIT Press.

Angeline, P. J. (1996b), "Two self-adaptive crossover operators for genetic programming," in *Advances in Genetic Programming 2*, P. J. Angeline and K. E. Kinnear, Jr. (Eds.), MIT Press.

Angeline, P. J. (1997), "An alternative to indexed memory for evolving programs with explicit state representations," in *Genetic Programming 1997: Proceedings of the Second Annual Conference*, J. R. Koza, K. Deb, M. Dorigo, D. B. Fogel, M. Garzon, H. Iba, and R. L. Riolo (Eds.), pp 423–430, Stanford University, CA, USA: Morgan Kaufmann.

Brave, S. (1996a), "The evolution of memory and mental models using genetic programming," in *Genetic Programming 1996: Proceedings of the First Annual Conference*, J. R. Koza, D. E. Goldberg, D. B. Fogel, and R. L. Riolo (Eds.), pp 261–266, Stanford University, CA, USA: MIT Press.

Brave, S. (1996b), "Using genetic programming to evolve recursive programs for tree search," in *Advances in Genetic Programming 2*, P. J. Angeline and K. E. Kinnear, Jr. (Eds.), Chapter 10, Cambridge, MA, USA: MIT Press.

Conrads, M., Nordin, P., and Banzhaf, W. (1998), "Speech sound discrimination with genetic programming," in *Proceedings of the First European Workshop on Genetic Programming*, W. Banzhaf, R. Poli, M. Schoenauer, and T. C. Fogarty (Eds.), LNCS 1391, Paris: Springer-Verlag.

Daida, J. (1996), "Algorithm discovery using the genetic programming paradigm: Extracting low-contrast curvilinear features from SAR images of arctic ice," in *Advances in Genetic Programming 2*, P. J. Angeline and K. E. Kinnear, Jr. (Eds.), Chapter 21, Cambridge, MA, USA: MIT Press.

Dellaert, F. and Beer., R. (1994), "Co-evolving body and brain in autonomous agents using a developmental model," in *Technical Report CES-94-16, Department of Computer Engineering and Science*, Case Western Reserve University, Cleveland, OH 44106.

Fogel, L., Angeline, P. J., and Fogel, D. (1995), "An evolutionary programming approach to self-adaptation on finite state machines," in *Proceedings of the 4th Annual Conference on Evolutionary Programming*, J. McDonnell, R. Reynolds, and D. Fogel (Eds.), MIT Press.

Holland, J. (1975), *Adaptation in Natural and Artificial Systems*, University of Michigan Press.

Holland, J. and Reitman, J. S. (1978), "Cognitive systems based on adaptive algorithms," in *Pattern Directed Inference Systems*, Academic Press.

Hopcroft, J. and Ullman, J. (1979), *Introduction to Automata Theory, Languages, and Computation*, Addison Wesley.

Kinnear, Jr., K. E. (1993), "Generality and difficulty in genetic programming: Evolving a sort," in *Proceedings of the 5th International Conference on Genetic Algorithms, ICGA-93*, S. Forrest (Ed.), pp 287–294, Morgan Kaufmann.

Koza, J. (1994), *Genetic Programming 2*, MIT Press.

Langdon, W. B. (1995), "Evolving data structures with genetic programming," in *Proceedings of the Sixth International Conference on Genetic Algorithms*, S. Forrest (Ed.), Pittsburgh, PA, USA: Morgan Kauffman.

Langdon, W. B. (1996), "Data structures and genetic programming," in *Advances in Genetic Programming 2*, P. J. Angeline and K. E. Kinnear, Jr. (Eds.), MIT Press.

Nguyen, T. and Huang, T. (1994), "Evolvable 3d modeling for model-based object recognition systems," in *Advances In Genetic Programming*, K. E. Kinnear, Jr. (Ed.), MIT Press.

Nordin, P. (1997), *Evolutionary Program Induction of Binary Machine Code and its Applications*, PhD thesis, der Universitat Dortmund am Fachereich Informatik.

Nordin, P. and Banzhaf, W. (1996), "Programmatic compression of images and sound," in *Genetic Programming 1996: Proceedings of the First Annual Conference*, J. R. Koza, D. E. Goldberg, D. B. Fogel, and R. L. Riolo (Eds.), pp 345–350, Stanford University, CA, USA: MIT Press.

Olsson, R. (1995), *Inductive Functional Programming using Incremental Program Transformation*, PhD thesis, University of Oslo.

O'Reilly, U.-M. (1995), *An Analysis of Genetic Programming*, PhD thesis, Carelton University, Ottawa-Carleton Institute for Computer Science, Ottawa, Ontario, Canada.

Poli, R. (1996a), "Discovery of symbolic, neuro-symbolic and neural networks with parallel distributed genetic programming," in *Technical Report CSRP-96-14, School of Computer Science, University of Birmingham*, University of Birmingham.

Poli, R. (1996b), "Genetic programming for image analysis," in *Genetic Programming 1996*, J. R. Koza, D. E. Goldberg, D. B. Fogel, and R. L. Riolo (Eds.), pp 363–368, Stanford University, CA, USA: MIT Press.

Rumelhart, D., Hinton, G., and Williams, R. (1986), "Learning internal represenations by error propogation," in *Parallel Distributed Processing*, Cambridge, MA, USA: MIT Press.

Sharman, K., Alcazar, A., and Li, Y. (1995), "Evolving signal processing algorithms by genetic programming," in *First International Conference on Genetic Algorithms in Engineering Systems: Innovations and Applications, GALESIA*.

Spector, L. and Luke, S. (1996), "Culture enhances the evolvability of cognition," in *Cognitive Science (CogSci) 1996 Conference Proceedings*.

Sutton, R. (1988), "Learning to predict by the methods of temporal differences," in *Proceedings of the International Conference on Machine Learning*, AAAI Press.

Tackett, W. A. (1993), "Genetic programming for feature discovery and image discrimination," in *Proceedings of the Fifth International Conference on Genetic Algorithms*, S. Forrest (Ed.), Morgan Kauffman.

Teller, A. (1994), "The evolution of mental models," in *Advances In Genetic Programming*, K. E. Kinnear, Jr. (Ed.), pp 199–220, MIT Press.

Teller, A. (1996), "Evolving programmers: The co-evolution of intelligent recombination operators," in *Advances in Genetic Programming 2*, K. E. Kinnear, Jr. and P. J. Angeline (Eds.), MIT Press.

Teller, A. (1998), *Algorithm Evolution with Internal Reinforcement for Signal Understanding*, PhD thesis, Computer Science Department, Carnegie Mellon University.

Teller, A. and Veloso, M. (1995), "Program evolution for data mining," in *The International Journal of Expert Systems. Third Quarter. Special Issue on Genetic Algorithms and Knowledge Bases.*, S. Louis (Ed.), pp 216–236, JAI Press.

Teller, A. and Veloso, M. (1997), "PADO: A new learning architecture for object recognition," in *Symbolic Visual Learning*, K. Ikeuchi and M. Veloso (Eds.), Oxford University Press.

Thrun, S. and Mitchell, T. (1994), "Learning one more thing," Technical Report CMU-CS-94-184, Computer Science Department, Carnegie Mellon Unversity.

Treleaven, P. C., Brownbridge, D. R., and Hopkins, R. P. (1982), "Data-driven and demand-driven computer architecture," *ACM Computing Surveys*, 14(1):93–143.

Watkins, C. J. (1989), *Learning from Delayed Rewards.*, PhD thesis, King's College.

Wilson, S. (1987), "Hierarchical credit allocation in a classifier system," in *Genetic Algorithms and Simulated Annealing*, Morgan Kaufman Publishers.

15 Inductive Genetic Programming with Immune Network Dynamics

Nikolay I. Nikolaev, Hitoshi Iba, and Vanio Slavov

This chapter presents an immune version of Genetic Programming (GP). This is a GP version that conducts progressive search controled by a dynamic fitness function. The new fitness function is based on analogy with a model of the biological immune system, such that the programs are viewed as lymphocyte clones that compete to recognize most of the examples, viewed as antigens. The programs are reinforced with rewards for matched important examples and stimulated to match different examples. Examples recognized by a small number of programs are considered important. The motivation for using the immune dynamics for GP navigation is to maintain a high population diversity and to achieve enhanced search performance. Empirical evidence for the efficacy of this immune version on practical inductive machine learning and time-series prediction tasks is provided.

15.1 Introduction

Genetic Programming (GP) [Koza, 1992; Iba and Sato, 1992; Banzhaf et al., 1998] is a stochastic search method suitable for addressing inductive learning tasks. Inspired by evolutionary processes in natural living organisms, the GP system maintains a population of programs to accomplish robust search. The search is considered robust when it locates a global, or nearly global, solution reliably. Such a behavior is not guaranteed, however, since the population is often trapped in local optima. If there are no intrinsic forces to push continuously the population on the search landscape, the system converges prematurely to a sub-optimal solution.

Recent studies into the principles of the biological immune system [Farmer et al.,1986; Bersini and Varela, 1991; Smith et al.,1993] provide innovative ideas about how to improve the search control and counteract early convergence to inferior solutions. They inspire us to develop an immune version of GP using the micro-mechanisms of the traditional GP and the dynamics of the immune system in order to achieve enhanced macroscopic performance. The motivation is the close similarity in the behavior of the immune system and the GP system: 1) they both perform search for generalizations of recognized patterns, that is, antigens or examples; and 2) they both use similar search mechanisms involving pattern matching, heuristic selection and modification of their hypothesis, namely antibodies or programs.

We employ an idiotypic network model of the immune system [De Boer and Hogeweg, 1989] and elaborate a dynamic fitness function which may be used in any GP implementation [Koza, 1992; Iba and Sato, 1992; Banzhaf et al., 1998]. The fitness function sustains progress in the sense of improving search by driving the programs to compete continuously via mutual behavioral interactions, and to pursue evolution of a program that recognizes most of the examples. This fitness function consists of two dynamic models that exert influence on each other: 1) a model for propagating programs recognizing more important examples, and stimulating the programs to match examples from different subsets; and 2) a model for changing the importance of examples in dependence of the number of programs that recognize it.

The fitness function navigates the search through the interactions by encouraging complementary programs considered as a network. The network connectivity is a source of diversity. The diversity is a spontaneous macroproperty that enables continuous search influenced by the importance of the examples. Program reinforcements by rewards for matched important examples occasionally provoke network perturbations which contribute to moving the population on the landscape and enable avoidance of premature convergence.

We perform comparative studies of the evolutionary search performance of an immune version of the GP system STROGANOFF [Iba et al., 1992, 1993, 1994], which differs from the original only in the use of the dynamic fitness function. STROGANOFF is implemented with programs representing multivariate, high order polynomials [Iba et al., 1992, 1993, 1994] but uses the micromechanisms of inductive GP (iGP) [Nikolaev and Slavov, 1998]: proportional selection, biased context-preserving mutation, and biased crossover. The results are analysed using two kinds of measures: 1) estimates of the learning accuracy by the mean squared error attained by the trees in the population, and 2) estimates of the population diversity by the number of clusters in the population. Empirical investigations show that the search control by immune dynamics improves the performance of GP on practical inductive machine learning and time-series prediction tasks.

This chapter presents the immune version of GP in section 15.2, and the counterparts from biological immune networks, and the elaborated dynamic fitness function. Section 15.3 describes the micromechanisms of iGP. In section 15.4 we study the performance of immune GP on machine learning and time-series prediction problems from practice. Finally, a discussion is made and conclusions are derived.

15.2   Immune Version of the GP System

GP systems are suitable for inductive learning as they allow rapid exploration of huge search spaces. The search space of a problem may be considered a *fitness landscape* on which the search is navigated [Jones, 1995]. The fitness function determines the landscape ruggedness, and has a great impact on the GP system performance. When the fitness function supports diversity in the population, the GP system usually has the capacity to flow continuously on the landscape and to improve. The presented research suggests that such robust GP performance can be achieved not only by stimulating the programs to recognize more unmatched examples, but also by stimulating the programs to recognize examples from different subsets. We show that this could be fulfilled with a formula describing the dynamics of an idiotypic network model of the biological immune system.

15.2.1 Biological Idiotypic Networks

The biological *idiotypic networks* recognize and learn foreign *antigens* [Farmer et *al.*, 1986; Perelson, 1989]. An idiotypic network consists of *lymphocyte clones* that are pairs of a lymphocyte cell and one type of antibody on its surface. A lymphocyte has attached only one type of antibody, which may recognize different antigens. Pattern recognition occurs when a region from the antibody structurally binds a region from the antigen with complementary shape. Biological theory [Jerne, 1974] reveals that the lymphocytes make protective antibodies which not only recognize antigens, but also recognize other types of antibodies to preserve their own specificity. The portion of the antibody with which it matches another antibody is called *idiotype*, hence the antibody *interactions* lead to formation of idiotypic networks.

The idiotypic network acquires an immune response[1] against external antigens by concentration-proportional *clonal selection* and *differentiation* (*somatic hypermutation*) mechanisms. This kind of immune learning includes the following phases [Perelson, 1989]: 1) generation of lymphocyte cells with encoded diverse antibody types from the gene segments in the bone marrow; 2) stimulation of the lymphocyte clones that bind a large amount of structurally related antigens to secrete free antibodies and to reproduce; 3) differentiation of some activated lymphocyte clones; and 4) clonal selection of lymphocyte clones.

The *concentration* of lymphocyte clones increases proportionally to their involvement in response to antigens, but it is also influenced by the antibody interactions. Lymphocyte clones participate in idiotypic interactions that can be stimulatory or suppressing [De Boer and Hogeweg, 1989]. In this way, the clones control their abilities to learn, and they self-regulate by mutual interactions. The stimulation of the lymphocyte clones suggests that cell activation through cross-linking of antibody will increase insofar as the concentration of its complementary antibody increases.

15.2.2 Computational Counterparts in GP

Motivated by the powerful learning abilities of the immune idiotypic networks, we incorporate their principles in GP in order to achieve robust search navigation. The idea is to simulate the way in which the immune system fosters lymphocytes that match more antigens while at the same time stimulating the lymphocytes to complement each other. A slightly more specific interpretation of complementarity is assumed here. We use complementarity to encourage competition between the programs for evolving one program that matches most of the examples, rather than programs which together cover the examples.

---

[1]Immune response to antigen means that there is at least a partial match between an antibody receptor region and a complementary shaped antigen.

We develop an immune version of a traditional inductive GP system. The novelty is in the elaboration of a dynamic fitness function by analogy with the biological immune system counterparts as follows: a lymphocyte clone corresponds to a program; the concentration of a lymphocyte clone is the fitness of the program; the interaction between two antigens is the complementarity in the recognition potential of two programs; the antigens correspond to examples; the antigen concentration is the importance of an example; the clonal selection process is associated with fitness proportional selection.

15.2.3   The Dynamic Fitness Function

The *dynamic fitness function* includes two models that influence each other: 1) a model of the program dynamics; and 2) a model of the examples' dynamics. The fitness of a program should increase when it recognizes more examples, as the concentration of a lymphocyte increases when it detects more antigens.

The fitness function for control of the immune version of inductive GP is elaborated upon a dynamic model describing the changes in the concentrations of the lymphocyte clones [De Boer and Hogeweg, 1989]. The *program dynamics* F_i^{n+1} is formed from a permanent quantity for initial supply, plus an amount proportional to the previous fitness F_i^n and proliferation due to arousal by recognized examples and evoked excitory interactions, without a constant death rate:

$$F_i^{n+1} = Z + F_i^n \cdot (\, p \cdot \text{Prol}(Ag_i^n, \text{Id}_i^n) - d \,)$$

where: Z is influx constant, d is turnover constant and p is proliferation constant;
$\quad Ag_i^n$ is the antigen score of the i-th program at generation n;
$\quad \text{Id}_i^n$ is the total anti-idiotype excitation of program i;
$\quad$ Prol is the proliferation function.

The *proliferation* Prol of a program i in the next generation according to this difference equation model depends not only on the recognized examples Ag_i^n, but also on the extent of its interactions Id_i^n with the other programs:

$$\text{Prol}(Ag_i^n, \text{Id}_i^n) = \frac{Ag_i^n + \text{Id}_i^n}{p_1 + Ag_i^n + \text{Id}_i^n}$$

where p_1 is a free constant parameter. The original proliferation function of the immune system is bell-shaped [De Boer and Hogeweg, 1989] but we use here only the exciting part of the bell-shaped curve. In this way programs with high idiotypic interactions are propagated to survive.

The antigen score of a program should account how many examples it matches and also it should depend on the importance of these eliciting examples. This is because the antigen of a lymphocyte clone depends on the number and on the specificity of the structurally related antigens that it binds. We define the *antigen score* Ag_i^n of program i as linearly proportional to the importance I_j^n of the examples R which it matches, $1 \leq j \leq R$, among all N_E examples, $R \leq N_E$:

$$Ag_i^n = \sum_{j=1, i \neq j}^{R} B_{ij} \cdot I_j^n$$

where the binding B_{ij} of a program i is 1 if the program recognizes the example j and 0 otherwise. Such a definition holds for discrete program outcomes, while for continuous outcomes it should be redefined (see section 15.4.4).

Our suggestion is that the program fitness dynamics should be in interplay with the dynamics of the examples. This resembles the objective of the biological immune system to recognize all antigens if possible. During the acquisition of an immune response, the idiotypic network topology changes to accommodate lymphocyte clones that match exceptional antigens. Making an association with the iGP system behaviour, if more programs recognize an example then it should become less attractive. Therefore, when a small number of unmatched exceptional examples remain, they have to reinforce these programs in the population which cover them, and so provoke perturbation of the search process. The *importance* I_e^n of an example e is defined as proportional to the number of programs in the population that correctly recognize it plus a term for constant recruitment γ_e:

$$I_e^{n+1} = I_e^n \cdot (\alpha - \sum_{j=1}^{N} B_{je} \cdot F_j^n / (F_{\max}^n \cdot N)) + \gamma_e$$

where α is a free constant parameter.

Specifying the program interactions A_{ij} is essential for driving the programs to compete and for supporting diversity. In the immune network the lymphocyte clones should be complementary in shape to antigens in order to defeat them. In context of inductive GP, this complementarity could be regarded as a behavioral characteristic. The programs will have complementary behaviour if the affinity accounts for the difference in their mutual learning potential. Two programs are considered behaviorally complementary when they recognize examples from disjoint sets. We define the *affinity* A_{ij} between two programs i and j as the set difference between the subset of examples which i recognizes and the subset which j recognizes:

$$A_{ij} = |E_i^n - E_j^n|$$

where E_i^n is the subset of examples correctly recognized by program i at generation n from all provided examples E: $E_i^n \subseteq E$, $E_j^n \subseteq E$.

The *network* comprises all programs in the population. We realize that the network is symmetric $A_{ij} = A_{ji}$ for $1 \leq i, j \leq N$, and also that the programs do not recognize self $A_{ii} = 0$. The affinity A_{ij} stimulates the programs to: 1) recognize more examples; and 2) match slightly overlapping sets of examples. Therefore, the fitness function with this affinity contributes for breeding distinct, non-similar programs. Such program interactions entail diversity in the population.

The idiotypic influence among the programs should estimate their mutual behavioral complementarity through the affinity interactions. The biological immune system uses such a factor to self-regulate so that the lymphocyte clones have together the power to detect and eliminate all the available antigens. We define the *anti-idiotype excitation* Id_i^n to favor a program i if its interaction A_{ij} with the other $1 \leq j \leq N$ programs in the population is high:

$$\text{Id}_i^n = (1/(N_E \cdot N)) \cdot \sum_{j=1, i \neq j}^{R} A_{ij} \cdot F_j^n$$

The evolution of the network topology determines the ability of the immune algorithm to conduct efficient search. It is important to reason how the network connectivity will correspond to the phases of evolutionary search. The GP system usually starts with a random initial population and the global excitation is large. When GP performs global search, the interactions should be relatively high indicating exploration of large landscape areas. During local search the wiring should be low as GP exploits landscape areas in the vicinities of the reached local optima. This holds even if there are a number of optima peaks located by the system.

In the experiments below we use reference values for the parameters in the fitness function as follows: $Z = 0.1$, $d = 0.5$, $p_1 = 0.25$, $p = 1.1$, $\gamma_e = 0.001$, and $\alpha = 1.025$. The initial fitness of the programs is calculated by solving the above difference equation for a steady state $F_i^0 = F_i^{n+1}$, which leads to the formula: $F_i^0 = Z(p_1 + 1)/(p_1 + 1 + d + dp_1 - p)$.

15.3   Micromechanisms of the Inductive GP

The immune inductive GP is developed with programs representing *multivariate trees* [Iba et al., 1992, 1993, 1994]. We use the following micromechanisms *fitness proportional selection, context-preserving mutation* and *crossover* operators, *biased* by the size of the programs [Nikolaev and Slavov, 1998]. Size proportional biasing of the application of the genetic operators is necessary in evolutionary algorithms with variable-length genomes to counteract the tree bloat phenomena [Langdon and Poli, 1998]. Such biased applications of the operators act as forces that guard against degenerated behavior by deporting the system to unseen landscape areas.

15.3.1   Inductive Learning and Regression

The GP method is useful for addressing inductive learning tasks. The problem of these tasks can be formulated as a multivariate regression problem. Given instantiated vectors of several independent variables, that is patterns $\mathbf{x}_i = \{x_{i1}, x_{i2}, ..., x_{il}\}$, and corresponding values $r_i \in \mathcal{R}$ of the dependent variable y_i, as predefined examples $E_i = \{(\mathbf{x}_i, y_i) | y_i = r_i \in \mathcal{R}\}$, the goal is to find a function mapping $y = f(\mathbf{x})$. This is a general definition since solving regression problems implies abilities for solving classification problems as well, where the dependent variable is discrete, often categorical: $E_i = \{(\mathbf{x}_i, y_i) | y_i = d_i \in \mathcal{N}\}$. In essence, GP is an evolutionary search paradigm suitable for learning a functional description that best approximates the dependent variable. The intention is to use this function for predicting real values associated with unknown example vectors.

15.3.2   Multivariate Trees

High-order multivariate polynomial regression models can be represented by trees with functions in the internal nodes, and independent variables in the leaves [Iba et al., 1992, 1993, 1994]. A *multivariate tree* hierarchy of non-linear polynomial combinations may capture very accurately the dependencies in the examples.

There are three important implementation issues in the construction of evolutionary GP systems with multivariate trees: 1) how to find the coefficients in the polynomials; 2) what kind of polynomials to use and with which variables; and 3) how to avoid overfitting with the provided examples.

Recent research on learning by inductive GP demonstrated results of high accuracies using binary multivariate trees with second-order polynomials [Iba et al., 1992, 1993, 1994]. The advantage of such trees is that they enable evaluation and finding of complex, high-order models for acceptable time by composing simple, second-order models with coefficients that are computed relatively fast. We adopt the multivariate tree regression model consisting of *cascaded quadratic polynomials* from the polynomial theory of complex systems [Ivakhnenko, 1971]:

$$y(\mathbf{x}) = \sum_{i=0}^{5} a_i z_i(\mathbf{x}) = a_0 z_0(\mathbf{x}) + a_1 z_1(\mathbf{x}) + a_2 z_2(\mathbf{x}) + a_3 z_3(\mathbf{x}) + a_4 z_4(\mathbf{x}) + a_5 z_5(\mathbf{x})$$

of terms: $z_0(\mathbf{x}) = 1$, $z_1(\mathbf{x}) = x_1$, $z_2(\mathbf{x}) = x_2$, $z_3(\mathbf{x}) = x_1 x_2$, $z_4(\mathbf{x}) = x_1^2$, and $z_5(\mathbf{x}) = x_2^2$. Considering the functions z_i as a vector $\mathbf{z} = (z_0(\mathbf{x}), z_1(\mathbf{x}), z_2(\mathbf{x}), z_3(\mathbf{x}), z_4(\mathbf{x}), z_5(\mathbf{x}))$, we may write:

$$y(\mathbf{x}) = \mathbf{a}^T \mathbf{z}(\mathbf{x})$$

A multivariate tree has such polynomials in the lowest functional nodes with leaf children, and independent variables in the leaves. Higher in the tree the same components are employed, where the variables may be outcomes of lower level polynomials: $z(xy)$ or $z(\mathbf{y}) = y_1 y_2$. Using these trees, polynomial approximation may be pursued by attempts to reduce the deviation when modelling data. According to the Group Method of Data Handling (GMDH) [Ivakhnenko, 1971] the polynomial coefficients at each node of the tree-like multilayer program structure are calculated in stepwise manner by the matrix formula:

$$\mathbf{a} = (\mathbf{Z}^T \mathbf{Z})^{-1} \mathbf{Z}^T \mathbf{y}$$

where $\mathbf{Z}$ is the 6×6 matrix of vectors $\mathbf{z}_i = \{z_{i0}, z_{i1}, ..., z_{i5}\}$, $i = 1..N_E$, and $\mathbf{y}$ is the output vector. This is known as a solution of the general least-squares fitting problem by the method of normal equations. The normal equations we solve using LU-decomposition [Press et al., 1992].

Following the GMDH algorithm, the evaluation of a tree-like polynomial starts from the lowest functional nodes, and then proceeding up to the tree root. The output vector at each step is used as independent variable vector for finding the coefficients in the next step higher in the tree. When a tree is modified, the coefficients must be recalculated to reflect the modification by mutation or crossover [Iba et al., 1993]. The recent implementations save some computations by using the old coefficients from the subtrees not affected by the genetic operators.

15.3.3   Context-Preserving Mutation

Inductive GP uses a *context-preserving mutation* operator [Nikolaev and Slavov, 1998]. It transforms a multivariate tree so that only the closest to the chosen mutation point neighboring vertices are affected. The elementary constituent submutations are: 1) substitution of a functional node by another one, or random substitution of a terminal; 2) insertion of a node as a parent of a subtree so that the subtree becomes leftmost child of the new node; and 3) deletion of a node only when no subtree below is to be cut.

The *biased mutation* operator for inductive GP performs context-preserving mutation with probability $p_m = m \cdot |g|^2$, where m is a free parameter [Goldberg et al., 1989]. This operator usually modifies large programs.

15.3.4   Crossover by Cut and Splice

The *biased crossover* for inductive GP splices two multivariate trees with probability $p_c = c/\sqrt{|g|}$, where c is a free parameter, and $|g|$ is size of tree g, or swaps them. The cut points are selected randomly. This operator produces offspring with larger size than their parents if the parents are of very small size.

The proper values for the free parameters m and c are identified with the autocorrelation function. These free parameters m and c serve as knobs with which one may regulate carefully the search efficiency [Nikolaev and Slavov, 1998].

15.4   Practical Induction by Immune Dynamics

15.4.1   Traditional and Immune Versions of iGP

The evolutionary performance of the immune version of GP is studied here in comparison with the traditional GP system STROGANOFF [Iba et al., 1993, 1994] that uses the multivariate tree representation from the previous section. STROGANOFF was implemented with the micromechanisms of inductive GP given above [Nikolaev and Slavov, 1998]: biased context-preserving mutation, biased crossover by cut and splice, and a stochastic complexity (MDL) fitness function with an improved complexity component:

$$F_{MDL} = k \cdot S_i^2 + \log(n_t + n_f) + n_t + n_t \cdot \log T + n_f + n_f \cdot \log F$$

where n_t are the leaves in the tree, n_f are the functional nodes, T are all terminals, F are all functions, k is a balancing parameter, and S_i^2 is the mean squared error:

$$S_i^2 = (1/N_E) \cdot \sum_{i=1}^{N_E} |y_i - y(\mathbf{x}_i)|^2$$

where y_i is the true outcome given with the i-th example, and $y(\mathbf{x}_i)$ is the estimated outcome from the program given the i-th input vector $\mathbf{x}$.

The only difference between STROGANOFF and the immune version is that the fitness in the immune iGP is calculated with the difference equation for F_i^{n+1}.

15.4.2   Performance Measures

The evolutionary performance of the traditional and the immune versions of inductive GP is evaluated with two kinds of measures: 1) estimates of the *learning accuracy*, and 2) estimates of the *population diversity*. The learning accuracy provides quantitative evidence for the development of the learning process. The diversity is a macroproperty that enhances the GP system potential to find highly fit programs.

The diversity can be analyzed with the *number of clusters* in the population [Bersini, 1997], computed using the K-means clustering algorithm [Hartigan and Wong, 1979]: split the current population of multivariate trees into groups by maximizing the tree-to-tree distance between them. The tree-to-tree distance here is the minimal number of context-preserving mutations necessary to produce one of the trees from the other [Nikolaev and Slavov, 1998].

With the experiments below we show that the immune version attains fitter programs and maintains higher population variety than the traditional inductive GP on machine learning and time-series prediction problem instances. All of the plots in the figures that follow are from the best runs, taken among the 1000 runs which were performed with each the immune iGP and STROGANOFF.

15.4.3   Machine Learning

Machine learning considers computational induction as a problem of finding a function f from provided $\{(\mathbf{x}_1, y_1), (\mathbf{x}_2, y_1), ..., (\mathbf{x}_N, y_C)\}$ examples. The task is to acquire such a function that will distinguish correctly unseen examples of the same classes. The dependent variable assumes discrete values, often denoting only several categories $y_i = d_i \in \mathcal{N}$, which are called classes.

The Glass recognition task is assumed as a benchmark machine learning problem. The goal is to learn the configuration of glass pieces collected after a car accident [Merz and Murphy, 1998]. The Glass data set includes $|E| = 214$ examples of 9 numeric features $E_i = \{(\mathbf{x}_i, y_i) | x_{i1} = r_1 \in \mathcal{R}, ..., x_{i9} = r_9 \in \mathcal{R}\}$, each associated with one of 6 classes: $y_1 = 1, y_2 = 2, ..., y_6 = 6$.

We compare inductive GP with the Non-linear Decision Trees algorithm (NDT) [Ittner and Schlosser, 1995] since it produces multivariate binary tree classifiers with quadratic polynomials of features in the nodes as inductive GP. This means that NDT is similar to inductive GP in that it also makes non-linear partitioning of the feature space. NDT differs in that it performs top-down induction of decision trees having the classes in their leaves. Several polynomials generalizing the examples are extracted from the decision tree by traversing it from the root to the leaves, while GP generates one polynomial. The NDT algorithm outperforms some of the best machine learning approaches [Ittner and Schlosser, 1995].

The presented results are derived using 10-fold cross validation: 10 disjoint subsets of 21 examples were formed, then the algorithms were trained 10 times using the outside $214 - 21$ examples of each partition and tested on the remaining 21 examples. We study the learning accuracy with the percentage of correctly recognized examples by the best tree. The best tree accuracies can be obtained from Table 15.1 by summation of the accuracies in the second column with the standard deviations in the third column. For example, the best tree found by the immune iGP from all 1000 runs was with 72.11% accuracy. One can see in Table 15.1 that the accuracies of the NDT trees deviate less, but the iGP may discover more accurate trees. An advantage of the two GP systems is that they derive smaller trees. NDT tends to overfit the examples due to the recursive partitioning of the examples.

Table 15.1
Learning accuracy of the best multivariate trees produced by the NDT, the immune iGP and the traditional STROGANOFF with the Glass recognition data

Approach	Best Tree Accuracy	Standard Deviation	Best Tree Size
NDT	67.43%	±2.53%	29
Immune inductive GP	68.22%	±3.89%	24
STROGANOFF	67.78%	±3.66%	25

The *learning performance* of the immune inductive GP and STROGANOFF may be analyzed with the curves given in Figure 15.1a,b. The mean squared error of the best tree recorded with the immune GP is occasionally perturbed by the system dynamics, which enables its progressive improvement. We note that after phases of local search between generations 350 − 540, 560 − 690, 720 − 770, the system conducts global search into different directions across the fitness landscape.

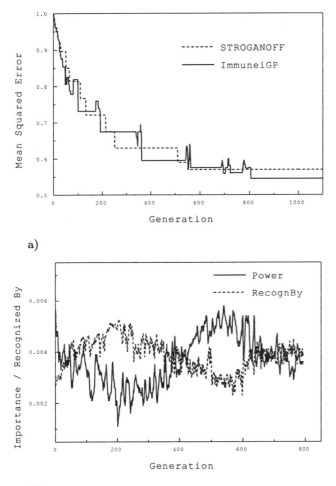

a)

b)

Figure 15.1
Learning accuracy: a) Mean squared error, of the best tree evolved by the immune iGP and STROGANOFF using *MaxSizeGP*=29, *PopSize*=60, and the Glass data, and b) Influence of a particular important example on the fitnesses of programs that recognize it

The reasons for such perturbations may be discovered by an experimental analysis of the changes in the examples' importance during a typical run of the immune iGP. We conducted an experiment with the immune iGP and selected a particular important example, in order to investigate how it is approached by the programs in the population in the sense of whether depending on its importance they are attracted to match it. Figure 15.1b shows the interplay between the changes of the importance of the selected important example and the number of programs in the population that recognize it. This figure displays that there is an inverse relation between the example's importance and the number of the programs in the population recognizing it. When more programs tend to recognize the example its power decreases, in the interval $20 - 200$ generation. After that, between $220 - 400$ generation, the programs begin to avoid this example since its importance has become low which means that it is no more so attractive. This causes again an increase of the example's importance, between generations $220 - 600$, as there are a small number of programs in the population that match it. Next, they strive to recognize it and decrease the example's importance again. Therefore, the changes in the importances of the examples really drive the programs to match more powerful examples and so contribute to reorientation of the evolutionary search.

The *population diversity* maintained by the immune iGP and STROGANOFF can be analyzed with the two plots in Figure 15.2. In Figure 15.2a we observe that the immune version of inductive GP sustains higher population diversity than STROGANOFF measured by the number of clusters of programs. Since the number of clusters is measured with the tree-to-tree distance characteristics between the tree-like programs in the population, one may assume that this is an estimate of the syntactic variety in the population during evolutionary search. It is interesting to note that the number of clusters during evolutionary search conducted by immune iGP slightly decreases when this system performs local search. This is evident from the horizontal line segments which correspond to the local search periods in Figure 15.1. The performance of the traditional inductive system STROGANOFF maintains almost 25% less clusters of programs.

Another measure of the diversity is the mean anti-idiotype excitation among the programs in the population (Figure 15.2b). The mean affinity shown in this figure presents the diversity from a different, semantic perspective as it estimates the variety in the recognition potential of the programs, or whether there are programs in the population with non-similar learning capacity. Figure 15.2b demonstrates that the mutual interactions between the programs in the immune iGP are occasionally perturbed. These could be considered search perturbations caused by changing the importances of some examples. The search obviously is kind of a shaken and next improves. This claim can be explained with the varying sloping down affinity curve on Figure 15.2b, which falls and raisings delimit approximately the same periods of local search between generations $380 - 580$, $590 - 680$, and $700 - 790$.

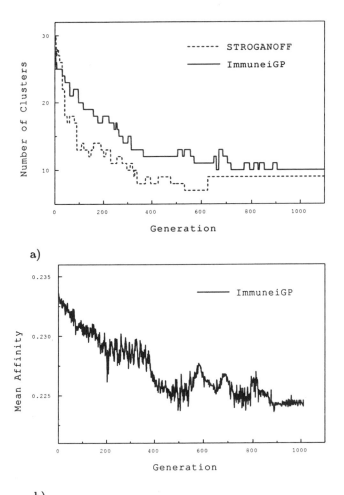

Figure 15.2
Population diversity: a) Clustering, recorded with the immune iGP and STROGANOFF using
MaxSizeGP=29 and *PopSize*=60, on the Glass data and b) Mean anti-idiotype excitation

15.4.4   Time-Series Prediction

Time-series prediction may also be regarded as an inductive problem. The task is to
identify the regularities among given series of points: $..., x^t, x^{t+1}, x^{t+2}, ...$, sampled
at discrete time intervals. This is accomplished by search for a series description
with only the most relevant from the available points, so that future points of

the series can be predicted. We assume an autoregressive model with non-linear polynomials, represented as multivariate trees. The available points are considered coordinates of the independent variable vector and serve as data for learning. The independent variable vectors $\mathbf{x}_i$ are created with embedding dimension k, and delay time $\tau = 1$ [Farmer and Sidorowich, 1987]:

$$\mathbf{x}_i = \{\ x^{t-(k-1)\cdot\tau}, x^{t-(k-2)\cdot\tau}, ..., x^t\}$$

that is window vectors from k nearest previous points starting at a point t. Dependent variable is the immediate next point to the starting $y_i = x^{t+1}$. Thus, examples of the kind $E_i = \{(\mathbf{x}_i, y_i)|y_i = r_i \in \mathcal{R}\}$ are formed. Difficulties in time-series prediction arise from the high dimensionalities of the series. That is why, the choice of the embedding dimension k and delay time τ are important design issues. We select empirically[2] embedding dimension $k = 10$, and delay time $\tau = 1$.

The immune iGP for time-series prediction is implemented with modified binding B_{ij} of a program i to recognized examples since the outcome $y(\mathbf{x}_j)$ is continuous:

$$B_{ij} = \begin{cases} 1 - S_i^2/S_A^2 & \text{if } S_{ij}^2 < S_A^2 \\ 0 & \text{otherwise} \end{cases}$$

where $S_{ij}^2 = |y_i - y(\mathbf{x}_j)|^2$ is the squared error between the outcome $y(\mathbf{x}_j)$ of program i given input $\mathbf{x}$, and y_i is the true outcome given with example j. The mean squared error S_i^2 is computed with the formula defined in section 15.4.1. The value of S_A^2 is calculated as the average mean squared error from all programs. The rationale is that the binding B_{ij} should be large enough in order to influence essentially the fitness function through the fitting error.

We used data series produced with the Mackey-Glass differential equation for prediction [Mackey and Glass, 1977]. This is an equation for simulating blood flood caused by the irregularity of the heart beats. Trajectories of 1400 points were generated with parameters: $a = 0.2, b = 0.1$, and three differential delays $\Delta = 17$, $\Delta = 23$, and $\Delta = 30$. The initial points in each of the cases were taken randomly. The first subseries of 1000 points were discarded. We considered the next 100 points for training, and the remaining 300 points for testing.

The plots in Figure 15.3 provide empirical evidence for the *learning performance* of the immune iGP and STROGANOFF. One observes that the immune iGP exhibits stable evolutionary performance, in the sense that it is able to search progressively. Despite some degradations in its performance, it continuously improves since the dynamics sustains the motion of the population on the fitness landscape.

---

[2]The theoretical studies advise to select embedding dimensions k corresponding to the concrete attractor dimensions D with the inequality $k \geq D + 1$ [Farmer and Sidorowich, 1987].

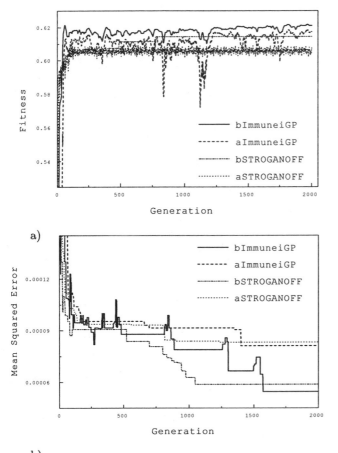

a)

b)

Figure 15.3
Learning accuracy: a) Average and best fitnesses, and b) Mean squared error, recorded with the immune iGP and STROGANOFF using $MaxSizeGP=29$, $PopSize=60$, and 100 points from the Mackey-Glass equation series derived with $\Delta = 17$

The phases of global and local search conducted by the immune version of GP can be clearly identified. During local search the mean squared error does not change, shown by the regions with horizontal lines in Figure 15.3b between generations $490 - 750, 820 - 1250, 1300 - 1500, 1540 - 2000$. These evidence for local search are supported by the horizontal slightly oscillating fitness values in the same generation intervals in Figure 15.3a. When global search is performed near generations $470, 780, 1275$, and 1520, the mean squared error sometimes fluctuates (Figure

15.3b), and after that there are sharp falls of the corresponding average and best fitnesses (Figure 15.3a). These sudden performance changes cause stepwise error decrease and finding more accurate best programs (Figure 15.3a,b). The traditional GP climbs on a local peak and remains there (after generation 1050 in Figure 15.3b), since the locally optimal program takes over the population.

Table 15.2
Learning accuracy, forecast and size of the best trees found by the immune iGP version and STROGANOFF, on Mackey-Glass equation series derived using: embedding dimension $k = 10$, delay time $\tau = 1$, and three differential delays Δ (the errors are in units of $1e - 5$)

	Mean Squared Error S_i^2		
	Best Tree TRAIN Error		
differential delay	$\Delta = 17$	$\Delta = 23$	$\Delta = 30$
Immune inductive GP	5.458376	8.137821	9.015442
STROGANOFF	5.870631	8.458412	9.527129
	Best Tree TEST Error		
Immune inductive GP	6.236278	8.852356	9.798612
STROGANOFF	6.762336	8.817821	10.153613
	Best Program Tree Size		
Immune inductive GP	$n_f = 10, n_t = 11$	$n_f = 11, n_t = 12$	$n_f = 13, n_t = 14$
STROGANOFF	$n_f = 9, n_t = 10$	$n_f = 11, n_t = 12$	$n_f = 12, n_t = 13$

In Table 15.2 we show the accuracies of the best trees from 1000 runs recorded with series derived with a slightly large embedding dimension, which amplifies the noise in the examples, but facilitates the comparison with other GP approaches to the same problem instance [Iba et al., 1993; Zhang et al., 1997; Mulloy et al., 1996]. We generated three series with different differential delays Δ and, thus, we produced three Mackey-Glass equation series of different complexities [Farmer and Sidorowich, 1987]. The first 17, respectively 23 and 30 points in each series, were randomly generated. The most frequently changing curve and hence most difficult to learn is the one obtained with $\Delta = 30$. It is visible that the immune version of iGP identifies solutions with higher approximation accuracy as well as predictability both on the training and on the testing subseries. The immune GP is stable as it shows abilities to search better in cases of data series with different complexities.

The lowest section of Table 15.2 displays the program sizes, given by the number of functional nodes n_f and terminal leaves n_t of the best multivariate tree found. The differences in the program complexities justify the accuracy deviations between the training and testing errors. The trees evolved by the traditional GP have a smaller number of functional nodes and terminal leaves, but they have lower accuracies. An advantage of the immune GP is in the high quality of the attained multivariate trees, and so suggest that the trees evolved by the immune GP are better approximators. Therefore, the experiments indicate that the immune iGP usually discovers best multivariate trees of larger size, which fit better the examples than predict. This, however, can be regulated by tuning the stoping criterion in the sense of number of generations to evolve.

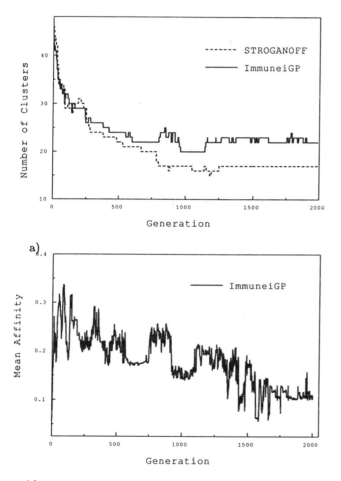

Figure 15.4
Population diversity: a) Clustering, recorded with the immune iGP and STROGANOFF using *MaxSizeGP*=29, *PopSize*=60, and 100 data points from the Mackey-Glass equation series derived with $\Delta = 17$; and b) Mean anti-idiotype excitation

We demonstrate in Figure 15.4a the changes of the *population diversity*. The numbers of clusters are taken during the same run for time-series prediction as above, in order to explain why the GP system behavior has the performance characteristics displayed in figures 15.3a and 15.3b. It seems that the immune version of iGP enforces the programs to occupy different fitness landscape areas, and keeps the population distributed. Initially, in the phase of global search the number of clusters is relatively high. During local search phases the number of clusters slightly diminishes and stays unchanged between $550 - 750$ and $900 - 1150$ generations. When the GP system performs global search the number of clusters increases and fluctuates. The traditional inductive GP has been deceived in the vicinity of some local optima after generation 1500 and further can not discover better solutions.

The network of programs in the immune version of iGP remembers examples by switching between different combinations of programs. That is why, the population diversity can be estimated by the evolution of the network connectivity since it influences the distribution of the search effort on different landscape areas. We evaluate the strength of idiotypic interactions with the affinities between the programs (Figure 15.4b). The high mean affinity in Figure 15.4b is an indication for the high diversity supported by the immune GP. It is interesting to observe that the affinity decreases between generations $550 - 750$ and $900 - 1150$, which makes us certain that search perturbations really occur during these periods.

15.5   Discussion

Understanding the intrinsic dynamics of the immune inductive GP is important for control of the evolutionary search carried by them.

The dynamics of the immune version of GP has three aspects [Farmer et *al.*, 1990]. The first aspect is the net topology dynamics. In our implementation we assumed that the network is symmetric and completely connected, but these are simplifications. The choice of programs for interaction should be suggested by an appropriate reformulation of the affinity formula. Theoretically, the network should comprise programs interacting with a small number of other programs. The affinity formula should not stimulate, however, formation of very sparse networks since they make it impossible for perturbations to occur.

The second aspect is the parameter dynamics. The large number of free parameters in the fitness formula creates difficulties for finding and tuning their values. The stability of the results is sensitive to these values, and the problem is whether the selected reference parameter values are the most relevant ones.

The third aspect is the concentration model dynamics of the lymphocyte-like programs. This dynamics is very difficult to analyze because of the bell-shaped character of the activating proliferation function.

15.6 Relevance to Other Works

The time-series prediction problem have been also addressed by many other GP systems [Oakley, 1994; Zhang et al., 1997; Mulloy et al., 1997]. All these GP systems use static fitness functions: Oakley [1994] uses the sum of squared errors, while Mulloy and colleagues [1997] use an adjusted version of the sum of squared errors. The Minimum Description Length (MDL) fitness function of Zhang, Ohm, and Muhlenbein [1997] is close to this which was employed in STROGANOFF in that it balances between the fitness and the program size, leading to high quality approximations. These static fitness functions, however, lack of intrinsic power to push the GP system to improve continuously its evolutionary search performance. This is because the static fitness functions do not have a reinforcing effect to counteract premature convergence to suboptimal programs.

An essential difference in the design of the above GP systems, the immune GP system and the STROGANOFF system is that the last two produce polynomials represented as specific cascaded multivariate trees. The polynomial coefficients in these specific multivariate trees are directly computed as least-squares solutions by the method of normal equations, which avoids the need to evolve them. Thus, the GP systems like STROGANOFF achieve very accuracte results trying only to evolve the basis polynomials which constitute the target polynomial.

Empirical investigations of the performance of the immune version and the GP version STROGANOFF have been presented [Iba et al., 1993]. The accuracies of the programs induced by the immune GP are slightly better than these of STROGANOFF. This is reasonable since the inductive learning problems that were used are known as hard benchmark instances for learning. The most significant result is that the immune dynamics reduces the probability of GP to become stuck in local optima. This impacts the GP system abilities to move continuously the population on the fitness landscape. Our hypothesis is that this robust performance of the immune version of GP, is due to two factors: 1) the rewarding program interactions; and 2) the reinforcing examples' importance changes. These provoke occasional network perturbations, and so contribute to the search reorientation toward different fitness landscape areas.

The presented fitness function is a dynamic model that distributes the population into niches [Horn and Goldberg, 1996]. This dynamic function makes coexistent in the population programs from different niches on the fitness landscape, which is a kind of fitness sharing. Fitness sharing means that the fitness of a program decreases if there are similar, slightly behaviorally different programs than it. In the immune GP the fitness sharing is implicit, and it is achieved through resource sharing with the affinity interactions. The immune dynamics via such affinity interactions encourages competition between the programs to cover more example resources from distinct resource niches, and does not divide the reward. Therefore, the immune

GP exhibits implicit niching like the classifier system of Horn and Goldberg [1996]. The immune GP differs in that the programs partially recognize the examples and mutually compete till one program individually attains a complete solution.

15.7   Conclusion

This chapter has proposed an inductive GP system navigated by a fitness function based upon a network model of the biological immune system. Viewing the learning as immunity phenomena, it is an attempt to employ the immune idiotypic networks as inductive computational mechanisms. The immune version of GP is not specific to any genetic mutation or crossover operators, and can be used for improving any traditional GP system. The implementation of the immune GP version is more sophisticated but features more learning power.

It has been reported that the immune GP system outperforms STROGANOFF in solving benchmark machine learning and time-series prediction tasks. We are inclined to think that the robust evolutionary behaviour will be retained if the same micromechanisms and dynamic fitness function are used. Because of computational efficiency reasons the immune GP will be particularly useful for machine learning tasks with close categorical examples distribution, and for time-series prediction tasks with close series size and embedding dimension to these studied here.

Further research should be directed toward deeper understanding of the computational properties and principles of this connectionist immune version of inductive Genetic Programming. Theoretical analysis should be made to clarify what this computer immune system can do.

Bibliography

Banzhaf, W., Nordin, P., Keller, R. E. and Francone, F. D. (1998). *Genetic Programming: An Introduction. On the Automatic Evolution of Computer Programs and Its Applications*. San Francisco, CA: Morgan Kaufmann.

Bersini, H. and Varela, F. (1991). Hints for Adaptive Problem Solving Gleaned from Immune Networks. In: Schwefel, H. P. and Mühlenbein, H. M. (eds.), *Proceedings of the First International Conference Parallel Problem Solving from Nature*, PPSN I, Berlin: Springer, 343-354.

Bersini, H. (1997). Frustration and Clustering in Biological Networks. In: Langdon, C. G. and Shimohara, T. (Eds.), *Artificial Life V: Proceedings of the of the Fifth International Workshop on the Synthesis and Simulation of Living Systems*, Cambridge, MA: The MIT Press.

De Boer, R. G. and Hogeweg, P. (1989). Idiotypic Networks Incorporating T-B Cell Cooperation. The Condition for Percolation. *Journal of Theoretical Biology*. 139, 17-38.

Farmer, J. D., Packard, N. H. and Perelson, A. S. (1986). The Immune System, Adaptation and Machine Learning. *Physica*, **22**D, 187-204.

Farmer, J. D. and Sidorowich, J. J. (1987). Predicting Chaotic Time Series. *Physical Review Letters,* **8***(59): 845-848.*

Farmer, J. D. (1990). A Rosetta Stone for Connectionism. *Physica,* **42**D, 153-187.

Goldberg, D., Korb, B. and Deb, K. (1989). Messy Genetic Algorithms: Motivation, Analysis and First Results. *Complex Systems,* **3**:493-530.

Hartigan, J. A. and Wong, M. A. (1979). A K-means clustering algorithm, *Applied Statistics,* **28***(1): 100-108.*

Horn, J. and Goldberg, D. E. (1996). Natural Niching for Evolving Cooperative Classifiers. In: Koza, J. R., Goldberg, D. E., Fogel, D. E. and Riolo, R. L. (Eds.), *Genetic Programming 1996: Proceedings of the First Annual Conference,* Cambridge, MA: The MIT Press, 553-564.

Iba, H. and Sato, T. (1992). Meta-level Strategy for Genetic Algorithms based on Structured Representations, In: *Proceedings of the Second Pacific Rim International Conference on Artificial Intelligence,* 548-554.

Iba, H., Kurita, T., de Garis, H. and Sato, T. (1993). System Identification using Structured Genetic Algorithms. In: Forrest, S. (Ed.), *Proceedings of the Fifth International Conference on Genetic Algorithms,* ICGA-93. San Mateo, CA: Morgan Kaufmann, 279-286.

Iba, H., de Garis, H. and Sato, T. (1994). Genetic Programming using a Minimum Description Length Principle. In: Kinnear, K. (Ed.), *Advances in Genetic Programming,* Cambridge, MA: The MIT Press, 265-284.

Ittner, A. and Schlosser, M. (1995). Non-Linear Decision Trees, In: Saitta, L. (Ed.), *Machine Learning: Proceedings of the 13th International Conference, ICML'96,* San Mateo, CA: Morgan Kaufmann, 252-257.

Ivakhnenko, A. G. (1971). Polynomial Theory of Complex Systems. *IEEE Trans. on Systems, Man, and Cybernetics.* **1** (4): 364-378.

Jerne, N. K. (1974). Towards a Network Theory of the Immune System. *Annual Immunology (Institute Pasteur),* **125** C, 373-389.

Jones, T. (1995). Evolutionary Algorithms, Fitness Landscapes and Search. PhD dissertation, Albuquerque, NM: The University of New Mexico.

Koza, J. R. (1992). *Genetic Programming: On the Programming of Computers by Means of Natural Selection.* Cambridge, MA: The MIT Press.

Langdon, W. B. and Poli, R. (1998). Genetic Programming Bloat with Dynamic Fitness, In: Banzhaf, W., Poly, R., Schoenauer, M. and Fogarty, T. (Eds.), *EuroGP'98: First European Workshop on Genetic Programming,* LNCS-1391, Springer, Berlin, 97-112.

Mackey, M. C. and Glass, L. (1977). Oscillation and Chaos in Physiological Control Systems. *Science,* **197**: 287-289.

Merz,C.J. and Murphy,P.M. (1998). UCI Repository of machine learning databases [www.ics.uci.edu/~mlearn/MLRepository.html], Irvine, CA: University of California, Dept. of Information and Computer Science.

Mulloy, B. S., Riolo, R. L. and Savit, R. S. (1996). Dynamics of Genetic Programming and Chaotic Time Series Prediction. In: Koza, J. R., Goldberg, D. E., Fogel, D. E. and Riolo, R. L. (Eds.), *Genetic Programming 1996: Proceedings of the First Annual Conference,* Cambridge, MA: The MIT Press, 166-174.

Nikolaev, N. and Slavov, V. (1998). Concepts of Inductive Genetic Programming, In: Banzhaf, W., Poly, R., Schoenauer, M. and Fogarty, T. (Eds.), *EuroGP'98: First European Workshop on Genetic Programming,* LNCS-1391, Springer, Berlin, 49-59.

Oakley, H. (1994). Two Scientific Applications of Genetic Programming: Stack Filters and Non-linear Equation Fitting to Chaotic Data. In: Kinnear, K. (Ed.), *Advances in Genetic Programming*, Cambridge, MA: The MIT Press, 369-389.

Perelson, A. S. (1989). Immune Network Theory. *Immunological Reviews*, **110**, 5-36.

Press, W. H., Flannery, B. P., Teukolsky, S. A. and Vetterling, W. T. (1992). *Numerical Recipes in C: The Art of Scientific Computing*, 2nd ed., Cambridge, England: Cambridge University Press.

Slavov, V. and Nikolaev, N. (1998). Immune Network Dynamics for Inductive Problem Solving. In: Eiben, A. E., Bäeck, T., Schoenauer, M. and Schwefel, H. P. (Eds.), *Parallel Problem Solving from Nature-PPSN V: 5th International Conference*, LNCS 1498, Springer: Berlin, 712-721.

Smith, R. E., Forrest, S. and Perelson, A. (1993). Searching for Diverse, Cooperative Populations with Genetic Algorithms. *Evolutionary Computation*, **1**(2): 127-149.

Zhang, B. -T., Ohm, P. and Mühlenbein, H. (1997). Evolutionary Induction of Sparse Neural Trees. *Evolutionary Computation*, **5**(2): 213-236.

16　A Self-Tuning Mechanism for Depth-Dependent Crossover

Takuya ITO, Hitoshi IBA and Satoshi SATO

There are three genetic operators: crossover, mutation and reproduction in Genetic Programming (GP). Among these genetic operators, the crossover operator mainly contributes to searching for a solution program. Therefore, we aim at improving the program generation by extending the crossover operator. The normal crossover selects crossover points randomly and destroys building blocks. We think that building blocks can be protected by swapping larger substructures. In our former work, we proposed a depth-dependent crossover. The depth-dependent crossover protected building blocks and constructed larger building blocks easily by swapping shallower nodes. However, there was problem-dependent characteristics on the depth-dependent crossover, because the depth selection probability was fixed for all nodes in a tree. To solve this difficulty, we propose a self-tuning mechanism for the depth selection probability. We call this type of crossover a "self-tuning depth-dependent crossover". We compare GP performances of the self-tuning depth-dependent crossover with performances of the original depth-dependent crossover. Our experimental results clarify the superiority of the self-tuning depth-dependent crossover.

16.1　Introduction

Recently Genetic Programming (GP) has been applied to various applications, e.g., a robot program [Koza, 1992a], a multi-agent task [Iba, 1997] and an image recognition [Iba et al., 1995]. In case of standard GP, it requires huge computational time to search for a solution program of a large scale problem. This is a critical problem when GP is applied to the large scale problem, such as the automatic generation of a practical program.

In many previous studies, it is shown that the crossover and the selection mechanism mainly contribute to generating a solution program in GP [Koza, 1992b, p. 599]. In this paper, we focus on the crossover operator and aim at generating computer programs efficiently by improving the crossover operator. "Efficient" means that reduction of the number of generations required to generate target programs.

A program structure in GP is generally a tree structure [1]. The normal crossover operator selects randomly a crossover point (node) regardless of its position within the tree structure. Thus, if the normal crossover operator destroys building blocks [2], it will result in the degradation of the search for a solution program.

Swapping a larger structure is one way to solve this difficulty. Because building blocks are larger protected by swapping structures. In our previous paper[Ito

---

[1] There are also a linear and a graph structure besides the tree structure[Banzhaf et al., 1998, pp.239–276]

[2] A "building block" is a pattern of genes in a contiguous section of a chromosome which, if present, confers a high fitness to the individual [Langdon, 1998, p. 238]

et al., 1998a], we proposed a "depth-dependent crossover", in which a crossover point is determined by a depth selection probability. The depth selection probability is the probability of selecting a depth to which is applied the crossover operator. The depth selection probability is higher for a node closer to a root node. The depth-dependent crossover protected building blocks and constructed larger building blocks easily by swapping higher nodes frequently. Through the use of the depth-dependent crossover, the computational time for the evolution was decreased for the boolean concept formation problems. However, there is a problem-dependent characteristic for the depth-dependent crossover, because the depth selection probability was fixed and given as a user-defined parameter. This explains why we could not show any advantage for the fitness performance for the ANT problem [Ito et al., 1998a].

We propose a self-tuning mechanism for the depth selection probability to avoid the difficulty mentioned above. We call this type of crossover a "self-tuning depth-dependent crossover". In case of the self-tuning depth-dependent crossover, each individual has a different depth selection probability. The depth selection probability of a selected individual is copied to the next generation. By using the self-tuning depth-dependent crossover, it is not required to set up beforehand the depth selection probability for a particular GP task.

The self-tuning is not necessarily the best strategy. If an optimal depth selection probability was known for one GP problem in advance, setting the optimal depth selection probability would be better than using the self-tuning mechanism. However, we do not know the optimal depth selection probability for each GP problem in general. Thus, it is required to design the self-tuning mechanism for the depth selection probability.

This paper is organized as follows. Section 16.2 explains the self-tuning mechanism for the depth-dependent crossover. Section 16.3 describes experiments in several tasks and compares GP performances of the self-tuning depth-dependent crossover with performances of the original depth-dependent crossover. Discussion is given in Section 16.4, followed by a conclusion and future work in Section 16.5.

16.2   A Self-Tuning Mechanism for Depth-Dependent Crossover

In case of the depth-dependent crossover[3], the depth selection probability is fixed (half of its parent node's probability). It is a user-defined parameter. If the depth selection probability is not set correctly, the crossover operator may not work well.

---

[3]Detailed description of the depth-dependent crossover is given in [Ito et al., 1998a]

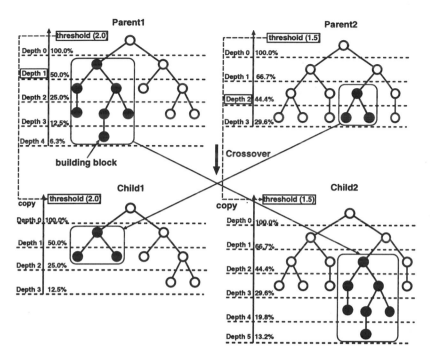

Figure 16.1
Self Tuning without Parameter Crossover. This method copies the depth selection probability of each parent to each child.

To solve this difficulty, we propose a self-tuning mechanism, in which each tree has a different depth selection probability. Then, each crossover point is determined by its depth selection probability. If an individual has a high depth selection probability, it is more likely that the crossover operator will select a shallower node. Therefore, on average, the selected subtrees will be bigger. On the contrary, if an individual has a low depth selection probability, the crossover will select a deeper node. So that, the selected subtrees will be smaller.

It is difficult to evaluate directly whether each depth selection probability is suitable for each tree structure or not. We do not have any evaluation criteria about the depth selection probability for each GP task. A high depth selection probability may be a good setting on one tree structure, whereas, a low depth selection probability may work well for another tree. In this self-tuning mechanism, we hypothesize that if the depth selection probability is effectively assigned to a tree

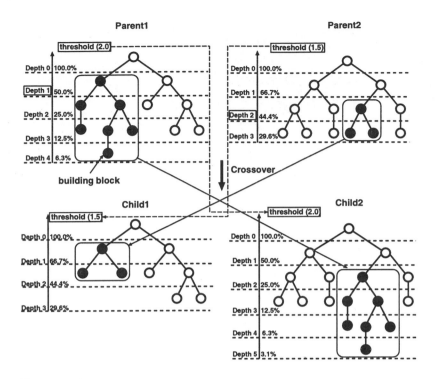

Figure 16.2
Self Tuning with Parameter Crossover. This method also swaps the depth selection probability of each parent when the selected subtrees are swapped.

structure suitably, the fitness of the tree structure is improved. According to this hypothesis, the depth selection probability of a desirable tree will be copied to the next generation. That is, the depth selection probability of the tree structure, which is selected by fitness selection, is also selected and inherited to the next generation. The advantage is that both the depth selection probability and the program fitness (i.e., program performance) are evaluated by means of fitness selection alone.

We introduce two methods for the above purpose. One is to copy the depth selection probability of each parent to each child (Fig. 16.1). Another method is to swap the depth selection probability (Fig. 16.2). In Fig. 16.1, black nodes means building blocks. The crossover point of each tree is determined by each depth selection probability. As a result of the crossover operator, two children with the same depth selection probability as their parents are generated. In case of child 2, if the depth selection probability is not swapped, it is easy to select a node of building blocks (i.e., black nodes) and to break building blocks. Because the depth selection probability of nodes within building blocks are higher (i.e., the probabilities of the depth 3, 4 and 5 are 29.6%, 19.8% and 13.2, respectively). The same is true of child 1 (i.e., the probability of the depth 2 is 25.0%).

In case of Fig. 16.2, the depth selection probability of each parent is also swapped when the selected subtrees are swapped. This method may work effectively for large building blocks. However, it may not be a good strategy for small building blocks. For instance, in case of Fig. 16.2, it is easy to protect building blocks of child 2 by swapping the depth selection probability. Because the depth selection probability of nodes within building blocks are low (i.e., the probabilities of the depth 3, 4 and 5 are 12.5%, 6.3% and 3.1%, respectively). However, in case of child 1, the depth selection probability of the node within a building block is high (i.e., the probability of depth 2 is 44.4%). Large building blocks of child 2 are protected, whereas small building blocks of child 1 are broken. Therefore, the method shown in Fig. 16.2 is a greedy method. We clarify differences of these methods (i.e, Fig. 16.1 and 16.2) in next section.

The above self-tuning mechanism for the depth-dependent crossover is realized as the following algorithm.

Pre-processing Assign a random depth selection probability between *min-probability* and *max-probability* for the tree initialization.

Crossover When applying the crossover operator, the following process is executed:

STEP 1. For parent1, determine the depth d for a selected tree using the depth selection probability of parent1.

STEP 2. For parent1, select randomly a node whose depth is equal to d in STEP1.

STEP 3. For parent2, determine the depth d for a selected tree using the depth selection probability of parent2.

STEP 4. For parent2, select randomly a node whose depth is equal to d in STEP3.

STEP 5. Swap the nodes chosen in STEP2 and STEP4.

STEP 6. Swap the depth selection probability (if the self tuning mechanism conducts parameter crossover, i.e., Fig. 16.2)

Table 16.1
Experimental Set Up

Setting	Crossover	Mutation
NORMAL	Random	Random
DD	Depth-Dependent	Random
SDD	Self-Tuning Depth-Dependent without Parameter Crossover (Fig. 16.1)	Random
SDD-XO	Self-Tuning Depth-Dependent with Parameter Crossover (Fig. 16.2)	Random

Mutation When applying the mutation operator, the following process is executed:

STEP 1. Mutate a selected tree randomly.

STEP 2. Mutate the depth selection probability of the selected tree between *min-probability* and *max-probability*.

We assign *min-probability* to 1.5 and *max-probability* to 2.0 in this paper (i.e., the depth selection probability of each tree ranges from 1.5 to 2.0). The self-tuning mechanism searches better depth selection probability for each tree between *min-probability* and *max-probability*. The mutation of the depth selection probability is to escape from a local minimum for the depth selection probability.

The probability of the crossover (and the mutation) of the depth selection is the same as the probability of the crossover (and the mutation) of the tree structure. This means that the depth selection probability is also swapped when tree structures are swapped with the same probability (the depth selection probability is also mutated when the tree structure is mutated).

16.3 Experimental Results

We have investigated the effectiveness of the self-tuning depth-dependent crossover for four GP problems. These problems are Boolean concept formation problems (i.e., the 11MX and the 4EVEN) the ANT and a robot problem. This section briefly explains the results of the 11MX, the ANT and the robot problem. Complete and detailed experimental results are described in [Ito, 1999]) Table 16.1 shows the experimental set up. For the sake of comparison, all experiments were conducted until a final generation, even if a solution was found during the evolution. Experimental results are shown on the average over twenty runs.

16.3.1 The 11MX problem

The task of the 11MX (11-multiplexor) problem is to generate a boolean function which decodes an address encoded in binary and returns the binary data value of the register at that address. The 11-multiplexor function has three binary-valued address lines (a_0, a_1, a_2) and eight data registers of binary values $(d_0, d_1, \cdots, d_7)$ [Koza, 1992b, p. 170]. The fitness of the 11MX is an error rate for total inputs. The used parameters are the same as [Ito et al., 1998a].

Fig. 16.3 shows the best and the average fitness. Note that the smaller, the better the fitness is. According to the best fitness performance curve, the **DD** shows an ability of which it searches a solution program quickly. The **SDD-XO** is slower than the **DD**, however, the **SDD-XO** shows the same fitness performance to the **DD** at the final generation. There was no difference between the **NORMAL** and the **SDD** on the best fitness. As for the average fitness, the **DD** gives the best performance among all crossover settings. Other three crossover settings show almost the same ability. We statistically examined the best and the average fitness performances at the final generation with the paired t-test [Freund and Wilson, 1992]. Table 16.2 shows the result of t-test. According to this test, we have confirmed that the **DD** was superior to the **NORMAL**, and that the **SDD-XO** was superior to the **NORMAL** in terms of the best and the average fitness values. However, we have not verified that the **SDD** was superior to the **NORMAL** in terms of the best and the average fitness values. Table 16.3 shows average numbers of hits and its standard deviation at the final generations over twenty runs. Note, if the solution program was acquired over twenty runs, the hits value is 1.0. On the contrary, if the solution program was not acquired over twenty runs at all, the value is 0.0. According to this table, both of the **DD** and the **SDD-XO** gave best performance among all crossover settings.

There was no difference between the **SDD-XO** and the **DD** in terms of the best fitness value as mentioned above. An advantage of the **SDD-XO** against the **DD** is to suppress the size of generated programs (i.e. trees). Fig. 16.4, 16.5 and 16.6 plot the depth of the tree, the number of function nodes and the number of terminal nodes with generations for the 11MX problem, respectively. The growth pattern of the tree depth of the **DD** shows the deepest trees among all crossover settings. On the contrary, the pattern of the **SDD-XO** shows the shallower trees than that of the **DD** (Fig. 16.4). The number of function nodes (and terminal nodes) was much larger with **DD** than that with **SDD-XO** (Fig. 16.5 and 16.6). By using the **DD**, a shallower node of the tree structure was selected more frequently. It frequently occurred that a small subtree in the shallower node of the tree structure was replaced

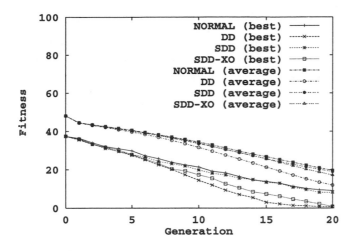

Figure 16.3
Experimental Results, means of twenty runs (11MX). The fitness of the 11MX is an error rate for total inputs. The "Best" means the fitness of best individual and the "average" indicates the average fitness of the population.

with a large subtree. In that case, the fitness of an individual which received a large subtree (individual 1) was improved because there were large building blocks in the received subtree. On the contrary, the fitness of an individual which received a small subtree (individual 2) was not improved because the size of building blocks in the received subtree was small. As a result, the size of the tree structure became large because individual 1 prospered in the population and individual 2 became extinct. Thus, the selection pressure which enlarged the tree size occurred in case of the **DD**. This phenomenon is called *bloat* [Langdon and Poli, 1997]. Angeline clarified that the crossover operator promoted unnecessary bloat by several experimental results [Angeline, 1998]. The **DD** induced the bloating phenomenon easily by means of the above reason.

There was a difference between the **SDD** and the **SDD-XO** in terms of the size of the tree structure. This difference was derived from difference of the depth selection probability of each individual. Fig. 16.7 and 16.8 show transitions of the depth selection probability during the evolution. The numbers of individuals (z axis) are accumulated values over twenty runs. For both cases, i.e., the **SDD** and the **SDD-XO**, the total depth selection probability at the initial generation (i.e.,

Table 16.2
Statistic t for the Best and the Average Fitness Values at the Final Generation (11MX).

Setting	Best	Average
DD (against **NORMAL**)	12.01	10.27
SDD (against **NORMAL**)	0.91	0.77
SDD-XO (against **NORMAL**)	9.91	3.21
SDD (against **DD**)	-11.74	-10.36
SDD-XO (against **DD**)	-0.42	-6.42
SDD-XO (against **SDD**)	12.22	2.62

Table 16.3
Average Numbers of Hits and Its Standard Deviation at the Final Generations over Twenty Runs (11MX). If the solution program was acquired over twenty runs, the hits value is 1.0. On the contrary, if the solution program was not acquired over twenty runs at all, the value is 0.0. Rank indicates a ranking of four crossover operators.

Setting	Hits	Standard Deviation	Rank
NORMAL	0.00	0.00	3
DD	0.70	0.46	1
SDD	0.00	0.00	3
SDD-XO	0.70	0.46	1

generation 0) was nearly same value (approximately 4000). This was because the depth selection probability of each individual was generated randomly. However, the number of individuals of lower depth selection probability was increased during the evolution in case of the **SDD** (Fig. 16.7). This means that crossover points were selected at deeper nodes more often. On the contrary, the depth selection probability became higher during the evolution by the **SDD-XO** (Fig. 16.8). This means that crossover points are often selected at shallower nodes. These phenomena were occurred on the other GP problems, i.e., the 4EVEN, the ANT and the robot problem [Ito, 1999].

The original depth-dependent and the self-tuning depth-dependent crossover have an effect that deep subtrees are swapped more often. This will result in the protection of building blocks. We can consider that the fitness performance may be improved because of this effect on the 11MX problem. Fig. 16.9 shows average absolute depth of swapped tree structures for the 11MX problem. According to this figure, average absolute depth of swapped subtrees for all crossover settings was shallow in the early generations. However, the **DD** swaps deeper subtrees as the evolution proceeds. The **SDD-XO** swapped shallower subtrees than the **DD**. On the contrary, there was no difference between the **SDD** and the **NORMAL**. These

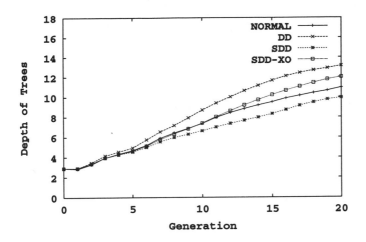

Figure 16.4
Depth of Trees (11MX)

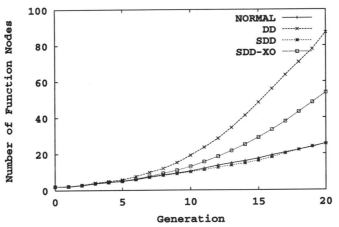

Figure 16.5
Number of Function Nodes (11MX)

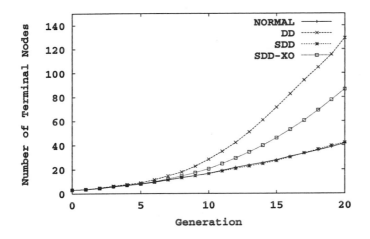

Figure 16.6
Number of Terminal Nodes (11MX)

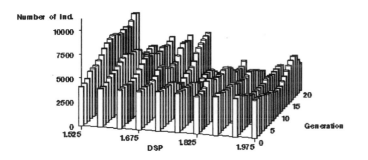

Figure 16.7
Transitions of the Depth Selection Probability (11MX, **SDD**) during the Evolution. DSP means depth selection probability. The numbers of individuals (z axis) are accumulated values over twenty runs.

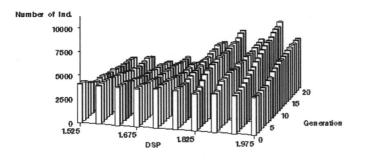

Figure 16.8
Transitions of the Depth Selection Probability (11MX, **SDD-XO**) during the Evolution. DSP means depth selection probability. The numbers of individuals (z axis) are accumulated values over twenty runs.

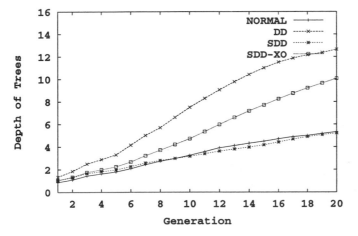

Figure 16.9
Average Absolute Depth of Swapped Tree Structure (11MX)

phenomena are also observed in the numbers of nodes of the swapped subtrees (see [Ito, 1999]). In case of the **DD**, this phenomenon was related to the tree growth and the fixed depth selection probability. In case of the **DD**, the depth selection probability of the crossover operator depended on an absolute tree depth, not a relative tree depth. Besides, the depth selection probability did not changed during the evolution. Due to these two factors, the depth of swapped subtrees became deeper gradually with the growth of the tree structure on the **DD**. A node of which was closer to the root node was selected frequently.

When we compare two particular crossover operators, we have to consider two factors, i.e., the fitness performance and the number of nodes. Even if the fitness is a good performance, we cannot insist that one crossover operator is better if tree structures become large. A large structure requires huge computer memory and computational time [Ito et al., 1998b]. The **DD** gave good performance in terms of the fitness performance, however, it induced the bloat and enlarged the tree structures. On the other hand, the **SDD-XO** did not only improve the fitness performance, but also suppressed the bloat. Thus, we can claim that the **SDD-XO** is superior than the **DD** on the 11MX problem.

16.3.2   The ANT problem

Next, we show experimental results on the ANT problem. The ANT problem is to generate a program to each as much food as possible given a limited amount of energy (400 units) [Koza, 1992b, p. 54]. The ANT can move forward, turn to the right and left. It consumes one unit of energy when it moves. The fitness of the ANT is the fraction of all available food that the ant could not eat. In other words, 1.0 means that the ant could not eat any of the 89 units of foods and 0.0 means that the ant could eat all the food within the limited energy. The used parameters were the same as [Ito et al., 1998a].

It is reported that this problem appears to be difficult because of the large number of sub-optimal peaks in the fitness landscape [Langdon and Poli, 1998] and the depth-dependent crossover was not effective on this problem [Ito et al., 1998a].

We conducted two types of experiments. In the first experiment, the maximum depth for a new tree is 10. In the second experiment, it is 5. We investigated how these different maximum depth values affect the performance of the **DD**, the **SDD** and the **SDD-XO**.

Fig. 16.10 plots the best and the average fitness values for the ANT problem of experiment 1 (i.e., the maximum depth for a new tree was 10). According to this figure, the **SDD-XO** gave the best performance on the best and the average

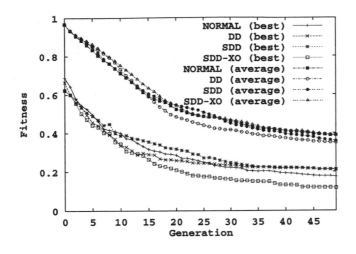

Figure 16.10
Experimental Results, means of twenty runs (ANT, Experiment 1, i.e., the maximum depth for a new tree is 10). The fitness of the ANT is a probability for which the ant could not eat 89 foods. The "Best" means the fitness of the best individual and the "average" indicates the average fitness of the population.

fitness values. On the contrary, there was no difference among the **NORMAL**, the **DD** and the **SDD** on the best fitness value. On the average fitness, there was no difference among all crossover settings. We examined these results using paired t-test and we have confirmed that the **SDD-XO** is superior to the **DD** and the **SDD** on the best value (Table. 16.4). On the hits measure, the **SDD-XO** give the best performance among all crossover settings (Table 16.5).

Fig. 16.11 plots the best and the average fitness values for the ANT problem of experiment 2 (i.e., the maximum depth for a new tree was 5). According to this figure, the **SDD-XO** also gave the best performance on the best fitness values. There was no difference between the **NORMAL** and the **DD** on the best fitness value. On the average fitness, the **SDD** gave the best performance among all crossover settings. We examined these results using paired t-test, and confirmed that the **SDD-XO** was better than the **DD** (Table. 16.4). On the hits measure, the **SDD-XO** gave the best performance among all crossover settings (Table 16.5).

As mentioned above, in case of the **NORMAL**, the number of the hits in experiment 2 (i.e., the maximum depth for a new tree is 5) was improved over experiment

Table 16.4

Statistic t for the Best and the Average Fitness Values at the Final Generation (ANT).

Setting	Experiment 1		Experiment 2	
	Best	Average	Best	Average
DD (against **NORMAL**)	-0.96	1.14	0.29	1.56
SDD (against **NORMAL**)	-0.82	-0.63	1.35	2.61
SDD-XO (against **NORMAL**)	1.34	0.06	1.69	1.26
SDD (against **DD**)	-0.03	-0.16	1.15	1.55
SDD-XO (against **DD**)	2.53	-0.89	1.78	0.09
SDD-XO (against **SDD**)	2.47	-0.90	0.59	-2.46

Table 16.5

Average Numbers of Hits and Its Standard Deviation at the Final Generations over Twenty Runs (ANT). If the solution program was acquired over twenty runs, the hits value is 1.0. On the contrary, if the solution program was not acquired over twenty runs at all, the value is 0.0. Rank indicates a ranking of four crossover operators.

Setting	Experiment 1			Experiment 2		
	Hits	Standard Deviation	Rank	Hits	Standard Deviation	Rank
NORMAL	0.15	0.36	2	0.20	0.40	4
DD	0.10	0.30	3	0.25	0.43	3
SDD	0.10	0.30	3	0.45	0.50	2
SDD-XO	0.35	0.48	1	0.60	0.49	1

1 (i.e., the maximum depth for a new tree is 10). However, these differences were small. In case of the other crossover settings (i.e., the **DD**, the **SDD** and the **SDD-XO**), the number of the hits in experiment 2 was superior to that in experiment 1 (Table 16.5).

These phenomena are related to the growth of the depth of the tree. Fig. 16.12 shows the depth of the tree of experiment 1 and that of experiment 2, respectively. According to this figure, the depth of the tree of experiment 1 was shallower than that of experiment 2 in the early generations. In case of experiment 1, the depth of the tree grows quickly as the evolution proceeds. On the contrary, in case of experiment 2, the depth of the tree became deep slowly during the evolution. At the last generation, the depth of the tree was almost same value (about 15) for both experiments. In case of experiment 2, the crossover operator generated building blocks effectively because the depth of the tree was shallow at early generations. On the contrary, the crossover operator was not so effective for experiment 1 because the initial tree depth was deep. This is a reason that the performances of the **DD**, the **SDD** and the **SDD-XO** are better for experiment 2 than for experiment 1.

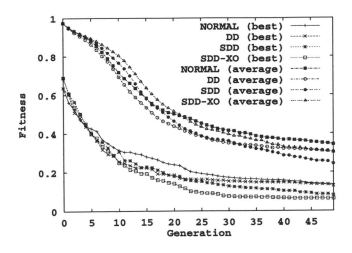

Figure 16.11
Experimental Results, means of twenty runs (ANT, Experiment 2, i.e., the maximum depth for a new tree is 5). The fitness of the ANT is a probability for which the ant could not eat 89 foods. The "Best" means the fitness of the best individual and the "average" indicates the average fitness of the population.

16.3.3 The robot problem

We verified the effectiveness of our proposed crossover operators on a robot problem. This is to show the feasibility of the depth-dependent crossover operators for a real-world task. An autonomous robot simulator was constructed (Fig. 16.13). The model is a behavior-based robot [Maes, 1993]. In this simulator, there are only five types of objects, i.e., the robot, a target object, a station, a wall and obstacles. (Fig. 16.14). The simulated robot has three types of sensors. They are eight bump sensors, an eye sensor and a beacon sensor (Table 16.6).

The robot task is to collect a target object (see [Ito, 1999] for the details). The robot can discriminate between the target object and obstacles by their colors.

As commonly used in most GP applications[Ito et al., 1996], the robot commands were considered as terminals, i.e., 0-argument function (Table 16.7). When each robot command is evaluated, one time-step is consumed and each command is evaluated until the total number of time-steps reaches a certain limitation, or the robot brings a target object to the station correctly. The maximum number of time-steps is set to be 300.

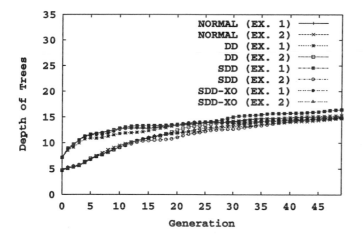

Figure 16.12
Depth of Trees (ANT, Experiments 1 and 2)

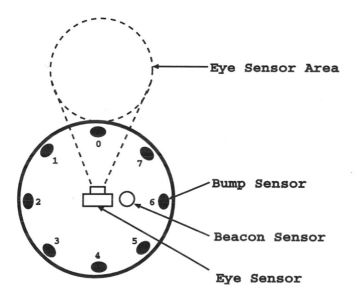

Figure 16.13
The Simulated Robot. The model is a behavior-based robot.

Table 16.6
Sensors of the Simulated Robot

Type	Number	Function
Bumped Sensor	8	Reports whether the robot bumps an object or not.
Eye Sensor	1	Reports the IDs of objects within the eye-sensor area.
Beacon Sensor	1	Reports the distance between the robot and the station when the station is within the robot's sensor range.

Table 16.7
Terminal Set (Robot)

ID	Type	Function
$0 \sim 5$	**GF**	Moves forward with the robot speed in its robot's direction. The robot speed is assumed to be constant.
6	**TR**	Makes the robot's body turn 10° to the right.
7	**TL**	Makes the robot's body turn 10° to the left.
8	**MCR**	Makes the eye sensor turn 10° to the right.
9	**MCL**	Makes the eye sensor turn 10° to the left.
10	**GP**	Grasps the target object within the robot's eye sensor area.

Table 16.8
Function Set (Robot)

ID	Type	Function
$0 \sim 7$	**(BS**ID **p0 p1)**	Evaluates p0 if the bumped ID-sensor reports collision, p1 otherwise.
8	**(AS p0 p1 p2)**	Evaluates p0 if the robot approaches the station, p1 if the robot goes away from the station, and p2 if the station is not within the beacon sensor range.
9	**(EWL p0 p1)**	Evaluates p0 if an wall within the eye-sensor area, p1 otherwise.
10	**(EBC p0 p1)**	Evaluates p0 if the obstacle is within the eye-sensor area, p1 otherwise.
11	**(ERC p0 p1)**	Evaluates p0 if the target object within the eye-sensor area, p1 otherwise.
12	**(ESN p0 p1)**	Evaluates p0 if an station is within the eye-sensor area, p1 otherwise.
13	**(PROG2 p0 p1)**	Evaluates sequentially two argument forms and returns the value of the second argument (p1).

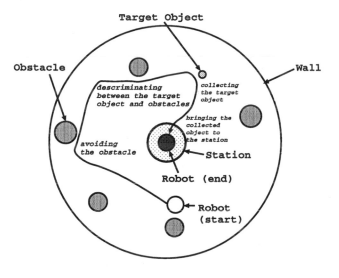

Figure 16.14
The Workspace of the Robot. There are only five types of objects, i.e., the robot, a target object, a station, a wall and obstacles on this workspace.

The robot does not move when **TR**, **TL**, **MCR**, **MCL** and **GP** commands are evaluated. If there is only one **GF** command in the terminal set, the robot will come to a stop too soon (this situation is called deadlock). To prevent this deadlock, the terminal set includes five **GF** commands.

In order to make the robot respond to its sensor inputs, the 14 functional nodes were introduced (Table 16.8).

The following fitness function is used for this robot task:

$$
Fitness = \begin{cases} dist(S, R_t) & \text{if the robot has the} \\ & \text{target object in hand} \\ dist(S, RC_t) + dist(R_t, RC_t) & \text{otherwise} \end{cases} \qquad (16.1)
$$

where S is the position of the station, R_t is the the position of the robot at t time step, RC_t is the the position of the target object at t time step, $dist(x, y)$ is the Euclidean distance between x and y.

Fig. 16.15 plots the best and the average fitness values for the robot problem (the used parameters were the same as [Ito, 1999]). According to this figure, the

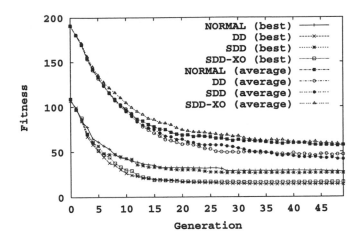

Figure 16.15
Experimental Results, means of twenty runs (Robot). The fitness of the Robot is derived from
equation 16.1. The "Best" means the fitness of the best individual and the "average" indicates
the average fitness of the population.

DD and the **SDD-XO** gave the best performance on the best fitness value. As for
the average fitness value, the **DD** gave the best performance.

Table 16.9 shows the result of t-test. We have confirmed that **DD** and **SDD-XO**
were superior to the **NORMAL** in terms of the best fitness value. On the average
fitness, the **DD** and the **SDD** were better than the **NORMAL**. However, we have
not verified that the **SDD-XO** was superior to the **NORMAL**.

Table 16.10 shows the averaged numbers of hits and its standard deviation at the
final generations over twenty runs. By using the **SDD-XO**, the solution program
was acquired for all twenty runs.

16.4   Discussion

We have hypothesized that, via a self tuning mechanism, if the depth selection
selection probability which is suitable for a tree structure is assigned to the tree
structure, a fitness of the tree structure is improved. We designed our self-tuning
mechanism in accordance with this hypothesis.

Our experimental results have shown that the **SDD-XO** gave good performance

Table 16.9
Statistic t for the Best and the Average Fitness Values at the Final Generation (Robot).

Setting	Best	Average
DD (against NORMAL)	3.34	2.40
SDD (against NORMAL)	0.28	3.15
SDD-XO (against NORMAL)	2.50	-0.09
SDD (against DD)	3.26	1.31
SDD-XO (against DD)	0.87	-2.44
SDD-XO (against SDD)	2.57	-3.43

Table 16.10
Average Numbers of Hits and Its Standard Deviation at the Final Generations over Twenty Runs (Robot). If the solution program was acquired over twenty runs, the hits value is 1.0. On the contrary, if the solution program was not acquired over twenty runs at all, the value is 0.0. Rank indicates a ranking of four crossover operators.

Setting	Hits	Standard Deviation	Rank
NORMAL	0.80	0.40	4
DD	0.95	0.22	2
SDD	0.95	0.22	2
SDD-XO	1.00	0.00	1

for all the four GP problems. For these problems, each individual has various kinds of depth selection probabilities in early generations because the probability was assigned randomly. However, the number of individuals with high depth selection probability increased gradually as the evolution proceeded (Fig. 16.8). As a result, the fitness performance was improved. According to Fig. 16.8, the self-tuning mechanism worked so as to search for building blocks during early generations and to protect completed building blocks in later generations. We believe that the SDD-XO will work for various GP problems due to this effect, i.e., adaptability.

16.5 Conclusion

The goal of this work was to consider an effective search method for applying GP to large scale problems. For this purpose, we proposed the self-tuning depth-dependent crossover. We verified experimentally the effectiveness of the crossover operation. As a result of experiments, the following points have been made clear:

1. The self-tuning depth-dependent crossover worked effectively for various GP problems, i.e., the 11MX, the 4EVEN, the ANT and the robot problem.

2. The self-tuning depth-dependent crossover suppressed the growth of the tree structure.

In this work, a gene structure of GP was a tree. Besides the tree structure, there are a linear and a graph structure [Banzhaf et al., 1998, pp.239–276]. These structures are quite different from the tree structure. The effectiveness of the depth-dependent crossover operations is not clear for these structures. The future research will evaluate depth-dependent crossover on these structures.

Acknowledgments

We would like to thank W. B. Langdon, Una-May O'Reilly and Peter J. Angeline for their helpful comments.

Bibliography

Angeline, P. J. (1998), "Subtree crossover causes bloat," in *Genetic Programming 1998: Proceedings of the Third Annual Conference*, J. R. Koza, W. Banzhaf, K. Chellapilla, K. Deb, M. Dorigo, D. B. Fogel, M. H. Garzon, D. E. Goldberg, H. Iba, and R. Riolo (Eds.), pp 745–752, University of Wisconsin, Madison, Wisconsin, USA: Morgan Kaufmann.

Banzhaf, W., Nordin, P., Keller, R. E., and Francone, F. D. (1998), *Genetic Programming – An Introduction; On the Automatic Evolution of Computer Programs and its Applications*, Morgan Kaufmann, dpunkt.verlag.

Freund, R. and Wilson, W. (1992), *Statistical Methods*, Academic Press, Inc.

Iba, H. (1997), "Multiple-agent learning for a robot navigation task by genetic programming," in *Genetic Programming 1997: Proceedings of the Second Annual Conference*, J. R. Koza, K. Deb, M. Dorigo, D. B. Fogel, M. Garzon, H. Iba, and R. L. Riolo (Eds.), pp 195–200, Stanford University, CA, USA: Morgan Kaufmann.

Iba, H., de Garis, H., and Sato, T. (1995), "Recombination guidance for numerical genetic programming," in *1995 IEEE Conference on Evolutionary Computation*, volume 1, p 97, Perth, Australia: IEEE Press.

Ito, T. (1999), *Efficient Program Generation by Genetic Programming*, PhD thesis, Japan Advanced Institute of Science and Technology, 1-1 Asahidai, Tatsunokuchi, Nomi, Ishikawa, 923-1292 Japan.

Ito, T., Iba, H., and Kimura, M. (1996), "Robustness of robot programs generated by genetic programming," in *Genetic Programming 1996: Proceedings of the First Annual Conference*, J. R. Koza, D. E. Goldberg, D. B. Fogel, and R. L. Riolo (Eds.), Stanford University, CA, USA: MIT Press, 321–326.

Ito, T., Iba, H., and Sato, S. (1998a), "Depth-dependent crossover for genetic programming," in *Proceedings of the 1998 IEEE World Congress on Computational Intelligence*, pp 775–780, Anchorage, Alaska, USA: IEEE Press.

Ito, T., Iba, H., and Sato, S. (1998b), "Non-destructive depth-dependent crossover for genetic programming," in *Proceedings of the First European Workshop on Genetic Programming*, W. Banzhaf, R. Poli, M. Schoenauer, and T. C. Fogarty (Eds.), volume 1391 of *LNCS*, pp 71–82, Paris: Springer-Verlag.

Koza, J. R. (1992a), "Evolution of subsumption using genetic programming," in *Proceedings of the First European Conference on Artificial Life. Towards a Practice of Autonomous Systems*, F. J. Varela and P. Bourgine (Eds.), pp 110–119, Paris, France: MIT Press.

Koza, J. R. (1992b), *Genetic Programming: On the Programming of Computers by Natural Selection*, Cambridge, MA, USA: MIT Press.

Langdon, W. B. (1998), *Data Structures and Genetic Programming: Genetic Programming + Data Structures = Automatic Programming!*, Boston: Kluwer.

Langdon, W. B. and Poli, R. (1997), "Fitness causes bloat," in *Second On-line World Conference on Soft Computing in Engineering Design and Manufacturing*, P. K. Chawdhry, R. Roy, and R. K. Pan (Eds.), Springer-Verlag London.

Langdon, W. B. and Poli, R. (1998), "Why ants are hard," in *Genetic Programming 1998: Proceedings of the Third Annual Conference*, J. R. Koza, W. Banzhaf, K. Chellapilla, K. Deb, M. Dorigo, D. B. Fogel, M. H. Garzon, D. E. Goldberg, H. Iba, and R. Riolo (Eds.), pp 193–201, University of Wisconsin, Madison, Wisconsin, USA: Morgan Kaufmann.

Maes, P. (1993), "Behavior-Based Artificial Intelligence," in *From Animals to Animats 2: Proceedings of the Second International Conference on Simulation of Adaptive Behavior (SAB-92)*, MIT Press.

17 Genetic Recursive Regression for Modeling and Forecasting Real-World Chaotic Time Series

Geum Yong Lee

This chapter explores several extensions to genetic programming for applications involving the forecasting of real world chaotic time series. We first used Genetic Symbolic Regression (GSR), which is the standard genetic programming technique applied to the forecasting problem in the same way that it is often applied to symbolic regression problems [Koza 1992, 1994]. We observed that the performance of GSR depends on the characteristics of the time series, and in particular that it worked better for deterministic time series than it did for stochastic or volatile time series. Taking a hint from this observation, an assumption was made in this study that the dynamics of a time series comprise a deterministic and a stochastic part. By subtracting the model built by GSR for the deterministic part from the original time series, the stochastic part would be obtained as a residual time series. This study noted the possibility that GSR could be used recursively to model the residual time series of rather stochastic dynamics, which may still comprise another deterministic and stochastic part. An algorithm called GRR (Genetic Recursive Regression) has been developed to apply GSR recursively to the sequence of residual time series of stochastic dynamics, giving birth to a sequence of sub-models for deterministic dynamics extractable at each recursive application. At each recursive application and after some termination conditions are met, the sub-models become the basis functions for a series-expansion type representation of a model. The numerical coefficients of the model are calculated by the least square method with respect to the predetermined region of the time series data set. When the region includes the latest data set, the model reflects the most recent changes in the dynamics of a time series, thus increasing the forecasting performance. This chapter shows how GRR has been successfully applied to many real world chaotic time series. The results are compared with those from other GSR-like methods and various soft-computing technologies such as neural networks. The results show that GRR saves much computational effort while achieving enhanced forecasting performance for several selected problems.

17.1 Problem Definition : Data Driven Model Building

The purpose of data driven model building in n-dimensional Euclidean space is to find the function $f : R^n \to R$ where the m data set $(R^n, R)_m$ is known. Rewriting the problem in terms of the time series analysis and forecasting literature [Casdagli 1993], we would like to find the function f in the following equation.

$$
\begin{aligned}
x_w^{(i)} &= f(\mathbf{x}_t^{(i)}) \\
\mathbf{x}_t^{(i)} &= \left(x_t, x_{t-\tau}, x_{t-2\tau}, \ldots, x_{t-(n-1)\tau} \right)^{(i)} \in R^n, and\ x_{t+T} \in R
\end{aligned}
\qquad (17.1)
$$

where $x_{TIME}^{(i)}$ is the time series value of the i-th data set at time *TIME*, t is current time, T is future time (also called lead time or prediction horizon), τ is delay time (also called lag time or lag spacing), and $\mathbf{x}_t^{(i)}$ is delay lag vector. $w = t + T$ is forecast time.

Note that $\mathbf{x}_t^{(i)}$ is a point in the n-dimensional state-space R^n reconstructed from a scalar time series. Pseudo code for the general data driven model building process is

1. Obtain the scalar time series data : x_0, x_1, x_2, ...
2. Analyze the data to get information about reasonable values of T, τ, n
3. Prepare the m data set from the reconstructed n-dimensional state-space, R^n
4. Build the model from the m data set through a method, such as GSR.

It is not guaranteed to obtain reasonable values of T, τ, n; they depend on the characteristics of the data set. Algorithms or methods to determine T, τ, n may be another area of research. Also, it should be noted that R^n should be sufficiently dense (large m) to the extent that time series dynamics is clearly depicted in the space.

17.2   Genetic Symbolic Regression and Data Driven Model Building

In this chapter, GSR is an ad hoc acronym for Genetic Symbolic Regression and refers to the standard genetic programming technique applied to a symbolic regression problem. Symbols may represent either complex concepts or simple values. GSR implements an elaborate set of symbolic operations designed to search possible combinations of symbolic elements, i. e. the *symbol space*, based on the principle of natural selection.

Our problem of finding the functional relationship or model in Eq. (17.1) is none other than finding the appropriate symbolic form through which we can understand and forecast the dynamics carried by the series of data set. GSR helps us in solving the situation that we have no information about the shape and domain of the symbol space, and the meaningful symbolic forms should be found within the limited computational resources.

17.3   A New Algorithm; Genetic Recursive Regression (GRR)

The newly proposed GRR has five (5) major mechanisms that are different from the standard GSR. They are the recursive regression, the series-expansion type representation of a regression model, the multiple populations to efficiently get basis functions of the regression model, the real-time update of the numerical coefficients in the regression model and the extensive use of the derived terminal set.

Figure 17.1 shows the overall flow of the Genetic Recursive Regression. See section 17.3.1 for the concepts and formulation of the recursive regression. Section 17.3.2 addresses how to integrate a regression model based on several basis functions obtained by GSR. Section 17.3.3, 17.3.4 and 17.3.5 address the parallel computational architecture, the adaptation of a model to the latest data and the derived terminal set, respectively.

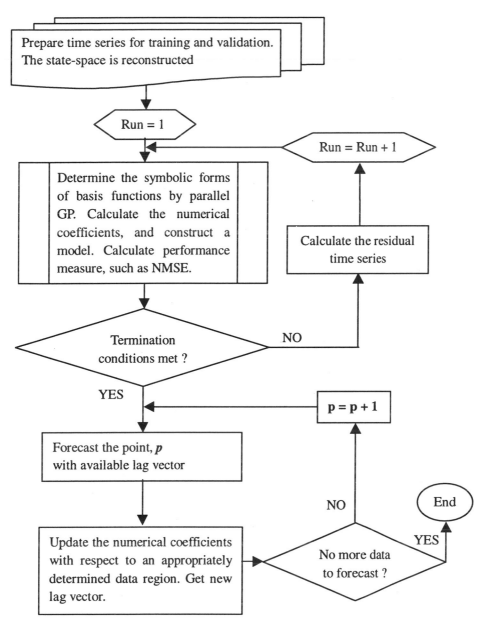

Figure 17.1

The overall flow of the proposed method, GRR to construct a regression model and forecasting with it.

17.3.1 Recursive Regression

It may be practical to assume that real world time series is somewhat deterministic, and somewhat stochastic in its dynamics. If a data set is from a system of purely physical characteristics, e. g. the $NH_3 - FIR$ laser [Hübner 1993], it is usually more deterministic than stochastic. On the other hand, a data set from highly volatile economic system or physiological system is more stochastic than deterministic.

When we tried GSR for various data sets, it was relatively easy to model and forecast deterministic time series than stochastic ones. In this chapter, it was assumed that the governing system dynamics of a given time series is composed of deterministic and stochastic part. That is,

$$f = f_{deterministic} + f_{stochastic} \qquad (17.2)$$

During study, it was confirmed that $f_{deterministic}$ is captured relatively easily at an early stage of GSR application. But, even with much increased computational efforts, it was very difficult to enhance the performance measure. If a data set is highly stochastic or volatile such as the foreign currency exchange rate, even the moderately performing $f_{deterministic}$ could not be obtained.

The solution was the recursive or the *zoom-in* regression. Let's see what this means in more detail. Recursion starts from zooming in on the difference or the residual time series $f - f_{deterministic} = f_{stochastic}$. The phrase 'zoom-in' comes from the fact that the modeling procedure is now applied to the residual time series of which order of magnitude is smaller than that of the original time series. The computational parameters remain unchanged from those used for obtaining $f_{deterministic}$. By the first recursive modeling procedure, we will have another pair of deterministic and stochastic part

$$f_{stochastic} = f_{deterministic}^{(1)} + f_{stochastic}^{(1)} \qquad (17.3)$$

When the desirable level of performance is not reached with the still available computational resources, the modeling procedure is restarted with respect to the residual time series from Eq. (17.3). And the process goes on over and over again.

Now, let v be the number of the applied recursive modeling procedure. Then, the recursive model building procedure is given by

$$f_{stochastic}^{(v)} = f_{deterministic}^{(v+1)} + f_{stochastic}^{(v+1)}, v = 0,1,2,3,... \qquad (17.4)$$

Note that Eq. (17.4) becomes Eq. (17.3) when v is 0. The left-hand-side of Eq. (17.3) is the first residual time series obtained by non-recursive modeling through GSR.

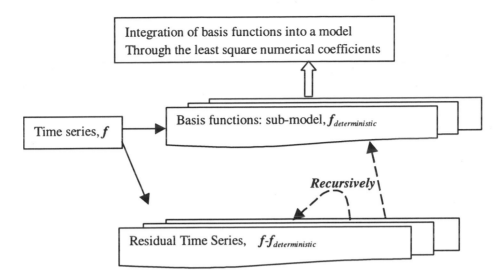

Figure 17.2

The concept of the recursive regression.

Figure 17.2 shows the concept of the recursive regression. $f_{deterministic}^{(0)}$ and $f_{deterministic}^{(v)}$ become basis functions that are to be integrated into a final regression model. See section 17.3.2.

17.3.2 Representation of the Regression Model as a Series Expansion

Usually, the standard GSR produces one symbolic form as a regression model. But, GRR involves several symbolic forms to use in the series-expansion type representation of the regression model.

Now, let $f_{deterministic}^{(0)} = g_1(\mathbf{x})$ be the symbolic form from the first application of the modeling procedure. At this stage, our regression model is written as

$$\alpha_0 + \alpha_1 g_1(\mathbf{x}) \tag{17.5}$$

where the numerical coefficients α_j are obtained by the least square method with respect to the training data set. If the second modeling procedure (= the first recursive regression) produces another symbolic form, say $f_{deterministic}^{(1)} = g_2(\mathbf{x})$, our regression model is now modified to

$$\alpha_0 + \alpha_1 g_1(\mathbf{x}) + \alpha_2 g_2(\mathbf{x}) \tag{17.6}$$

Since the numerical coefficients are re-calculated when there is any new symbolic form, the coefficient symbols in Eq. (17.5) and Eq. (17.6) do not necessarily have the same numerical values. The final representation of our model would be

$$f \cong \alpha_0 + \alpha_1 g_1(\mathbf{x}) + \alpha_2 g_2(\mathbf{x}) + \dots = \sum_j \alpha_j g_j(\mathbf{x}) \tag{17.7}$$

The recursive modeling procedure can be considered as the gradual effort to find basis functions or sub-models $g_j(\mathbf{x})$ for the deterministic behavior remaining in the residual time series, $f_{stochastic}^{(v+1)} = f_{stochastic}^{(v)} - f_{deterministic}^{(v+1)}$.

17.3.3 Parallel Computational Architecture

Since each population can designate the best symbolic form as the model, a modeling procedure will produce only one basis function if it uses only a single population. However, GRR uses multiple populations to produce as many basis functions as there are populations undergoing evolution.

In fact, GRR is based on a parallel architecture to find multiple basis functions in one modeling procedure. Because of the limited computational resources to search the vast symbol space, we can not find a correct symbolic form for the dynamics of a given data set by applying only once the modeling procedure. There will be enormous variations in the attributes of the symbolic forms that are only partially or locally successful for identifying the time series dynamics.

Integration of the various locally successful symbolic forms is done as follows: let P the number of populations, then there will be P symbolic forms found for the first modeling procedure, that is, we have $g_{1,1}(\mathbf{x})$, $g_{1,2}(\mathbf{x}), g_{1,3}(\mathbf{x}), \dots$, $g_{1,P}(\mathbf{x})$. With these, the parallel version of Eq. (17.7) is

$$\alpha_0 + \sum_{p=1}^{P} \alpha_{1,p} g_{1,p}(\mathbf{x}) \tag{17.8}$$

And the final regression model can be rewritten as

$$f \cong \alpha_0 + \sum_{j=1}^{J} \sum_{p=1}^{P} \alpha_{j,p} g_{1,p}(\mathbf{x}) \tag{17.9}$$

In Eq. (17.8) and Eq. (17.9), the first subscripts stand for the modeling procedure, and the second subscripts stand for the number of the population.

There is a point to note for determining a basis function in Eq. (17.9). The best individual from a population replaces an existing individual of a special population called *super population* at each generation if and only if its fitness excels that of the individual being replaced. Otherwise, it is simply discarded. The number of the best individuals in the super population remains unchanged.

No individuals of the super population are engaged in the evolutionary processes of the *ordinary populations*. Only the individuals that survived the whole generations can become the basis functions in Eq. (17.9). In this context, the super population is different from something like the *multi-agent team* , e.g. [Luke 1996]; agents or team members are somehow engaged in the evolutionary processes. See section 17.4.2 for more detail.

17.3.4 Adaptive Update of the Numerical Coefficients.

Once the basis functions along with numerical coefficients are determined with respect to the training data set, the modeling procedure is over. An ideal model may be the one that forecasts data for any region of the given time series. However, usually our model is far from the ideal one for several reasons. For example, the limited number of data in the training region may not contain sufficient information to build an ideal model. Moreover, the dynamics of real world chaotic time series are generally largely time dependent.

Therefore, the forecasting performance of a model becomes poorer for a region that is distant from the training region. The simplest way to achieve forecasting performance in the remote region as good as those attainable for the training region may be to build a new model using the latest data region as a new training region. But the new model should be built in time to become a meaningful forecaster for the given time series.

This chapter explores more timesaving approach. The numerical coefficients are updated adaptively with respect to the newly available data set, so that as much latest information as possible is reflected in the model to enhance the forecasting performance. This may correspond to tuning up or adaptation of the existing model to the latest system dynamics.

17.3.5 Derived Terminal Set

An arbitrary function can be expressed as a series expansion with the basis orthogonal functions and the corresponding numerical coefficients. Taking a hint from this fact, we introduce a derived terminal set (DTS) and examine whether it can contribute to improving performance of a regression model when the model is expressed as a series expansion, like Eq. (17.9). DTS is obtained by applying an orthogonal function to a state-space coordinate variable x_j .

$$T = [T_i(x_t),\ \ T_i(x_{t-\tau}),\ \ T_i(x_{t-2\tau}),\ \ ...,\ \ T_i(x_{t-(n-1)\tau})] \tag{17.10}$$

where $T_i(x_j)$ is, in this chapter, $T_{i,j} = \cos[i \times \arccos(x_j)]$ or the Tschebyshev function of order i applied to the state-space coordinate variable x_j. We include DTS above in the terminal set along with the set of the normal state-space coordinate variables, $x_t, x_{t-\tau}, x_{t-2\tau}, ..., x_{t-(n-1)\tau}$ and a terminal which generates a random number between 0.0 and 1.0.

17.4 Implementation Issues

17.4.1 Fitness Assignment

Each symbolic form, i.e. individual in a population is assigned a value called *the fitness,* which measures how well the symbolic form fits the data set. In this chapter, the fitness value is the inverse of either NMSE (Normalized Mean Squared Error) or CV (Coefficient of Variation) calculated with respect to a predetermined subset, i.e. a region of the given time series. They are defined by

$$CV(\rho) = \frac{1}{\bar{x}} \left[(1/\rho) \sum_{i=1}^{\rho} \left(x^{(i)} - \tilde{x}^{(i)} \right)^2 \right]^{\frac{1}{2}} \tag{17.11}$$

$$NMSE(\rho) = \frac{\sum_i \left(x^{(i)} - \tilde{x}^{(i)} \right)^2}{\sum_i \left(x^{(i)} - \bar{x} \right)^2} \approx \frac{1}{\hat{\sigma}^2} \frac{1}{\rho} \sum_i \left(x^{(i)} - \tilde{x}^{(i)} \right)^2 = \frac{1}{\hat{\sigma}^2} MSE \tag{17.12}$$

where $\tilde{x}^{(i)}$, $x^{(i)}$ are the predicted and the observed numerical values for the i-th datum. $\bar{x}$ and $\hat{\sigma}^2_\Omega$ denote the sample average and sample variance of the observed values in the predetermined subset of data [Weigend 1993]. ρ is the number of data points over which CV or NMSE is calculated. *MSE* stands for Mean Squared Error.

17.4.2 Super Population and Migration between Multiple Populations

By the evolutionary processes, we hope there is an overall increase in the performance or the fitness. But, also true is that good enough attributes (= structures and contents of symbolic forms) in one generation might be subject to destruction later through the blind application of the genetic symbolic operations. So, there is a need to keep the good enough attributes safely.

In addition to multiple populations undergoing evolution, GRR has a special-purpose population called the super population of which sole service is to store desirable attributes.

At the end of each generation, the best symbolic form is selected from each evolving populations. The size of the super population is equal to the number of such *ordinary* populations. Once the super population is full at a generation, any newly selected symbolic form after the generation is allowed to replace the existing one in the super population if and only if its fitness excels that of at least one individual in the super population.

No individuals at a generation in the super population are transferred to or *injected into* the ordinary populations; they only represent the best individuals that survived up to the generation. This means that they do not involve themselves in the evolutionary processes of the ordinary populations. Therefore, we should differentiate the super population from the concept of elitism [Goldberg 1989]. An elite individual or the multi-agent team member [Luke 1996] is somehow engaged in the evolutionary processes.

Obviously, we need to avoid any semantic replication in the super population. For example, $(+ x_3 (\sin (/ x_1 x_1)))$ is an example of semantic replications possible for $(+ x_3 (\sin 1.0)) = x_3$. Individuals of the super population after the last generation become the basis functions, Eq. (17.9). If there is any semantic replication among basis functions, it should be avoided before computing the numerical coefficients.

After operations to breed offspring are over, migrations occur between the ordinary popluations. In this chapter, the total number of migration operation is fixed to 1 % of the total number of individuals in all populations. Single migration is based on four random numbers. The first and second ones are to identify two populations between which a migration operation occurs. The third random number is compared with the migration probability, 0.02 here. The fourth random number is to identify an individual to replace. No migration to and from the super population is allowed.

17.4.3 Dealing with Absurd Attributes of a Symbolic Form

Symbolic forms sometimes contain mathematically or computationally absurd or nonsense attributes. Division-by-zero or negative values given to a function which requires only positive argument(s) results in the mathematical absurdity. Computational absurdity occurs when the attributes result in overflow or underflow for given computing systems.

For these cases, the numerical equivalent of the attributes is arbitrarily given, and the performance measures of the symbolic form are reduced by one hundred (100) times. This policy gives a definite penalty to the symbolic form for having the absurdity. By the reduced performance measures, their chances of being selected as parents to breed offspring become very small.

17.4.4 Division of the Data Set: Training, Validation and Prediction Regions

There are three regions in the time series data. That is, T, V, and P regions. The region T is called the "training region", and comes first. Symbolic forms are constructed through the application of the evolutionary symbolic computation with respect to the region T.

Coming next is the V region or the "validation region". When a regression model captures spurious information in the T region such as noise, the forecasting performance becomes low in the "prediction" or P region even if its performance in the T region was high. The problem is termed as *over-fitting*. See [Zhang 1993], [Smith 1993] for details. To prevent the over-fitting or over-training, the performance of any model constructed by the training data is evaluated with respect to the validation region.

When the validation performance deteriorates as compared to that in the former modeling procedure, the modeling procedure stops on the assumption that the model has started to capture spurious or excessive information such as noise or disturbance. This is the so-called *early stopping policy* [Geman 1992]. Also see [Weigend 1991].

The last region is called the "prediction" or P region. And, it is the region where the real effectiveness of the constructed model is manifested. Unless otherwise specified, the number of data points in T, V, and P region was 200, 100, 100 respectively for all time series that were applied in this chapter.

17.4.5 Termination Conditions

There may be two kinds of termination conditions. One is set by the limit on the computational resources; after the predetermined number of the generation is passed, the process of searching attributes of symbolic forms is terminated. The other one is natural; if the desired level of model performance, i.e. the performance criteria is achieved, there is no need to continue. For example, if NMSE or CV is 0.01 for a given data set, the model is sufficiently good and the modeling procedure stops. Deterioration in the validation performance also stops the procedure, see section 17.4.4.

17.4.6 Some Manipulations on the Raw Data

A DTS element $T_i(x_j)$ of Eq. (17.10) is defined on the interval $[-1, 1]$. Therefore, the raw interval or $[minimum, maximum]$ of any state-space coordinate variable x_j should be modified to $[-1, 1]$. It is done by the following equation.

$$y_j = ax_j + b, \quad a = \frac{2}{\left(x_j^{n-\max} - x_j^{n-\min}\right)}, \quad b = -\left(1 + \frac{2x_j^{n-\min}}{\left(x_j^{n-\max} - x_j^{n-\min}\right)}\right) \quad (17.13)$$

Then, $T_i(x_j) \Rightarrow T_{i,j} = \cos[i \times \arccos(y_j)] = \cos[i \times \arccos(ax_j + b)]$. The minimum and maximum values of the raw data, $x_j^{n-\min}$ and $x_j^{n-\max}$, should be determined for all regions of a data set. If they are determined only for the training region, values less than $x_j^{n-\min}$ or greater than $x_j^{n-\max}$ result in values less than -1 or values greater than 1, respectively, by Eq. (17.13). This situation causes mathematical absurdities. See section 17.4.3.

Let $x_j^{\min}$ and $x_j^{\max}$ be the minimum and the maximum of the variable x_j encountered in the training region. In this chapter, they are expanded by the following equations.

$$x_j^{n-\min} = x_j^{\min} - \eta(x_j^{\max} - x_j^{\min}) = (1+\eta)x_j^{\min} - \eta x_j^{\max}$$
$$x_j^{n-\max} = x_j^{\max} + \eta(x_j^{\max} - x_j^{\min}) = (1+\eta)x_j^{\max} - \eta x_j^{\min} \qquad (17.14)$$

Therefore, the expanded effective interval $[x_j^{n-\min}, x_j^{n-\max}]$ is $2\eta + 1$ times broader than the raw $[x_j^{\min}, x_j^{\max}]$. In this chapter, the expansion ratio is arbitrarily set to $\eta = 2$.

17.5 Application to Real World Chaotic Time Series

17.5.1 Benchmarking

GRR was benchmarked with respect to three points of view. The effects of introducing DTS are not mentioned in this benchmarking, but discussed in the next section where GRR is applied to more stochastic time series. See section 17.5.2.2. We can see evident effects of DTS for stochastic time series. The three points of view are

1. How effective is the adaptive update of the numerical coefficients; for this, a new terminology "impact step" is introduced. The impact step γ is the number of data points between the data point to predict and the last data point of the region with respect to which the coefficients are updated. To predict x_t, the numerical coefficients in Eq. (17.7) or Eq. (17.9) are updated with data $x_{t-\gamma-200} \sim x_{t-\gamma}$. The performance was observed with $\gamma = 1, \quad 2, \quad 4, \quad 6, \quad 8, \quad 12, \quad 15, \quad 20, \quad 30, \quad 40$.
2. How effective is the parallel architecture; this was assessed by comparing the performances from single population with those from multiple populations.
3. How effective is the recursion; this was assessed by observing the performances with and without recursive regression.

17.5.1.1 Data and Computational Settings

For the benchmarking purpose, the time series data set generated by solving the Mackey-Glass equation was used, [Oakeley 1994]. The Mackey-Glass equation simulates the nonlinear dynamics of the human blood flow, and is written by

$$\frac{dx_t}{dt} = \frac{bx_{t-\Delta}}{1+\left(x_{t-\Delta}\right)^c} - ax_t \qquad \Rightarrow \qquad x_{t+1} = x_t + \frac{bx_{t-\Delta}}{1+\left(x_{t-\Delta}\right)^c} - ax_t \qquad (17.15)$$

In Eq. (17.15), the constants are a = 0.1, b = 0.2, c = 10, and Δ = 30. To generate time series, the first 40 random seeds are prepared in the range [0.5, 1.5]. For the numerical values after the *40*-th datum, Eq. (17.15) was used.

GRR was benchmarked with three groups of computations. Each group has ten (10) computations, identified by ID's like *c##* where ## is the computation number. See Table 17.1 for details. The total number of symbolic forms allowed is 4500 in all computations, *c1 ~ c30*, for the sake of fair evaluation of the three points of view. Early termination could reduce the number. For the division of the data set, see section 17.4.4.

17.5.1.2 Benchmarking Results and Discussion

We applied GRR ten times for each computations *c1 ~ c30*. And the best model from a computation was taken for inter-comparisons between *c1 ~ c30*.

Effects of the Adaptive Update of the Numerical Coefficients

The allowed number of modeling procedures was 5; the first modeling procedure followed by four recursive modeling procedures. Note that all applications of GRR to the first group computations, *c1 ~ c10*, stopped only after the first recursion because the termination condition of NMSE (0.01 in the region *T*) had been met.

The performances of the best models in each computation are summarized in Table 17.2. Each numerical entry represents the NMSE value after the first recursion. First, observe the remarkable performance for every computation. The model was almost exact in capturing the dynamics carried by the time series data.

Table 17.1
Computational settings for benchmarking purpose, see section 17.5.1. There are three computation groups. For parameters that are not specified in this table, see Table 17.6.

	1st Group	2nd Group	3rd Group
Computation ID	*c1 ~ c10*	*c11 ~ c20*	*c21 ~ c30*
No. of Runs allowed	5	5	1
Population Size	15	30	30
No. of Populations	5	1	5
Generation Limit	12	30	30
Description	Recursion with multiple populations	Recursion with single population	No recursion with multiple populations

Table 17.2

NMSE values from the 1st group computations, see Table 17.1. γ is the impact step, section 17.5.1. In this table, NT = NMSE in Region T, NV = NMSE in Region V, NP = NMSE in Region P; Section 17.4.4

	c1	c2	c3	c4	c5	c6	c7	c8	c9	c10
γ	1	2	4	6	8	12	15	20	30	40
NT	0.00345	0.00767	0.00437	0.00345	0.00767	0.00437	0.01083	0.00586	0.00345	0.00767
NV	0.00526	0.01038	0.00401	0.00563	0.01100	0.00407	0.01378	0.01027	0.00493	0.01071
NP	0.00203	0.01060	0.00419	0.00228	0.01216	0.00450	0.00913	0.00544	0.00195	0.00693

Since the first group computations stopped only after the first recursive modeling procedure, the computational effort was only 1800 = the consumed modeling procedure 2 × the number of populations 5 × the population size 15 × the number of generation 12.

Although the performances vary with the computations: 0.00345 (*c1*, *c4*, *c9*), 0.00437 (*c3*, *c6*), 0.00586 (*c8*), 0.00767 (*c2*, *c5*, *c10*), and 0.01083 (*c7*), we can see that the better the performance in the training region, the better the performances in the validation and the prediction region.

Eq. (17.15) shows that the dictating variables are x_{t-1} and x_{t-30}. It is interesting to note that the impact step γ of 1 and 30 (*c1* and *c9*) resulted in the highest performances in all data regions. These observations with respect to the impact step γ were generally true for both the second group of computations (*c11* ~ *c20*) and the third group of computations (*c21* ~ *c30*).

Effects of the Parallel Architecture

The effectiveness of the parallel architecture or the multiple populations can be seen by comparing the performances between the first group computations (*c1* ~ *c10*) and the second group computations (*c11* ~ *c20*). Again, only the best models from each computations of the second group were taken for comparisons. Table 17.3 summarizes the comparison.

Except the row for γ, each entry represents a relative value between the two groups. Now, let NMSE (*c##*, *D*) represent the NMSE obtained in *c##* for the data region *D*. Then, the entry in the row *Ratio of NT* crossing the column *c11 vs. c1* is the NMSE (*c11*, *T*) divided by NMSE (*c1*, *T*).

Except the impact steps of 2, 8, 15, 20 and 40, the ratios of *NT*, *NV* and *NP* are greater than 1.0. To take the computational efforts (CE) into account, the ratios of *NT*, *NV* and *NP* should be multiplied by *Ratio of* CE. They become greater than 1.0 except the impact step of 15 and 40. This means that the NMSE values are larger in the second group computations than those in the first group computations.

Table 17.3

Performance comparisons between the 1st and 2nd group computations, see Table 17.1. Effects of the parallel computational architecture can be seen. CE (Computational Efforts) is the total number of symbolic forms evaluated to make a model.

2nd Group →	c11	c12	c13	c14	c15	c16	c17	c18	c19	c20
vs.	vs.	vs.	vs.	vs.	vs.	vs.	vs.	vs.	vs.	vs.
1st Group →	c1	c2	c3	c4	c5	c6	c7	c8	c9	c10
γ	1	2	4	6	8	12	15	20	30	40
Ratio of **CE**	2	2	2	2	2	2.5	1	2.5	2	1
Ratio of *NT*	1.61	0.63	3.56	2.74	0.93	3.90	0.6	0.97	1.57	0.73
Ratio of *NV*	1.80	0.80	5.13	2.36	0.85	4.60	0.88	0.43	2.00	0.83
Ratio of *NP*	4.58	0.50	4.20	3.16	0.55	3.70	0.81	0.92	3.90	0.66

Effects of the Recursive Model Building

As discussed earlier, GRR allows multiple modeling procedures. The first modeling procedure is just a standard GSR. But, from the second modeling procedure, the modeling procedure can be considered as the recursive procedure. See Eq. (17.2) ~ Eq. (17.4), and Figure 17.2. To see how effective the recursive modeling procedure is, the model performances with and without recursion are compared in Table 17.4 between the first group and the third group computations.

The large values of the ratios of *NT*, *NV* and *NP* in this table show that NMSE's are much smaller in the first group computations as compared to those in the third group computations. Since no recursive modeling procedure is allowed in the third group computations, these enhanced performances, i.e. smaller NMSE's must come from the recursive modeling procedures.

Table 17.4

Performance comparisons between the 1st and 3rd group computations, see Table 17.1. Effects of the recursive model building can be clearly seen.

3rd Group →	c21	c22	c23	c24	c25	c26	c27	c28	c29	c30
vs.	vs.	vs.	vs.	vs.	vs.	vs.	vs.	vs.	vs.	vs.
1st Group →	c1	c2	c3	c4	c5	c6	c7	c8	c9	c10
γ	1	2	4	6	8	12	15	20	30	40
Ratio of **CE**	2.5	2.5	2.5	2.5	2.5	2.5	2.5	2.5	2.5	2.5
Ratio of *NT*	4.95	3.77	3.91	4.95	13.9	24.5	1.58	2.91	4.95	13.9
Ratio of *NV*	3.28	2.98	4.49	3.24	11.3	29.7	1.26	1.59	3.34	9.90
Ratio of *NP*	7.00	2.75	3.54	6.55	4.43	12.1	1.56	2.53	6.08	5.55

When we take the ratios of the computational efforts into account, the ratios of *NT*, *NV* and *NP* become even greater; they should be multiplied by the entries in the corresponding columns crossing the row *Ratio of* **CE**. Also note that the recursive modeling procedure is much more effective than the parallel computational architecture; compare the foregoing two tables concerning them.

17.5.2 Real World Chaotic Time Series

17.5.2.1 Data and Computational Settings

The Complex Systems Summer School at the Santa Fe Institute planned a competition for time series analysis and prediction in the summer of 1990. Among the vast library of time series data, five representative data sets were selected and distributed through ftp for competition participants who used their own methods to predict designated hidden region. The data are available from ftp.santafe.edu/pub/Time-Series. [Weigend 1993] discusses the results and various methods used by successful participants of *Santa Fe Competition.*

ASHRAE (American Society for Heating, Refrigerating, and Air-conditioning Engineers) held a seminar on June 1993, Denver, Colorado to discuss and award the results of *ASHRAE Competition.*

For the competition, a vast range of time series data for weather and actual energy consumption such as electricity or hot water in a building is given to participants. See ftp.cs.colorado.edu/pub/energy-shootout for more details. Table 17.5 lists the data sources from Santa Fe and ASHRAE competitions.

In table 17.5, the data for intensity fluctuation of the far infra red NH_3 laser and for the surface brightness of a white dwarf star, PG1195 were generated from physics system, and they were analyzed to be rather deterministic or stationary. Other data are more stochastic or non-stationary. At the stochastic extreme is the currency exchange rate. [Weigend 1993] discusses the data characteristics in more detail.

For most time series data sets, the competitions required to use *the runaway extension* of the forecast data. The runaway extension means that the long-term forecasts should be based on the lag vectors available from the short-term forecasts by the same forecasters.

The performance measures from GRR are based on *the update extension* [Smith 1993] of the forecast data, in which the future forecast extension is free to use the true time series available up to the time that is T steps past from the data point to forecast.

Computational settings for this section are summarized in Table 17.6. Note that the crossover operation was allowed at any points in a tree. For mutation, a terminal symbol was simply replaced with another terminal symbol, and a function symbol was replaced with another function symbol that requires same number of arguments.

Table 17.5
This study uses time series data from Santa Fe [Weigend 1993] and ASHRAE competitions, section 17.5.2.1

Sources	Data	Description
ASHRAE Competition	Solar flare flux	Solar beam isolation flux data measured with respect to five different solar positions were given in the competition
	WBEC	Data for the whole energy-consumption data in a building (WBEC) and for the weather data outside the building were given
Santa Fe Competition	Laser intensity	Intensity fluctuation of the far infra red NH_3 laser. The data were analyzed to be deterministic since
	Heart rate of a human patient	Time series data for the heart rate, chest volume, blood oxygen concentration and EEG of a patient. Only the heart rate data were tackled in this study
	Currency exchange rate	Currency exchange rate between Swiss franc vs. US $. The data are highly non-stationary or stochastic.
	Particle position	Time-dependent position of a quantum particle in 4D potential well
	Star	Time series data observed for surface brightness of a white dwarf star, PG1195. The data are also deterministic

Table 17.6
Computational settings for genetic programming paradigm and time series modeling. See section 17.4 for other implementation issues of GRR. One run means either standard GSR or recursive GSR. If any termination condition, section 17.4.5, has been met, the actual number of run becomes smaller than that given here.

Settings for genetic programming paradigm	Number of populations	5
	Population size	30
	Generation limit	9
	Number of runs	5
	Function set	$+,-,\times,/,sin,cos,exp,log,expt$
	Terminal set	State-space coordinate variables, DTS,
	Crossover fraction	0.8
	Depth of a tree	Initial 6, after-crossover 18
	Mutation fraction	0.1
	Reproduction fraction	0.1
	Migration probability	0.02
	Migrating individuals	1% of total individuals
Settings for time series modeling	Terminating NMSE	0.01
	Delay time	1
	Lag time	1
	Embedding dimension	1 or 4
	Number of data points	400
	Data region T	First 200 data
	Data region V	Next 100 data after region T
	Data region P	Last 100 data after region V

17.5.2.2 Results and Discussion

Depending on the characteristics of the time series data set, the computational efforts and the obtained performances were quite different. For example, the solar beam isolation flux and the fluctuations in the laser intensity were relatively easy to model and predict. That is, higher performance was possible with smaller computational efforts. The highly stochastic or volatile time series were very difficult.

Table 17.7 summarizes NMSE's obtained by GRR with the computational settings given in Table 17.6. The impact step was 1. For ASHRAE Competition, *Multivariate* means the usual time series modeling and forecasting problem, Eq. (17.1) for each time series, e.g. the solar beam isolation flux. This multivariate problem was not required in the ASHRAE Competition.

The competition required only the univariate analysis; see section 17.5.2.1 for details. n stands for the usual embedding dimension. The names of the time series data sets are reduced ad hoc for formatting purpose. See section 17.5.2.1 for details on them. We can see that the stochastic time series such as the human patient heart rate, the currency exchange rate, etc are much more difficult to tackle.

For stochastic data, the large embedding resulted in poorer performance while the performances generally improved for deterministic data. Simplistically assumed values of n, τ and T might have caused much more uncertainties for stochastic time series. We suspect that, with no correct information about n, τ and T available, a model based on smaller embedding dimension could be better for highly non-stationary dynamics.

Table 17.7

Summary of GRR application to real world chaotic time series data sets.

Time Series			*NT*	*NV*	*NP*
ASHRAE Competition (CV)	Solar	Multivariate	0.005	0.001	0.002
		Univariate	0.008	0.024	0.017
	WBEC	Multivariate	0.032	0.039	0.054
		Univariate	0.004	0.003	0.018
Santa Fe Competition (NMSE)	Laser	$n = 1$	0.007	0.018	0.015
		$n = 4$	0.0014	0.0027	0.0043
	Heart	$n = 1$	0.0654	0.1895	0.1651
		$n = 4$	0.1783	0.2587	0.3547
	Currency	$n = 1$	1.542	1.666	1.247
		$n = 4$	8.364	7.878	15.39
	Particle	$n = 1$	0.0233	0.0325	0.0756
		$n = 4$	0.6986	0.3544	0.1543
	Star	$n = 1$	0.0055	0.0075	0.0331
		$n = 4$	0.0016	0.0013	0.0017

Table 17.8
NMSE values with and without the derived terminal set, DTS. DTS has positive effects in particular on stochastic time series such as the heart rate and the currency exchange rate.

Time Series		NMSE (100) , Region P	
		Without DTS	With DTS
ASHRAE Competition	Solar	0.002	0.002
	WBEC	0.021	0.018
Santa Fe Competition	Laser ($n = 4$)	0.0042	0.0043
	Heart rate ($n = 1$)	8.021×10^6	0.1651
	Currency ($n = 1$)	35.887	1.247
	Particle ($n = 1$)	12.543	0.0756
	Star ($n = 4$)	0.0035	0.0017

Effects of the Derived Terminal Set (DTS)

To see the effects of DTS, GRR was applied to each of the time series used in section 17.5.1 and 17.5.2 with and without DTS. Table 17.8 shows selected results.

Observe that DTS has minimal effects for the deterministic time series. For the stochastic time series, DTS has positive effects, improving the performance measures. It may be temporarily safe to say that DTS does contribute to the model performances. The reasons why DTS has positive effects on the stochastic time series are not clear yet. Various kinds of DTS should be examined to have a conclusion.

17.5.3 Comparisons with Earlier Works

17.5.3.1 ASHRAE and Santa Fe Competitions

The model's forecasting performance recordings for the two time series data sets from each competition are compared with those of the best winners in the ASHRAE and Santa Fe Competitions, and summarized in the following table. The performance measures for comparisons were calculated for the same number of prediction data points.

Recall that GRR proposed here is based on the update extension while the very most participants used the runaway extension methods. Direct comparisons based on the runaway extension are topics for further study.

With the simplistic assumptions on the characteristics of time series and the small quantity (200) of data used to build a model, the runaway extension method is not applicable. As [Smith 1993] showed, the runaway extension is best successful when there is a sufficient data to build a dense state-space [Kailath 1980]. Coarsely reconstructed state-space, as was done in this study, results in the poor forecasts especially for stochastic time series. Table 17.9 is only for numerical comparisons between the best winners of the competitions and GRR.

Table 17.9

NMSE values for four time series data. Recall that the competitions required the runaway extension of the forecast data while GRR in this study was based on the update extension. See [Smith 1993].

	Time Series	Best Winner	This Study (GRR)
ASHRAE	Solar Beam Isolation Flux	0.0240	0.002
Competition	WBEC	0.14084	0.01804
Santa Fe	Intensity of the laser light	0.023	0.00433
Competition	Position of the quantum particle	0.086	0.0756

The performance measure for the first two time series was CV, and was NMSE for the last two times series. Numerically, it seems that GRR outperforms the best winners of the two competitions. However, it might be misleading at this stage if we say that GRR is superior to the methods used in the competitions, e. g. the highly sophisticated neural networks developed by Eric A. Wan [Wan 1993], the best winner of Santa Fe competition.

17.5.3.2 Mackey-Glass Equation

[Casdagli 1989], [Oakeley 1994] and [Iba 1994] also used the time series generated from Mackey-Glass equation, Eq. (17.15) to test their methods. The results by GRR were compared with those earlier works. See Table 17.10. Except the number of data points, computational settings were same as those used for section 17.5.2.

Since each of the earlier works used different performance measures, the performance measure NMSE of this study were converted to the corresponding performance measures. In Table 17.10, *GRR-c* is a variant of GRR. That is, the numerical coefficients obtained with respect to the region T are used to predict the time series. No adaptive update of the numerical coefficients is made.

Table 17.10

Comparisons of NMSE's between the works by Casdagli, Oakeley, and GRR. For the numerical values, See Table 17.4, p. 386 of [Oakeley 1994]. GRR-c stands for the constant-coefficient version of GRR. We can see that GRR-c and GRR worked better than earlier works. Comparing GRR-c and GRR reveals that the adaptive update of the numerical coefficients in Eq. (17.7) and (17.9) does improve the forecast performances.

Performance	Earlier works		This study	
Measures	[Casdagli 1989]	[Oakeley 1994]	GRR-c	GRR
NMSE(20)	0.0631	0.0311	0.0247	0.0187
NMSE(30)	0.1585		0.069	0.0085
NMSE(40)	0.316	0.158	0.181	0.0039
NMSE(50)	0.631	0.371	0.258	0.0025
NMSE(60)	0.990	0.6170	0.266	0.0046

See how much the performance was improved with GRR. Moreover, the computational efforts in the earlier works were much more than GRR. The computational efforts for GRR was only 5 (Number of populations) × 2 (Number of Modeling Procedure consumed; allowed was 5)× 30 (Population Size)× 9 (Generation Limit) = 2700, which is only fraction as compared with the earlier works. See Table 17.3, [Oakeley 1994].

[Iba 1994] used MSE (Mean Squared Error) as the performance measure. Δ is 17 for Iba. Table 17.11 compares MSE's with increasing computational efforts. Note that 6750 is the limit on the computational efforts set for GRR. Comparing MSE's for the testing data at 6750 (GRR-c) and 13890 [Iba 1994] reveals that GRR-c outperforms [Iba 1994] $0.01261/1.033 \times 10^{-4} = 122$ times better. Moreover, if we consider the ratio of the computational efforts, $13890/6750 = 2.06$, the figure goes up to $122 \times 2.06 = 250$.

17.6 Conclusion and Issues Remaining

This chapter examined a new method to model chaotic time series through the application of evolutionary symbolic computation. And, if we use the update extension of the forecast data, the method GRR performed very well especially for deterministic dynamics or a time series that is deterministic.

The major originality of GRR lies in the recursive regression scheme through which multiple basis functions are derived. Based on the assumption that the dynamics of a time series comprise the stochastic part and the deterministic part, GRR has been quite successfully applied to many real world chaotic time series data sets of which modeling and forecasting were very difficult using the standard GSR.

It is interesting to note that a method known as *stochastic modeling* [Tong 1990] introduces a variety of noise terms for treating the stochastic dynamics of time series. Then, the modeling procedure is a systematic approach to minimize the noise terms or *errors*, they say, in a model. See [Tong 1990] for more details.

In the field of quantum mechanics, there is a theory or method called the *perturbation theory* to get solutions for very complex system equation that usually does not allow for an exact solution. The system for a time series might have such complex system equation.

Perturbation theory assumes that a solution to complex system equation is a sum of the unperturbed and the perturbed contribution. See [Rae 1992] and [Nayeh 1993] for more details. This is somewhat similar to our assumption here that a complex dynamics of real world chaotic time series comprise the deterministic part and the stochastic part, Eq. (17.2). It would be interesting if we try to interpret or improve GRR in the context of the various perturbation techniques to get the unperturbed *Hamiltonian* of a complex system.

Table 17.11

Comparison of the constant coefficient version of the proposed method, GRR-c with works by [Iba 1994]. For this table, the training region was the first 100 data of time series generated from Eq. (17.15) with $\Delta = 17$: The next 400 data were given for testing. Except the number of data, all other computational settings were the same as those given in Table 17.6.

Computational Efforts	Mean Squared Error			
	This Study (GRR-c)		[Iba 1994]	
	Training Data	Testing Data	Training Data	Testing Data
1350	2.632×10^{-3}	2.021×10^{-3}		
2700	2.935×10^{-4}	3.698×10^{-4}		
4050	2.931×10^{-4}	3.738×10^{-4}		
5400	9.932×10^{-5}	2.262×10^{-4}		
6750	4.219×10^{-5}	1.033×10^{-4}		
13980			0.01215	0.01261
104400			4.7×10^{-6}	5.06×10^{-6}

For tuning-up of a regression model, the numerical coefficients of the model were simply updated with respect to a predetermined number of data set of which last datum is γ, called the impact step, behind the datum to forecast. However, if there is plenty of data such that a sufficiently dense state-space is possible, the numerical coefficients should be updated with respect to *the nearest k neighbors* in the state-space [Casdagli 1993]. From the preliminary study, it was observed that the forecasting performance does depend on the number of the nearest neighbors. The dependency becomes more severe for stochastic time series than for deterministic time series.

Along with the numerical coefficients, the basis functions should also be updated. If sufficient computational resources are available, the basis functions could be updated with respect to newly available time series data. For an on-line or real-time forecasting of a time series, the update speed should be at least the one that can allow the new basis functions to be used in time. The update time of 6 hours is nonsense if the forecasting should be done in less than 1 hour or less.

Even if the basis functions are updated in a timely manner, it may still be a problem to update the regression model. We should have systematic selection algorithms for basis functions from the *old* and the newly updated basis functions.

GRR may be more powerful if it is combined with some kinds of time series characterization technologies. For example, detailed information about the lead time, the embedding dimension, and the delay time for a given time series is extremely important to have a successful model. Various chaos-qualifying technologies will also be very helpful. Fractal dimension is a good guide to reconstruct a state-space.

This study used the raw time series data. It is meaningful if we manipulate or represent the time series data differently. Normalization or appropriate data manipulation such as the first difference transformation [Chatfield 1989] might be helpful. The very most participants in the Santa Fe and ASHRAE competitions used the somehow manipulated data rather than the raw data. Also, we suspect that any normalization techniques to set limits on the minimum and maximum values of a model, e.g. between −1 and 1, should also be explored for the runaway extension.

For demonstrative comparisons between many time series of different characteristics, GRR was run in this study with only fixed computational parameters of genetic programming such as the crossover probability, the mutation probability, the migration probability between multiple populations, Table 17.6. The parents were selected only in proportion to the fitness values. Other selection policies were not examined. The initial and the after-crossover depth of trees were also fixed. Only the Tschebyshev function was used to make the derived terminal set. Detailed studies on effects of these parameters and policies are necessary. In addition, full-scale computational experiments are necessary to study the runaway extension of the forecast data with GRR.

Acknowledgments

I'd like to thank Professor John R. Koza of Stanford University for his encouragement. I would like to thank Professor Lee Spector of Hampshire College who fixed every spelling and grammatical bugs in my manuscript. Of course, any remaining errors are my responsibility.

Bibliography

Casdagli, M. C. (1989), "Nonlinear prediction of chaotic time series," *Physics D*. 35: 335 – 356

Casdagli, M. C. (1993) and A. S. Weigend, "Exploring The Continuum Between Deterministic And Stochastic Modeling," in *Time Series Prediction-Forecasting the Future and Understanding the Past*, A. S. Weigend, and N. A. Gershenfeld, Eds., SFI Studies in the Science of Complexity, Vol. XV, 347-366, Addison-Wesley Publishing Co.

Chatfield, C. (1989), *The Analysis of Time Series*, 4th ed. London : Chapman and Hall.

Geman, S. (1992)   et al, "Neural Networks And The Bias / Variance Dilemma," *Neural Computation*, **4**, 1-58.

Gershenfeld, N. A. (1993) and A. S. Weigend, "The Future Of Time Series : Learning and Understanding," in *Time Series Prediction-Forecasting the Future and Understanding the Past*, A. S. Weigend, and N. A. Gershenfeld, Eds., SFI Studies in the Science of Complexity, Vol. XV, 1-70, Addison-Wesley Publishing Co.

Goldberg, D. E. (1989), *Genetic Algorithms in Search, Optimization, and Machine Learning*, Addison-Wesley Publishing Co.

Hübner, U (1993) et al, "Lorenz-Like Chaos In NH_3 Lasers (Data Set A)," in *Time Series Prediction-Forecasting the Future and Understanding the Past*, A. S. Weigend, and N. A. Gershenfeld, Eds., SFI Studies in the Science of Complexity, Vol. XV, 73-104, Addison-Wesley Publishing Co.

Iba, H. (1994) et al, "Genetic Programming Using A System Identification, " *ETL-TR-94-11*, Electrotechnical Lab., Japan.

Kailath, T (1980), Linear Systems, Englewood Cliffs, NJ: Prentice Hall.

Koza, J. R. (1992), *Genetic Programming*, MIT Press.

Koza, J. R. (1994), *Genetic Programming* II, MIT Press.

Luke, S. (1996) and Spector L., "Evolving Teamwork and Coordination with Genetic Programming", *Genetic Programming 1996: Proceedings of the First Annual Conference*, pp. 150-156,   MIT Press, 28-31 July 1996.

Nayeh, A. H. (1993) and Nayfeh, A. H., *Introduction to Perturbation Techniques*, John Wiley & Sons.

Oakeley, H. (1994), "Two Scientific Application Of Genetic Programming: Stack Filters And Non-Linear Equation Fitting To Chaotic Data", in *Advances in Genetic Programming*, Kenneth E. Kinnear Jr., Eds. MIT Press, 369-389.

Smith, L. A. (1993), "Does A Meeting In Santa Fe Imply Chaos ?," in *Time Series Prediction-Forecasting the Future and Understanding the Past*, A. S. Weigend, and N. A. Gershenfeld, Eds., SFI Studies in the Science of Complexity, Vol. XV, 323-343, Addison-Wesley Publishing Co.

Rae, A. I. M. (1992), *Quantum Mechanics*, 3rd Edition, University of Birmingham, UK. IOP Publishing Ltd.

Tong, H. (1990), *Nonlinear Time Series Analysis: A Dynamical Systems Approach*. Oxford: Oxford University Press.

Wan, E. A. (1993), "Time Series Prediction by Using a Connectionist Network with Internal Delay Lines," in *Time Series Prediction-Forecasting the Future and Understanding the Past*, A. S. Weigend, and N. A. Gershenfeld, Eds., SFI Studies in the Science of Complexity, Vol. XV, 195-217, Addison-Wesley Publishing Co.

Weigend, A. S. (1991) and D. E. Rumelhart, "The effective Dimension of the Space of Hidden Units.", in *Proceedings of International Joint Conference on Neural Networks, Singapore*, 2069-2074. Piscataway, NY: IEEE Service Center.

Weigend, A. S. (1993) and N. A. Gershenfeld, Eds., Time *Series Prediction-Forecasting the Future and Understanding the Past*, SFI Studies in the Science of Complexity, Vol. XV, Addison Wesley Publishing Co

Zhang, X. (1993) and Jim Hutchinson, "Simple Architectures on Fast Machines : Practical Issues In Nonlinear Time Series Prediction," in *Time Series Prediction-Forecasting the Future and Understanding the Past*, A. S. Weigend, and N. A. Gershenfeld, Eds., SFI Studies in the Science of Complexity, Vol. XV, 219-241, Addison-Wesley Publishing Co.

18 Co-evolutionary Fitness Switching: Learning Complex Collective Behaviors Using Genetic Programming

Byoung-Tak Zhang and Dong-Yeon Cho

Genetic programming provides a useful paradigm for developing multiagent systems in the domains where human programming alone is not sufficient to take into account all the details of possible situations. However, existing GP methods attempt to evolve collective behavior immediately from primitive actions. More realistic tasks require several emergent behaviors and a proper coordination of these is essential for success. We have recently proposed a framework, called *fitness switching*, to facilitate learning to coordinate composite emergent behaviors using genetic programming. *Co-evolutionary fitness switching* described in this chapter extends our previous work by introducing the concept of coevolution for more effective implementation of fitness switching. Performance of the presented method is evaluated on the table transport problem and a simple version of simulated robot soccer problem. Simulation results show that coevolutionary fitness switching provides an effective mechanism for learning complex collective behaviors which may not be evolved by simple genetic programming.

18.1 Introduction

Evolving complex collective behaviors is an interesting problem for distributed intelligence and artificial life. Some tasks can be done faster or more easily by dividing them up among many agents. Other tasks may not only be solved better by using multiple agents, but can only be effectively solved, by using teams of agents working together [Kube and Zhang, 1993; Mataric, 1996].

Several attempts have been made to use genetic programming to evolve cooperative behavior of a group of simple robotic agents. [Koza, 1992] and [Bennett III, 1996] used genetic programming to evolve a common program that controls foraging for food by ants. [Haynes et al., 1995] showed that programs for solving a predator-prey problem can be generated by genetic programming without any deep domain knowledge. [Luke and Spector, 1996] explored various strategies for evolving teams of agents in the Serengeti world, a simple predator-prey environment. [Iba, 1997] studied three different breeding strategies (homogeneous, heterogeneous, and coevolutionary) for cooperative robot navigation. Genetic programming was also used in agent based computing. [Qureshi, 1996] demonstrated that it is possible to evolve agents that communicate and interact with each other to solve a global problem.

Most of these studies have attempted to evolve emergent collective behavior immediately from primitive actions. However, more realistic complex tasks require more than one emergent behavior and a proper coordination of these is essential for successful accomplishment of the task. In real applications, it is common to use externally imposed structures to reduce the complexity of learning [Digney, 1996]. For example, [Langdon, 1998] and [Bruce, 1995] show that evolving a list took much less effort if broken into 2 tasks, one following the other.

In previous work [Zhang and Cho, 1998] we have introduced a framework, called *fitness switching*, that facilitates evolution of composite emergent behaviors using genetic programming. In fitness switching, different parts of a genetic tree are responsible for different behaviors and for each of the subtrees a basis fitness function is defined. The complex behavior is produced by dynamically changing fitness types from a pool of fitness functions. *Coevolutionary fitness switching* described in this chapter is an extension of fitness switching in which multiple subtrees are coevolved in a single GP run.

Our approach is different from other heterogeneous breeding schemes [Luke and Spector, 1996; Iba, 1997] in which different subtrees represent different *agents*. In coevolutionary fitness switching, different subtrees represent different *behaviors* of a single agent which need to be coordinated. The basic idea behind this approach is that fitness functions are a fundamental mechanism that guides the evolutionary process. It is motivated by progressive learning, i.e. learning easier tasks first and then harder tasks, which is a well-proven method in pedagogy [Zhang and Hong, 1997]. As will be discussed later, coevolutionary fitness switching can be considered as a method that enhances scalability of genetic programming by enabling the designer to incorporate problem structure while preserving essential explorative and automatic programming capability of genetic programming.

The chapter is organized as follows. Section 18.2 describes the general framework for coevolutionary fitness switching. Section 18.3 evaluates the effectiveness of the framework on the table transport task, a multiagent cooperation task. Section 18.4 shows application results on simulated robotic soccer. Section 18.5 discusses our results and further work.

18.2 Genetic Programming with Coevolutionary Fitness Switching

Genetic programming is an automatic programming method that finds the most fit computer programs by means of natural selection and genetics [Koza, 1992; Langdon, 1998; Banzhaf et al., 1998]. A population of computer programs are generated at random. They are evolved to better programs using genetic operators. The ability of the program to solve the problem is measured as its fitness value.

In genetic programming, the computer programs are usually represented as *trees* or LISP S-expressions. The tree consists of elements from the function set and the terminal set. Typically, terminal symbols provide values to the GP program while function symbols perform operation on their input, which are either terminals or output from other functions. Therefore, terminals should be evaluated earlier than functions; that is, bottom-up evaluations are performed. For multiagent control, functions denote sensing of environments and terminals denotes actions to be taken. Thus functions first should determine the state of environment and then actions described by terminals are taken; that is, top-down evaluations are performed. An illustrative example of the genetic program for multiagent control is shown in Figure 18.1.

Fitness switching is a method designed for evolving complex group behaviors using genetic programming [Zhang and Cho, 1998]. The procedure for applying fitness switching to a specific problem can be summarized as follows:

1. Define the primitive actions for the problem domain. These are the terminal set, i.e. the actions executed by the agents to solve the problem.

2. Define a small number of micro-behaviors

$$\mathcal{B} = \{B_1, B_2, \cdots, B_n\},$$

that constitute the original problem-solving behavior.

3. Define a fitness function for each micro-behavior. Together they make the pool of fitness functions

$$\mathcal{F} = \{f_1, f_2, \cdots, f_n\}.$$

4. Design a sequence of micro-behaviors or their combinations to achieve the target behavior:

$$S_t = S_{t-1} \oplus B_t,$$

where $\oplus$ denotes the append operator and S_0 is the empty sequence, i.e. $S_0 = \langle\rangle$. The corresponding sequence of fitness functions are defined as

$$F_t = F_{t-1} \oplus f_t,$$

where $F_0 = \langle\rangle$.

5. Define the structure of a genetic program A as having n subtrees, A^i ($i = 1, \cdots, n$), immediately under the root node.

$$A = (A^1, A^2, \cdots, A^n).$$

6. Apply genetic programming to evolve S_t, $t = 1, \cdots, n$ in sequence. The first subtree A^1 is executed on the given problem and the fitness of this subtree is evaluated using its fitness function f_1. Then the second subtree A^2 is executed and evaluated. Likewise, other subtrees are executed and evaluated sequentially. After that, the fitness of the program A, $F(A)$, is calculated (Figure 18.2).

The method is called fitness switching since evolution is guided by fitness functions switched from simpler ones to more complex ones. If multiple subtrees are coevolved, then the method is referred to as *coevolutionary fitness switching*.

In coevolutionary fitness switching, each subtree A^i is responsible for one micro-behavior B_i and fitness measures are switched within a single generation. Fitness of programs is measured at each generation as follows:

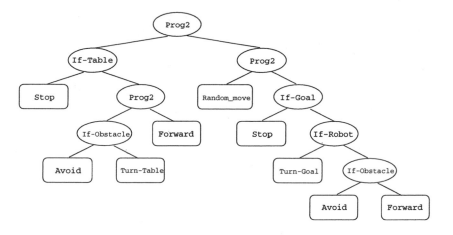

Figure 18.1
An example of genetic program for controlling the behavior of a robot. The left subtree means "If the table is nearby then stop, else do [if an obstacle is nearby then avoid it, otherwise turn to the table] and move forward." Likewise, the right subtree encodes a control program for the robot which is executed after the left subtree.

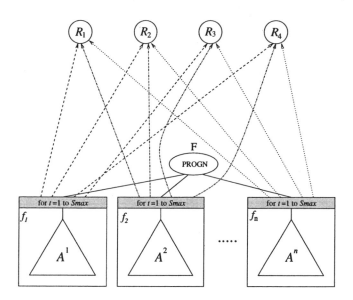

Figure 18.2
Schematic diagram for genetic programming with coevolutionary fitness switching. For multiagent control, each subtree A^i represents a control program for a micro-behavior of each robot R_j. The fitness of subtree A^i is assigned by executing it S_{max} times and measuring the goodness of its behavior by fitness function f_i.

```
Procedure CoevolutionaryFitnessSwitching()
  Pop = Initialize()
  For each generation g = 1 to G
      For each individual A ∈ Pop
          F(A) = 0
          For each subtree t = 1 to n
              For i = 1 to S_max
                  Execute(A^t)
              EndFor
              Calculate f_t
              F(A) = F(A) + f_t
          EndFor
      EndFor
      Pop = Select(Pop, |Pop|/2)
      NewPop = { }
      For each selection step s = 1 to |Pop|/2
          Select A1 and A2 from Pop based on F
          (C1, C2) = CrossoverMutation(A1, A2)
          NewPop = NewPop ∪ {C1, C2}
      EndFor
      Pop = NewPop
  EndFor
  Return(A_best = Best(Pop))
EndProcedure
```

Figure 18.3
Procedure for genentic programming with coevolutionary fitness switching. Each subtree A^i is responsible for a single micro-behavior and fitness measures are switched within a single generation to coordinate a sequence of micro-behaviors to evolve macro-behaviors. (See text for more details.)

1. Execute the first subtree A^1 for S_{max} times and measure its fitness by f_1.

2. Execute the second subtree A^2 for S_{max} times and measure its fitness by f_2.

3. Execute other subtrees and measure their fitness sequentially.

4. The fitness of the program $A = (A^1, A^2, \cdots, A^n)$ is defined as $F(A) = \sum_{i=1}^{n} f_i$.

The advantage of this method is the ability of concurrent evolution of primitive cooperative behaviors and their coordination.

A more formal description of this procedure is given in Figure 18.3. The initial population is created with random individuals. Then, the fitness values of individual A_i at generation t for the training set D, $F_t^{(i)} := E(D|A_i)$, are evaluated as described above. Based on the adaptive Occam method [Zhang et al., 1997] a complexity term was used in all experiments to penalize large trees:

$$F(i) = E(D|A_i) + \beta C(A_i),$$

where $C(A_i)$ is the complexity measured in the number of nodes in tree A_i and β is a small constant. This measure is based on the minimum description length (MDL) principle, i.e. it encourages to induce models that have the minimal total code length:

$$A_{best} = \arg\min_{A_i}\{L(D|A_i) + L(A_i)\},$$

where $L(A_i)$ is the code length for model description and $L(D|A_i)$ is the code length for data description using the model.

We used (μ, λ) uniform ranking selection, i.e., the best μ individual assigned a selection probability of $\frac{1}{\mu}$, while the rest are discarded:

$$p_s(A_i) = \begin{cases} \frac{1}{\mu}, & 1 \le i \le \mu \\ 0, & \mu < i \le \lambda. \end{cases}$$

In experiments $\frac{\mu}{\lambda} = 0.5$, i.e. the best 50% of the population are deterministically selected into the mating pool. Two parents in the mating pool are selected at random to generate two offspring by crossover and mutation.

The crossover operator selects a subtree from A_i^k of the first parent A_i and swap it with a subtree selected from the A_j^k in the second parent A_j. If the depth of the offspring tree exceeds the depth limit, crossover is performed again. Then, the mutation operator changes a node symbol according to the mutation rate. A terminal node is replaced by another terminal node and a nonterminal node by a different nonterminal.

The genetic operators are applied repeatedly until offspring of population size are produced. After generating all offspring, the best two of the parents population replace two individuals selected at random from the offspring population (2-elitism). This completes one generation and the process is repeated for G generations.

There are two simple implementational variants of fitness switching. One is *naive evolution* in which each micro-behavior is performed using the whole genetic program tree. Naive evolution is one extreme on which most existing GP studies are based. This method is very efficient in memory usage since the same tree is shared by multiple behaviors. A disadvantage is that this representation is difficult to coordinate multiple cooperative behaviors. An alternative method for implementing fitness switching is *sequential evolution*. Here each subtree A^i is responsible for one micro-behavior B_i. Subtree A^i is evolved by a GP run and then the best program for this run is used to evolve the next GP run for evolving the subtree A^{i+1}. This is another extreme in which the coordination is hard-coded both in representation and in evolutionary process. Sequential evolution approach seems the most practical in solving tasks which can be clearly decomposed into a sequence of independent subtasks. But most of the interesting problems that need emergent computations do not belong to this class of problems.

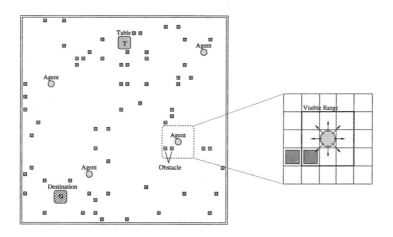

Figure 18.4
Table transport problem. There is one table, one destination, four robotic agents and a fixed number of obstacles.
The robots can move in 8 directions and have a limited visual field of range 1 in all 8 directions. The table and
destination are assumed to be observable by the agents from any position.

18.3   Results on Table Transport

The different GP approaches have been experimentally compared on table transport problem. This problem consists of an $n \times m$ grid world, a single table T and four robotic agents
as shown in Figure 18.4. A specific location G is designated as the destination. All 6 initial
locations are chosen randomly. The goal of the robots is to transport the table to the destination G. The robots need to move in a herd since the table is too heavy and large to be
transported by single robots.

This problem requires at least two emergent behaviors, i.e. homing and herding, to
be executed in sequence. The four robots need first to get together around the object to
transport, i.e. homing, and then transport it in team to the destination, i.e. herding. Though
in a different context, [Werner and Dyer, 1993] have studied the herding behavior. In this
task, a group of robot agents must cooperate to achieve the goal.

The fitness switching method is applied to the table transport problem. This task can
be considered as a composition of two following cooperative behaviors: homing and herding. Thus the sequence of micro-behaviors is $\mathcal{B} = \langle B_1, B_2 \rangle$, where $B_1 = homing$ and
$B_2 = herding$. The sequence of fitness functions is $\mathcal{F} = \langle f_1, f_2 \rangle$, where f_1 measures
the fitness of the homing behavior to the table and f_2 measures the fitness of the herding
behavior for transporting the table to the goal. Better programs are defined to have lower

Table 18.1
Symbols used for fitness definition.

Symbol	Description
X_r	x-axis distance between target and robot r
Y_r	y–axis distance between target and robot r
S_r	number of steps moved by robot r
C_r	number of collisions made by robot r
M_r	distance between starting and final position of r
A_r	penalty for moving away from other robots
c_i	coefficient for factor i
K	positive constant ($K = 40$)

fitness values as follows:

$$f_1 \quad = \quad \sum_{r=1}^{4} \{c_1 \max(X_r, Y_r) + c_2 S_r + c_3 C_r - c_4 M_r + K\} \tag{18.1}$$

$$f_2 \quad = \quad \sum_{r=1}^{4} \{c_1 \max(X_r, Y_r) + c_2 S_r + c_3 C_r - c_4 M_r + c_5 A_r + K\} \tag{18.2}$$

where the subscript r denotes the index for robots. Typical values of c_i are $c_1 = 5.0$, $c_2 = 0.25, c_3 = 1.0, c_4 = 3.0$, and $c_5 = 0.25$. The definitions of the symbols used in these equations are summarized in Table 18.1. The constant K is used to normalize the fitness values to be positive (this does not change the selective chance of the individuals.) The target position for homing behavior is the initial position of the table T while the target position for herding behavior is the destination G of the table.

The objective of a GP run is to find a multi-robot algorithm that, when executed by each robot in a group of 4 robots, causes efficient table transport behavior in group. The terminals and functions used for GP are listed in Table 18.2. The function set consists of six primitives: IF-OBSTACLE, IF-ROBOT, IF-TABLE, IF-GOAL, PROG2 and PROG3. The terminal set consists of six primitive actions: FORWARD, AVOID, RANDOM-MOVE, TURN-TABLE, TURN-GOAL and STOP. If FORWARD or RANDOM-MOVE cause a robot to run into obstacles, other robots or edges of the world, then the robot remains the current position. We assume that all primitive actions take the same time for execution and the robots have a mixture of local and global sensors. Local sensors (e.g., infra-red sensors) are used for IF-OBSTACLE and IF-ROBOT. Global sensors are used for IF-TABLE and IF-GOAL. An example of genetic program is shown in Figure 18.1. Table 18.3 summarizes the experimental setup for genetic programs. We enforce a maximum tree depth of 10 to avoid generating overly large structures.

Each fitness case represents a world of 32 by 32 grid on which there are four robots, 64 obstacles, and the table to be transported. A total of 20 different, randomly generated training cases were used. A total of 20 different worlds were also used for evaluating the

Table 18.2
Terminals and functions of GP-trees for the table transport problem.

	Symbol	Description
Terminals	FORWARD	Move one step forward in the current direction.
	AVOID	Check clockwise and make one step in the first direction that avoids collision.
	RANDOM-MOVE	Move one step in the random direction.
	TURN-TABLE	Make a clockwise turn to the nearest direction of the table.
	TURN-GOAL	Make a clockwise turn to the nearest direction of the goal.
	STOP	Stay at the same position.
Functions	IF-OBSTACLE	Check collision with obstacles.
	IF-ROBOT	Check collision with other robots.
	IF-TABLE	Check if the table is nearby (within the range of one cell.)
	IF-GOAL	Check if the destination is nearby (within the range of one cell.)
	PROG2, PROG3	Evaluate two (or three) subtrees in sequence.

Table 18.3
Parameters used in the experiments for the table transport problem.

Parameter	Value
Population size	100
Max generation	200
Crossover rate	0.9
Mutation rate	0.1
Max tree depth	10

generalization performance of evolved programs. The training and test cases differ in the initial positions of the robots and the locations of the table, destination and obstacles.

All the robots use the same control program. In evaluating the fitness of robots we made a complete run of the program for one robot, before the fitness of another is measured. This is an efficient way of measuring the fitness, but is different from the real situation in which robots are moving at the same time. This is an advantage of subgoal evolution. Sequential execution of the program can detect various behavior patterns of parallel execution if a sufficient number of training cases are used.

Figure 18.5 shows the change in fitness values during a GP run with coevolutionary fitness switching: The fitness of a tree A is measured by $F(A) = f_1(A) + f_2(A)$, where $f_1(A)$ is the fitness for homing and $f_2(A)$ is the fitness for herding. A rapid decrease in fitness indicates the fast improvement in cooperative behavior.

We examined the evolution process of cooperative behavior by analyzing the performance of best programs at each generation. Shown in Figure 18.6 are the performance at generations $g = 1, 10, 14, 71$. At $g = 1$, a program was evolved that successfully moves some of the robots toward the table. But, no herding behavior was achieved. At $g = 10$ the robots tend to move toward the goal position but no group behavior is observed. At $g = 14$, three of the robots learned the herding behavior but one failed. This is possible

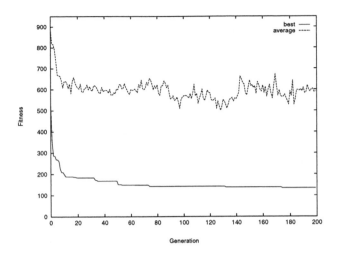

Figure 18.5
Evolution of fitness values during a GP run: (solid line) best fitness for each generation, (dotted line) average fitness for the individuals in each generation. Lower fitness means better individuals. A rapid decrease in fitness indicates fast improvement in cooperative behavior for table transport.

since, though having the same control program, the robots see different local environments. It took the robots 71 generations to learn perfect homing (i.e., every robot arrives at the table) and herding behaviors to transport the table to the destination.

Genetic programming with coevolutionary fitness switching was able to learn to solve the transport problem for more than one environments. The generality of the evolved programs was verified by running them on test environments. Figure 18.7 shows the behaviors of the robots for the test cases. Shown is the performance for four test cases out of 20. The composite cooperative behaviors can be observed: The robots start at their initial positions, getting together to the table (homing), moving in a herd to the goal (herding), and finally arriving at the destination (transporting).

The performance of genetic programs was measured by the number of hits: the number of times all the robots reached the destination. Figure 18.8 shows the change in the number of hits during the run.

Table 18.4 compares the number of hits for the three fitness switching methods described in the previous section. We made 10 runs for each method and measures the average values and their standard deviations. It is interesting to note that the naive approach only succeeded on 0.4 fitness cases in average out of 20 test cases in each run. As expected the fitness switching with sequential evolution, the most engineered version, was the best in number of hits for training and test. The coevolutionary switching method was competitive to the sequential switching in number of hits for both training and test performance. Relatively small values of standard deviation suggest that the results are statistically significant.

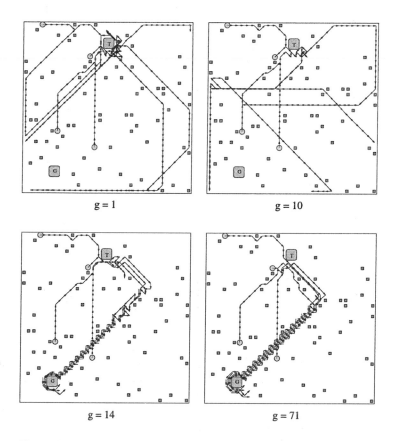

g = 1   g = 10

g = 14   g = 71

Figure 18.6
Trajectories of robots controlled by the best programs in the population. At generation one, three out of four robots succeeded in homing to the table (T), but they failed to arrive at the goal (G) position. At generation 10, all the robots succeeded in homing but still failed in herding. As generation goes on ($g = 14$, $g = 71$), they show successful homing and herding behaviors.

Table 18.4
Comparison of different evolution methods in terms of the number of hits for table transport. Experiments have been performed on 20 fitness cases for training and test, respectively. The values are averaged over ten runs. Also shown are the standard deviation. Coevolutionary fitness switching is competitive to sequential evolution, the most problem-specific approach, while the naive evolution method fails to solve this problem.

Method	Number of Hits	
	Training	Test
Naive	0.3 ± 0.458	0.4 ± 0.663
Sequential	15.1 ± 2.982	13.0 ± 1.949
Coevolution	13.9 ± 2.737	11.9 ± 2.546

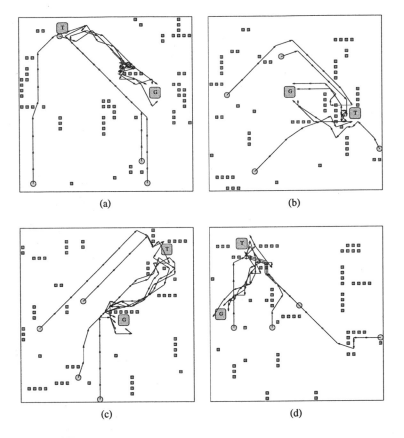

(a) (b)

(c) (d)

Figure 18.7
Trajectory of robots running the best program for the 4 test cases out of 20. Though the environments are different, robots have successfully performed homing and herding behaviors to transport the table to the destination. Here the environments have wall-like obstacles whose position and length were generated randomly.

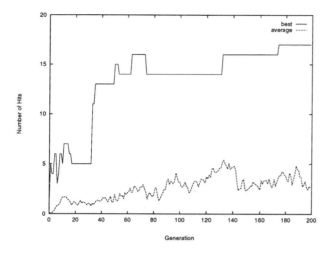

Figure 18.8
Number of hits vs. generation for a typical run. Despite the elitism, best fitness (and the number of hits) can decrease since the control programs have random moves as their primitive actions.

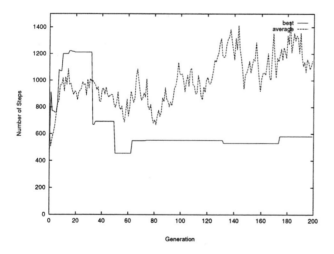

Figure 18.9
Average number of steps vs. generation. The solid line shows the number of steps taken by a group of 4 robots using the best program. The dotted line shows the average number of steps for a group of 4 robots, average taken over all the programs in the population.

Table 18.5
Comparison of the number of steps taken by a group of four robots for table transport. Shown are average values with standard deviation for the training set and test set, respectively. Also shown are the tree size in terms of the number of nodes. Coevolutionary fitness switching achieved competitive performance to the sequential evolution using more smaller programs.

Method	Average Number of Steps		Tree Size
	Training	Test	(#Nodes)
Naive	327.75 ± 156.11	697.18 ± 200.19	36.9 ± 15.34
Sequential	671.69 ± 140.01	523.39 ± 132.39	60.5 ± 21.95
Coevolution	553.72 ± 122.88	538.47 ± 107.75	37.8 ± 11.90

Figure 18.9 shows the evolution of the average number of steps made by four robots for 20 different training environments. The number of steps for a robot is defined as the number of primitive actions taken during the execution of the program. Shown are the best-of-generation and population-average values. Table 18.5 compares the performance of three different methods for fitness switching. The values given are the average number of steps made by a group of four robots for 20 different environments for training and test. Since genetic programs are shared for two micro-behaviors in naive evolution, robots have tried to remain around the table or destination. Thus, the average number of steps for training cases was very small, but they did not achieve the goal. In contrast, the most engineered sequential evolution method obtained the largest average number of steps because the control programs were fully evolved to fit the training cases. In the coevolutionary method, the average number of steps for training and test cases was moderate, indicating relatively reliable fitting to both the training data and the test data. It should be mentioned that, compared to the number of hits (Table 18.4), the standard deviation of the performance is relatively large. The table also shows the size of programs evolved by each method. The program evolved by coevolutionary fitness switching was the most sparse consisting of 37.8 nodes in average.

18.4 Application to Robotic Soccer

Robot soccer is an interesting challenge for artificial intelligence research on autonomous agents and multiagent learning [Kitano et al., 1997]. It involves two adversary teams of cooperative agents. To achieve the ultimate goal, each team needs to cooperate with teammates but its cooperation is hindered by the opponent team. Agents also need to generate subgoals, such as passing or intercepting the ball, and have to collaborate to achieve them in harmony with others. As the teammates and opponents are moving around in the field, the environment is dynamically changing. It is almost impossible for humans to develop a soccer program that takes into account every possible situation [Kitano et al., 1997].

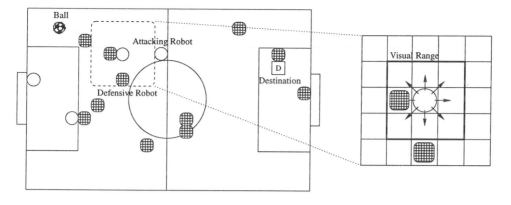

Figure 18.10
The environment for the dash-and-dribble problem. There are two teams and a ball in the 22 × 14 grid field. Attacking robots can move in 8 directions and have a limited visual field of range 1 to each movable direction.

We demonstrate the effectiveness of coevolutionary fitness switching in the context of a particular aspect of soccer game in the RoboCup domain [Cho and Zhang, 1998]. A fuller application of genetic programming to RoboCup Simulation League is reported in [Luke et al., 1997]. We focus on the dash-and-dribble behavior: given the ball position and its destination, a team of robot players is to approach to the ball and dribble it to the destination. In this task, a group of robot agents should cooperate to accomplish the task, otherwise they will get the ball intercepted by the opponent team.

We consider a soccer field of 22 × 14 grid points (Figure 18.10). There are two teams of robots and a ball in the field. The target position of the ball is given as D. Each team consists of 11 players. The objective of the attacking team, T_A, is to dash to and dribble the ball to the destination. The objective of the opponent team, T_B, is to hinder this attack.

The dash-and-dribble behavior is useful in several situations. The dashing behavior is used in a defensive mode; team T_A needs to dash to the ball to intercept the ball of the opponent team. The dribble behavior is required to pass the ball to the destination. In both cases group behaviors are required so that the respective behavior is performed effectively, that is, not to be intercepted by the opponents. Since not all players of team T_A need to take part in the attacking dash-and-dribble, we consider in the experiments the case of four attacking players. In contrast, all of the 11 opponent players are considered as obstacles.

The attacking robots move forward in the current direction (N, E, S, W, NE, SE, SW, NW) or remain in the current position. The defensive robots do not move, that is, remain in the current position (they are regarded as obstacles). The attacking robots are all have the same sensors and actuators (homogeneous agents) and have a limited visual field of range 1 to each movable direction.

Table 18.6
The terminal and function set used in the dash-and-dribble problem. This is similar to Table 18.2.

	Symbol	Description
Terminals	FORWARD	Move one step forward in the current direction.
	AVOID	Check the surrounding region and make one step in the first direction possible.
	RANDOM-MOVE	Make a movement in the random direction.
	TURN-BALL	Make a clockwise turn to the nearest direction of the ball.
	TURN-DESTINATION	Make a clockwise turn to the nearest direction of the destination.
	STOP	Make no step and remain in the current position.
Functions	IF-OPPONENT	Return true if an opponent is adjacent to the current block, else false.
	IF-MATE	Return true if a mate is adjacent, else false.
	IF-BALL	Return true if a ball is adjacent, else false.
	IF-Destination	Return true if the destination is adjacent, else false.
	PROG2	Execute two subtrees in sequence.
	PROG3	Evaluate three subtrees in sequence.

The attacking robots activate their control program to run a team trial. At the beginning of the trial, they have different positions and orientations which are chosen randomly. During a trial they should approach and move the ball to the destination in cooperation with others.

This problem has similarities to the table transport problem (TTP) in several aspects. Dashing to the ball can be considered as a homing behavior in TTP, and dribbling the ball to the destination can be regarded as a herding behavior in TTP. In our experiments there are four robots which perform the given task and eleven defensive robots. The terminals and functions used in the dash-and-dribble problem are shown in Table 18.6. Fitness functions for dash and dribble behaviors are similar to Equation (18.1) and (18.2) except for the target positions. A total of 20 training cases are used for evolving programs. A total of 20 different worlds are used for evaluating the generalization performance of the evolved programs. Other parameter values are the same as in the previous section (Table 18.3).

Figure 18.11 shows the evolution of fitness values during a GP run. A rapid decrease in fitness during early generations indicates a fast improvement in cooperative behavior. The training resulted in a program tree whose depth is 8 and the number of nodes is 37 in the 187th generation. Figure 18.12 shows the change in the number of hits during the run. The number of steps needed for dash-and-dribble behavior is shown in Figure 18.13.

The generality of the programs evolved was verified by running them on test environments. Figure 18.14 shows the behavior of the robots to some test cases. Though the environments are different, robots successfully perform the dash-and-dribble behavior. Table 18.7 compares the performance of three methods for the training and test cases. The naive evolution failed to find the appropriate control program. The sequential evolution showed the best results in number of hits for both cases. The coevolutionary fitness switching was competitive to the sequential method.

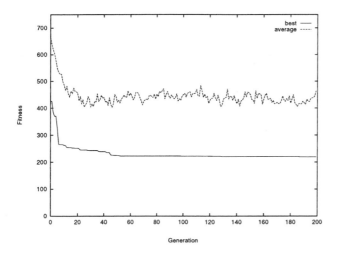

Figure 18.11
Evolution of fitness values during a GP run for the dash-and-dribble behavior: (solid line) best fitness for each generation, (dotted line) average fitness for the individuals in each generation. Lower fitness means better individuals.

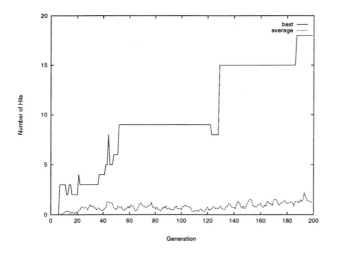

Figure 18.12
Number of hits vs. generation for the dash-and-dribble behavior. Despite the elitism, the number of hits can decrease the control programs have random moves as their primitive actions.

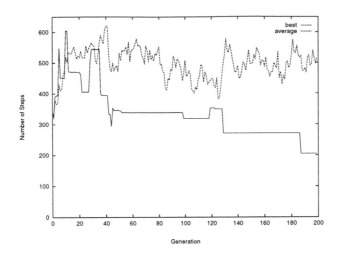

Figure 18.13
Number of steps vs. generation for the dash-and-dribble behavior. The solid line shows the number of steps taken by a group of 4 robots using the best program. The dotted line shown the average number of steps for a group of 4 robots, average taken over all the programs in the population.

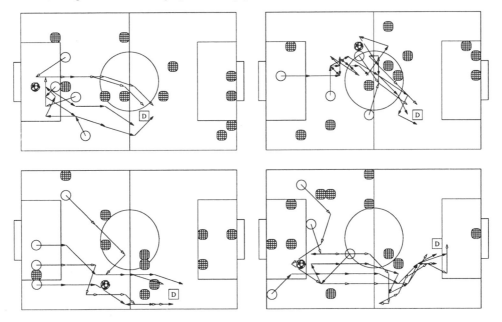

Figure 18.14
Trajectories of robots running the evolved programs on the 4 test cases. Robots successfully dashed to the ball and dribbled it to the destination D.

Table 18.7
Results for the training and test cases on the dash-and-dribble problem. The values are averaged over ten runs. Also shown are the standard deviation.

Method	Number of Hits	
	Training	Test
Naive	0.0 ± 0.000	0.0 ± 0.000
Sequential	17.0 ± 2.366	13.9 ± 1.700
Coevolution	13.0 ± 3.162	10.9 ± 3.673

18.5   Conclusions

We described a method for evolving composite cooperative behaviors of multiple robotic agents. This method, called coevolutionary fitness switching, is based on a pool of fitness functions which are defined to reflect the problem structure but without too much need for domain knowledge. The method was motivated by the observation that, while GP is able to evolve emergent behaviors, the evolution can be more efficient if the program structure and sometimes the evolution strategy is constrained to match the problem structure.

In the context of the table transport problem we have experimentally shown that coevolution with fitness switching can solve a class of tasks which we were not able to efficiently solve using simple genetic programming. Simulation results also show that, compared with the carefully designed sequential evolution method, the coevolutionary fitness switching is competitive in training and test performance. We also observed that coevolutionary fitness switching generally produced more smaller solution trees. It seems that coevolutionary fitness switching has the effect of avoiding overfitting to one specific behavior, thus resulting in small trees, while sequential evolution tends to find large trees overfit to specific subgoals.

The method was also applied to learn the dash-and-dribble behavior for soccer robots. Here each genetic program consists of several subroutines which are coordinated to perform the entire task. Each subroutine is responsible for a group behavior and it is evolved by a specific fitness function. The coevolutionary fitness switching method is then used to coordinate the evolution of the complex macro behaviors from the primitive micro-behaviors. Our experimental results demonstrate that it is feasible to evolve by genetic programming some complex group behaviors which are useful for solving specific aspects of robotic soccer games.

Acknowledgements

This research was supported in part by the Korea Science and Engineering Foundation (KOSEF) under grants 96-0102-13-01-3 and 981-0920-350-2. Thanks to William B. Langdon and Peter J. Angeline for comments on the previous versions of this paper.

Bibliography

Banzhaf, W., Nordin, P., Keller, R. E., and Francone, F. D. (1998), *Genetic Programming – An Introduction; On the Automatic Evolution of Computer Programs and its Applications*, Morgan Kaufmann.

Bennett III, F. H. (1996), "Automatic creation of an efficient multi-agent architecture using genetic programming with architecture-altering operations," in *Genetic Programming 1996: Proceedings of the First Annual Conference*, J. R. Koza, D. E. Goldberg, D. B. Fogel, and R. L. Riolo (Eds.), pp 30–38, Stanford University, CA, USA: MIT Press.

Bruce, W. S. (1995), *The Application of Genetic Programming to the Automatic Generation of Object-Oriented Programs*, PhD thesis, School of Computer and Information Sciences, Nova Southeastern University, 3100 SW 9th Avenue, Fort Lauderdale, Florida 33315, USA.

Cho, D.-Y. and Zhang, B.-T. (1998), "Learning soccer-robot cooperation strategies using genetic programming," Technical Report SCAI-98-009, Artificial Intelligence Lab (SCAI), Dept. of Computer Engineering, Seoul National University.

Digney, B. L. (1996), "Emergent hierarchical control structures: Learning reactive/hierarchical relationships in reinforcement environments," in *Proceedings of the Fourth International Conference on Simulation of Adaptive Behavior: From animals to animats 4*, P. Maes, M. J. Mataric, J.-A. Meyer, J. Pollack, and S. W. Wilson (Eds.), pp 363–372, Cape Code, USA: MIT Press.

Haynes, T., Sen, S., Schoenefeld, D., and Wainwright, R. (1995), "Evolving a team," in *Working Notes for the AAAI Symposium on Genetic Programming*, E. V. Siegel and J. R. Koza (Eds.), pp 23–30, MIT, Cambridge, MA, USA: AAAI.

Iba, H. (1997), "Multiple-agent learning for a robot navigation task by genetic programming," in *Genetic Programming 1997: Proceedings of the Second Annual Conference*, J. R. Koza, K. Deb, M. Dorigo, D. B. Fogel, M. Garzon, H. Iba, and R. L. Riolo (Eds.), pp 195–200, Stanford University, CA, USA: Morgan Kaufmann.

Kitano, H., Asada, M., Kuniyoshi, Y., Noda, I., Osawa, E., and Matsubara, H. (1997), "Robocup: A challenge problem for ai," *AI Magazine*, 18(1):73–85.

Koza, J. R. (1992), *Genetic Programming: On the Programming of Computers by Natural Selection*, Cambridge, MA, USA: MIT Press.

Kube, C. R. and Zhang, H. (1993), "Collective robotics: From social insects to robots," *Adaptive Behavior*, 2(2):189–218.

Langdon, W. B. (1998), *Data Structures and Genetic Programming: Genetic Programming + Data Structures = Automatic Programming!*, Boston: Kluwer.

Luke, S., Hohn, C., Farris, J., Jackson, G., and Hendler, J. (1997), "Co-evolving soccer softbot team coordination with genetic programming," in *Proceedings of the First International Workshop on RoboCup, at the International Joint Conference on Artificial Intelligence*, H. Kitano (Ed.), pp 115–118.

Luke, S. and Spector, L. (1996), "Evolving teamwork and coordination with genetic programming," in *Genetic Programming 1996: Proceedings of the First Annual Conference*, J. R. Koza, D. E. Goldberg, D. B. Fogel, and R. L. Riolo (Eds.), pp 150–156, Stanford University, CA, USA: MIT Press.

Mataric, M. J. (1996), "Learning in multi-robot systems," in *Adaptation and Learning in Multi-Agent Systems*, G. Weiss and S. Sen (Eds.), volume 1042 of *LNCS*, pp 152–163, Springer-Verlag.

Qureshi, A. (1996), "Evolving agents," in *Genetic Programming 1996: Proceedings of the First Annual Conference*, J. R. Koza, D. E. Goldberg, D. B. Fogel, and R. L. Riolo (Eds.), pp 369–374, Stanford University, CA, USA: MIT Press.

Werner, G. M. and Dyer, M. G. (1993), "Evolution of herding behavior in artificial animals," in *From Animals to Animats 2: Proceedings of the Second International Conference on Simulation of Adaptive Behavior*, J. A. Meyer, H. L. Roitblat, and S. W. Wilson (Eds.), pp 393–399, Honolulu, Hawaii, USA: MIT Press.

Zhang, B.-T. and Cho, D.-Y. (1998), "Fitness switching: Evolving complex group behaviors using genetic programming," in *Genetic Programming 1998: Proceedings of the Third Annual Conference*, J. R. Koza, W. Banzhaf, K. Chellapilla, K. Deb, M. Dorigo, D. B. Fogel, M. H. Garzon, D. E. Goldberg, H. Iba, and R. Riolo (Eds.), pp 431–438, University of Wisconsin, Madison, Wisconsin, USA: Morgan Kaufmann.

Zhang, B.-T. and Hong, Y.-J. (1997), "A multiple neural architecture for evolving collective robotic intelligence," in *Proceedings of 1997 International Conference on Neural Information Processing*, N. Kasabov, R. Kozma, K. Ko, R. O'Shea, G. Coghill, and T. Gedeon (Eds.), pp 971–974, University of Otago, Dunedin, New Zealand: Springer.

Zhang, B.-T., Ohm, P., and Mühlenbein, H. (1997), "Evolutionary induction of sparse neural trees," *Evolutionary Computation*, 5(2):213–236.

19 Evolving Multiple Agents by Genetic Programming

Hitoshi Iba

This paper presents the emergence of the cooperative behavior for multiple agents by means of Genetic Programming (GP). Our experimental domains are multi-agent test beds, i.e., the robot navigation task and the Tile World. The world consists of a simulated robot agent and a simulated environment which is both dynamic and unpredictable. In our previous paper, we proposed three types of strategies, i.e, homogeneous breeding, heterogeneous breeding, and co-evolutionary breeding, for the purpose of evolving the cooperative behavior. We use the heterogeneous breeding in this paper. The previous Q-learning approach commonly used for the multi-agent task has the difficulty with the combinatorial explosion for many agents. This is because the state space for Q-table is so huge for the practical computer resources. We show how successfully GP-based multi-agent learning is applied to multi-agent tasks and compare the performance with Q-learning by experiments. Thereafter, we conduct experiments with the evolution of the communicating agents. The communication is an essential factor for the emergence of cooperation. This is because a collaborative agent must be able to handle situations in which conflicts arise and must be capable of negotiating with other agents to reach an agreement. The effectiveness of the emergent communication is empirically shown in terms of the robustness of generated GP programs.

19.1 Introduction

This paper applies GP in order to evolve multiple agents and shows that the cooperative behavior emerges as a result of evolution. There are three main motivations for us to realize GP-based multi-agent learning.

First, there have been many approaches to adaptive agents. For instance, reinforcement learning, i.e., Q-learning, is often used for multi-agent tasks [Tan93], [Sen et al.95]. However, most of these straightforward approaches scale poorly to more complex multi-agent learning problems, because the state space for each learning agent grows exponentially in the number of its partner agents engaged in the joint task [Ono97],[Rosca96]. On the other hand, GP searches for the combination of input variables so as to reduce the computational complexity. We will explain the comparative study in Section 4.

Secondly, many breeding strategies, e.g. homogeneous strategy, heterogeneous strategy, and co-evolutionary strategy, are proposed and compared for the multi-agent learning method. Thus, we can use a different strategy for a particular task by using evolutionary learning. For instance, [Bull97] described the key feature of the co-evolving strategy as "genetic joining" i.e., hereditary endosymbioses, and observed that it worked best in terms of mean performance due to their reduction in the effects of the partner variance (see [Iba96],[Iba97] and [Bull97] for the details of the comparative studies).

The third motivation comes from the communication issue. The communication is an essential factor for the emergence of cooperation. This is because a collaborative agent must be able to handle situations in which conflicts arise and must be capable of negotiating with other agents to reach an agreement [Chu-Carroll *et al.*95]. [Benda *et al.*88] introduced the following three types of relationship between agents:

1. Communicating agents (Type A), i.e., one agent is capable of requesting data from another agent.

2. Negotiating agents (Type B), i.e., in addition to the above data request, agents can negotiate with each other about their movements.

3. Controlling agents (Type C), i.e., an agent can exert control over another agent.

However, it is not easy to design agents with the above communication protocols by humans, because many factors, such as synchronization, communication costs, and transmission channel, have to be considered beforehand. There have been relatively few studies on the adaptive agents with such higher-level communication as types B and C. GP is suitable for representing these communication protocols. In Section 5, we use ACL (Agent Communication Language) to show the evolvability of communicating agents.

The rest of this paper is structured as follows. Section 2 describes the experimental domains used in this paper, i.e., the robot navigation task and the Tile World. Section 3 explains different breeding strategies for multi-agent learning. In section 4, GP performance is compared with Q-learning. We introduce communication commands in section 5 and conduct experiments with communicating agents. Section 6 discusses our approach, followed by some conclusions in Section 7.

19.2   Example Tasks

There are some benchmark problems for the multi-agent research. We use two target tasks in this paper.

First task is a robot navigation domain. Consider a robot navigation task for four agents (Fig.19.1). The world consists of a rectangular grid (i.e., 10×10), on which agents (denoted as Ai, $i = 0, 1, \cdots$) and some obstacles (#) can be placed. Each object occupies one cell of the grid. The agent can move up, down, left, and right unless doing so would cause it to run into the world's boundaries or an obstacle. The agents' goal is to find the optimal path in a grid world, from given starting locations to their respective goals (denoted as Gi in the figure). A possible optimal path for A0 is shown in the figure as a dotted line. The goal of the multi-agent team is for each agent to move quickly to their respective goal locations without

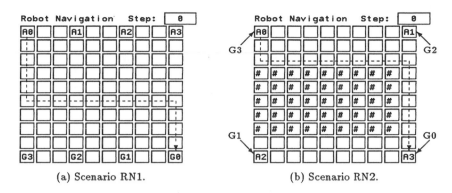

(a) Scenario RN1. (b) Scenario RN2.

Figure 19.1
The Robot Navigation.

colliding with other agents and walls. In Scenario RN1, the obstacles are the other agents alone. This is an example of loosely-coupled interactions [Sen *et al.*95].

In order to apply GP to evolving an agent's program in the robot navigation, we use the basic terminal and nonterminal sets shown in Table 19.1[1] . In the table, a symbol without any argument is a terminal symbol.

What is required by a GP tree program is to tell how to move an agent, i.e., right, left, up, down and stay. Thus, the wrapper (i.e., the mapping between the output of a parse tree and the action to be taken) is applied to the output of the GP tree so as to decide the agent's move. The mapping between vectors and actions is determined as follows: If the norm of the vector $\vec{v}$ is less than or equal to the parameter Radius, then STAY where you are. Otherwise, move 1 step RIGHT, UP, LEFT or DOWN depending on the direction of $\vec{v}$, i.e., when $\vec{v}$ is between $[-\frac{\pi}{4}, +\frac{\pi}{4}]$, $[+\frac{\pi}{4}, +\frac{3\pi}{4}]$, $[+\frac{3\pi}{4}, +\frac{5\pi}{4}]$ and $[+\frac{5\pi}{4}, +\frac{7\pi}{4}]$, respectively. We set the Radius parameter to 1.0. For instance, if the output of a GP tree is a vector $\binom{5}{10}$, then the agent's move is UP as the result of the wrapper.

The second experimental domain is the Tile World, which is a multi-agent test bed that consists of simulated robot agents and a simulated environment which is both dynamic and unpredictable [Pollack *et al.*90], [Hanks *et al.*93]. The world also consists of a rectangular grid, on which agents (denoted as Ai, $i = 0, 1, \cdots$), some tiles (T), some obstacles (#), and some holes (\/) can be placed (see Fig.19.2(a)). Each object occupies one cell of the grid. The agent can move up, down, left, and right unless doing so would cause it to run into the world's boundaries or an obstacle. When a tile is in a cell adjacent to the agent, the agent can push the tile by moving in its direction. The agents' goal is to push all tiles into the holes. The

---

[1] The usage of these symbols is motivated by the study reported by [Luke *et al.*96]. Luke studied evolving teamwork by GP for a pursuit game, in which the world is a continuous 2-dimensional area.

Table 19.1
Basic GP Terminals and Functions (Robot Navigation).

Name	#Args.	Description
Goal	0	The directional vector by which to move the agent toward its goal.
last	0	The last vector of the GP output for the agent. If this is the first move, then returns a random vector.
Agi	0	The directional vector by which to move the agent toward the i-th nearest agent.
V1	0	A unit vector, i.e., $\binom{1}{0}$.
Rand	0	A random vector.
+	2	Add two vectors.
-	2	Subtract two vectors.
*2	1	Multiply the magnitude of a vector by 2.
/2	1	Divide a vector by 2.
->90	1	Rotate a vector clockwise 90 degrees.
inv	1	Invert a vector, i.e., if the input is v, then return $-v$.
if_dot	4	Evaluate the first and second arguments. If their dot product is greater than 0, then evaluate and return the third argument, else evaluate and return the fourth argument.
if>=	4	Evaluate the first and second arguments. If the magnitude of the first argument is greater than the magnitude of the second argument, then evaluate and return the third argument, else evaluate and return the fourth argument.

simple interaction is shown in Fig.19.2(a). This is an example of strongly-coupled interactions (i.e. the constraints on movement are so severe) [Goldman *et al.*94]. For either agent to accomplish its goal, it would need to carry out a large number of movements to perform its own task. For example, for A0 alone to fill holes with two tiles, it needs to move 17 steps (assuming A1 is not on its way). Similarly, A1 alone would need to move 26 steps to finish its task. However, if they work together, they can finish their task by going 12 steps (see [Iba96] for how GP evolved this optimal behavior). We have chosen the same basic terminal/functional symbols shown in Table 19.1 for this task, except that Hole and Tile terminals are used in stead of Goal terminal. The Tile terminal returns the vector from the agent to the nearest tile and the Hole returns the vector from the agent to the nearest hole.

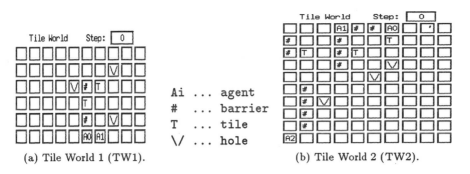

(a) Tile World 1 (TW1).   (b) Tile World 2 (TW2).

Figure 19.2
The Tile World.

19.3 Fitness Assignment and Breeding Strategies

Fitness functions need to be designed carefully so that they satisfy the following requirements:

Requirement 1   Give a high score to a GP program which makes each agent achieve its own goal.

Requirement 2   Give a higher score to a GP program which finishes the whole task quickly.

Requirement 3   If any agents have not achieved the goals after the execution of a GP program, give a higher score when they have contributed to their goals more.

In order to meet the above requirements, we use the following fitness derivation for a GP tree T. This algorithm includes three user-defined parameters, i.e., $Bonus$, C_T, and $Speed\_UP$. The meaning of these parameters is explained later.

Step 1   Set $Step\_Time := 51$, $Fitness := 0.0$.

Step 2   Evaluate T and move agents according to the result of the wrapper.

Step 3   If an agent achieves its goal, then

$$Fitness := Fitness + Bonus \times FT, \tag{19.1}$$

where FT is the number of agents that have achieved the goals at this step.

Step 4 If all agents achieve their goals, then

$$Fitness := Fitness + Speed\_UP \times Step\_Time, \qquad (19.2)$$

and return *Fitness*.

Step 5 $Step\_Time := Step\_Time - 1.$

Step 6 If *Step_Time* is zero, then

$$Fitness \quad := \quad Fitness \qquad\qquad\qquad\qquad (19.3)$$
$$+C_T \times \sum_{ag \in AG} \{d(st(ag), gl(ag)) - d(cr(ag), gl(ag))\},$$

where *AG* is the set of remaining agents. Return *Fitness*.

Step 7 Go to **Step 2**.

Initially, the maximum number of evaluations is set to 51 (**Step 1**). In **Step 3**, the value of *Bonus* is added to the fitness if an agent achieves its goal, which satisfies **Requirement 1**. If all agents achieve their goals, i.e., the task is completed, the fitness value is increased with the remaining *Step_Time* (**Step 4**). This meets the above **Requirement 2**. In **Step 6**, $d(x, y)$ means the distance of x and y. $st(ag)$, $cr(ag)$, and $gl(ag)$ are the original position, the current position, and the destination (i.e., the goal for the robot navigation task and the nearest tile for the Tile World) for an agent ag. Thus, $\{d(st(ag), gl(ag)) - d(cr(ag), gl(ag))\}$ equals the motion distance of an agent ag toward its goal. Therefore, the equation (19.3) means that the fitness is more increased if the remaining agents have been moved nearer to their destination after the execution of the program, which satisfies the above **Requirement 3**.

We have chosen the *Bonus*, *Speed_UP*, and C_T parameters as 3000.0, 80.0 and 100.0, respectively. Since we use the tournament selection, (see Table 19.2), the absolute values of these parameters are not important. However, the *Bonus* parameter should be larger than the second term of the equation (19.3), so that GP searches for a program which completes the task at first. The task completion is defined as follows:

1. For the robot navigation task, each agent reaches its own goal.

2. For the Tile World task, all tiles are put into the holes.

19.4   Comparison with Reinforcement Learning

This section compares the performance of multi-agent Q-learning and GP for the robot navigation domain (see Appendix 19.A for the details of multi-agent Q-learning).

Let us take a straightforward approach for the navigation task (Fig.19.1(a)). The simple table entry x for Q-table, i.e., Q_large, would be as follows:

$$x \in \{(me, g_x, g_y, a_{1x}, a_{1y}, a_{2x}, a_{2y}, a_{3x}, a_{3y}, last)\}, \qquad (19.4)$$

where me is the agent number (i.e., 0,1,2,3), $\binom{gx}{gy}$ is a relative vector to its own goal, and $\binom{a_{ix}}{a_{iy}}$ is a relative vector to the other three agents. The variables gx, gy, a_{ix}, a_{iy} range from -9 to +9. $last$ is the last move of the agent, i.e., STAY, RIGHT, LEFT, UP, and DOWN. Therefore, the size of this state space is

$$5 \times 4 \times 18^8 \approx 10^{11}. \qquad (19.5)$$

This number is so huge for the practical computer resources that Q-learning often fails in the task for many agents. [Ono97] proposed a remedy called Modular Q-learning, in which each learning modular focused on one agent and its particular partner. However, the effectiveness of this method relies on the modular decomposability of the problem, which is not known beforehand.

An alternative way is to shrink the search space. For instance, since the minimum distance seems more important for avoiding the collision, we can choose the following state representation Q_small:

$$x \in \{(g_x, g_y, amin_x, amin_y, last)\}, \qquad (19.6)$$

where $(amin_x, amin_y)$ is a relative vector to the nearest agent. The same sort of perceptual representation was chosen for a different problem [Tan93]. However, this state space representation requires the problem-specific knowledge, which is not always available.

During each trial, a sequence of actions is executed so as to update Q-table. The trial is terminated either when the task is completed, i.e., when all agents are moved to their goals, or when a fixed number of actions are tried. For the sake of comparison, we set this number to be 51, which is equal to the $Evals$ value described in Section 2. After each trial, all agents are displaced at the initial positions and the next trial is started again with the updated Q-table. One trial in Q-learning corresponds to one fitness evaluation of a GP individual. Thus, the Q-learning performance of N trials is comparable with that of GP at the generation of g, provided that the following equation is satisfied:

Table 19.2
The Experimental Setup for sgpc1.1.

GP Parameters	
max_generation	100
population_size	2000
steady_state	0
grow_method	GROW
tournament_K	6
selection_method	TOURNAMENT
max_depth_after_crossover	17
max_depth_for_new_trees	5
max_mutant_depth	4
crossover_any_pt_fraction	0.7
crossover_func_pt_fraction	0.1
fitness_prop_repro_fraction	0.1

$$N = pop_{size} \times g, \tag{19.7}$$

where pop_{size} is the population size of GP. We regard N/pop_{size} as the generation of Q-learning.

With these preparations, we have conducted the experiment with the previous scenario RN1 by using GP and Q-learning. The Q-learning parameters were set at $\beta = 0.8$, $\gamma = 0.9$, and $T = 0.4$ (see [Tan93] for details). Fig.19.3 plots the best standard fitness (i.e., that which was derived from eqs.(19.1),(19.2), and (19.3)) with generations, averaged over 20 runs. The fitness values of GP-based agents are also shown. We used the heterogeneous breeding by GP with the parameters shown in Table19.2. Q-learning (Homo.) represents that agents share the Q-table, whereas each agent uses a different Q-table in case of Q-learning (Hetero.). As can be seen from the figure, the agents gave poorer results with Q-learning. At most three agents learned to reach their goals with Q-learning. We played with Q-learning parameters in several other ways, only to observe the similar result.

The difficulty of Q-learning seems to be due to the above-mentioned representational issue. The appropriate design of the state space is difficult for this task because of its high dimensionality. Although the total set of sensor inputs, i.e., GP terminals, is provided, yet it is not easy to distinguish between essential terminals and useless ones. A part of terminals may be combined to construct an effective Q-table, but its combination is not known beforehand. On the other hand, in case of GP, essential terminals are expected to be adaptively chosen and functionally com-

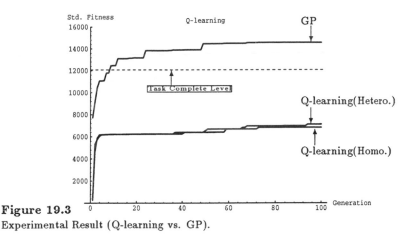

Figure 19.3
Experimental Result (Q-learning vs. GP).

bined as a result of the tree evolution. Thus, we think the superiority of GP-based multi-agent learning has been confirmed by this experiment.

19.5   Evolving Agents with Communication

19.5.1   Evolving Controlling Agents

For the navigation task, we use communication commands such as SEND or RE-CEIVE, by which an agent can tell another agent to stop or move. The SEND_i functional symbol takes two arguments and returns its second value (i.e. a two-dimensional vector). As a side effect, SEND_i sends its first argument to the i-th nearest agent as a command. The RECEIVE function returns the evaluated result of the command message, if any, which has been sent to itself by the SEND_i command. The message list is an FIFO (i.e., first in, first out) queue. If no message is sent, then the RECEIVE function returns its argument by default. The function symbols introduced for the communication are shown in Table 19.3. SEND_iY, SEND_iS, and SEND_iR macros send commands such as YIELD (i.e., the receiver moves to one of its adjacent empty cell), STOP (i.e., the receiver stays at its current position) and RANDOM (i.e., the receiver moves randomly). These commands are commonly used for the motion control. Thus, in addition to the SEND_i and RE-CEIVE primitives, we introduce these macros for the sake of improving efficiency.

We have conducted comparative experiments so as to confirm the effectiveness of the communication. The heterogeneous strategy was applied for evolving agents without communication (i.e., with GP functions and terminals shown in Table 19.1) and for evolving communicating agents (i.e., Table 19.1 and Table 19.3). The used

Table 19.3

GP Functions for Communication (Controlling Agents).

Name	#Args.	Description
Send_i	2	Send its first argument to the i-th nearest agent as a command. Return its second argument.
Send_iY	1	Send the YIELD command to the i-th nearest agent. Return its argument.
Send_iS	1	Send the STOP command to the i-th nearest agent. Return its argument.
Send_iR	1	Send the RANDOM command to the i-th nearest agent. Return its argument.
Receive	1	Receive a message as a command. If no message is received, return its argument by default.

parameters are shown in Table 19.2. We chose 6 training and 3 testing scenarios, which are similar to Fig.19.1(b). They were modified to constitute a variety of examples in several ways, by rotating or widening a passage. The total number of the training and testing data were 24 and 9, respectively. The fitness of a program is the averaged fitness over the various training cases.

Fig.19.4(a) shows the result of experiments. The figure plots the best fitness value with generations, averaged over 10 runs. The fitness value of $4 \times Bonus (= 12000.0)$ is given to a GP tree which completes the task i.e., moves all agents to the goals. Thus, on the average, GP reaches a solution around 60 generations for the communicating agents, whereas agents without communication could not solve the task after 100 generations. Note the superiority of the communicating agents for the testing cases as well as for the training cases.

The poor performance of non-communicating agents results from the lack of appropriate generalization. They could adapt to a certain situation and memorize it as a specialized cognitive map. But they failed to generalize it so as to cope with multiple cases. For instance, the following programs were acquired in one run:

```
Agent0: (if>= Ag1 V1 Goal (inv Goal))
Agent1: (if>= Ag1 (*2 V1) Goal (inv Goal))
Agent2: (if>= Ag1 (*2 (*2 V1)) Goal (inv Goal))
Agent3: (if>= Ag1 V1 Goal (inv Goal))
```

These programs realize a form of cooperation, in the sense that an agent moves to its goal if the other agents are further than some threshold (i.e., (if>= Ag1 ***)).

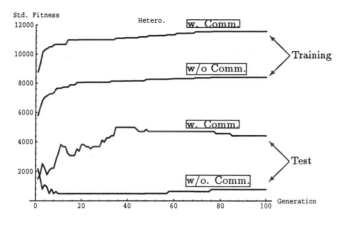

Figure 19.4
Experimental Results (Robot Navigation Task).

If the nearest agent is close, it gives way by moving in the direction opposite to its goal (i.e., (inv Goal)). Although this strategy succeeded in some limited situations, the agents failed to solve a complicated task.

On the other hand, agents with communication were able to solve the various tasks. For instance, the programs shown in Table 19.4 were acquired in one run at the generation of 56. These programs scored the standard fitness of 13520.0, which means that they solved most of the training cases. Fig.19.5 shows the emergent behavior of these agents for Training #3. The key features of these programs are as follows:

1. Agent0 and Agent2 are receivers, which always give way if they receive a message.

2. Agent3 is a receiver if the nearest agent is far, i.e., | Ag1 |≥| V1 | ⇒ Receive. It sends a yield message otherwise, because (if>= Ag1 V1 (Receive Goal) V1) returns V1 and (if>= V1 V1 (Send1_Y Goal) ***) always returns the third argument (Send1_Y Goal).

3. Agent1 moves to its goal if the nearest agent is further than the goal. Otherwise, unless it has received any message, it sends a yield message to its nearest agent. If it has received any message, execute the received command.

As can be seen in the behavior of A3 from Step9 to Step19 (Fig.19.5), if an agent receives a message, it stops moving or gives way. As a result of this effective communication, agents cooperate with each other to avoid the deadlock situation in the narrow path.

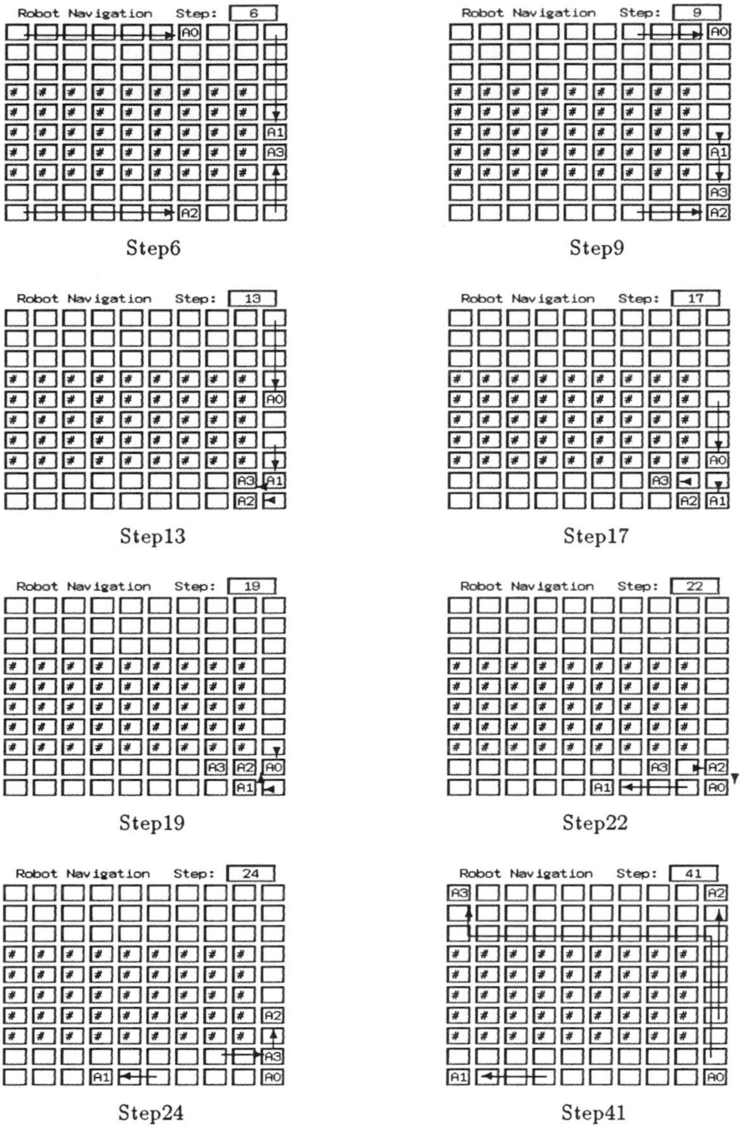

Figure 19.5
Emergent Behavior with Communication.

Table 19.4
Acquired Trees for Heterogeneous Strategy.

Agent Name	Tree
Agent0:	(Receive Goal)
Agent1:	(if>= Goal Ag1 (if>= (Receive Goal) (Send1_Y Goal)) (if>= (if>= Goal Goal (Receive Goal)) Goal) (Send1 Goal Goal) (*2 (Receive Goal)) (Receive Goal)) Goal) Goal)
Agent2:	(Receive Goal)
Agent3:	(if>= (if>= Ag1 V1 (Receive Goal) V1) V1 (Send1_Y Goal) (if>= Ag1 Goal Goal (Receive Goal)))

The above experimental results have shown that the communicating agents complete the training tasks more effectively, i.e., the evolved program is more robust. It is also suggested that the GP-based adaptive learning resulted in establishing the effective job separation among the communicating agents.

19.5.2 Evolving Negotiating Agents

A number of researchers in DAI use various protocols developed in economics and game theory to evaluate the multi-agent interaction. In the simplest case, the agent requesting a service offers a specific reward for the completion of a task. The task may be completed by a set of agents, who need to negotiate how to divide the reward. Dividing the total amount equally might not be fair if the agents made different contributions. If there are many agents (or sets of agents) that may complete the task, the requester might try to minimize its cost by seeking multiple bids or holding an auction. There are a number of alternatives that have different properties and may be applicable or preferred in different situations [Genesereth et al.97].

We use ACL (Agent Communication Language) for the Tile World in order to evolve the negotiation among agents. ACL consists of three parts, i.e., its vocabulary, an inner language called KIF (Knowledge Interchange Format), and an outer language called KQML (Knowledge Query and Manipulation Language). The vocabulary of ACL is listed in a large and open-ended dictionary of words appropriate to common application areas. Each word in the dictionary has an English description used by humans in understanding the meaning of the word. The dictionary is open-ended to allow for the addition of new words within existing areas and in new application areas. Full specifications are available, and parts of the language are making their way through various standards organizations (see [Genesereth et al.97] for details).

Now consider the modified Tile World shown in Fig.19.2(b). Agent 0's goal is to fill hole H0, while agent 1's and 2's need to fill holes H1 and H2, respectively. To fill its hole, agent 1 needs to do 17 steps. Agents can cooperate and help each other to reduce the cost of achieving their goals. There are several kinds of joint plans that the agents can execute for the reduction.

We use ACL-like commands shown in Table 19.5 for agents to negotiate with each other. The experimental results have shown that the effective communication emerged among the agents so that they negotiate with each other to reduce the cost of achieving their own goals. For instance, the programs shown in Table 19.6 were acquired in one run. We observed that Agent0 and Agent2 negotiated with each other while Agent1 tried to achieve its goal by itself.

The above result shows that GP has formed a 3-agent coalition, i.e., {{Agent0, Agent2}, {Agent1}}. This coalition structure means that there are two coalitions, one consisting of Agent0 and Agent2, and the other consisting only of Agent1. When two agents form a coalition, they are coordinating their actions. The utility of an agent from a joint plan that achieves his goal is defined as the difference between the cost of achieving his goal alone and the cost of his part of the joint plan [Zlotkin et al.91]. In general, n-agent coordination mechanisms can be used when any sub-group of agents may engage in task exchange to the exclusion of others. [Zlotkin et al.94] showed that a simple and rational coalition was formed by means of cryptographic techniques. However, this method assumes certain characteristics of the task domain, i.e., sub-additivity. The sub-additive task domain means that, by combining sets of tasks, we may reduce (and can never increase) the total cost, as compared with the sum of the costs of achieving the sets separately. Unfortunately, many task domains do not have this property. In some case, there is no knowing whether the domain has this property or not. The above experimental result has shown that a certain coalition was established by means of GP, which requires no particular conditions for the coalition formation. Therefore, we believe GP-based multi-agent learning can provide an effective coordination method for a broader range of task domains. Further research will consider the applicability and feasibility of GP in this direction.

19.6 Discussion

19.6.1 Evolving Other Types of Communicating Agents

In this paper, we introduced communication commands of types B for the robot navigation domain (Section 5.1) and C for the Tile World (Section 5.2). Other types of communication can be defined as well. For example, [Werner et al.91] presented a simulation, in which a population of artificial organisms evolved low-

Table 19.5

GP Functions for Communication (Negotiating Agents).

Name	#Args.	Description
Propose_i	1	Send a proposal to the i-th nearest agent. The proposal is that the sender gives some of the sender's reward (the ratio is given by the first argument) to the receiver if the receiver achieves the sender's goal. Return the Tile vector.
Accept_i	0	Accept the i-th nearest agent's proposal and send the acceptance message. Return the Hole vector.
Reject_i	0	Reject the i-th nearest agent's proposal and send the rejection message. Return the Tile vector.

Table 19.6

Acquired Trees for Negotiating Agents.

Agent Name	Tree
Agent0:	(+ (inv (if>= last (- (+ (if>= (Propose_2 0.3259680) last (Accept_2) (if>= (Accept_1) (Propose_2 0.3260016) (Reject_2) Ag0)) (Accept_2)) (- Ag1 (if>= last (if>= Ag0 (Reject_0) (Reject_2) (Reject_0)) (Propose_0 0.3261200) (Propose_0 0.217209)))) (- (- (Accept_0) (Accept_2)) (Accept_0)) (+ Hole (+ Tile (+ Hole (- Ag1 (Reject_0))))))))) (->90 Tile))
Agent1:	(if_dot Tile (if_dot last (->90 (if>= (+ Ag1 Ag0) Tile Hole Ag1)) (inv (Reject_1)) Hole) [-1.076370,-0.553187] last)
Agent2:	(if_dot (if_dot Ag1 Tile Ag2 (inv (if>= Ag0 (if>= (Propose_0 0.3563) Ag1 (+ (if>= (Reject_0) Ag0 Ag0 Ag1) Ag0) (if>= (if>= (Reject_0) (+ Ag1 (Propose_2 0.02550)) (- (Propose_0 0.979331) (Accept_0)) (- Ag0 (Accept_0))) (Accept_0) (if>= (Propose_1 0.541944) Ag0 (if>= (Accept_0) (Reject_0) (Propose_0 0.582183) (Accept_0)) (Propose_0 0.918706)) (Propose_2 0.235540)) (Accept_1)) (+ Ag1 (+ (if>= Ag1 (Propose_1 0.980090) (if>= (Propose_1 0.289795) Ag0 (Propose_1 0.000803) Ag0) (Reject_0)) (if>= (+ (Accept_1) (Accept_1)) (Reject_0) (if>= (Reject_0) (Propose_1 0.093556) (Accept_0) (Accept_0)) (if>= (Propose_1 0.966526) (Propose_1 0.947458) (Reject_0) Ag1))))))) Ag2 (*2 (/2 Tile)))

level communication protocols for mate finding. They showed how the organisms generated and interpreted meaningful signals as a result of evolution. For the pursuit problem, we used a communication command of type A and empirically confirmed the evolvability of the communicative cooperation of this type [Iba97]. In this experiment, agents were assumed to have a limited visibility. In most cases, agents without communication were unable even to get closer to the prey. On the other hand, the communicating agents succeeded in enclosing the prey.

The effective communication and its learnability for a specific task remain to be seen in DAI. We have shown the emergence of communication among agents so as to increase the robustness of a generated GP program. The evolvability of various types of communication for other problem domains is our future research concern.

19.6.2 Q-learning and Genetic Programming

The previous result has shown the difficulty with Q-learning approach for the multi-agent task. The state space for Q-table may become so huge in case of many agents. This paper presented a GP-based approach to avoid the above problem. We have also proposed an extension of multi-agent reinforcement learning with GP. This is to integrate GP-based adaptive search with Q-learning so as to shrink the search space. The established system is called QGP, i.e., Q-learning with Genetic Programming. The salient features of QGP are as follows:

1. GP searches for the combination of input variables, i.e., constructs an effective Q-table entry.

2. Q-learning updates Q-values for each Q-table, i.e., a GP individual. These values are inherited from generation to generation.

3. The fitness of GP is derived from the reinforcement reward given by Q-learning.

We showed how successfully QGP was applied to the robot navigation task [Iba98]. Our QGP is based upon a selectionist approach [Steels97], in the sense that a structure comes into existence by variation or construction and is tested as a whole for the fitness (i.e., the reinforcement reward) in the environment. We believe that QGP leads to the effective integration of two learning paradigms, i.e., Q-learning and GP.

19.6.3 Related Work

[Teller94] realized an indexed memory in GP and studied the evolution of agents with mental models. He evolved programs that could solve a problem of pushing blocks up against the boundaries of a world. [Andre95] extended this idea to realize MAPMAKER, a method for the automatic generation of agents that discovered information about their environment, encoded this information for later use, and created simple plans utilizing the stored mental models. He applied his method to a "gold" collection problem, in which one part of a program made a map of the world and stored it in memory, and the other part used this map to find the gold. These works are closely related to our robot navigation domain, because both tasks require the effective map making and its usage. However, their work did not necessarily aim at the multi-agent cooperation.

As for multi-agent learning, Koza used GP to evolve sets of seemingly simple rules that exhibit an emergent behavior. The goal was to genetically breed a common computer program, when simultaneous executed by all the individuals in a group of independent agent, i.e., the homogeneous breeding, that causes the emergence of beneficial and interesting higher-level collective behavior [Koza 92]. [Fogarty *et al.*95] studied the evolution of the multiple communicating classifier systems in the heterogeneous environment of a distributed control system for a walking robot.

They introduced the "symbiosis" analogy to realize a macro-level operator to the evolution of heterogeneous species and showed the effectiveness of their approach empirically. But they failed to observe the evolution of a "superorganism" by their experiments. They also investigated the evolution of multiple fuzzy controllers in the homogeneous environment of a distributed control system for a communication network. Haynes proposed an approach to the construction of cooperation strategies based on GP for a group of agents [Haynes *et al.*95],[Haynes *et al.*96]. He experimented in the predator-prey domain, i.e., the pursuit game, and showed that the GP paradigm could be effectively used to generate apparently complex cooperation strategies without any deep domain knowledge. [Luke *et al.*96] examined three breeding strategies (clones, free and restricted) and three coordination mechanisms (none, deictic sensing, and named-based sensing) for evolving teams of agents in the Serengeti world, a simple predator/prey environment. The terminal and function symbols in Table 19.1 have been partly motivated by the study reported by this work. They studied evolving a teamwork by GP for the pursuit game, in which the world is a continuous 2-dimensional area.

19.7 Conclusion

This paper described the emergence of cooperative behavior based on GP and showed the following points:

1. The effectiveness of GP-based method was shown by the comparative experiment with Q-learning.

2. GP was successfully applied to multi–agent test beds, i.e., the robot navigation task and the Tile World. We have confirmed that the cooperative behavior emerged

by means of GP.

3. The evolvability of communicative cooperation has been shown. The robustness of a generated GP program was increased with the emergent communication.

The experimental results showed the effective emergence of cooperation in many difficult situations. A more general way to validate the evolutionary scheme is our future concern. Another important topic is to apply our approach to a real-world problem. We have attempted to evolve a robust robot programming in a real world situation [Ito *et al*.96]. This research focused on the robustness of a single robot. We are currently working on the extension of this framework to realize the evolution of a group of robots.

19.A Multi-agent reinforcement learning

This appendix briefly explains multi-agent reinforcement learning (see [Tan93] for details).

Each agent uses the one-step Q-learning algorithm. Given a current state x and an available actions a_i, a Q-learning agent selects each action a with a probability given by the Boltzmann distribution:

$$p(a_i \mid x) = \frac{e^{Q(x,a_i)/T}}{\sum_{k \in actions} e^{Q(x,a_i)/T}}, \tag{19.8}$$

where T is the temperature parameter that adjusts the randomness of decisions. The agent then executes the action, receives an immediate reward r, moves to the next state y.

In each time step, the agent updates $Q(x,a)$ by recursively discounting future utilities and weighting them by a positive learning rate β:

$$Q(x,a) \Longleftarrow Q(x,a) + \beta(r + \gamma V(y) - Q(x,a)). \tag{19.9}$$

Where $\gamma(0 \leq \gamma < 1)$ is a discount parameter, and $V(x)$ is given by:

$$V(x) = \max_{b \in actions} Q(x,b). \tag{19.10}$$

$Q(x,a)$ is updated only when taking action a from state x. Selecting actions stochastically by $p(a_i \mid x)$ ensures that each action will be evaluated repeatedly. In general, the $Q(x,a)$ value is kept as a multi-dimensional table, which we call a Q-table. Two types of multi-agent reinforcement learning algorithms have been proposed [Weiβ93], i.e., heterogeneous learning and homogeneous learning. In the former case, each agent uses and updates a different Q-table, whereas all agents share a common Q-table in the latter.

For the robot navigation task, the reward r is defined by following the same principle described in Section 3. According to **Requirement 1**, the bonus reward is given when an agent is moved to a goal. When the task is completed, the reward proportional to the remaining time steps is provided, which meets **Requirement 2**. If an action causes an agent to get closer to its goal, a little reward is given, which satisfies **Requirement 3**.

Bibliography

Andre,D., The Automatic Programming of Agents that Learn Mental Models and Create Simple Plans of Action, in *Proc. of the 14th International Joint Conference on Artificial Intelligence*, 1995

Benda,M., Jagannathan,V., and Dodhiawalla,R., On Optimal Cooperation of Knowledge Sources, in *Proceedings of the 1988 Workshop on Distributed Artificial Intelligence*, May 1988

Bull,L., Evolutionary Computing in Multi-agent Environments: Partners, in *Proc. of the 7th International Conference on Genetic Algorithms (ICGA97)*, 1997

Chu-Carroll,J., and Carberry,S., Communicating for Conflict Resolution in Multi-Agent Collaborative Planning, in *Proceedings of the First International Conference on Multi-Agent Systems (ICMAS95)*, 1995

Fogarty,T., Bull,L., and Carse,B., Evolving Multi-Agent Systems, in *Genetic Algorithms in Engineering and Computer Science*, Winter G., Pèriaux,J., Galàn,M. and Cuesta,P. (eds), John Wiley & Sons, 1995

Genesereth,R., and Ketchpel,S.P., Software Agents, 1997

Goldman,C.V. and Rosenshein,J.S. Emergent Coordination through the use of Cooperative State-Changing Rules, in *Proceedings of the 12th National Conference on Artificial Intelligence*, 1994

Hanks,S., Pollack,M.E., and Cohen,P.R., Benchmarks, Test Beds, Controlled Experimentation, and the Design of Agent Architectures, In *AI Magazine*, Winter, 1993

Haynes, T., Wainwright,R., and Sen,S., Evolving a Team, In *Working Notes of the AAAI-95 Fall Symposium on Genetic Programming*, AAAI Press, 1995

Haynes, T. and Sen,S., Learning Cases to Compliment Rules for Conflict Resolution in Multiagent Systems, In *International Journal of Human Computer Studies*, 1996

Iba,H., Emergent Cooperation for Multiple Agents using Genetic Programming, in *Parallel Problem Solving form Nature IV (PPSN96)*, 1996

Iba,H., Multiple-Agent Learning for Robot Navigation Task by Genetic Programming, *Genetic Programming 1997 (GP97)*, 1997

Iba,H., Multiple-Agent Reinforcement Learning with Genetic Programming, *Genetic Programming 1998 (GP98)*, 1998

Ito,T., Iba,H. and Kimura,M., Robot Programs Generated by Genetic Programming, Japan Advanced Institute of Science and Technology, IS-RR-96-0001I, in *Genetic Programming 96*, 1996

Rosca,J.., Ballard,D.H., Discovery of Subroutines in Genetic Programming, in *Advances in Genetic Programming II*, MIT Press, 1996

Koza, J., Genetic Programming, On the Programming of Computers by means of Natural Selection, MIT Press, 1992

Koza, J., Genetic Programming II, Automatic Discovery of Reusable Programs, MIT Press, 1994

Luke,S. and Spector,L., Evolving Teamwork and Coordination with Genetic Programming, in Genetic Programming 96, MIT Press, 1996

Steels,L., Perceptually Grounded Meaning Creation, in *Proc. Second International Conference on Multi-Agent Systems (ICMAS96)*, 1997

Ono,N., Fukumono,K., A Modular Approach to Multi-Agent Reinforcement Learning, in *Distributed Artificial Intelligence Meets Machine Learning*, Weiβ,G. (ed.), Springer, 1997

Pollack,M.E. and Ringuette,M., Introducing the Tileworld: Experimentally Evaluating Agent Architectures, in *Proceedings of the 8th National Conference on Artificial Intelligence*, 1990

Sen,S. and Sekaran,M., Multiagent Coordination with Learning Classifier Systems, in *Adaption and Learning in Multi-Agent Systems*, Weiβ,G. and Sen,S. (eds.), Springer, 1995

Tan,M., Multi-Agent Reinforcement Learning: Independent vs. Cooperative Agents, in *Proceedings of the Tenth International Conference on Machine Learning*, pp.330–337, 1993

Teller,A., The Evolution of Mental Models, in *Advances in Genetic Programming*, 1994

Weiβ,G., Learning to Coordinate Actions in Multi-Agent Systems, in *Proceedings of the Thirteenth International Joint Conference on Artificial Intelligence*, pp.311–316, 1993

Werner,G.M. and Dyer,M.G., Evolution of Communication in Artificial Organisms, in *Artificial Life II*, Langton,C.G., Taylor,C., Farmer,J.D. and Rasmussen,S. (eds.), Addison-Wesley, 1991

Zlotkin,G., and Rosenschein,J.S., Cooperation and Conflict Resolution via Negotiation among Autonomous Agents in Noncooperative Domains, in *IEEE Transactions on Systems, Man and Cybernetics*, 21(6), pp.1317-1324, 1991

Zlotkin,G., and Rosenschein,J.S., Coalition, Cryptography, and Stability: Mechanisms for Coalition Formation in Task Oriented Domains, in *Proc. 12th National Conference on Artificial Intelligence (AAAI94)*, 1994

Index